815+
Enhanced ACT®
Practice Questions

By the Staff of The Princeton Review

PrincetonReview.com

Penguin
Random
House

The Princeton Review Publishing Team
Rob Franek, Editor-in-Chief
David Soto, Senior Director, Data Operations
Stephen Koch, Senior Manager, Data Operations
Deborah Weber, Director of Production
Jason Ullmeyer, Production Design Manager
Jennifer Chapman, Senior Production Artist
Selena Coppock, Director of Editorial
Aaron Riccio, Director, Editorial Admissions Content
Orion McBean, Senior Editor
Meave Shelton, Senior Editor
Laura Rose, Editor
Isabelle Appleton, Editorial Assistant

Penguin Random House Publishing Team
Tom Russell, VP, Publisher
Alison Stoltzfus, Senior Director, Publishing
Emily Hoffman, Managing Editor
Mary Ellen Owens, Assistant Director of Production
Suzanne Lee, Senior Designer
Eugenia Lo, Publishing Assistant

For customer service, please contact **editorialsupport@review.com**, and be sure to include:

- full title of the book
- ISBN
- page number

Acknowledgments

The Princeton Review would like to extend very special thanks to our contributing authors: Kenneth Brenner, Cat Healey, Sara Kuperstein, Amy Minster, Scott O'Neal, Harrison Foster, Beth Hollingsworth, Kevin Keogh, Christine Lindwall, Sweena Mangal, Sionainn Marcoux, Robert Otey, Elizabeth Owens, Gabby Peterson, Kathy Ruppert, Suzanne Wint, Cindy Cannizzo, Chris Chimera, Stacey Cowap, Lori DesRochers, Anne Goldberg-Baldwin, Spencer LeDoux, Jomil London, Dave MacKenzie, Jason Morgan, Alice Swan, Jess Thomas, Cynthia Ward, and Jimmy Williams.

We are also grateful to Jennifer Chapman, Liz Dacey, and Sarah Litt for their careful attention to every page.

Finally, special thanks to Adam Robinson, who conceived of and perfected the Joe Bloggs approach to standardized tests, and many of the other successful techniques used by The Princeton Review.

Contents

Get More (Free) Content
at **PrincetonReview.com/prep**

As easy as 1·2·3

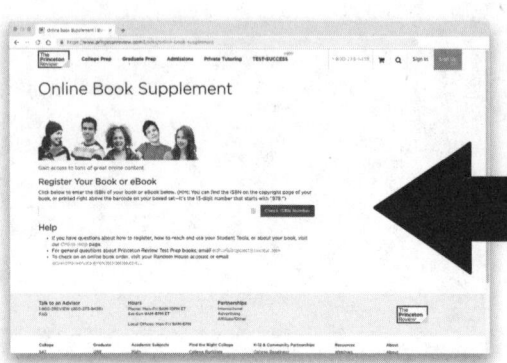

1 Go to PrincetonReview.com/prep or scan the **QR code** and enter the following ISBN to register your book:
9780593518014

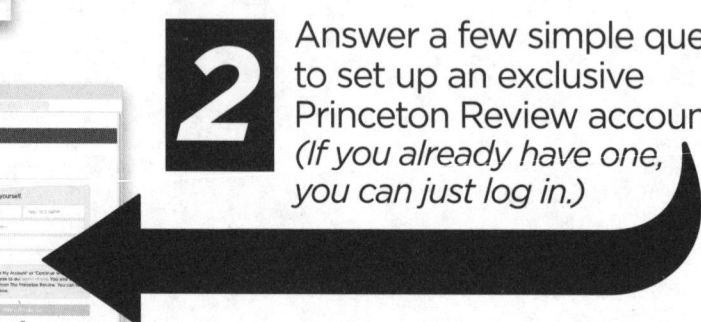

2 Answer a few simple questions to set up an exclusive Princeton Review account. *(If you already have one, you can just log in.)*

3 Enjoy access to your **FREE** content!

Once you've registered, you can...

- Get our take on any recent or pending updates to the ACT

- Take Test 2, a fully digital Enhanced ACT with a built-in timer, a score report, and full answer explanations

- Take a fully digital version of Test 1 (also in this book) for additional practice with the online ACT format; includes a score report and full explanations

- Get valuable advice about the college application process, including tips for writing a great essay and where to apply for financial aid

- If you're still choosing between colleges, use our searchable rankings of *The Best 391 Colleges* to find out more information about your dream school

- Check to see if there have been any corrections or updates to this edition

Need to report a potential **content** issue?

Contact **EditorialSupport@review.com** and include:

- full title of the book
- ISBN
- page number

Need to report a **technical** issue?

Contact **TPRStudentTech@review.com** and provide:

- your full name
- email address used to register the book
- full book title and ISBN
- Operating system (Mac/PC) and browser (Chrome, Firefox, Safari, etc.)

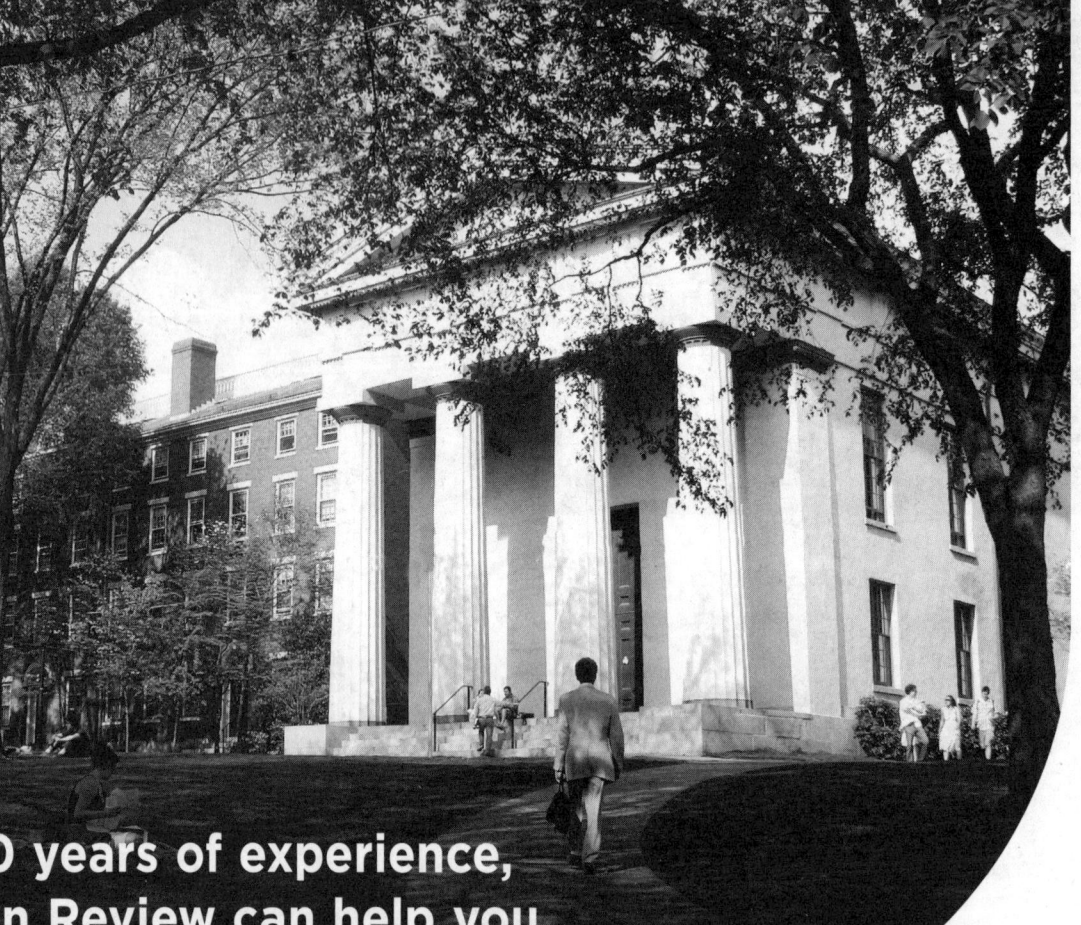

Introduction

So you think you need more practice? Well, we have tons of practice right here for you. We have created a variety of drills and practice ACT sections to help you get your best possible score on this beast of a test! After all, the harder you practice, the better off you'll be on test day.

Since you probably know the basics of how the test is conducted, we'll spare you that information. What we will give you here is a breakdown of the "tests" on the Enhanced ACT, available for all national test-takers starting in September 2025 and all school day test-takers in spring of 2026.

1. English Test (35 minutes—50 questions)

In this section, you'll see an essay on the left side of the page or screen. For most questions, some words will be underlined or highlighted. You'll be asked to choose whether that portion of the text or one of three alternatives is most grammatically acceptable or fulfills a certain goal. There will be six or seven passages in all, each with either five or ten questions. The English Test covers topics in grammar, punctuation, sentence structure, and rhetorical skills.

2. Math Test (50 minutes—45 questions)

These are the regular, multiple-choice math questions you've been doing all your life. The easier questions tend to come in the beginning and the difficult ones in the end, but the folks at the ACT try to mix in easy, medium, and difficult problems throughout the Math Test. About 80% of the content is what ACT calls "Preparing for Higher Mathematics," which includes high school-level concepts in areas such as functions, geometry, and statistics. The remainder of the questions are "Integrating Essential Skills," which are math concepts from before high school. Finally, less than 20 percent of the questions in those two categories will be "Modeling" questions, which is ACT's term for word problems.

3. Reading Test (40 minutes—36 questions)

In this section, there will be four reading passages of varying length, with the longest coming in at about 800 words each—the average length of a *People* magazine article but maybe not as interesting. There is usually one literary narrative passage followed by three informational passages that will cover topics in social sciences, humanities, and natural science. One of the passages is made up of two shorter pieces on a similar topic instead of one long article. After reading each passage, you have to answer 9 questions.

4. Optional Science Test (40 minutes—40 questions)

Very little scientific knowledge is necessary for the Science Test. You won't need to know the chemical makeup of hydrochloric acid or any formulas, but you may see some questions about basic scientific knowledge. You will see 6 or 7 passages and, in most of those, you will be asked to understand scientific information presented in graphs, charts, tables, and research summaries. In addition, you will have to make sense of one disagreement between two to four scientists. Some schools require you to take Science, while others don't. Even if a college doesn't require Science, though, it may be required or recommended if you plan to pursue a science-related major. Do your research. If you're absolutely sure that you don't need a Science score for any school you plan to apply to, feel free not to take the Science. On the other hand, if even one school you're interested in requires it, you'll need to take the ACT with Science.

5. Optional Writing Test (40 minutes)

The ACT contains an "optional" Writing Test featuring a single essay. Few schools require the "ACT Test with Writing" version of the test anymore. You should obviously take it if you're applying to one of the schools that does require it, and if you're unsure where you're going to apply, it's probably a good idea to take it in case you end up needing it. You will be asked to write an essay stating your position on a given prompt that the test-writers deem "relevant" to high school students. Your essay will be read by two different readers. Each will give your essay a score between 1 and 6 in each of four domains (leading to four different subscores from 2–12). Your writing score is then calculated by averaging the four 2–12 subscores and rounding to the nearest whole point for a total score of 2–12.

If you are unsure about any of the sections or if you want more strategies for conquering these kinds of questions, you can find more information at PrincetonReview.com or you can review our comprehensive guide, *ACT Prep*.

What you should also know is that the key to raising your ACT score does not lie in memorizing dozens of math theorems, the periodic table of elements, or obscure rules of English grammar. There's more to mastering this test than just improving math, verbal, and science skills. At its root, the ACT measures academic achievement. It doesn't pretend to measure your analytic ability or your intelligence. The people at ACT admit that you can increase your score by preparing for the test, and by spending just a little extra time preparing for the ACT, you can substantially change your score on the ACT (and the way colleges look at your applications). After all, out of all the elements in your application "package," your ACT score is the easiest to change.

That being said, we have included in this book a variety of drills to help you master the content of the ACT. Rest assured that these tests and questions are modeled closely on actual ACT exams and questions, with the proper balance of questions reflective of what the ACT actually tests.

At the beginning of this book, you'll find one complete ACT practice test. After you've taken that test, score it to learn your strengths and weaknesses. Next in the book, you will find drills that are designed to reinforce the essential English, math, reading, and science skills that will serve you throughout the rest of the ACT. Work through these in the order that makes the most sense to you. Practice in areas that were difficult for you on the first test so that you can improve your scores in your weaker areas. Also, make sure to continue to hone your skills in your strong areas to maximize their impact on your composite score. Mix it up as you go through the content, doing some practice in each subject each week of your prep period. Once you are ready to take another test, you will find one online in your Student Tools, so make sure to register your book (see page x for instructions).

A final thought before you begin: the ACT does not predict your ultimate success or failure as a human being. No matter how high or how low you score on this test initially, and no matter how much you may increase your score through preparation, you should never consider the score you receive on this or any other test a final judgment of your abilities. When it's all said and done, we know you'll get into a great school and that you'll have an incredible experience there.

We wish you the best of luck, even though you won't need it after all this practicing!

The Princeton Review

How to Approach the ACT Online Test

In this chapter, you'll learn what to expect on the ACT Online Test, including how to apply its computer-based features and our strategies to the question types in each section—English, Math, Reading, Science, and Writing. If you are taking the pencil-and-paper test, this chapter can still help you with some ACT strategies.

*If you plan to take a school-day ACT test in October 2025, you should know that your test will be the legacy version of the test. It won't be until spring of 2026 that students taking school-day ACT tests will see the shorter, "enhanced" version of the test. However, both versions test the same concepts.

WHAT IS THE ACT ONLINE TEST?

The ACT Online Test is the ACT that you take on a computer, rather than with a pencil and paper. Despite the name, you can't take the ACT from the comfort of your own home; instead, you'll have to go to a testing center (possibly your high school) and take the test on one of the center's computers.

The ACT Online Test has the same overall structure, timing, and number of questions as the pencil-and-paper ACT*. The scoring, score range, and scoring method are also the same. If the ACT Online Test is basically the same as the pencil-and-paper ACT, who would take the ACT Online Test?

WHO TAKES THE ACT ONLINE TEST?

ACT has been offering computer-based versions of the ACT since about 2016. The first students to take the ACT on the computer were students taking the test at school. Schools and school districts decided whether to give the test on the computer.

Since 2018, all students taking the ACT outside of the United States have taken the test on a computer (except for those students with accommodations requiring the use of a traditional pencil-and-paper test).

With the move to the shorter "enhanced" ACT that was announced in 2024 and first implemented in April 2025, ACT committed to offering students in the United States the option of taking the ACT Online Test instead of the traditional pencil-and-paper version. Not all testing centers will offer online testing, however, so students who prefer this option may need to travel farther to their chosen test site. ACT has committed to expanding online testing to as many test centers as possible.

ACT Retesting and Superscoring

If you are happy with the score you receive from a single test administration, you will still have the option to send just that score to colleges. If your score in one or more sections is not as high as you'd like, you should take the ACT again. As soon as you do, ACT will produce a "superscore," which is the average of your best scores from each subject from multiple test attempts. Since the composite of any test taken after September 2025 is based only on the scores for English, Math, and Reading, the superscore will be based on the scores in these three subjects. Scores for the optional Science and Writing Tests will not affect the composite score or the superscore, but they will be listed on the score report. Note that not all colleges accept a superscored ACT, as some will take your highest score instead, so make sure to research what is required at the schools to which you are applying.

ACT ONLINE TEST FEATURES

So, besides the obvious fact that it's taken on a computer, what are the differences between taking the ACT on the computer and taking it on paper? Let's start with what you can't do on the ACT Online Test. You can't "write" on the screen in a freehand way. You're limited in how you're able to mark the answer choices, and each question appears on its own screen (so you can't see multiple questions at one glance). You will also be given scratch paper or a small "whiteboard" and dry erase pen with which to make notes and do work.

So, what features does the ACT Online Test have? It depends a bit on where you are testing, as there are slight differences between the platform used for national test date administrations and the one used for state or district testing. Here are the main features of the national test date platform.

- Timer
    - You can hide the timer by clicking the eye symbol to the right of it.
    - There is a 5-minute warning toward the end of each test. There is no audible signal at the 5-minute warning, only a small indicator in the upper-right corner of the screen.
- Index tool
    - You can use this tool to navigate directly to any question in the section.
    - The Index opens on the right side of the screen.
    - Opening the Index narrows the width of the question on the left side of the screen.
    - If the question is associated with a passage, the question will move from being on the right side of the passage to appearing below the passage.
    - In the Index, you can filter the questions by Flagged, Answered, and Unanswered.
- Flag tool
    - You can flag a question on the question screen.
    - Flagging a question has no effect besides marking the question for your own purposes.
- Answer Eliminator
    - Answer choices can be "crossed off" on-screen.
    - An answer choice that's been eliminated cannot be chosen and must be "un-crossed-off" first by clicking the answer choice.
- Magnifier
    - You can use this to magnify specific parts of the screen.
- Line Reader
    - This tool covers part of the screen. There is an adjustable window you can use to limit what you can see.
    - This is an excellent tool if you need an aid to help you focus on specific parts of the text or figure.
    - However, not everyone will find this tool useful, so do not feel obligated to use it!
    - Note that you cannot highlight the text in the window of the Line Reader.

Don't Forget Your Online Tests!
For practice with ACT Online Test features and functionality, make sure to take the online practice ACTs that accompany this book. Register your book at PrincetonReview.com/prep to access a fully digital version of Test 1 (which is also in this book) as well as Test 2 (online only). See page x for details.

- Answer Masking
  - ○ This tool hides the answer choices of a question.
  - ○ Answers can be revealed one at a time.
- Highlighter
  - ○ You can use this tool to highlight parts of passage text, question text, or answer text.
  - ○ You cannot highlight within figures.
  - ○ If you highlight in a passage with multiple questions, your highlights will only show up on that question. (In other words, if you make a highlight in the passage for one question, that highlight will not show up on the passage when you are looking at any other question.)
  - ○ Hitting the Clear button or closing the highlighter tool removes your highlights.
- Contrast
  - ○ Next to the Tools menu is a Contrast Menu.
  - ○ The general contrast settings are default, high color contrast, high color contrast inverted, and low color contrast.
  - ○ Color blindness contrasts include black on cream, black on light blue, black on magenta, white on black, light yellow on royal blue, and gray on green.
- The Writing Test is typed, rather than written by hand.

If you are taking the ACT at school as part of state or district testing, these tools will be similar but may go by different names (for example, the school-day platform has a Bookmark tool rather than a Flag tool). Additionally, at the time of this writing, the calculator included in the school-day testing platform is a graphing calculator, while the one in the Saturday-testing platform is a scientific calculator.

HOW TO APPROACH THE ACT ONLINE TEST

The strategies mentioned in this chapter are thoroughly discussed in our comprehensive guide, *ACT Prep*, so be sure to pick up a copy of that book if you have not already done so. These approaches were created in reference to the pencil-and-paper format, but they still apply to the ACT Online Test with some adjustments. This chapter assumes your familiarity with these strategies and will show you how to make the best use of them given the tools available in the computer-based format.

You will also want to incorporate some computer-based practice into your prep plan. Registration of this book online includes one full enhanced ACT test. Additionally, ACT's website has practice sections for each of the four multiple-choice parts of the test and for the essay. We recommend that you do this practice toward the end of your preparation (and close to your test date) to give yourself an opportunity to practice what you've learned on a platform similar to the one you'll be using on the day of the test.

If you are planning to take the ACT online, you should practice as if you're doing all your work on the computer, even when you're working in a physical book. Use a highlighter, but don't use the highlighter on any figures (as the ACT Online Test won't let you do so). For most of your practice, you will want to write your notes on the page but off to the side of the question, as if those notes are on scratch paper. This will allow you to review your work carefully after you finish testing. When you are taking your final practice test, you can do all your work on a separate sheet of paper or a whiteboard, as you would on the official test.

Also, remember that our approaches work. Don't get misled by ACT's instructions on the day of the test—the test-writers' way of approaching the test won't give you the best results!

Overall

Your Personal Order of Difficulty (POOD) and Pacing goals will be the same on the ACT Online Test as on the pencil-and-paper version. Because it is easy to change your answers, put in a guess answer when skipping a Later or Never question. Use the Flag tool on the Later questions so you can jump back easily (using the Index on the right side of the screen, where you can filter by Flagged, Answered, and Unanswered questions).

Process of Elimination (POE) is still a vital approach. On both the paper-and-pencil ACT and the ACT Online Test, there are more wrong answers than correct ones. Eliminating ones you know are wrong helps you to save time, avoid trap answers, and make a better guess if you have to. On the ACT Online Test, you cannot write on the test, but you can use the Highlighter tool. Turn on these tools (and the Line Mask, if desired) at the beginning of the English section and use them throughout.

ENGLISH

The Basic Approaches to all types of English questions are the same on the computerized and the paper versions of the ACT. For either format, you may want to highlight or underline the key words in the question stem to help yourself focus on the task at hand. When you decide to skip a question to come back to it Later (for example, a question asking for the introduction to the topic of the passage before you've read any part of the passage), flag the question so you can easily jump back to it before moving on to the next passage. When you have five minutes remaining, flag your current question and use the Index tool to make sure you've put in guesses for any questions that you haven't done, then return to your spot and work until time runs out.

> **Remember!**
> Your goal is to get the best possible score on the ACT. ACT's goal is to assign a number to you that (supposedly) means something to colleges. Focus on your goal!

For a comprehensive review of all sections of the ACT and the strategies mentioned throughout this chapter, check out our book *ACT Prep*.

When you work questions about grammar you can use the Highlighter tool to help you focus on the key parts of the text. Let's see an example:

Use the tools available to help you focus on the key portions of the text. Practice with a highlighter when you're working on paper (instead of underlining with your pencil).

Sneaking down the corridor, the agent, taking care not to alert the guards, spotting the locked door.

Which choice makes the sentence most grammatically acceptable?

- ○ **A.** **No Change**
- ○ **B.** spot
- ○ **C.** are spotting
- ○ **D.** spots

Here's How to Crack It

Verbs are changing in the answer choices, so the question is testing subject-verb agreement. The verb must be consistent with the subject. *The agent* is the subject; highlight it:

Sneaking down the corridor, the agent, taking care not to alert the guards, spotting the locked door.

Which choice makes the sentence most grammatically acceptable?

- ○ **A.** **No Change**
- ○ **B.** spot
- ○ **C.** are spotting
- ○ **D.** spots

The agent is singular, so the verb must be singular. Eliminate (B) and (C), as both are plural. *Spotting* cannot be the main verb of a sentence, so eliminate (A). The correct answer is (D).

Similarly, the Highlighter tool is helpful on questions that state a specific goal. Use the tool on both the passage and the question to help you focus on the relevant parts of each.

As it's name suggests, the Indian fantail is not native to North America. In fact, its establishment here was quite accidental. In 1926, the San Diego Zoo acquired four pythons from India for its reptile exhibit. The long trip from India required, that, the pythons be provided with food for the journey, and a group of unfortunate fantails was shipped for just that purpose. Two lucky fantails survived, and their beautiful appearance caused the San Diego Zoo to keep and breed them for the public to see. Eventually, some of the animals escaped captivity and developed populations in the wild, all thanks to those two birds!

Given that all the choices are true, which one provides the most relevant and specific information at this point in the essay?

- ⊙ **A.** **No Change**
- ⊙ **B.** and they have quite an appetite.
- ⊙ **C.** because no one wanted them to starve.
- ⊙ **D.** and they are quite picky in what they'll eat.

Here's How to Crack It

The question asks for the *most relevant and specific information*. Highlight those words in the question. The first sentence of the paragraph focuses on the *Indian fantail*, and the sentence after the underlined portion discusses *Two lucky fantails*. The final sentence discusses *the animals* that escaped. Highlight these words in the paragraph.

Your screen should look like this:

As it's name suggests, the Indian fantail is not native to North America. In fact, its establishment here was quite accidental. In 1926, the San Diego Zoo acquired four pythons from India for its reptile exhibit. The long trip from India required, that, the pythons be provided with food for the journey, and a group of unfortunate fantails was shipped for just that purpose. Two lucky fantails survived, and their beautiful appearance caused the San Diego Zoo to keep and breed them for the public to see. Eventually, some of the animals escaped captivity and developed populations in the wild, all thanks to those two birds!

Given that all the choices are true, which one provides the most relevant and specific information at this point in the essay?

- ⊙ **A.** **No Change**
- ⊙ **B.** and they have quite an appetite.
- ⊙ **C.** because no one wanted them to starve.
- ⊙ **D.** and they are quite picky in what they'll eat.

Use POE, focusing on whether the choice is consistent with the highlights in the passage. The sentence as written discusses *a group of unfortunate fantails*; keep (A). Choices (B), (C), and (D) do not talk about the Indian fantail; instead, they focus on the pythons. This is inconsistent with the goal of the sentence and the content of the paragraph; eliminate those answers. The correct answer is (A).

MATH

First off, you'll still need to bring your calculator to the ACT Online Test—which is a good thing! You're already comfortable with your personal calculator, so there will be one less thing to worry about on the day of the test. The online version of the ACT will have a built-in calculator. Try to practice with that before test day to see what it can do.

> **Write It Down!**
> It is tempting to do all your work in your head. Don't fall into this trap! It's easier to make mistakes when you're not writing down your work, and you'll often have to "go back" if you don't have something written down. Use your scratch paper or whiteboard!

When choosing questions to do Later, flag the question so you can easily navigate back to it after doing your Now questions. Do put in a guess answer when doing so; you don't want to accidentally leave a question blank! When there are five minutes remaining, finish the question you're working on, flag it (so you can find your spot easily), and then put in a guess for every unanswered question. Then you can go back to working until time runs out.

Use the Highlighter tool to highlight what the question is actually asking, especially in Word Problems. Of course, you'll want to use your scratch paper or whiteboard when working the steps of a math problem (don't do the work in your head!).

ACT Online Geometry Basic Approach

Because you can't write on the screen, the Basic Approach for Geometry questions needs a few slight tweaks:

1. Draw the figure on your scratch paper or whiteboard (copy if it's provided; draw it yourself otherwise). If the figure would be better drawn differently from the way ACT has drawn it (for instance, a similar triangles question), redraw the figure in a way that will help you answer the question.

2. Label the figure you drew with the information from both ACT's figure and the question.

3. Write down any formulas you need and fill in the information you know.

Let's see how that works on a question.

In the figure shown, triangle *ABC* is similar to triangle *DEF* with *B* corresponding to *E* and *C* corresponding to *F*. What is the length of *EF* ?

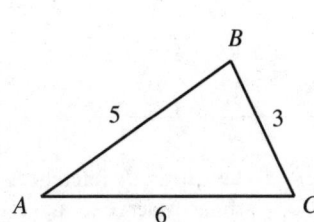

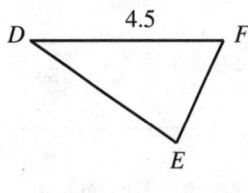

○ **A.** 1.5
○ **B.** 2.25
○ **C.** 3
○ **D.** 4

Here's How to Crack It

The question asks for the length of *EF*, so highlight that in the question. Follow the Geometry Basic Approach. Start by drawing the figure on your scratch paper or whiteboard. Because the triangles are similar, redraw triangle *DEF* to be oriented the same way as *ABC*. Label your figure with the given information.

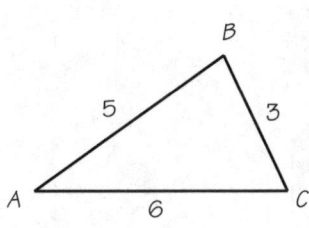

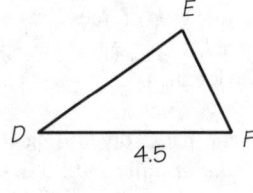

Write down the equation you need and fill in the necessary information. *AC* corresponds to *DF*, and *BC* corresponds to *EF*. Set up a proportion: $\dfrac{AC}{DF} = \dfrac{BC}{EF}$. Fill in the information from your figure: $\dfrac{6}{4.5} = \dfrac{3}{x}$, where *x* is equal to *EF*. Cross-multiply to get $6x = 3(4.5)$, or $6x = 13.5$. Divide both sides by 6 to get $x = 2.25$. The correct answer is (B).

READING

First off, there are a few differences between the pencil-and-paper ACT and the ACT Online Test. In the ACT Online Test, there are no line references; rather, the relevant part of the text is highlighted. The passage will also "jump" to the highlighted text if it's off the screen when you go to that question. This may disorient you at first: be prepared for this to happen.

Let's see an example.

...protested every step. We could still run, but, Hook worried, for how long? In a cross-country race, only a team's top five runners score, and we weren't those five. Our job was to finish ahead of as many of our rival teams' top fives as we could.

Leah was a senior that year, my freshman year. All season, she'd been counting down to this last race, praying her body wouldn't say *No*. She and I joked that we needed to go to the Knee Store and pick out new knees, ones that wouldn't crack and pop and burn all the time. It was hard to watch a teammate in that much pain, but Leah was a trooper, never slacking from workouts, never stopping to walk, never losing sight of the next person in front of her to catch.

The crack of the starter's pistol sent us surging out of that little crop of trees and onto the race course. I hollered, "See you at the Knee Store!" Behind me, she laughed.

The pack stayed tight through the first quarter-mile, and I was surrounded by so many bodies I couldn't think. I just ran, putting one foot in front of the other, trying not to fall. Trying to look beyond the jostling mass surrounding me, I could barely...

The narrator's references to the Knee Store primarily serve to suggest that:

- **A.** Leah wishes to buy better knee supports.
- **B.** the narrator and Leah use humor to cope with their pain.
- **C.** the narrator desires to learn more about her injury.
- **D.** Leah's injuries, unlike the narrator's, have become unbearable.

Reading on a computer screen can be disorienting. Make sure to do at least some of your practice online.

Here's How to Crack It

The question asks what the *references to the Knee Store...suggest*. The references to the *Knee Store* are highlighted in the text. Note that the text has shifted down to the highlighted portions. The window indicates that Leah and the narrator *joked that we needed to go to the Knee Store*. Leah *laughed* after the narrator referred to the Knee Store. Therefore, the answer should be consistent with joking and laughing. Choice (A) takes the reference too literally; eliminate (A). "Humor" is consistent with the text's references to *joked* and *laughed*; keep (B). There's no indication of the narrator's goal to *learn more about her injury*, nor does the text support the idea that Leah's injuries *have become unbearable*, eliminate (C) and (D). The correct answer is (B).

When you have five minutes remaining, flag your current question and use the Index tool to make sure you've put in guesses for any questions that you haven't done. Then return to your spot and work until time runs out. If you've just started or finished a passage, click through the questions to look for Easy to Find questions in the remaining time, and don't forget to put in guesses for any question you don't answer!

The biggest difference between the ACT Online Test and the paper-and-pencil ACT is that you can only see one question on the screen at a time. Rather than looking over the questions at a glance, you must click from question to question. This feature means that the Reading Basic Approach (covered below) needs to be modified in order to be as time efficient as possible.

ACT Online Reading Basic Approach

1. **Preview**
    Read only the blurb—do not go through and map the questions. Instead, write the question numbers on your scratch paper or whiteboard to prepare to Work the Passage.

2. **Work the Passage**
    This step is *even more* optional on the ACT Online Test than on the pencil-and-paper ACT. You haven't mapped the questions, and your highlights only show up on one question. If you do decide to Work the Passage, ensure that you're getting through the passage in 2–3 minutes. More likely, you'll find it best to just skip this step and move on to the questions after reading the blurb and setting up your whiteboard.

> You don't get points for reading—only for answering questions correctly. Determine whether Working the Passage helps you answer questions correctly and quickly.

3. **Select and Understand a Question**
    When Selecting a Question, if a question is Easy to Find (a portion of the text is highlighted or you Worked the Passage and know where in the passage the content you need is), do it Now. Understand the question, and then move on to Step 4. If the question is not Easy to Find (in other words, you don't immediately know where in the passage to go), write down the question's lead words on your whiteboard, next to the question number. Include EXCEPT/LEAST/NOT if the question includes those words. If there are no lead words, flag the question.

    After you do all the questions with highlights, then Work the Passage, scanning actively for your lead words. Once you find a lead word, do the corresponding question. After answering the questions with lead words, finish with the flagged questions.

4. **Read What You Need**
    Find the 5–10 lines you need to answer the question. Remember that only the quotation will be highlighted—the answer is not necessarily highlighted. You must read the lines before and after the highlighted portion to ensure that you find the correct answer to the question. If you find the Line Mask tool helpful, use it to frame your window.

5. **Predict the Correct Answer**

As you read, look for evidence for the answer to the question in your window and highlight it using the highlighter tool. (You can highlight text that ACT has already highlighted—the color will change to "your" highlighting color.) As always, base your prediction on the words in the passage as much as possible.

6. **Use POE**

Use the Answer Eliminator tool to narrow the answer choices down to one answer. If the question is an EXCEPT/LEAST/NOT question, instead write ABCD on your whiteboard and mark each answer T or F for True or False (or Y or N for Yes or No) and choose the odd one out.

Dual Reading Approach

The questions for Dual Reading passages usually start with the questions about Passage A, then those about Passage B, then those about both passages. Each question should include an indicator for the passage the question refers to. Work each passage separately, answering all the Passage A questions you plan to answer before moving on to the Passage B questions.

You should also write down the main idea of each passage on your scratch paper or whiteboard —either after Working the Passage or after finishing the questions on that passage. That will aid you in answering the questions about both passages.

SCIENCE

The overall approach to the Science Test is the same on the ACT Online Test as it is on the traditional pencil-and-paper version. There are a few small adjustments to make, but the overall strategy remains the same.

The Flag tool is very important when identifying Later passages and questions. On a Later passage, flag the first question, then put a guess answer for every question on the passage. Make a note on your scratch paper or whiteboard of the first question in the passage so that you can easily jump back to the passage.

When working a Now passage, you may still encounter a Later question. For these stand-alone Later questions, flag the question but don't put in an answer. When you get to the end of a passage, check the Index on the right side of the screen to make sure you have answered every question up to that point.

Science Basic Approach

There are a few small changes to the Science approach when taking the ACT Online Test.

1. **Work the Figures**

You can't highlight the figures. Experiment with taking quick notes about the variables, units, and trends on your scratch paper or whiteboard and determine whether it helps you find the needed information quickly.

2. **Work the Questions**

Highlight the words and phrases from the figures in the question to help guide you to the relevant information.

3. **Work the Answers**

Use the Answer Eliminator tool to work POE on answer choices with multiple parts.

Let's look at an example.

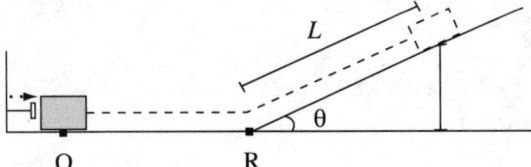

A block is placed on a frictionless horizontal surface at point Q. The block is pushed with a plunger and given initial velocity v along the horizontal surface. At point R, the block slides up a ramp with coefficient of friction f to a maximum distance L along the ramp. The distance between points Q and R is 1.0 m.

Figure 1

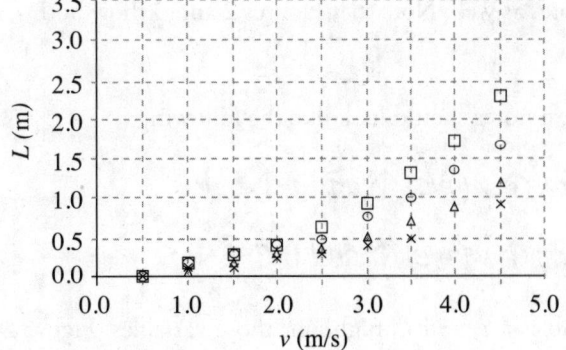

Figure 2, below, shows how L varies with v for different f on a ramp with $\theta = 20°$. Figure 3 (on the following page) shows how L varies with v for different θ on a ramp with $f = 0.1$.

Figure 2

Key	
Marker	f
□	0.15
○	0.30
△	0.60
×	0.90

Scrolling Passages
Most passages in Science will require scrolling down to see all the figures. Look for a scroll bar for every passage!

Figure 3

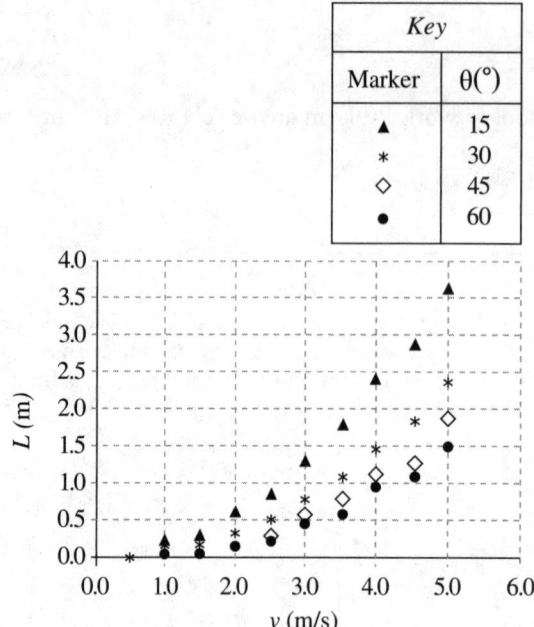

Key	
Marker	θ(°)
▲	15
✳	30
◇	45
●	60

If $f = 0.90$ for the sliding block and $v = 5.5$ m/s, L will most likely be closest to which of the following?

- **A.** 0.3 m
- **B.** 0.7 m
- **C.** 1.5 m
- **D.** 3.0 m

Here's How to Crack It

Start by Working the Figures. Figure 1 shows the points Q and R and variables L and θ, but there are no numbers or trends. Figure 2 shows a direct relationship between L (m) and v (m/s); mark this on your scratch paper or whiteboard. Furthermore, the legend gives values of f; as f increases, L decreases. Mark these relationships on your notes. Figure 3 also shows a direct relationship between L (m) and v (m/s); the legend, however, gives θ (°). As θ increases, L decreases. Put these on your notes as well. Note that Figures 2 and 3 show both L and v; Figure 2 has f, whereas Figure 3 has θ.

Your scratch paper or whiteboard notes should look like the following:

Figure 2: L (m) ↑ v (m/s) ↑ and f ↑ L ↓

Figure 3: L (m) ↑ v (m/s) ↑ and θ ↑ L ↓

The question refers to the variables f, v, and L; highlight those variables. Figure 2 has all three variables. The highest value of v given in the figure is 4.5, so start there and use the trend to make a prediction about a v of 5.5. At $v = 4.5$ and $f = 0.90$, L is approximately 0.9. The trend is increasing, so a v of 5.5 must result in an L value of greater than 0.9; eliminate (A) and (B).

An *L* value of 3.0 would be higher than any value already in Figure 2, and extending the trend for the line created by the f = 0.90 marks would not result in L increasing to 3.0 by the time v reaches 5.5; eliminate (D). Although you can't physically extend the line because it's on a computer screen, it may be a good idea to use your finger or the edge of your scratch paper to trace where you would draw on the screen. The correct answer is (C).

You'll still approach the passage that's all or mostly text as if it is a Reading passage. Unlike in Reading, you will want to Map the Questions during the Preview step, as there will not be a group of questions about each passage like there is in the Dual Reading passage. Instead, the questions will not be asked in any particular order, so use your scratch paper or whiteboard to map out which scientist(s) or experiment(s) each question refers to. As with the other sections, at the five-minute warning, flag your question, put in your guess answers on any unanswered question, and then keep working until time runs out.

WRITING

As you have probably guessed, you'll be typing the Writing Test on the ACT Online Test. But before we get to writing the essay, there are a few minor points to note about the format of this test on the computer.

First, you may not be able to highlight when Working the Prompt or Perspectives, so be sure to write notes on your scratch paper or whiteboard. Second, in the past, ACT has given the prompt and perspectives on one screen, then repeated them on the screen that contains a text box. If this is the case, feel free to do your work on the screen within the text box. If you're used to making your essay outlines on a computer, you can use the text box to do so here, as long as you remember to delete any notes before the section comes to an end.

When writing the essay, all the same points apply to both the pencil-and-paper and online tests (have a clear thesis, make and organize your arguments in a way that is easy to follow, etc.). When you have 5 minutes left, quickly type up a conclusion paragraph (if you haven't already), and then go back and finish up your body paragraph ideas. It's more important to have a conclusion than it is to have perfect body paragraphs. Finally, spend a minute or two at the end to quickly fix any obvious typos or grammatical issues.

When you practice the Writing Test at home, type your essay in a word processing program instead of writing it by hand. Be sure to turn off spell check, as the ACT may not provide it, so you don't want to rely on it.

That's it! Everything you've learned for the pencil-and-paper ACT can be applied to the ACT Online Test with a few small tweaks. You've got this!

Test 1

This practice ACT is provided in two formats: pencil-and-paper and digital. To take the digital version, see page x for instructions on how to access your online content, which also includes Test 2.

Note: some style elements in this test—and the drills that follow—may differ slightly from those you'll encounter on test day. These are superficial discrepancies that should not affect your test-taking experience.

Please turn to page 75 to find the bubble sheet for this test.

ENGLISH TEST
35 Minutes—50 Questions

DIRECTIONS: In the passages that follow, certain words and phrases are underlined and numbered. In the right-hand column, you will find alternatives for the underlined part. You are to choose the best answer to each question. If you think the original version is best, choose "**No Change.**"

You will also find questions about a section of the passage, or about the passage as a whole. These questions do not refer to an underlined portion of the passage, but rather are identified by a number or numbers in a box.

For each question, choose the alternative you consider best and fill in the corresponding oval on your answer document. Read each passage through once before you begin to answer the questions that accompany it. For many of the questions, you must read several sentences beyond the question to determine the answer. Be sure that you have read far enough ahead each time you choose an alternative.

PASSAGE I

Apay'uq Moore's Artistic Celebration of Yup'ik Culture

When Yup'ik artist Apay'uq Moore, inspired by her desire to protect her Alaskan homeland from an invasive mining operation, created her first acrylic on canvas paintings in 2001, many people advised her that a career in art was <u>impactful.</u> However, painting colorful depictions of the Yup'ik way of life

1. The writer wants to emphasize the negative reaction that many people had toward Moore's career aspirations. Which choice best accomplishes that goal?
   - **A. No Change**
   - **B.** dynamic.
   - **C.** transformative.
   - **D.** impractical.

<u>are allowing</u> Moore to establish herself as a successful artist. By

2. Which choice makes the sentence most grammatically acceptable?
   - **F. No Change**
   - **G.** allow
   - **H.** has allowed
   - **J.** have allowed

infusing her art with her deep <u>connection to her heritage that she is strongly linked to,</u> Moore has also become a prominent cultural ambassador for her people.

3. Which choice is least redundant in context?
   - **A. No Change**
   - **B.** connection to her heritage,
   - **C.** connecting link to her heritage,
   - **D.** connection to her and her ancestors' heritage,

GO ON TO THE NEXT PAGE.

Later, Moore gained notoriety for her canvas work, she
——
4
extended her creative reach by painting large murals. Viewed
by many people, her murals, which depict powerful imagery
of traditional activities alongside stunning Alaskan landscapes,

have represented her commitment to showcasing the beauty
                                     ——————
                                        5
and vitality of her heritage. Through these public works, Moore
captures the spirit of the Yup'ik way of life in a way that reso-
nates deeply with viewers, fostering a greater understanding and
appreciation of her culture.

Indeed, Moore's stylistic representations often pay homage
——
                                        6
to other famous Indigenous artists. As a committed sustenance
————————————————————————
           6
fisher herself, she honors the importance of salmon to her
people's survival and identity. In her dynamic art, she often portrays scenes of the arduous life cycle of salmon. Upon returning

to freshwater after years in the ocean, the females lay eggs in its
                                          ———————————————————
                                                  7
own location of birth. Through such depictions, Moore highlights the challenges of sustaining longstanding salmon fishing

traditions, incorporating her distinctive vibrant color schemes,
—————————————————
        8
to celebrate the resilience of the Yup'ik people.

Through her passion for art, Apay'uq Moore stays at
                                              ————————
                                                 9
pushing awareness of Yup'ik culture and the unique landscapes
———————
   9
of Alaska. Her work invites viewers to connect with the values

4. Which choice makes the sentence most grammatically
   acceptable?
   F. **No Change**
   G. After
   H. Within a few years,
   J. **Delete** the underlined text.

5. Which choice is clearest and most precise in context?
   A. **No Change**
   B. justifying
   C. exaggerating
   D. vilifying

6. Given that all the choices are accurate, which one provides
   the best transition from the preceding paragraph to this
   paragraph?
   F. **No Change**
   G. Besides her colorful paintings and murals, Moore has
      occasionally designed logos, hats, and even T-shirts.
   H. Complementing her portrayals of nature, Moore is also
      an advocate for traditional Yup'ik subsistence fishing.
   J. Moore's commitment to educating others about the
      practices and beliefs of her ancestors is extraordinary.

7. Which choice makes the sentence most grammatically
   acceptable?
   A. **No Change**
   B. female lay eggs in it's
   C. female lays eggs in their
   D. female lays eggs in its

8. Which choice makes the sentence most grammatically
   acceptable?
   F. **No Change**
   G. traditions who incorporate
   H. traditions, which incorporate
   J. traditions that incorporate

9. Which choice most effectively maintains the essay's tone?
   A. **No Change**
   B. keeps on blowing up
   C. persists in showing off
   D. continues to expand

GO ON TO THE NEXT PAGE.

of her people—for example, the importance of community and
the harmony between humans and nature—while preserving
Yup'ik traditions in visual form.

10. Which choice makes the sentence most grammatically
acceptable?

F. **No Change**
G. people for example, the importance of community,
H. people, for example, the importance of community
J. people for example—the importance of community

Trota: A Myth No More

The *Trotula*, a collection of medical texts, was consulted
by doctors for centuries. Published in the Italian city of Salerno,
home of the most renowned medical school in Medieval Europe,
the work covers mainly gynecology and obstetrics. Its name
comes from Trota of Salerno and, it turns out, she was a physician
cited in one of the texts as a famous authority on these subjects.

11. Which choice makes the sentence most grammatically
acceptable?

A. **No Change**
B. a physician from Salerno named Trota, she was
C. Trota of Salerno, a physician
D. Trota of Salerno, she was a physician

Her identity as a historical person, long doubted, by scholars
was recently re-established through textual comparison of
Trotula with other medieval medical manuscripts.

Although it is unknown when or where Trota was born,

historians now know that she studied, working in Salerno
during the 12th century. The city owed much to its location on
the Mediterranean: the same sea routes that generated wealth
from trading also carried Greek and Arabic medical books
unavailable in other parts of Western Europe. This unique
access to accumulated knowledge helped Salerno's medical

12. Which choice makes the sentence most grammatically
acceptable?

F. **No Change**
G. doubted by scholars
H. doubted by scholars—
J. doubted by scholars,

13. Which choice best helps indicate that Trota was a medical
practitioner as well as a student?

A. **No Change**
B. worked as a student
C. studied and worked
D. studied for a job

GO ON TO THE NEXT PAGE.

school to be better than other similar establishments in the
region. For several years, Trota explored the school's extensive
collection of literature and gained professional experience

by treating the city's sick. However, she earned the title of
Magistra, or instructor, and authored a textbook on practical
medicine.

Despite her accomplishments and fame, Trota faded from
history—but not forever.

14. Which choice most effectively maintains the essay's tone?

  F. **No Change**
  G. tower above
  H. stay ahead of the pack of
  J. surpass

15. Which transition word or phrase is most logical in context?

  A. **No Change**
  B. Eventually,
  C. In other words,
  D. Nevertheless,

PASSAGE III

Nostalgia on Aisle 3

[1]

Every summer, we took a trip to Maine to visit family. We'd always stop at the same grocery store. I'd bring my
daughter, she would ride in the shopping cart as I steered

us around the store with so many aisles that were full of different snacks that always managed to grab her attention. Here we
are at the same store, but she isn't a kid anymore and seems
more interested in her phone, which she stares at blankly as

we walk down the cereal aisle. Glancing behind me, I see that
she's still following me, and then in the corner of my eye I
notice something bright and red. [A]

16. Which choice makes the sentence most grammatically
    acceptable?

  F. **No Change**
  G. who would ride
  H. whose ridden
  J. whom would ride

17. Which choice makes the sentence most grammatically
    acceptable?

  A. **No Change**
  B. us, around the store with so many aisles that were,
  C. us around the store with so many aisles, that were,
  D. us around the store, with so many aisles that were

18. Which choice is least redundant in context?

  F. **No Change**
  G. see that she's still following me, more interested
     in looking at her phone than shopping,
  H. look down the cereal aisle and see that she's still
     following me,
  J. can see that she's no longer a kid, though she is
     still trailing behind me,

GO ON TO THE NEXT PAGE.

[2]

A package of dyed-red hot dogs <u>radiate</u> brightly from the
₁₉
shelf. My daughter and I used to laugh so much at these "red
snapper" hot dogs. [B] I have heard a couple of different explanations for how this practice of dyeing hot dogs started. One
story says it was as a marketing tactic to make the hot dogs
more eye-catching—<u>another involves color-coding foods that
were nearing their expiration date.</u> My daughter used to say
₂₀
that they were painted that way so that they wouldn't get lost

as easily. <u>In addition,</u> I prefer her version.
₂₁

[3]

When I hold up the hot dogs, I see the excited recognition

light up her eyes as she <u>sees our old favorite food that she
recognizes.</u> She starts filming the hot dogs with her phone,
₂₂
explaining the mystery of the food's color. [C] She pretends
to interview me and asks me why they are red. Holding up the
hot dogs as a pretend microphone, I answer her questions. [D] I
sometimes feel I can't keep up with how fast time is passing,
but <u>here in this moment, as we relive those summers past, I feel
time slow down a bit.</u>
₂₃

[4]

Time still does pass. With every year, I feel like things are
changing faster and faster. As I look at my daughter about to
start her third year of college, I can hardly believe how different
our lives look now. But some things—like our jokes about a hot

19. Which choice makes the sentence most grammatically acceptable?

A. No Change
B. shines
C. have radiated
D. shine

20. If the writer were to delete the underlined text (adjusting the punctuation as needed), the paragraph would primarily lose:

F. details that indicate what color the hot dogs are.
G. details about the process of dyeing hot dogs.
H. information that reveals the narrator's feelings about the hot dogs.
J. information about an alternative explanation for the origin of the red hot dogs.

21. Which transition word or phrase is most logical in context?

A. No Change
B. As stated,
C. In summary,
D. Needless to say,

22. Which choice is least redundant in context?

F. No Change
G. glimpses our old favorite food.
H. excitedly notices that I am holding our old favorite food item.
J. recognizes that I am showing her the bright red hot dogs.

23. Given that all the choices are accurate, which one most effectively leads into the rest of the essay?

A. No Change
B. many other shoppers look over at us and laugh along with the impromptu play.
C. she and I still have several more items to find in other parts of the store.
D. we have not yet determined for certain the true reason behind the hot dogs' bright red color.

GO ON TO THE NEXT PAGE.

dog with a funny hue—have stayed the same. [24]

24. At this point, the writer is considering adding the following accurate sentence:

> Maine is not the only state in the country that has bright red hot dogs.

Should the writer make this addition?

F. Yes, because it reveals that the hot dogs at the grocery store are not unique.
G. Yes, because it makes clear that the narrator knows more information about the hot dogs.
H. No, because it fails to say which other states have bright red hot dogs.
J. No, because it draws the focus away from the narrator's reflections on the passage of time.

Question 25 asks about the preceding passage as a whole.

---

25. The writer wants to add the following sentence to the essay:

> Why were they bright red?

The sentence would most logically be placed at:

A. Point A in Paragraph 1.
B. Point B in Paragraph 2.
C. Point C in Paragraph 3.
D. Point D in Paragraph 3.

PASSAGE IV

The End of Late Fines

[1]

Public libraries provide a valuable service by letting community members borrow books and other media. [A] In an attempt to make sure that the items are returned, many libraries have a late fee system. If an item isn't returned by the due date, a small amount of money is charged each day the item is overdue.

26. Which choice is clearest and most precise in context?

F. **No Change**
G. Since
H. Although
J. While

GO ON TO THE NEXT PAGE.

A late fine <u>such that</u> may be a small amount of money can lead
to the suspension of a person's library account. [B] While

libraries <u>want, and need</u> people to return items, libraries also
seek to combat social inequity by removing barriers to access.

[2]

In an attempt to increase accessibility, several libraries over
the years have temporarily suspended or completely eliminated
library fines. The late fine was eliminated in part due to the
disproportionate <u>affect it has</u> on community members who live
in low-income neighborhoods. Youth and families in particular
are impacted by the financial penalties. When libraries have
gone fine-free, patrons who hadn't used these libraries for years

started visiting again. [C] <u>Since eliminating</u> late fines for overdue items has also led to an increase in library card signups and
annual renewals.

[3]

Late fines were originally implemented because people
thought that there needed to be a consequence for not returning
library items. The belief was that people would not be motivated
to return library items without a monetary punishment.
<u>Surprisingly,</u> many libraries that ran amnesty campaigns

<u>(when library fees are forgiven)</u> or ended late fines altogether

27. Which choice makes the sentence most grammatically
acceptable?

  A. **No Change**
  B. that
  C. when it
  D. **Delete** the underlined text.

28. Which choice makes the sentence most grammatically
acceptable?

  F. **No Change**
  G. want and, need
  H. want—and need—
  J. want and need—

29. Which choice makes the sentence most grammatically
acceptable?

  A. **No Change**
  B. affect they have
  C. effect they have
  D. effect it has

30. Which choice makes the sentence most grammatically
acceptable?

  F. **No Change**
  G. Eliminating
  H. Following the elimination of
  J. By eliminating

31. Which transition word is most logical in context?

  A. **No Change**
  B. Obviously,
  C. Specifically,
  D. Fittingly,

32. If the writer were to delete the underlined text, the essay
would primarily lose:

  F. an argument for libraries to end late fines.
  G. an example of an amnesty campaign run by a library.
  H. a description of the types of library fines forgiven.
  J. an explanation of what an amnesty campaign is.

GO ON TO THE NEXT PAGE.

have had high rates of returned items. [D] There are still consequences if people do not return the library's items 33 .

[4]

While not every public library has eliminated late fines,
those that have done so are encouraging more people from their
communities to use the resources these libraries offer. This is
important because a library's services go beyond the materials it
lends out: many

libraries, which offer support for daily living and job-searching,
such as skill classes and access to the internet.

33. At this point, the writer is considering adding the following parenthetical phrase:

(such as temporary account suspension or replacement fees for lost items)

Given that the information is accurate, should the writer make this addition here?

A. Yes, because it gives specific examples of items that are returned late.
B. Yes, because it provides more details about the consequences of not returning items.
C. No, because it overshadows the positive changes that libraries have made.
D. No, because it is irrelevant to the paragraph's focus on the community impacts of late fines.

34. Which choice makes the sentence most grammatically acceptable?

F. **No Change**
G. libraries, offering
H. libraries offer
J. libraries make offering

Question 35 asks about the preceding passage as a whole.

35. The writer wants to add the following sentence to the essay:

This consequence may make people less likely to use the library.

For the sake of logic and cohesion, the sentence should be placed at:

A. Point A in Paragraph 1.
B. Point B in Paragraph 1.
C. Point C in Paragraph 2.
D. Point D in Paragraph 3.

GO ON TO THE NEXT PAGE.

PASSAGE V

The Venus Flytrap's Unique Feeding Habits

Native to the East Coast of the United States, the Venus flytrap (*Dionaea muscipula*) is an insect- and arachnid-eating plant that preys on its victims using a surprising mechanism.
36

The plant's unique morphology—including hinged leaves and trigger hairs—allows the plant to act more predatorial than other plant species. 37 The carnivorous plant's leaves serve as "jaws," which can vary from approximately one to four inches in length, that can be triggered to shut in as little as one-tenth of a second when prey lands on sensitive trigger hairs.

The precise deployment of the Venus flytrap's jaws requires two distinct stimulations of trigger hairs, which perform

similarly to human reflexes. The plant operates the mechanism
38
by registering that prey is touching a trigger hair,

then waits for a second trigger hair to be activated, and
39
snapping shut to trap the prey. This multi-step process avoids triggering the trap for dust or other non-edible particles, which would waste valuable energy. The trap is sprung via a generated action potential involving calcium ions, which is similar to the

36. Which choice makes the sentence most grammatically acceptable?

   F. **No Change**
   G. on they're
   H. as if on it's
   J. on it's

37. If the writer were to delete the phrase "including hinged leaves and trigger hairs" from the preceding sentence (adjusting the punctuation as needed), the sentence would primarily lose:

   A. general facts that clarify the type of prey the Venus flytraps hunt.
   B. general facts that describe the exact mechanism of the Venus flytrap's trap.
   C. specific details that identify some of the unusual morphological features of the plant.
   D. specific details that explain the speed of the Venus flytrap's reflexes.

38. The writer wants to illustrate the mechanism of the trigger hairs by making a technical comparison to a specific feature of human anatomy. Which choice best accomplishes this goal?

   F. **No Change**
   G. a mouth chomping on a burger.
   H. highly sensitive nerve receptors in human skin.
   J. muscles stressing out.

39. Which choice makes the sentence most grammatically acceptable?

   A. **No Change**
   B. it waits
   C. to wait
   D. waiting

GO ON TO THE NEXT PAGE.

process that allows a human to reflexively <u>recoil when touching</u>[40]
<u>something hot or sharp.</u>[40]

The unique hunting method of the Venus flytrap can be compared to snap traps often used for pest control. These traps deploy a snapping mechanism very quickly to ensnare and contain a rodent.

40. Which choice is least redundant in context?

F. **No Change**
G. respond when touching something hot or sharp and react to the pain.
H. recoil involuntarily from the pain of touching something too hot or sharp.
J. activate the pain reflex automatically after touching something hot or sharp.

PASSAGE VI

Sharing Uyghur Culture Through Food

On a chilly evening in Arlington, Virginia, diners tuck in to <u>prepared</u>[41] noodles with colorful vegetables, steamed dumplings stuffed with beef and pumpkin, and <u>something with eggplant.</u>[42] For some, the experience is nothing more than a hot meal after a long day. For the local Uyghur immigrant population, however, dining at Bostan is comforting and nostalgic—and even political. The restaurant's owner, Mirzat Salam, came to the United States <u>(a Turkic ethnic minority group of the Xinjiang</u>[43] <u>region in Northwest China)</u>[43] as an asylum-seeker when the Chinese government began imprisoning Uyghurs in a purported effort to assimilate them into mainstream Chinese culture. At Bostan, Uyghurs like Salam who have fled to the United States can find community and preserve the culture that is imperiled at home.

41. The writer is considering revising the underlined text to the following:

> hand-pulled

Should the writer make this revision?

A. Yes, because the revision emphasizes the chef's desire to minimize food costs by preparing food manually.
B. Yes, because the revision introduces the idea that the food has been made with special care.
C. No, because the original word more specifically describes the type of noodles served at the restaurant.
D. No, because the original word reinforces the idea that although the noodles have been made by the restaurant, they may not be made to order.

42. Which choice best maintains the stylistic pattern of descriptions established earlier in the sentence?

F. **No Change**
G. spicy eggplant salad.
H. some salad.
J. eggplant salad that has been served.

43. The best placement for the underlined text would be:

A. where it is now.
B. after the word *asylum-seeker*.
C. after the word *government*.
D. after the word *Uyghurs*.

GO ON TO THE NEXT PAGE.

Uyghur cuisine bears a resemblance to Turkish, Chinese, and Middle Eastern food, given that the Uyghurs were once a nomadic people, traveled throughout Asia and eventually
₄₄

adopted the religion of Islam. In traditional Uyghur medicine, a specific diet is recommended depending on an individual's age
₄₅
and nature. With some of the most common dishes being lamb
₄₅
or beef kebabs, roasted mutton, and a chicken dish called *polo*,

Uyghur dishes tend to be spicy. Noodles are also common,
₄₆
and the cooks at Bostan prepare five different types by hand. Long, round noodles are featured in *lagmen*, one of the most traditional Uyghur dishes, which also includes stir-fry meat and

vegetables and can be an hours-long process to make.
₄₇

Salam never planned to become a restaurateur. For example,
₄₈
he actually attended medical school in Xinjiang. Now, though,
₄₈
he's proud of his contribution to his new country and recognizes the importance of providing a gathering place for people who

44. Which choice makes the sentence most grammatically acceptable?

F. **No Change**
G. people of whom
H. people who
J. people in which

45. The writer is considering deleting the underlined sentence. Should the sentence be kept or deleted?

A. Kept, because it provides additional context for why certain components of the cuisine are used.
B. Kept, because it compares traditional Uyghur medical practices with modern ones.
C. Deleted, because it adds a detail that is irrelevant to the paragraph's focus on the elements of Uyghur cuisine.
D. Deleted, because it detracts from the paragraph's exploration of the various types of Eurasian cuisines.

46. Which choice most clearly builds on the information provided earlier in the sentence about common elements of Uyghur dishes?

F. **No Change**
G. Uyghurs usually eat at home rather than at restaurants.
H. Uyghur food is more suitable for meat-eaters than for vegetarians.
J. Uyghur dishes are often prepared by experienced chefs.

47. Which choice makes the sentence most grammatically acceptable?

A. **No Change**
B. hour's-longest
C. hour's-long
D. hours'-long

48. Which transition word or phrase, if any, is most logical in context?

F. **No Change**
G. Consequently, he
H. He
J. On the other hand, he

GO ON TO THE NEXT PAGE.

may never be able to return <u>to their homeland.</u>
₄₉

49. Which choice makes the sentence most grammatically acceptable?

  A. **No Change**
  B. to that place.
  C. there.
  D. to it.

[50] Salam is not only bringing together members of his community but also increasing awareness of Uyghur culture among people who may not otherwise have been exposed to it.

50. Which of the following true statements, if added here, would best build on the ideas presented in this paragraph and connect to the final sentence of the essay?

  F. Salam plays traditional Uyghur music in his restaurant to accompany the traditional menu.
  G. For Uyghurs, having a place to meet others from the same cultural background makes adjusting to a new country easier.
  H. Salam first cooked food in another Uyghur restaurant in Fairfax, Virginia, before opening his own restaurant.
  J. At Bostan, non-Uyghurs can become acquainted with Uyghur culture and educate themselves on the treatment of Uyghurs in Xinjiang.

END OF TEST 1
STOP! DO NOT TURN THE PAGE UNTIL TOLD TO DO SO.

MATHEMATICS TEST
50 Minutes—45 Questions

DIRECTIONS: Solve each problem, choose the correct answer, and then fill in the corresponding oval on your answer document.

Do not linger over problems that take too much time. Solve as many as you can; then return to the others in the time you have left for this test.

You are permitted to use a calculator on this test. You may use your calculator for any problems you choose, but some of the problems may best be done without using a calculator.

Note: Unless otherwise stated, all of the following should be assumed:

1. Illustrative figures are **not** necessarily drawn to scale.
2. Geometric figures lie in a plane.
3. The word "line" indicates a straight line.
4. The word "average" indicates arithmetic mean.

1. In an elite marathon runner's training, total mileage consists of miles run at or faster than marathon pace and miles run slower than marathon pace. The table shows miles run at or faster than marathon pace and total mileage for an elite marathon runner for each of 3 consecutive years.

Running at or faster than marathon pace			
Year	# Runs	Total miles	Miles/Month
2002	294	2,645	220.4
2003	179	1,614	134.5
2004	128	1,150	95.8
Total mileage			
Year	Total runs	Total miles	Miles/Month
2002	414	3,725	310.4
2003	458	4,122	343.5
2004	554	4,982	415.2

In 2004, how many miles of the runner's total mileage were miles run slower than marathon pace?

A. 1,012
B. 2,972
C. 3,832
D. 3,850

2. A 24-hour day is how many times as long as 60 seconds?

F. 30
G. 365
H. 720
J. 1,440

DO YOUR FIGURING HERE.

GO ON TO THE NEXT PAGE.

DO YOUR FIGURING HERE.

3. A student reads a pages per day for d days and then reads b pages per day for $2d$ days. In terms of a, b, and d, how many pages did the student read?

  A. $ad + 2b$
  B. $ad + 2bd$
  C. $2ad + 2bd$
  D. $2abd^2$

4. The graph shows the number of people visiting a museum during the first 5 months of the year. How many people need to visit the museum during June for the mean of the first 6 months to equal the mean of the first 5 months?

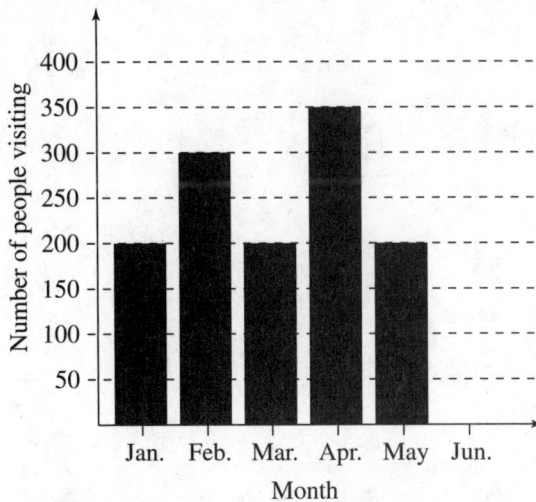

  F.   0
  G. 200
  H. 250
  J. 500

5. A graduation cap is tossed upward. It is f feet above the ground s seconds after it has been thrown. The relationship between f and s is given by the equation $f = 60s - 17s^2$, where $0 \le s \le 3.5$. How many feet above the ground is the cap 3 seconds after it is thrown?

  A.   27
  B.   41
  C.   80
  D. 163

GO ON TO THE NEXT PAGE.

6. The highest and lowest test scores of five students in Mr. Canyon's science class are listed in the chart. Which student had the greatest range of scores?

	High	Low
Alicia	93	76
Brandon	91	79
Cleo	99	81
David	74	56
Emily	89	70

F. Alicia
G. Brandon
H. Cleo
J. Emily

7. Nita, Craig, and Chris catch a total of 300 fish on their trip. If Chris catches 45% of the fish and Craig catches 25 fish, what fraction of the 300 fish does Nita catch?

A. $\dfrac{23}{30}$

B. $\dfrac{1}{2}$

C. $\dfrac{7}{15}$

D. $\dfrac{1}{3}$

8. Given that $f(x) = 4x^2$ and $g(x) = 3 - \dfrac{x}{2}$, what is the value of $f(g(4))$?

F. 1
G. 4
H. 16
J. 64

GO ON TO THE NEXT PAGE.

DO YOUR FIGURING HERE.

9. In the grid shown, each small square has a side length of 1 unit. In the shaded region, each vertex lies on a vertex of a small square. What is the area, in square units, of the shaded region?

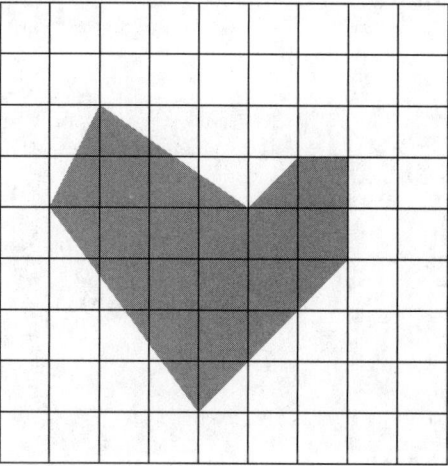

- **A.** 35
- **B.** 24
- **C.** 19
- **D.** 13

10. A ramp rises 6 inches for each 24 inches of horizontal run. This ramp rises how many inches for 62 inches of horizontal run?

- **F.** $15\frac{1}{2}$

- **G.** $20\frac{2}{3}$

- **H.** 44

- **J.** 248

11. What is the value of $y^x + (2x - 2y)$ when $x = 2$ and $y = -3$?

- **A.** 1
- **B.** 7
- **C.** 16
- **D.** 19

GO ON TO THE NEXT PAGE.

12. The day a clothing store puts out a batch of brand-name T-shirts it sells 95 shirts at $4.10 per shirt. However, each day the shirts are on the rack, the store reduces the price of the shirts by $0.02 and consequently sells 1 additional shirt with each price reduction. If x represents the number of $0.02 price reductions, which of the following expressions represents the amount of money, in dollars, that the store will take in daily in sales of these brand-name T-shirts?

F. $(4.10 - 2x)(95 + x)$
G. $(4.10 + 0.02x)(95 + x)$
H. $(4.10 - 0.02x)(95 + x)$
J. $(4.10 - 0.02x)(95 + 0.02x)$

13. The expression $x^2 - 7x + 12$ is equivalent to:

A. $(x - 4)(x - 3)$
B. $(x - 4)(x + 3)$
C. $(x - 6)(x - 2)$
D. $(x - 6)(x + 2)$

14. If $x = 5$ and $y = 2$, then $\dfrac{xy}{70} + \dfrac{9}{5(x + y)} + \dfrac{1}{x + y} = ?$

F. $\dfrac{19}{35}$

G. $\dfrac{1}{2}$

H. $\dfrac{4}{7}$

J. $\dfrac{5}{28}$

15. The minutes and seconds on a 60-minute digital timer are represented by 3 or 4 digits. What is the *largest* product that can be obtained by multiplying the digits in one of these representations?

(Note: When the timer displays 16:15, the product of the digits is $(1)(6)(1)(5) = 30$.)

A. 90
B. 2,025
C. 3,481
D. 6,561

GO ON TO THE NEXT PAGE.

16. The area of the square in the figure shown is 324 square centimeters, and the two small isosceles right triangles are congruent. What is the combined area, in square centimeters, of the two small triangles?

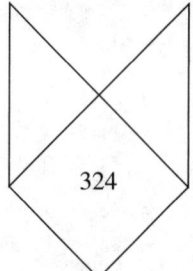

324

- **F.** 108
- **G.** 162
- **H.** 324
- **J.** 648

17. For what value of x, if any, is the equation $(x-1)^2 = (x-7)^2$ true?

- **A.** -4
- **B.** -1
- **C.** 4
- **D.** There is no value of x for which the equation is true.

18. $\triangle ABC$, shown in the standard (x,y) coordinate plane, is equilateral with vertex A at $(0,w)$ and vertex B on the x-axis as shown. What are the coordinates of vertex C?

- **F.** $(w, 2w)$
- **G.** $(w\sqrt{3}, w)$
- **H.** $(w\sqrt{3}, 2w)$
- **J.** $(2w, w\sqrt{3})$

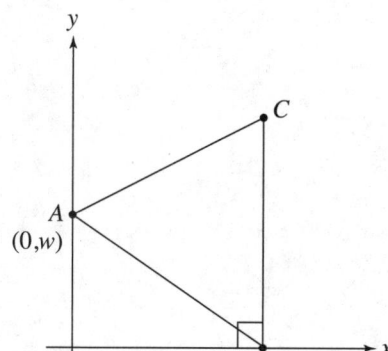

19. The diagonal of a square quilt is $4\sqrt{2}$ feet long. What is the area of the quilt in square feet?

- **A.** $16\sqrt{2}$
- **B.** 16
- **C.** $4\sqrt{2}$
- **D.** 4

GO ON TO THE NEXT PAGE.

DO YOUR FIGURING HERE.

20. A painter needs to reach the top of a tall sign in the middle of a flat and level field. He uses a ladder of length x to reach a point on the sign 15 feet above the ground. The angle formed where the ladder meets the ground is noted in the figure as θ. Which of the following relationships must be true?

   F. $\sin\theta = \dfrac{15}{x}$

   G. $\cos\theta = \dfrac{15}{x}$

   H. $\tan\theta = \dfrac{15}{x}$

   J. $\dfrac{\sin\theta}{\cos\theta} = \dfrac{15}{x}$

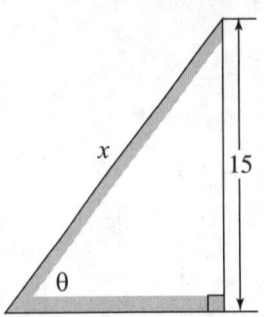

21. The equation $\sqrt{45+a} + \sqrt{a} = 15$ is true for what real value of a ?

   A. 9
   B. 25
   C. 36
   D. 64

22. Two hoses attached to separate water sources are available to fill a cylindrical swimming pool. If both hoses are used, the time it will take to fill the pool can be represented by the following equation: $\dfrac{1}{T_1} + \dfrac{1}{T_2} = \dfrac{1}{T_c}$, where T_1 and T_2 represent the time needed for hoses 1 and 2, respectively, to fill the pool on their own, and T_c represents the time needed for hoses 1 and 2 to fill the pool working together. If hose 1 alone can fill the pool in exactly 20 minutes and hose 2 alone can fill the pool in exactly 60 minutes, how many minutes will it take to fill the pool if both hoses work simultaneously?

   F. 3
   G. 10
   H. 15
   J. 18

GO ON TO THE NEXT PAGE.

DO YOUR FIGURING HERE.

23. A 5-sided die, which has sides 2, 3, 4, 5, and 6, is thrown. What is the probability that the die will NOT land on a prime-numbered face?

A. $\dfrac{4}{5}$

B. $\dfrac{3}{5}$

C. $\dfrac{2}{5}$

D. $\dfrac{1}{5}$

24. For $f(x,y) = 7x + 9y$, what is the value of $f(x,y)$ when $y = \left(\dfrac{5}{x}\right)^2$ and $x = 3$?

F. $\dfrac{68}{3}$

G. $\dfrac{214}{9}$

H. 36

J. 46

25. What is the length, in coordinate units, of a diagonal of a square in the standard (x,y) coordinate plane with vertices at points (0,0), (4,0) and (4,4) ?

A. 3

B. 4

C. $4\sqrt{2}$

D. $4\sqrt{3}$

26. What is the value of a if $\log_4 a = 3$?

F. 120

G. 64

H. $4\sqrt{3}$

J. $\sqrt[4]{3}$

GO ON TO THE NEXT PAGE.

27. A certain 18-quart stockpot is filled completely with water and exposed to a heat source so that the water boils away at a constant rate. The water remaining in the stockpot can be approximated by the following equation: $y = 18 - 0.2x$, where x is the number of minutes that the pot has been heated for $0 \le x \le 90$, and y is the number of quarts remaining in the pot. According to this equation, which of the following statements is true about this stockpot?

A. After 0.2 minutes, 1 quart of water has boiled away.
B. After 1 minute, 0.2 quarts of water has boiled away.
C. After 18 minutes, 0.2 quarts of water has boiled away.
D. After 18 minutes, 1 quart of water has boiled away.

28. The volume of a right circular cone with the bottom removed to create a flat base can be calculated with the following equation: $V = \dfrac{1}{3}\pi h(R^2 + r^2 + Rr)$, where h represents the height of the shape and R and r represent its radii, as shown in the figure:

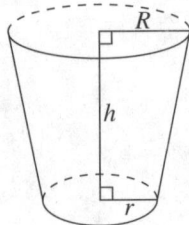

This formula can be used to determine the capacity of a large coffee mug. Approximately how many cubic inches of liquid can the cup shown hold if it is filled to the brim and its handle holds no liquid?

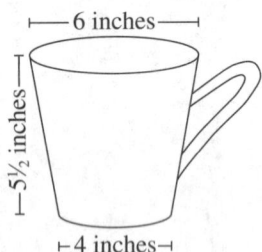

F. 19
G. 105
H. 109
J. 438

GO ON TO THE NEXT PAGE.

DO YOUR FIGURING HERE.

29. Which of the following is the set of real solutions for the equation $9x + 12 = 3(3x + 4)$?

A. The set of all real numbers

B. $\{0,1\}$

C. $\left\{-\dfrac{4}{3}\right\}$

D. The empty set

30. The expression $\dfrac{\dfrac{\dfrac{3}{4}}{\dfrac{3}{4} - \dfrac{2}{3}}}{\dfrac{3}{4} - \dfrac{2}{3} + \dfrac{1}{2}}$ equals:

F. $\dfrac{3}{28}$

G. $\dfrac{4}{21}$

H. $\dfrac{28}{3}$

J. $\dfrac{108}{7}$

31. For all nonzero real numbers a, b, and c, what is the value of $a^0 + b^0 + c^0$?

A. Undefined
B. 0
C. 1
D. 3

32. In the figure shown, $ABCD$ is a rectangle, $AB = AE$, and $E, F, G,$ and H lie on $\overline{AD}$. Of the angles BEA, BFA, BGA, BHA, and BDA, which one has the greatest tangent?

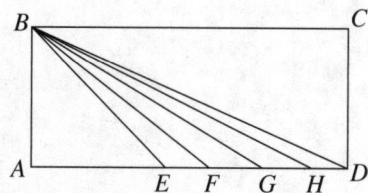

F. $\angle BEA$
G. $\angle BFA$
H. $\angle BGA$
J. $\angle BDA$

GO ON TO THE NEXT PAGE.

33. The graph of $y = f(x)$ is shown in the standard (x,y) coordinate plane.

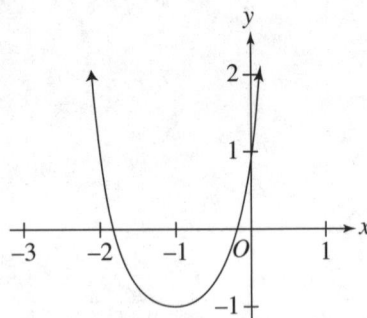

If $y = f(x)$ is to be reflected across the line $y = x$, which of the following graphs represents the result?

A.

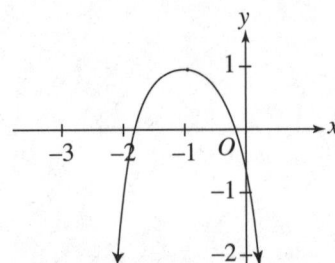

B.

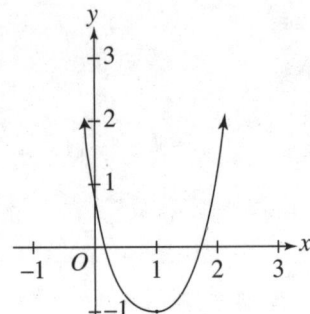

C.

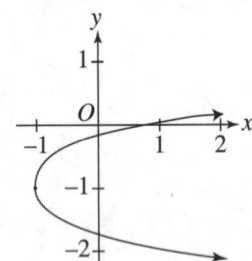

D.

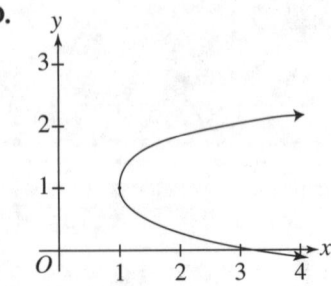

GO ON TO THE NEXT PAGE.

DO YOUR FIGURING HERE.

34. For each positive integer k, let k_o be the sum of all positive odd integers less than k. For example, $6_o = 5 + 3 + 1 = 9$ and $7_o = 5 + 3 + 1 = 9$. What is the value of $17_o \times 4_o$?

   F.   16
   G. 144
   H. 256
   J. 816

35. If $(a,-3)$ is on the graph of the equation $x - 4y = 14$ in the standard (x,y) coordinate plane, then $a = $?

   A. $-\dfrac{17}{4}$
   B. -2
   C.   2
   D. 26

36. For all $t > 1$, $f(t) = \dfrac{t^2 - 1}{t - 1} - t$. Which of the following is true about $f(t)$?

   F. It increases in proportion to t.
   G. It increases in proportion to t^2.
   H. It decreases in proportion to t.
   J. It remains constant.

37. Points $(2,-2)$ and $(3,10)$ lie on the same line in the standard (x,y) coordinate plane. What is the slope of this line?

   A. 12
   B.   8
   C. $\dfrac{1}{12}$
   D. -8

38. Which of the following gives the equation for the circle in the standard (x,y) coordinate plane with a center at $(4,-8)$ and a circumference of 10π coordinate units?

   F. $(x - 4)^2 + (y + 8)^2 = 25$
   G. $(x - 4)^2 + (y + 8)^2 = 100$
   H. $(x + 8)^2 + (y - 4)^2 = 25$
   J. $(x + 8)^2 + (y - 4)^2 = 100$

GO ON TO THE NEXT PAGE.

39. For some x and y that satisfy the equation $xy = -x^2$, which of the following is FALSE?

DO YOUR FIGURING HERE.

   A. $x\left(\dfrac{1}{y}\right) = -1$

   B. $x^2\left(\dfrac{1}{y^2}\right) = 1$

   C. $x^2 = y^2$

   D. $x^3 - y^3 = 0$

40. Rectangle $ABCD$ lies in the standard (x,y) coordinate plane with corners at $A(4,2)$, $B(6,-1)$, $C(1,-4)$, and $D(-1,-1)$, and is represented by the 2×4 matrix $\begin{bmatrix} 4 & 6 & 1 & -1 \\ 2 & -1 & -4 & -1 \end{bmatrix}$. $ABCD$ is then translated, with the corners of the translated rectangle represented by the matrix $\begin{bmatrix} 1 & 3 & -2 & -4 \\ n & -3 & -6 & -3 \end{bmatrix}$. What is the value of n ?

   F.   0
   G.   −1
   H.   −2
   J.   −3

41. Whenever $a > 0$, which of the following real number line graphs represents the solutions for x to the inequality $|x - a| \leq 3$?

   A.

        $-a-3$ $a-3$ $a+3$

   B.

        $-a-3$ $a-3$ $a+3$

   C.

        $-a-3$ $a-3$ $a+3$

   D.

        $-a-3$ $a-3$ $a+3$

GO ON TO THE NEXT PAGE.

42. Three different functions are defined in the table.

Symbol	Function	Description
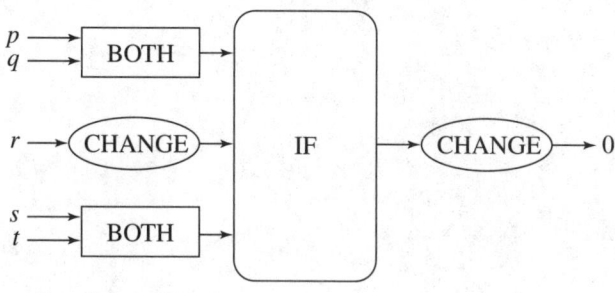 BOTH	BOTH	If both inputs are 1, the output will be 1. If both inputs are 0, the output will be 0. If both inputs are different, the output will be 0.
1st → 2nd → IF 3rd →	IF	If the first input is 1, the output will be the second input. If the first input is 0, the output will be the third input.
→ CHANGE →	CHANGE	If the input is 1, the output is 0. If the input is 0, the output is 1.

The diagram shown uses three functions. The only values for p, q, r, s, and t are 1 and 0. Which of the following inputs (p, q, r, s, t) will produce the output 0 ?

p → BOTH →
q →

r → CHANGE → IF → CHANGE → 0

s → BOTH →
t →

F. (0,1,1,0,1)
G. (0,1,1,1,1)
H. (0,0,1,0,1)
J. (1,0,1,0,0)

43. Whenever x and y are both integers, what is $(6.0 \times 10^x)(5.0 \times 10^y)$ expressed in scientific notation?

A. 30.0×100^{xy}
B. 30.0×10^{xy}
C. $3.0 \times 10^{x+y+1}$
D. 3.0×10^{xy}

GO ON TO THE NEXT PAGE.

44. The points P, Q, R, and S lie in that order on a straight line. The midpoint of $\overline{QS}$ is R and the midpoint of $\overline{PS}$ is Q. The length of $\overline{QR}$ is x feet and the length of $\overline{PQ}$ is $4x - 16$ feet. What is the length, in feet, of $\overline{PS}$?

DO YOUR FIGURING HERE.

F. 32
G. 20
H. 16
J. 8

45. The circle shown has an area of 64π cm². A central angle with measure $24°$ intercepts minor $\overset{\frown}{CD}$. What is the length of minor $\overset{\frown}{CD}$, in centimeters?

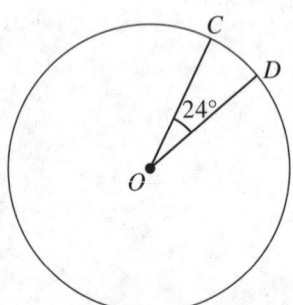

A. $\dfrac{1}{8}\pi$

B. $\dfrac{1}{4}\pi$

C. $\dfrac{16}{15}\pi$

D. $\dfrac{8}{3}\pi$

END OF TEST 2
STOP! DO NOT TURN THE PAGE UNTIL TOLD TO DO SO.
DO NOT RETURN TO THE PREVIOUS TEST.

THIS PAGE IS INTENTIONALLY LEFT BLANK.

READING TEST
40 Minutes—36 Questions

DIRECTIONS: There are several passages in this test. Each passage is followed by several questions. After reading a passage, choose the best answer to each question and fill in the corresponding oval on your answer document. You may refer to the passages as often as necessary.

Passage I

LITERARY NARRATIVE: This passage is adapted from the novel *The Joy Luck Club* by Amy Tan (© 1989 by Amy Tan).

On a cold spring afternoon, while walking home from school, I detoured through the playground at the end of our alley. I saw a group of old men, two seated across a folding table playing a game of chess, others smoking pipes, eating
5 peanuts, and watching. I ran home and grabbed Vincent's chess set, which was bound in a cardboard box with rubber bands. I also carefully selected two prized rolls of Life Savers. I came back to the park and approached a man who was observing the game.

10 "Want to play?" I asked him. His face widened with surprise and he grinned as he looked at the box under my arm.

"Little sister, been a long time since I play with dolls," he said, smiling benevolently. I quickly put the box down next to him on the bench and displayed my retort.

15 Lau Po, as he allowed me to call him, turned out to be a much better player than my brothers. I lost many games and many Life Savers. But over the weeks, with each diminishing roll of candies, I added new secrets. Lau Po gave me the names. The Double Attack from the East and West Shores. Throwing
20 Stones on the Drowning Man. The Sudden Meeting of the Clan. The Surprise from the Sleeping Guard. The Humble Servant Who Kills the King. Sand in the Eyes of Advancing Forces. A Double Killing Without Blood.

There were also the fine points of chess etiquette. Keep
25 captured men in neat rows, as well-tended prisoners. Never announce "Check" with vanity, lest someone with an unseen sword slit your throat. Never hurl pieces into the sandbox after you have lost a game, because then you must find them again, by yourself, after apologizing to all around you. By the end
30 of the summer, Lau Po had taught me all he knew, and I had become a better chess player.

A small weekend crowd of Chinese people and tourists would gather as I played and defeated my opponents one by one. My mother would join the crowds during these outdoor
35 exhibition games. She sat proudly on the bench, telling my admirers with proper Chinese humility, "Is luck."

A man who watched me play in the park suggested that my mother allow me to play in local chess tournaments. My mother smiled graciously, an answer that meant nothing. I
40 desperately wanted to go, but I bit back my tongue. I knew she would not let me play among strangers. So as we walked home I said in a small voice that I didn't want to play in the local tournament. They would have American rules. If I lost, I would bring shame on my family.

45 "Is shame you fall down nobody push you," said my mother.

During my first tournament, my mother sat with me in the front row as I waited for my turn. I frequently bounced my legs to unstick them from the cold metal seat of the fold-
50 ing chair. When my name was called, I leapt up. My mother unwrapped something in her lap. It was her chang, a small tablet of red jade which held the sun's fire. "Is luck," she whispered, and tucked it into my dress pocket. I turned to my opponent, a fifteen-year-old boy from Oakland. He looked at
55 me, wrinkling his nose.

As I began to play, the boy disappeared, the color ran out of the room, and I saw only my white pieces and his black ones waiting on the other side. A light wind began blowing past my ears. It whispered secrets only I could hear.

60 "Blow from the South," it murmured. "The wind leaves no trail." I saw a clear path, the traps to avoid. The crowd rustled. "Shhh! Shhh!" said the corners of the room. The wind blew stronger. "Throw sand from the East to distract him." The knight came forward ready for the sacrifice. The wind
65 hissed, louder and louder. "Blow, blow, blow. He cannot see. He is blind now. Make him lean away from the wind so he is easier to knock down."

"Check," I said, as the wind roared with laughter. The wind died down to little puffs, my own breath.

70 My mother placed my first trophy next to a new plastic chess set that the neighborhood Tao society had given to me. As she wiped each piece with a soft cloth, she said, "Next time win more, lose less."

"Ma, it's not how many pieces you lose." I said. "Some-
75 times you need to lose pieces to get ahead."

GO ON TO THE NEXT PAGE.

"Better to lose less, see if you really need."

At the next tournament, I won again, but it was my mother who wore the triumphant grin.

"Lost eight piece this time. Last time was eleven. What I
80 tell you? Better off lose less!" I was annoyed, but I couldn't say anything.

I attended more tournaments, each one farther away from home. I won all games, in all divisions. The Chinese bakery downstairs from our flat displayed my growing collection of
85 trophies in its window, amidst the dust-covered cakes that were never picked up. The day after I won an important regional tournament, the window encased a fresh sheet cake with whipped-cream frosting and red script saying, "Congratulations, Waverly Jong, Chinatown Chess Champion." Soon after
90 that, a flower shop, headstone engraver, and funeral parlor offered to sponsor me in national tournaments. That's when my mother decided I no longer had to do the dishes. Winston and Vincent had to do my chores.

1. The point of view from which the passage is told is best described as that of a:

   A. first-person narrator, present in the story, who interacts with other characters.
   B. first-person narrator, not present in the story, who describes interactions that happened in the past.
   C. third-person narrator, present in the story, who describes the motivations and emotions of multiple characters.
   D. third-person narrator, not present in the story, who describes the motivations and emotions of one central character.

2. The passage as a whole can best be described as an exploration of the:

   F. relationships a girl develops with the various children and adults she meets in the park throughout the summer.
   G. internal struggle of a daughter to balance her personal desires with her mother's expectations.
   H. challenges faced by immigrants adjusting to new environments while maintaining traditional values.
   J. progression of a girl's skill in chess and her performance in tournaments.

3. The passage most strongly suggests that a crucial aspect of the narrator's success, in terms of her chess game, is her:

   A. ruthless determination.
   B. keen strategizing.
   C. unmerited confidence.
   D. family legacy.

4. In lines 47–59, the narrator's mental state once the chess match with the boy begins could be described as:

   F. focused.
   G. generally carefree.
   H. completely distracted.
   J. uninterested.

5. In the passage, the mother's second utterance of "Is luck" to the narrator at the tournament, compared to her first utterance of it to the onlookers at the park, could be characterized as:

   A. more superstitious in its tone.
   B. more doubtful in its tone.
   C. more confident in its tone.
   D. more reassuring in its tone.

6. According to the passage, the narrator's mother believes that her chang will bring:

   F. retribution to her daughter's opponent.
   G. warmth of the sun to her daughter.
   H. good fortune in the chess tournament.
   J. comfort from her ancestors.

7. One main point of lines 37–44 is that:

   A. the narrator believes her mother's actions contribute to her success in tournaments.
   B. the narrator feels torn between wanting to please her mother and her desire for independence.
   C. the narrator's mother is more concerned with the number of pieces lost than the overall outcome of the game.
   D. the narrator wishes her mother would recognize her personal achievements beyond winning.

8. In the passage, the chess knowledge that the narrator possesses is most directly compared to:

   F. an unseen sword.
   G. a light wind.
   H. a roll of Life Savers.
   J. a cardboard box.

9. The passage suggests that one way those in Waverly's community show their support for the narrator's growing success is:

   A. the businesses in the area suggest taking people to her matches to cheer her on.
   B. the businesses in the area offer to sponsor her in national chess tournaments.
   C. the Chinese bakery hangs a large red congratulatory banner across the window.
   D. the Chinese bakery shows its admiration by keeping Waverly's trophies from getting dusty.

GO ON TO THE NEXT PAGE.

Passage II

INFORMATIONAL: This passage is adapted from the article "Crafting Locality" from the Library of Congress Collection *Tending the Commons: Folklife and Landscape in Southern West Virginia.* "Ramps" are greens with a strong garlic flavor that are in the same family as chives, leeks, and onions.

Historically, in these mountains, female sociality has flourished around the gathering and processing of greens and other wild produce. On the heels of ramps, a host of other greens start popping up: dandelions, poke, shawnee lettuce,
5　woolen britches, creasies, and lamb's tongue. And around these, women have fashioned women's worlds. "That was the big deal when everybody used to go green picking," said Carrie Lou Jarrell, of Sylvester, on another occasion. "That was the event of the week. Mrs. Karen Thomas would come
10　up and she always brought Jessie Graybill with her, and then Miss Haddad would come, and most of the time Maggie Wriston came with her. And usually Sylvia Williams was always there to do green picking with them. I knew from the time I came into the world that she was just a good friend. But that
15　was the thrill of my life to get to go with all of these women, because they talked about good stuff."

Such talk is one means of crafting locality. It catches people up into a dense fabric of kinship and community and fastens that fabric to places and events in the mountains.
20　Through such talk the women enunciate their place in the hills, a place remarkable not only for its biodiversity, but for the interweaving of biodiversity and community life. In the Ramp House the women laugh over how Violet Dickens once mistook sassafras tea for bacon grease and poured it
25　over the frying ramps: "We need you to come season the ramps," Mabel kidded her the other day. They compare the aromas of poke and collard greens, and marvel at how window screens get black with flies when you're cooking them. They wonder where the creasies (dry land cress) are
30　growing this year, and Jenny points out that creasies won't grow unless you till the soil.

The salient feature of ramps is the smell. The Menominee Indians called it "pikwute sikakushia": the skunk. "Shikako," their name for a large ramp patch that once flourished in
35　northern Illinois, has been anglicized to *Chicago*: "the skunk place." Our chopping of leaves is filling the air with aromatic organosulphur compounds, characteristic of members of the allium family but carried to extremes in ramps and their consumers. Some have seen in this practice of restoring the
40　body while emitting a sulphurous odor a rite of death and resurrection, serendipitously coinciding with Easter. Actually with ramps the motif appears to be breath and insurrection. Liberating organosulfides seems to comprise, if not a rite of inversion, at least a delicious form of backtalk: the country
45　backtalking the city, the improper backtalking propriety. The efforts of official institutions to quell this annual olfactory uprising have been rehearsed at every ramp supper I've attended.

"Let me get this down so I can move on," said John Flynn at the 1995 Ramp Supper. "We did not eat ramps. There
50　were very strong women in my family who did not like the odor. Also, if you ate ramps and went to school, they sent you home because of the odor. There were a lot of authoritarians in the school, so you didn't do a lot of ramp eating. Someone might get up the guts to do it once, but they didn't do it twice.
55　The odor was the issue." Ways of annulling the odor creep into ramp talk.

"I like them raw," said Jess Duncan, of Sylvester, "like you'd eat a hot pepper or something with a sandwich."

"Fried potatoes, pinto beans," added Pat Canterbury.

60　"You can't beat them," said Jess, "and they don't stink if you don't eat very many of them."

"They do too," said Pat.

"If you eat them with a sandwich, they don't," Jess insisted. "My wife's never complained."

65　"Now, if you're confined close," cautioned Bob Daniel, of Dry Creek, one morning in Syble's Bed and Barn, "say in an office with people, I'm sure it would offend people like that, but in my line of work I don't think I bother anybody with them."

70　"If you don't like the smell," laughed Mae Bongalis, "go the other way. Stay at your house!"

Behind the powerful aroma it appears there really is something good for what ails you. Ramps have long been recommended for their germicidal and toning effects. The
75　beliefs that ramps are good for the heart, that they thin and purify the blood and that they relieve the common cold are widespread. Scientific research suggests that such faith in ramps is well-placed. The allicin (diallylsulfide oxide) in ramps, which has antibiotic properties, has been linked
80　with reduced rates of cancer. Ramps are higher in vitamin C than oranges. They contain cepaenes, which function as antithrombotic agents. Ramps also contain flavonoids and other antioxidants that are free-radical scavengers.

As the first of the wild foods to appear, ramps satisfy the
85　body's craving for living food at the end of a winter filled with produce that's been dried, canned, frozen, or shipped from faraway places. "They used to say," said Jenny Bonds, "that people that lived out like we did didn't live near grocery stores, so they said in the springtime you always need green
90　things, like vegetables. So they said in the springtime the country people got ramps, that was our spring tonic."

GO ON TO THE NEXT PAGE.

10. The primary purpose of the passage is to:

   F. explain the properties of a vegetable and its role in the activities of a community.
   G. highlight the medicinal properties of wild greens like ramps.
   H. describe how women influence biodiversity in mountain regions.
   J. explore the cultural and social significance of food gathering in rural communities.

11. The main idea of the second paragraph (lines 17–31) is that:

   A. ramps are the only greens that are culturally significant in the mountain communities.
   B. the women who gather greens form a competitive bond rather than a cooperative one.
   C. preparing greens provides a social occasion where women bond over shared experiences.
   D. the women sometimes mistakenly season the frying ramps and lightheartedly joke about such mishaps.

12. It can reasonably be inferred from the passage that Bob Daniel's line of work most likely involves:

   F. working in an office.
   G. talking to many people.
   H. shipping and receiving.
   J. being alone or outside.

13. The information in lines 22–26 primarily functions to:

   A. highlight the difficulties women face when learning to gather greens.
   B. emphasize how regional foods have shaped local culture.
   C. illustrate the humor and camaraderie that can accompany food preparation.
   D. describe the importance of certain foods in traditional mountain diets.

14. The twelfth paragraph (lines 72–83) differs from the rest of the passage in that it:

   F. emphasizes the medicinal properties of ramps.
   G. weighs the pleasure of eating ramps against the social effects of their odor.
   H. highlights the historical significance of ramps.
   J. argues against the locals' belief that ramps are beneficial for health.

15. According to the passage, the fact that ramps contain more organosulphur compounds compared to other members of the allium family results in:

   A. a reputation for having medicinal properties.
   B. an increased popularity in modern culinary dishes.
   C. an effort from local officials to discourage ramp dinners.
   D. a particularly strong odor that contributes to their distinctiveness.

16. In the passage, the author compares community as it is formed in the mountains of West Virginia to a:

   F. woven fabric.
   G. field of greens.
   H. cycle of life.
   J. spring tonic.

17. The passage author most likely mentions that ramps contain more vitamin C than oranges to:

   A. emphasize that ramps offer more nutritional benefits than oranges.
   B. suggest that ramps can be a substitute for oranges in a balanced diet.
   C. explain why ramps became so popular in West Virginia as a medicinal food.
   D. highlight the nutritional benefits of ramps by comparing them to a more familiar source of vitamin C.

18. As it is used in line 13, the word *green* most nearly means:

   F. weeds.
   G. plants.
   H. coloration.
   J. eco-friendly.

GO ON TO THE NEXT PAGE.

Passage III

INFORMATIONAL: Passage A is adapted from the article "Graffiti as a Form of Contentious Political Participation" by Lisa K. Walder and Betty A. Dobratz (© 2013 by John Wiley and Sons). Passage B is from the blog post "Street Art and Graffiti: A Personal Reflection from the Heart of Urban Art" by Miguel Ángel Sánchez Martos (© 2025 by Miguel Ángel Sánchez Martos).

Passage A by Lisa K. Walder and Betty A. Dobratz

Graffiti comes from the Italian word *sgraffiato* for scratching or cutting stone and may consist of images and/or words—"virtually anything that is drawn, painted, etched, scratched, or scribbled on any surface visible to the public"—and can
5 be produced with writing instruments, spray paint, or sharp instruments for etching. Graffitists often use walls but also might take advantage of "street furniture" such as bus stops, traffic lights, benches, utility housing and the like. Sometimes the choice of street furniture is part of the message.

10 We define political graffiti as containing ideas or values designed to influence public opinion, policy, or government decision making. Unlike tags, political graffiti carries a specific oppositional message in that it "presents opinions against governments, institutions, authorities, politicians,
15 majorities, etc." Political graffiti often "reflect[s] current social conditions and community concerns" and is counter hegemonic.

Street art is considered a sub-genre of graffiti writing. Murals as street art have long been associated with the
20 Chicano movement with over a thousand murals created in Los Angeles since 1965. Murals have been studied in other locations including Gaza and Brazil. [A] mural expressing nationalistic pride [is] located in Plaza de Mayo, Buenos Aires, Argentina, a well-known political site beginning with
25 the May 25, 1810 revolution for independence and a frequent location for demonstrations including, since 1977, a weekly protest by the mothers of missing children who disappeared during the military dictatorship's "Dirty War."

Within the graffiti genre, a hierarchy exists with street
30 art accorded a higher status compared to graffiti writing. This often is reflected in the differential legal treatment of street art. In Atlanta, street art is encouraged and legally sanctioned as a means of sprucing up an urban environment. Simultaneously, Atlanta has also stepped up efforts to discourage illegal
35 graffiti by assigning police officers to track down offenders who face fines if caught. Another sign of differential status is those who define themselves as either street artists or graffiti writers. Lewisohn explains, "If you had a degree you did street art as opposed to graffiti." The transforming legal
40 status of graffiti from always illegal to sometimes legal may have implications for its political utility because increasing legitimacy potentially undermines its effectiveness.

Passage B by Miguel Ángel Sánchez Martos (Saturno)

My foray into graffiti began with a deep need for expression and an irresistible attraction to the clandestine world
45 of graffiti writers. Inspired by the artists I saw around me, I started tagging everywhere. I wanted to be like them, living that life full of adrenaline and excitement. I spent nights painting letters on the city walls, with panic and laughter as my constant companions. This quickly became my daily routine.

50 I clearly remember spending hours at home, drawing my first sketches while listening to Ice T or House Of Pain. These moments of creative solitude were as important as the nocturnal escapades. What did I feel during those times? I felt a deep connection to something larger than myself, an
55 underground current of creativity and rebellion that pulled me ever deeper. I had no doubt that I belonged to that link called graffiti. The graffiti writers, with their philosophy and modus operandi, were my tribe. Their codes of conduct and the camaraderie we shared made me feel that I perfectly fit
60 that label. Graffiti was more than an activity; it was an identity and a way of life.

However, despite having rarely done letters—mostly characters—I never saw this as an obstacle to being part of a world where letters reign supreme. In graffiti, those who paint
65 characters are recognized just as much as those who paint letters, thanks to their unique style. This is one of the codes of graffiti, one of its fundamental pillars: a war of styles where each artist is valued for their skill and creativity, regardless of their chosen form of expression.

70 Over time, through a natural evolution driven by practice and introspection, I began to explore new forms of expression. My works evolved from simple tags to more complex characters and figures. Initially, I continued painting in illegal and dark environments, barely illuminated by distant street-
75 lights. What changed within me? Something began to shift. The authenticity of graffiti, that essence that had drawn me in and led me to the world of hip hop, started to transform.

GO ON TO THE NEXT PAGE.

19. According to Passage A, one indication that street art is considered to have a higher status than graffiti writing is that street art:

A. is usually created in private spaces.
B. does not focus on making political statements.
C. has sometimes received endorsement from municipalities.
D. focuses exclusively on creating murals.

20. Based on Passage A, it can reasonably be inferred that the authors view graffiti as:

F. an upsetting sight.
G. seemingly harmless but actually quite damaging.
H. admired by academics but less so by artists.
J. a controversial art form.

21. Based on Passage A, which statement best captures the relationship between street artists and law enforcement in Atlanta?

A. Street art is legally sanctioned in Atlanta.
B. Street artists have denounced the actions of law enforcement.
C. Street artists know about the efforts of law enforcement but are not bothered by them.
D. Law enforcement officers and street artists face similar challenges.

22. Which of the following details does the author of Passage B highlight as one that can distinguish the styles of different graffiti artists?

F. The fact that some artists use bright colors
G. The graffiti's intended audience
H. The form of expression
J. The location of the graffiti

23. As it is used in line 46, the word *tagging* most nearly means:

A. monitoring.
B. categorizing.
C. mentioning on social media.
D. painting.

24. In the context of Passage B, the main point of lines 50–61 is that the author was:

F. struggling to understand the complex philosophies behind the graffiti culture he was joining.
G. viewing his connection to the graffiti community as a source of personal identity and belonging.
H. disillusioned with the graffiti scene after realizing it was mostly about fame and recognition.
J. primarily interested in the technical aspects of graffiti, such as mastering lettering styles.

25. Compared to Passage A, Passage B focuses more on:

A. the author's own experience with graffiti.
B. the distinction between graffiti and street art.
C. examples of the political power of street art.
D. street furniture.

26. Which of the following elements of Passage A is not included in Passage B?

F. An explanation of how other types of artists view graffiti art
G. A description of a mural's connection to politics
H. A distinction between types of graffiti artists
J. A reference to the illegal nature of graffiti

27. The authors of both passages would most likely agree with the idea that graffiti art:

A. is difficult to categorize.
B. allows artists to condemn corrupt governments and their officials.
C. allows for self-expression in a variety of ways.
D. is more problematic than street art.

GO ON TO THE NEXT PAGE.

Passage IV

INFORMATIONAL: This passage is from the article "A New Connection between the Gut and Brain" by Jonathan D. Grinstein (© 2018 by Scientific American).

It is well known that a high salt diet leads to high blood pressure, a risk factor for an array of health problems, including heart disease and stroke. But over the last decade, studies across human populations have reported the association
5 between salt intake and stroke irrespective of high blood pressure and risk of heart disease, suggesting a missing link between salt intake and brain health.

Interestingly, there is a growing body of work showing that there is communication between the gut and brain, now
10 commonly dubbed the gut–brain axis. The disruption of the gut–brain axis contributes to a diverse range of diseases, including Parkinson's disease and irritable bowel syndrome. Consequently, the developing field of gut–brain axis research is rapidly growing and evolving. Five years ago, a couple
15 of studies showed that high salt intake leads to profound immune changes in the gut, resulting in increased vulnerability of the brain to autoimmunity—when the immune system attacks its own healthy cells and tissues by mistake, suggesting that perhaps the gut can communicate with the
20 brain via immune signaling.

Now, new research shows another connection: immune signals sent from the gut can compromise the brain's blood vessels, leading to deteriorated brain heath and cognitive impairment. Surprisingly, the research unveils a previously
25 undescribed gut–brain connection mediated by the immune system and indicates that excessive salt might negatively impact brain health in humans through impairing the brain's blood vessels regardless of salt's effect on blood pressure.

This research proposes new therapeutic targets for coun-
30 tering stroke—the second leading cause of death worldwide—and cognitive dysfunction. Reducing salt intake is applicable to people around the globe, as nearly every adult consumes too much salt: on average 9–12 grams per day or around twice the recommended maximum level of intake (5 grams) by the
35 World Health Organization.

The researchers used mice, and found that immune responses in the small intestines set off a cascade of chemical responses, reaching the brain's blood vessels, reducing blood flow to the cortex and hippocampus, two brain regions crucial
40 for learning and memory. This, in turn, brought a decline in tests of cognitive performance. The impairment in learning and memory was clear even in the absence of high blood pressure; they observed that the gut is reacting to the salt overload and directing immune signals that lay the basis for deterioration
45 throughout the brain's vital vascular complex and compromise

cognitive function. While this study has only been carried out on research animals so far, the scientists believe it's likely that much of the same applies to people.

Lowering salt intake has been shown to have beneficial
50 effects to overall health, so the researchers wanted to know whether these effects extend to this newly identified signaling cascade that begins in the gut and targets the brain's blood vessels to, ultimately, affect cognitive function. When the mice were returned to a normal diet after being on a high salt diet,
55 the detrimental health effects caused by excess salt intake were erased. A pharmacological intervention that disrupted the immune signals also reversed the effects.

The implications of this newly identified gut–brain connection extend to several autoimmune disorders, including
60 multiple sclerosis, rheumatoid arthritis, psoriasis, and inflammatory bowel disease, that have been shown to activate the same immune signaling pathway implicated in this study. These autoimmune disorders have a high stroke risk and are linked to poorly functioning blood vessels in the nervous
65 system. This research is also a demonstration that what we eat affects how we think, and that seemingly isolated parts of the body can play vital roles in brain health. These results motivate research on how everyday stressors to our digestive systems and blood vessels might change the brain and, con-
70 sequently, how we see, and experience, the world.

GO ON TO THE NEXT PAGE.

28. In the context of the passage, what associations have researchers found between salt intake and cognitive function?

    F. Researchers have found that there is a direct link between salt intake and cognitive function.
    G. Researchers have found that there is a link between salt intake and cognitive function only when high blood pressure also occurs.
    H. Researchers have found that there is no relationship between salt intake and cognitive function.
    J. Researchers have found that the gut operates independently from the brain.

29. Which of the following statements best summarizes research regarding the therapeutic implications of lowering salt intake as presented in lines 49–57?

    A. It indicates that reducing salt intake could prevent strokes and cognitive decline, which are linked to gut health.
    B. It indicates that salt intake does not affect brain function and is unrelated to stroke, which is affected by cardiovascular health.
    C. It indicates that treatment plans for autoimmune disorders should focus solely on pharmaceutical interventions, which can reverse effects of high salt intake.
    D. It indicates that a new diet plan that involves increased salt consumption will improve brain health, which is related to blood vessel size.

30. The main purpose of lines 8–20 is to:

    F. provide information about how increased salt intake directly damages brain cells.
    G. introduce the expanding research on the process by which the gut communicates with the brain.
    H. highlight the specific ways salt intake causes changes in the immune system's role in brain health.
    J. detail the mechanism that causes high salt intake to lead to increased vulnerability to heart disease.

31. According to the passage, the research on the mice revealed a decline in cognitive performance due to salt intake affecting the:

    A. cerebellum and medulla.
    B. cortex and hippocampus.
    C. occipital lobe and frontal cortex.
    D. thalamus and hypothalamus.

32. In the context of the passage, the statement in lines 46–48 ("While...people.") mainly serves to:

    F. prove that the findings in mice have already been applied directly to humans.
    G. suggest that the research on salt and brain health is irrelevant to human health.
    H. indicate that further research on salt and brain health might produce similar findings in humans.
    J. suggest that salt has no effect on human brain health.

33. According to the passage, when the mice were returned to a normal diet after being on a high-salt diet, the mice then:

    A. developed permanent cognitive impairment.
    B. displayed increased blood pressure.
    C. exhibited a more active gut–brain signaling pathway.
    D. experienced a reversal of the detrimental health effects.

34. In the context of the passage, the detail that impairment in learning and memory was evident even in the absence of high blood pressure provides support for the claim that cognitive impairment:

    F. is affected by high salt intake.
    G. is only caused by high blood pressure.
    H. requires both high salt intake and high blood pressure.
    J. is unaffected by diet.

35. According to the passage, the average salt intake of adults worldwide is:

    A. 5 grams per day.
    B. 5–10 grams per day.
    C. 9–12 grams per day.
    D. 18–24 grams per day.

36. Based on the passage, the phrase "a cascade of chemical responses" (lines 37–38) is most likely meant to be read:

    F. figuratively; the chemical responses are massive in scope and awe-inspiring.
    G. figuratively; the chemical responses flow elegantly like a water in a waterfall.
    H. literally; the chemical responses occur slowly at first and then gain momentum.
    J. literally; the chemical responses happen one by one, in sequence.

END OF TEST 3.
STOP! DO NOT TURN THE PAGE UNTIL TOLD TO DO SO.
DO NOT RETURN TO A PREVIOUS TEST.

SCIENCE TEST

40 Minutes—40 Questions

DIRECTIONS: There are several passages in this test. Each passage is followed by several questions. After reading a passage, choose the best answer to each question and fill in the corresponding oval on your answer document. You may refer to the passages as often as necessary.

You are **not** permitted to use a calculator on this test.

Passage I

A group of students studied the frictional forces involved on stationary objects.

In a series of experiments, the students used rectangular shaped objects of various materials that all had identical masses. One end of a plastic board coated with a polymer film was fastened to a table surface by a hinge so the angle θ between the board and table could be changed, as shown in Figure 1.

Figure 1

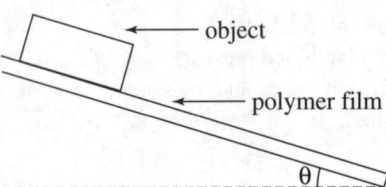

Objects were placed on the opposite end of the board, and the angle θ at which the object started to slide was recorded. The tangent of this angle represents the coefficient of static friction between the object and the polymer surface. This coefficient is proportional to the force required to move a stationary object. Higher coefficients mean that greater forces of friction must be overcome to initiate movement.

The dimensions of the objects gave them 3 distinct *faces* of unequal area as shown in Figure 2. Unless otherwise stated, the objects were placed on the ramp with Face A down.

Figure 2

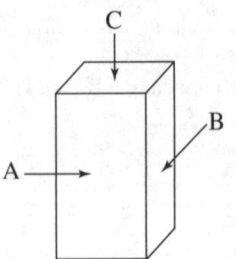

Experiment 1

Four objects made of different materials were placed on the ramp at a temperature of 25°C. The ramp was gradually raised and as soon as the object started to move, the angle θ of the ramp was recorded in Table 1.

Table 1	
Object material	θ (degrees)
Granite	12.1
Copper	16.8
Wood	22.0
Brick	31.1

Experiment 2

The procedure for Experiment 1 was repeated with the wooden object, varying which face was placed down on the ramp. Results were recorded in Table 2.

Table 2	
Face	θ (degrees)
A	22.0
B	22.0
C	22.0

GO ON TO THE NEXT PAGE.

Experiment 3

The procedure for Experiment 1 was repeated with the wooden object, varying the temperature of the polymer ramp. Results for 5 temperatures were recorded in Table 3.

Table 3	
Temperature (°C)	θ (degrees)
0	18.5
25	22.0
50	25.4
75	29.0
100	32.5

Experiment 4

The procedure for Experiment 1 was repeated with multiple wooden objects. For each trial, the objects were stacked on top of each other before raising the ramp. The angle θ where the stack started to slide was recorded in Table 4.

Table 4	
Number of objects	θ (degrees)
2	22.0
3	22.0
4	22.0

1. If the procedure used in Experiment 3 had been repeated at a temperature of 62.5°C, the angle required for the object to start moving down the ramp most likely would have been closest to which of the following?

   A. 27.2 degrees
   B. 29.2 degrees
   C. 30.3 degrees
   D. 31.4 degrees

2. Suppose the students had placed the 4 objects used in Experiment 1 on the ramp when it was flat and pushed each of the objects, such that the amount of force applied to each object gradually increased until it moved. Based on the results of Experiment 1, the object made of which material would most likely have taken the *greatest* amount of force to start moving?

   F. Brick
   G. Wood
   H. Copper
   J. Granite

3. Based on the results of Experiments 1 and 4, what was the effect, if any, of the weight of the object on the coefficient of static friction?

   A. The coefficient of static friction always increased as the object's weight increased.
   B. The coefficient of static friction always decreased as the object's weight increased.
   C. The coefficient of static friction increased and then decreased as the object's weight increased.
   D. The coefficient of static friction was not affected by the weight of the object.

4. Which of the following is the independent variable in Experiment 2?

   F. Angle of ramp
   G. Face
   H. Object Material
   J. Temperature

5. Which of the following ranks the different types of objects used, in order, from the material that presented the greatest resistance to movement to the material that presented the least resistance to movement?

   A. Granite, copper, wood, brick
   B. Brick, wood, copper, granite
   C. Granite, wood, brick, copper
   D. Copper, wood, granite, brick

6. Suppose the procedure in Experiment 1 were repeated in a new trial with the granite block placed with Face C against the polymer surface of the ramp. Based on the results in Tables 1 and 2, the force required to move the stationary block in the new trial would be:

   F. less than the force required to move the block in Experiment 1 because the force is directly proportional to the surface area.
   G. the same as the force required to move the block in Experiment 1 because the force is directly proportional to the surface area.
   H. less than the force required to move the block in Experiment 1 because the force is directly proportional to the coefficient of static friction.
   J. the same as the force required to move the block in Experiment 1 because the force is directly proportional to the coefficient of static friction.

GO ON TO THE NEXT PAGE.

Passage II

Ethanolamines are compounds that contain both alcohol (–OH or HO–) and amine (–NH$_3$, –RNH$_2$, –R$_2$NH, or –R$_3$N) subgroups. They remove weakly acidic gases from the atmosphere of enclosed spaces such as on a submarine. An example is the use of *monoethanolamine* (MEA) to remove CO$_2$ from the atmosphere as shown in Figure 1.

Figure 1

$$2 \text{ MEA (liquid)} + CO_2\text{(gas)} \xrightarrow{H_2O} \text{(MEA)COO}^-\text{(aqueous)} + \text{(MEA) H}^+\text{(aqueous)} + \text{heat}$$

If the temperature rises sufficiently, ethanolamines will release any absorbed acidic gases back into the environment, creating a potential hazard.

Scientists studied the absorption properties of 2 ethanolamines (MEA and DEA).

Experiment 1

At 0°C and 1 atmosphere (atm) pressure, 1 mole (6.02×10^{23} molecules) of MEA was spread at the base of a reaction vessel containing CO$_2$ gas at a concentration of 1,000 parts per million (ppm). As the CO$_2$ was absorbed, its ambient concentration decreased. The *scrub time* (time for CO$_2$ concentration to drop to at least 10 ppm) was measured. Longer scrub times indicate a slower rate of absorption. The experimental procedure was repeated at varying temperatures and for DEA, with results recorded in Table 1.

Temperature (°C)	Scrub time (msec)	
	MEA	DEA
0	11,400	8,600
5	11,150	8,410
10	11,025	8,315
15	10,925	8,240
20	10,850	8,190
25	10,790	8,145
30	10,740	8,105
35	10,700	8,075

Table 1

Experiment 2

The scrub times of MEA for different acidic gases were measured using the procedures of Experiment 1 at 26°C (see Table 2). Each of the gases listed is toxic and poses a significant safety hazard if its concentration becomes elevated within an enclosed space.

Table 2

Gas	Formula	Scrub time (msec)
Hydrogen chloride*	HCl	8,500
Hydrogen cyanide	HCN	14,400
Hydrogen sulfide	H$_2$S	12,200
Sulfur dioxide	SO$_2$	8,930
Sulfur trioxide	SO$_3$	9,120

*Hydrogen chloride forms gaseous hydrochloric acid upon contact with atmospheric humidity.

GO ON TO THE NEXT PAGE.

7. In which of the following ways was the procedure of Experiment 2 different from that of Experiment 1? In Experiment 2:

   A. only MEA was used; in Experiment 1, only DEA was used.

   B. only DEA was used; in Experiment 1, only MEA was used.

   C. temperature was held constant; in Experiment 1, the temperature was varied.

   D. temperature was varied; in Experiment 1, the temperature was held constant.

8. If, in Experiment 1, an additional trial were done at 12°C, the scrub times (in msec) for MEA and DEA would most likely be closest to which of the following?

	MEA	DEA
F.	10,805	8,370
G.	10,985	8,285
H.	11,000	8,365
J.	11,025	8,315

9. Based on the information in the passage, which of the following is a possible chemical formula for an ethanolamine?

   A. $HO-(CH_2)_2-NH_3$

   B. $HO-(CH_2CF_2)_2-CH_3$

   C. $H_3C-(CH_2)_4-NH_3$

   D. $H_3N-(CH_2CHCl)_2-NH_3$

10. A scientist claims that under the same conditions, DEA will always absorb CO_2 at a faster rate than will MEA. Do the results of Experiment 1 support this claim?

   F. No; at all temperatures tested, the scrub time for DEA was more than that for MEA.

   G. No; at all temperatures tested, the scrub time for MEA was more than that for DEA.

   H. Yes; at all temperatures tested, the scrub time for DEA was more than that for MEA.

   J. Yes; at all temperatures tested, the scrub time for MEA was more than that for DEA.

11. Based on the results of Experiment 2, which acidic gas had the slowest absorption by MEA at 26°C ?

   A. HCl

   B. HCN

   C. H_2S

   D. SO_2

12. Which of the following correctly identifies a reactant and a product for a reaction that occurred in Experiment 1 ?

	reactant	product
F.	MEA	CO_2
G.	DEA	Heat
H.	CO_2	H_2O
J.	DEA	H_2O

GO ON TO THE NEXT PAGE.

Passage III

Pepsin is an enzyme in humans that catalyzes the digestion of proteins, like the milk protein *casein*, into smaller subunits called peptides.

The researchers prepared a solution of casein, a solution of *anserine* (a small peptide), a solution of pepsin, and various *buffer solutions* (solutions maintaining a constant pH). The following experiments were conducted using these solutions.

Experiment 1

Seven solutions were prepared in test tubes using a 5 mL solution buffered to pH 3.0. Different amounts of casein, anserine, and pepsin solutions were added to each tube, and then diluted to 10 mL with the buffer solution, so that the final pH in each test tube would be 3.0. Each tube was incubated at a constant temperature for 15 minutes, and then was monitored to determine whether there was any activity by pepsin (see Table 1).

Table 1					
Trial	Casein (mL)	Anserine (mL)	Pepsin (mL)	Temperature (°C)	Pepsin Activity
1	1	1	1	30	No
2	1	1	1	35	Low
3	1	1	1	40	High
4	1	0	1	40	High
5	0	1	1	40	No
6	0	0	1	40	No
7	1	1	1	45	No

Experiment 2

Seven solutions were prepared in test tubes according to the same procedure as in Trial 3 of Experiment 1, and each test tube was diluted with different buffer solutions of varying pH (see Table 2).

Table 2		
Trial	pH	Pepsin activity
8	2.5	high activity
9	3.0	high activity
10	3.5	high activity
11	4.0	low activity
12	4.5	low activity
13	5.0	low activity
14	5.5	no activity

GO ON TO THE NEXT PAGE.

13. Suppose Trial 10 were repeated, but the researcher forgot to add the anserine. Would the solution show any pepsin activity?

    A. Yes, because Trial 6 shows no pepsin activity.
    B. Yes, because Trial 4 shows high pepsin activity.
    C. No, because Trial 6 shows no pepsin activity.
    D. No, because Trial 4 shows high pepsin activity.

14. Pepsin is most likely to be found in which of the following organs?

    F. Kidney
    G. Heart
    H. Stomach
    J. Spinal cord

15. Which of the following is the most likely reason that Trials 3 and 4 show high levels of pepsin activity, while Trial 5 shows no pepsin activity?

    A. Pepsin activity is dependent on both casein and anserine.
    B. Pepsin activity is blocked by anserine.
    C. Pepsin is able to digest casein, but not anserine.
    D. Pepsin is able to digest anserine, but not casein.

16. According to the results from Experiment 1, which of the following trials are most likely to contain undigested casein?

    F. Trials 1 and 7 only
    G. Trials 5, 6, and 7 only
    H. Trials 1, 3, 4, and 7 only
    J. Trials 1, 5, 6, and 7 only

17. The experimental conditions for Trial 3 are most similar to those for which of the following trials?

    A. Trial 9
    B. Trial 11
    C. Trial 13
    D. Trial 14

18. A researcher hypothesized that pepsin would digest proteins at the fastest rates in the least acidic solutions. Do the results from Experiment 2 support this hypothesis?

    F. Yes; Trial 8 shows high pepsin activity.
    G. Yes; Trial 14 shows high pepsin activity.
    H. No; Trial 8 shows no pepsin activity.
    J. No; Trial 14 shows no pepsin activity.

GO ON TO THE NEXT PAGE.

Passage IV

A group of researchers performed the following study in order to investigate declines in primarily carnivorous polar bear populations in the Arctic over a 10-year period.

Study

The researchers obtained previously collected data from several areas previously identified as polar bear habitats. From this data, the researchers selected sixty 5 km × 5 km blocks that do not overlap with one another. The blocks were selected to fall into six groups, each with a different set of conditions selected in order to conform to criteria for listing animals as threatened species. Previous research has indicated that Arctic sea ice and available food are among the factors which may affect polar bear populations.

Table 1 identifies each of the groups utilized in the study. Conditions other than the ones listed were considered to be normal.

Table 1	
Group	Conditions
1	These areas had significantly decreased populations of marine mammals consumed by polar bears.
2	These areas had significantly increased populations of seaweed commonly consumed by marine mammals.
3	These areas had been subject to excess thawing of Arctic sea ice.
4	These areas were subject to the same conditions as Groups 1 and 3.
5	These areas were subject to the same conditions as Groups 2 and 3.
6	These areas represent unaffected polar bear habitat.

Data for each of the plots was collected, and the population density of polar bears was calculated in terms of adult polar bears/km². Table 2 shows the population density of the blocks in Group 6.

Table 2	
Area label	Population density of Group 6 areas (polar bears/km²)
A	0.93
B	2.10
C	0.21
D	0.72
E	0.88
F	0.72
G	0.91
H	0.53
I	1.12
J	0.74

The data collected was analyzed to find the *average population density ratio* for each group. The researchers defined the average population density ratio of a given group as being equal to the result of the following expression:

$$\frac{\text{average population density of the group's areas}}{\text{average population density of Group 6 areas}}$$

Figure 1 shows the average population density ratio of Groups 1–5.

Figure 1

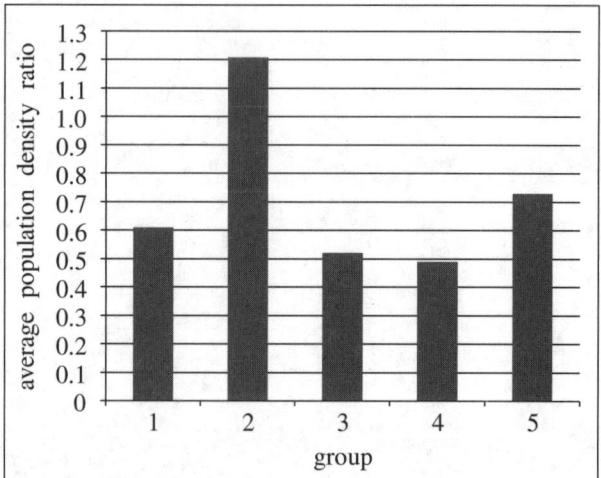

GO ON TO THE NEXT PAGE.

19. Which of the following statements provides the best explanation for why the researchers collected data for Group 6 in their study?

    A. Group 6 provided data indicating the types of predators that most threaten polar bears in their natural habitat.

    B. Group 6 provided a standard by which the other groups could be compared in order to determine how each set of conditions affected polar bear populations.

    C. Group 6 provided a means by which the researchers could carefully identify and select the conditions for the remaining five groups.

    D. Group 6 provided a means of determining the greatest number of polar bears that would be likely to survive in an area of 25 km².

20. Which of the following correctly ranks Groups 1–5 from the group where the conditions are *most* conducive to polar bear population density in the study to the group where the conditions are *least* conducive?

    F. Group 1, Group 2, Group 3, Group 4, Group 5

    G. Group 4, Group 3, Group 1, Group 5, Group 2

    H. Group 2, Group 5, Group 1, Group 3, Group 4

    J. Group 2, Group 1, Group 5, Group 3, Group 4

21. Which of the following is most likely an organism that the researchers identified as exhibiting a significantly decreased population when defining Group 1 ?

    A. Polar bear
    B. Salmon
    C. Seal
    D. Snowy owl

22. Before performing their analysis of the data, the researchers developed four different hypotheses. Each one of the four hypotheses below is supported by the results of the study EXCEPT:

    F. Declining prey populations have a greater effect on polar bear populations than the melting of Arctic sea ice.

    G. The melting of Arctic sea ice has a greater effect on polar bear populations than declining prey populations.

    H. Declining prey populations have had some effect on polar bear populations.

    J. The melting of Arctic sea ice has had some effect on polar bear populations.

23. According to the information in the passage and Table 2, which of the following is closest to the total number of polar bears found in all ten areas of Group 6 ?

    A. 10
    B. 45
    C. 90
    D. 225

GO ON TO THE NEXT PAGE.

Passage V

A *solution* results from dissolving a *solute* into a *solvent*. The van 't Hoff factor (*i*) is the number of moles (1 mole = 6.02 × 10²³ entities such as molecules, ions, or atoms) of particles produced in solution for every 1 mole of solute dissolved.

The temperature at which a solution changes state from liquid to solid is the *freezing point*. Two scientists observed that the freezing point of H_2O decreased after adding KCl to it. To explore this further, they conducted an experiment and each scientist provided separate explanations of the results.

Experiment

One mole each of fructose, KCl, and $MgCl_2$ were separately dissolved in 1 kg of pure water. The concentration of each solution was thus 1.0 mole/kg. In addition, 1 kg of pure water only was placed in a fourth container. The containers were placed in a cooling device. The temperature was gradually decreased, and the freezing point of each solution was recorded. The results are shown in Table 1.

Table 1				
Solution	Solute	*i*	Solution properties	Freezing point
1	—	—	Pure water only	0°C
2	fructose	1	1 dissolved neutral particle	–1.9°C
3	KCl	2	2 dissolved charged particles (K^+ and Cl^-)	–3.8°C
4	$MgCl_2$	3	3 dissolved charged particles (Mg^{2+} and 2 Cl^-)	–5.7°C

Scientist 1

For a solvent to freeze, its molecules must arrange in an orderly fashion relative to each other. When a solute is added, the dissolved solute molecules are attracted to the solvent molecules by the intermolecular force of charge. The attraction of the solute particles to the solvent particles interferes with the orderly arrangement of solvent molecules, and the net effect is that the freezing point is lowered. This decrease in freezing point is related only to the charge of the solute particles and occurs with solutes that form charged particles in solution.

Scientist 2

The freezing point of a solvent is the temperature at which the liquid and solid states of that solvent have equivalent energetic potentials. Below the freezing point, the solvent has a lower energetic potential in the solid state. When a solute is dissolved in a solvent, the energetic potential of the liquid phase is decreased more than the energetic potential of the solid phase. Because of the different energetic potentials, it takes a larger drop in temperature for the liquid to freeze. Thus, the size of the decrease in freezing point is in direct proportion with the van 't Hoff factor. This decrease in freezing point is related only to the concentration of particles, not to the identity or properties of each individual particle.

GO ON TO THE NEXT PAGE.

24. Which of the solutions shown in Table 1 contained ions?

    F. Solution 1 only
    G. Solutions 1 and 2 only
    H. Solutions 3 and 4 only
    J. Solutions 2, 3, and 4 only

25. The freezing point of benzene is lowered with the addition of the solute naphthalene ($C_{10}H_8$), which has no charge. According to the information in the passage, this observation *disagrees* with the explanation provided by:

    A. Scientist 1, who argued that only charged particles can have an effect on the freezing point of a solution.
    B. Scientist 1, who argued that any solute is capable of increasing the stability of the liquid phase of a solvent.
    C. Scientist 2, who argued that only charged particles can have an effect on the freezing point of a solution.
    D. Scientist 2, who argued that any solute is capable of increasing the stability of the liquid phase of a solvent.

26. With which of the following statements about solutes would both scientists agree? Adding to a liquid a substance that has:

    F. a positive or negative charge will decrease the liquid's freezing point.
    G. a positive or negative charge will increase the liquid's freezing point.
    H. no charge will decrease the liquid's freezing point.
    J. no charge will increase the liquid's freezing point.

27. Of the following diagrams, which best illustrates how Scientist 1 would describe the results after a charged solute (•) has been added to H_2O (×) ?

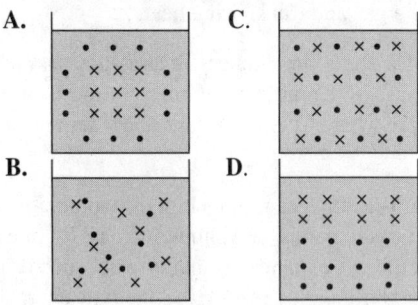

28. Do the scientists offer different explanations for the impact of a solute's physical properties, such as solute charge, on the decrease in freezing point of a solution?

    F. Yes; Scientist 1 states that solute physical properties have an impact, but Scientist 2 states they do not.
    G. Yes; Scientist 2 states that solute physical properties have an impact, but Scientist 1 states they do not.
    H. No; both scientists state that solute physical properties have an impact on solution freezing point.
    J. No; neither Scientist discusses the impact of solute physical properties on solution freezing point.

29. Assume the following for the addition of a substance to a pure liquid: k is a constant, ΔT is the decrease in freezing point, and i is the van 't Hoff factor. Which of the following equations is most consistent with Scientist 2's explanation?

    A. $\Delta T = k/i$
    B. $\Delta T = ki^2$
    C. $\Delta T = k/i^2$
    D. $\Delta T = ki$

GO ON TO THE NEXT PAGE.

Passage VI

Figure 2

A *Carnot heat engine* is an engine which runs by compressing and expanding a gas and transferring heat.

Figures 1 and 2 show the changes in pressure, P, and volume, V, that occur as two Carnot heat engines, A and B, run. For every gas, $PV = \Omega T$, where Ω is a constant and T represents the temperature.

The cycle begins as the gas is at its highest temperature and pressure. First, the gas expands, so volume increases while pressure decreases. As the gas expands, it can do work, such as pushing a piston. After the gas has run out of thermal energy and can no longer do work, it is at its lowest temperature and pressure. At this point, the gas begins to be compressed. As the gas is compressed, pressure increases while volume decreases. Once the pressure and volume reach a certain point, the temperature begins to rise again. In every Carnot heat engine, the gas ends at the same pressure, temperature, and volume as it began, thus completing a cycle.

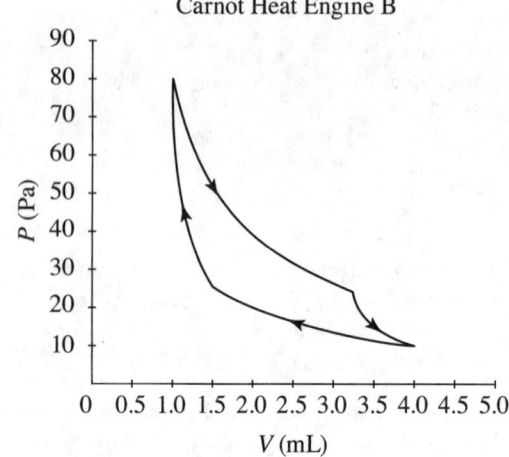

Figure 1

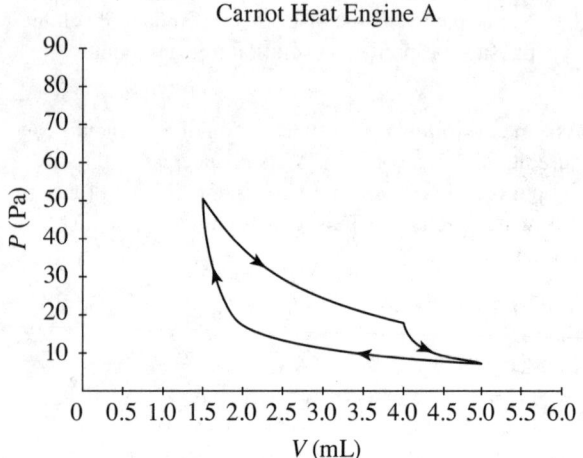

GO ON TO THE NEXT PAGE.

30. At which of the following volumes and pressures does the gas in Carnot heat engine B have the highest temperature?

   F. $V = 1.0$ mL and $P = 80$ Pa
   G. $V = 2.0$ mL and $P = 20$ Pa
   H. $V = 3.5$ mL and $P = 15$ Pa
   J. $V = 4.0$ mL and $P = 10$ Pa

31. According to Figure 2, for Carnot heat engine B, when V was decreasing from its largest value and had a value of 2.0 mL, P had a value closest to:

   A. 10 Pa.
   B. 20 Pa.
   C. 40 Pa.
   D. 70 Pa.

32. For Carnot heat engine A, the minimum value of P was obtained at a V closest to:

   F. 0.5 mL.
   G. 2.0 mL.
   H. 4.0 mL.
   J. 5.0 mL.

33. Consider the largest value of V and the smallest value of V in Figure 2. How are these values related?

   A. The smallest value of V is -4 times the largest value of V.
   B. The smallest value of V is $\frac{1}{8}$ times the largest value of V.
   C. The smallest value of V is $\frac{1}{4}$ times the largest value of V.
   D. The smallest value of V is 4 times the largest value of V.

34. The *reversible isothermal expansion* step of a Carnot heat engine cycle takes place when P is decreased from its highest value and V is increased from its lowest value. According to Figure 1, the *reversible isothermal expansion* step for Carnot heat engine A begins when V is closest to:

   F. 1.5 mL.
   G. 2.25 mL.
   H. 3.0 mL.
   J. 3.5 mL.

GO ON TO THE NEXT PAGE.

Passage VII

The pH at which a protein is uncharged is called its *isoelectric point (pI)*. As the surrounding pH decreases, proteins gain an increasing positive charge. As the surrounding pH increases, proteins gain an increasingly negative charge. In *gel electrophoresis*, a mixture of proteins can be separated based on their relative charge. The proteins are first dissolved in a solvent and then placed at the starting point of an agarose gel. A current is applied to the gel and the proteins migrate different distances according to their charge (see Figure 1).

Figure 1

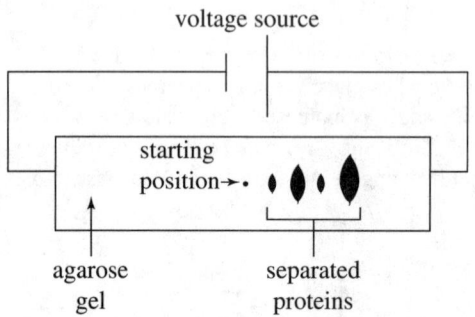

The following experiments were done to determine how varying the pH of a solvent affects the separation of proteins with gel electrophoresis. Table 1 shows the isoelectric points of the proteins and the pH values of the solvents used.

Table 1	
Protein	*pI*
A	8.2
B	7.4
C	6.8
D	5.9
Solvent	pH
1	8.9
2	9.6
3	10.2

Experiment 1

A special paper 150 mm long is treated with an agarose gel. Electrodes were attached on each end and wired to a 100-volt source. A 150 μg mixture of proteins A–D was added to Solvent 1 to make a 200 μL solution. The solution was placed at the starting point of the gel and allowed to separate for 60 minutes. The density of the separated proteins was plotted as a percentage over their distance traveled. The procedure was repeated for Solvents 2 and 3 and the results presented in Figure 2.

Figure 2

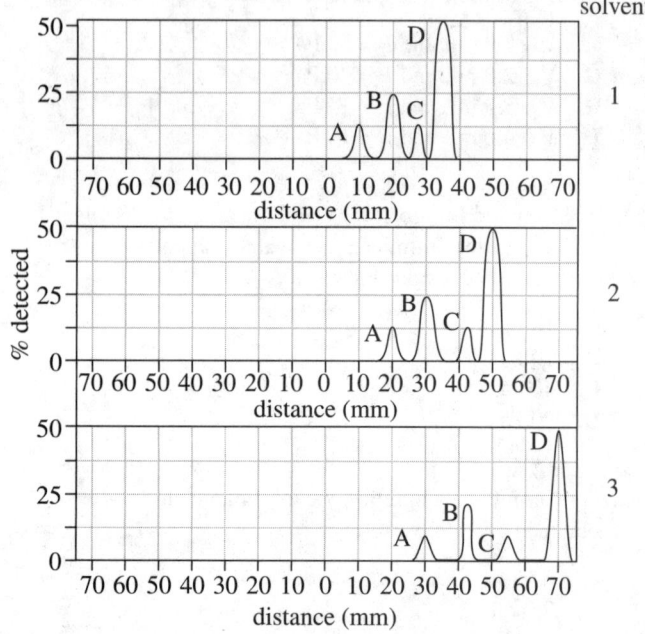

Experiment 2

The procedures of Experiment 1 were repeated after reversing the electrode attachments on the voltage source. Results are shown in Figure 3.

Figure 3

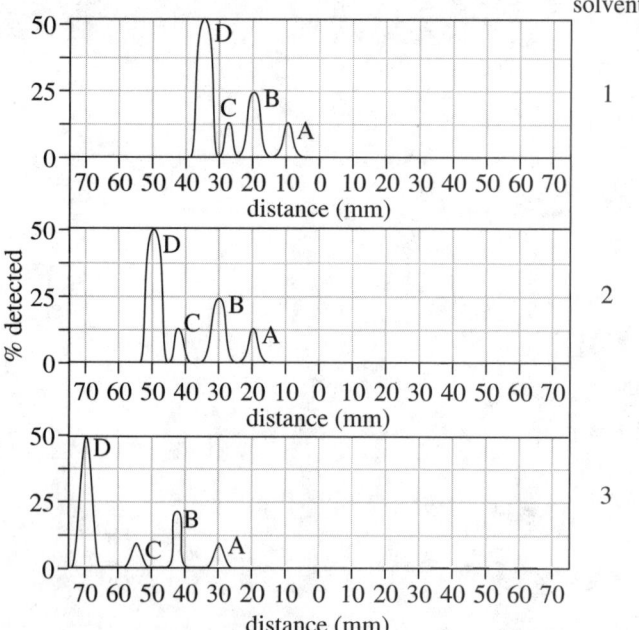

GO ON TO THE NEXT PAGE.

35. In Experiment 2, when Solvent 2 was used, the majority of Protein D migrated a distance from the starting point closest to:

   A. 15 mm.
   B. 35 mm.
   C. 50 mm.
   D. 65 mm.

36. Suppose that Experiment 1 were repeated using a solvent with a pH of 8.4. The migration distance of Protein A would most likely peak at:

   F. less than 10 mm.
   G. between 10 mm and 20 mm.
   H. between 20 mm and 30 mm.
   J. greater than 30 mm.

37. Protein L has an isoelectric point (pI) of 6.6. The results of Experiments 1 and 2 would be most similar to the plots shown in Figures 1 and 2 if, in each trial, Protein L were added to the protein mixture after removing:

   A. Protein A.
   B. Protein B.
   C. Protein C.
   D. Protein D.

38. The *resolution* of gel electrophoresis decreases as the overall distance between the peaks on the density plot decreases. Based on the results of Experiments 1 and 2, which of the following sets of conditions had the lowest resolution for the separation?

	Experiment 1	Experiment 2
F.	Solvent 1	Solvent 1
G.	Solvent 2	Solvent 3
H.	Solvent 3	Solvent 1
J.	Solvent 3	Solvent 3

39. Suppose that Experiment 1 will be repeated using Solvent 2, but Protein Y ($pI = 7.1$) is added to the overall mixture. Which of the following best predicts the order of migration distances of the 5 proteins, from shortest to longest?

   A. D, C, Y, B, A
   B. D, Y, C, B, A
   C. A, Y, B, C, D
   D. A, B, Y, C, D

40. In Experiment 2, for Solvent 2, at the migration distance where Protein B returned to its 0% migration detection, the percent of Protein A that migrated using Solvent 3 was closest to:

   F. 0%.
   G. 25%.
   H. 50%.
   J. 75%.

END OF TEST 4
STOP! DO NOT RETURN TO ANY OTHER TEST.

Directions

This is a test of your writing skills. You will have forty (40) minutes to read the prompt, plan your response, and write an essay in English. Before you begin working, read all material in this test booklet carefully to understand exactly what you are being asked to do.

You will write your answer on the lined pages in the answer document provided. Your writing on those pages will be scored. You may use the unlined pages in this test booklet to plan your essay. Your work on these pages will not be scored.

Your essay will be evaluated based on the evidence it provides of your ability to:

- clearly state your own perspective on a complex issue and analyze the relationship between your perspective and at least one other perspective

- develop and support your ideas with reasoning and examples

- organize your ideas clearly and logically

- communicate your ideas effectively in standard written English

Lay your pencil down immediately when time is called.

DO NOT OPEN THIS BOOK UNTIL YOU ARE TOLD TO DO SO.

Composition paper for the essay can be found beginning on page 79.

Cell Phones While Driving

In only a short time, the use of cell phones, or "smartphones," has significantly increased. In direct relation, problems with their use at certain times have also risen. While driving, people use the smartphone for various activities such as texting, searching the Internet, or mapping a route with GPS. Certain studies suggest that operating a vehicle while using a cell phone is almost as severe, if not the same, as driving while intoxicated. Certain parts of the world have banned talking on the phone while driving, whereas regulations in the United States currently vary from state to state.

Read and carefully consider these perspectives. Each suggests a particular way of thinking about the conflict between driving with a cell phone and both public and personal safety.

Perspective One	Perspective Two	Perspective Three
Teenage drivers are more likely to use phones in cars. Teens are already the highest-risk drivers, so a cell-phone ban would decrease reckless driving at a proportionately higher rate among the most dangerous group.	There will always be distractions. Anything—other passengers, commotion outside, news interruptions on the radio—might distract a driver. Rather than ban cell phones, spend time teaching drivers how to better handle interferences.	Holding a cell phone while driving is dangerous. One hand is not on the steering wheel, which can significantly hinder the reaction time one needs to deal with an occurrence. In the case of an emergency, having one hand unavailable will slow the driver's reaction time and increase the chance of an accident.

Essay Task

Write a unified, coherent essay in which you evaluate multiple perspectives on the usage of cell phones while driving. In your essay, be sure to:

- clearly state your own perspective on the issue and analyze the relationship between your perspective and at least one other perspective
- develop and support your ideas with reasoning and examples
- organize your ideas clearly and logically
- communicate your ideas effectively in standard written English

Your perspective may be in full agreement with any of the others, in partial agreement, or wholly different. Whatever the case, support your ideas with logical reasoning and detailed, persuasive examples.

ACT Diagnostic Test Form

USE A SOFT LEAD NO. 2 PENCIL ONLY.
(Do NOT use a mechanical pencil, ink,
ballpoint, correction fluid, or felt-tip pen.)

E-MAIL: _____

PHONE NO.: _____
(Print)

SCHOOL: _____

CLASS OF: _____

IMPORTANT: Please fill in these boxes exactly
as shown on the back cover of your tests book.

2. TEST FORM

3. TEST CODE

⓪ ⓪ ⓪ ⓪
① ① ① ①
② ② ② ②
③ ③ ③ ③
④ ④ ④ ④
⑤ ⑤ ⑤ ⑤
⑥ ⑥ ⑥ ⑥
⑦ ⑦ ⑦ ⑦
⑧ ⑧ ⑧ ⑧
⑨ ⑨ ⑨ ⑨

ALL examinees must complete Blocks A, B, C, and D – please print.

A   NAME, MAILING ADDRESS, AND TELEPHONE
(Please print.)

Last Name   First Name   MI (Middle Initial)

House Number & Street (Apt. No.); or PO Box & No.; or RR & No.

City   State/Province   ZIP/Postal Code

/

Area Code   Number   Country

B   MATCH NAME
(First 5 letters of last name)

ⓐ ⓐ ⓐ ⓐ ⓐ
Ⓑ Ⓑ Ⓑ Ⓑ Ⓑ
Ⓒ Ⓒ Ⓒ Ⓒ Ⓒ
Ⓓ Ⓓ Ⓓ Ⓓ Ⓓ
Ⓔ Ⓔ Ⓔ Ⓔ Ⓔ
Ⓕ Ⓕ Ⓕ Ⓕ Ⓕ
Ⓖ Ⓖ Ⓖ Ⓖ Ⓖ
Ⓗ Ⓗ Ⓗ Ⓗ Ⓗ
Ⓘ Ⓘ Ⓘ Ⓘ Ⓘ
Ⓚ Ⓚ Ⓚ Ⓚ Ⓚ
Ⓛ Ⓛ Ⓛ Ⓛ Ⓛ
Ⓜ Ⓜ Ⓜ Ⓜ Ⓜ
Ⓝ Ⓝ Ⓝ Ⓝ Ⓝ
Ⓞ Ⓞ Ⓞ Ⓞ Ⓞ
Ⓟ Ⓟ Ⓟ Ⓟ Ⓟ
Ⓠ Ⓠ Ⓠ Ⓠ Ⓠ
Ⓡ Ⓡ Ⓡ Ⓡ Ⓡ
Ⓢ Ⓢ Ⓢ Ⓢ Ⓢ
Ⓣ Ⓣ Ⓣ Ⓣ Ⓣ
Ⓤ Ⓤ Ⓤ Ⓤ Ⓤ
Ⓥ Ⓥ Ⓥ Ⓥ Ⓥ
Ⓦ Ⓦ Ⓦ Ⓦ Ⓦ
Ⓧ Ⓧ Ⓧ Ⓧ Ⓧ
Ⓨ Ⓨ Ⓨ Ⓨ Ⓨ
Ⓩ Ⓩ Ⓩ Ⓩ Ⓩ

C   MATCH NUMBER

① ① ① ①   ① ① ① ①
② ② ② ②   ② ② ② ②
③ ③ ③ ③   ③ ③ ③ ③
④ ④ ④ ④   ④ ④ ④ ④
⑤ ⑤ ⑤ ⑤   ⑤ ⑤ ⑤ ⑤
⑥ ⑥ ⑥ ⑥   ⑥ ⑥ ⑥ ⑥
⑦ ⑦ ⑦ ⑦   ⑦ ⑦ ⑦ ⑦
⑧ ⑧ ⑧ ⑧   ⑧ ⑧ ⑧ ⑧
⑨ ⑨ ⑨ ⑨   ⑨ ⑨ ⑨ ⑨
⓪ ⓪ ⓪ ⓪   ⓪ ⓪ ⓪ ⓪

D   DATE OF BIRTH

Month		Day	Year
○ January			
○ February			
○ March		① ①	① ①
○ April		② ②	② ②
○ May		③ ③	③ ③
○ June		④	④ ④
○ July		⑤	⑤ ⑤
○ August		⑥	⑥ ⑥
○ September		⑦	⑦ ⑦
○ October		⑧	⑧ ⑧
○ November		⑨	⑨ ⑨
○ December		⓪	⓪ ⓪

Marking Directions: Mark only **one** oval for
each question. Fill in response completely.
Erase errors cleanly without smudging.

Correct mark: ○ ● ○ ○

- -

Do NOT use these *incorrect* or *bad* marks.

Incorrect marks: ⊘ ⊗ ⊖ ⊙
Overlapping mark: ○ ○ ◑◐ ○
Cross-out mark: ○ ○ ⊗ ○
Smudged erasure: ○ ○ ◐ ○
Mark is too light: ◌ ○ ○ ○

BOOKLET NUMBER

① ① ① ① ① ①
② ② ② ② ② ②
③ ③ ③ ③ ③ ③
④ ④ ④ ④ ④ ④
⑤ ⑤ ⑤ ⑤ ⑤ ⑤
⑥ ⑥ ⑥ ⑥ ⑥ ⑥
⑦ ⑦ ⑦ ⑦ ⑦ ⑦
⑧ ⑧ ⑧ ⑧ ⑧ ⑧
⑨ ⑨ ⑨ ⑨ ⑨ ⑨
⓪ ⓪ ⓪ ⓪ ⓪ ⓪

FORM

Print your
3-character
Test Form in
the boxes
above and
fill in the
corresponding
oval at the
right.

BE SURE TO FILL IN THE CORRECT FORM OVAL.

PRE ○

THIS PAGE IS INTENTIONALLY LEFT BLANK.

The Princeton Review
Diagnostic ACT Form

TEST 1: ENGLISH

1 Ⓐ Ⓑ Ⓒ Ⓓ	11 Ⓐ Ⓑ Ⓒ Ⓓ	21 Ⓐ Ⓑ Ⓒ Ⓓ	31 Ⓐ Ⓑ Ⓒ Ⓓ	41 Ⓐ Ⓑ Ⓒ Ⓓ
2 Ⓕ Ⓖ Ⓗ Ⓙ	12 Ⓕ Ⓖ Ⓗ Ⓙ	22 Ⓕ Ⓖ Ⓗ Ⓙ	32 Ⓕ Ⓖ Ⓗ Ⓙ	42 Ⓕ Ⓖ Ⓗ Ⓙ
3 Ⓐ Ⓑ Ⓒ Ⓓ	13 Ⓐ Ⓑ Ⓒ Ⓓ	23 Ⓐ Ⓑ Ⓒ Ⓓ	33 Ⓐ Ⓑ Ⓒ Ⓓ	43 Ⓐ Ⓑ Ⓒ Ⓓ
4 Ⓕ Ⓖ Ⓗ Ⓙ	14 Ⓕ Ⓖ Ⓗ Ⓙ	24 Ⓕ Ⓖ Ⓗ Ⓙ	34 Ⓕ Ⓖ Ⓗ Ⓙ	44 Ⓕ Ⓖ Ⓗ Ⓙ
5 Ⓐ Ⓑ Ⓒ Ⓓ	15 Ⓐ Ⓑ Ⓒ Ⓓ	25 Ⓐ Ⓑ Ⓒ Ⓓ	35 Ⓐ Ⓑ Ⓒ Ⓓ	45 Ⓐ Ⓑ Ⓒ Ⓓ
6 Ⓕ Ⓖ Ⓗ Ⓙ	16 Ⓕ Ⓖ Ⓗ Ⓙ	26 Ⓕ Ⓖ Ⓗ Ⓙ	36 Ⓕ Ⓖ Ⓗ Ⓙ	46 Ⓕ Ⓖ Ⓗ Ⓙ
7 Ⓐ Ⓑ Ⓒ Ⓓ	17 Ⓐ Ⓑ Ⓒ Ⓓ	27 Ⓐ Ⓑ Ⓒ Ⓓ	37 Ⓐ Ⓑ Ⓒ Ⓓ	47 Ⓐ Ⓑ Ⓒ Ⓓ
8 Ⓕ Ⓖ Ⓗ Ⓙ	18 Ⓕ Ⓖ Ⓗ Ⓙ	28 Ⓕ Ⓖ Ⓗ Ⓙ	38 Ⓕ Ⓖ Ⓗ Ⓙ	48 Ⓕ Ⓖ Ⓗ Ⓙ
9 Ⓐ Ⓑ Ⓒ Ⓓ	19 Ⓐ Ⓑ Ⓒ Ⓓ	29 Ⓐ Ⓑ Ⓒ Ⓓ	39 Ⓐ Ⓑ Ⓒ Ⓓ	49 Ⓐ Ⓑ Ⓒ Ⓓ
10 Ⓕ Ⓖ Ⓗ Ⓙ	20 Ⓕ Ⓖ Ⓗ Ⓙ	30 Ⓕ Ⓖ Ⓗ Ⓙ	40 Ⓕ Ⓖ Ⓗ Ⓙ	50 Ⓕ Ⓖ Ⓗ Ⓙ

TEST 2: MATHEMATICS

1 Ⓐ Ⓑ Ⓒ Ⓓ	11 Ⓐ Ⓑ Ⓒ Ⓓ	21 Ⓐ Ⓑ Ⓒ Ⓓ	31 Ⓐ Ⓑ Ⓒ Ⓓ	41 Ⓐ Ⓑ Ⓒ Ⓓ
2 Ⓕ Ⓖ Ⓗ Ⓙ	12 Ⓕ Ⓖ Ⓗ Ⓙ	22 Ⓕ Ⓖ Ⓗ Ⓙ	32 Ⓕ Ⓖ Ⓗ Ⓙ	42 Ⓕ Ⓖ Ⓗ Ⓙ
3 Ⓐ Ⓑ Ⓒ Ⓓ	13 Ⓐ Ⓑ Ⓒ Ⓓ	23 Ⓐ Ⓑ Ⓒ Ⓓ	33 Ⓐ Ⓑ Ⓒ Ⓓ	43 Ⓐ Ⓑ Ⓒ Ⓓ
4 Ⓕ Ⓖ Ⓗ Ⓙ	14 Ⓕ Ⓖ Ⓗ Ⓙ	24 Ⓕ Ⓖ Ⓗ Ⓙ	34 Ⓕ Ⓖ Ⓗ Ⓙ	44 Ⓕ Ⓖ Ⓗ Ⓙ
5 Ⓐ Ⓑ Ⓒ Ⓓ	15 Ⓐ Ⓑ Ⓒ Ⓓ	25 Ⓐ Ⓑ Ⓒ Ⓓ	35 Ⓐ Ⓑ Ⓒ Ⓓ	45 Ⓐ Ⓑ Ⓒ Ⓓ
6 Ⓕ Ⓖ Ⓗ Ⓙ	16 Ⓕ Ⓖ Ⓗ Ⓙ	26 Ⓕ Ⓖ Ⓗ Ⓙ	36 Ⓕ Ⓖ Ⓗ Ⓙ	
7 Ⓐ Ⓑ Ⓒ Ⓓ	17 Ⓐ Ⓑ Ⓒ Ⓓ	27 Ⓐ Ⓑ Ⓒ Ⓓ	37 Ⓐ Ⓑ Ⓒ Ⓓ	
8 Ⓕ Ⓖ Ⓗ Ⓙ	18 Ⓕ Ⓖ Ⓗ Ⓙ	28 Ⓕ Ⓖ Ⓗ Ⓙ	38 Ⓕ Ⓖ Ⓗ Ⓙ	
9 Ⓐ Ⓑ Ⓒ Ⓓ	19 Ⓐ Ⓑ Ⓒ Ⓓ	29 Ⓐ Ⓑ Ⓒ Ⓓ	39 Ⓐ Ⓑ Ⓒ Ⓓ	
10 Ⓕ Ⓖ Ⓗ Ⓙ	20 Ⓕ Ⓖ Ⓗ Ⓙ	30 Ⓕ Ⓖ Ⓗ Ⓙ	40 Ⓕ Ⓖ Ⓗ Ⓙ	

The Princeton Review
Diagnostic ACT Form

TEST 3: READING

1 Ⓐ Ⓑ Ⓒ Ⓓ	7 Ⓐ Ⓑ Ⓒ Ⓓ	13 Ⓐ Ⓑ Ⓒ Ⓓ	19 Ⓐ Ⓑ Ⓒ Ⓓ	25 Ⓐ Ⓑ Ⓒ Ⓓ	31 Ⓐ Ⓑ Ⓒ Ⓓ
2 Ⓕ Ⓖ Ⓗ Ⓙ	8 Ⓕ Ⓖ Ⓗ Ⓙ	14 Ⓕ Ⓖ Ⓗ Ⓙ	20 Ⓕ Ⓖ Ⓗ Ⓙ	26 Ⓕ Ⓖ Ⓗ Ⓙ	32 Ⓕ Ⓖ Ⓗ Ⓙ
3 Ⓐ Ⓑ Ⓒ Ⓓ	9 Ⓐ Ⓑ Ⓒ Ⓓ	15 Ⓐ Ⓑ Ⓒ Ⓓ	21 Ⓐ Ⓑ Ⓒ Ⓓ	27 Ⓐ Ⓑ Ⓒ Ⓓ	33 Ⓐ Ⓑ Ⓒ Ⓓ
4 Ⓕ Ⓖ Ⓗ Ⓙ	10 Ⓕ Ⓖ Ⓗ Ⓙ	16 Ⓕ Ⓖ Ⓗ Ⓙ	22 Ⓕ Ⓖ Ⓗ Ⓙ	28 Ⓕ Ⓖ Ⓗ Ⓙ	34 Ⓕ Ⓖ Ⓗ Ⓙ
5 Ⓐ Ⓑ Ⓒ Ⓓ	11 Ⓐ Ⓑ Ⓒ Ⓓ	17 Ⓐ Ⓑ Ⓒ Ⓓ	23 Ⓐ Ⓑ Ⓒ Ⓓ	29 Ⓐ Ⓑ Ⓒ Ⓓ	35 Ⓐ Ⓑ Ⓒ Ⓓ
6 Ⓕ Ⓖ Ⓗ Ⓙ	12 Ⓕ Ⓖ Ⓗ Ⓙ	18 Ⓕ Ⓖ Ⓗ Ⓙ	24 Ⓕ Ⓖ Ⓗ Ⓙ	30 Ⓕ Ⓖ Ⓗ Ⓙ	36 Ⓕ Ⓖ Ⓗ Ⓙ

TEST 4: SCIENCE

1 Ⓐ Ⓑ Ⓒ Ⓓ	8 Ⓕ Ⓖ Ⓗ Ⓙ	15 Ⓐ Ⓑ Ⓒ Ⓓ	22 Ⓕ Ⓖ Ⓗ Ⓙ	29 Ⓐ Ⓑ Ⓒ Ⓓ	36 Ⓕ Ⓖ Ⓗ Ⓙ
2 Ⓕ Ⓖ Ⓗ Ⓙ	9 Ⓐ Ⓑ Ⓒ Ⓓ	16 Ⓕ Ⓖ Ⓗ Ⓙ	23 Ⓐ Ⓑ Ⓒ Ⓓ	30 Ⓕ Ⓖ Ⓗ Ⓙ	37 Ⓐ Ⓑ Ⓒ Ⓓ
3 Ⓐ Ⓑ Ⓒ Ⓓ	10 Ⓕ Ⓖ Ⓗ Ⓙ	17 Ⓐ Ⓑ Ⓒ Ⓓ	24 Ⓕ Ⓖ Ⓗ Ⓙ	31 Ⓐ Ⓑ Ⓒ Ⓓ	38 Ⓕ Ⓖ Ⓗ Ⓙ
4 Ⓕ Ⓖ Ⓗ Ⓙ	11 Ⓐ Ⓑ Ⓒ Ⓓ	18 Ⓕ Ⓖ Ⓗ Ⓙ	25 Ⓐ Ⓑ Ⓒ Ⓓ	32 Ⓕ Ⓖ Ⓗ Ⓙ	39 Ⓐ Ⓑ Ⓒ Ⓓ
5 Ⓐ Ⓑ Ⓒ Ⓓ	12 Ⓕ Ⓖ Ⓗ Ⓙ	19 Ⓐ Ⓑ Ⓒ Ⓓ	26 Ⓕ Ⓖ Ⓗ Ⓙ	33 Ⓐ Ⓑ Ⓒ Ⓓ	40 Ⓕ Ⓖ Ⓗ Ⓙ
6 Ⓕ Ⓖ Ⓗ Ⓙ	13 Ⓐ Ⓑ Ⓒ Ⓓ	20 Ⓕ Ⓖ Ⓗ Ⓙ	27 Ⓐ Ⓑ Ⓒ Ⓓ	34 Ⓕ Ⓖ Ⓗ Ⓙ	
7 Ⓐ Ⓑ Ⓒ Ⓓ	14 Ⓕ Ⓖ Ⓗ Ⓙ	21 Ⓐ Ⓑ Ⓒ Ⓓ	28 Ⓕ Ⓖ Ⓗ Ⓙ	35 Ⓐ Ⓑ Ⓒ Ⓓ	

The Princeton Review
Diagnostic ACT Form

ESSAY

Begin your essay on this side. If necessary, continue on the opposite side.

Continue on the opposite side if necessary.

The Princeton Review
Diagnostic ACT Form

Continued from previous page.

The Princeton Review
Diagnostic ACT Form

Continued from previous page.

The Princeton Review
Diagnostic ACT Form

Continued from previous page.

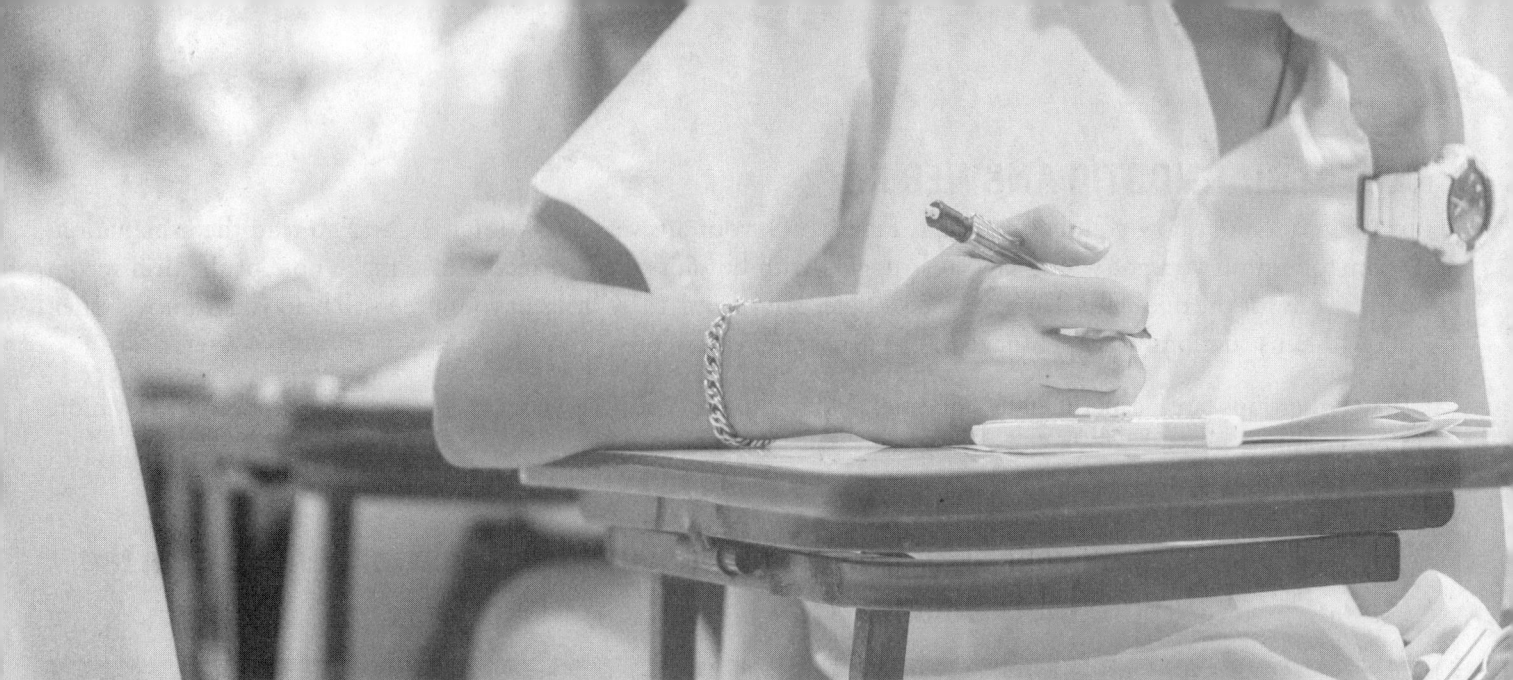

Test 1
Answers and
Explanations

TEST 1: DIAGNOSTIC ANSWER KEY

Let's take a look at how you did on Test 1. First, check your answers below (Step 1), and go read the explanations for any questions you got wrong or you struggled with but answered correctly. Also make note of the drill recommendations for the questions that gave you trouble; prioritizing these drills in your prep will help you improve. Then, follow the instructions in Step 2 (page 89) to determine your score.

*These questions are "experimental" questions that do not count towards your score. See page 89 for more information.

STEP 1 » Check your answers and mark any correct answers with a ✔ in the appropriate column.

English									○
Q #	Ans.	✔	Chapter	Drill # (Q #)	Q #	Ans.	✔	Chapter	Drill # (Q #)
1	D		English Drills	1 (1, 3, 6), 2 (3, 10), 3 (2, 3), 5 (10), 6 (2), 7 (10), 8 (2), 9 (3, 9, 10) 10 (10), 12 (9, 10), 14 (6)	14	J		English Drills	3 (4), 8 (7)
2	H		English Drills	1 (2), 10 (3), 11 (4)	15	B		English Drills	1 (5), 5 (8), 6 (5), 11 (6), 12 (5) 13 (6)
3	B		English Drills	1 (7), 4 (2, 8), 5 (1, 9), 6 (9), 7 (5), 8 (1), 9 (2, 4), 10 (1, 5), 12 (8)	16	G		English Drills	1 (4, 10), 2 (4, 8, 9), 5 (7), 6 (3), 7 (6), 11 (1, 3, 5), 13 (7)
4	G		English Drills	1 (5), 5 (8), 6 (5), 11 (6), 12 (5) 13 (6)	17	A		English Drills	1 (8), 2 (6), 4 (6), 9 (7), 14 (4)
5	A		English Drills	2 (1), 3 (7), 4 (5), 5 (2, 6), 6 (6), 7 (1, 3, 7), 10 (2)	18	F		English Drills	1 (7), 4 (2, 8), 5 (1, 9), 6 (9), 7 (5), 8 (1), 9 (2, 4), 10 (1, 5), 12 (8)
6	H		English Drills	4 (7, 10), 5 (4), 7 (8), 8 (10), 10 (9), 11 (2), 12 (7)	19	B		English Drills	1 (2), 10 (3), 11 (4)
7	D		English Drills	8 (9), 13 (2), 14 (2)	20	J		English Drills	5 (3), 8 (5), 9 (8), 10 (4), 11 (8), 13 (1)
8	F		English Drills	1 (4, 10), 2 (4, 8, 9), 5 (7), 6 (3), 7 (6), 11 (1, 3, 5), 13 (7)	21	D		English Drills	1 (5), 5 (8), 6 (5), 11 (6), 12 (5) 13 (6)
9	D		English Drills	3 (4), 8 (7)	22	G		English Drills	1 (7), 4 (2, 8), 5 (1, 9), 6 (9), 7 (5), 8 (1), 9 (2, 4), 10 (1, 5), 12 (8)
10	F		English Drills	1 (8), 2 (6), 4 (6), 9 (7), 14 (4)	23	A		English Drills	8 (10)
11	C		English Drills	1 (4, 10), 2 (4, 8, 9), 5 (7), 6 (3), 7 (6), 11 (1, 3), 13 (7)	24	J		English Drills	2 (5), 3 (6), 6 (4, 8, 10), 7 (2), 9 (6), 12 (3, 4), 13 (5), 14 (1, 5)
12	J		English Drills	4 (10), 6 (1), 7 (4), 8 (6), 9 (5), 12 (1, 2, 6), 14 (3, 9)	25	B		English Drills	7 (9), 11 (10)
13	C		English Drills	1 (1, 3), 2 (10), 5 (10), 7 (10), 8 (2), 9 (3, 10), 10 (10), 12 (9, 10)	26	F		English Drills	2 (1), 3 (7), 4 (5), 5 (2, 6), 6 (6), 7 (1, 3, 7), 10 (2)

Q #	Ans.	✔	Chapter	Drill # (Q #)	Q #	Ans.	✔	Chapter	Drill # (Q #)
27	B		English Drills	1 (4, 10), 2 (4, 8, 9), 5 (7), 6 (3), 7 (6), 11 (1, 3, 5), 13 (7)	39	D		English Drills	5 (5), 10 (8)
28	H		English Drills	1 (8), 2 (6), 4 (6), 9 (7), 14 (4)	40	F		English Drills	1 (7), 4 (2, 8), 5 (1, 9), 6 (9), 7 (5), 8 (1), 9 (2, 4), 10 (1, 5), 12 (8)
29	D		English Drills	3 (9), 4 (9), 11 (7)	41*	B		English Drills	2 (5), 3 (6), 6 (4, 8, 10), 7 (2), 9(6), 12 (3, 4), 13 (5), 14 (1, 5)
30	G		English Drills	1 (4, 10), 2 (4, 8, 9), 5 (7), 6 (3), 7 (6), 11 (1, 3, 5), 13 (7)	42*	G		English Drills	1 (1, 3, 6), 2 (3, 10), 3 (2, 3), 5 (10), 6 (2), 7 (10), 8 (2), 9 (3, 9, 10) 10 (10), 12 (9, 10)
31	A		English Drills	1 (5), 5 (8), 6 (5), 11 (6), 12 (5) 13 (6)	43*	D		English Drills	3 (8), 4 (4), 7 (9), 8 (4), 11 (9), 13 (9), 14 (8, 10)
32	J		English Drills	5 (3), 8 (5), 9 (8), 10 (4), 11 (8), 13 (1)	44*	H		English Drills	1 (4, 10), 2 (4, 8, 9), 5 (7), 6 (3), 7 (6), 11 (1, 3, 5), 13 (7)
33	B		English Drills	2 (5), 3 (6), 6 (4, 8, 10), 7 (2), 9(6), 12 (3, 4), 13 (5), 14 (1, 5)	45*	C		English Drills	1 (9), 2 (2), 6 (7), 13 (10)
34	H		English Drills	1 (4, 10), 2 (4, 8, 9), 5 (7), 6 (3), 7 (6), 11 (1, 3, 5), 13 (7)	46*	H		English Drills	7 (8), 8 (10), 10 (9)
35	B		English Drills	7 (9), 11 (10)	47*	A		English Drills	4 (3)
36	F		English Drills	8 (9), 13 (2), 14 (2)	48*	H		English Drills	1 (5), 5 (8), 6 (5), 11 (6), 12 (5) 13 (6)
37	C		English Drills	5 (3), 8 (5), 9 (8), 10 (4), 11 (8), 13 (1)	49*	A		English Drills	4 (5), 13 (3)
38	H		English Drills	1 (1, 3, 6), 2 (3, 10), 3 (2, 3), 5 (10), 6 (2), 7 (10), 8 (2), 9 (3, 9, 10) 10 (10), 12 (9, 10), 14 (6)	50*	J		English Drills	7 (8), 8 (10), 10 (9)

					Mathematics				
Q #	Ans.	✔	Chapter	Drill	Q #	Ans.	✔	Chapter	Drill
1	C		Math Drills	Statistics and Probability Drill 1	24	J		Math Drills	Functions Drill 1
2	J		Math Drills	Integrating Essential Skills Drill 1	25	C		Math Drills	Geometry Drill 1
3	B		Math Drills	Algebra Drill 1	26	G		Math Drills	Functions Drill 2
4	H		Math Drills	Statistics and Probability Drill 1	27*	B		Math Drills	Functions Drill 1
5	A		Math Drills	Functions Drill 1	28	H		Math Drills	Geometry Drill 1
6	J		Math Drills	Statistics and Probability Drill 1	29	A		Math Drills	Algebra Drill 2
7*	C		Math Drills	Integrating Essential Skills Drill 1	30	J		Math Drills	Algebra Drill 2
8	G		Math Drills	Functions Drill 2	31	D		Math Drills	Number and Quantity Drill 1
9	C		Math Drills	Integrating Essential Skills Drill 3	32	F		Math Drills	Geometry Drill 2
10	F		Math Drills	Geometry Drill 1	33	C		Math Drills	Integrating Essential Skills Drill 2
11	D		Math Drills	Algebra Drill 1	34	H		Math Drills	Number and Quantity Drill 2
12	H		Math Drills	Integrating Essential Skills Drill 2	35	C		Math Drills	Geometry Drill 1
13	A		Math Drills	Algebra Drill 1	36	J		Math Drills	Functions Drill 2
14	F		Math Drills	Algebra Drill 1	37	A		Math Drills	Geometry Drill 1
15	B		Math Drills	Number and Quantity Drill 1	38	F		Math Drills	Geometry Drill 2
16*	H		Math Drills	Geometry Drill 1	39	D		Math Drills	Number and Quantity Drill 2
17	C		Math Drills	Algebra Drill 1	40*	F		Math Drills	Integrating Essential Skills Drill 3
18	H		Math Drills	Integrating Essential Skills Drill 1	41	D		Math Drills	Integrating Essential Skills Drill 1
19	B		Math Drills	Geometry Drill 1	42	G		Math Drills	Functions Drill 2
20	F		Math Drills	Geometry Drill 2	43	C		Math Drills	Number and Quantity Drill 2
21	C		Math Drills	Algebra Drill 2	44	F		Math Drills	Integrating Essential Skills Drill 3
22	H		Math Drills	Integrating Essential Skills Drill 1	45	C		Math Drills	Geometry Drill 2
23	C		Math Drills	Statistics and Probability Drill 1					

Q #	Ans.	✔	Chapter	Drill(s)	Q #	Ans.	✔	Chapter	Drill(s)
				Reading					
1*	A		Reading Drills	Craft and Structure	19	C		Reading Drills	Craft and Structure
2*	J		Reading Drills	Key Ideas and Details	20	J		Reading Drills	Key Ideas and Details
3*	B		Reading Drills	Key Ideas and Details	21	A		Reading Drills	Key Ideas and Details
4*	F		Reading Drills	Key Ideas and Details	22	H		Reading Drills	Key Ideas and Details
5*	D		Reading Drills	Key Ideas and Details	23	D		Reading Drills	Craft and Structure
6*	H		Reading Drills	Key Ideas and Details	24	G		Reading Drills	Key Ideas and Details
7*	B		Reading Drills	Key Ideas and Details	25	A		Reading Drills	Integration of Knowledge and Ideas
8*	G		Reading Drills	Key Ideas and Details	26	G		Reading Drills	Integration of Knowledge and Ideas
9*	B		Reading Drills	Key Ideas and Details	27	C		Reading Drills	Integration of Knowledge and Ideas
10	F		Reading Drills	Craft and Structure	28	F		Reading Drills	Key Ideas and Details
11	C		Reading Drills	Key Ideas and Details	29	A		Reading Drills	Key Ideas and Details
12	J		Reading Drills	Key Ideas and Details	30	G		Reading Drills	Craft and Structure
13	C		Reading Drills	Craft and Structure	31	B		Reading Drills	Key Ideas and Details
14	F		Reading Drills	Key Ideas and Details	32	H		Reading Drills	Craft and Structure
15	D		Reading Drills	Key Ideas and Details	33	D		Reading Drills	Key Ideas and Details
16	F		Reading Drills	Key Ideas and Details	34	F		Reading Drills	Integration of Knowledge and Ideas
17	D		Reading Drills	Craft and Structure	35	C		Reading Drills	Key Ideas and Details
18	G		Reading Drills	Key Ideas and Details	36	J		Reading Drills	Integration of Knowledge and Ideas

				Science						
Q #	Ans.	✔	Chapter	Drill(s)	Q #	Ans.	✔	Chapter	Drill(s)
1	A		Science Drills	Look It Up	21	C		Science Drills	Outside Knowledge
2	F		Science Drills	Later	22	F		Science Drills	Later
3	D		Science Drills	Later	23	D		Science Drills	Later
4	G		Science Drills	Look It Up	24	H		Science Drills	Multiple Viewpoints
5	B		Science Drills	Later	25	A		Science Drills	Multiple Viewpoints
6	J		Science Drills	Later	26	F		Science Drills	Multiple Viewpoints
7*	C		Science Drills	Look It Up	27	B		Science Drills	Multiple Viewpoints
8*	G		Science Drills	Look It Up	28	F		Science Drills	Multiple Viewpoints
9*	A		Science Drills	Look It Up	29	D		Science Drills	Multiple Viewpoints
10*	J		Science Drills	Later	30	F		Science Drills	Look It Up
11*	B		Science Drills	Look It Up	31	B		Science Drills	Look It Up
12*	G		Science Drills	Later	32	J		Science Drills	Look It Up
13	B		Science Drills	Later	33	C		Science Drills	Look It Up
14	H		Science Drills	Outside Knowledge	34	F		Science Drills	Later
15	C		Science Drills	Later	35	C		Science Drills	Look It Up
16	F		Science Drills	Later	36	F		Science Drills	Look It Up
17	A		Science Drills	Look It Up	37	C		Science Drills	Look It Up
18	J		Science Drills	Outside Knowledge	38	F		Science Drills	Look It Up
19	B		Science Drills	Later	39	D		Science Drills	Look It Up
20	H		Science Drills	Look It Up	40	F		Science Drills	Look It Up

STEP 2 ≫ To determine your score, follow the instructions below.

Step A

Determine the number of correct, scored questions in each section. On the Enhanced ACT, some "experimental" items are embedded in each section and will not count toward your score. For Test 1, these questions are marked with an asterisk on the previous chart, but here is a recap.

> English questions 41 through 50
> Math questions 7, 16, 27, and 40
> Reading questions 1 through 9
> Science questions 7 through 12

Excluding any correct answers you got on the above experimental questions, count the number of remaining correct answers for each section and record the number in the space provided for your raw score on the Score Conversion Worksheet below.

Step B

Using the Score Conversion Chart on the next page, convert your raw scores on each section to scaled scores.

Score Conversion Worksheet		
Section	**Raw Score**	**Scaled Score**
English	_____/40	_____
Math	_____/41	_____
Reading	_____/27	_____
Science	_____/34	_____

The optional Science section is not part of the composite score, but if you take that section, your Science score will be reported separately.

To compute your ACT composite score, add the scaled scores for English, Math, and Reading, then divide the total by 3.

Sum of English, Math, and Reading: _____

Divided by 3: _____

This is your ACT composite score.

Step C

To grade your essay, see the Essay Checklist and an example of a top-scoring essay online on your Student Tools.

SCORING YOUR PRACTICE EXAM

Scaled Score	Raw Scores				Scaled Score
	English	**Math**	**Reading**	**Science**	
36	40	40–41	27	34	36
35	38–39	39	26	33	35
34	37	38	25	32	34
33	—	36–37	—	31	33
32	36	35	24	—	32
31	—	34	—	30	31
30	35	33	23	29	30
29	34	32	—	28	29
28	33	31	22	27	28
27	32	29–30	—	26	27
26	31	28	21	24–25	26
25	30	26–27	20	23	25
24	29	25	19	21–22	24
23	27–28	24	18	19–20	23
22	26	23	17	18	22
21	25	22	16	17	21
20	23–24	21	—	16	20
19	22	20	15	15	19
18	21	18–19	14	13–14	18
17	20	16–17	13	12	17
16	19	13–15	12	11	16
15	17–18	11–12	11	10	15
14	16	8–10	10	—	14
13	14–15	6–7	9	9	13
12	13	5	8	8	12
11	11–12	4	7	6–7	11
10	8–10	—	6	5	10
9	7	3	5	4	9
8	6	—	4	—	8
7	5	2	—	3	7
6	4	—	3	—	6
5	3	1	—	2	5
4	2	—	2	—	4
3	—	—	1	1	3
2	1	—	—	—	2
1	0	0	0	0	1

SCORE CONVERSION CHART

TEST 1 ENGLISH ANSWERS AND EXPLANATIONS

Passage I

1. **D** The question is asking to *emphasize the negative reaction that many people had toward Moore's career aspirations*, so eliminate answers that are not *negative*. Choice (A), *impactful*, would be positive toward a career in art, so eliminate it. Choices (B) and (C) are also more positive or neutral toward an art career, so eliminate them. Choice (D), *impractical*, is the only *negative* answer because it suggests that this career isn't a good idea. The correct answer is (D).

2. **H** The question asks about grammar, so look at the answers to see what's changing. Verbs are changing in the answer choices, so identify the subject. The subject of this verb is the act of *painting*, which is singular. Eliminate any answers that are plural: (F), (G), and (J). Choice (H) is the only singular answer. The correct answer is (H).

3. **B** The question is asking for the *least redundant* answer, so eliminate answers that are overly wordy or repeat information given earlier. Eliminate (A) because the phrase *that she is strongly linked to* is not necessary because the sentence is already referring to *her deep connection*, which implies a strong link. Choice (B) is short, so keep it. Eliminate (C) because it's redundant and overly wordy compared to (B); a *link* is something that inherently connects, so *connecting* doesn't need to be stated. Eliminate (D) because there is no reason to add *her ancestors*, given that her *heritage* already indicates the existence of ancestors. The correct answer is (B).

4. **G** The question asks about grammar, so look at the answers to see what's changing. Transitions are changing in the answer choices, and there is also the option to delete, so try that first. Deleting the transition produces a run-on sentence because it contains two complete ideas separated by only a comma, which isn't allowed. Eliminate (J). Next, consider the remaining options. With (F) and (H), the transition is separated from the rest of the sentence with a comma, making the transition unnecessary information. These options also result in two complete ideas separated with only a comma. Eliminate (F) and (H). Choice (G) makes the first part of the sentence an incomplete idea, which allows the incomplete and complete ideas to then be connected with the comma alone, which is acceptable. Therefore, the correct answer is (G).

5. **A** The question is asking for the *clearest and most precise* answer, so use Process of Elimination. Choice (A) works because *showcasing* matches with the other ideas in the passage suggesting that Moore is a *cultural ambassador* and *captures the spirit* of her people's way of life, so keep (A). Eliminate (B) because it's inconsistent with the passage; there is no evidence that Moore needs to *justify*, or defend, her heritage. Eliminate (C) because *exaggerating* is a negative word, and the passage never suggests that Moore's depictions go too far. Eliminate (D) because *vilifying* means "portraying negatively," which also doesn't match the positive tone of the text. The correct answer is (A).

6. **H** The question is asking to provide *the best transition from the preceding paragraph to this paragraph*, so identify the ideas from the two paragraphs. The preceding paragraph is about Moore's *murals* and how they represent her culture. This paragraph discusses Moore's identity as a *committed sustenance*

fisher and how she depicts salmon fishing in her art. Eliminate (F) because *other famous Indigenous artists* aren't mentioned in either paragraph. Eliminate (G) because nothing related to *logos, hats, and even T-shirts* is mentioned in either paragraph. Keep (H) because *her work as an artist* relates back to the previous paragraph and *advocate for…fishing* relates to this paragraph. Eliminate (J) because while both paragraphs touch on how her work reaches beyond her community, there is no specific mention that she is *educating* people; furthermore, this answer doesn't shift from the topic of the previous paragraph to that of this one. The correct answer is (H).

7. **D** The question asks about grammar, so look at the answers to see what's changing. Nouns and pronouns are changing in the answer choices, so eliminate answers that are inconsistent or contain an error. Eliminate (A) because *females* is plural and *its* is singular, which is inconsistent. Eliminate (B) because *it's* means "it is," which is not correct in this context. Eliminate (C) because *female* is singular and *their* is plural. Keep (D) because *female* is singular and *its* is also singular, so they agree. The correct answer is (D).

8. **F** The question asks about grammar, so look at the answers to see what's changing. The punctuation after *traditions* and the structure of the phrase after it are changing. Use Process of Elimination to identify answers that don't produce a complete sentence or make a logical error. Keep (F) because it doesn't contain any errors. Eliminate (G) because *who* is only used for people, but *traditions* aren't people. Eliminate (H) because it suggests that the *traditions* are incorporating *vibrant color schemes*, which doesn't provide a logical meaning; it's her art that is colorful. Eliminate (J) for the same reason; it also describes the traditions themselves as incorporating vibrant color schemes rather than the art. The correct answer is (F).

9. **D** The question is asking for the answer that will maintain *the essay's tone*, so consider the tone of the essay and eliminate options that are inconsistent. The essay's tone is academic and praises Moore's work. Eliminate any answer that doesn't match. Eliminate (A) because it's inconsistent with the academic tone of the passage. Eliminate (B) because *blowing up* is overly casual and not a precise way of describing what Moore does. Eliminate (C) because while *persists* is consistent with the tone, *showing off* has a negative tone that is inconsistent with the passage's positivity. Keep (D) because it's not overly casual and offers a precise description of what Moore does. The correct answer is (D).

10. **F** The question asks about grammar, so look at the answers to see what's changing. Punctuation is changing in the answer choices, so consider the structure of the sentence. The part after the word *people* begins with *for example*, and the phrase *for example* should be set off with punctuation before and after because it's unnecessary information. Eliminate (G) and (J). Comparing (F) and (H), they both put a comma after *for example*, but (F) has a dash before it. The sentence contains a dash later on in the sentence, so consider whether the entire phrase is unnecessary. It says *for example, the importance of community and the harmony between humans and nature*. This is an unnecessary phrase, with the main meaning of the sentence being *Her work invites viewers to connect with the values of her people while preserving Yup'ik traditions in visual form*. Thus, because the phrase has a dash after it, it needs a dash before in order to separate the unnecessary example from the rest of the sentence. Eliminate (H). The correct answer is (F).

Passage II

11. **C** The question asks about grammar, so look at the answers to see what's changing. The structure of the wording is changing, so look to eliminate answers that don't produce a complete sentence. Choice (A) contains two complete ideas (*Its name comes from Trota of Salerno* and *it turns out, she was a physician cited…as a famous authority…*) connected with only the word *and*. This isn't allowed, as a FANBOYS word can connect two complete ideas only if there is a comma before it. Eliminate (A). Choice (B) makes the same error, so eliminate (B). Choice (C) makes the second part an incomplete idea, so it works with the comma. Keep (C). Eliminate (D) because it also creates two complete ideas with only a comma in between. The correct answer is (C).

12. **J** The question asks about grammar, so look at the answers to see what's changing. Punctuation before and after *by scholars* is changing, so identify whether there is a reason to use punctuation before or after the phrase. In the sentence, there is a comma before the word *long* that separates an unnecessary phrase. The phrase is *long doubted by scholars*, referring to her *identity as a historical person*. Since there is a comma before the phrase, there must also be a comma after. Eliminate (G) and (H). Choice (F) separates only *long doubted*, but without this phrase, the sentence would read "Her identity as a historical person by scholars," which isn't correct. Eliminate (F). The correct answer is (J).

13. **C** The question is asking for the answer that will *indicate that Trota was a medical practitioner as well as a student*, so eliminate any answer that doesn't fulfill this goal. Choice (A) is unclear because the word *working* could refer only to what she did as a student, so eliminate (A). Choice (B) suggests that her work was done as a student, so this wouldn't suggest both roles. Eliminate (B). Choice (C) refers to two separate activities—studying and working—and therefore could more clearly indicate the two different roles. Keep (C). Choice (D) uses the word *studied* to refer to something Trota did *for a job*, which wouldn't suggest that she was a student. Eliminate (D). The correct answer is (C).

14. **J** The question is asking for the answer that will maintain *the essay's tone*, so consider the tone of the essay and eliminate options that are inconsistent. The essay's tone is somewhat formal and factual. Eliminate any answer that doesn't match. All four answers relate to the idea of this medical school being superior to others. Choice (J) is clear and somewhat formal, so keep it. In comparison, (F) is more casual, so eliminate it. Choices (G) and (H) are also more casual and less precise than (J), so eliminate them. The correct answer is (J).

15. **B** The question is asking for a *logical* transition, so identify the relationships between the ideas. The previous sentence refers to Trota's *several years* of researching and *treating the city's sick*. This sentence describes what she logically would have done after that: earning a title and authoring a textbook. Eliminate any answer that doesn't match this relationship. Eliminate (A) and (D) because the ideas don't contrast with each other. Keep (B) because it accurately captures the time-change relationship. Eliminate (C) because this sentence is not merely restating the idea from the previous sentence; it's indicating additional things Trota did later on. The correct answer is (B).

Passage III

16. **G**   The question asks about grammar, so look at the answers to see what's changing. Pronouns and verbs are changing in the answer choices, so eliminate anything that isn't consistent with the passage. Eliminate (F) because it creates two complete ideas (*I'd bring my daughter* and *she would ride in the shopping cart…*) separated by only a comma, which isn't allowed. Keep (G) because changing *she* to *who* makes the second part of the sentence incomplete and therefore able to be connected to the complete idea with a comma. Eliminate (H) because *whose* is a possessive pronoun, but the word after it (*ridden*) is a verb and therefore can't be possessed. Eliminate (J) because *whom* is an object pronoun, but a subject pronoun is needed. The correct answer is (G).

17. **A**   The question asks about grammar, so look at the answers to see what's changing. Commas are changing in the answer choices, so read the sentence and use Process of Elimination to determine whether and where any commas are needed. Keep (A) because it doesn't have any commas and there isn't a clear need for commas. Eliminate (B) because *steered us* shouldn't be separated from *around the store*, as they are part of the same thought. Eliminate (C) because a comma shouldn't be used between *that were* and *full of different snacks*, as they are part of the same idea. Eliminate (D) because there is no reason to put a comma before *with*. The correct answer is (A).

18. **F**   The question is asking for the *least redundant* answer, so eliminate answers that are overly wordy or repeat information given earlier. Keep (F) because it's the shortest answer and works in the sentence. Eliminate (G) because the previous sentence already said that she *seems more interested in her phone*. Eliminate (H) because the previous sentence says *as we walk down the cereal aisle*, so this idea doesn't need to be repeated. Eliminate (J) because the previous sentence already said that *she isn't a kid anymore*. The correct answer is (F).

19. **B**   The question asks about grammar, so look at the answers to see what's changing. Verbs are changing in the answer choices, so identify the subject. The subject of the verb is *package*, which is singular, so eliminate (A), (C), and (D), which are all plural. Keep (B) because it's singular. The correct answer is (B).

20. **J**   The question is asking what the paragraph *would primarily lose* if the underlined text were deleted, so try reading the paragraph with and without the underlined text to identify the difference. The first part of the sentence offers one explanation for why the hot dogs are bright red. The underlined text provides a second possible explanation. Eliminate (F) because the underlined portion doesn't specify the *color of the hot dogs*. Eliminate (G) because nothing about the *process* is mentioned in the underlined portion. Eliminate (H) because the explanation doesn't involve the *narrator's feelings*. Keep (J) because *alternative explanation* matches with the role of the underlined text. The correct answer is (J).

21. **D**   The question is asking for a *logical* transition word, so consider the relationships between the ideas. The previous sentence gives the daughter's explanation for the bright red hot dogs. This sentence states that the narrator prefers this explanation. Eliminate (A) because while these ideas do agree, this sentence isn't an additional point; it's responding to the previous idea rather than adding on to it. Eliminate (B) because this idea of the author's preferred explanation wasn't *stated* already.

Eliminate (C) because this sentence isn't a summary of the previous ideas. Keep (D) because the narrator's affection for the daughter in the first two paragraphs makes it unsurprising that they prefer the daughter's explanation. The correct answer is (D).

22. **G** The question is asking for the *least redundant* answer, so eliminate answers that are overly wordy or repeat information given earlier. Eliminate (F) because the phrase *that she recognizes* is redundant with *recognition* earlier in the sentence. Keep (G) because it's short and doesn't contain anything redundant. Eliminate (H) because *excitedly* is redundant with *excited* and *that I am holding* is redundant with *When I hold up the hot dogs*. Eliminate (J) because *recognizes* is redundant with *recognition*. The correct answer is (G).

23. **A** The question is asking for the answer that *most effectively leads into the rest of the essay*, so read the next paragraph to determine what topic the answer should lead into. The following paragraph is about time passing and what has changed or stayed the same. Keep (A) because *I feel time slow down* is consistent with the topic of the rest of the essay. Eliminate (B), (C), and (D) because they don't reference the passage of time that is the focus of the last part of the essay. The correct answer is (A).

24. **J** The question is asking whether a sentence should be added. Consider how it does or does not relate to the surrounding text. The last paragraph focuses on the parent's reminiscence of time passing as the daughter has grown up. The new sentence references other states having bright red hot dogs. Although that might be related to the topic of the passage as a whole, it's not consistent with the focus of this paragraph, so the sentence should not be added. Eliminate (F) and (G). Next, eliminate (H) because even if it said which states have these hot dogs it would still not be consistent with the last paragraph. Keep (J) because it relates to consistency, so it accurately states why this sentence shouldn't be added at this point in the passage. The correct answer is (J).

25. **B** The question is asking where the new sentence should be added, so consider the content of the new sentence and use Process of Elimination to determine where it fits. The new sentence asks why *they* were bright red. The sentence should go in a part of the passage where *they* clearly refers back to the hot dogs. Eliminate (A) because at this point there is no clear word for *they* to refer back to. Keep (B) because *they* would refer back to *hot dogs* and the following sentences offer possible answers to the question. Eliminate (C) because this sentence would incorrectly separate two ideas that belong together (the daughter pretending to do an interview and asking her parent why the hot dogs are red). Additionally, the word *they* would be referring back to *the food's color*, which isn't correct. Eliminate (D) because the sentence after this point shifts to a different topic about time passing, so it's not appropriate to add this question before that idea. The correct answer is (B).

Passage IV

26. **F** The question is asking for the *clearest and most precise* answer, so use Process of Elimination. Keep (F) because *If* suggests a hypothetical cause-and-effect idea that is supported by the context of the sentence. Eliminate (G) because it assumes that *an item* isn't returned by the due date, which is not as logical as the hypothetical situation implied by (F). Eliminate (H) and (J) because they are opposite-direction transitions and therefore don't match with the cause-and-effect idea implied by the sentence. The correct answer is (F).

27. **B** The question asks about grammar, so look at the answers to see what's changing. Connecting words are changing in the answers, and there is also the option to delete, so try that first. Without the underlined phrase, the sentence reads *A late fine may be a small amount of money can lead to the suspension of a person's library account.* This doesn't work because it contains two verbs (*may be* and *can*) for the subject (*fine*) that aren't connected by the word *and*, so eliminate (D). Next, compare the other options. Eliminate (A) because *such that* does not produce a complete sentence. Keep (B) because *that* makes a phrase (*that may be a small amount of money*) that describes *A late fine* and produces a complete sentence. Eliminate (C) because it wrongly suggests that only when a late fine is a *small amount of money* can it lead to account suspension, which isn't logically supported. The correct answer is (B).

28. **H** The question asks about grammar, so look at the answers to see what's changing. Punctuation around the words *and need* is changing, so read the sentence and consider what punctuation is needed. Choice (F) puts commas around the entire phrase *and need people to return items*, suggesting that it is unnecessary to the sentence, but removing the phrase makes the sentence say *While libraries want libraries also seek…*, which isn't correct. Eliminate (F). Choice (G) makes the unnecessary phrase *need people to return items*, making the rest of the sentence say *While libraries want and libraries also seek…*, which isn't correct, so eliminate (G). Choice (H) makes *and need* unnecessary, leaving the rest of the sentence to say *While libraries want people to return items, libraries also…*, which does provide a clear and correct meaning, so keep (H). Choice (J) puts a single dash after need, but there is no other dash in the sentence, so this can only work if the part before the dash is a complete idea, which it isn't. Eliminate (J). The correct answer is (H).

29. **D** The question asks about grammar, so look at the answers to see what's changing. There is a choice between *affect* and *effect* as well as between *it* and *they*. The sentence is referring to *the disproportionate* affect/effect, so because of the word *the*, this word should be a noun. The noun form of the word is "effect," so eliminate (A) and (B). Next consider the pronoun. The pronoun here refers back to *The late fine*, which is singular, so eliminate (C), which is plural. The correct answer is (D).

30. **G** The question asks about grammar, so look at the answers to see what's changing. The structure of the beginning of the sentence is changing, so look to eliminate any answer that doesn't produce a complete sentence. Eliminate (F) because with the word *Since* at the beginning, this is not a complete idea. Keep (G) because it makes *Eliminating* the subject of the sentence with the verb being *has…led* and thus produces a complete idea. Eliminate (H) and (J) because neither produces a complete sentence. The correct answer is (G).

31. **A** The question asks for a *logical* transition, so consider the relationships between ideas. The previous sentence states that it was believed that people wouldn't return library items *without a monetary punishment*. This sentence says that when libraries forgave fees or ended late fines, there were *high rates of returned items*. These ideas contrast with each other because this sentence is contrary to what was expected. Eliminate (B), (C), and (D) because they are all same-direction transitions. Choice (A) is appropriate because it would be surprising for the outcome to be different from what people believed it would be. The correct answer is (A).

32. **J** The question is asking what the essay would *lose* if the underlined text were deleted, so read the paragraph with and without the underlined portion to identify what would be lost. The underlined portion defines what *amnesty campaigns* are. Eliminate (F) because this portion doesn't explicitly make an argument. Eliminate (G) because the underlined portion offers a definition, not an *example*. Eliminate (H) because the underlined portion doesn't describe any *types* of fines that are forgiven. Keep (J) because it matches with the function of the underlined portion. The correct answer is (J).

33. **B** The question is asking whether a new phrase should be added, so consider the content of the new phrase and whether it is consistent with the surrounding text. While the sentence still works without the phrase, the phrase does expand on what the *consequences* could be. Use Process of Elimination. Eliminate (A) because the new phrase gives examples of *consequences*, not of *items*. Keep (B) because the new phrase does do this. Eliminate (C) because adding examples of consequences wouldn't *overshadow the positive changes*. Eliminate (D) because this paragraph is not focused on *the community impacts of late fines*. The correct answer is (B).

34. **H** The question asks about grammar, so look at the answers to see what's changing. The punctuation and phrasing of the verb are changing in the answers, so check each option to see whether it produces a complete sentence. Choice (F) creates an unnecessary phrase beginning with *which* but does not finish the idea of what *many libraries* do, so eliminate (F). Choice (G) does the same thing, so eliminate it. Choice (H) makes the idea state *many libraries offer support…*, which completes the idea, so keep (H). Choice (J) states that libraries *make offering support* but does not finish the thought of what libraries *make* offering support do, so eliminate (J). The correct answer is (H).

35. **B** The question is asking where the new sentence should go, so consider the content of the new sentence and use Process of Elimination to determine where it fits. The new sentence refers to *This consequence*, so it should follow a mention of a consequence. Eliminate (A) because no *consequence* is mentioned in the sentence before. Keep (B) because the previous sentence refers to *suspension of a person's library account*, which would be a consequence for not returning materials. Eliminate (C) because the previous sentence refers to people visiting these libraries again, which isn't consistent with the new sentence's statement that people would be *less likely* to visit. Eliminate (D) because there is no *consequence* mentioned in the sentence before that would make people less likely to use the library. The correct answer is (B).

Passage V

36. **F** The question asks about grammar, so look at the answers to see what's changing. Pronouns are changing in the answer choices, so identify the word the pronoun refers back to, which is *plant*. This word is singular, so eliminate any answer that is plural: (G). Then, consider the use of apostrophes. The word *it's* means "it is," which is not the intended meaning here because the word is meant to state that the *victims* belong to the *plant*. Thus, eliminate (H) and (J). The correct possessive spelling is *its*. The correct answer is (F).

37. **C** The question is asking what would be lost if the phrase were deleted, so read the sentence with and without the phrase to see what changes. Without the phrase, the sentence doesn't specify what is *unique* about the plant's *morphology*. Use Process of Elimination. Eliminate (A) because no *type of prey* is mentioned in the phrase. Eliminate (B) because the phrase mentions only two aspects of the morphology and not the *exact mechanism* of the trap. Keep (C) because it accurately identifies the content of the underlined phrase. Eliminate (D) because the underlined phrase doesn't mention anything related to *speed*. The correct answer is (C).

38. **H** The question is asking for the answer that will *illustrate the mechanism of the trigger hairs by making a technical comparison to a specific feature of human anatomy*. Use Process of Elimination to eliminate any answer that doesn't fully meet this goal. Choice (F) mentions a *feature of human anatomy* that could be compared to the trigger hairs, so keep it. Eliminate (G) because this is not a *technical comparison*. Choice (H) is similar to (F) but is more specific, so keep it. Choice (J) mentions a *feature of human anatomy* but is not *technical*, so eliminate it. Compare (F) and (H). Of the two, (H) is more *technical* and more *specific*. Eliminate (F). The correct answer is (H).

39. **D** The question asks about grammar, so look at the answers to see what's changing. The form of the verb is changing in the answer choices, so look for a complete sentence. Notice that the last part of the sentence says *then snapping*, so the sentence is providing a series of events in the form of a list. All list items should be in the same format. Thus, the first item in the list is *registering*, and the underlined verb should be consistent with *registering* and *snapping*. Eliminate (A), (B), and (C) because they aren't consistent with these verbs. The correct answer is (D).

40. **F** The question is asking for the *least redundant* answer, so eliminate answers that are overly wordy or repeat information given earlier. Choice (F) doesn't have any obvious redundancies, so keep it. Choice (G) is similar but adds *and react to the pain*. The phrase *respond when touching something hot or sharp* already implies a reaction to pain, so this answer is redundant. Eliminate (G). Choice (H) adds *involuntarily* and *from the pain*, but these additional words are repetitive with the words *recoil* and *hot or sharp*, so eliminate (H). Choice (J) adds the word *automatically*, but a *reflex* is already automatic, so eliminate it due to redundancy. The correct answer is (F).

Passage VI

41. **B** The question is asking whether the word *prepared* should be revised to read *hand-pulled*. Read the sentence both ways and consider whether the change is an improvement. Stating that the noodles are *prepared* does not really provide any particular information, whereas *hand-pulled* gives them a more specific and potentially positive description. Use Process of Elimination. Eliminate (A) because while *preparing food manually* matches with *hand-pulled*, there is no evidence that the reason for doing this is *to minimize food costs*. Keep (B) because making noodles by hand matches with *special care* and the positive tone of the revision. Eliminate (C) because *prepared* is less specific, not more specific. Eliminate (D) because *prepared* doesn't provide any information about whether the noodles are *made by the restaurant* or *made to order*. The correct answer is (B).

42. **G** The question is asking for an answer that *best maintains the stylistic pattern of descriptions established earlier in the sentence*. Identify the pattern in the sentence. The other items are *hand-pulled noodles with colorful vegetables* and *steamed dumplings stuffed with beef and pumpkin*. These are both positive and specific descriptions of the dishes, so eliminate answers that aren't consistent. Eliminate (F) because *something* is not specific like the other list items. Keep (G) because it's specific about the type of dish. Eliminate (H) because *some salad* isn't as specific as (G). Eliminate (J) because there is no reason to say *that has been served*, and it's also less specific than (G). The correct answer is (G).

43. **D** The question is asking for the *best placement for the underlined text*, so try it in all four options and eliminate any that don't produce a clear meaning. Eliminate (A) because *the United States* is not *a Turkic ethnic minority group*. Eliminate (B) because *an asylum-seeker* refers to an individual, not a *minority group*. Eliminate (C) because *the Chinese government* is an institution, not a *minority group*. Keep (D) because *the Uyghurs* could refer to an *ethnic minority group*. The correct answer is (D).

44. **H** The question asks about grammar, so look at the answers to see what's changing. The punctuation and possible pronoun after *people* is changing in the answer choices, so look for a complete sentence. Choice (F) puts a comma after *people*, making the phrase after it describe the Uyghurs. The verbs in this phrase, *traveled* and *adopted*, aren't in the right form to produce this unnecessary phrase, so eliminate (F). Eliminate (G) because the preposition *of* shouldn't be used after *people* in this context. Keep (H) because it creates the phrase *who traveled...and adopted* to describe the Uyghurs, which works. Eliminate (J) because people should be referred to with "who" and not *which*. The correct answer is (H).

45. **C** The question is asking whether the sentence should be deleted, so consider the content of the sentence and that of the surrounding text. The underlined sentence describes the Uyghurs' use of diets for medical purposes. While the paragraph is discussing what the Uyghurs often eat, the topics of *Uyghur medicine* and *a specific diet* based on one's *age and nature* doesn't directly connect with the rest of the paragraph. Therefore, the sentence should be deleted. Eliminate (A) and (B). Next, compare (C) and (D). Choice (C) provides a good reason to delete the sentence, so keep it. Eliminate (D) because the paragraph doesn't explore *the various types of Eurasian cuisines*; it focuses on Uyghur cuisine. The correct answer is (C).

46. **H** The question is asking for an answer that *builds on the information provided earlier in the sentence about common elements of Uyghur dishes.* Look to see what information was provided: it mentions common dishes of *lamb or beef kebabs, roasted mutton, and a chicken dish called polo.* Eliminate any answer not consistent with this information. Choice (F) is not consistent because none of the dishes were described as being *spicy,* so eliminate it. Eliminate (G) because the sentence didn't mention eating at home versus at *restaurants.* Keep (H) because only meat dishes were mentioned, so this answer is consistent. Eliminate (J) because the sentence doesn't mention anything related to *experienced chefs.* The correct answer is (H).

47. **A** The question asks about grammar, so look at the answers to see what's changing. Apostrophes and wording are changing in the answer choices, so consider whether any apostrophes are needed. The meaning of the sentence is that *lagmen* takes hours to make. Therefore, *hours* should be plural and not possessive. Eliminate (B), (C), and (D) because they are all possessive. The correct answer is (A).

48. **H** The question is asking about a *logical* transition, so consider the relationships between ideas. There is also the option to use no transition, so try that first. The previous sentence states that Salam didn't plan to open a restaurant, and this sentence says that he *attended medical school* in the past. These ideas work without a transition, so keep (H), but consider the other options. This sentence isn't an example of the previous sentence, so eliminate (F). This sentence also isn't a consequence of the one before, so eliminate (G). Choice (J) uses a contrasting transition, and while there is a contrast between Salam's current career and his past education, these two sentences are both about the idea of him not starting out in the restaurant business, so they agree with each other. Eliminate (J). The correct answer is (H).

49. **A** The question asks about grammar, so look at the answers to see what's changing. Pronouns and nouns are changing in the answer choices, so eliminate answers that are unclear. Choice (A) provides a clear meaning, so keep it. Choice (B) says *that place,* but the only *place* that is mentioned in this sentence is *his new country;* this part of the sentence is about not being able to return to a previous home, so eliminate (B). Choices (C) and (D) also do not clearly refer to where the Uyghurs came from. The correct answer is (A).

50. **J** The question is asking for an answer that would *build on the ideas presented in this paragraph and connect to the final sentence of the essay.* Identify the ideas already stated in the paragraph as well as the topic of the final sentence. The first part of the paragraph touches on Salam's background and his pride in *providing a gathering place* for Uyghurs. The last sentence of the passage mentions that he is *bringing together members of his community* and also *increasing awareness of Uyghur culture among people who may not otherwise have been exposed to it.* Eliminate any answer that doesn't connect with both of these ideas. Choice (F) doesn't relate to either idea, so eliminate it. Choice (G) refers back to the idea of *providing a gathering place* from the previous sentence but doesn't lead into the idea in the final sentence, so eliminate it. Choice (H) doesn't relate to either idea from the last paragraph, so eliminate it. Choice (J) relates to the idea of what Salam does at Bostan and introduces the idea about customers who are *non-Uyghurs* and can learn about Uyghur culture, as stated in the last sentence. This fulfills the goal from the question, so keep (J). The correct answer is (J).

TEST 1 MATH ANSWERS AND EXPLANATIONS

1. **C** The question asks for the number of miles the runner ran slower than the marathon pace in 2004. Subtract the number of miles run at or faster than marathon pace during 2004 from the number of total miles run in 2004. This becomes 4,982 – 1,150 = 3,832. The correct answer is (C).

2. **J** The question asks for the length of a 24-hour day in seconds. Convert the numbers into like units using conversion factors. There are 60 seconds in 1 minute, and since there are 60 minutes in 1 hour, multiply 24 hours × $\dfrac{60 \text{ minutes}}{1 \text{ hour}}$ to find that there are 1,440 minutes in 24 hours. The correct answer is (J).

3. **B** The question asks for the number of pages the student read. Since the student reads at two different rates in the given period, multiply each rate by the number of days the student read at that rate and then add the rates together to find the total. This becomes $(a \times d) + (b \times 2d) = ad + 2bd$. Choice (A) omits the d in the second term, and (C) applies the 2 to both terms. Choice (D) multiplies the two terms instead of adding them. The correct answer is (B).

4. **H** The question asks for the number of visitors needed in June to keep the six-month average the same as the five-month average. Use the graph to find the total number of visitors in each of the first five months; then find the average by adding the five numbers together and dividing by 5 to get (200 + 300 + 200 + 350 + 200) ÷ 5 = 250. For the six-month average to remain the same as this current average, the total in June must equal the current average of 250. Confirm this by testing the value in (H) and finding the new average, which is (200 + 300 + 200 + 350 + 200 + 250) ÷ 6 = 250. The correct answer is (H).

5. **A** The question asks for the height of the graduation cap after 3 seconds of flight. Use the provided equation to solve for f when $s = 3$. The equation becomes $f = 60(3) - 17(3^2) = 180 - 153 = 27$ feet. The correct answer is (A).

6. **J** The question asks which student had the greatest range in test scores. Alicia's score range is 93 − 76 = 17 points. Brandon's score range is 12 points, Cleo's score range is 18 points, and Emily's score range is 19 points. Thus, Emily's score range is the greatest. Choice (G) gives the *smallest* range in test scores. The correct answer is (J).

7. **C** The question asks for the fraction of fish that Nita caught. Subtract the number of fish caught by Craig and Chris to find how many fish Nita caught. Find Chris's total by multiplying 300 by 45% to get 300 × 0.45 = 135. Since Chris caught 135 fish and Craig caught 25, Nita must have caught 300 − 135 − 25 = 140 fish. Convert this value into a fraction by putting it over the total number of fish caught and then reduce: $\dfrac{140}{300} = \dfrac{7}{15}$. The correct answer is (C).

8. **G** The question asks for the value of a compound function, so work from the inside out. Find the value of $g(4)$ and substitute it into the function given for $f(x)$. The value of $g(4) = 3 - \dfrac{4}{2} = 3 - 2 = 1$, and the value of $f(1) = 4(1)^2 = 4$, (G). Choice (F) stops at the value of $g(4)$ and (J) finds $f(4)$. Choice (H) makes a math error while solving the functions. The correct answer is (G).

9. **C** The question asks for the area of the shaded region. Estimate by calculating the area of a 6 × 6 square surrounding the shaded figure and then counting and subtracting the unshaded squares within that 36-unit area: roughly 18 squares. Subtract to get 36 – 18 = 18. The closest answer to this estimate is 19. The correct answer is (C).

10. **F** The question asks for the total rise of the 62-inch ramp. Because the question asks about the rise after two different horizontal runs, sketch one run of 24 with a ramp of 6. Sketch a second run of 62 and a ramp of x. Make each a triangle by drawing a third line from the top of the ramp to the end of the run. The two triangles have three congruent angles, so they're similar. To solve, set up a proportion of rise/run. The proportion is $\dfrac{6}{24} = \dfrac{x}{62}$. Cross-multiply to get $24x = 372$. Divide both sides by 24 to find that $x = 15.5$. The correct answer is (F).

11. **D** The question asks for the value of the expression for a given x and y. Substitute the given values of x and y into the expression and simplify, using the rules of order of operations (PEMDAS). The expression becomes $(-3)^2 + [(2 \times 2) - (2 \times -3)] = 9 + [4 - (-6)] = 9 + (4 + 6) = 19$. Choice (B) drops the second negative sign in the final term, subtracting 6 from 4 instead of adding. Choice (A) subtracts 9 from 10 in the last step instead of adding. Choice (C) finds the value of xy in the first term of the expression instead of y^x. The correct answer is (D).

12. **H** The question asks for the expression that gives the total amount of money earned selling T-shirts. Multiply the price by the number of shirts sold to find the earnings for a given day. The price of the shirt would start at $4.10 and be reduced by increments of $0.02, which can be written as $(4.10 - 0.02x)$. Eliminate (F), which reduces the price of the shirt by increments of $2 instead of $0.02, and eliminate (G), which adds $0.02 to the price instead of subtracting from it. The question states that the number of shirts sold will increase by 1 for each $0.02 decrease in price, so eliminate (J), which increases the number of shirts sold by only 0.02. The correct answer is (H).

13. **A** The question asks for an equivalent expression. To factor $x^2 - 7x + 12$, find two numbers that multiply to +12 and add to –7. Those numbers are –4 and –3. The factored expression is $(x - 4)(x - 3)$. The correct answer is (A).

14. **F** The question asks for the value of an expression given x and y. Substitute the values given for x and y in the equation: $\frac{5(2)}{70} + \frac{9}{5(5+2)} + \frac{1}{5+2} = \frac{10}{70} + \frac{9}{35} + \frac{1}{7}$. Find a common denominator for all of the fractions by looking at the smallest multiple of 70, 35, and 7: this number is 70. The equation becomes $\frac{10}{70} + \frac{18}{70} + \frac{10}{70} = \frac{38}{70} = \frac{19}{35}$. To avoid having to simplify all these fractions, another approach would be to find the decimal answer on a calculator and compare it to the decimal versions of the answers. The correct answer is (F).

15. **B** The question asks for the largest possible product of the digits displayed on a timer. To find the greatest possible product, first determine the largest number of minutes and seconds possible, which is 59:59. After that, the timer will roll over to its maximum value of 60:00. Multiply the digits together to get $(5)(9)(5)(9) = 2{,}025$. Choice (A) results from $(5 \times 9) + (5 \times 9)$, and (C) takes the product of $(59)(59)$ instead of separating the values into digits first. Choice (D) assumes the largest display to be 99:99, which it cannot be because, as the problem states, this is only a 60-minute timer. The correct answer is (B).

16. **H** The question asks for the area of two congruent triangles. The area of the square is 324, so each side is 18. Since the two right triangles are isosceles, their respective bases and heights are congruent. For each of the triangles, $A = \frac{1}{2}bh = \frac{1}{2}(18)(18) = 162$. There are two triangles, so the total area is $162 \times 2 = 324$. Choice (G) gives the area of only one triangle, and (J) gives the area of the entire figure. Choice (F) assumes 324 to be the area of the entire figure and divides by three, assuming that the three smaller shapes are equal in area. The correct answer is (H).

17. **C** The question asks for the value of x that is true for the given equation. Rewrite the equation as $(x - 1)(x - 1) = (x - 7)(x - 7)$ and multiply everything out to get $x^2 - 2x + 1 = x^2 - 14x + 49$. Subtract x^2 from each side to get $-2x + 1 = -14x + 49$. Add $14x$ to each side to get $12x + 1 = 49$. Subtract 1 from each side to get $12x = 48$. Divide both sides by 12 to get $x = 4$. Another approach would be to try the answers in the equation. When $x = 4$, the equation becomes $(4 - 1)^2 = (4 - 7)^2$. This simplifies to $(3)^2 = (-3)^2$ or $9 = 9$, making the equation true. The correct answer is (C).

18. **H** The question asks for the coordinates of point C. Draw a horizontal line at point A to split $\angle BAC$ in half, creating two 30°-60°-90° triangles. The y-value at point A, which is w, is equal to the y-value halfway between points B and C, so the y-value at point C is twice as big: $2w$. Eliminate (G) and (J) where the y-value is not $2w$. The ratio of the sides of a 30°-60°-90° triangle is $1:\sqrt{3}:2$ from smallest to largest, so the length of the leg adjacent to the 30° angle is $\sqrt{3}$ times the length of the shorter leg, or $w\sqrt{3}$. Choice (F) neglects to multiply the x-value by $\sqrt{3}$. The correct answer is (H).

19. **B** The question asks for the area of a square quilt. The diagonal of a square makes two triangles with angle measures 45°, 45°, and 90°, and sides in the proportion $x:x:x\sqrt{2}$. Since the hypotenuse of one of the triangles is $4\sqrt{2}$, the legs of that triangle, which are also the sides of the square, measure 4 feet. The area of the square is $side^2 = 4^2 = 16$ feet^2. The correct answer is (B).

20. **F** The question asks for a true trigonometric relationship for the given triangle. Use SOHCAHTOA to remember the trigonometric relationships. Given an angle θ, the side opposite θ, and the hypotenuse, use the sine function, which is $\sin\theta = \dfrac{\text{opposite}}{\text{hypotenuse}}$. Here, that becomes $\sin\theta = \dfrac{15}{x}$, which matches (F). Choices (G) and (H) confuse cosine and tangent with sine. Choice (J) contains $\dfrac{\sin\theta}{\cos\theta}$, which is equal to tan θ, making (J) the same answer as (H). The correct answer is (F).

21. **C** The question asks which value of a is true for the given equation. Test the answer choices in the equation. Test (B): $a = 25$ and the equation becomes $\sqrt{45+25} + \sqrt{25} = \sqrt{70} + 5$, which is approximately 13.4. Since this answer is smaller than 15, eliminate (A) and (B). Test (C): when $a = 36$, the equation becomes $\sqrt{45+36} + \sqrt{36} = \sqrt{81} + 6$, which simplifies to $9 + 6$ and equals 15. The correct answer is (C).

22. **H** The question asks for the total time required to fill the pool using both hoses together. To solve, enter the data into the given equation and solve using a common denominator. The equation becomes $\dfrac{1}{20} + \dfrac{1}{60} = \dfrac{3}{60} + \dfrac{1}{60} = \dfrac{4}{60} = \dfrac{1}{15}$, so T_c, the combined time, is 15 minutes. Choice (F) divides the two numbers given. Choices (G) and (J) make calculation errors. The correct answer is (H).

23. **C** The question asks for the probability that the die will NOT land on a prime-numbered face. The numbers 2, 3, and 5 are prime, while 6 and 4 are not. The probability that the die will NOT land on a prime number is 2 non-prime numbers out of 5 total numbers, or $\dfrac{2}{5}$. Choice (B) is the probability that the die WILL land on a prime-numbered face. The correct answer is (C).

24. **J** The question asks for the value of the function when using the provided values for x and y. Find y by substituting $x = 3$: $y = \left(\dfrac{5}{3}\right)^2 = \dfrac{25}{9}$. Now find the value of $7x + 9y$, which is $7 \times 3 + 9 \times \dfrac{25}{9} = 21 + 25 = 46$. The answers in (F) and (G) may result from forgetting to square the fraction or to multiply it by 9. Choice (H) comes from not squaring the $\dfrac{5}{3}$. The correct answer is (J).

25. **C**   The question asks for the length of a diagonal for the square. Start drawing the square by plotting the three provided points. Now, add in the missing fourth corner, which would logically go at (0, 4). Next, draw in the diagonal from (0, 0) to (4, 4) or from (0, 4) to (4, 0). Since the diagonal of a square will divide the square into two 45-45-90 triangles, use the standard $x:x:x\sqrt{2}$ ratio of sides in a 45-45-90 triangle to find the length of the hypotenuse. Because the length of each side of the square is 4, the hypotenuse of the triangle must be $4\sqrt{2}$. Choice (B) gives the length of a side of the square, and (D) applies the side ratios of a 30-60-90 triangle instead of a 45-45-90. The correct answer is (C).

26. **G**   The question asks for the value of a in the logarithm. Apply the definition of a logarithm to rewrite the equation as $4^3 = a$ and evaluate to find that $a = 64$. Choices (H) and (J) incorrectly rewrite the logarithm. The correct answer is (G).

27. **B**   The question asks which statement is true based on the given equation. An easy way to answer this question is to test each answer choice to find the pair of numbers that satisfies the equation. Choice (A) becomes $y = 18 - 0.2(0.2) = 17.96$ quarts left in the pot, so $18 - 17.96 = 0.04$ quart of water has boiled away. This isn't equal to the 1 quart in the answer, so eliminate (A). For (B), $y = 18 - 0.2(1) = 17.8$, so 0.2 quart has boiled away. This matches the information in the answer. The correct answer is (B).

28. **H**   The question asks for the total amount of liquid that the cup can hold. The second figure shows that the small and large diameters of the coffee cup are 4 and 6, respectively, so the radii are 2 and 3. Plugging the numbers into the equation given results in $V = \frac{1}{3}\pi(5.5)(3^2 + 2^2 + 3\times 2) = \frac{1}{3}\pi(5.5)(19) \approx 109$. Choice (F) is the portion of the equation inside the parentheses, and (G) neglects to multiply by $\frac{1}{3}\pi$. Choice (J) plugs the diameters into the equation instead of the radii. The correct answer is (H).

29. **A**   The question asks for the set of values that satisfies the given equation. Choices (A) and (D) are clues that the two sides of the equation are either always equal or never equal, and simplifying the right side of the equation to $9x + 12$ shows that the two sides are indeed the same. Since $9x + 12$ will equal itself for all real numbers, the correct answer is (A).

30. **J**   The question asks for a simplified form of the compound fraction. The order of operations requires simplifying the fractions grouped in each of the three parts of the fraction as a first step, so begin with the fractions in the numerator. The denominator of that fraction, $\frac{3}{4} - \frac{2}{3}$, becomes $\frac{9}{12} - \frac{8}{12}$ and equals $\frac{1}{12}$. Since dividing by a fraction is the same as multiplying by the reciprocal, the entire

numerator of the expression becomes $\dfrac{3}{4} \div \dfrac{1}{12} = \dfrac{3}{4} \times \dfrac{12}{1}$, which equals 9. Now simplify the denomi-

nator: $\dfrac{3}{4} - \dfrac{2}{3} + \dfrac{1}{2} = \dfrac{9}{12} - \dfrac{8}{12} + \dfrac{6}{12} = \dfrac{7}{12}$. Find the solution to the full expression by dividing 9 by

$\dfrac{7}{12}$, which becomes $9 \div \dfrac{7}{12} = 9 \times \dfrac{12}{7} = \dfrac{108}{7}$. The other answers to this question confuse the order of

operations or represent common calculator errors. The correct answer is (J).

31. **D** The question asks for the value of the given expression. Any nonzero number raised to the 0 power = 1. So $a^0 = 1$, $b^0 = 1$, and $c^0 = 1$. Since $1 + 1 + 1 = 3$, the correct answer is (D).

32. **F** The question asks which angle has the largest tangent value. Use SOHCAHTOA to remember that $\tan\theta = \dfrac{\text{opposite}}{\text{adjacent}}$. For each of the angles, the opposite side is AB. Since AB is constant for each angle, the length of the adjacent side is all that matters when determining which angle has the greatest tangent value. The angle with the shortest adjacent side, $\angle BEA$, has the greatest tangent. Choice (J) gives the smallest tangent value instead of the greatest one. The correct answer is (F).

33. **C** The question asks what the function of the graph would look like if reflected along the line $y = x$. To reflect a graph over this line, switch the x- and y-coordinates of the function: point V at $(-2, 1)$ becomes $(1, -2)$, point Z at $(0, 1)$ becomes $(1, 0)$, and point X at $(-1, -1)$ stays the same. Sketch these points into a new graph and match to an answer. Choice (A) reflects the graph across the x-axis, and (B) reflects the graph across the y-axis. Choice (D) reflects the graph but moves the vertex from $(-1, -1)$ to $(1, 1)$. The correct answer is (C).

34. **H** The question asks for the sum of two numbers that have first been run through the provided function. Follow the rule given in the question to find $17_o = 15 + 13 + 11 + 9 + 7 + 5 + 3 + 1 = 64$ and $4_o = 3 + 1 = 4$. So $17_o \times 4_o = 64 \times 4 = 256$. Choice (F) is $17_o \div 4_o$. Choice (G) is 72×2, which mistakenly adds all the even values less than the two numbers instead of the odd ones. Choice (J) adds together both the odd and even values less than k. The correct answer is (H).

35. **C** The question asks for the value of a, which is the x-value of the equation when $y = -3$. There's no need to graph the equation or to put it into $y = mx + b$ form. Substitute a into the equation for x and -3 into the equation for y. The equation becomes $a - 4(-3) = 14$ or $a + 12 = 14$. Therefore, $a = 2$. Choice (A) is the result of substituting a for y and -3 for x. Choice (D) is the result of a sign error when substituting to get $a - 12 = 14$. The correct answer is (C).

36. **J** The question asks for a description of the function. Substitute values to see what happens as t grows larger. When $t = 2$, $f(t) = \dfrac{2^2 - 1}{2 - 1} - 2 = 1$. When $t = 3$, $f(t) = \dfrac{3^2 - 1}{3 - 1} - 3 = 1$. Even when $t = 1{,}000$, $f(t) = \dfrac{1{,}000^2 - 1}{1{,}000 - 1} - 1{,}000 = 1$. Choices (F), (G), and (H) mirror terms from the question but do not accurately describe what happens as t changes. Using algebra to simplify the equation

also shows that the function always equals 1: $f(t) = \dfrac{t^2 - 1}{t - 1} - t = \dfrac{(t-1)(t+1)}{(t-1)} - t = (t+1) - t = 1$.

The correct answer is (J).

37. **A** The question asks for the slope of a line containing the two given points. Use the slope formula, $m = \dfrac{y_2 - y_1}{x_2 - x_1}$, plugging in the provided values to get $\dfrac{10 - (-2)}{3 - 2} = \dfrac{10 + 2}{1} = \dfrac{12}{1} = 12$. Choice (C) reverses the numerator and denominator of the slope formula, and (B) and (D) confuse positive and negative signs when subtracting or dividing. The correct answer is (A).

38. **F** The question asks for the standard equation for the circle with the given properties. The equation of a circle with center (h, k) and radius r is defined as $(x - h)^2 + (y - k)^2 = r^2$. Here, $h = 4$ and $k = -8$. Eliminate (H) and (J), which flip the values of h and k. To find the radius, use the circumference 10π given in the problem. $C = \pi d = 10\pi$, so the diameter is 10. The radius is half of that, or 5, so to complete the equation, $r^2 = 25$. Choice (G) squares the diameter instead of the radius. The correct answer is (F).

39. **D** The question asks which equation is false for values that satisfy the given equation. Choose values for x and y that make the given statement true. For example, if $x = 2$, then $2y = -(-2^2)$, which simplifies to $2y = -4$, and results in $y = -2$. Now use these values to test out the answer choices. Choice (A) becomes $2\left(\dfrac{1}{-2}\right) = -1$, which is true. Since the question asks about a statement that is false, eliminate (A). For (B), the equation becomes $2^2\left(\dfrac{1}{(-2)^2}\right) = 1$ or $\dfrac{4}{4} = 1$. Eliminate (B). Choice (C) becomes $(2)^2 = (-2)^2$ or $4 = 4$. Eliminate (C). Choice (D) must be false, and indeed the equation $(2)^3 - (-2)^3 = 0$ becomes $8 - (-8) = 0$ or $16 = 0$. The correct answer is (D).

40. **F** The question asks for the value of n in the second matrix. Compare the points of the original rectangle with the first matrix to see that the x values of A, B, C, and D run along the top row and their y-values run along the bottom row. By this logic, the value of n in the second matrix represents the y-coordinate of A after it is translated. Since translating a figure moves each corner of the figure over equal distances along the x- and y-axes, compare the y-coordinates in the first matrix to the known y-coordinates in the second matrix. Each y value is decreased by 2 ($-1 - 2 = -3$, $-4 - 2 = -6$, and $-1 - 2 = -3$) when it is translated into the second matrix, so n must be $2 - 2 = 0$. The correct answer is (F).

41. **D** The question asks for the number line graph of an absolute value inequality. First, use Process of Elimination. When an absolute value function is less than a given number, its solution is an "and": the answer would state that x is greater than one number and also less than another, and when graphed, this solution would be a single line with two defined end points. Choices (A) and (C)

give "or" solutions, which would work only if the given absolute value function was *greater* than a particular number: eliminate them. Now, begin solving the inequality by first considering the positive case of the absolute value, $x - a \leq 3$. This simplifies to $x \leq a + 3$, an endpoint which is not part of (B) but is part of (D). The correct answer is (D).

42. **G** The question asks for a possible set of inputs that yields a final output of 0. Start from the output 0. Since a CHANGE function needs to have input 1 to get output 0, the output of the IF function needs to be a 1. A 1 is the output of an IF function either if the first input is 1 and the second input is 1, or if the first input is 0 and the third input is 1. The first input could be 1 if both p and q are 1; however, no answer choices contain p and q values that are both 1. Therefore, p and q could be either 0 and 1, or 1 and 0, or 0 and 0, to yield an output of 0. This doesn't eliminate any answer choices. Since the first input of the IF function is 0, the second input could be either 1 or 0, so the input of the next CHANGE function doesn't matter. However, s and t must both be 1, since the output of the BOTH function must be a 1 in order to make the third term in the IF function a 1. Choice (G) is the only answer choice that has s and t both as 1. The correct answer is (G).

43. **C** The question asks for the value of two terms multiplied together when expressed in scientific notation. Use Process of Elimination. Since scientific notation requires the lead term be a number between 1 and 10, eliminate (A) and (B). When multiplying two exponential numbers with like bases, the exponents should be added together, not multiplied, so eliminate (D). The correct answer is (C).

44. **F** The question asks for the length of $\overline{PS}$. Start by drawing a line and filling in the provided information. If $\overline{QR}$ has a length of x feet and R is the midpoint of $\overline{QS}$, $\overline{RS}$ is the same length as $\overline{QR}$. As $\overline{QS} = \overline{QR} + \overline{RS}$, $\overline{QS} = x + x = 2x$. Since $\overline{PQ} = 4x - 16$, and Q is the midpoint of $\overline{PS}$, $\overline{PQ} = \overline{QS}$ and $2x = 4x - 16$. Simplify this equation to find that $-2x = -16$ and $x = 8$. To find the total length of $\overline{PS}$, substitute $x = 8$ into the algebraic measures of $\overline{PQ}$ and $\overline{QS}$ and add the results. When $x = 8$, $4x - 16 + 2x = 4(8) - 16 + 2(8) = 32 - 16 + 16 = 32$. The correct answer is (F).

45. **C** The question asks for the length of a minor arc on the given circle. Find the radius of the circle using the area formula: $A = \pi r^2$. For this circle, the formula becomes $64\pi = \pi r^2$ and $r = 8$. To find the length of a minor arc, first find the circumference of the circle: $C = 2\pi r = 2\pi(8) = 16\pi$. The minor arc is $\frac{24}{360} = \frac{1}{15}$ of the circumference of the circle. Therefore, the length of the minor arc is $\overset{\frown}{CD} = \left(\frac{1}{15}\right)(16\pi) = \frac{16}{15}\pi$. Choice (A) attempts to use the radius of the circle, 8, to find the fractional part of the circle. Choice (B) is similar to (A) but uses half of the radius. Choice (D) is the area divided by the central angle. The correct answer is (C).

TEST 1 READING ANSWERS AND EXPLANATIONS

Passage I

1. **A**   The question asks for the point of view from which the passage is told. Because this is a general question, it should be done after all the specific questions. The narrator refers to herself as "I" throughout the story, so she is a first-person narrator. Eliminate (C) and (D). The narrator is both *present in the story* and does interact *with other characters* such as her mother and Lau Po, so keep (A). Since the narrator is *present in the story*, eliminate (B). The correct answer is (A).

2. **J**   The question asks what idea the whole passage explores. Because this is a general question, it should be done after all the specific questions. While the narrator learns from Lau Po, whom she met in the park, no other *relationships...with the various children and adults* she met in the park are mentioned, so eliminate (F). The contrast between the *mother's expectations* and the narrator's *personal desires* is primarily discussed only in the seventh paragraph and is not a subject of *the passage as a whole*, so eliminate (G). The passage does not focus on *challenges faced by immigrants*, so eliminate (H). The passage does discuss the narrator's efforts to improve her chess game and her performance in chess tournaments, which is consistent with (J). The correct answer is (J).

3. **B**   The question asks for a crucial aspect of the narrator's success when it comes to her chess game. Because this is a general question, it should be done after all of the specific questions. The narrator is not described as *ruthless*, or unforgiving, so eliminate (A). The narrator does learn many chess strategies from Lau Po in the fourth and fifth paragraphs and uses them in the tenth and eleventh paragraphs to win a match in a tournament, which is consistent with (B). The narrator does not boast or portray confidence that she has not earned, so eliminate (C). While the narrator's family is discussed, it's not stated that her *family legacy* has an impact on her chess game, so eliminate (D). The correct answer is (B).

4. **F**   The question asks how the narrator's mental state could be described once her chess match with the boy begins. The tenth paragraph states that *As I began to play, the boy disappeared, the color ran out of the room, and I saw only my white pieces and his black ones waiting on the other side.* This evidence implies that the narrator is focused, which is consistent with (F). She is not *carefree, distracted*, or *uninterested*, as she is engaged during the match and taking it seriously, so eliminate (G), (H), and (J). The correct answer is (F).

5. **D**   The question asks how the mother's second utterance of saying "*Is luck*" could be characterized when compared to the first instance. The sixth paragraph contains the first instance of "*Is luck*" as the mother's attempt to downplay her daughter's performance to other observers, even though the mother is proud. The second instance of the mother saying "*Is luck*" is in the ninth paragraph and is connected with the mother giving the daughter her *chang*, which is a jade tablet, before a tournament match. The ninth paragraph does not describe the mother as *more*, or less, *superstitious* than the sixth paragraph, so eliminate (A). The mother is not described as having become more *doubtful* of her daughter's ability in either instance, so eliminate (B). The mother is also never described

as growing *more confident* in her daughter in the second instance, so eliminate (C). Choice (D) is most consistent with the passage as the second time she says *"Is luck,"* she is not attempting to appear humble as she did the first time but is rather handing her daughter her *chang* as a symbol of good luck prior to the daughter's tournament match. The correct answer is (D).

6.   **H**   The question asks for something the mother believes her *chang* will give to her daughter. The ninth paragraph states that the mother says the *chang…"Is luck."* The paragraph does not discuss the narrator's opponent being someone she is seeking *retribution*, or revenge, against, so eliminate (F). The mother's *chang* is said to hold the *sun's fire* but not that it will literally warm the daughter, so eliminate (G). The *chang* isn't said to be connected to the mother's or narrator's *ancestors*, so eliminate (J). The mother does say that the *chang…"Is luck,"* so keep (H). The correct answer is (H).

7.   **B**   The question asks for the main point of lines 37–44, which is the seventh paragraph. The text states that *I desperately wanted to go, but I bit back my tongue. I knew she would not let me play among strangers*, so the main focus is on a disconnect between what the daughter and the mother each want. The text does not discuss how much *success* the daughter has in tournaments, so eliminate (A). Choice (B) references that there is a difference between what the mother wants and what the daughter wants, so keep (B). Only later in the passage does the mother talk about the *number of pieces lost*, so eliminate (C). None of the author's *personal achievements* are discussed in lines 37–44, so eliminate (D). The correct answer is (B).

8.   **G**   The question asks for what the chess knowledge that the narrator possesses could be best compared to. Because this is a general question, it should be done after all the specific questions. Use lead words from the answers to find each reference in the passage. In the fifth paragraph, an *unseen sword* refers to a specific piece of advice the narrator receives from Lau Po rather than her *chess knowledge* as a whole, so eliminate (F). The tenth and eleventh paragraphs use the *light wind* as a metaphor for the narrator's thoughts and strategy during the chess match, so keep (G). In the first paragraph, a *roll of Life Savers* was something the narrator brought with her to the park, so eliminate (H). Also in the first paragraph, a *cardboard box* is what the narrator's brother Vincent's chess set was kept in, so eliminate (J). The correct answer is (G).

9.   **B**   The question asks for one way that those in the narrator's community show support for the narrator's growing success. Since the narrator's success is discussed later in the passage, look in the final few paragraphs for this information. The last paragraph states that *The day after I won an important regional tournament, the window encased a fresh sheet cake with whipped-cream frosting and red script saying, "Congratulations, Waverly Jong, Chinatown Chess Champion." Soon after that, a flower shop, headstone engraver, and funeral parlor offered to sponsor me in national tournaments.* These businesses do not *suggest taking people to her matches to cheer* the narrator on, so eliminate (A). Three different businesses offer to sponsor the narrator, so keep (B). The *Chinese bakery* made a *sheet cake* for the narrator rather than a *large red congratulatory banner*, so eliminate (C). It was the display cakes in the window of the Chinese bakery that were *dust-covered*, not the narrator's trophies, so eliminate (D). The correct answer is (B).

Passage II

10. **F** The question asks for the primary purpose of the passage. Because this is a general question, it should be done after all the specific questions. The second half of the passage discusses the *properties* of ramps, while the first half describes the community and kinship between the women who work with them, which supports (F). The *medicinal properties of ramps* are only discussed in one paragraph towards the end of the passage, so eliminate (G). While *biodiversity* and *women* are mentioned in the second paragraph, the passage doesn't claim that the women *influence* the biodiversity of the region in any way. Only one rural community is discussed in the passage, and the focus is more on the properties of ramps and the interactions among the people who work with ramps in that community, so eliminate (J). The correct answer is (F).

11. **C** The question asks for the main idea of the second paragraph (lines 17–31). The paragraph states that *Such talk is one means of crafting locality. It catches people up into a dense fabric of kinship and community and fastens that fabric to places and events in the mountains*, so the focus of the paragraph is on the people in the community and how they bond with each other. The paragraph states that the community is a place that is *remarkable…for its biodiversity* and that *ramps, poke, collard greens*, and *creasies* are all topics of discussion as far as food goes, so eliminate (A). The paragraph discusses *a dense fabric of kinship* and the women are not said to compete with one another, so eliminate (B). Besides the *dense fabric of kinship* between the women, the passage states that the women *compare the aromas of poke and collard greens, and marvel at how window screens get black with flies when you're cooking them*, so keep (C). Only one instance of *mistakenly* seasoning the *frying ramps* is mentioned and it's not the main idea of the paragraph, so eliminate (D). The correct answer is (C).

12. **J** The question asks for what Bob Daniel's line of work most likely involves. Bob Daniel mentions in the tenth paragraph that *if you're confined close…in an office with people, I'm sure it would offend people like that, but in my line of work I don't think I bother anybody with them*. Therefore, Bob does not work in a confined space or likely interact with a lot of people, so eliminate (F) and (G). There's not enough evidence in the passage to determine a specific role for Bob such as *shipping and receiving*, so eliminate (H). Bob's comments imply that he likely works either *alone* or *outside*, so keep (J). The correct answer is (J).

13. **C** The question asks for the primary function of lines 22–26, which is in the second paragraph. The text serves as an example of the how *such talk* catches people up into a *dense fabric of kinship and community*, which is stated earlier in the paragraph. The text is about a mistake while cooking, not *difficulties* while gathering food, so eliminate (A). The text does not describe *local culture* but just one interaction among a group of women, so eliminate (B). The women *laugh* and *kid* Violet Dickens for an error she made when seasoning ramps, which supports (C). The text does not discuss how important *ramps* are in the *diet* of the people who live in the community, so eliminate (D). The correct answer is (C).

14. **F** The question asks how the twelfth paragraph differs from the rest of the passage. The paragraph starts by claiming that *Behind the powerful aroma it appears there really is something good for what ails you. Ramps have long been recommended for their germicidal and toning effects*. This indicates

that the focus of the passage is no longer on how ramps smell but how they might be beneficial medically and physically. The passage goes on to state that ramps are *linked with reduced rates of cancer* and *contain flavonoids and other antioxidants*, all of which is consistent with (F). The *social effects* of the odor of ramps are discussed in the dialogue before lines 72–83, so eliminate (G). The paragraph does not explain why ramps carry *historical significance* but rather their medical and nutritional significance, so eliminate (H). This portion of the text does not claim what the *locals* do or do not believe about ramps, so eliminate (J). The correct answer is (F).

15. **D** The question asks for something that results from ramps having more organosulphur compounds than other members of the allium family. The third paragraph states that *Our chopping of leaves is filling the air with aromatic organosulphur compounds, characteristic of members of the allium family but carried to extremes in ramps and their consumers*, meaning that ramps have a stronger smell, or aroma, due to these organosulphur compounds than other members of their family. The organo-sulphur compounds discussed in the third paragraph are not said to be connected to the medicinal properties of ramps, which are discussed later in the passage. Eliminate (A). Ramps are only discussed in the context of a community in mountainous West Virginia, not as used in *modern culinary dishes*, so eliminate (B). The *efforts of official institutions* mentioned in the third paragraph actually occur at *ramp suppers* and are therefore not about discouraging ramp dinners, so eliminate (C). The information given in this paragraph is most consistent with (D), so keep it. The correct answer is (D).

16. **F** The question asks for something that the author compares the West Virginia mountain community to. The community is discussed most directly in the second paragraph, where the author states that *Such talk…catches people up into a dense fabric of kinship and community and fastens that fabric to places and events in the mountains.* This could be similar to a *woven fabric*, so keep (F). The *field of greens* is most closely referenced in the first paragraph, where it's described as something the women physically interact with rather than a symbol of their community, so eliminate (G). While the passage makes references to *biodiversity* and *community life* being interwoven in the third para-graph, it does not state that the West Virginia community is like a *cycle of life*, so eliminate (H). The *spring tonic* is discussed in the last paragraph as a way to understand how the people in the community view ramps but not as a metaphor for the community itself, so eliminate (J). The cor-rect answer is (F).

17. **D** The question asks why the author most likely mentions that ramps contain more vitamin C than oranges. The comparison between ramps and oranges is found in the second-to-last paragraph. While the passage explains that *Ramps are higher in vitamin C than oranges,* it does not claim that ramps offer *more nutritional benefits* than oranges or *can be a substitute for oranges* in diets. It only indicates that ramps have more of one specific thing, so eliminate (A) and (B). The passage does not state that ramps having more vitamin C is why they became so *popular in West Virginia*, so eliminate (C). The comparison is made as part of a paragraph discussing the medical and nutri-tional benefits of ramps, and oranges are generally a more commonly known food than ramps, which supports (D). The correct answer is (D).

18. **G** The question asks what the word *green* most nearly means. In the first paragraph, this word is related to an activity undertaken by several different women in a community. The activity is described earlier in the passage as picking wild produce such as ramps, dandelions, poke, shawnee lettuce, woolen britches, and creasies, so look for an answer that means something like "wild produce." The passage does not claim the women are weeding, which is usually associated with removing an unwanted plant rather than harvesting a wanted one, so eliminate (F). A word like *plants* could match "wild produce," so keep (G). Choices (H) and (J) both offer alternate meanings of the word *green* that do not fit in this context, so eliminate them both. The correct answer is (G).

Passage III

19. **C** The question asks for evidence that indicates that street art is considered to have a higher status than graffiti art. The last paragraph of Passage A states that *a hierarchy exists with street art accorded a higher status compared to graffiti writing. This often is reflected in the differential legal treatment of street art.* So, the primary difference between how the two are treated is based on legality. Passage A states that both *graffiti* and *street art* are done in public space, not private, so eliminate (A). Graffiti and street art are both associated with *political statements* in the second and third paragraphs, respectively, so eliminate (B). The passage states that *In Atlanta, street art is encouraged and legally sanctioned as a means of sprucing up an urban environment*, which is consistent with (C). While murals are called street art in the third paragraph, the passage doesn't claim that murals are the only form of street art, so eliminate (D). The correct answer is (C).

20. **J** The question asks how the authors of Passage A view graffiti. Because this is a general question, it should be done after all the specific questions for Passage A. The authors of Passage A do not directly criticize graffiti as *upsetting* or *damaging*, so eliminate (F) and (G). The authors also don't make a comparison between how positively *academics* and *artists* view graffiti, so eliminate (H). The authors of Passage A claim in the last paragraph that *political graffiti carries a specific oppositional message* and that *Atlanta has also stepped up efforts to discourage illegal graffiti by assigning police officers to track down offenders who face fines if caught*, so they would agree that the art form is not without controversy, which supports (J). The correct answer is (J).

21. **A** The question asks for the relationship between street artists and law enforcement in Atlanta. In the last paragraph, the passage states that *In Atlanta, street art is encouraged and legally sanctioned as a means of sprucing up an urban environment.* Choice (A) states that street art *is legally sanctioned in Atlanta*, so keep (A). The opinion of street artists in Atlanta towards law enforcement, either positive, negative, or neutral, is not offered in the final paragraph of Passage A, so eliminate (B) and (C). The passage does not argue that *law enforcement officers* and *street artists* in Atlanta face any *similar challenges*, so eliminate (D). The correct answer is (A).

22. **H** The question asks for which detail can distinguish the styles of graffiti artists. Different styles are discussed in the third paragraph of Passage B, which states that there is *a war of styles where each artist is valued for their skill and creativity, regardless of their chosen form of expression* and states that

those who paint characters are recognized just as much as those who paint letters, thanks to their unique style. The paragraph does not claim that graffiti artists use *bright colors* (this would be outside knowledge), so eliminate (F). The passage focuses on an artist's connection to graffiti but never discusses his *intended audience*, so eliminate (G). The information related to styles relates directly to the artists' form of expression, so keep (H). While the passage does discuss the *location* some graffiti is painted such as *city walls*, this isn't identified as something that can *distinguish the styles of different graffiti artists* from each other, so eliminate (J). The correct answer is (H).

23. **D**   The question asks what the word *tagging* most nearly means. In the first paragraph, this word describes an activity undertaken by the author of the passage. In the first paragraph of Passage B, the author states that *I spent nights painting letters on the city walls*, so look for an answer that means something like "painting." Choices (A) and (B) focus on the concept of "tagging" as something that relates to science or data collection, so eliminate them both. Similarly, (C) uses "tagging" as it's used in *social media*, not art. Choice (D) is a direct match for "painting," so keep it. The correct answer is (D).

24. **G**   The question asks for the main point of lines 50–61, which is the second paragraph of Passage B. The paragraph states that *Graffiti was more than an activity; it was an identity and a way of life*, and the rest of the paragraph offers evidence of this connection that the author feels to graffiti. The paragraph indicates that the author understood the principles of the group he was joining and was clear about his choice, so eliminate (F). The main idea at the end of the paragraph is consistent with (G), so keep it. The author speaks of his experiences as a graffiti writer positively, not negatively, so eliminate (H). The text focuses on the *connection*, *philosophy*, and *camaraderie* experienced by the author rather than the *technical aspects of graffiti*, so eliminate (J). The correct answer is (G).

25. **A**   The question asks for something that Passage B focuses more on than Passage A. Eliminate any answer choice that misrepresents either passage. Passage B is about the specific experiences of a graffiti artist, the author, whereas Passage A compares graffiti art to street art, so keep (A). Passage A is the passage that mentions *the distinction between graffiti and street art* (Paragraphs 3 and 4), examples of *the political power of street art* (Paragraphs 2 and 3), and *street furniture* (Paragraph 1), so eliminate (B), (C), and (D). The correct answer is (A).

26. **G**   The question asks for which element of Passage A is not included in Passage B. Eliminate any answer choice that misrepresents either passage. Neither passage discusses how *other types of artists* besides graffiti artists view graffiti art, so eliminate (F). Passage A spends part of the third paragraph discussing a mural's presence at a site where political events have taken place, whereas Passage B does not discuss murals at all, so keep (G). Passage B does make a *distinction between types of graffiti artists*, discussing those who paint characters and those who paint letters, so eliminate (H). Both passages discuss the *illegal nature of graffiti* in their respective final paragraphs, so eliminate (J). The correct answer is (G).

27. **C**   The question asks what idea the authors of both passages would most likely agree with. Eliminate any answer choice that misrepresents either passage. Both passages spend time defining graffiti and some of its parameters, so eliminate (A). Passage B does not discuss graffiti as a political tool at all

while Passage A does not directly claim that it is used to *condemn* corrupt governments or individuals, so eliminate (B). The second paragraph of Passage A and all of Passage B discuss how artists express themselves using graffiti, which supports (C). Only Passage A mentions street art and compares graffiti to street art as being *more problematic*, so eliminate (D). The correct answer is (C).

Passage IV

28. **F**   The question asks for what researchers have found the association between cognitive function and salt intake to be. These terms are first discussed together in the third paragraph, which states that *excessive salt might negatively impact brain health in humans through impairing the brain's blood vessels*. This supports that there may be a *direct link* between salt intake and cognitive function, so keep (F). The third paragraph states that this link exists *regardless of salt's effect on blood pressure*, so eliminate (G) and (H). The second paragraph states that *there is communication between the gut and brain*, so eliminate (J). The correct answer is (F).

29. **A**   The question asks which statement best summarized the research regarding the therapeutic implications of lowering salt intake as presented in lines 49–57, which is the sixth paragraph. The paragraph states that *Lowering salt intake has been shown to have beneficial effects to overall health*, and the research involving the mice shows that *When the mice were returned to a normal diet after being on a high salt diet, the detrimental health effects caused by excess salt intake were erased*. Because these detrimental health effects are stated in the fourth paragraph to be *stroke* and *cognitive dysfunction*, or decline, keep (A). The passage indicates that salt intake does *affect brain function*, so eliminate (B). The text does not advocate for *pharmaceutical interventions*—it only discusses a pharmaceutical intervention that had the same effect as lowering salt intake might—so eliminate (C). Eliminate (D) because it suggests a positive link between *increased salt consumption* and improved *brain health*, which is the opposite of the correlation given in the passage. The correct answer is (A).

30. **G**   The question asks for the main purpose of lines 8–20, which is the second paragraph. Since the paragraph begins by stating that *there is a growing body of work showing that there is communication between the gut and brain*, the primary purpose of the paragraph must be to explain more about that growing body of work. The paragraph discusses how *high salt intake* affects the gut but not directly how it *damages brain cells* or causes *changes in the immune system's role*, so eliminate (F) and (H). Choice (G) is consistent with the topic introduced by the first sentence of the paragraph, so keep it. The link between increased salt intake and *heart disease* is discussed in the first paragraph, not this one, so eliminate (J). The correct answer is (G).

31. **B**   The question asks what parts of the mice's anatomy were affected by salt intake, which caused a decline in the mice's cognitive performance. The reference to mice is first found in the fifth paragraph, which states that *immune responses in the small intestines set off a cascade of chemical responses, reaching the brain's blood vessels, reducing blood flow to the cortex and hippocampus*. Eliminate (A), (C), and (D), and keep (B). The correct answer is (B).

32. **H** The question asks what the statement in lines 46–48 mainly serves to do. The statement says that *While the study has only been carried out on research animals so far, scientists believe it's likely that much of the same applies to people.* Therefore, the statement is intended to indicate that people will probably experience the same negative cognitive effects from increased salt intake and a reduction in those negative cognitive effects from reduced salt intake, as did the mice. Because this is only a belief of the scientists, this means it has not *already been applied directly to humans*, so eliminate (F). Since it's *likely that much of the same applies to people*, it would be relevant to, not *irrelevant* to or have *no effect* on, human health or human brain health, so eliminate (G) and (J). Choice (H) is consistent with the statement, so keep it. The correct answer is (H).

33. **D** The question asks what happened to the mice when they were returned to a normal diet after being on a high-salt diet. This is discussed in the sixth paragraph, which states that after this change, *the detrimental health effects caused by excess salt intake were erased.* Since both (A) and (B) state that the mice instead suffered negative consequences rather than positive results, eliminate them. While the *gut-brain signaling pathway* is implied to be affected by the high salt diet in the fifth paragraph, it's not explicitly stated that this pathway became *more active* when the diet was returned to normal, so eliminate (C). The passage states that *the detrimental health effects caused by excess salt intake were erased*, which supports (D). The correct answer is (D).

34. **F** The question asks what claim is supported by the detail that impairment in learning and memory was evident even in the absence of high blood pressure. The fifth paragraph states that the *impairment in learning and memory was clear even in the absence of high blood pressure*, and that the *gut is reacting to the salt overload and directing immune signals that…compromise cognitive function.* This evidence supports the claim that salt intake can impair cognitive things like learning and memory even when someone does not have high blood pressure. Choice (F) is consistent with this relationship between *cognitive impairment* and *high salt intake*, so keep it. High blood pressure does not need to be present for salt intake to affect cognitive function, so eliminate (G) and (H). The impairment in cognitive function is linked to *high salt intake*, a dietary issue, several times in the passage, so eliminate (J). The correct answer is (F).

35. **C** The question asks for what the average salt intake of adults worldwide is. This information is found in the fourth paragraph, which states that the salt intake of people around the globe is *on average 9–12 grams per day*, so eliminate (A), (B), and (D), and keep (C). The correct answer is (C).

36. **J** The question asks how the phrase *a cascade of chemical responses* (lines 37–38) should be read. This information can be found in the fifth paragraph, which states that *immune responses in the small intestines set off a cascade of chemical responses, reaching the brain's blood vessels, reducing blood flow to the cortex and hippocampus, two brain regions crucial for learning and memory.* The paragraph does not go on to claim that this cascade is an *awe-inspiring* or elegant process, so eliminate (F) and (G). The passage does not indicate the relative speed of each response, so eliminate (H). The phrasing of the cascade suggests a sequence of cause and effects, which supports (J). The correct answer is (J).

TEST 1 SCIENCE ANSWERS AND EXPLANATIONS

Passage I

1. **A** The question asks for the angle of the ramp if Experiment 3 had been repeated at a temperature of 62.5°C. Look at Table 3 and find where 62.5°C would fit in with the existing data. As temperature increases in Table 3, the angle also increases. A temperature of 62.5°C would fall between 50°C and 75°C, so the angle for 62.5°C would fall between 25.4 and 29.0. Eliminate (B), (C), and (D). The correct answer is (A).

2. **F** The question asks which material would have taken the *greatest amount of force to start moving*, based on the results of Experiment 1. Look at the results of Experiment 1. Table 1 lists the different materials in order of increasing angle. The object made of brick required the largest ramp angle before any movement took place, which means it is most resistant to movement. Therefore, the brick object would also require the greatest amount of force to start moving on a flat surface. Eliminate (G), (H), and (J). The correct answer is (F).

3. **D** The question asks for the effect of the weight of the object on the *coefficient of static friction*, based on the results of Experiments 1 and 4. Look at the results of Experiments 1 and 4. Table 1 lists the different materials in order of increasing ramp angle. Table 4 lists the number of objects and the ramp angle. Experiment 4 used only wooden objects, so compare the angle for wood in Table 1 with the results in Table 4. In all cases, the angle is 22.0. Because adding more objects does not change the results, choose the answer that indicates no change. Eliminate (A), (B), and (C). The correct answer is (D).

4. **G** The question asks for the independent variable in Experiment 2. In Experiment 2, the researchers varied which face was placed down on the ramp and measured the angle of the ramp. Eliminate (H) and (J) as neither of these variables are seen in Experiment 2. The *independent variable*, sometimes called the manipulated variable, is the variable that is directly manipulated by researchers. Eliminate (F) as the angle was measured but not directly manipulated by the researchers. Only the face was directly varied by the researchers. The correct answer is (G).

5. **B** The question asks for a list of different materials, from *greatest resistance to movement to least resistance to movement*. Find the experiment that varies the materials and look at the results. Table 1 lists the different materials in order of increasing ramp angle. An increased angle indicates greater resistance to movement, so brick, which has the greatest angle, has the most resistance to movement. Eliminate (A), (C), and (D). Note that (A) has the materials listed in order from least resistance to greatest resistance, the opposite of what the question asks. The correct answer is (B).

6. **J** The question asks about the force required to move the stationary block if *Experiment 1 were repeated with the granite block placed with Face C against the surface of the ramp*. Look at Tables 1 and 2. According to Table 2, the angle at which the object started to slide was identical, no matter which face of the block was placed down on the ramp. This means that if Experiment 1 were

repeated with the granite block on Face C, the force required to move the block would be the same as if it were on Face A. Eliminate (F) and (H). Since the blocks start to slide at the same angle regardless of what face of the block is placed down on the ramp, the surface area of the block is not important in determining the force required for movement. Eliminate (G). The true determinant of the force is the coefficient of friction. The correct answer is (J).

Passage II

7. **C**   The question asks in what way the procedure of Experiment 2 differed from that of Experiment 1. Both (C) and (D) mention temperature. Look for the word *temperature* in the descriptions of Experiments 1 and 2. According to the description of Experiment 1, *the experimental procedure was repeated at varying temperatures,* and according to the description of Experiment 2, the same procedures were repeated but this time at *26°C.* Eliminate (D) because it states that *temperature was varied* in Experiment 2 and *in Experiment 1, the temperature was held constant,* which is incorrect. Choice (C) accurately represents the data. Eliminate (A) and (B) because both *MEA* and *DEA* were used in Experiment 1. The correct answer is (C).

8. **G**   The question asks for the *scrub times (in msec) for both MEA and DEA* if *an additional trial were done at 12°C* in Experiment 1. Look at the results of Experiment 1 in Table 1. As temperature increases, the scrub times for both MEA and DEA decrease. Draw a horizontal line across the table where 12°C would fall, in between 10°C and 15°C. The scrub time for MEA would fall between 10,925 and 11,025 msec. Eliminate (F) because the scrub time listed for MEA is out of range. Keep (G) and (H) because the scrub times listed for MEA are within range. Eliminate (J) because the scrub time listed for MEA is equivalent to that of a trial done at 10°C. According to Table 2, the scrub time for DEA at 10°C is 8,315 and at 15°C it is 8,240, so the scrub time for DEA at 12°C must be between those values. Eliminate (H) because the time listed is out of range. The correct answer is (G).

9. **A**   The question asks for *a possible chemical formula for an ethanolamine,* based on the information in the passage. Paragraph 1 states that *ethanolamines are compounds that contain both alcohol (–OH or HO–) and amine (–NH$_3$, –RNH$_2$, –R$_2$NH, or –R$_3$N) subgroups.* Both (A) and (B) contain HO– so keep them. Eliminate (C) and (D) because neither contains –OH or HO–. Eliminate (B) because it does not contain –NH$_3$, –RNH$_2$, –R$_2$NH, or –R$_3$N. The correct answer is (A).

10. **J**   The question asks whether the results of Experiment 1 support the following claim: *DEA will always absorb CO$_2$ at a faster rate than will MEA.* Look at the results of Experiment 1 as listed in Table 1. *CO$_2$* is not present in Table 1, so look for *CO$_2$* in the description of Experiment 1. The passage defines *scrub time* as the *time for CO$_2$ concentration to drop at least 10 ppm.* Table 1 shows that the scrub time of MEA is always more than that of DEA. The passage states that *longer scrub times indicate a slower rate of absorption.* Therefore, the claim is supported; *DEA will always absorb CO$_2$ at a faster rate than will MEA.* Eliminate (F) and (G) because they say *no.* Although (H) states that the claim is supported, its explanation is opposite. Only (J) states that the claim is supported and that *the scrub time for MEA was more than that for DEA.* The correct answer is (J).

11. **B** The question asks *which acidic gas had the slowest absorption by MEA at 26°C,* according to Experiment 2. Look for the word *absorption* in the passage. The description of Experiment 1 states that *longer scrub times indicate a slower rate of absorption.* Look at Table 2. The formula with the longest scrub time is HCN. The correct answer is (B).

12. **G** The question asks for a reactant and a product from the reaction in Experiment 1. Experiment 1 studies either MEA or DEA, and, according to the formula in Figure 1, is mixed with gaseous CO_2. Since all of the answer choices list MEA, DEA, or CO_2 as potential reactants, this doesn't help eliminate any answers. However, refer to Figure 1 for the possible products of Experiment 1. None of the listed products is water (H_2O), so eliminate (H) and (J). Additionally, CO_2 is not a product—it's a reactant, so eliminate (F) as well. The only correct product shown in Figure 1 is heat. Therefore, the correct answer is (G).

Passage III

13. **B** The question asks whether there would be any pepsin activity if Trial 10 were repeated without anserine. Trial 10 has high pepsin activity, but Table 2 does not give any information about *anserine.* The passage indicates that all trials in Table 2 were prepared *according to the same procedure as Trial 3,* so look at Trial 3. In Trial 3, equal amounts of casein and anserine were used, the temperature was 40°C, and the pepsin activity was high. Look at the trials listed in the answer choices to help answer this question. In Trial 4, anserine was eliminated from the reaction while the temperature remained constant, and the pepsin activity remained high. This indicates that at 40°C, the activity of pepsin is unaffected by the addition of anserine; eliminate (C) and (D). Trial 6 is not relevant to this question, because it removes casein as well as anserine, which is not what the question specifies; eliminate (A). The correct answer is (B).

14. **H** The question asks in which organ *pepsin is most likely to be found.* Look for the key word *pepsin* in the passage. Paragraph 1 states that *pepsin is an enzyme in humans that catalyzes the digestion.* Eliminate (F), (G), and (J) because those organs are not found in the digestive system. The correct answer is (H).

15. **C** The question asks for the reason that *Trial 5 shows no pepsin activity,* while *Trials 3 and 4 show high levels of pepsin activity.* Look at Trials 3–5 in Table 1. Because the answer choices are based on *casein* and *anserine,* look at those columns in Table 1. *Casein* is present in Trials 3 and 4 but not in Trial 5, so its absence could explain the lack of pepsin activity in Trial 5. Use this knowledge to eliminate (D). *Anserine* is present in Trials 3 and 5 but not in Trial 4, so its presence could not provide the explanation for why Trial 3 and Trial 4 have high levels of pepsin activity. Use this knowledge to eliminate (A) and (B). The correct answer is (C).

16. **F** The question asks which *trials are most likely to contain undigested casein,* according to the results of Experiment 1. Look at the results of Experiment 1, found in Table 1. Only Trials 1–4 and 7 used solutions that contained *casein,* so eliminate (G) and (J) because the solutions of Trials 5 and 6 did

not contain *casein*. Paragraph 1 states that *pepsin is an enzyme in humans that catalyzes the digestion of proteins, like the milk protein casein.* Look at Table 1. In Trials 1 and 7, there was *no pepsin activity,* which means the *casein* did not get digested. In Trials 3 and 4, there was a *high* level of *pepsin activity,* which means *casein* did get digested; eliminate (H). The correct answer is (F).

17.   **A**   The question asks which trial's experimental conditions were most similar to those of Trial 3. Look at Table 1. The *pepsin activity* for Trial 3 is *high.* All of the trials listed in the answers are in Table 2, so look at Table 2. Only Trials 8–10 had *high pepsin activity.* Eliminate (B), (C), and (D) because they had either *low activity* or *no activity* at all. The correct answer is (A).

18.   **J**   The question asks if the results for Experiment 2 support the hypothesis that pepsin digests proteins fastest in the least acidic solutions. The results for Experiment 2 are shown in Table 2. Table 2 shows that Trial 8 has high pepsin activity, so eliminate (H) as this is the opposite of what is shown in Table 2. Table 2 also shows that Trial 14 has no activity, so eliminate (G), which incorrectly states that Trial 14 has high pepsin activity. Choosing between (F) and (J) requires some outside knowledge. On a pH scale, all values less than 7 are acidic, with the lower values corresponding to higher acidity. Therefore, the *least* acidic values in Table 2 would be the pH values closest to 7. Trial 14 is the least acidic pH shown in Table 2. Since Trial 14 shows no pepsin activity, this data does not support the hypothesis that the least acidic solutions would have the highest digestion rates. Eliminate (F). The correct answer is (J).

Passage IV

19.   **B**   The question asks why the researchers collected data for Group 6. Look at the information given for each group in Table 1. Group 6 is described as *unaffected polar bear habitat.* There is no information about *predators that most threaten polar bears,* so eliminate (A). A *standard by which the other groups could be compared* could describe Group 6, because there were no unusual factors in the Group 6 habitat; keep (B). Because the Group 6 habitat had no unusual factors, it could not have helped the researchers *identify and select the conditions for the remaining five groups;* eliminate (C). Figure 1 shows that Group 2 had a higher population density than Group 6 did, so Group 6 does not show *the greatest number of polar bears that would be likely to survive in an area of 25 km².* Eliminate (D). The correct answer is (B).

20.   **H**   The question asks for a list of Groups 1–5 in order from *most conducive to polar bear population density* to *least conducive.* Figure 1 gives data about population density for Groups 1–5, so eliminate any answers that don't match the data in Figure 1. Group 2 has the highest population density ratio, so it should be first on the list; eliminate (F) and (G). Group 5 has the second highest population density, so eliminate (J). Note that (G) has the groups listed in order from *least* to *greatest,* the opposite of what the question asks. The correct answer is (H).

21. **C** The question asks for the organism with a decreased population in Group 1. Look at the information given for Group 1 in Table 1. Group 1 was in areas that *had significantly decreased populations of marine mammals consumed by polar bears*. Eliminate (B) and (D) because neither the *salmon* nor *snowy owl* is a mammal. Polar bears do not eat polar bears, so eliminate (A). The correct answer is (C).

22. **F** The question asks which hypothesis is not supported by the results of the study. When a question asks which answer is **not** in the passage, eliminate answers that **are** in the passage. Group 1 had *declining prey populations* as described in (H), and Figure 1 indicates that Group 1 had lower than average population density: the formula above Figure 1 shows that the *population density ratio* in Figure 1 is calculated by dividing each group's average population density by the average population density of Group 6, the unaffected habitat. A population density ratio of less than 1 shows a decline in population, while a ratio of greater than 1 shows an increase. Group 1 thus effectively answers the question in (H); eliminate (H). Group 3 had *melting Arctic sea ice* as described in (G), and the population density ratio in Figure 1 is lower for Group 3 than it is for Group 1, which had *declining prey populations*. The question in (G) is answered, so eliminate (G). Choice (F) presents the opposite hypothesis of the one in (G); since (G) is correct, (F) must be incorrect. Keep (F). Group 3's population density ratio is less than 1, which effectively answers the question in (J), so eliminate (J). The correct answer is (F).

23. **D** The question asks *which of the following is closest to the total number of polar bears found in all ten areas of Group 6*. Table 2 shows the population density for all 10 blocks in Group 6. The population density in Table 2 is expressed as the number of polar bears per km^2, but according to the passage, each block measured in the study represents a 5 km by 5 km area, or 25 km^2. Start by examining Area A in Table 2, which has a population density of 0.93. This can be rounded to about 1 polar bear per km^2. However, since each block is actually 25 km^2, there are approximately 25 polar bears in Area A. Repeat this logic with Area B, which has a population density of about 2 polar bears per km^2, to find that there are about 50 polar bears in Area B. So far, there are 75 total polar bears in Areas A and B alone. Eliminate (A) and (B). There are still eight more areas to be calculated, so there must be many more polar bears than 90. Eliminate (C). The correct answer is (D).

Passage V

24. **H** The question asks which of the solutions shown in Table 1 contained ions. An *ion* is a positively or negatively charged molecule. According to Table 1, Solution 1 contained only pure water, so it has no charged particles. Eliminate (F) and (G) because they include Solution 1. Table 2 also shows that Solution 2 only contained neutral particles. Eliminate (J) as Solution 2 did not contain ions. Solutions 3 and 4 both contained charged particles, so the correct answer is (H).

25. **A** The question asks which scientist's explanation is in disagreement with the following observation: *the freezing point of benzene is lowered with the addition of the solute naphthalene ($C_{10}H_8$), which has no charge.* Look at Scientist 1's explanation in paragraph 4. It states that a *decrease in freezing point is related only to the charge of the solute particles.* This disagrees with the observation in the question stem, so eliminate (C) and (D). Eliminate (B) because it erroneously states that Scientist 1 believes that **any** *solute is capable of increasing the stability of the liquid phase of a solvent.* The correct answer is (A).

26. **F** The question asks which statements both Scientists 1 and 2 would agree with. Check each answer choice against the information in the passage. Look at Scientist 1's explanation in paragraph 4. It states that a *decrease in freezing point is related only to the charge of the solute particles;* eliminate (H) because it states that *no charge will decrease the liquid's freezing point.* Eliminate (G) and (J) because they mention *increase* in a liquid's freezing point and neither scientist discussed this. The correct answer is (F).

27. **B** The question asks which diagram *best illustrates how Scientist 1 would describe the results after a charged solute has been added to H_2O.* Look at Scientist 1's explanation in paragraph 4, which states, *when a solute is added the...charge...interferes with the orderly arrangement of solvent molecules.* Eliminate (A), (C), and (D) because they all show *orderly arrangements of the solvent molecules.* Choice (B) has no order to the arrangement of molecules. The correct answer is (B).

28. **F** The question asks whether *the scientists offer different explanations for the impact of a solute's physical properties, such as solute charge, on the decrease in freezing point of a solution.* Look at Scientist 1's explanation in paragraph 4. It states that a *decrease in freezing point is related only to the charge of the solute particles,* so Scientist 1 does discuss the *impact of...charge on the decrease in freezing point.* Eliminate (G) and (J) because they say that Scientist 1 does not say such properties have an impact. Look at Scientist 2's explanation in paragraph 5. It states that a *decrease in freezing point is related only to the concentration of particles, not to the identity or properties of each individual particle.* Since Scientist 2 disagrees that physical properties play a role in decreasing freezing point, eliminate (H). The correct answer is (F).

29. **D** The question asks which equation *is most consistent with Scientist 2's explanation,* assuming that k *is a constant,* ΔT *is the decrease in freezing point, and* i *is the van 't Hoff factor.* Look for the key words *van 't Hoff factor* in Scientist 2's explanation. Scientist 2 states that *the size of the decrease in freezing point is in direct proportion with the van 't Hoff factor.* Eliminate (A) and (C) because they both show inverse proportions. Eliminate (B) because it shows a direct proportion with the square of the van 't Hoff factor. Choice (D) shows a direct proportion between the decrease in freezing point and the van 't Hoff factor. The correct answer is (D).

Passage VI

30. **F** The question asks at which volume and pressure the gas in Carnot heat engine B will have the highest temperature. According to the first sentence of Paragraph 3 of the passage, the cycle begins when the gas is *at its highest temperature and pressure*. Refer to Figure 2 to study Carnot heat engine B. The highest pressure point on this graph is at 80 Pa when the volume is at 1.0 mL. This point, therefore, also represents the point of the highest temperature. The correct answer is (F).

31. **B** The question asks for the value of *P* under certain conditions according to Figure 2. Read the question carefully and look up the given values on Figure 2. The question specifies *when V was decreasing from its largest value*. *V* is on the *x*-axis of Figure 2, and its largest value is at 4.0. Look at the arrows on the lines on the graph to determine when *V* was *decreasing*. The left, or lower, part of the graph has arrows pointing to the left, which gives decreasing values for *V,* so look at the lower line on the graph. The question asks for the value of *P* when *V* is 2.0, so find 2.0 on the *x*-axis. Draw a line up to the lower part of the graph; then draw a horizontal line to the *y*-axis to find the value of *P*, which is about 20. The correct answer is (B).

32. **J** The question asks for the value of *V* when *P* was at its minimum for engine A. Engine A is shown in Figure 1, so look at Figure 1. First, determine the minimum value of *P*. *P* is on the *y*-axis, and its minimum is about 7.5 Pa. Draw a vertical line from this lowest point to the *x*-axis to determine the value of *V,* which is about 5.0. The correct answer is (J).

33. **C** The question asks for the relationship between the largest and smallest values of *V* in Figure 2. Look at Figure 2. *V* is on the *x*-axis; its minimum value is 1.0 mL, and its maximum value is 4.0 mL. Eliminate (A) because the minimum value is not negative. Eliminate (B) because $\frac{1}{8}$ of 4.0 is 0.5. Eliminate (D) because it says the smallest value is larger than the largest value. The correct answer is (C).

34. **F** The question asks for the value of *V* when the *reversible isothermic expansion* begins for engine A. The question defines the *reversible isothermic expansion* as the time *when P is decreased from its highest value and V is increased from its lowest value*. Engine A is shown in Figure 1, so look at Figure 1. The *highest value* for *P* and the *lowest value* for *V* both occur at the same point, at the upper left of the graph. Draw a vertical line from that point to the *x*-axis to determine the value of *V* at that point. *V* is 1.5 mL. The correct answer is (F).

Passage VII

35. C   The question asks *what distance from the starting point Protein D migrated* to *when Solvent 2 was used,* according to Experiment 2. Look at the results of Experiment 2 and locate the graph that corresponds to Solvent 2. The *distance* of Protein D is 50 mm. The correct answer is (C).

36. F   The question asks at which value *the migration distance of Protein A would most likely peak* if *Experiment 1 were repeated using a solvent with a pH of 8.4.* First, look at Table 1, which shows pH. The pH of this new solvent is slightly less than the pH of Solvent 1. Next, look at the results of Experiment 1. As the pH of each solvent increases, the distance Protein A travels also increases. Therefore, *the migration distance of Protein A would most likely peak* at a shorter distance than it did in Solvent 1, which was 10 mm. Eliminate (G), (H), and (J) because they contain values that are greater than 10 mm. The correct answer is (F).

37. C   The question asks which protein could be replaced by Protein L, which has an isoelectric point (*pI*) of 6.6, while keeping the results of Experiments 1 and 2 similar to the plots shown in Figures 2 and 3. Look at Table 1, which shows *pI*. The isoelectric point of Protein L is most similar to that of Protein C, so if it were replaced by Protein L, the results would be similar as well. The correct answer is (C).

38. F   The question asks which solvents displayed the *lowest resolution,* according to the results of Experiments 1 and 2. The question specifies that resolution *decreases as the overall distance between the peaks on the density plot decreases.* The *overall distance between the peaks* in Solvent 1 is 25 mm in both figures. The *overall distance between the peaks* in Solvent 2 is 30 mm in both figures. The *overall distance between the peaks* in Solvent 3 is 40 mm in both figures. Therefore, the *lowest resolution* occurs in Solvent 1 in both experiments. The correct answer is (F).

39. D   The question asks for a list of proteins, from shortest migration to longest, when Protein Y with a *pI* of 7.1 is added to Solvent 2 in Experiment 1. Look at Table 1. The *pI* of Protein Y falls between Proteins B and C. Look at the results of Experiment 1. For each solvent, the migration path from shortest to longest is A, B, C, D. As a result, the new order should be A, B, Y, C, D. The correct answer is (D).

40. F   The question asks for *the percent of Protein A that migrated using Solvent 3, at the migration distance where Protein B returned to its 0% migration detection* in Solvent 2, in Experiment 2. Look at the results of Experiment 2 when Solvent 2 was used. Protein B returns to 0% migration detected at 35 mm. Now locate 35 mm on the graph of data from when Solvent 3 was used. At 35 mm, the *percent of Protein A that migrated* was 0. The correct answer is (F).

TEST 1 ESSAY CHECKLIST

☐ Clearly state your own perspective.

☐ Reference the ideas of all 3 perspectives.

☐ Use examples to explain your point of view.

☐ Have 2–3 body paragraphs with 5–7 sentences each.

☐ Have an introduction and a conclusion paragraph.

☐ Write neatly.

☐ Use a formal tone and a mature level of vocabulary.

☐ Avoid spelling and grammar errors.

English Drills

HOW TO APPROACH THE ENGLISH PASSAGES

This section of the book contains 14 realistic English passages, each followed by explanations. We recommend starting by completing the passages untimed in order to focus on your strategy and ability to apply the rules that are tested. After completing each passage, carefully review the corresponding explanations and evaluate what you did well and what you can do to avoid making the same mistakes next time. Then, apply those corrections to your next passage.

Don't do all of the passages in one or two sittings. Try to spread them out over several days or weeks to allow time for your corrections to stick.

Once you have improved your accuracy, then work on speed. If you would like to time yourself in a way that is realistic to the amount of time given on the test, allot 7 minutes for each passage.

ENGLISH PASSAGE DRILL 1

Roast Done Right

Just like sculpting the *Venus de Milo* or painting the Sistine Chapel, preparing a delicious meal is an art. Even the seemingly mundane pot roast can be a true masterpiece. Nothing can be more rewarding to a cook than the <u>sign</u> of a roast done right.
1

Cooking a delicious roast with vegetables <u>require</u> three
2
things: the freshest ingredients, a slow-cooker, and good tim-ing. My friend Eric goes to the butcher shop just after its 5 A.M. delivery to snatch up the best cuts of meat, then heads to the local farmer's market. He fills his canvas shopping bag with ripe red tomatoes, crisp yellow onions, and round red potatoes. The tastiest vegetables are the results of natural sunshine and of a farmer's careful tending.

With supplies in tote, Eric heads to the kitchen. While the beef marinates in garlic and spices, he chops the colorful array of fresh vegetables. Eric <u>slowly places the vegetables</u> around
3

the meat in the slow-cooker's pot, <u>he alternates</u> rings of bright
4
orange carrots and chunks of red potatoes. He sprinkles in sliced onions and herbs until the ingredients nearly spill over the top. Like many cooks, Eric has a secret, final ingredient: a splash of red wine for flavor.

1. The writer would like to convey the distinct scent of a properly cooked roast. Given that all the choices are true, which best accomplishes the writer's goal?

   A. **No Change**
   B. swirling rush of robust aromas
   C. fine textures of vegetables and meats
   D. diners' eager expectation

2. Which choice makes the sentence most grammatically acceptable?

   F. **No Change**
   G. have required
   H. requiring
   J. requires

3. The writer wishes to emphasize Eric's attention to detail in making his pot roast. Given that all the choices are true, which one best accomplishes the writer's goal?

   A. **No Change**
   B. is very careful when pouring the vegetables
   C. meticulously layers the evenly cut vegetables
   D. arranges the vegetables in a kind of order

4. Which choice makes the sentence most grammatically acceptable?

   F. **No Change**
   G. he has alternated
   H. alternates
   J. alternating

At least, it's time to cram the lid onto the heaping potful
<u>5</u>
of ingredients and turn on the cooker. The temperature inside

the <u>pot rises slowly as the contents stew</u> in their natural juices.
<u>6</u>
The roast will take six to eight hours to cook, but after an hour

or two, the first spicy scents start <u>wafting through the kitchen.</u>
<u>7</u>
A few hours later, the rich, juicy smell of beef begins to escape.

Every half <u>hour, using a long, meat thermometer</u> Eric reads the
<u>8</u>
temperature of the roast and carefully examines the stewing

contents. He doesn't want it overcooked or undercooked but

"just right." ⌷9⌷

<u>Lift</u> the finished roast out of the pot to serve, the tender
<u>10</u>
meat plops juicily onto our plates in generous servings. He tops

it off with zesty, steaming vegetables. Eric is obviously proud

to share his work of art, and his friends are more than willing to

eat it.

5. Which transition word or phrase is most logical in context?

   A. No Change
   B. Prior to that,
   C. Today,
   D. At this point,

6. Given that all the choices are true, which one provides the most specific sensory detail and maintains the style and tone of the essay?

   F. No Change
   G. rises slowly but surely, stewing
   H. rises slowly to a lazy, bubbling boil, stewing the savory contents
   J. increases to about 200 degrees Fahrenheit to stew the contents

7. Which choice is least redundant in context?

   A. No Change
   B. drifting through the air to make the whole kitchen smell.
   C. wafting and floating through the whole kitchen.
   D. wafting through the air of the kitchen.

8. Which choice makes the sentence most grammatically acceptable?

   F. No Change
   G. hour, using a long meat thermometer,
   H. hour using a long meat thermometer
   J. hour, using a long meat thermometer;

9. The writer is considering deleting the preceding sentence. Should it be kept or deleted?

   A. Kept, because it provides a reason for Eric's diligent attention to the temperature.
   B. Kept, because it reinforces the fact that roasts are typically done cooking after 8 hours.
   C. Deleted, because it puts the focus on Eric and his cooking, rather than the roast.
   D. Deleted, because it doesn't provide enough information about temperature's effects on the roast.

10. Which choice makes the sentence most grammatically acceptable?

   F. No Change
   G. As he lifts
   H. When you lift
   J. Lifting

ENGLISH PASSAGE DRILL 1 EXPLANATIONS

1. **B** The question is asking for the answer that would *convey the distinct scent of a properly cooked roast,* so eliminate any answers that don't fulfill this goal. The *sign* does not include any reference to *scent,* so eliminate (A). Choice (B) mentions *aromas,* which is consistent with *scent,* so keep (B). Neither the *textures of vegetables and meats* nor the *diners' eager expectation* addresses the idea of *scent,* so eliminate (C) and (D). The correct answer is (B).

2. **J** The question asks about grammar, so look at the answers to see what's changing. Verbs are changing in the answer choices, so identify the subject: *Cooking.* As a subject, this word is singular, so eliminate (F) and (G) because they are both plural. Next, consider the form of the verb. The part of the sentence before the colon needs to be an independent clause, so the main verb can't be in *-ing* form. Eliminate (H) because it doesn't produce a complete sentence. The correct answer is (J).

3. **C** The question is asking for the answer that would *emphasize Eric's attention to detail in making his pot roast,* so eliminate any answers that don't fulfill this goal. The word *slowly* could be consistent with *attention to detail,* but there could be other reasons for slowness; eliminate (A). The idea that Eric *is very careful* could be consistent with *attention to detail,* but the word *meticulously* and the phrase *finely cut vegetables* in (C) more clearly convey *attention to detail.* Eliminate (B) and keep (C). The phrase *a kind of order* does not clearly convey *attention to detail,* so eliminate (D). The correct answer is (C).

4. **J** The question asks about grammar, so look at the answers to see what's changing. Subjects and verbs are changing in the answer choices, so look for independent clauses. The first part of the sentence, *Eric slowly places the vegetables around the meat in the slow-cooker's pot,* is an independent clause. It's followed by a comma, so the part after the comma cannot be an independent clause since two independent clauses can't be connected by only a comma. Eliminate (F) and (G) because they both make the second part of the sentence an independent clause. Although (H) doesn't have a subject, the verb *alternates* isn't in the right form to make a describing phrase that can go after a comma. Eliminate (H). Choice (J) correctly produces the unnecessary phrase that follows the comma. The correct answer is (J).

5. **D** The question is asking for a *logical* transition, so identify the relationships between the ideas. The preceding sentence identifies Eric's *final* ingredient, and this sentence states what Eric does once all of the ingredients have been added. Therefore, a time-change transition is needed. Eliminate (A) because it's not related to time. Next, eliminate (B) because the phrase *it's time* suggests that this event is occurring after Eric has added the ingredients, not *Prior to that*. Eliminate (C) because there is no evidence of a change from the past to today. Keep (D) because *At this point* shows that the action of closing the lid happens once all the ingredients have been added. The correct answer is (D).

6. **H** The question is asking for the answer that would provide *the most specific sensory detail,* so eliminate any answers that don't fulfill this goal. Neither (F) nor (G) gives a *sensory detail,* so eliminate them both. Choice (H) describes the *lazy, bubbling boil,* which evokes a visual sense of the pot, and the word *savory* evokes a smell. Keep (H). Choice (J) does not include any *sensory detail,* so eliminate (J). The correct answer is (H).

7. **A** The question is asking for the *least redundant* answer, so eliminate answers that are overly wordy or repeat information given earlier. The nonunderlined portion of the sentence mentions *scents,* so there is no need to use the word *smell*; eliminate (B). *Wafting* and *floating* mean the same thing in this context, so there is no need to use both words; eliminate (C). Choices (A) and (D) both express the same idea, but (A) is more concise, given that *wafting* implies being in *the air.* Eliminate (D). The correct answer is (A).

8. **G** The question asks about grammar, so look at the answers to see what's changing. Commas and a semicolon around the phrase *using a long meat thermometer* are changing, so consider whether any punctuation is needed. The first part of the sentence, *Every half hour, using a long meat thermometer,* is not an independent clause. A semicolon can only be used between two independent clauses, so eliminate (J). The phrase *using a long meat thermometer* is not necessary to the main meaning of the sentence, so it should be set off by commas. Eliminate (H) because it lacks commas. Choice (F) lacks a comma after the unnecessary phrase; eliminate (F). The correct answer is (G).

9. **A** The question is asking whether a sentence should be deleted, so consider the content of the sentence and the surrounding context. The paragraph focuses on cooking the pot roast, and the sentence in question gives a reason that *Eric reads the temperature,* as described in the previous sentence. The sentence in question is therefore consistent with the paragraph and should not be deleted; eliminate (C) and (D). Choice (A) accurately describes the sentence. The sentence does not reinforce *that roasts are typically done cooking after 8 hours,* so eliminate (B). The correct answer is (A).

10. **G** The question asks about grammar, so look at the answers to see what's changing. Subjects and verbs are changing in the answer choices, so eliminate answers that don't produce a complete sentence. In (F), the first part of the sentence, *Lift the finished roast out of the pot to serve,* is an independent clause. The second part of the sentence, *the tender meat plops juicily onto our plates in generous servings,* is also an independent clause. A comma on its own cannot be used between two independent clauses, so eliminate (F). Changing the verb to *lifting* means that the first part of the sentence is no longer an independent clause, but it is now a descriptive phrase that would suggest that the *tender meat* is lifting something, which isn't logical; eliminate (J). Choices (G) and (H) have different pronouns. The story is about how *Eric* makes the roast, and there is no mention of *you* in the passage. Eliminate (H). The correct answer is (G).

ENGLISH PASSAGE DRILL 2

Hats: On My Head, On My Mind

I do not remember how I came to like wearing a hat. Friends view it as an odd habit of mine, since so few of them wear hats. I think my fondness for hats comes down to the desire to <u>compare</u> what type of person I am. Telling the world
₁
what kind of person resides directly below its brim is one of the principal jobs of any hat.

Even if we are not supposed to judge a book by its cover, we very often judge people by their hats. $\boxed{2}$ In a narrow sense, a top hat indicates to all that you are a magician, just as a mortarboard and tassel tell the world you just graduated. More generally, a cowboy hat may say you are the strong, silent type, while a beret suggests you are artistic and creative. Hats show up in our figures of speech as well. Home is where you hang your hat, while declaring your desire to win a position is throwing your hat into the ring. How could anyone not want to wear a hat, <u>especially because it makes your hair messy?</u>
₃

A hat can do even more in everyday life. <u>Deserving</u> con-
₄
gratulations, I say that my hat is off to them—and then I can literally do exactly that. When someone has exciting news for me, he can tell me to hold on to my hat. If the news has to be kept secret, I can promise to keep it under my hat. He could even tell

1. Which choice is clearest and most precise in context?

   A. **No Change**
   B. create
   C. proclaim
   D. investigate

2. The writer is considering deleting the preceding sentence from the essay. Should the sentence be kept or deleted?

   F. Kept, because it establishes the theme of this paragraph, the ways in which hats symbolize things about people and their actions.
   G. Kept, because it establishes the narrator's love of hats.
   H. Deleted, because the information it contains is contradicted in the previous sentence.
   J. Deleted, because the narrative is more interesting if readers are left to draw their own conclusions about the ways in which they personally interpret hats.

3. Given that all the choices are true, which one most strongly reinforces the author's attitude toward hats as it has been conveyed up to this point in the essay?

   A. **No Change**
   B. when it may cost a substantial amount?
   C. although you may forget one in a restaurant?
   D. when it can do so much?

4. Which choice makes the sentence most grammatically acceptable?

   F. **No Change**
   G. As they are deserving
   H. When people deserve
   J. To deserve

me to remain calm and not be a mad hatter. ☐5

Maybe the real reason I like wearing a hat, however, has to do with getting away from everyday life. What I find so interesting is the possibility of using a hat, to make myself more like someone very different from my everyday self. A fedora helps

me to think of me as more of a street-smart tough-guy private eye. Another hat, appropriately battered, helps me feel like a

daring adventurer his search for fabulous treasures will succeed against all odds.

On my last birthday, my family that gave me a Napoleon hat. I wonder, what are they trying to tell me?

5. At this point, the writer is considering adding the following true statement:

> "Mad hatter" properly refers to the many nineteenth-century hat makers who suffered extensive neurological damage after they were exposed to the toxic mercury fumes then utilized in hat construction.

Should the writer make this addition here?

A. Yes, because it helps support the idea that the author has affection for hats.
B. Yes, because it provides a striking parallel between the author's interest in hats and Lewis Carroll's.
C. No, because many individuals in the nineteenth century besides hat makers were exposed to poisonous fumes.
D. No, because its historical explanation of the scientific origins of the image of mad hatters does not fit with the essay to this point.

6. Which choice makes the sentence most grammatically acceptable?

F. **No Change**
G. possibility of using a hat
H. possibility, of using a hat
J. possibility, of using a hat,

7. Which choice makes the sentence most grammatically acceptable?

A. **No Change**
B. myself
C. my own self
D. I

8. Which choice makes the sentence most grammatically acceptable?

F. **No Change**
G. whose
H. pursing a
J. making a

9. Which choice makes the sentence most grammatically acceptable?

A. **No Change**
B. are those who
C. were among who
D. **Delete** the underlined portion.

Question 10 asks about the preceding passage as a whole.

10. Suppose one of the writer's goals had been to indicate that items of clothing can be used to communicate things, literally and figuratively, about their wearers. Would this essay have fulfilled that goal?

    F. Yes, because the essay reveals that the narrator uses hats to express his feelings and present himself as different kinds of people.

    G. Yes, because the essay reveals that hats have been symbols of royalty and power for centuries.

    H. No, because the essay indicates that the narrator prefers to wear hats from popular culture instead of history.

    J. No, because the essay establishes that the narrator's attitude toward hats may not be shared by his family and friends.

ENGLISH PASSAGE DRILL 2 EXPLANATIONS

1. **C** The question is asking for the *clearest and most precise* answer, so use Process of Elimination. With (A), the sentence does not finish the thought to compare whom the narrator is comparing himself to, so eliminate (A). Eliminate (B) because the phrase *create what type of person I am* doesn't have a clear meaning. Keep (C) because *proclaim* means "tell others," and it's logical that the narrator might like telling others *what type of person he is*. Although (D) is grammatical, it's less logical that a hat would help you *investigate* who you are than that it would help you show others your personality, as in (C). Eliminate (D). The correct answer is (C).

2. **F** The question is asking whether a sentence should be deleted, so consider the content of the sentence and the surrounding context. The paragraph gives examples of how a hat visually expresses something about its wearer, so the sentence is consistent; eliminate (H) and (J). The sentence does not discuss *the narrator's love of hats,* so eliminate (G). The sentence does, as (F) says, establish *the theme of this paragraph.* The correct answer is (F).

3. **D** The question is asking for an answer that best *reinforces the author's attitude toward hats as it has been conveyed up to this point,* so eliminate any answers that don't fulfill this goal. There is no discussion of whether a hat *makes your hair messy,* so eliminate (A). There is also no discussion of the *cost* of hats, so eliminate (B). The author does not mention the potential to *forget* a hat, so eliminate (C). The essay up to this point discusses the many different things a hat can communicate about a person, so keep (D). The correct answer is (D).

4. **H** The question asks about grammar, so look at the answers to see what's changing. Subjects and verbs are changing within a describing phrase, so eliminate any answer that doesn't produce a clear and correct meaning. With (F), the sentence describes the narrator as *Deserving congratulations.* However, the context suggests that other people (referred to later in the sentence as *them*) are being congratulated. Eliminate (F). Choice (J) makes a similar error, so eliminate it. Comparing (G) and (H), choice (G) uses a pronoun, *they,* that doesn't clearly refer back to anyone from the paragraph. In contrast, (H) uses a specific noun, *people.* Eliminate (G). The correct answer is (H).

5. **D** The question is asking whether a sentence should be added to the end of the paragraph, so consider the content of the sentence and the surrounding context. The paragraph focuses on the meanings of different expressions that include references to hats. The new sentence gives a history of one of these phrases but is not consistent with the overall paragraph, so it should not be added. Eliminate (A) and (B). The number of *individuals in the nineteenth century* who *were exposed to poisonous fumes* is not relevant to the paragraph, so eliminate (C). Choice (D) correctly states that the new sentence *does not fit with the essay.* The correct answer is (D).

6. **G** The question asks about grammar, so look at the answers to see what's changing. Commas around the phrase *of using a hat* are changing, so consider whether any punctuation is needed. The phrase *of using a hat* is necessary to the main meaning of the sentence, so it should not be set off by commas; eliminate (J). There is no reason to put a comma after either *possibility* or *hat,* as neither of these commas separates distinct ideas in the sentence; eliminate (F) and (H). The correct answer is (G).

7. **B** The question asks about grammar, so look at the answers to see what's changing. Pronouns are changing in the answer choices, so identify who or what the pronoun refers back to and use Process of Elimination. The sentence is describing how the narrator thinks of himself, since it says *helps me to think of…*, so the reflexive pronoun *myself* is needed here. Eliminate (A) and (D). Although (C) is also reflexive, (B) is more concise, so eliminate (C). The correct answer is (B).

8. **G** The question asks about grammar, so look at the answers to see what's changing. Nouns and pronouns are changing in the answer choices, so eliminate any answer that doesn't produce a complete sentence. With (F), the sentence contains two separate independent clauses (*Another hat…helps me feel like a daring adventurer* and *his search for fabulous treasures will succeed…*) with no punctuation in between, which isn't allowed. Eliminate (F). Keep (G) because it produces a complete sentence with no errors. Both (H) and (J) create a describing phrase beginning with an *-ing* verb, but the word *that* would need to be included later on in the sentence to go along with the verb *will succeed*. Eliminate (H) and (J). The correct answer is (G).

9. **D** The question asks about grammar, so look at the answers to see what's changing. Connecting words are changing in the answer choices, and there is also the option to delete, so consider complete sentences. Start with the option to delete. With this choice, the sentence says *On my last birthday, my family gave me a Napoleon hat*. This produces a complete sentence with no errors, so keep (D). Adding *that* would make the sentence incomplete, so eliminate (A). Although (B) does produce a complete sentence, there's no reason to add the additional words, so eliminate (B). For (C), it's not correct to say *were among who*, so eliminate (C). The correct answer is (D).

10. **F** The question is asking whether the essay indicates that *items of clothing can be used to communicate things, literally and figuratively, about their wearers,* so consider the overall focus of the essay. This essay discusses both the literal and figurative messages hats can send, so it is consistent with this idea; eliminate (H) and (J). The narrator of the essay does discuss how he *uses hats to express his feelings and present himself as different kinds of people,* so keep (F). The essay never discusses that *hats have been symbols of royalty and power,* so eliminate (G). The correct answer is (F).

ENGLISH PASSAGE DRILL 3

A Diamond in the Rough

Beginning around 1963, when cassette recorders with built-in microphones first became available for purchase, amateur songwriters were able to record songs that <u>had been formerly</u> undocumented. One guitarist and saxophonist, Bruce Diamond, recorded nearly a hundred songs from his home in Lexington, Kentucky. Recently, hundreds of these rough recordings have been re-mastered. They have captured the attention of musicologists for a number of reasons.

First, <u>it is seemingly apparent that Diamond's songs were</u> influenced by many different popular artists of the day. One song sounds very similar to a complicated jazz song by Charlie Parker. However, another song is the opposite, sounding like the straightforward rock of Buddy Holly. The lyrics are very similar to Holly's as well, <u>and one is led to wonder what inspired them.</u>

One music critic observed that Diamond found it <u>completely effortless</u> to switch back and forth between very different musical genres.

1. Which choice makes the sentence most grammatically acceptable?
   A. **No Change**
   B. have been formerly
   C. are now being
   D. are formerly

2. Which of the following choices provides the most stylistically effective and concise wording here?
   F. **No Change**
   G. there is the impression given by Diamond's songs that he was
   H. Diamond's songs suggest that he was
   J. it is the impression Diamond's songs give that he was

3. Given that all the choices are true, which of the following would best provide further detail about the lyrical subject matter?
   A. **No Change**
   B. dealing mostly with dating and automobiles.
   C. and he mostly uses rhymed couplets and alliteration.
   D. which are easy to understand because of Diamond's enunciation.

4. Which choice most effectively maintains the essay's tone?
   F. **No Change**
   G. super easy
   H. to be a cinch
   J. not too tricky

Diamond's recordings are noteworthy for their unique artistic voice—an interesting combination of jazz, bluegrass, and gospel styles. In one piece, Diamond starts with a soulful intro leading into an upbeat verse that provides an interesting contrast to the mournful opening. Diamond seems to express in this song that he has overcome some emotional wounds but that it remains conflicted. [6]
                                      5

Since sources of music from major music towns such
        7
as New Orleans, Detroit, and Nashville are abundant, little is known about Lexington's music scene because the town lacked

a real recording studio. Therefore, Diamond's songs in a city
                                                        8
like Lexington offer music historians a rare taste of the musical
    8
culture in the 1960s. No one knows how much Diamond was

effected by other musicians in Lexington, but he did perform
    9
regularly at local venues. Some things, though, are for sure: he

5. Which choice makes the sentence most grammatically acceptable?

   A. **No Change**
   B. he remains conflicted.
   C. they were conflicted.
   D. he is conflicting.

6. At this point, the writer is thinking of adding the following sentence:

   > We have all experienced sad events and know very well what it is like to feel a sense of conflict.

   Should the writer make this addition here?

   F. Yes, because it shows the writer's compassionate feelings toward Diamond's difficult situation.
   G. Yes, because it adds extra emphasis to the subject matter of one of Diamond's most well-known songs.
   H. No, because it strays from the paragraph's main focus on Diamond's unique songwriting voice.
   J. No, because it encourages readers to think about sad events in their own lives.

7. Which choice is clearest and most precise in context?

   A. **No Change**
   B. Unless
   C. While
   D. If

8. The best placement for the underlined portion would be:

   F. where it is now.
   G. after the word *historians*.
   H. after the word *taste*.
   J. after the word *culture*.

9. Which choice makes the sentence most grammatically acceptable?

   A. **No Change**
   B. affected by
   C. affected with
   D. effected with

has recorded an interesting portfolio of songs, and <u>he may soon</u>
₁₀

<u>be a famous saxophonist.</u>
₁₀

10. Given that all the choices are true, which of the following would provide the best conclusion to this essay in relation to one of its main points?

F. **No Change**
G. now Diamond's work provides scholars with an example of Lexington's music.
H. he probably never had to buy another cassette recorder.
J. he may have performed in other cities besides Lexington.

ENGLISH PASSAGE DRILL 3 EXPLANATIONS

1. **A**   The question asks about grammar, so look at the answers to see what's changing. Verbs are changing in the answer choices, so identify the subject: *songs*. All of the answers work with this subject, so consider tense. The sentence is referring to songs being *undocumented* prior to the release of *cassette recorders with built-in microphones*. Thus, past tense is needed. Eliminate (C) and (D) because they are both in present tense. Keep (A) because it's in past perfect tense and accurately refers to a past event that occurred before another past event. Eliminate (B) because the tense that uses *have* suggests something that goes up to the present, rather than something that occurred in the past and has ended. The correct answer is (A).

2. **H**   The question is asking for the answer that *provides the most stylistically effective and concise wording,* so eliminate any answers that don't fulfill this goal. The words *seemingly* and *apparent* in (F) mean the same thing, so there is no need to use both. Eliminate (F). Choices (G), (H), and (J) all have the same meaning, but (H) is most concise. Eliminate (G) and (J). The correct answer is (H).

3. **B**   The question is asking for the answer that provides *detail about the lyrical subject matter,* so eliminate any answers that don't fulfill this goal. Wondering *what inspired* the lyrics does not say anything about the *subject,* so eliminate (A). *Dating and automobiles* does give more information about *subject matter,* so keep (B). Neither *rhymed couplets and alliteration* nor *Diamond's enunciation* gives detail about *subject matter,* so eliminate (C) and (D). The correct answer is (B).

4. **F**   The question is asking for a choice that *maintains the essay's tone,* so consider the overall tone of the essay and eliminate any answer that is inconsistent. The essay's tone is academic, but not overly so, and praising toward Diamond. Keep (F) because there is nothing noticeably wrong with it. Eliminate (G), (H), and (J) because *super, cinch,* and *tricky,* are overly casual for the somewhat formal tone of the essay. The correct answer is (F).

5. **B**   The question asks about grammar, so look at the answers to see what's changing. Pronouns are changing in the answer choices, so identify who or what the pronoun refers back to: *Diamond.* Diamond should be referred to as "he," so eliminate (A) and (C). Eliminate (D) because the contrasting emotions mentioned in the paragraph are better described as Diamond being *conflicted* than himself being *conflicting.* The correct answer is (B).

6. **H**   The question is asking whether a sentence should be added to the end of the paragraph, so consider the content of the sentence and the surrounding context. The paragraph focuses on Diamond's *unique artistic voice.* The new sentence discusses what *We have all experienced,* so it is not consistent. Eliminate (F) and (G). Keep (H) because it correctly states that the new sentence *strays from the paragraph's main focus.* The new sentence may encourage *readers to think about sad events in their own lives,* but that is not consistent with the paragraph; eliminate (J). The correct answer is (H).

7. **C**   The question is asking for the *clearest and most precise* answer, and the answers contain transitions, so consider the relationship between ideas. The first part of the sentence says *sources of music from major music towns…are abundant,* and the second part of the sentence says *little is known about Lexington's music scene.*

These ideas disagree, so eliminate (A) because it's a same-direction transition. Then, eliminate (B) and (D) because a cause-and-effect relationship isn't supported here. Choice (C) is a contrasting transition, which is appropriate in this sentence. The correct answer is (C).

8. **J** The question is asking for the *best placement for the underlined portion,* so try the phrase in each spot and eliminate any that don't offer a logical meaning. Choice (F) describes the *songs* as being in Lexington, which isn't logical, so eliminate (F). With (G), the *historians* are *in a city like Lexington,* but there is no clear reason it would make sense to describe historians this way. Eliminate (G). Choice (H) says *a rare taste in a city like Lexington,* which is unclear because the sentence needs to say what it's a *taste* of. Eliminate (H). Choice (J) says *Diamond's songs offer music historians a rare taste of the musical culture in a city like Lexington,* which provides a logical meaning because the previous sentence states that *little is known about Lexington's music scene.* The correct answer is (J).

9. **B** The question asks about grammar, so look at the answers to see what's changing. The answer choices contain phrases with "affect" and "effect," so determine which is needed. A verb is needed here, so eliminate (A) and (D) because "effect" is a noun. The correct phrase is "affected by," not *affected with,* so eliminate (C). The correct answer is (B).

10. **G** The question is asking for the answer that provides *the best conclusion to this essay,* so consider the essay's *main points.* The essay is about Bruce Diamond's *recordings* and why they are *noteworthy.* Eliminate (F) because, while the uncovering of the tapes may bring more attention to Diamond, the focus of the essay is on how the tapes reveal information about *musical culture* rather than about Diamond's own playing. Keep (G) because it is consistent with the essay's focus on how Diamond's recordings provide information about the music scene in Lexington. Whether Diamond ever *had to buy another cassette recorder* is not relevant to the passage, so eliminate (H). The passage focuses on only Lexington, not *other cities,* so eliminate (J). The correct answer is (G).

ENGLISH PASSAGE DRILL 4

Going Underground

[1] When I left my home in rural Missouri to attend college in New York City, I didn't consider myself a veteran subway rider. [2] Luckily, I was able to overcome this fear by having my first trip by subway guided by a neighbor named Sasha. [3] He had grown up in Manhattan, so he was familiar with the dense, intricacy subway routes.
                                                                                    1

[4] During his childhood, he had taken the subway almost every
                                                  2
day as a child with his family, so I was encouraged to set off with him to learn the ins and outs of the New York subways.

[5] Because of my family's warnings, I was afraid to take the
                                    3

subway at first. ⁴

Sasha led me down the steps from the busy street to our nearest stop. I couldn't decide whether to buy my token from the imposing-looking woman on the left or the imposing-looking woman on the right, but Sasha confidently tugged me right up to them. I managed to squeak out, "Canal Street,
                      5
please," and the woman scooped up my change and slipped a token through the window slot.

I couldn't tell which platform to descend to. After a little searching, though, I saw the sign that read "Canal St.," and
          6

1. Which choice makes the sentence most grammatically acceptable?

   A. **No Change**
   B. dense, intricate
   C. intricately, dense
   D. dense intricacy

2. Which choice is least redundant in context?

   F. **No Change**
   G. He had been starting to take
   H. His childhood was spent taking
   J. He had taken

3. Which choice makes the sentence most grammatically acceptable?

   A. **No Change**
   B. familys' warnings,
   C. families' warnings
   D. families warnings,

4. For the sake of the logic and coherence of this paragraph, Sentence 5 should be placed:

   F. where it is now.
   G. after Sentence 1.
   H. before Sentence 3.
   J. before Sentence 4.

5. Which choice is clearest and most precise in context?

   A. **No Change**
   B. the one on the left.
   C. her.
   D. the women.

6. Which choice makes the sentence most grammatically acceptable?

   F. **No Change**
   G. searching though:
   H. searching, though
   J. searching, though:

Sasha and I walked down to our platform. I felt very conspicuous standing on the platform, waiting for our train to arrive.
7
Sasha distracted me by pointing out a performer across the

tracks. At first, I was confused like a whirlwind in my mind
8
about what the man was doing. Then I saw that he was juggling
all kinds of objects: milk crates, thick books, and even bowling
balls. I wondered if he would of been there when we returned.
9

When we were seated on the train, Sasha looked at me with
a pleased expression, I suppose, he was proud of how well he
10
had served as a guide. When we arrived at our station and rode
up the escalator toward the street, I felt as though I had been
exploring an undiscovered continent and was emerging from
fantastic caverns. I'll always remember my first subway ride,
when "going underground" took on a new meaning.

7. Given that all of the choices are true, which one most effectively introduces the action in this paragraph while suggesting the narrator's discomfort in her new surroundings?
   A. **No Change**
   B. Sasha's stylish boots clicked on the floor as he walked ahead of me.
   C. Although it wasn't rush hour yet, quite a few people stood waiting on the platform.
   D. Sasha explained that the first subway line in New York City opened in 1904.

8. Which choice is least redundant in context?
   F. **No Change**
   G. confused with uncertainty and curiosity
   H. confused by the initial lack of understanding
   J. confused

9. Which choice makes the sentence most grammatically acceptable?
   A. **No Change**
   B. would be
   C. should be
   D. could of been

10. Which choice makes the sentence most grammatically acceptable?
    F. **No Change**
    G. expression I suppose
    H. expression. I suppose
    J. expression, however, I suppose

ENGLISH PASSAGE DRILL 4 EXPLANATIONS

1. **B** The question asks about grammar, so look at the answers to see what's changing. Commas and wording are changing in the answer choices, so eliminate any answer with incorrect wording or punctuation. The words *dense* and *intricate* are used to describe *subway routes* in the sentence, so they must be adjectives or adverbs. The word *intricacy* is a noun, and therefore it cannot be used to describe another noun; eliminate (A) and (D). The word *intricately* in (C) is an adverb, and could be used to describe the adjective *dense,* but there is no need to separate those two words with a comma; eliminate (C). Choice (B) appropriately uses a comma between two adjectives that both describe the same noun. The correct answer is (B).

2. **J** The question is asking for the *least redundant* answer, so eliminate answers that are overly wordy or repeat information given earlier. The nonunderlined portion of the sentence specifies that the action in the underlined portion happened when Sasha was *a child,* so there is no need to repeat that idea. Eliminate (F) and (H). There is no need for the word *starting* in the sentence, so eliminate (G). Choice (J) is concise and makes the meaning of the sentence clear. The correct answer is (J).

3. **A** The question asks about grammar, so look at the answers to see what's changing. Apostrophes and commas are changing in the answer choices, so consider whether either is needed. A noun with an apostrophe shows possession. Since the *warnings* belong to the *family,* an apostrophe is needed in this sentence; eliminate (D). Choice (B) is an incorrect version of the plural possessive, so eliminate (B). Between (A) and (C), it is possible that the narrator has just one family or multiple families, but a comma is needed after the phrase, so eliminate (C). The correct answer is (A).

4. **G** The question is asking where a sentence should go, so consider the content of the sentence and that of the surrounding sentences in the paragraph. Sentence 5 mentions the *family's warnings* and that the narrator *was afraid to take the subway.* Sentence 4 is about Sasha, the neighbor who taught the narrator how to ride the subway, which is not consistent with the *family's warnings* at the beginning of Sentence 5; eliminate (F). Sentence 2 says that the narrator *was able to overcome this fear.* The phrase *this fear* must refer back to something, and the narrator's being *afraid* at the end of Sentence 5 provides that reference. Choice (G) accurately places Sentence 5 before Sentence 2. The correct answer is (G).

5. **B** The question is asking for the *clearest and most precise* answer, so use Process of Elimination. The underlined portion refers to the person Sasha *tugged* the narrator to, between the *woman on the left* and the *woman on the right.* Although it's possible that the narrator was pulled toward both of them, the next sentence mentions *the woman,* so (A) doesn't work. Eliminate (A) as well as (D), which makes a similar error. Choice (B) makes it clear which woman the narrator approached, so keep (B). Eliminate (C) since it is not clear which woman *her* refers to. The correct answer is (B).

6. **F** The question asks about grammar, so look at the answers to see what's changing. Punctuation before and after *though* is changing in the answer choices, so consider whether any punctuation is needed. The first part of the sentence, *After a little searching, though,* is not an independent clause, so eliminate (G) and (J) because a colon can only come after an independent clause. Both (F) and (H) put a comma before *though,* but there must also be a comma after this unnecessary word, so eliminate (H). The correct answer is (F).

7. **A** The question is asking for the answer that *most effectively introduces the action in this paragraph while suggesting the narrator's discomfort in her new surroundings,* so eliminate any answers that don't fulfill this goal. Choice (A) states that the narrator *felt very conspicuous* (meaning "noticeable"), which is consistent with the idea of *discomfort,* so keep (A). Both (B) and (D) focus on *Sasha,* rather than on *the narrator's discomfort,* so eliminate them. Eliminate (C) because it focuses on *people…on the platform* and not on *the narrator's discomfort.* The correct answer is (A).

8. **J** The question is asking for the *least redundant* answer, so eliminate answers that are overly wordy or repeat information given earlier. Both *uncertainty* and *lack of understanding* mean the same thing as *confused,* so there is no need to repeat those ideas. Eliminate (G) and (H). The phrase *like a whirlwind in my mind* does not make the meaning of the sentence clearer, so eliminate (F). Choice (J) is concise and makes the meaning of the sentence clear. The correct answer is (J).

9. **B** The question asks about grammar, so look at the answers to see what's changing. Wording changes in the answer choices, so eliminate any answer that isn't correctly worded. The phrases *could of* and *would of* are incorrect spellings of the contractions "could've" (could have) or "would've" (would have) and are therefore both wrong. Eliminate (A) and (D). *Should* means "ought to," and *would* expresses the possibility of something happening. *Would* is the appropriate word in this context. Eliminate (C). The correct answer is (B).

10. **H** The question asks about grammar, so look at the answers to see what's changing. Connecting punctuation is changing in the answer choices, so look for a complete sentence. The first part of the sentence says *When we were seated on the train, Sasha looked at me with a pleased expression,* which is an independent clause. The second part of the sentence says *I suppose he was proud of how well he had served as a guide,* which is also an independent clause. Eliminate (F) and (J) because commas alone can't link two independent clauses. Eliminate (G) because a lack of punctuation can't link two independent clauses. Keep (H) because a period can separate the independent clauses into individual sentences. The correct answer is (H).

ENGLISH PASSAGE DRILL 5

Black Holes—Astronomy's Great Mystery

Black holes are <u>likely and possibly</u> the most fascinating
¹
topic facing contemporary astronomy. The concept of a black
hole—a region of space with such an intense gravitational pull
that nothing can escape—is truly the stuff of science fiction.
Albert Einstein's general theory of relativity predicted the
existence of black holes, but he thought of his prediction as
an error to be corrected, not a predictor of one of the strangest
astronomical phenomena yet discovered.

<u>Because</u> Einstein didn't live to see it, the universe proved
²
the accuracy of his calculations in 1970, when Cygnus X-1 was
discovered about 7,000 light-years from Earth. It is about 8.7
times as massive as our Sun yet has a diameter of only about
50 km. When you consider that the diameter of the Sun could
accommodate over 100 Earths, it becomes clear that fitting
a mass almost nine times greater than that into a diameter of
about 31 miles is truly remarkable. ☐3

<u>How do these amazingly dense objects come into exis-</u>
⁴
<u>tence?</u> There are several theories to explain the process. The
⁴
most popular hypothesis suggests that black holes are fairly

common and <u>involving</u> the disintegration of massive stars
⁵

---

1. Which choice is least redundant in context?

  A. No Change
  B. very probably to be
  C. possibly
  D. a possible likeness of being

2. Which choice is clearest and most precise in context?

  F. No Change
  G. Although
  H. Since
  J. Given that

3. If the writer were to delete the preceding sentence, the paragraph would primarily lose:

  A. a description that explains the purpose of studying black holes.
  B. information that helps the reader grasp the size of black holes by presenting it in understandable terms.
  C. a reference that explains how the black hole is compressed into such a small size.
  D. an unnecessary detail, because this information is repeated later in the passage.

4. Which choice provides the most effective transition from the previous paragraph to the new paragraph?

  F. No Change
  G. Why should we study black holes at all?
  H. Is the Sun going to collapse and become a black hole?
  J. What are the effects of such massive gravitational pull?

5. Which choice makes the sentence most grammatically acceptable?

  A. No Change
  B. is involving
  C. will involve
  D. involves

<u>close</u> the end of their lifecycle.
⁶

Other theorists <u>suggesting</u> that black holes are the result of
⁷
a galactic game of bumper cars. The universe is teeming with

neutron stars, which are not sufficiently massive to create black

holes. <u>Likewise,</u> on occasion these stars will actually collide
⁸
with each other and together become massive enough to form a

black hole.

Perhaps the most bizarre theory made about these phenom-

ena involves the existence of "micro" or "mini" black holes.

These peculiar items are very small, astronomically speaking.

They have a mass far less than that of our Sun, and, frankly, the

scientific community <u>cannot explain and articulate fully</u> how
⁹
stars with so little mass could have formed black holes. That is

a question for future generations of scientists to explore.

6. Which choice is clearest and most precise in context?
   F. **No Change**
   G. near
   H. about
   J. into

7. Which choice makes the sentence most grammatically
   acceptable?
   A. **No Change**
   B. has been suggesting
   C. will suggest
   D. suggest

8. Which transition word or phrase is most logical in context?
   F. **No Change**
   G. Similarly,
   H. However,
   J. In addition,

9. Which choice is least redundant in context?
   A. **No Change**
   B. cannot explain or describe in any detail
   C. cannot explain
   D. not only cannot explain but also can't describe

> Question 10 asks about the preceding passage as a
> whole.

10. Suppose the writer's goal had been to write a brief
    essay about how Einstein's skepticism stopped scientific
    inquiry into the existence of black holes. Would this essay
    successfully fulfill that goal?
    F. Yes, because black holes were not discovered until
       after Einstein's death.
    G. Yes, because no other scientists were mentioned by
       name as doing research into the subject.
    H. No, because Einstein later decided that black holes
       did exist and encouraged the scientific community to
       search for them.
    J. No, because the essay does not discuss how Einstein's
       doubt affected the inquiries of other scientists.

ENGLISH PASSAGE DRILL 5 EXPLANATIONS

1. **C** The question is asking for the *least redundant* answer, so eliminate answers that are overly wordy or repeat information given earlier. The words *likely* and *possibly* mean the same thing in this context, so there is no need to use both; eliminate (A) and (D). Choices (B) and (C) express the same idea, but (C) is more concise. Eliminate (B). The correct answer is (C).

2. **G** The question is asking for the *clearest and most precise* answer, and the answers contain transitions, so consider the relationship between ideas. The first part of the sentence says *Einstein didn't live to see it*, and the second part mentions the proof of *his calculations*. These ideas contrast, so eliminate (F), (H), and (J), which are all same-direction transitions. Choice (G) is an opposite-direction transition. The correct answer is (G).

3. **B** The question is asking what the paragraph would *lose* if the preceding sentence were deleted, so try reading the paragraph with and without the sentence to see what the difference is. The sentence describes the mass and size of a black hole in terms of the sizes of Earth and the Sun. There is no mention of the *purpose of studying black holes,* so eliminate (A). Choice (B) accurately describes the sentence, so keep (B). The sentence says that a black hole is compressed into a small space, but it does not explain *how* it's compressed, so eliminate (C). The information is not repeated later in the passage, so eliminate (D). The correct answer is (B).

4. **F** The question is asking for the *most effective transition from the previous paragraph to the new paragraph,* so identify the content of the two paragraphs. The previous paragraph discusses the discovery of a specific black hole and describes the *remarkable* nature of black holes in general. The new paragraph describes a theory of how black holes are formed. Choice (F) is consistent with both paragraphs, so keep it. Neither paragraph discusses *why* black holes should be studied, so eliminate (G). Neither paragraph discusses the possibility of *the Sun* becoming *a black hole,* so eliminate (H). Neither paragraph discusses *the effects of such massive gravitational pull,* so eliminate (J). The correct answer is (F).

5. **D** The question asks about grammar, so look at the answers to see what's changing. Verbs are changing in the answer choices, so identify the subject. The subject could be either *hypothesis* or *black holes*, so begin by considering verb form. With either subject, the underlined verb needs to be consistent in form and tense with the other verb connected to it with the word *and*: either *suggests* or *are*. Choice (A), *involving*, isn't consistent with *suggests* or *are*, so eliminate it. Choice (B) could match with the subject *hypothesis* but isn't consistent in form with *suggests*, so eliminate (B). Choice (C) is not consistent with *suggests* or *are*, whereas *involves* and *suggests* are in the same form and tense. Eliminate (C). The correct answer is (D).

6. **G**   The question is asking for the *clearest and most precise* answer, so use Process of Elimination. Although it would be fine to say "close to the end," *close the end* isn't correct, so eliminate (F). Choice (G), *near the end of their lifecycle*, works, so keep it. Choice (H) doesn't work because it lacks the word "at"; eliminate (H). Eliminate (J) because *into the end of their lifecycle* isn't a correct phrasing. The correct answer is (G).

7. **D**   The question asks about grammar, so look at the answers to see what's changing. Verbs are changing in the answer choices, so identify the subject: *theorists*. This noun is plural, so eliminate (B) because it's singular. Next, consider form and tense. Eliminate (A) because the *-ing* verb does not produce a complete sentence. Choice (C) is in future tense, but it's not logical that the sentence would speculate about what theorists *will suggest*. Eliminate (C). Choice (D) is in present tense, which is consistent with the next sentence. The correct answer is (D).

8. **H**   The question is asking for a *logical* transition, so identify the relationships between the ideas. The preceding sentence discusses *stars* that are *not sufficiently massive to create black holes*. This sentence says that *these stars will…collide…and together become massive enough to form a black hole*. These ideas contrast with each other. Eliminate (F), (G), and (J) because they are all transitions that indicate agreement. Only (H) is a contrasting transition. The correct answer is (H).

9. **C**   The question is asking for the *least redundant* answer, so eliminate answers that are overly wordy or repeat information given earlier. *Articulate* and *describe* mean the same thing as *explain* in this context, so there is no need to use more than one of these words; eliminate (A), (B), and (D). Choice (C) is concise and makes the meaning of the sentence clear. The correct answer is (C).

10. **J**   The question asks whether the essay describes *how Einstein's skepticism stopped scientific inquiry into the existence of black holes*, so consider the overall focus of the essay. Although the essay mentions at the beginning that Einstein thought his prediction was *an error to be corrected*, most of the essay is about current knowledge and theories of black holes, so (F) and (G) are not consistent with the purpose stated in the question. There is no indication in the essay that *Einstein later decided that black holes did exist*, so eliminate (H). Choice (J) accurately describes the essay. The correct answer is (J).

ENGLISH PASSAGE DRILL 6

An Argument for E-Waste Recycling

Drive through any suburb in the United States today, and it's hard to miss the bins, that have become companions to America's trashcans. Recycling has become commonplace, as people recognize the need to care for the environment. Yet most people's recycling consciousness extends only as far as paper,

bottles, and cans. People seldom find themselves confronted with the growing phenomenon of e-waste.

E-waste proliferates as the techno-fashionable constantly upgrade to the most cutting-edge devices, which the majority of them end up in landfills. It's estimated that Americans discard approximately seven million tons of TVs, computers, cell phones, and other electronics each year. Unless we can find a safe alternative, this e-waste may leak into the ground and poison the water with dangerous toxins. [4]

Consequently, e-waste often contains reusable silver, gold, and other electrical conductors. Recycling these materials reduces environmental impact by reducing both landfill waste and the need to mine such metals.

1. Which choice makes the sentence most grammatically acceptable?

   A. **No Change**
   B. bins that have become companions,
   C. bins, which have become companions,
   D. bins that have become companions

2. Which choice would most effectively begin this sentence so that it emphasizes a lack of awareness of this problem?

   F. **No Change**
   G. Many in our communities simply don't realize the dangers of
   H. A majority of local governments are assiduously studying
   J. Little attention is paid by the people in our neighborhoods to

3. Which choice makes the sentence most grammatically acceptable?

   A. **No Change**
   B. devices that
   C. devices, and
   D. devices after

4. At this point, the writer is considering adding the following phrase to the end of the preceding sentence, adjusting the punctuation accordingly:

   such as lead, mercury, and arsenic

   Should the writer add the phrase here?

   F. Yes, because it adds specific details clarifying which toxins are leaking.
   G. Yes, because it supports the idea that landfills have too much waste.
   H. No, because it doesn't specify how dangerous these toxins are.
   J. No, because it would be redundant in a paragraph that has already mentioned which toxins e-waste contains.

5. Which transition word is most logical in context?

   A. **No Change**
   B. Particularly,
   C. Moreover,
   D. However,

A growing number of states have adopted laws to prohibit
———————————————————————
6

dumping e-waste. Despite this, less than a quarter of this refuse

will reach legitimate recycling programs. [7] Some companies

advertising safe disposal in fact merely ship the waste to

developing countries, where it still ends up in landfills. [8]

Nevertheless, the small but growing number of cities and

corporations that do handle e-waste responsibly represent

progress and a real step forward toward making the world a
————————————————————
9

cleaner, better place for us all. [10]

6. Which choice is clearest and most precise in context?

   F. **No Change**
   G. Adoptions are growing in state
   H. States have growingly adopted
   J. Growing states have adopted numbers of

7. The writer is considering deleting the preceding sentence from this paragraph. Should the sentence be kept or deleted?

   A. Kept, because it provides a logical transition between the first and last sentences of the paragraph.
   B. Kept, because it provides meaningful statistics.
   C. Deleted, because it adds no new information to the paragraph.
   D. Deleted, because it would be redundant, given that the next sentence explains that some companies don't recycle.

8. At this point, the author is considering adding the following sentence:

   These organizations hamper progress by unsafely disposing of waste in an out-of-sight, out-of-mind location.

   Would this be a relevant addition to make here?

   F. Yes, because it completes the idea expressed in the preceding sentence.
   G. Yes, because it paints such organizations in a negative light.
   H. No, because it contradicts the following sentence.
   J. No, because it introduces a tangential point.

9. Which choice is least redundant in context?

   A. **No Change**
   B. a real step forward in the progress moving
   C. progress
   D. real forward-stepping progress

10. At this point, the writer is considering adding the following sentence:

    Today, pollution is one of the most dangerous forces threatening our environment, and the government must work to regulate its effects.

    Should the writer add this sentence here?

    F. Yes, because it adds important details that suggest recycling is not the only concern of environmentalists.
    G. Yes, because it provides additional information discussing the impact of recycling programs in urban areas.
    H. No, because it digresses from the article's main point about e-waste and related recycling issues.
    J. No, because government regulation is a complicated and controversial topic addressed elsewhere in the passage.

ENGLISH PASSAGE DRILL 6 EXPLANATIONS

1. **D**   The question asks about grammar, so look at the answers to see what's changing. Punctuation around the phrase *that have become companions* is changing in the answer choices, so consider whether any punctuation is needed. Phrases beginning with *that* are necessary to the meaning of the sentence and don't get punctuation around them, so eliminate (A). Eliminate (B) and (C) because a comma shouldn't be used after the phrase, since *to America's trashcans* is part of the same idea. The correct answer is (D).

2. **G**   The question is asking for the answer that *emphasizes a lack of awareness of this problem* (that is, the problem of e-waste), so eliminate any answers that don't fulfill this goal. *Assiduously studying* means "paying a lot of attention," so eliminate (H). It's possible that the fact that *People seldom find themselves confronted with* the problem (as (F) says) or that *Little attention is paid by the people* (as (H) says) could mean they *lack awareness*, but the idea in (G), that people *don't realize the dangers*, more directly matches the idea of *a lack of awareness*. Eliminate (F) and (J). The correct answer is (G).

3. **C**   The question asks about grammar, so look at the answers to see what's changing. Punctuation and connecting words are changing in the answer choices, so consider complete sentences. The phrase *of them* in the second part of the sentence refers back to *devices*, so it's not correct to also have the connecting word *which* to refer back to the devices. Eliminate (A). Eliminate (B) for the same reason, as *that* would also refer back to *devices*. Keep (C) because the sentence does contain two independent clauses (*E-waste proliferates as the techno-fashionable constantly upgrade to the most cutting-edge devices* and *the majority of them end up in landfills*), and a comma with a coordinating conjunction such as *and* can connect two independent clauses. Eliminate (D) because the sentence doesn't express a time change. The correct answer is (C).

4. **F**   The question is asking whether a phrase should be added to the end of the sentence, so consider the content of the phrase and the sentence. The sentence talks about the *dangerous toxins* that e-waste produces, and the new phrase gives examples of those toxins. The new phrase is consistent with the sentence, so eliminate (H) and (J). Choice (F) accurately states that the new phrase *adds specific details*. There is no indication that *landfills have too much waste,* so eliminate (G). The correct answer is (F).

5. **C**   The question is asking for a *logical* transition, so identify the relationships between the ideas. The end of the previous paragraph discusses the dangers of e-waste. The new paragraph discusses the *reusable* materials that e-waste contains, offering another reason that e-waste shouldn't be trashed. These ideas agree, so eliminate (D). Choice (A) doesn't work because this paragraph isn't a consequence of the previous information; eliminate (A). Eliminate (B) because this paragraph isn't offering a more specific idea from what was previously mentioned. Choice (C) works because this paragraph gives an additional point supporting why e-waste shouldn't go to landfills. The correct answer is (C).

6. **F** The question is asking for the *clearest and most precise* answer, so use Process of Elimination. Choice (F) makes it clear that the *number of states* that *have adopted laws* is *growing*, so keep (F). It is not *Adoptions* that are *growing*, so eliminate (G). The word *growing* is not meant to describe the verb *adopted* as it does in (H); eliminate (H). It is the *number of states* that is growing rather than the *states* themselves, so eliminate (J). The correct answer is (F).

7. **A** The question is asking whether a sentence should be deleted, so consider the content of the sentence and the surrounding context. The paragraph focuses on how little e-waste is recycled, and the sentence gives more information on that topic. It should not be deleted, so eliminate (C) and (D). The sentence does *provide a logical transition between the first and last sentences of the paragraph*, so keep (A). The sentence does provide a *statistic*, but it is more important as a transition between the idea of increasing *laws to prohibit dumping e-waste* in the first sentence and the idea that *Some companies…merely ship the waste to developing countries, where it still ends up in landfills* in the last sentence. Eliminate (B). The correct answer is (A).

8. **F** The question is asking whether a sentence should be added, so consider the content of the sentence and the surrounding context. The paragraph focuses on how little e-waste is recycled, and the new sentence gives further details about the companies described in the last sentence. It is therefore consistent with the paragraph and should be added; eliminate (H) and (J). Keep (F) because it accurately describes the new sentence. The paragraph already *paints such organizations in a negative light*, so that is not a good reason to add the new sentence. Eliminate (G). The correct answer is (F).

9. **C** The question is asking for the *least redundant* answer, so eliminate answers that are overly wordy or repeat information given earlier. The phrase *step forward* means the same thing as *progress* in this context, so there is no need to use both terms. Eliminate (A), (B), and (D). Choice (C) is concise and makes the meaning of the sentence clear. The correct answer is (C).

10. **H** The question is asking whether a sentence should be added, so consider the content of the sentence and the surrounding context. The passage focuses on e-waste, while the subject of the new sentence is *pollution*. It is therefore not consistent and should not be added; eliminate (F) and (G). Choice (H) accurately states that the new sentence *digresses from the article's main point*; keep (H). The passage does not extensively discuss *government regulation*, so eliminate (J). The correct answer is (H).

ENGLISH PASSAGE DRILL 7

Building a Beauty Empire

In 1867, on a farm in tiny Delta, Louisiana, a daughter was born to former enslaved people Minerva and Owen Breedlove. Little did anyone realize that Sarah Breedlove, orphaned at age six, would grow up to become one of the most successful African-American entrepreneurs in history. [2]

Widowed at twenty with a daughter, Breedlove supported herself as a laundress in St. Louis for the next eighteen years. In 1905, she came up with an idea that would revolutionize the cosmetics industry. By ten years, she would not only oversee a vast financial empire but also become one of the best-known women in the United States.

Breedlove invented a scalp conditioning and healing formula. She undertook countless journeys to sell her formula door-to-door. As well as in churches and lodges. She dubbed herself Madame C. J. Walker, taking the name of her second husband, Charles J. Walker, who worked in the newspaper publishing business and who also lived in St. Louis.

1. Which choice is clearest and most precise in context?
   A. **No Change**
   B. by
   C. under
   D. for

2. At this point, the writer is considering adding the following true statement:

   > Also born in Louisiana, Louis Armstrong went on to exert a similarly powerful influence on 1920s American culture as a jazz trumpeter.

   Should the writer add this sentence here?
   F. Yes, because it's important to know that other influential people were born in Louisiana besides the woman portrayed in this essay.
   G. Yes, because this reference shows that music was important during this period.
   H. No, because the role Louis Armstrong played in 1920s culture is irrelevant to the main topic of this essay.
   J. No, because the 1920s were not significant years in American history.

3. Which choice is clearest and most precise in context?
   A. **No Change**
   B. Up to
   C. Within
   D. Before

4. Which choice makes the sentence most grammatically acceptable?
   F. **No Change**
   G. door-to-door; as
   H. door-to-door, as
   J. door-to-door: as

5. Which choice is least redundant in context?
   A. **No Change**
   B. a man who lived in St. Louis and who worked in newspaper publishing.
   C. a St. Louis newspaper executive.
   D. a newspaper publishing businessman who was very well known in the St. Louis area.

Walker taught her methods to other <u>women, they</u> focused
₆

on sales and became known as the "Walker Agents." <u>Below</u>
₇
Walker's supervision, these agents became familiar sights in
their white shirts and black skirts. Walker called them "scalp
specialists" and hair and beauty "culturists" to emphasize the
professional nature of the treatments.

[1] <u>In 1913, she traveled to the Caribbean and to Central
America, but before that</u> Walker concentrated on improving
₈
the manufacture of her products. [2] One of the first of these
charitable acts was her generous $1,000 donation to the city's
YMCA. [3] In 1910, she established the Walker Company
headquarters in Indianapolis. [4] Chosen because it was then
the largest inland manufacturing city in the country, Indianapolis became both Walker's home and the first beneficiary of her
social activism and dedication to charitable causes. $\boxed{9}$

Upon her death in 1919, "Madame Walker"—now often
regarded as the richest self-made woman in the United States
during her lifetime—donated two-thirds of her company's net
profit to charitable causes.

6. Which choice makes the sentence most grammatically
   acceptable?

   F. **No Change**
   G. women, who
   H. women, with whom
   J. women those

7. Which choice is clearest and most precise in context?

   A. **No Change**
   B. Above
   C. As
   D. Under

8. Given that all the choices are true, which one provides the
   most effective transition from the preceding paragraph to
   this new one?

   F. **No Change**
   G. After her daughter built a magnificent townhome in an
      exclusive Manhattan neighborhood,
   H. In addition to training a small "army" of agent-
      operators,
   J. When Walker had designed a special Walker Method
      treatment for celebrated dancer Josephine Baker,

9. For the sake of the logic and coherence of this paragraph,
   Sentence 2 should be placed:

   A. where it is now.
   B. before Sentence 1.
   C. after Sentence 3.
   D. after Sentence 4.

> Question 10 asks about the preceding passage as a
> whole.

10. Suppose the writer's goal had been to write a brief essay
    focusing on the development of the beauty industry in
    the early part of the twentieth century. Would this essay
    successfully accomplish this goal?

    F. Yes, because the essay focuses on the beauty indus-
       try of the 1920s, during which Madame C. J. Walker
       became wealthy.
    G. Yes, because the essay describes how Walker invented
       a new formula to facilitate hair growth and treat scalp
       problems.
    H. No, because the essay focuses mainly on Sarah
       Breedlove Walker and her place in the history of
       American business and culture.
    J. No, because the essay describes other events taking
       place during this time that were more significant.

ENGLISH PASSAGE DRILL 7 EXPLANATIONS

1. **A** The question is asking for the *clearest and most precise* answer, so use Process of Elimination. The phrase *born to former enslaved people* makes it clear that *Minerva and Owen Breedlove* were the parents, so keep (A). Both *born by* and *born under* would indicate location, which is not what this sentence discusses; eliminate (B) and (C). *Born for* would indicate a purpose, which is not what this sentence discusses; eliminate (D). The correct answer is (A).

2. **H** The question is asking whether a sentence should be added, so consider the content of the sentence and the surrounding context. The paragraph introduces *Sarah Breedlove,* who is the main subject of the passage. *Louis Armstrong* is not consistent with this focus, so the sentence should not be added. Eliminate (F) and (G). Choice (H) accurately states that *the role Louis Armstrong played in 1920s culture is irrelevant to the main topic of this essay.* The question of whether *the 1920s* were *significant* is not relevant to this essay, so eliminate (J). The correct answer is (H).

3. **C** The question is asking for the *clearest and most precise* answer, so use Process of Elimination. The phrase *By ten years* isn't a correct phrasing, so eliminate (A). Although *Up to ten years* could be a phrase, it can't appear as a transition at the beginning of a sentence, so eliminate (B). Keep (C) because *Within ten years* correctly states that it took only ten years for Breedlove to accomplish a great deal. Eliminate (D) because *Before ten years* on its own can't begin the sentence. The correct answer is (C).

4. **H** The question asks about grammar, so look at the answers to see what's changing. Punctuation is changing in the answer choices, so look for independent clauses. The first part of the sentence, *She undertook countless journeys to sell her formula door-to-door,* is an independent clause. The second part, *as well as in churches and lodges,* is not an independent clause. Eliminate (F) and (G) because a period and a semicolon can only be used between two independent clauses. Eliminate (J) because a colon can only be used when the second part elaborates on the first, which isn't the case here. A comma is needed. The correct answer is (H).

5. **C** The question is asking for the *least redundant* answer, so eliminate answers that are overly wordy or repeat information given earlier. Choice (C) is the shortest answer and offers a clear meaning, so keep it. The remaining answers use more words to say the same thing, so eliminate (A), (B), and (D) because they are not as concise as (C). The correct answer is (C).

6. **G**   The question asks about grammar, so look at the answers to see what's changing. Connecting words are changing in the answer choices, so look for a complete sentence. With (F), the sentence contains two independent clauses separated by only a comma, which isn't allowed, so eliminate (F). Choice (J) makes a similar error, with the sentence containing two independent clauses with no punctuation at all between them, so eliminate (J). Comparing (G) and (H), the subject pronoun *who* is needed rather than the object pronoun *whom* because the pronoun is the subject for the verb *focused*. Eliminate (H). The correct answer is (G).

7. **D**   The question is asking for the *clearest and most precise* answer, so use Process of Elimination. It's correct to say that the *agents* were *Under Walker's supervision*, so keep (D), but the phrase *Below Walker's supervision* isn't correct, so eliminate (A). Likewise, *Above Walker's supervision* and *As Walker's supervision* aren't correct phrasings. Eliminate (B) and (C). The correct answer is (D).

8. **H**   The question is asking for the *most effective transition from the preceding paragraph to this new one,* so identify the content of the two paragraphs. The previous paragraph discusses the *"Walker Agents,"* and the new paragraph describes the establishment of the Walker Company's headquarters in Indianapolis. Walker's travel to *the Caribbean and to Central America* is not consistent with either paragraph, so eliminate (F). Sarah's *daughter* is also not relevant to either paragraph, so eliminate (G). Choice (H) provides an effective transition between the agents and other achievements of the Walker Company. *Josephine Baker* is not consistent with either paragraph, so eliminate (J). The correct answer is (H).

9. **D**   The question is asking where a sentence should go, so consider the content of the sentence and that of the surrounding sentences in the paragraph. Sentence 2 refers to *these charitable acts,* so it must come after a sentence that introduces the idea of *charitable acts.* Sentence 4 describes Walker's *dedication to charitable causes,* so Sentence 2 must come after Sentence 4. The correct answer is (D).

10. **H**   The question asks whether the essay focuses *on the development of the beauty industry in the early part of the twentieth century,* so consider the overall focus of the essay. The essay focuses on one beauty entrepreneur, not on the entire *industry,* so it is not consistent with the idea in the question. Eliminate (F) and (G). Choice (H) accurately describes the essay. The passage does not *describe other events taking place during this time,* so eliminate (J). The correct answer is (H).

ENGLISH PASSAGE DRILL 8

A Tale of Two Uncles

[1] As my uncle and I finished our dinners, we were hardly saying a word. [2] For the most part, it was a very ordinary birthday celebration. [3] After we had my favorite meal, my uncle made me his famous banana split sundae for dessert. [4] Banana splits are best with two scoops of chocolate ice cream, in my opinion. [5] Normally, my uncle would get very excited watching me eat dessert and make wishes for the coming year. [6] However, as our spoons clinked, his mood turned sad. [7] I knew the source of our agreement: today was my eighteenth

birthday and next month I'd be at boot camp. [3]

He said that joining the army he had some strong reservations about me rather than going to college. I told him that I believed my father, who was killed serving in the Polish army,

would have been proud of my decision. [5] My uncle responded that my father would have felt even better about me staying out of harm's way. In fact, my uncle continued, the reason that we moved to the United States was so that I would be more protected than I had been in Poland. I think my uncle also found it surprising that I would want to join the U.S. army.

---

1. Which choice is least redundant in context?

   A. **No Change**
   B. celebration, just like always.
   C. celebration with nothing abnormal.
   D. celebration and traditional.

2. Which choice best conveys the idea that the narrator and the uncle feel a sense of unresolved discomfort?

   F. **No Change**
   G. quandary
   H. tension
   J. intention

3. Which of the following sentences is LEAST relevant to the theme of the passage and could therefore be deleted?

   A. Sentence 2
   B. Sentence 3
   C. Sentence 4
   D. Sentence 6

4. The best placement for the underlined portion would be:

   F. where it is now.
   G. after the word *reservations*.
   H. after the word *me*.
   J. after the word *than*.

5. If the writer were to delete the phrase "who was killed serving in the Polish army" (and the surrounding commas) from the preceding sentence, the paragraph would primarily lose:

   A. nothing, since this information is mentioned elsewhere in the paragraph.
   B. evidence that the narrator's father was considered a brave man.
   C. a necessary detail that supports the logical flow of ideas in the paragraph.
   D. an explanation of why the narrator is unwilling to join the Polish army.

He often asked <u>me</u>—why I would risk my life for a country that
₆
was not my homeland. I told him that I considered America my

new homeland. He was <u>shocked.</u>
₇

   He began reminding me of my Polish upbringing. My
uncle has as many stories about my childhood <u>than I do.</u> When
₈
my uncle finished reminiscing, I assured him that I still love

Poland and will never lose sight of <u>it's</u> influence on me.
₉
However, America gave my uncle an opportunity when an
engineering firm in Pittsburgh offered him a job seven years

ago. <u>After we immigrated to America,</u> I became exposed to the
₁₀
cultural attitudes, social customs, and economic possibilities
of growing up as an American child. My time in America has
given me a deep love for it and loyalty to it. As we finished our
dessert, I asked my uncle to make peace with my decision to
defend Uncle Sam.

6. Which choice makes the sentence most grammatically
   acceptable?

   F. **No Change**
   G. me,
   H. me
   J. me:

7. Which choice most effectively maintains the essay's tone?

   A. **No Change**
   B. indubitably shaken.
   C. freaking out.
   D. displaying a stricken look upon his face.

8. Which choice makes the sentence most grammatically
   acceptable?

   F. **No Change**
   G. as I do.
   H. then I do.
   J. **Delete** the underlined portion and end the sentence
       with a period.

9. Which choice makes the sentence most grammatically
   acceptable?

   A. **No Change**
   B. its'
   C. its
   D. their

10. Given that all of the choices are accurate, which one
    provides the most effective and logical transition from the
    preceding sentence to this one?

    F. **No Change**
    G. Pittsburgh being the biggest city in Pennsylvania,
    H. He is a very well-respected engineer, and
    J. Although I have visited Philadelphia, Pittsburgh is
        where

ENGLISH PASSAGE DRILL 8 EXPLANATIONS

1. **A** The question is asking for the *least redundant* answer, so eliminate answers that are overly wordy or repeat information given earlier. Choice (A) is concise and makes the meaning of the sentence clear, so keep (A). The phrase *just like always* means the same thing as *ordinary,* which is in the non-underlined portion of the sentence. There is no need to repeat this idea, so eliminate (B). The words *with nothing abnormal* and *traditional* also mean the same thing as *ordinary* in this context, so eliminate (C) and (D). The correct answer is (A).

2. **H** The question is asking for the answer that would convey *the idea that the narrator and the uncle feel a sense of unresolved discomfort,* so eliminate any answers that don't fulfill this goal. Eliminate (F) because it's a positive word. Eliminate (G) because a *quandary* is a problem and doesn't necessarily imply *discomfort* or a conflict between the two people (for example, they could be dealing with a problem together). Keep (H) because *tension* matches with *unresolved discomfort* between one another. Eliminate (J) because an *intention* is a goal, which doesn't match the purpose in the question. The correct answer is (H).

3. **C** The question is asking which sentence is *LEAST relevant to the theme of the passage and could therefore be deleted,* so consider the overall theme of the passage and identify a sentence that is inconsistent. The paragraph describes the *ordinary birthday celebration* that the narrator had with their uncle just before leaving for boot camp. Sentence 2 introduces the idea that the dinner mentioned in the first sentence was for a *birthday,* and the phrase *For the most part* sets up the idea that there is something slightly unusual about this dinner. Sentence 2 is relevant to the passage, so eliminate (A). Sentence 3 gives details about what the narrator and the uncle ate for dinner, and introduces the *dessert,* which is the turning point in the uncle's mood. Sentence 3 is relevant to the passage, so eliminate (B). Sentence 4 gives a general opinion about *banana splits* that is not relevant to the particular dinner described in the paragraph, so keep (C). Sentence 6 describes the shift in mood that was set up by the phrase *For the most part* in Sentence 1. Sentence 6 is relevant, so eliminate (D). The correct answer is (C).

4. **H** The question is asking for the *best placement for the underlined portion,* so try the phrase in each spot and eliminate any that don't offer a logical meaning. Where it is now, the underlined phrase describes the uncle, but it is the narrator who is *joining the army,* so eliminate (F). Choice (G) makes the same error, so eliminate (G) as well. Choice (H) appropriately places the phrase after the word *me,* to make it clear that it is the narrator who is *joining the army,* so keep (H). Choice (J) makes the comparison, indicated by *rather than* between *me* (that is, the narrator) and *joining the army.* These two things are not similar to each other and therefore cannot be compared. Eliminate (J). The correct answer is (H).

5. **C** The question is asking what the paragraph would *lose* if the phrase were deleted, so try reading the paragraph with and without the phrase to see what the difference is. The phrase is a descriptive phrase that gives more information about the narrator's *father.* The information is not *mentioned elsewhere in the paragraph,* so eliminate (A). The phrase does not state that the father was *considered a brave man,* so eliminate (B). The phrase provides a detail about the father that makes clear both why the narrator thinks his father *would have been proud* and why the uncle thinks that the father *would have felt even better about* the narrator's *staying out of harm's way,* so (C) gives an accurate description of the phrase. There is no discussion of the narrator's joining *the Polish army,* so eliminate (D). The correct answer is (C).

6. **H** The question asks about grammar, so look at the answers to see what's changing. Connecting punctuation is changing in the answer choices, so look for a complete sentence. The first part of the sentence says *He often asked me*, and the second part states what the uncle asked. There is no need for punctuation to separate these ideas since the second part is a continuation of the first. Eliminate (F), (G), and (J). The correct answer is (H).

7. **A** The question is asking for a choice that *maintains the essay's tone*, so consider the overall tone of the essay and eliminate any answer that is inconsistent. The essay's tone is personal but not overly informal. Keep (A) because it doesn't have any clear issues. Eliminate (B) because *indubitably* is too formal to be consistent with the essay's tone. Eliminate (C) because it's too casual. Eliminate (D) because it's overly wordy and formal compared to (A). The correct answer is (A).

8. **G** The question asks about grammar, so look at the answers to see what's changing. Phrasing changes in the answer choices, and there is also the option to delete, so find the context and use Process of Elimination. The beginning of the sentence sets up a comparison, *My uncle has as many stories,* that is left incomplete if the underlined portion is deleted. Eliminate (J). The second part of the comparison must be consistent with the first part. Because the comparison starts with *as*, it must also end with *as*. Eliminate (F) and (H). The correct answer is (G).

9. **C** The question asks about grammar, so look at the answers to see what's changing. Pronouns and apostrophes are changing in the answer choices, so find the word the pronoun refers back to: *Poland*. This word is singular, so eliminate (D), which is plural. Eliminate (B) because it's not a word at all. Choice (A), *it's*, means "it is," which doesn't work in this context. The sentence is referring to the *influence* of Poland, so a possessive pronoun is needed. Eliminate (A). The correct answer is (C).

10. **F** The question is asking for the *most effective and logical transition from the preceding sentence to this one*, so identify the content of the two sentences. The preceding sentence says that *America gave my uncle an opportunity,* and this sentence lists the things the narrator was *exposed to…as an American child*. Choice (F) maintains the focus of both sentences on *America,* so keep (F). *Pittsburgh* is not mentioned in either sentence, so eliminate (G) and (J). The uncle's job is also not mentioned in either sentence, so eliminate (H). The correct answer is (F).

ENGLISH PASSAGE DRILL 9

Not the Same Old Song and Dance

After graduating from college, I began living and working in China. I poured myself into work, finding that enduring the same 12-hour workdays as several of my Chinese coworkers was just as difficult <u>as to adapt</u> to Chinese culture.

¹

<u>All the while, at the same time,</u> I slowly taught myself more Chinese with a language CD and forced myself to interact at local places. The easiest way to adapt, however, had been

²

<u>right under my nose</u> the entire time.

³

All I had to do was spend time with my coworkers outside of work. One night, I accepted my coworkers' invitation, knowing this would be an important step in learning the Chinese way of life. The ensuing night would prove to be quite <u>memorable and unforgettable.</u>

⁴

We began the evening with dinner. I proudly requested to order since I had learned quite a lot of food vocabulary. Everyone <u>seemed surprised,</u> and impressed by the variety of dishes I could order. Our post-dinner destination was a karaoke house

⁵

(KTV), a very popular form of entertainment in China. [6]

1. Which choice makes the sentence most grammatically acceptable?

   A. **No Change**
   B. when adapting
   C. as having adapted
   D. as adapting

2. Which choice is least redundant in context?

   F. **No Change**
   G. All the while,
   H. All while at the same time,
   J. While all the time was the same,

3. Which choice would most clearly and effectively express the obviousness of the best method of adaptation?

   A. **No Change**
   B. noticeable
   C. doubtful
   D. obscure

4. Which choice is least redundant in context?

   F. **No Change**
   G. memorable and hard to forget.
   H. as memorable as can be.
   J. memorable.

5. Which choice makes the sentence most grammatically acceptable?

   A. **No Change**
   B. seemed surprised
   C. seemed, surprised
   D. seemed; surprised

6. At this point, the writer is considering adding the following true statement:

   Karaoke did not originate in China.

   Should the writer add this sentence here?

   F. Yes, because it supports the fact that karaoke is very popular despite being an import.
   G. Yes, because it adds to the international flavor of the essay.
   H. No, because it simply repeats a detail stated earlier in the essay.
   J. No, because it doesn't add to the focus of this paragraph.

The experience was accompanied by <u>embarrassment as</u> karaoke
                                              7
often provides, but mine did not come from singing.

    I decided to playfully chant a song's number, thirty-eight,
but I chanted only three and eight. What I failed to realize was
that the Chinese words for *three* and *eight* together make a rude
slang term. My Chinese friends could only assume I had just
unreasonably insulted one of them. [8] After much confusion
and a difficult explanation on my part, the matter was resolved,

and everyone had a good laugh over it. I certainly learned a
valuable lesson about differences in slang. [9] My experience
with my co-workers was the first of many cultural

lessons I would learn by <u>simply being social in a foreign envi-</u>
                                                            10
<u>ronment.</u>
   10

7. Which choice makes the sentence most grammatically
   acceptable?

   A. **No Change**
   B. embarrassment as,
   C. embarrassment, as
   D. embarrassment, as,

8. If the preceding sentence were deleted, the essay would
   primarily lose:

   F. a repetition of the main point of the essay.
   G. another example of slang errors between languages.
   H. a contrast with the paragraph's opening sentence.
   J. a detail of how the party reacted to the author's mis-
      take.

9. If the writer wanted to emphasize the benefits of learning
   slang expressions in a new language, which of the
   following true statements should be added at this point?

   A. Slang differences are difficult to understand.
   B. Slang is a popular way to communicate.
   C. Learning about other slang differences can help to
      avoid cultural misunderstandings.
   D. Daily conversation among peers often includes slang.

10. Which choice would best summarize the main point of the
    essay as illustrated by the narrator's miscommunication
    experience?

    F. **No Change**
    G. intentionally insulting a local person in a foreign coun-
       try.
    H. enjoying nightlife in a foreign country.
    J. studying a foreign language in an isolated environment.

ENGLISH PASSAGE DRILL 9 EXPLANATIONS

1. **D**   The question asks about grammar, so look at the answers to see what's changing. Connecting words and verb forms are changing in the answer choices, so consider complete sentences. The underlined portion is the second part of a comparison. The verb in the first part of the comparison is *enduring*, so the underlined verb should also have an *-ing* ending. Eliminate (A) because it does not have an *-ing* ending. Eliminate (C) because there is no need for the extra word *having*. The difference between (B) and (D) is *when* versus *as*. *As* makes the comparison consistent with the non-underlined phrase *just as difficult,* so eliminate (B). The correct answer is (D).

2. **G**   The question is asking for the *least redundant* answer, so eliminate answers that are overly wordy or repeat information given earlier. *All the while* and *at the same time* mean the same thing, so there is no need to use both terms. Eliminate (F) and (H). The additional words in (J) do not make the meaning of the sentence clearer, so eliminate (J). Choice (G) is concise and makes the meaning of the sentence clear. The correct answer is (G).

3. **A**   The question is asking for the answer that would best *express the obviousness of the best method of adaptation,* so eliminate any answers that don't fulfill this goal. Neither *doubtful* nor *obscure* is consistent with the idea of *obvious,* so eliminate (C) and (D). *Noticeable* could mean *obvious,* but *right under my nose* is a stronger statement of *obviousness.* Eliminate (B). The correct answer is (A).

4. **J**   The question is asking for the *least redundant* answer, so eliminate answers that are overly wordy or repeat information given earlier. *Memorable* and *unforgettable* or *hard to forget* mean the same thing in this context, so there is no need to use both terms. Eliminate (F) and (G). The additional words in (H) do not make the meaning of the sentence clearer, so eliminate (H). Choice (J) is concise and makes the meaning of the sentence clear. The correct answer is (J).

5. **B**   The question asks about grammar, so look at the answers to see what's changing. Punctuation is changing in the answer choices, so consider whether any punctuation is needed. Choice (D) puts a semicolon after *seemed,* but a semicolon can only be used between two independent clauses, and *Everyone seemed* isn't an independent clause. Eliminate (D). Similarly, a comma followed by the coordinating conjunction *and* can also only be used between two independent clauses, but the second half of the sentence (*impressed by the variety of dishes I could order*) isn't an independent clause, so eliminate (A). There is no need for a comma after *seemed,* as the second part of the sentence continues the idea begun in the first part. Eliminate (C). The correct answer is (B).

6. **J**   The question is asking whether a sentence should be added, so consider the content of the sentence and the surrounding context. The paragraph discusses what the narrator and friends did on the night the narrator first went out with them. Although they went to a *karaoke house,* the origins of karaoke are not relevant to the paragraph. Eliminate (F) and (G). The new sentence does not repeat *a detail stated earlier,* so eliminate (H). Choice (J) accurately states that the new sentence *doesn't add to the focus of this paragraph.* The correct answer is (J).

7. **C** The question asks about grammar, so look at the answers to see what's changing. Commas are changing in the answer choices, so consider whether any commas are needed. The word *as* cannot be removed from the sentence on its own, so it should not be set off by commas; eliminate (D). The entire phrase *as karaoke often provides* is not necessary to the main meaning of the sentence, so it should be set off from the rest of the sentence with commas. Eliminate (A) and (B) because neither has a comma before *as*. The correct answer is (C).

8. **J** The question is asking what the essay would *lose* if the sentence were deleted, so try reading the paragraph with and without the sentence to see what the difference is. The sentence says that the narrator's friends *could only assume I had just unreasonably insulted one of them.* This is not *a repetition of the main point of the essay*, so eliminate (F). Eliminate (G) because the sentence describes the friends' reaction to the narrator's error; it does not give *another example of slang errors.* Eliminate (H) because there is no *contrast* between this sentence and *the paragraph's opening sentence.* Choice (J) accurately states that the sentence describes *how the party reacted to the author's mistake.* The correct answer is (J).

9. **C** The question is asking for the answer that would *emphasize the benefits of learning slang expressions in a new language*, so eliminate any answers that don't fulfill this goal. Choice (A) says that slang is *difficult to understand*, which is not a *benefit*, so eliminate (A). Choices (B) and (D) both discuss how frequently slang is used, which could be understood as a *benefit*. Choice (C) states that understanding slang *can help to avoid cultural misunderstandings*, which is a direct statement of a *benefit.* Eliminate (B) and (D) because (C) more directly matches the purpose stated in the question. The correct answer is (C).

10. **F** The question is asking for the answer that would *summarize the main point of the essay*, so consider the essay's main point. The essay is about how the narrator learned a cultural lesson by making a mistake while spending time with friends. The narrator was *being social* when the mishap took place, so keep (F). The narrator did not *intentionally insult* anyone, so eliminate (G). It may have been at night that the mishap took place, but the focus of the passage was more on the narrator interacting with friends than on the time of day; eliminate (H). The narrator was not *in an isolated environment*, so eliminate (J). The correct answer is (F).

ENGLISH PASSAGE DRILL 10

Life in the Bike Lane

When I was growing up, I used to ride my bike all the time, which provided a certain amount of freedom. When I finally got my driver's license, I felt that my old bike was part of a previous chapter in my life. For the next few years, I gleefully drove even the distances smallest in length.
₁

Then I moved out on my own and found that the car had
₂
less allure. I didn't have bundles of money to throw around, and

in my new city, bundles of money was exactly what I needed to
₃
use the car with any regularity. Gas cost much more per gallon than I was used to, and what would've been a quick 30-minute drive where I grew up easily became a two-hour drive because

of all the traffic in this new place! [4]

After I couldn't take any more, I resolved and decided
₅
that the next time I visited my parents, I would find my bike.

1. Which choice is least redundant in context?

   A. **No Change**
   B. shortest and smallest distances.
   C. distances that were short, not long.
   D. shortest distances.

2. Which choice is clearest and most precise in context?

   F. **No Change**
   G. myself out
   H. myself in
   J. in

3. Which choice makes the sentence most grammatically acceptable?

   A. **No Change**
   B. weren't exacting
   C. was exact
   D. were exactly

4. If the writer were to delete the phrase "in this new place" (placing an exclamation point after the word *traffic*), this sentence would primarily lose:

   F. a contrast to the phrase "where I grew up" in the same sentence.
   G. factual information regarding the purpose of the author's move.
   H. a contrast to the phrase "a quick 30-minute drive" in the same sentence.
   J. a logical connection to the place mentioned in the first paragraph.

5. Which choice is least redundant in context?

   A. **No Change**
   B. resolution in my deciding
   C. resolved
   D. decidedly resolved

I entered the attic with a flashlight, <u>even if I fought</u> off fear
and cobwebs in equal measure. I felt overwhelming joy once I
located my old bike, which was amplified when I returned to my

own place and began <u>by riding</u> the bike around town. I had been

freed from expensive gas, traffic jams, and <u>having been freed</u>
<u>from the</u> interminable wait at the bus stop!

I realized then that I had regained that freedom I had
enjoyed so much when I was younger. Now, this freedom had
taken on a different character: <u>it wasn't just freedom of move-</u>
<u>ment anymore.</u> Now it was freedom from constraints that
prevented me from doing what I wanted to do in the city and
had me sitting in traffic or spending all my hard-earned cash on
gas. I had moved out of the fast lane and into the bike lane, and
I was finally able to get the most out of my new life.

6. Which choice makes the sentence most grammatically
   acceptable?

   F. **No Change**
   G. fighting
   H. because I fought
   J. and had fought

7. Which choice makes the sentence most grammatically
   acceptable?

   A. **No Change**
   B. to riding
   C. to ride
   D. with riding

8. Which choice makes the sentence most grammatically
   acceptable?

   F. **No Change**
   G. freed from the
   H. the
   J. from the freeing of the

9. Given that all of the following are true, which one would
   provide the most effective transition to the following
   sentence?

   A. **No Change**
   B. not a character as in a play, but more in the sense of a
      "type."
   C. I had resolved to ride my bike any distance shorter
      than ten miles.
   D. I had to get the brakes fixed before I could use it a lot.

Question 10 asks about the preceding passage as a
whole.

---

10. Suppose the writer had intended to write a brief essay
    detailing the transportation options for visitors to a major
    city. Would this essay successfully fulfill the writer's goal?

    F. Yes, because the writer discusses biking, driving, and
       taking the bus in detail.
    G. Yes, because this essay deals with the ways in which
       the city would have fewer traffic jams if more people
       were to ride bikes.
    H. No, because the essay focuses instead on the writer's
       personal feelings about biking and driving in the city.
    J. No, because the essay deals primarily with the conve-
       nience of driving and its superiority over other forms
       of transportation.

ENGLISH PASSAGE DRILL 10 EXPLANATIONS

1. **D** The question is asking for the *least redundant* answer, so eliminate answers that are overly wordy or repeat information given earlier. *Shortest* and *smallest* express the same idea, so there is no need to use both words; eliminate (B). *Not long* means the same thing as *shortest,* so there is no need to use both those terms; eliminate (C). Including the phrase *in length* does not make the meaning of the sentence clearer, so eliminate (A). Choice (D) is concise and makes the meaning of the sentence clear. The correct answer is (D).

2. **F** The question is asking for the *clearest and most precise* answer, so use Process of Elimination. The correct idiom is to "move out on my own," not to "move in on my own," so eliminate (H) and (J). The reflexive pronoun *myself* should be used only if *I* is both the subject and object of the verb. In this sentence, *I* is the subject of *moved out,* but there is no object. There is no reason to use *myself,* so eliminate (G). The correct answer is (F).

3. **D** The question asks about grammar, so look at the answers to see what's changing. Verbs and describing words are changing in the answers, so start by identifying the subject: *bundles.* This word is plural, so eliminate (A) and (C) because *was* is singular. For (B), the phrase *bundles of money weren't exacting what I needed* doesn't provide a clear meaning, whereas (D) does. Eliminate (B). The correct answer is (D).

4. **F** The question is asking what the sentence would *lose* if the phrase were deleted, so try reading the sentence with and without the phrase to see what the difference is. The phrase refers to a specific *place.* Choice (F) accurately describes the role of the phrase; the first part of the sentence describes a *quick...drive where I grew up,* which is contrasted to *a two-hour drive...in this new place.* Keep (F). The phrase does not describe *the purpose of the author's move,* so eliminate (G). The phrase *two-hour drive* contrasts with *a quick 30-minute drive,* but the phrase in question is not about time; eliminate (H). *The place mentioned in the first paragraph* is where the author grew up, not *this new place;* eliminate (J). The correct answer is (F).

5. **C** The question is asking for the *least redundant* answer, so eliminate answers that are overly wordy or repeat information given earlier. *Resolved* and *decided* mean the same thing in this context, so there is no need to use both words. Eliminate (A), (B), and (D). Choice (C) is concise and makes the meaning of the sentence clear. The correct answer is (C).

6. **G** The question asks about grammar, so look at the answers to see what's changing. Verb forms and connecting words are changing in the answer choices, so consider complete sentences. The first part of the sentence says that the narrator *entered the attic with a flashlight,* and the second part describes the narrator fighting *fear and cobwebs.* There is no contrast between the two parts of the sentence, so eliminate (F), which contains the contrasting transition *even if.* There is also no causal relationship between the two parts of the sentence, so eliminate *because* in (H). The verb tense in (J) is not consistent with the simple past tense verb *entered* in the non-underlined portion of the sentence; eliminate (J). Choice (G) uses *fighting* to make it clear that the second part of the sentence describes what the narrator did when they *entered the attic.* The correct answer is (G).

7. **C** The question asks about grammar, so look at the answers to see what's changing. Verb forms and connecting words are changing in the answer choices, so consider complete sentences. Although *began by* and *began with* are correct phrasings, they can be used only to refer to the first step in a process, but no process is mentioned here, so eliminate (A) and (D). The phrase *began to riding* isn't correct, so eliminate (B). Choice (C) works, so keep it. The correct answer is (C).

8. **H** The question asks about grammar, so look at the answers to see what's changing. Wording is changing in the answer choices, so consider how the options fit in the context of the sentence. The sentence contains a list of things the narrator *had been freed from.* The items in the list are *expensive gas, traffic jams,* and *the interminable wait at the bus stop.* The phrase *freed from* at the beginning of the list refers to all three things, so there is no need to repeat it. Eliminate (F), (G), and (J). Choice (H) is concise and makes the items in the list consistent with one another. The correct answer is (H).

9. **A** The question is asking for the *most effective transition to the following sentences,* so identify the content of the following sentences. This sentence introduces the idea of *freedom* with a *different character.* The following sentence describes the new character of the freedom. Choice (A) describes what *this freedom* had been previously, so it is consistent with both sentences. Keep (A). Choice (B) describes what the narrator means by *character,* which is not relevant to the second sentence; eliminate (B). Choices (C) and (D) both refer to the narrator's bike but do not mention anything about *freedom.* Eliminate (C) and (D). The correct answer is (A).

10. **H** The question asks whether the essay details *the transportation options for visitors to a major city,* so consider the overall focus of the essay. The essay focuses on the narrator's transportation options, not on *visitors to a major city,* so it is not consistent with the idea in the question. Eliminate (F) and (G). Choice (H) accurately describes the essay. The passage does not discuss the *superiority* of *driving,* so eliminate (J). The correct answer is (H).

ENGLISH PASSAGE DRILL 11

Man's Best Friend

[1]

Archaeologists have found evidence of domesticated dogs as far back as 6500 BCE in Mesopotamia and 8300 BCE in what is now North America. [A] Some historians suggesting [1] that dogs as a species evolved into something close to their current form as many as 100,000 years ago, and many historians estimate that dogs were first domesticated as many as 15,000 years ago. There are over 800 different breeds of dogs and many [2] more that cannot be classified into a single breed. [2]

[2]

Although dogs have been bred and domesticated for many [3] reasons throughout history, the primary reason for their

breeding in ancient times was their usefulness as hunting com- [4] panions. Dogs were also often used as protectors;

whose primary responsibility was to sit in front of a residence [5] or place of gathering and scare away would-be robbers and evildoers. [B]

1. Which choice makes the sentence most grammatically acceptable?
   - **A. No Change**
   - B. to suggest
   - C. having suggested
   - D. suggest

2. Given that all of the choices are true, which one would most effectively conclude this paragraph while leading into the main focus of the next paragraph?
   - **F. No Change**
   - G. Even since these early times, people have recognized the importance of keeping domesticated dogs.
   - H. Many argue that the dog has been as important to the unfolding of human history as has the horse.
   - J. The dog is a major subspecies of the wolf, and many features of its biological makeup are still similar to those of the wolf.

3. Which choice makes the sentence most grammatically acceptable?
   - **A. No Change**
   - B. However, dogs
   - C. As a result, dogs
   - D. Dogs

4. Which choice makes the sentence most grammatically acceptable?
   - **F. No Change**
   - G. were
   - H. have been
   - J. are

5. Which choice makes the sentence most grammatically acceptable?
   - **A. No Change**
   - B. his
   - C. their
   - D. who

[3]

[1] More recently, <u>by way of example,</u> dogs have been seen
                              6
more as companions and family members. [2] From this date
forward, the dog has increasingly filled the role of domesticated

pet, and there are no <u>fewer then</u> 74 million owned dogs in the
                              7
United States. [3] Inspired by the ideas of the Enlightenment,

people's attitudes toward dogs began to take on a more personal

character. ⟨8⟩ [4] Dogs came to be prized for their loyalty, and

as early as 1855, the American English phrase "man's best

friend" was already common. ⟨9⟩

[4]

It should be no surprise, then, that people have come to

think of their dogs more and more as near-human members of

their families. [C] Think about all the roles that dogs play in

our lives—they are not just our pets and "best friends"; they are

also necessary to law enforcement, firefighters, and the visually

impaired, to name just a few. [D] Although it may seem at first

that dogs are just lazy pets, in actuality they are really much

more than that.

6. Which transition word or phrase is most logical in context?

    F. **No Change**
    G. as a consequence,
    H. by contrast,
    J. moreover,

7. Which choice makes the sentence most grammatically acceptable?

    A. **No Change**
    B. less then
    C. lesser than
    D. fewer than

8. If the writer were to delete the phrase "take on a more personal character" from the preceding sentence and replace it with the word "change," the essay would primarily lose:

    F. an important description of a dog-breeding technique.
    G. a detail that indicates how attitudes toward dogs have changed.
    H. information that emphasizes the historical importance of dogs.
    J. nothing, since this detail is the topic of the preceding paragraph.

9. For the sake of logic and coherence, Sentence 2 should be placed:

    A. where it is now.
    B. before Sentence 1.
    C. after Sentence 3.
    D. after Sentence 4.

Question 10 asks about the preceding passage as a whole.

---

10. Upon reviewing notes for this essay, the writer comes across some information and composes the following sentence, incorporating that information:

    > Furthermore, many ancient civilizations, Greek and Egyptian among them, used trained war dogs to aid them in battle.

    For the sake of logic and coherence of the essay, this sentence should be placed at:

    F. Point A in Paragraph 1.
    G. Point B in Paragraph 2.
    H. Point C in Paragraph 4.
    J. Point D in Paragraph 4.

ENGLISH PASSAGE DRILL 11 EXPLANATIONS

1. **D** The question asks about grammar, so look at the answers to see what's changing. Verb forms are changing in the answer choices, so consider complete sentences. The subject of the sentence is *historians*, and the underlined portion represents the main verb of the independent clause. Eliminate (A) and (C) because an *-ing* verb can't be the main verb in an independent clause. Likewise, eliminate (B) because a "to" verb can't be a main verb. The correct answer is (D).

2. **G** The question is asking for the answer that would *conclude this paragraph while leading into the main focus of the next paragraph,* so identify the content of the two paragraphs. This paragraph discusses archaeological and historical evidence of dogs, and the next paragraph discusses the reasons that dogs *have been bred and domesticated.* The number of different breeds is not consistent with these ideas, so eliminate (F). *Early times* is consistent with this paragraph, while *the importance of keeping domesticated dogs* leads into the next paragraph, so keep (G). *The horse* is not relevant to either paragraph, so eliminate (H). The *biological makeup* of the dog and its similarity to that of *the wolf* is not relevant to either paragraph, so eliminate (J). The correct answer is (G).

3. **A** The question asks about grammar, so look at the answers to see what's changing. Ways to begin the sentence with or without a transition are changing in the answers, so consider complete sentences. The second part of the sentence, *the primary reason for their breeding…was their usefulness as hunting companions*, is an independent clause. Since the two halves are separated with a comma, the first part must not be an independent clause. Eliminate (B), (C), and (D) because they all make the first part of the sentence an independent clause, and two independent clauses can't be connected with a comma alone. The correct answer is (A).

4. **F** The question asks about grammar, so look at the answers to see what's changing. Verbs are changing in the answer choices, so identify the subject: *reason*. This word is singular, so eliminate (G), (H), and (J), which are all plural. The correct answer is (F).

5. **C** The question asks about grammar, so look at the answers to see what's changing. Pronouns are changing in the answer choices, so identify the word the pronoun refers back to: *Dogs*. This word is plural, so eliminate (B) because it's singular. Next, consider the sentence construction. It has a semicolon, so both parts of the sentence must be independent clauses. Eliminate (A) and (D) because they don't create an independent clause after the semicolon. The correct answer is (C).

6. **H**   The question is asking for a *logical* transition, so identify the relationships between the ideas. The preceding sentence discusses dogs' roles as *protectors*. This sentence says that they were *seen more as companions and family members* in a later time period. There is a contrast between these two ideas, so eliminate (F), (G), and (J), all of which contain transitions that indicate agreement between ideas. Choice (H) appropriately indicates a contrast. The correct answer is (H).

7. **D**   The question asks about grammar, so look at the answers to see what's changing. The words *less*, *lesser*, and *fewer* are changing, as are *then* and *than*. *Then* is used to indicate time, while *than* is used in a comparison. There is a comparison in this sentence, so *than* is the appropriate word. Eliminate (A) and (B). The difference between (C) and (D) is *lesser* versus *fewer*. *Fewer* is the idiomatically correct word in this context, so eliminate (C). The correct answer is (D).

8. **G**   The question is asking what the essay would *lose* if the phrase were deleted, so try reading the sentence with and without the phrase to see what the difference is. The phrase gives more details about how *people's attitudes toward dogs* changed. Eliminate (F) because there is nothing about *dog-breeding* in the phrase. Choice (G) accurately describes the phrase, so keep (G). The phrase does not discuss the *historical importance* of dogs, so eliminate (H). The phrase does not repeat *the topic of the preceding paragraph,* so eliminate (J). The correct answer is (G).

9. **D**   The question is asking where a sentence should go, so consider the content of the sentence and that of the surrounding sentences in the paragraph. Sentence 2 refers to a date (*From this date forward*), so it must come after some mention of a specific date. From the options, only Sentence 4 includes a date (*1855*), so Sentence 2 must come after Sentence 4. The correct answer is (D).

10. **G**   The question is asking where the new sentence should go, so consider the content of the sentence and that of the surrounding sentences in each of the four spots. The new sentence says that *ancient civilizations… used trained war dogs to aid them in battle*. Paragraph 1 discusses archaeological and historical evidence of dogs, but not their roles, so eliminate (F). Paragraph 2 discusses the roles of dogs, and in particular their roles as *hunting companions* and *protectors*. The new sentence is consistent with these ideas, so keep (G). Paragraph 4 discusses dogs' part in modern society, so eliminate (H) and (J). The correct answer is (G).

ENGLISH PASSAGE DRILL 12

André Bazin's New Wave

Film critic André Bazin published his first piece in 1943 and pioneered a new way of writing about <u>film, he</u> championed
¹
the idea that cinema was the "seventh art," every bit as

deserving as the more respected arts <u>of: architecture,</u> poetry,
²
dance, music, painting, and sculpture. Many before Bazin's time thought of the cinema as a simple extension of another art form: theater. In fact, in many early writings about film, it is not

uncommon to hear the authors speak of film. ☐3 Bazin, though, sought to show that the cinema had every bit as much crafts-manship as any of the other six arts. From this fundamental belief came what was possibly Bazin's greatest contribution to

film criticism: *auteur* theory. ☐4

1. Which choice makes the sentence most grammatically acceptable?

   A. **No Change**
   B. film. He
   C. film he
   D. film. Although he

2. Which choice makes the sentence most grammatically acceptable?

   F. **No Change**
   G. of, architecture,
   H. of architecture,
   J. of, architecture

3. The writer is considering adding the following phrase to the end of the preceding sentence (deleting the period after the word film):

   > as a second-class substitute for the "legitimate theater."

   Should the writer make this addition there?

   A. Yes, because it clarifies the sentence to show more specifically how some critics talked about film.
   B. Yes, because it helps the reader to understand more clearly the subjects of Bazin's writing.
   C. No, because it fails to maintain this paragraph's focus on cinema.
   D. No, because it speaks disparagingly about the practice of filmmaking.

4. At this point the writer is considering adding the following true statement:

   > Bazin's work is available in a text commonly read in Film Studies classes, the collection *What Is Cinema*?

   Should the writer make this addition here?

   F. Yes, because it maintains the essay's focus on an important figure in French film criticism.
   G. Yes, because it gives a good sense of the type of reading students can expect in Film Studies classes.
   H. No, because it interrupts the discussion of a specific theory of Bazin's.
   J. No, because other information in the essay suggests that this statement is untrue.

Auteur is the French word for *author*, and it suggests that every film is "authored" by a single mind. Bazin was among the first to discuss films and the practice of cinema in general as the masterwork of directors, rather than of screenwriters or actors. With *auteur* theory, <u>nonetheless,</u> Bazin created a new way of
₅

looking at films, and his early <u>works on</u> such influential direc-
₆
tors as Orson Welles, Vittorio de Sica, and Jean Renoir—remain, to this day, pioneering works of film criticism that are studied

and emulated by film critics today. [7]

Bazin's greatest achievement was the strong impression he left on a young generation of French filmmakers and critics who came on to the international scene <u>all over the world</u> just
₈

a year after Bazin's death. In 1959, two films <u>changed the</u>
₉
<u>landscape of international filmmaking:</u> François Truffaut's *The*
₉
400 Blows and Jean-Luc Godard's *Breathless*. In each film, the director took Bazin's emphasis on *auteur* filmmaking to heart, and in every frame, the viewer is reminded of the director's presence by the overwhelming stylistic personality of the shots and scenes. Today, there are legions of filmmakers whose inspiration can in some way be traced back to Bazin.

5. Which transition word or phrase, if any, is most logical in context?

   A. **No Change**
   B. meanwhile,
   C. still,
   D. **Delete** the underlined portion.

6. Which choice makes the sentence most grammatically acceptable?

   F. **No Change**
   G. works, on
   H. works: on
   J. works—on

7. Which of the following sentences, if added here, would effectively conclude this paragraph and introduce the topic of the next?

   A. Bazin himself never made any films, but he always preferred the Italian Neorealist style.
   B. While Bazin's magazine was the place to read about classic films, Henri Langlois's *Cinematheque* was the place to see them.
   C. Despite these great written achievements, Bazin's true and lasting influence lay elsewhere.
   D. Many film critics working in the later part of the twentieth century, such as Christian Metz and Gilles Deleuze, are clearly indebted to Bazin.

8. Which choice is least redundant in context?

   F. **No Change**
   G. in all parts of the world
   H. in every nation and country
   J. **Delete** the underlined portion.

9. Which choice would most effectively guide readers to understand the great importance of the two films discussed?

   A. **No Change**
   B. came out around the same time:
   C. joined the long list of films shot primarily in Paris:
   D. were created by directors who knew Bazin personally:

Question 10 asks about the preceding passage as a whole.

10. Suppose the author intended to write an essay that illustrates how the writings of one film critic have had an influence beyond the realm of film criticism. Would this essay successfully fulfill that goal?

F. Yes, because the essay describes Bazin's influence on the six arts of architecture, poetry, dance, music, painting, and sculpture.

G. Yes, because the essay describes Bazin's influence on both film criticism and filmmaking.

H. No, because the essay discusses auteur theory and French films in general.

J. No, because the essay states that Bazin's greatest achievements were as a filmmaker.

ENGLISH PASSAGE DRILL 12 EXPLANATIONS

1. **B** The question asks about grammar, so look at the answers to see what's changing. Connecting punctuation is changing in the answers, so look for independent clauses. The first part of the sentence, *Film critic André Bazin published his first piece in 1943 and pioneered a new way of writing about film,* is an independent clause. The second part of the sentence, *he championed the idea that cinema was…every bit as deserving as the more respected arts…,* is also an independent clause. Two independent clauses must be separated by some type of punctuation other than a comma, so eliminate (A) and (C). Choice (B) appropriately uses a period to separate two independent clauses. Adding the word *Although* to the beginning of the second part of the sentence makes it into a dependent clause. A period can only be used between two independent clauses, so eliminate (D). The correct answer is (B).

2. **H** The question asks about grammar, so look at the answers to see what's changing. Commas and a colon are changing in the answer choices, so consider whether any punctuation is needed. The first part of the sentence, *He championed the idea that cinema was the "seventh art," every bit as deserving as the more respected arts of,* is not an independent clause. A colon can only be used after an independent clause, so eliminate (F). There is no need to use a comma after *of,* so eliminate (G) and (J). Choice (H) appropriately uses a comma after *architecture* because it is the first item in a list. The correct answer is (H).

3. **A** The question is asking whether a phrase should be added, so consider the content of the phrase and the surrounding context. The sentence discusses how *the authors speak of film* in *early writings about film.* The new phrase gives more detail about the way in which *the authors speak of film,* so it should be added; eliminate (C) and (D). Choice (A) accurately describes the phrase, so keep (A). The phrase does not mention *the subjects of Bazin's writings,* so eliminate (B). The correct answer is (A).

4. **H** The question is asking whether a sentence should be added, so consider the content of the sentence and the surrounding context. The paragraph discusses the important ideas in Bazin's *film criticism.* The new sentence names a book in which Bazin's writings are published. The name of this book is not relevant to the important ideas in the writings, so the sentence should not be added. Eliminate (F) and (G). Choice (H) accurately states that the new sentence *interrupts the discussion of a specific theory of Bazin's,* so keep (H). There is no indication that *this statement is untrue,* so eliminate (J). The correct answer is (H).

5. **D** The question is asking for a *logical* transition, if one is needed, so identify the relationships between the ideas. The preceding sentence states that Bazin was *among the first* to do something, and this sentence states that *Bazin created a new way of looking at films.* There is no contrast between these ideas, so eliminate (A), (B), and (C) because they all contain contrasting transitions. No transition is necessary. Choice (D) is concise and makes the meaning of the sentence clear. The correct answer is (D).

6. **J** The question asks about grammar, so look at the answers to see what's changing. Punctuation is changing in the answer choices, so look at the rest of the sentence and determine whether any punctuation is needed. When there is a dash in the answer choices, look at the non-underlined portion of the sentence to see whether there is another dash in the sentence. There is a dash in the non-underlined portion, after *Jean Renoir.* The phrase *on such influential directors as Orson Welles, Vittorio de Sica, and Jean Renoir* contains a

list of names that is not necessary to the main meaning of the sentence. It should therefore be set off from the sentence by either commas or dashes both before and after the phrase. Since the non-underlined dash cannot be changed, the beginning punctuation must also be a dash. Eliminate (F), (G), and (H). The correct answer is (J).

7. **C**   The question is asking for an answer that would *conclude this paragraph and introduce the topic of the next*, so identify the topics of both paragraphs. This paragraph states that Bazin's early writings are *pioneering works of film criticism that are studied and emulated by film critics today*. The following paragraph says that *Bazin's greatest achievement was the strong impression he left on a young generation of French filmmakers and critics*. Neither paragraph discusses *the Italian Neorealist style*, so eliminate (A). Neither paragraph mentions *Henri Langlois's* Cinematheque either, so eliminate (B). Choice (C) mentions both Bazin's *great written achievements* and his *true and lasting influence*, so it is consistent with both paragraphs. Keep (C). Choice (D) mentions some *film critics* who were influenced by Bazin, which is consistent with this paragraph but not with the next one. Eliminate (D). The correct answer is (C).

8. **J**   The question is asking for the *least redundant* answer, so eliminate answers that are overly wordy or repeat information given earlier. The underlined portion describes *the international scene*. *International* means *all over the world* or *in every nation and country*, so there is no need to repeat that idea. Eliminate (F), (G), and (H). Choice (J) is concise and makes the meaning of the sentence clear. The correct answer is (J).

9. **A**   The question is asking for the answer that would *most effectively guide readers to understand the great importance of the two films discussed*, so eliminate any answers that don't fulfill this goal. The phrase *changed the landscape of international filmmaking* indicates that the films were of *great importance*, so keep (A). When the films *came out* has nothing to do with their *importance*, so eliminate (B). Where the films were *shot* also is unrelated to their importance, so eliminate (C). Whether the directors *knew Bazin personally* similarly has nothing to do with the films' *importance;* eliminate (D). The correct answer is (A).

10. **G**   The question asks whether the essay *illustrates how the writings of one film critic have had an influence beyond the realm of film criticism*, so consider the overall focus of the essay. The essay discusses the writings of Bazin and his influence on both film critics and directors, so it is consistent with this idea. Eliminate (H) and (J). The passage does not discuss *Bazin's influence on the six arts*, so eliminate (F). Choice (G) accurately describes the passage. The correct answer is (G).

ENGLISH PASSAGE DRILL 13

Preventing Biblioemergencies

Before I move next week, I will unwillingly return the books that I have checked out from the library. Sadly, I never even opened a couple of them, and returning them will be painfully abrupt. ☐1

I know that I have plenty of other books to read. Still, whenever I return a book, I get that feeling of *what if*: What if I run out of books? Some friends of mine recently coined the term *biblioemergency* to describe just such a situation. A *biblioemergency* is when an avid reader, such as myself, discovers that she has nothing left to read. To me, <u>its</u> a disaster.
2

Ever since childhood, I've made it a point to carry at least one extra book, sometimes two or more. People ask me why I can't just make do with one book in my bag. But, I always point out, what if I finish <u>them</u>? What would I do then? I think this
3
all comes from a habit developed at an early age. Whenever my mother took me to a store or to an appointment, she brought along books. <u>As soon as I got fidgety,</u> she'd supply me with
4
a new book to keep me entertained. ☐5 Now as an adult, I

1. If the writer were to delete the words *unwillingly*, *sadly*, and *painfully* from this paragraph, the paragraph would primarily lose:
   A. evidence undermining the author's later assertion that she loves to read.
   B. the sense that the author is unhappy about her move.
   C. an explanation of the motive behind the writer's intended actions.
   D. its emphasis on the writer's reluctance to part with any books.

2. Which choice makes the sentence most grammatically acceptable?
   F. No Change
   G. theirs
   H. they're
   J. it's

3. Which choice makes the sentence most grammatically acceptable?
   A. No Change
   B. the book I'm reading?
   C. it?
   D. those?

4. Which choice makes the sentence most grammatically acceptable?
   F. No Change
   G. I got fidgety
   H. After fidgeting,
   J. Getting fidgety,

5. At this point, the author is considering adding the following sentence:

   > The best ones were the ones that had both pictures and words.

   If the information is taken to be true, should the author make this addition here?
   A. Yes, because it gives more information that is relevant to the previous comment.
   B. Yes, because it adds a detail that explains the main idea of the paragraph.
   C. No, because it contradicts information given in an earlier paragraph.
   D. No, because it is offensive and irrelevant to the passage as a whole.

neverthe<u>less</u> find it nearly impossible to wait patiently unless I
₆
have reading material.

      [1] When I've run out of books in the past, <u>finding</u> myself
₇
reading the backs of cereal boxes or the labels on my clothes.
[2] Even though I will have to return my books to the library, I

plan to <u>packing</u> at least four or five in my carry-on luggage, as I
₈
do every time I travel. [3] That, my friend, is an experience I

never need to repeat. [4] If that sounds like a hassle, imagine the

alternative. ☐ 9

6. Which transition word is most logical in context?

  F. **No Change**
  G. coincidentally
  H. conversely
  J. consequently

7. Which choice makes the sentence most grammatically acceptable?

  A. **No Change**
  B. being that I've found
  C. I've found
  D. having found

8. Which choice makes the sentence most grammatically acceptable?

  F. **No Change**
  G. have been packing
  H. pack
  J. be packing

9. Which of the following sequences of sentences makes this paragraph the most logical?

  A. **No Change**
  B. 2, 4, 1, 3
  C. 3, 1, 2, 4
  D. 4, 1, 2, 3

Question 10 asks about the preceding passage as a whole.

---

10. Upon reviewing the essay, the writer is considering removing the final paragraph. Should that paragraph be kept or deleted?

  F. Kept, because it returns to the opening idea and provides a conclusion.
  G. Kept, because it reveals the writer's true motivation for refusing to return the books.
  H. Deleted, because it distracts from the focus of the passage.
  J. Deleted, because it repeats information already given without adding any new elements.

ENGLISH PASSAGE DRILL 13 EXPLANATIONS

1. **D** The question is asking what the paragraph would *lose* if the words were deleted, so try reading the paragraph with and without the words to see what the difference is. The words in question are all adverbs that describe how the narrator feels about the prospect of returning her books. The words do not *undermine the author's…assertion that she loves to read*, so eliminate (A). They do not express feelings about the narrator's *move*, so eliminate (B). The words describe what the author is going to do, but they do not give her *motive*, so eliminate (C). Choice (D) accurately states that the words convey *the writer's reluctance to part with any books*. The correct answer is (D).

2. **J** The question asks about grammar, so look at the answers to see what's changing. Pronouns are changing in the answer choices, so identify the word the pronoun refers back to: *A biblioemergency*. This word is singular, so eliminate (G) and (H), which are both plural. Choice (F), *its*, is a possessive pronoun, but there is no noun directly after that this pronoun could be possessing. Eliminate (F). Choice (J) means "it is," which is correct in this context. The correct answer is (J).

3. **B** The question asks about grammar, so look at the answers to see what's changing. Pronouns and nouns are changing in the answer choices, so consider what is clearest and most consistent. There is no plural noun that the underlined pronoun could refer to, so eliminate (A) and (D) because *them* and *those* are both plural. *It* could refer to *one extra book*, but *the book I'm reading* gives a clearer idea of the narrator's meaning. Eliminate (C). The correct answer is (B).

4. **F** The question asks about grammar, so look at the answers to see what's changing. Phrasing at the beginning of the sentence is changing in the answer choices, so eliminate any option that is incorrectly phrased or doesn't make a complete sentence. Choice (F) doesn't contain any errors, so keep it. Choice (G) is missing a connecting word or punctuation between two independent clauses, so eliminate it. Both (H) and (J) incorrectly describe the mother as the one fidgeting, so eliminate them. The correct answer is (F).

5. **A** The question is asking whether a sentence should be added, so consider the content of the sentence and the surrounding context. The paragraph discusses how the narrator's mother gave her books to keep her *entertained* when she was a child. The new sentence describes the books the narrator liked as a child. Although the sentence is not absolutely necessary to add to the paragraph, neither of the reasons given in (C) or (D) is accurate: the new sentence does not *contradict information given in an earlier paragraph*, and it is not *offensive*. Eliminate (C) and (D). Choice (A) accurately states that the new sentence *gives more information that is relevant to the previous comment*, so keep (A). The new sentence does not *explain the main idea of the paragraph*, so eliminate (B). The correct answer is (A).

6. **J** The question is asking for a *logical* transition so identify the relationships between the ideas. The preceding sentence discusses how the narrator's mother would *supply* her *with a new book to keep* her *entertained* when they had to wait someplace. The sentence with the transition states that *Now* the narrator finds it *nearly impossible to wait patiently unless* she has *reading material*. These ideas agree, so eliminate (F) and (H) because they're both contrast transitions. Next, eliminate (G) because the paragraph is implying that the narrator's

dependence on books is a result of the *habit developed at an early age*, not merely a coincidence. Choice (J) appropriately connects the two ideas with *consequently,* which indicates that the idea in the second sentence is a result of the previous idea. The correct answer is (J).

7.   **C**   The question asks about grammar, so look at the answers to see what's changing. Subjects and verbs are changing in the answer choices, so consider complete sentences. The first part of the sentence, *When I've run out of books in the past,* isn't an independent clause. Thus, the second part of the sentence must be an independent clause because every sentence needs at least one independent clause. The second part needs a subject and a verb in order to be an independent clause, so eliminate (A) and (D) because they don't contain a subject. Choice (B) begins the phrase with *being that,* which doesn't produce an independent clause. Eliminate (B). The correct answer is (C).

8.   **H**   The question asks about grammar, so look at the answers to see what's changing. Verb forms are changing in the answer choices, so consider complete sentences. The part before the underlined portion says *I plan to,* so the verb needs to be in the right form to follow *to*. The phrase *to packing* isn't correct, so eliminate (F). The sentence is addressing future plans, so eliminate (G) because it refers to something in the past. Comparing (H) and (J), *be packing* is not consistent with the other verb in the sentence, *do,* so eliminate (J). The correct answer is (H).

9.   **B**   The question is asking for the *most logical* sequence of sentences, so look for clues indicating sentences that must go before or after one another. Sentence 4 says *If that sounds like a hassle,* so look for something that could be a *hassle* that must come before Sentence 4. Sentence 2 says *I plan to pack at least four or five* books *in my carry-on luggage,* which *sounds like a hassle,* so Sentence 4 must come directly after Sentence 2; eliminate (A) and (D). Sentence 3 also refers to something that came before: *That…is an experience I never need to repeat.* Sentence 1 describes such an experience: *I've found myself reading the backs of cereal boxes or the labels on my clothes.* Sentence 3 should therefore come after Sentence 1; eliminate (C). The correct answer is (B).

10.   **F**   The question is asking whether the *final paragraph* should be removed, so consider the content of this paragraph along with that of the rest of the essay. The passage focuses on the reasons the narrator always carries books with her. The final paragraph is consistent with this idea, so it should be kept; eliminate (H) and (J). The idea of returning *books to the library* does return *to the opening idea,* so keep (F). The paragraph says that the narrator will *return* the *books to the library*, not that she will refuse *to return the books,* so eliminate (G). The correct answer is (F).

ENGLISH PASSAGE DRILL 14

The Space Race

In the 1960s, the Russians and the Americans were in a fierce political competition with one another, and this competition was the backdrop for the explosive race to the Moon. [1] However, a longer-lasting, and some say more important, achievement has been the development of the International Space Station.

The International Space Station was not created overnight. It can trace <u>it's</u> lineage back to
                                   2

Salyut 1, the very first space station launched in 1971 by the
          3
Russians. In most respects, *Salyut 1* was actually a failure. For

example, before <u>plummeting, to Earth, it</u> orbited the planet for
                                   4
less than six months and was plagued by mechanical problems that ultimately resulted in the deaths of three cosmonauts.

1. The writer is considering adding the following clause to the end of the preceding sentence (replacing the period after *Moon* with a comma):

   > because both the Russians and the Americans wanted to reach the Moon first.

   Should the writer add this phrase here?

   A. Yes, because it specifies that both groups were competing.
   B. Yes, because it emphasizes to the reader the ultimate goal of the race.
   C. No, because it is clear from earlier in the sentence that both groups were competing to reach the Moon.
   D. No, because it provides additional information that distracts the reader from the primary focus of the passage.

2. Which choice makes the sentence most grammatically acceptable?

   F. **No Change**
   G. its'
   H. its
   J. their

3. Which choice makes the sentence most grammatically acceptable?

   A. **No Change**
   B. *1* the
   C. *1*; the
   D. *1*. The

4. Which choice makes the sentence most grammatically acceptable?

   F. **No Change**
   G. plummeting to Earth, it
   H. plummeting to Earth. It
   J. plummeting to Earth; it

[5] Yet, the *Salyut* experiment proved that extraterrestrial habitation was possible and allowed the Russians to develop other, more technically successful space stations in the years that

followed, the most famous of which was called *Mir*. [6]

Not to be outdone, the Americans looked to the mixed success the Russians enjoyed with *Salyut 1* and launched their own space station in 1973 called Skylab. Like the Russian space station, however, Skylab also had operational difficulties. Hit by debris, severe damage was suffered by it during the launch
                            7
and was inoperable until astronauts repaired it during numerous spacewalks. Once it was repaired, astronauts focused on

conducting mainly scientific experiments, and three separate
            8

crews successfully docked there throughout 1973 and 1974.
                                                        9
Though additional missions had been planned, none were ever
9
launched, and Skylab fell back to Earth in 1979 after about six years in orbit.

5. The writer is considering adding the following clause to the end of the preceding sentence (replacing the period after the word cosmonauts with a comma):

    who were honored as heroes at their funerals.

   Should the writer add this clause here?

   A. Yes, because it was not the cosmonauts' fault that they were killed.
   B. Yes, because it provides information that is not mentioned elsewhere in the passage.
   C. No, because it distracts the reader from the main focus of the paragraph.
   D. No, because no description of the funeral is provided.

6. Which of the following true statements, if added here, would best point out how successful *Mir* was?

   F. *Mir* orbited Earth for 14 years and hosted more than two dozen long-duration crews.
   G. The name *Mir* actually means *peace* in Russian.
   H. Unfortunately, Russian cosmonauts would stay on *Mir* for so long that they were unable to walk when they returned to Earth.
   J. *Mir* fell to Earth in 2001 and ended in a way reminiscent of *Salyut 1*'s fate thirty years earlier.

7. Which choice makes the sentence most grammatically acceptable?

   A. **No Change**
   B. it suffered severe damage
   C. severely damaged it suffered
   D. it was suffering from severe damage

8. The best placement for the underlined portion would be:

   F. where it is now.
   G. after the word *Once*.
   H. after the word *focused*.
   J. after the word *three*.

9. Which choice makes the sentence most grammatically acceptable?

   A. **No Change**
   B. 1974 though
   C. 1974, though
   D. 1974 though,

[1] This space station was successfully launched in 2000 and has hosted more than 67 crews from numerous countries since then. [2] In the 1990s, the end of the Cold War allowed the two nations to work together on the goal of achieving a sustainable habitat in outer space. [3] The Russian stations *Salyut* and *Mir* and the American Skylab laid the groundwork for the International Space Station. [10]

10. Which of the following sequences of sentences will make this paragraph most logical?

    F. **No Change**
    G. 1, 3, 2
    H. 2, 1, 3
    J. 2, 3, 1

ENGLISH PASSAGE DRILL 14 EXPLANATIONS

1. **C**   The question is asking whether a phrase should be added, so consider the content of the phrase and the surrounding context. The sentence describes how *the Russians and the Americans were in a fierce political competition with one other,* which provided *the backdrop for the explosive race to the Moon.* The new phrase repeats the idea of *competition,* so there is no need to add it. Eliminate (A) and (B). Choice (C) accurately states that *it is clear from earlier in the sentence that both groups were competing to reach the Moon,* so keep (C). The new phrase does not *distract the reader from the primary focus of the passage,* so eliminate (D). The correct answer is (C).

2. **H**   The question asks about grammar, so look at the answers to see what's changing. Pronouns are changing in the answer choices, so identify the word the pronoun refers back to: *It.* This word is singular, so eliminate (J). Next, eliminate (G) because this isn't a real word. Choice (F), *it's,* means "it is," which is not appropriate in this context. Eliminate (F). Choice (H), *its,* is a possessive pronoun, and the sentence is referring to the *lineage* of the International Space Station. The correct answer is (H).

3. **A**   The question asks about grammar, so look at the answers to see what's changing. Connecting punctuation is changing in the answer choices, so look for independent clauses. The first part of the sentence, *It can trace its lineage back to Salyut 1,* is an independent clause. The second part of the sentence, *the very first space station launched in 1971 by the Russians,* is not an independent clause. Both periods and semicolons can only be used between two independent clauses, so eliminate (C) and (D). The second part of the sentence is a descriptive phrase that is not necessary to the main meaning of the sentence, so it should be set off from the first part of the sentence by a comma. Eliminate (B). The correct answer is (A).

4. **G**   The question asks about grammar, so look at the answers to see what's changing. Connecting punctuation is changing in the answer choices, so look for independent clauses. The first part of the sentence, *For example, before plummeting to Earth,* is not an independent clause. Both periods and semicolons can only be used between two independent clauses, so eliminate (H) and (J). The phrase *to Earth* is necessary to the first part of the sentence, so it should not be set off by commas; eliminate (F). The correct answer is (G).

5. **C**   The question is asking whether a phrase should be added, so consider the content of the phrase and the surrounding context. The sentence describes the failure of *Salyut 1.* The new phrase states that the *cosmonauts who were killed on Salyut 1 were honored as heroes at their funerals.* The main focus of the sentence is the space station, not the cosmonauts, so the new phrase is not consistent and should not be added. Eliminate (A) and (B). Choice (C) accurately states that the phrase *distracts the reader from the main focus of the paragraph,* so keep (C). It is true that *no description of the funeral is provided,* but as *the funeral* is not consistent with the focus of the sentence, (D) does not provide an accurate reason not to include the phrase. Eliminate (D). The correct answer is (C).

6. **F**   The question is asking for the answer that would *best point out how successful Mir was,* so eliminate any answers that don't fulfill this goal. Choice (F) describes things that could be understood as successes, so keep (F). What *the name Mir…means* has nothing to do with success, so eliminate (G). Both the fact that *Russian cosmonauts…were unable to walk when they returned to Earth* and that *Mir fell to Earth* are negatives rather than successes, so eliminate (H) and (J). The correct answer is (F).

7. **B**   The question asks about grammar, so look at the answers to see what's changing. The order of the words is changing in the answer choices, so eliminate any answer that is overly wordy, creates an error, or is unclear. The sentence starts with the descriptive phrase *Hit by debris*. This phrase modifies the underlined portion, so the first noun in the underlined portion must be something that was *Hit by debris*. *Severe damage* could not have been *Hit by debris,* so eliminate (A). *Severely damaged* is another descriptive phrase that cannot be described by the opening phrase, so eliminate (C). *It* refers to *Skylab*, which could have been *Hit by debris,* so keep (B) and (D). The difference between (B) and (D) is the verb tense. A verb must be consistent in tense with the rest of the sentence. The other verbs in the sentence, *was* and *repaired,* are in simple past tense, so the underlined verb should also be in simple past tense. Choice (B) is in simple past tense. There is no need for the *-ing* ending, so eliminate (D). The correct answer is (B).

8. **H**   The question is asking for the *best placement for the underlined portion,* so try the word in each spot and eliminate any that don't offer a logical meaning. *Mainly* is an adverb that means "for the most part." There is no indication that the *experiments* were anything other than *scientific,* so eliminate (F). Adverbs can be used to describe verbs or adjectives, but not nouns, so *mainly* cannot describe *it;* eliminate (G). It makes sense to say that the *astronauts focused* "for the most part" *on conducting scientific experiments,* so keep (H). There is no indication that the *crews* were anything other than *separate,* so eliminate (J). The correct answer is (H).

9. **A**   The question asks about grammar, so look at the answers to see what's changing. Connecting punctuation is changing in the answer choices, so look for independent clauses. The first part of the sentence, *Once it was repaired...astronauts focused mainly on conducting scientific experiments, and three separate crews successfully docked there throughout 1973 and 1974,* is an independent clause. The second part of the sentence, *Though additional missions were planned, none were ever launched, and Skylab fell back to Earth in 1979 after about six years in orbit,* is also an independent clause. Two independent clauses must be separated by some type of punctuation other than a comma, so eliminate (B), (C), and (D). Choice (A) appropriately uses a period to separate the two independent clauses. The correct answer is (A).

10. **J**   The question is asking for the *most logical* sequence of sentences, so look for clues indicating sentences that must go before or after one another. Sentence 1 mentions *This space station,* so it must come after a reference to a space station. Sentence 3 mentions the *International Space Station,* so Sentence 1 must come after Sentence 3; eliminate (F), (G), and (H). The correct answer is (J).

Math Drills

NUMBER AND QUANTITY

These questions test your ability to work with numbers and apply your knowledge of the underlying concepts. Topics include real numbers, imaginary numbers, exponents, matrices, and vectors. A subcategory of Preparing for Higher Math, Number and Quantity questions make up 10–12% of the ACT Math Test.

There are two Number and Quantity Drills on the following pages, with easy to medium questions in the first drill and medium to hard questions in the second drill.

NUMBER AND QUANTITY DRILL 1

1. For integers x and y such that $xy = 14$, which of the following is NOT a possible value of x ?

   A. 2
   B. −7
   C. −8
   D. −14

2. Which of the following numbers is an imaginary number?

   F. $\sqrt{64}$

   G. $-\dfrac{4}{\sqrt{3}}$

   H. $-\sqrt{-64}$

   J. $-\sqrt{64}$

3. A geometric sequence has as its first 4 terms, −0.125, 1, −8, and 64. What is the 5th term of this sequence?

   A. 512
   B. −55
   C. −73
   D. −512

4. The difference of two integers is 6. The sum of the same two integers is 42. What is the lesser of the two integers?

   F. 18
   G. 19
   H. 23
   J. 24

5. Four matrices are given. Which of the following matrix products is undefined?

$$A = \begin{bmatrix} 3 \\ 2 \end{bmatrix} \qquad B = \begin{bmatrix} 1 & 8 \\ 7 & 3 \end{bmatrix}$$

$$C = \begin{bmatrix} 4 & 8 \\ 1 & 7 \end{bmatrix} \qquad D = \begin{bmatrix} 5 & 6 \\ 1 & 9 \\ 8 & 3 \end{bmatrix}$$

   A. BA
   B. BD
   C. CB
   D. DA

6. Vectors $\overrightarrow{WX}$ and $\overrightarrow{YZ}$ are shown in the standard (x,y) coordinate plane. Which of the following is the unit vector notation of the vector $\overrightarrow{WX} + \overrightarrow{YZ}$?

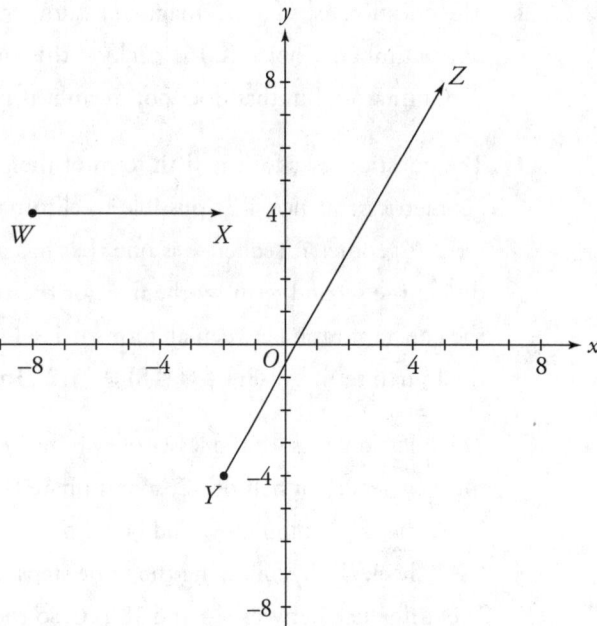

   F. $-8\mathbf{i} + 8\mathbf{j}$
   G. $-1\mathbf{i} + 8\mathbf{j}$
   H. $5\mathbf{i} + 12\mathbf{j}$
   J. $13\mathbf{i} + 12\mathbf{j}$

7. If a, b, and c are positive prime numbers, in the equation $a - b = c$, either b or c must represent which number?

   A. 13
   B. 11
   C. 5
   D. 2

8. A pair of numbers share a least common multiple (LCM) of 168. The larger number in the pair is 84. What is the greatest value the other number in the pair can have?

   F. 2
   G. 8
   H. 42
   J. 56

NUMBER AND QUANTITY DRILL 1 EXPLANATIONS

1. **C**   The question asks which value of *x* would NOT yield an integer solution for *y*. Try to use each of the answer choices as values for *x* and find a value of *y* for which *xy* = 14. In (A), if *x* = 2, *y* = 7. In (B), if *x* = –7, *y* = –2. In (D), if *x* = –14, *y* = –1. Only (C) does not have a complementary integer value for *y*. The correct answer is (C).

2. **H**   The question asks for an imaginary number. Taking the square root of a negative number yields an imaginary number. Choice (G) is tricky—this number is not *rationalized* (that is, it has a square root in the denominator), but that does not mean it is not a *real number*. The correct answer is (H).

3. **D**   The question asks for the fifth term of the geometric sequence. Even without knowing the definition of a geometric sequence, it is possible to eliminate (A) because a negative number must come next in the pattern. A geometric sequence is one that has a constant ratio between its terms. To find this constant ratio, divide the second term by the first (or the third by the second, the fourth by the third, etc.). In this case, the constant ratio between all terms is $1 \div (-0.125) = (-8) \div 1 = -8$. To find the fifth term, simply multiply the fourth term by -8: $64 \times (-8) = -512$. The correct answer is (D).

4. **F**   The question asks for the lesser of two integers with a difference of 6 and a sum of 42. The smaller number must be less than half of 42, so eliminate (H) and (J). Test the remaining answers. If the smaller number is 19, the larger number would be $42 - 19 = 23$. Since the difference between 23 and 19 is not 6, eliminate (G). Check (F) by following the same steps. If 18 is the smaller number, the larger number is $42 - 18 = 24$. The difference between 24 and 18 is 6, so the correct answer is (F).

5. **B**   An undefined matrix product is the result of attempting to multiply two matrices with incompatible dimensions. In order to multiply matrices, the number of columns in the first matrix must equal the number of rows in the second matrix. Because the dimensions are given as rows by columns (*A* is 2×1, *B* and *C* are both 2×2, and *D* is 3×2), the trick is that the middle numbers of the matrices must be the same. For (A), matrix *B* is 2×2, and matrix *A* is 2×1, so multiplying these together is $(2 \times 2)(2 \times 1)$. The middle numbers are the same, so this multiplication is possible. Eliminate (A) because the question asks for the product that's not possible. Choice (B) is $(2 \times 2)(3 \times 2)$. The middle numbers do not match, so this product is undefined. The correct answer is (B).

6. **J**   Unit vector notation is another way of describing the components of a vector. In two dimensions, **i** is the unit vector for the vector with components (1, 0), and **j** is the unit vector for the vector with components (0, 1). When measuring the components of a vector in the (*x, y*) coordinate plane, measure the displacement from the beginning of the vector to the end. Vector $\overrightarrow{WX}$ has components going 6 units directly to the right from point *W* to point *X*, so its components are (6, 0). Vector $\overrightarrow{YZ}$ goes 7 units right and 12 units up, so its components are (7, 12). Therefore, vector $\overrightarrow{WX} + \overrightarrow{YZ}$ will have components (6 + 7, 0 + 12), or (13, 12). In unit vector notation, the *x*-component becomes the coefficient on **i**, and the *y*-component becomes the coefficient on **j**. Therefore, the unit vector notation of $\overrightarrow{WX} + \overrightarrow{YZ}$ is 13**i** + 12**j**. The correct answer is (J).

7. **D** The question asks for the number that must be part of the given equation. Test the prime numbers from the answer choices in the equation. Since all the numbers in the equation $a - b = c$ must be positive prime numbers, the only possible result for c can be 2 (for example, $13 - 11 = 2$, and $7 - 5 = 2$). The only exceptions to $c = 2$ are $5 - 2 = 3$, $13 - 2 = 11$, and $7 - 2 = 5$. Even so, the only number common to all of these equations is 2. The correct answer is (D).

8. **J** The question asks for a number in a pair with a *least common multiple (LCM) of 168*. If 168 is a *multiple* of a given number, that number will be a factor of 168. Check each answer to see if it is a factor of 168. Start with (J), 56, since the question asks for the *greatest value*. The result is $\frac{168}{56} = 3$. Since 3 is a whole number, 168 is a multiple of 56. Check that 56 and 84 do not have a common multiple less than 168: the first two multiples of 84 are 84 and 168, and 84 is not a multiple of 56. Thus, 168 is the least common multiple of 84 and 56. The correct answer is (J).

NUMBER AND QUANTITY DRILL 2

1. What is the sequence of a, b, and c from greatest to least if
$a = \dfrac{5}{6} + \dfrac{6}{5}$, $b = \dfrac{3}{5} + \dfrac{5}{3}$, and $c = 3 - 1$?

   A. $c > a > b$
   B. $b > c > a$
   C. $b > a > c$
   D. $a > b > c$

2. The 12 numbers on a circular clock are equally spaced around the edges of the clock. Belinda chooses an integer, n, that is greater than 1. Beginning at a randomly chosen number, Belinda goes around the circle counterclockwise and paints in every nth number. She continues going around and around the clock, painting in every nth number, until all twelve numbers on the clock are painted. Which of the following could have been Belinda's integer n ?

   F. 2
   G. 3
   H. 7
   J. 9

3. If a is a factor of 32 and b is a factor of 45, the product of a and b could NOT be which of the following?

   A. 1
   B. 54
   C. 80
   D. 288

4. At the company YouGroove, 35 employees work in the sales department and 50 employees work in the operations department. Of these employees, 15 work in both the sales and the operations departments. How many of the 110 employees at YouGroove do NOT work in either the sales or the operations departments?

   F. 10
   G. 20
   H. 35
   J. 40

5. If $a^4 = 17,850,625$, which of the following is true for a ?

   A. $10 < a < 100$
   B. $100 < a < 1,000$
   C. $1,000 < a < 10,000$
   D. $10,000 < a < 100,000$

6. How many 4-letter orderings, where no letters are repeated, can be made using the letters of the word BADGERS ?

   F. 4
   G. 7
   H. 256
   J. 840

7. Which of the following expressions is equivalent to the expression $[f(f-1)(f-2) \dots (1)]^g$ for all positive integer values of f and g ?

   A. $(f!)^g$
   B. $(g!)^f$
   C. $(g^f)!$
   D. $(f+g)!$

8. The determinant of the matrix $\begin{bmatrix} 6 & x \\ 7 & 3 \end{bmatrix}$ has a value of -17. What is the value of x ?

   F. -35

   G. -5

   H. 5

   J. $\dfrac{59}{3}$

THIS PAGE IS INTENTIONALLY LEFT BLANK.

NUMBER AND QUANTITY DRILL 2 EXPLANATIONS

1. **C** The question asks for a comparison of variables representing expressions with fractions. Perform the calculation for each variable's expression, finding common denominators and using a calculator when necessary. The expression for c is the easiest to calculate, as it is simply $c = 3 - 1 = 2$. The expression for a becomes $a = \frac{5}{6} + \frac{6}{5} = \frac{25}{30} + \frac{36}{30} = \frac{61}{30}$. Use a calculator to determine that this is $2.0\overline{3}$. Because this is larger than 2, eliminate (A) and (B) as they indicate that $c > a$. The expression for b becomes $b = \frac{3}{5} + \frac{5}{3} = \frac{9}{15} + \frac{25}{15} = \frac{34}{15}$. Use a calculator to determine that this is $2.2\overline{6}$. Because this is larger than $2.0\overline{3}$, eliminate (D) which indicates that $a > b$. The correct answer is (C).

2. **H** The question asks for the value of n that would allow Belinda to paint in all 12 numbers on the clock. Draw the circular clock and mark 12 evenly spaced points on it, and start trying out the numbers for n in the given problem. Choose any starting point—let's say 2 for this example. Starting at 2 and painting in every second number, as in (F), the numbers painted in the first revolution will be 4, 6, 8, 10, 12; in the second revolution, they will be 2, 4, 6, 8, 10, 12. In other words, if the integer n is 2, then there is no way that all of the numbers on the face of the clock will be painted. Choices (G) and (J) all create the same issue. Only (H), $n = 7$, will fill in all of the numbers on successive revolutions. The correct answer is (H).

3. **B** The question asks which number could NOT be the result of multiplying together a factor from each of the two given numbers. Start by factoring the two given numbers, being careful not to forget that every real number has 1 and itself as factors. The factors of 32 are 32, 16, 8, 4, 2, and 1; the factors of 45 are 45, 15, 9, 5, 3, and 1. Now test the answers by seeing if one number taken from each list can be multiplied together to equal the answer. Choice (A) is 1×1, (C) is 16×5, and (D) is 32×9. Since there is no factor of 32 that can be multiplied by a factor of 45 to equal 54, the correct answer is (B).

4. **J** The question asks for the number of employees who do NOT work in either operations or sales. To solve this problem, use the group formula: $Total = Group_1 + Group_2 - Both + Neither$. This becomes $110 = 35 + 50 - 15 + Neither$. This simplifies to $110 = 70 + Neither$, so $Neither = 40$, (J). Choice (F) erroneously subtracts all the smaller values from the total number of employees; (G) subtracts employees working in both departments from the number of employees in sales; and (H) subtracts employees working in both departments from the number of employees in operations. The correct answer is (J).

5. **A** The question asks which inequality is true for a given an equation involving a. There are variables in the answer choices, so plug in. Start in the middle of the answer choices and try 1,000 because it is between (B) and (C). Plug this into the equation to get $1,000^4 = 1,000,000,000,000$. This is too large, so eliminate (C) and (D). Next, try 100, which is between (A) and (B). Plug this into the equation to get $100^4 = 100,000,000$. This is still too large, so eliminate (B). The correct answer is (A).

6. **J** The question asks for the number of possible orderings for any four letters in the word BADGERS. First, determine how many possible options there are for each of the four positions. Since there are seven total letters in BADGERS, any of the seven letters could be the first in the new four-letter combination. Since letters cannot be repeated, there are only six possible options for the second letter in the combination, five possible options for the third, and four possible options for the fourth. To find the total number of combinations, multiply together the number of possible options for each of the four positions to get $7 \times 6 \times 5 \times 4$ = 840 orderings. The correct answer is (J).

7. **A** The question asks for an equivalent form of the provided expression. There are variables in the answer choices, so plug in. Keep the numbers small due to all of the exponents and use the ! button on a calculator to do the hard work. Make $f = 3$ and $g = 2$. Plug in these numbers until the last term in the brackets is equal to 1. The given expression becomes $[3(3 - 1)(3 - 2)]^2$. This simplifies to $[3(2)(1)]^2$ or $[6]^2$, which is 36. This is the target value, circle it. Now plug $f = 3$ and $g = 2$ into the answer choices to see which one matches the target value. Choice (A) becomes $(3!)^2$, which is 6^2 or 36. This matches the target, so keep (A), but check the other answers just in case. Choice (B) becomes $(2!)^3 = 2^3 = 8$. Eliminate (B). Choice (C) becomes $(2^3)!$ or 8!, which is 40,320. Eliminate (C). Choice (D) becomes $(2 + 3)!$ or 5!, which is 120. Eliminate (D). The correct answer is (A).

8. **H** The question asks for the value of x given the *determinant of the matrix*. For any matrix in the form $\begin{bmatrix} a & b \\ c & d \end{bmatrix}$, the determinant is defined as $ad - bc$. Use this definition to plug in the known values. In the given matrix, $a = 6$, $b = x$, $c = 7$, and $d = 3$. Thus, the determinant becomes $-17 = (6)(3) - (x)(7)$. This simplifies to $-17 = 18 - 7x$. Subtract 18 from both sides of the equation to get $-35 = -7x$, then divide both sides by -7 to get $5 = x$. The correct answer is (H).

ALGEBRA

Algebra questions on the ACT test your ability to solve various types of equations or inequalities, find solutions to systems of equations or inequalities, and model word problems as equations or inequalities. A subcategory of Preparing for Higher Math, Algebra questions make up 17–20% of the ACT Math Test.

There are two Algebra Drills on the following pages, with easy to medium questions in the first drill and medium to hard questions in the second drill.

ALGEBRA DRILL 1

1. What is the value of x when $\dfrac{4x}{5} + 7 = 6$?

   A. $-\dfrac{4}{5}$

   B. -1

   C. $-\dfrac{5}{4}$

   D. -5

2. A beaker contains one ounce of Solution A and n ounces of Solution B. The salt content of each ounce of Solution A is 3.1 grams, and the salt content of each ounce of Solution B is 2.3 grams. If the beaker has a total salt content of 10 grams, which of the following models the salt content of the beaker?

   F. $2.3n = 3.1n + 10$
   G. $2.3n = 3.1 + 10$
   H. $2.3n + 3.1n = 10$
   J. $2.3n + 3.1 = 10$

3. What is the value of $4 + 3^{x-y}$ when $x = 3$ and $y = -1$?

   A. 13
   B. 16
   C. 30
   D. 85

4. Carla has 5 times as many notebooks as her brother does. If they have 42 notebooks between them, how many notebooks does Carla have?

   F. 30
   G. 35
   H. 37
   J. 47

5. Pat's Pastries baked 80 apple pies and 50 loaves of apple bread to be sold at a 2-day Fall Festival. The pies were sold for $25 each and the loaves of bread were sold for $10 each. Which of the following expressions gives the total amount of money, in dollars, collected from selling all of the apple pies and b of the loaves of bread?

   A. $35b$
   B. $b + 80$
   C. $10b + 1{,}250$
   D. $10b + 2{,}000$

6. In the equation $\dfrac{3^{3n}}{9^2} = 3^2$, what is the value of n?

   F. 1
   G. 2
   H. 4
   J. 81

7. Kunal, a pharmacist, sorted bottles of medicine in a box at the end of the day, and then he left the office for the evening. The next day, he realized he lost the piece of paper that had the quantities of the different packages in the box. He recalled that there were only 12-dose and 24-dose count bottles of medicine. He also remembered that there were 48 bottles in the box with a total of 720 doses. How many 24-dose count bottles of medicine were in the box?

   A. 4
   B. 12
   C. 36
   D. 52

8. The Crestview High School student body is made up only of freshmen, sophomores, juniors, and seniors. 25% of the students are freshmen, 35% are sophomores, and 20% are juniors. If no student can be considered to be in two classes, and there are 150 seniors, how many students make up the Crestview High School student body?

   F.   500
   G.   600
   H.   750
   J.   1,500

9. $(2 - 4t + 5t^2) - (3t^2 + 2t - 7)$ is equivalent to:

   A. $2t^2 - 6t + 9$
   B. $2t^2 - 2t + 9$
   C. $8t^2 - 6t - 5$
   D. $8t^4 - 6t^2 - 5$

10. If $y = 6$ and $y = -3$ are solutions to the equation $y^2 - 3y + p = 0$, what is the value of p?

   F.   18
   G.   3
   H.   -3
   J.   -18

11. Which of the following is equivalent to $(x^4 - 4)(x^4 + 4)$?

   A. $x^8 - 16$
   B. $x^8 + 16$
   C. $x^{16} - 16$
   D. $x^8 - 8x^4 - 16$

12. What is the solution to the equation $9x - (3x - 1) = 3$?

   F. -3

   G. $\dfrac{1}{3}$

   H. $\dfrac{2}{3}$

   J.   3

ALGEBRA DRILL 1 EXPLANATIONS

1. **C** The question asks for the value of x, so isolate the variable. First subtract 7 from both sides to get $\frac{4x}{5} = -1$. Next, multiply both sides by 5 to get $4x = -5$. Finally, divide both sides by 4 to get $x = -\frac{5}{4}$. Choice (A) is the reciprocal of the correct answer. Choices (B) and (D) are partial answers. The correct answer is (C).

2. **J** The question asks for an equation that models a specific situation. Translate the information into bite-sized pieces and eliminate after each piece. One piece of information says that there is *one ounce of Solution A* in the beaker. Look for other information about Solution A. The question states that *the salt content of Solution A is 3.1 grams*. The salt content provided by Solution A is 3.1 per ounce for one ounce, or just 3.1 grams. The 3.1 should not be multiplied by n. Eliminate (F) and (H). Compare the remaining answer choices. The difference between (G) and (J) is the side of the equation that contains 3.1. The question states that the total salt content is 10 grams. This includes the 3.1 grams from Solution A plus the 2.3 grams per ounces from Solution B. The 3.1 should not be added to the 10, so eliminate (G). The correct answer is (J).

3. **D** The question asks for the value of the expression for the given values of x and y. Plug in the values given into the expression, using order of operations (PEMDAS). Start with the exponent: $4 + 3^{(3-(-1))} = 4 + 3^4 = 4 + 81 = 85$. Choice (A) confuses the signs in the exponent, and (B) multiplies 3×4 instead of finding 3^4. Choice (C) subtracts 1 from the whole expression, instead of treating it as part of the exponent. The correct answer is (D).

4. **G** The question asks for the number of notebooks Carla has. Set up an equation. If Carla's brother has x notebooks, Carla has $5x$ notebooks, and $5x + x = 42$. To find x, first add like terms to get $6x = 42$; then divide both sides by 6 to get $x = 7$. That means that Carla has $5(7) = 35$ notebooks. Alternatively, use the answer choices to solve this problem: since the answers represent the number of notebooks Carla has, divide the answers by 5 to determine how many notebooks her brother has. Then add that number to the original answer and choose the one that totals 42. A calculation error of $x = 6$ leads to (F). Choices (H) and (J) add and subtract numbers from the problem without answering the question. The correct answer is (G).

5. **D** The question asks for the expression that represents the total amount of money Pat's Pastries earned selling pie and bread. Add the products of 80 pies sold at $25 each and b loaves of bread sold at $10 each to get $(80 \times 25) + (b \times 10) = 2,000 + 10b$. Choice (C) finds the price of 50 pies instead of 80, and (B) gives the number of baked goods sold. Choice (A) finds the price of b loaves of bread and b apple pies. The correct answer is (D).

6. **G** The question asks for the value of the variable n in an equation with exponents. When dealing with questions about exponents, remember the MADSPM rules. The DS part of the acronym indicates that Dividing matching bases means to Subtract the exponents. In order to do this, a common base is needed.

Rewrite 9 as 3^2. The equation becomes $\dfrac{3^{3n}}{\left(3^2\right)^2} = 3^2$. The denominator now uses the PM part of the acronym, which means that to raise a base number with an exponent to another Power, Multiply the exponents. The equation now becomes $\dfrac{3^{3n}}{3^4} = 3^2$. Now subtract the exponents to get $3^{3n-4} = 3^2$. The exponents on the bases are equal, which means that $3n - 4 = 2$. Add 4 to both sides of the equation to get $3n = 6$. Divide both sides by 3 to get $n = 2$. This question can also be solved by plugging in the answers. It may be necessary to try a few answers on a calculator, but that may be a more straightforward approach than solving. Either way, the correct answer is (G).

7. **B** The question asks for a value in a model of a specific situation. Since the question asks for a specific value and the answers contain numbers in increasing order, plug in the answers. Begin by labeling the answers as "24 doses" and start with (C), 36. If there are 36 bottles with 24 doses in each bottle, those bottles contain 36(24) = 864 doses. There were only 720 doses altogether, so this is too many. Eliminate (C). There must be fewer of the 24-dose bottles to have a smaller total number of doses, so eliminate (D) as well. Try (B), 12. If there are 12 bottles with 24 doses in each bottle, those bottles contain 12(24) = 288 doses. There were 48 bottles, so with 12 of the 24-dose bottles, there would be 48 − 12 = 36 of the 12-dose bottles. These bottles would have 36(12) = 432 doses. Together, the two types of bottles would have 288 + 432 = 720 doses. This matches the information in the question, so stop here. The correct answer is (B).

8. **H** The question asks for the total number of students at Crestview High School. First find what percentage of students are seniors. Since the percentage of students who are not seniors is 25 + 35 + 20 = 80, the remaining 20% of the students are seniors. Since there are 150 seniors, 150 is 20% of the total number of students. Now put the numbers into an equation: 150 = 0.20 × *total*. Divide both sides by 0.20 to find that the total is 750. Choice (G) miscalculates 150 to be 25% of the total, and (F) miscalculates it to be 30% of the total. Choice (J) resembles the number of students but does not use the information given. The correct answer is (H).

9. **A** The question asks for an equivalent form of the given expression. Distribute the minus sign throughout the parentheses before combining like terms: $(2 − 4t + 5t^2) − (3t^2 + 2t − 7) = 2 − 4t + 5t^2 − 3t^2 − 2t + 7 = 2t^2 − 6t + 9$. The other choices all confuse signs in calculating. Choice (D) also adds the exponents of the terms. The correct answer is (A).

10. **J** The question asks for the value of a constant in an equation given the solutions. To find the constant p, plug one of the solutions into the equation for y and solve for p. Plug $y = 6$ into the equation to get $(6)^2 − 3(6) + p = 0$. The equation becomes 36 − 18 + p = 0. Simplify to get 18 + p = 0. Subtract 18 from both sides of the equation to get $p = −18$. The correct answer is (J).

11. **A** The question asks for the answer that is equivalent to the expression given in the question. In order to multiply factors, use FOIL (First, Outer, Inner, Last). Remember to *add* exponents when multiplying numbers with the same base and watch the signs carefully. The expression becomes $x^8 + 4x^4 - 4x^4 - 16 = x^8 - 16$. Choice (C) multiplies the exponents instead of adding them. Choices (B) and (D) confuse the signs. The correct answer is (A).

12. **G** The question asks for the solution to the equation. First distribute the minus sign through the parentheses to get $9x - 3x + 1 = 3$. Combine the terms on the left and subtract 1 from both sides to get $6x = 2$. Divide both sides by 3 to find that $x = \dfrac{1}{3}$. Choice (H) does not distribute the parentheses, and (F) and (J) divide incorrectly. The correct answer is (G).

ALGEBRA DRILL 2

1. Which of the following values of x does NOT satisfy the inequality $|x - 3| \geq 12$?

   A. -15
   B. -9
   C. 9
   D. 15

2. What is the matrix product $\begin{bmatrix} -1 & 0 & 1 \end{bmatrix} \begin{bmatrix} x \\ y \\ z \end{bmatrix}$?

   F. $\begin{bmatrix} -x & 0 & x \\ -y & 0 & y \\ -z & 0 & z \end{bmatrix}$

   G. $\begin{bmatrix} -x & -y & -z \\ 0 & 0 & 0 \\ x & y & z \end{bmatrix}$

   H. $\begin{bmatrix} -xz \end{bmatrix}$

   J. $\begin{bmatrix} z-x \end{bmatrix}$

3. Three dogs—an Akita, a beagle, and a collie—each have been given several chew toys by their owners. The beagle has five times as many toys as the Akita and collie have together, and the collie has three fewer toys than the Akita. If the Akita has a toys and the beagle has b toys, what is the relationship between a and b ?

   A. $b = a - 3$
   B. $b = 5a$
   C. $b = 10a - 15$
   D. $b = 10a + 15$

4. Which of the following is a COMPLETE factorization of the expression $12b^2c + 6bc + 3b$?

   F. $4bc + 2c + 1$
   G. $3b(9bc + 2c + 1)$
   H. $3b(4bc + 2c + 1)$
   J. $3b(4bc + 2c)$

5. What is the y-coordinate of the solution of the following system, presuming the system has a solution?

   $$8x + y = 30$$
   $$8x + 4y = 96$$

   A. 1
   B. 19
   C. 22
   D. The system has no solution.

6. In a Spanish class there are m students, of which n did NOT pass the last exam. Which of the following is a general expression for the fraction of the class that did receive a passing grade?

   F. $\dfrac{m-n}{m}$

   G. $\dfrac{m-n}{n}$

   H. $\dfrac{n-m}{n}$

   J. $\dfrac{n-m}{m}$

7. What is the solution set of $\sqrt[5]{x^2 + 4x} = 2$?

   A. $\{4\}$
   B. $\{-4, 8\}$
   C. $\{-8, 4\}$
   D. $\{-2, \pm 2\sqrt{2}\}$

8. Which of the following defines the solution set for the system of inequalities given?

$$0 > 3x - 6$$
$$-4 < x$$

   F. $x < 2$
   G. $-4 < x < 18$
   H. $-4 < x < -2$
   J. $-4 < x < 2$

9. The inequality $|a - 3| > 9$ is satisfied by the same set of values for a as which of the following inequalities:

   A. $a < -6$ or $a > 6$
   B. $a < -6$ or $a > 12$
   C. $a < -12$ or $a > 6$
   D. $a < -12$ or $a > 12$

10. If it can be determined, what is the least value of the expression $\dfrac{a}{a+b}$ given $a \geq 10$ and $2 \leq b \leq 5$?

   F. $\dfrac{5}{6}$

   G. $\dfrac{2}{3}$

   H. $\dfrac{1}{3}$

   J.   Cannot be determined from the given information

11. If $-6 \leq a \leq -4$ and $3 \leq b \leq 7$, what is the maximum value of $|a - 2b|$?

   A. 11
   B. 18
   C. 20
   D. 42

12. If A, x, and y are all distinct numbers, and $A = \dfrac{xy - 2}{x - y}$, which of the following represents x, in terms of A and y ?

   F. $\dfrac{Ay - 2}{A - y}$

   G. $\dfrac{A - 2}{x - 1}$

   H. $\dfrac{A - y}{x - y}$

   J. $\dfrac{Ay - 2}{A + y}$

ALGEBRA DRILL 2 EXPLANATIONS

1. **C**   The question asks for the value that does NOT satisfy the given inequality, so eliminate answers that **do** satisfy it. One approach to this problem is to test all the answer choices. When 9 is put in as the value of x, the result is $|9 - 3| \geq 12$, which becomes $6 \geq 12$. This is false. Alternatively, solve algebraically. The inequality becomes two expressions: $x - 3 \geq 12$ or $x - 3 \leq -12$. Solve by adding 3 to both sides of both inequalities to get $x \geq 15$ or $x \leq -9$. Only (C) does not fit these ranges. The other choices either place the inequality signs in the wrong direction or confuse the positive/negative values within the absolute value. The correct answer is (C).

2. **J**   Start by determining the size of the product matrix. The first matrix has dimensions 1×3, and the second matrix has dimensions 3×1. The product matrix will have the same number of rows as the first matrix and the same number of columns as the second matrix. In other words, the product matrix will have the outside values of the two dimensions. Therefore, the product matrix will have dimensions 1×1; eliminate (F) and (G). To multiply the matrices, find the dot product. Multiply each element in the row of the first matrix by its corresponding element in the column of the second matrix; then add the products. Therefore, the dot product is $(-1 \times x) + (0 \times y) + (1 \times z)$, which is $-x + 0 + z$, or $z - x$. The correct answer is (J).

3. **C**   The question asks for an equation relating to the relationship between two sets of dog toys. There are variables in the answer choices, so plug in. Make $a = 5$, the number of toys the Akita has. The question states that *the collie has three fewer toys than the Akita*, so the collie has $5 - 3 = 2$ toys. The question also states that *the beagle has five times as many toys as the Akita and collie have together*. This means that $b = 5(5 + 2) = 5(7) = 35$. Now check the answer choices using $a = 5$ and $b = 35$ to see which equation is true. Choice (A) becomes $35 = 5 - 3$ or $35 = 2$. This is not true, so eliminate (A). Choice (B) becomes $35 = 5(5)$ or $35 = 25$. Eliminate (B). Choice (C) becomes $35 = 10(5) - 15$, which is $35 = 50 - 15$ or $35 = 35$. This is true, but check (D) just in case. Choice (D) becomes $35 = 10(5) + 15$, which is $35 = 50 + 15$ or $35 = 65$. Eliminate (D). The correct answer is (C).

4. **H**   The question asks for a complete factorization of the expression. Consider each element of the three terms and factor if possible. Look first at the coefficients: 12, 6, and 3 are all divisible by 3, so factor out a 3 to get $3(4b^2c + 2bc + b)$. Now consider the b terms: since each of the three terms contains a b, factor out a b to get $3b(4bc + 2c + 1)$. Since there is not a c in all three terms, this variable cannot be factored out. The correct answer is (H).

5. **C**   The question asks for the y-coordinate of the solution to the system. Since each equation contains an $8x$, use the elimination method to solve for y. Subtract the first equation from the second.

    $$8x + 4y = 96$$
    $$\underline{- (8x + y = 30)}$$
    $$0x + 3y = 66$$

    Divide both sides of the equation $3y = 66$ by 3 to find that $y = 22$. Choice (A) gives the value of the x-coordinate in the system. The correct answer is (C).

6. **F** The question asks for a fraction of the students. A fraction is a part/whole relationship, so this fraction is equal to $\frac{\text{\# of students who passed}}{\text{total \# of students}}$. If there are m students in the class, m must be the denominator, so eliminate (G) and (H). The number of students who received a passing grade is calculated by subtracting the number who didn't pass the last exam, n, from the total number of students, m. Choice (J) would give a negative fraction, which is not possible. The correct answer is (F).

7. **C** The question asks for the solution set to the given equation. To isolate x, first raise both sides of the equation to the fifth power to get rid of the fifth root: $\left(\sqrt[5]{x^2 + 4x}\right)^5 = 2^5$ becomes $x^2 + 4x = 32$. Then, subtract 32 from both sides to get a standard quadratic form: $x^2 + 4x - 32 = 0$. Factor the quadratic to get $(x + 8)(x - 4) = 0$. Set each factor equal to 0 and solve to find that $x = -8$ or $x = 4$. Alternatively, try the answers in the equation to determine all those that work. Choice (A) gives only one of the possible values for x. Choice (B) reverses the signs. Choice (D) is the result of taking away the radical but squaring the 2, rather than raising it to the fifth power, and then using the quadratic formula. The correct answer is (C).

8. **J** The question asks for the solution set for the system of inequalities. Manipulate the first given inequality to get x alone on one side. Subtract $3x$ from both sides to get $-3x > -6$. Then divide both sides by -3 to get $x < 2$. Don't forget to flip the inequality sign when dividing both sides by a negative number. Combine the first inequality with the second to get $-4 < x < 2$. Choice (F) gives the solution to only the first inequality. Choices (G) and (H) make errors in manipulating the first inequality. The correct answer is (J).

9. **B** The question asks for the set of values satisfied by an inequality. There are variables in the answer choices, so plug in. Pick a number that is in some answer choice ranges but not others to try in the inequality. Make $a = 7$. The inequality becomes $|7 - 3| > 9$, which simplifies to $|4| > 9$ or $4 > 9$. This is not true, so 7 does not satisfy the inequality. Eliminate (A) and (C) because they include 7. The difference between the remaining answer choices is whether a is less than -6 or -12. Try a number between those values such as $a = -7$. The inequality becomes $|-7 - 3| > 9$, which simplifies to $|-10| > 9$ or $10 > 9$. This is true, so -7 satisfies the inequality. Eliminate (D) because it does not include this value. The correct answer is (B).

10. **G** The question asks for the least value of an expression given limits on the variables in the expression. Because all the values must be positive, the fraction will be smallest when the denominator is as large as possible. Therefore, b should be the largest value possible, which is 5. If this isn't obvious, try plugging in a few values for b to see what happens. Let $a = 10$ and $b = 2$. The expression becomes $\frac{10}{10+2} = \frac{10}{12} = \frac{5}{6}$. Now try $b = 5$. The expression becomes $\frac{10}{10+5} = \frac{10}{15} = \frac{2}{3}$. The expression

has a smaller value when b is larger, so keep $b = 5$ and plug in values for a to see what happens as a changes in value. The calculations already got $\frac{2}{3}$ as a possible answer, so eliminate (F), which is larger than $\frac{2}{3}$. Plug in a larger number for a. Let $a = 15$. The expression becomes $\frac{15}{15+5} = \frac{15}{20} = \frac{3}{4}$. This is larger than $\frac{2}{3}$. Increasing the value of a only causes the fraction to increase. Therefore, $\frac{2}{3}$ is the smallest possible value for the fraction. The correct answer is (G).

11. **C** The question asks for the maximum value of the expression. Pair together various combinations of the smallest and largest possible values for a and b. Then test those pairs in the expression $|a - 2b|$. Using $a = -6$ and $b = 3$ gives $|-6 - 2(3)|$, which reduces to $|-12|$ and yields 12. Since this value is greater than 11, eliminate (A). Now try $a = -6$ and $b = 7$: this gives $|-6 - 2(7)|$ and solves to $|-20| = 20$. Since 20 is greater than 18, eliminate (B). Neither of the two remaining combinations ($a = -4$, $b = -3$ and $a = -4$, $b = 7$) gives a value for $|a - 2b|$ that is larger than 20, so the correct answer is (C).

12. **F** The question asks for the value of x in terms of A and y. To solve algebraically, begin with the original equation $A = \frac{xy - 2}{x - y}$ and multiply both sides by $(x - y)$ to get $A(x - y) = xy - 2$. Distribute the A to get $Ax - Ay = xy - 2$, and then get both terms that contain an x to the same side of the equation. Adding Ay to both sides gives $Ax = xy - 2 + Ay$, and subtracting xy from both sides gives $Ax - xy = Ay - 2$. Factor the x out on the left side to get $x(A - y) = Ay - 2$, and divide both sides by $(A - y)$ to get $x = \frac{Ay - 2}{A - y}$. It is also possible to solve this question by substituting numerical values for the three variables: for example, if x is set equal to 4 and y is set equal to 3, then $A = \frac{(4)(3) - 2}{4 - 3} = 10$. Substitute $y = 3$ and $A = 10$ into the answer choices, and only (F) equals the value that was assigned to x, which was $x = 4$. The correct answer is (F).

FUNCTIONS

The ACT tests several types of functions—including linear, exponential, and logarithmic—in the contexts of solving, modeling, and graphing. A subcategory of Preparing for Higher Math, Functions questions make up 17–20% of the ACT Math Test.

There are two Functions Drills on the following pages, with easy to medium questions in the first drill and medium to hard questions in the second drill.

FUNCTIONS DRILL 1

1. A function f is defined by $f(x,y) = x - (xy - y)$. What is the value of $f(8,6)$?

 A. −46
 B. −34
 C. 46
 D. 50

2. The second term of an arithmetic sequence is −2, and the third term is 8. What is the first term?

 (Note: An arithmetic sequence has a common difference between consecutive terms.)

 F. −12

 G. −10

 H. $\dfrac{1}{2}$

 J. 3

3. A cellular phone company unveiled a new plan for new customers. It will charge a flat rate of $100 for initial connection and service for the first two months, and $60 for service each subsequent month. If Bob subscribes to this plan for one year, how much does he pay in total for the year?

 A. $600
 B. $700
 C. $800
 D. $820

4. For the first several weeks after hiring a private tutor, Teddy's score on a standardized test increased slowly. As Teddy began to understand the concepts more clearly, though, his standardized test scores improved more rapidly. After several more weeks, Teddy stopped working with his tutor and his scores did not improve any more. Which of the following graphs could represent all of Teddy's standardized test scores as a function of time, in weeks, after he hired a private tutor?

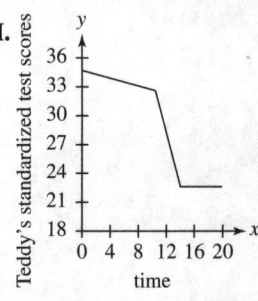

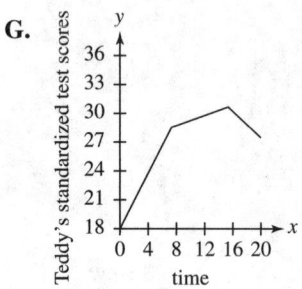

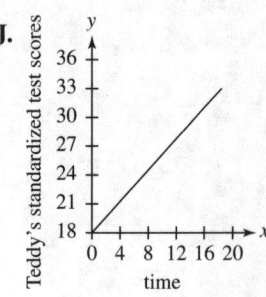

5. For $x = 2$, what is the value of $j(x) + k(x)$ when $j(x) = 4(3)^x$ and $k(x) = \dfrac{6}{x}$?

 A. 27
 B. 33
 C. 39
 D. 147

6. The percent P of a population that has completed 4 years of college is given by the function $P(t) = -0.001t^2 + 0.4t$, where t represents time, in years. What percent of the population has completed four years of college after 20 years, to the nearest tenth?

 F. 0.1
 G. 7.6
 H. 8.0
 J. 160.0

7. On April 8th, a flower at Blooming Acres Florist was 15.0 centimeters tall. On April 16th, the flower was 17.4 centimeters tall. If the flower grew at a constant rate, on what day was the flower 16.5 centimeters tall?

   A. April 12th
   B. April 13th
   C. April 14th
   D. April 15th

8. Given $g(x) = 4x^2 - 8x + 2$, what is the value of $g(-5)$?

   F. −138
   G. −58
   H. 142
   J. 442

9. In a certain sequence of numbers, each term after the 1st term is the result of adding 2 to the previous term and multiplying that sum by 3. If the 4th term in the sequence is 186, what is the 2nd term?

   A. 2
   B. 4
   C. 18
   D. 60

10. Aleksandra began collecting model airplanes in May of 2025. The number of model airplanes that she owns in each month can be modeled by the function $A(m) = 2m + 2$, where $m = 0$ corresponds to May. Using this model, how many model airplanes would you expect Aleksandra to own in December of 2025?

    F. 2
    G. 14
    H. 16
    J. 18

11. A restaurant decides on the following production model, $N = x^2 - 600x - 160,000$, where N is the number of ounces of flour the restaurant purchases each month, based on the number of ounces, x, the restaurant uses during the preceding month. According to this model, what is the greatest quantity of flour, in number of ounces, that the restaurant can use during a month, without having to purchase any new flour the next month?

    A. 800
    B. 550
    C. 400
    D. 350

FUNCTIONS DRILL 1 EXPLANATIONS

1. **B**   The question asks for the value of the function for the provided values of *x* and *y*. Substitute 8 and 6 for *x* and *y*, respectively, into the equation $f(x,y)$ to get $f(8,6) = 8 - [(8 \times 6) - 6] = 8 - 42 = -34$. Choices (A), (C), and (D) are wrong because they do not distribute the negative correctly. The correct answer is (B).

2. **F**   The question asks for the first term of the arithmetic sequence. First, calculate the difference of the third and second terms: $8 - (-2) = 10$. The first term, therefore, is the second term minus the difference: $(-2) - 10 = -12$. Choice (G) is a variation of the actual common difference, rather than the value of the first term. Choice (H) calculates the first term in a geometric, rather than arithmetic, sequence. Choice (J) incorrectly uses –2 as the first term and calculates what would then be the second. The correct answer is (F).

3. **B**   The question asks for the total cost of Bob's cell phone plan over a single year. Because the flat rate of $100 includes the first two months, Bob will be billed $60/month for only 10 months out of the year. The total cost is $100 + $60 (10) = $700, so (B) is correct. Choice (A) is the result of mistakenly charging $100 for every two-month period. The flat rate applies only for the first two months. Choice (C) incorrectly charges the flat rate twice for the first two months. Choice (D) adds 12, rather than 10, months of service charges to the flat rate. The correct answer is (B).

4. **F**   The question asks which graph matches the description of Teddy's test scores. Use Process of Elimination. Teddy's standardized test scores do not decrease at any point, so eliminate (G). Nor do they *only* increase—at the end, his scores leveled off and neither increased nor decreased, so eliminate (J). Since these scores level off at the end, not in the middle, eliminate (H). Only (F) gives an accurate representation of scores that increase slowly, then increase quickly, and then remain constant. The correct answer is (F).

5. **C**   The question asks for the sum of two functions for a given value of *x*. In function notation, the number inside the parentheses is the *x*-value that goes into the function, and the value that comes out of the function is the *y*-value. To get $j(2)$, plug $x = 2$ into the *j* function to get $j(2) = 4(3)^2 = 4(9) = 36$. To get $k(2)$, plug $x = 2$ into the *k* function to get $k(2) = \dfrac{6}{2} = 3$. To get $j(2) + k(2)$, add the values together to get $36 + 3 = 39$. The correct answer is (C).

6. **G**   The question asks for the value of the given function after a certain amount of time. To find the percent, *P*, substitute 20 for *t* to calculate $-0.001(20)^2 + 0.4(20) = 7.6$. Choice (F) is the rounded value of 0.076%, which is not equivalent to 7.6%. Choice (H) may be the result of not paying attention to the order of operations (PEMDAS) or distribution of the negative sign. Choice (J) results if t^2 and *t* are switched. The correct answer is (G).

7. **B** The question asks for the day on which the flower reached a certain height. Work through the problem one step at a time. Find the flower's growth rate by dividing the total growth by the number of days: $\frac{17.4 - 15.0}{16 - 8} = \frac{2.4}{8} = 0.3$ cm per day. To find when the flower was 16.5 cm tall, first determine how much it has grown since April 8: $16.5 - 15 = 1.5$ cm. Then find how many days it took to grow that much by dividing the growth by the rate to get $\frac{1.5 \text{ cm}}{0.3 \text{ cm/day}} = 5 \text{ days}$. The day that is 5 days after April 8 is April 13. The correct answer is (B).

8. **H** The question asks for the value of the function when $x = -5$. Substitute -5 for x in the function and solve: $4(-5)^2 - 8(-5) + 2$ becomes $4(25) - (-40) + 2$. This simplifies to $100 + 40 + 2$ and ultimately equals 142. Choice (J) incorrectly applies the order of operations for $4x^2$ by multiplying first and then squaring the result. Choice (G) mistakenly gives the value of -5^2 as -25, and (F) repeats this mistake and confuses positive and negative signs for the second term. The correct answer is (H).

9. **C** The question asks for the second term in the sequence. Try the answer choices to see which one matches the information in the question. For (C), if the second term is 18, then the third term is $(18 + 2) \times 3 = 60$, and the fourth term is $(60 + 2) \times 3 = 186$. Alternatively, work backward: if the fourth term is 186, then the third term is $(186 \div 3) - 2 = 60$, and the second term is $(60 \div 3) - 2 = 18$. Choices (B) and (D) are the 1st and 3rd terms of the sequence, respectively. The correct answer is (C).

10. **H** The question asks for the number of model airplanes that Aleksandra would own by December 2008. To solve for the function, determine the value of m in December. Since December is 7 months after May and $m = 0$ in May, $m = 7$ in December. Substitute 7 for m in the function to get $A(7) = 2(7) + 2$, so Aleksandra will have 16 model airplanes. Choice (F) is the number of airplanes she had in May. Choices (G) and (J) both substitute incorrect values for m in the equation when solving. The correct answer is (H).

11. **A** The question asks for the greatest quantity of flour the restaurant could use in a month without needing to purchase any new flour for the next month. Since N represents the amount of flour the restaurant would need to purchase, set $N = 0$ and test the possible answer choices. The question asks for the greatest quantity that satisfies the equation, so start with (A), which is $x = 800$. Substituting this value into the equation $0 = x^2 - 600x - 160{,}000$ gives $0 = 800^2 - 600(800) - 160{,}000$, which simplifies to $0 = 640{,}000 - 480{,}000 - 160{,}000$ and ultimately yields $0 = 0$. Because 800 satisfies the equation and is the largest available value, the correct answer is (A).

FUNCTIONS DRILL 2

1. Which of the following defines a function g from R onto S given the sets shown?

    $R = \{0, 1, 2, 3, 4\}$

    $S = \{-4, 1, 6, 11, 16\}$

    A. $g(x) = x - 4$
    B. $g(x) = 3x + 2$
    C. $g(x) = 3x + 4$
    D. $g(x) = 5x - 4$

2. The costs of tutoring packages of different lengths, given in quarter hours, are shown in the table.

Number of quarter hours	8	10	12	20
Cost	$200	$230	$260	$380

    Each cost consists of a fixed charge and a charge per quarter hour. What is the fixed charge?

    F. $15
    G. $23
    H. $80
    J. $120

3. When $f(a) = a^2 + 2a + 5$, what is the value of $f(a + b)$?

    A. $a^2 + b^2 + 2ab + 5$

    B. $a^2 + b^2 + 2a + 2b + 5$

    C. $(a + b)^2 + a + b + 5$

    D. $(a + b)^2 + 2a + 2b + 5$

4. The graph of $y = f(x)$ is shown in the standard (x,y) coordinate plane.

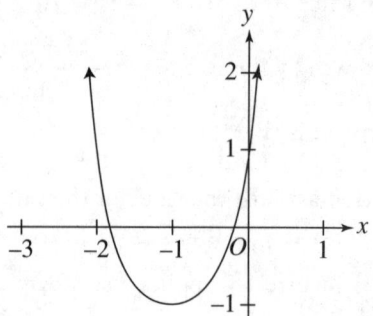

The function $y = f(x)$ can be classified as one of which of the following types of functions?

    F. Trigonometric
    G. Quadratic
    H. Absolute value
    J. Cubic

5. As shown, a paint ball is shot at the ceiling, striking it at an angle. The measure of that angle is given as x.

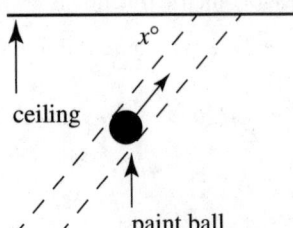

The paint from the paintball makes an oval shape on the ceiling. The maximum length and width of the oval can be measured and used to calculate angle x with the formula

$\sin x = \dfrac{length_{max}}{width_{max}}$. The paintball stain is shown. At

approximately what angle did the paintball that made the stain strike the ceiling?

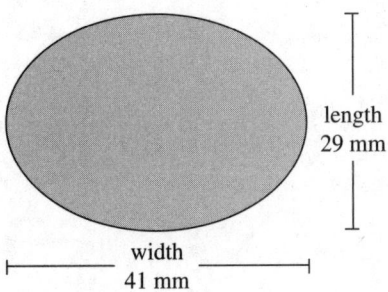

A. 15°
B. 30°
C. 45°
D. 120°

6. Consider the exponential equation $y = \dfrac{p^{(x+1)}}{K}$, where K and p are positive real constants and x is a positive real number. The value of y decreases as the value of x increases if and only if which of the following statements about p is true?

F. $0 < p < 1$
G. $1 < p < 2$
H. $p > 0$
J. $p > 1$

7. If $f(x) = \sqrt{x}$ and the composite function $f(g(x)) = \sqrt{4x^2 - 5}$, which of the following could be $g(x)$?

A. $\sqrt{4x^4 - 5}$
B. $\sqrt{16x^4 - 25}$
C. $2x^2 - 25$
D. $4x^2 - 5$

8. Whenever a, b, and c are positive real numbers, which of the following expressions is equivalent to

$\log_4 a - 2\log_8 b + \dfrac{1}{2}\log_4 c$?

F. $\log_4 a\sqrt{c} - \log_8 b^2$

G. $\log_4 \dfrac{ac}{2} - \log_8 2b$

H. $\log_4 \dfrac{a\sqrt{c}}{b}$

J. $\log_4(a - c) - \log_8 b^2$

9. A function $f(x)$ is defined as even if and only if $f(x) = f(-x)$ for all real values of x. Which one of the following graphs represents an even function $f(x)$?

    A.

    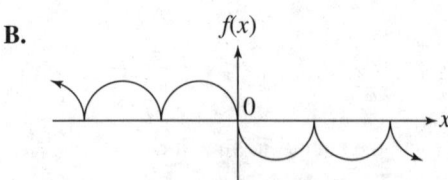

    B.

    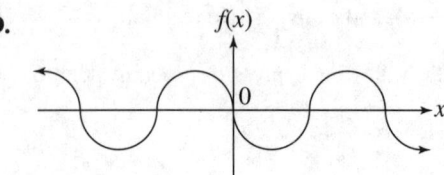

    C.

    ![graph C]

    D.

    ![graph D]

10. Which of the following trigonometric functions has an amplitude of 3 ?

    (Note: The *amplitude* of a trigonometric function is $\frac{1}{2}$ the nonnegative difference between the maximum and minimum values of the function.)

    F. $f(x) = \dfrac{1}{3} \sin x$

    G. $f(x) = \cos 3x$

    H. $f(x) = 3 \tan x$

    J. $f(x) = 3 \cos x$

11. If function f is defined by $f(x) = -2x^3$, then what is the value of $f(f(1))$?

    A. −16
    B. −8
    C.   8
    D.   16

FUNCTIONS DRILL 2 EXPLANATIONS

1. **D** The question asks for the definition of a function between two data sets. The question says *R onto S*, which means the *R* data set is the input and the *S* data set is the output. There are variables in the answer choices, so plug in. Choose corresponding numbers from both data sets and test each equation. Make $x = 0$ in *R*, so the corresponding value of -4 in *S* is the target value for $g(x)$. Now plug $x = 0$ into the answer choices to see which one matches the target value. Choice (A) becomes $g(0) = (0) - 4 = -4$. This matches the target value, so keep (A), but check the remaining answer choices just in case. Choice (B) becomes $g(0) = 3(0) + 2 = 0 + 2 = 2$. Eliminate (B). Choice (C) becomes $g(0) = 3(0) + 4 = 0 + 4 = 4$. Eliminate (C). Choice (D) becomes $g(0) = 5(0) - 4 = 0 - 4 = -4$. Keep (D). Since two answers still work, test another input and output. Make $x = 1$ in *R* and the target value $g(x) = 1$ in *S*. Choice (A) becomes $1 - 4 = -3$. Eliminate (A). Choice (D) becomes $5(1) - 4 = 5 - 4 = 1$. Keep (D). The correct answer is (D).

2. **H** The question asks for the fixed charge for the tutoring packages shown in the table. First, determine the cost per quarter hour using the rate formula: $\text{rate} = \dfrac{\text{change in cost}}{\text{change in quarter-hours}}$. Pick two different packages to set up the equation $\dfrac{\$230 - \$200}{10 - 8} = \dfrac{\$30}{2}$ to find the rate that is $15 per quarter-hour. Now use the 8-quarter-hour package to set up the equation fixed cost $+ \$15 \times 8 = \$200$ to find that the fixed cost is $80. Choice (G) finds the rate for the 10-quarter-hour package without a fixed cost. Choice (J) is a partial answer. The correct answer is (H).

3. **D** The question asks for the value of the function. Substitute $(a + b)$ into the function for *a* to get $f(a + b) = (a + b)^2 + 2(a + b) + 5$. Distribute the 2 to get $f(a + b) = (a + b)^2 + 2a + 2b + 5$. The correct answer is (D).

4. **G** The question asks which type of function $f(x)$ represents. Use Process of Elimination. The function does not repeat in a wave-like pattern, so it is not trigonometric: eliminate (F). An absolute value function forms a V pattern instead of a U-shaped one, so eliminate (H). Cubic functions are not vertically symmetrical, so eliminate (J). The correct answer is (G).

5. **C** The question asks for the measure of the angle at which the paint ball strikes the ceiling, identified by $x°$. There is a formula provided, so plug in the given values. The formula is $\sin x = \dfrac{length_{max}}{width_{max}}$ and the relevant measurements are 29 for the length and 41 for the width. The formula becomes $\sin x = \dfrac{29}{41} \approx 0.707$. Take the inverse sine of both sides of the equation to get $\sin^{-1}(\sin x) = \sin^{-1}(0.707)$, which becomes $x \approx 45°$. The correct answer is (C).

6. **F** The question asks for the possible values of p such that y will decrease as x increases. Since $(x + 1)$ will never be a negative exponent, increasing this exponent will always increase the value of a number greater than 1 and decrease the value of a real number between 0 and 1. The problem stipulates that p must be positive, so if y decreases as x increases, p must be a fractional constant less than 1. If this isn't clear, pick some numbers for the variables that fit the requirements and try them in the equation to see what happens. The correct answer is (F).

7. **D** The question asks for the definition of a function. In function notation, the value inside the parentheses is the x-value that goes into the function, and the value that comes out of the function is the y-value. In this case, $g(x)$ is the input for $f(x)$. Since $f(x)$ is defined as $\sqrt{x}$, try the answer choices. Put each one under a square root and choose the one that matches $\sqrt{4x^2 - 5}$. Only (D) works. Taking the square root of the expressions in any of the other answer choices does not result in the correct expression. The correct answer is (D).

8. **F** The question asks for an equivalent form of the logarithmic expression. To combine logarithms (logs), the bases must be the same, so eliminate (H). Group the first and last terms together, since they have common bases, to get $\log_4 a + \frac{1}{2}\log_4 c - 2\log_8 b$. The Laws of Logarithms state that $c\log_b x = \log_b x^c$, so the expression becomes $\log_4 a + \log_4 c^{\frac{1}{2}} - \log_8 b^2$. Eliminate (G) because it multiplies b by 2 instead of squaring it. A fractional power represents a root, so $\log_4 a + \log_4 \sqrt{c} - \log_8 b^2$. Eliminate (J), which does not include $\sqrt{c}$. The Laws of Logs also state that $\log_b x + \log_b y = \log_b xy$, so the expression becomes $\log_4 a + \log_4 \sqrt{c} = \log_4 a\sqrt{c}$. The correct answer is (F).

9. **A** The question asks which graph represents an even function. An even function is defined in the question as a function for which the value of $f(x) = f(-x)$. This means that $f(x)$ has the same value for both x and $-x$. If the graph of an even function is folded along the y-axis, the two sides of the graph will be mirror reflections of each other. Choices (B), (C), and (D) are odd functions, in which $f(-x) = -f(x)$ for all values of x. Odd functions rotate 180° about the point (0, 0). The correct answer is (A).

10. **J** The question asks which of the given trigonometric functions has an amplitude of 3. First, $\tan x$ does not have an amplitude, so eliminate (H). Second, multiplying the entire function by a constant stretches the graph vertically and changes the amplitude. Both $\sin x$ and $\cos x$ alone have amplitudes of 1. Multiplying the functions $\sin x$ or $\cos x$ by a constant will make the amplitude equal to that constant. Altering the *angle,* as in (G), does not change the amplitude of the function—it changes the *period*. The correct answer is (J).

11. **D** The question asks for the value of a compound function. To deal with compound functions, the trick is to work inside out. First, determine the value of the inside: $f(1) = -2(1)^3 = -2$. The value of $f(1)$ becomes the new x-value for the outside f function, so determine $f(-2) = -2(-2)^3 = -2(-8) = 16$. A negative number raised to an odd integer stays negative; (A) and (B) are wrong because they confuse the signs. Choice (C) is the result of multiplying $f(x)$ by $f(x)$, which is not the correct operation for compound functions. The correct answer is (D).

GEOMETRY

Geometry on the ACT involves two- and three-dimensional shapes, key formulas, and relationships among figures. A subcategory of Preparing for Higher Math, Geometry questions make up 17–20% of the ACT Math Test.

There are two Geometry Drills on the following pages, with easy to medium questions in the first drill and medium to hard questions in the second drill.

GEOMETRY DRILL 1

1. In the hiking trail shown, X marks the trail's halfway point. If $\overline{YZ}$ measures 24 kilometers and is $\frac{1}{3}$ the length of $\overline{XZ}$, what is the total length, in kilometers, of the trail?

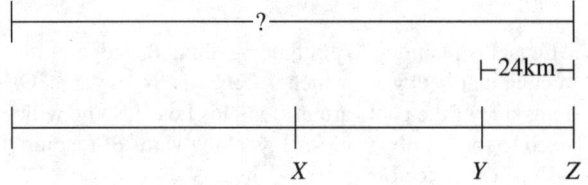

A. 144
B. 104
C. 96
D. 72

2. The perimeter of a square is 36 inches. What is the area of the square, in square inches?

F. 6
G. 9
H. 36
J. 81

3. A trapezoidal driveway has the dimensions, in yards, given in the figure shown. What is the area, in square yards, of the driveway?

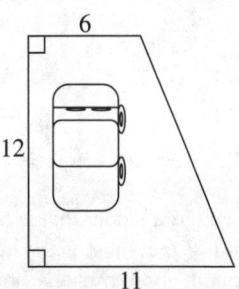

A. 42
B. 72
C. 102
D. 156

4. In cubic meters, what is the volume of a large cube whose edges each measure 6 meters in length?

F. 18
G. 36
H. 108
J. 216

5. What is the slope of a line that has a coordinate point of $(11,-2)$ and crosses the x-axis at $(4,0)$ when the line is graphed in the standard (x,y) coordinate plane?

A. $-\dfrac{7}{2}$

B. $-\dfrac{2}{7}$

C. $\dfrac{1}{4}$

D. $\dfrac{4}{13}$

6. A right triangle contains an angle with a measure of θ. If $\cos \theta = \dfrac{12}{13}$ and $\tan \theta = \dfrac{5}{12}$, what is the value of $\sin \theta$?

F. $\dfrac{5}{13}$

G. $\dfrac{13}{5}$

H. $\dfrac{12}{5}$

J. $\dfrac{12}{\sqrt{313}}$

7. In the figure shown, the circle with center O is tangent to $\overline{AE}$, $\overline{BD}$, $\overline{CF}$, and $\overline{DE}$. The measure of angle $\angle BDE$ is 75° and the measure of $\angle DEA$ is 105°.

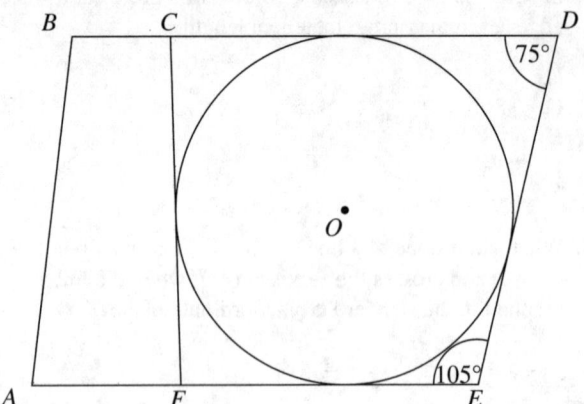

The lines in which of the following pairs of lines are necessarily parallel?

   I. $\overline{AB}$ and $\overline{DE}$

   II. $\overline{BD}$ and $\overline{AE}$

   III. $\overline{CF}$ and $\overline{DE}$

A. II only
B. III only
C. I and II only
D. I, II, and III

8. $\overline{QR}$ is intersected by $\overline{ST}$ at the point U, as shown by the figure. If $\angle QUT$ has a measure of $(8x - 22)°$, and $\angle SUR$ has a measure of $(6x + 18)°$, what is the measure of $\angle QUS$?

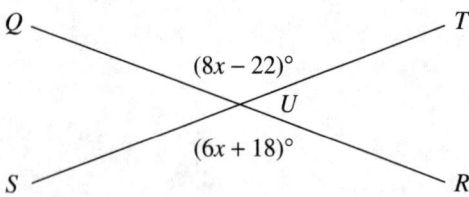

F. 24°
G. 42°
H. 96°
J. 156°

9. Point C (1,2) and point D (7,–10) lie in the standard coordinate plane. What are the coordinates of the midpoint of $\overline{CD}$?

A. (3,–6)
B. (4,–4)
C. (4,–6)
D. (7,–4)

10. Michael is planning to put fencing along the edge of his rectangular backyard, which is 22 yards by 16 yards. One long side of the backyard is along his house, so he will need to fence only 3 sides. How many yards of fencing will Michael need?

F. 54
G. 60
H. 76
J. 352

11. In the figure shown, points A, B, C, and D are collinear, and distances marked are in feet. Rectangle $ADEG$ has an area of 48 square feet. What is the area, in square feet, of the trapezoid $BCEF$?

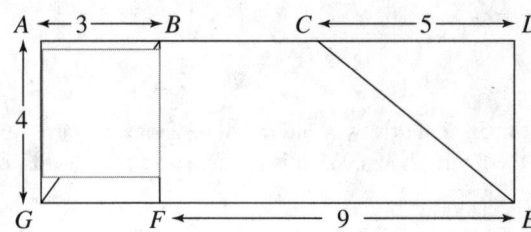

A. 16
B. 20
C. 26
D. 36

12. The playground equipment shown has a ladder that is 6 feet tall and a diagonal slide that is 7 feet long. If the ladder makes a right angle with the ground, approximately how many feet is the base of the slide from the base of the ladder?

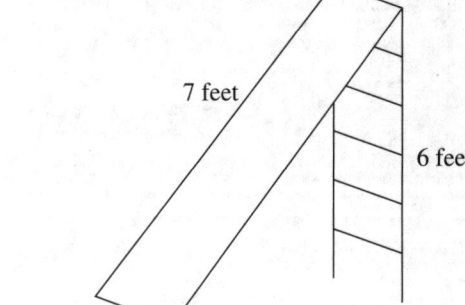

F. 2
G. 4
H. 6
J. 8

GEOMETRY DRILL 1 EXPLANATIONS

1. **A** The question asks for the total length of the trail. Since $\overline{YZ}$ is $\frac{1}{3}$ the length of $\overline{XZ}$, $\overline{XZ}$ is $3 \times 24 = 72$ kilometers. Since X is the halfway point of the trail, the trail's entire length is twice $\overline{XZ}$, or $72 \times 2 = 144$ kilometers. The correct answer is (A).

2. **J** The question asks for the area of a square. The formula for the area of a square is $A = s^2$, so first find the length of a side, based on the perimeter given. The formula for the perimeter of a square is $P = 4s$. That means that $36 = 4s$; divide both sides of the equation by 4 to get $s = 9$. Use the side length in the area formula to get $A = 9^2 = 81$. The correct answer is (J).

3. **C** The question asks for the area of the driveway. To find the area of the trapezoid, split it into a rectangle with dimensions of 12 and 6 and a triangle with a height of 12 and a base of 5; then add the areas of the two smaller shapes. This becomes $A = (6)(12) + \frac{1}{2}(5)(12) = 72 + 30 = 102$. Choice (B) gives the area of only the rectangular portion, and (A) gives the perimeter of the whole figure. Choice (D) finds the hypotenuse of the triangle and multiplies it by the height of the triangle. The correct answer is (C).

4. **J** The question asks for the volume of the cube. The formula for the volume of a cube is $V = s^3$. In this case, $s = 6$, so the volume is 216. Choice (F) finds $s \times 3$; (G) finds the area of a square with sides of 6; and (H) finds $s^2 \times 3$. The correct answer is (J).

5. **B** The question asks for the slope of a line. The slope of a line is defined as the change in y over the change in x, or $slope = \frac{y_2 - y_1}{x_2 - x_1}$. Plug in the values of the points in the question to get $m = \frac{0 - (-2)}{4 - 11} = \frac{2}{-7} = -\frac{2}{7}$. The correct answer is (B).

6. **F** The question asks for the value of a trigonometric function. The trigonometric functions sine, cosine, and tangent have to do with right triangles, so draw a right triangle. Label one angle that is not the right angle as θ. Write out SOHCAHTOA to remember the trig definitions. The CAH part defines cosine as $\cos = \frac{adjacent}{hypotenuse}$. Since $\cos\theta = \frac{12}{13}$, label the adjacent side as 12 and the hypotenuse as 13. The TOA part defines tangent as $\tan = \frac{opposite}{adjacent}$. Since $\tan\theta = \frac{5}{12}$, label the opposite side as 5. The question asks for the value of $\sin\theta$. The SOH part defines sine as $\sin = \frac{opposite}{hypotenuse}$, so take the side opposite angle θ and place it over the length of the hypotenuse to get $\sin\theta = \frac{5}{13}$. The correct answer is (F).

7. **A** The question asks which of the line pairs must be parallel based on the provided information. Because ∠*DEA* measures 105° and ∠*BDE* measures 75°, and the sum of these angles is 180°, $\overline{BD}$ and $\overline{AE}$ are parallel. Eliminate (B) because it does not include II. Since there is no way to determine the measures of ∠*ABD* or ∠*BAE*, it cannot be concluded that $\overline{AB}$ and $\overline{DE}$ are parallel. Therefore, eliminate (C) and (D). The correct answer is (A).

8. **G** The question asks for the measure of an angle on a figure. No information is given about ∠*QUS*, so see what else can be determined. The figure has the expressions already labeled on it, so move on to the next step. Since angles opposite each other are equal, set the two expressions equal to each other to get $8x - 22 = 6x + 18$. Add 22 to both sides of the equation to get $8x = 6x + 40$. Next, subtract $6x$ from both sides of the equation to get $2x = 40$. Divide both sides of the equation by 2 to get $x = 20$. Plug $x = 20$ into one of the expressions to get the measure of the large angle: $8(20) - 22 = 160 - 22 = 138°$. This is the measure of the large angles ∠*QUT* and ∠*SUR*. The question asks for the measure of the smaller angle. There are 180° in a line, so subtract 138 from 180 to get $180 - 138 = 42°$. The correct answer is (G).

9. **B** The question asks for the coordinates of the midpoint. To find the midpoint of a line, take the average of the x-coordinates $\left(\dfrac{x_1 + x_2}{2}\right)$ and the average of the y-coordinates $\left(\dfrac{y_1 + y_2}{2}\right)$ of the endpoints. The midpoint here is $\left(\dfrac{1 + 7}{2}, \dfrac{2 + (-10)}{2}\right) = (4, -4)$. Choices (A) and (D) incorrectly average the x-coordinates. Choice (C) incorrectly averages the y-coordinates. The correct answer is (B).

10. **F** The question asks for the required amount of fencing. Draw a picture and label it with the information provided in the question.

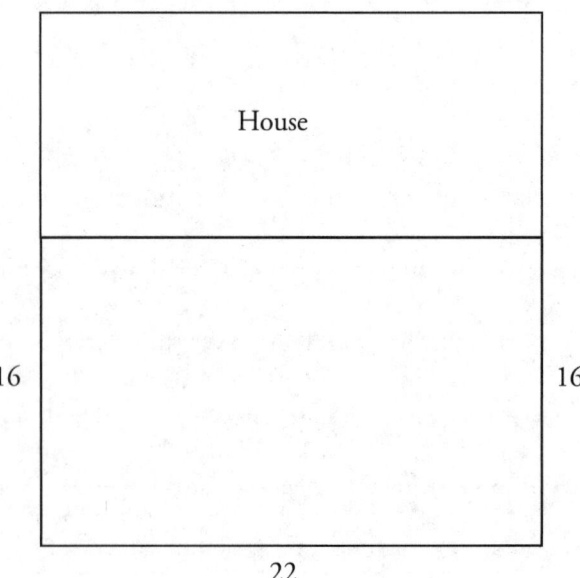

Add the lengths of the two short sides of the backyard and one long side: $16 + 16 + 22 = 54$. Choice (G) is the sum of two long sides and one short side. Choice (H) is the perimeter of the backyard, but the problem says the fencing is needed only on 3 sides. Choice (J) is the area of the backyard. The correct answer is (F).

11.   **C**   The question asks for the area of trapezoid *BCEF*. To find the area of the trapezoid *BCEF*, subtract the area of triangle *CDE* from the area of rectangle *BDEF*. The area of a rectangle is $A = lw$, so the area of *BDEF* is $(9)(4) = 36$ square feet. The area of a triangle is $A = \frac{1}{2}bh$, so the area of triangle *CDE* is $\frac{1}{2}(5)(4) = 10$ square feet. The area of trapezoid *BCEF* is $36 - 10 = 26$ square feet. Choice (A) is incorrect because it finds the area of the square with sides *BC* and *BF*. Choice (D) is incorrect because it is solving only for the area of the rectangle *BDEF*. The correct answer is (C).

12.   **G**   The question asks for the distance between the end of the slide and the ladder. Draw a line along the bottom of the figure to indicate this distance, and label it *x*. The question indicates that the ladder is at a right angle with the ground, so use the Pythagorean Theorem $(a^2 + b^2 = c^2)$ to solve $6^2 + x^2 = 7^2$, which becomes $36 + x^2 = 49$. Subtract 36 from both sides of the equation to get $x^2 = 13$; then take the square root of both sides to get $\sqrt{13}$, which rounds to 4. The correct answer is (G).

GEOMETRY DRILL 2

1. In a certain isosceles triangle, the measure of the vertex angle is four times the measure of each of the base angles. What is the measure, in degrees, of the vertex angle?

   A. 30°
   B. 60°
   C. 120°
   D. 150°

2. The triangle shown has a hypotenuse with a length of 13 feet. The measure of ∠A is 20° and the measure of ∠B is 70°. Which of the following is closest to the length, in feet, of $\overline{BC}$?

   (Note: sin 70° ≈ 0.9397
   cos 70° ≈ 0.3420
   tan 70° ≈ 2.747)

   F. 4.4
   G. 5.0
   H. 12.2
   J. 35.7

   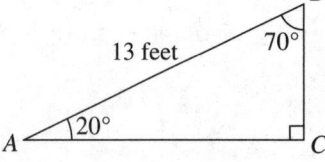

3. Which of the following could be the equation of a line that passes through the points (−2,−7) and (2,17) in the standard (x,y) coordinate plane?

   A. $x + y = 6$
   B. $5x − 2y = 7$
   C. $6x − y = −5$
   D. $9x − 2y = −16$

4. An artist wants to cover the entire outside of a rectangular box with mosaic tiles. The dimensions of the box shown are given in centimeters. If each tile is exactly one square centimeter, and the artist lays the tiles with no space between them, how many tiles will he need?

   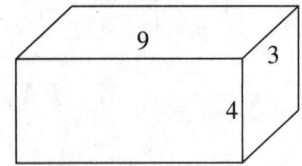

   F. 75
   G. 96
   H. 126
   J. 150

5. As shown in the figure, a skateboard ramp leading from the top of a boulder is 10 feet long and forms a 32° angle with the level ground. Which of the following expressions represents the height, in feet, of the boulder?

   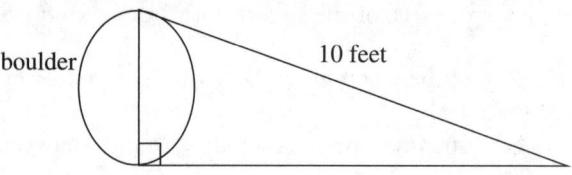

   A. 10 tan 32°

   B. $\dfrac{\sin 32°}{10}$

   C. $\dfrac{10}{\cos 32°}$

   D. 10 sin 32°

6. Given the two points in the standard (x,y) coordinate plane (3,2) and (−1,9), what is the distance between them in coordinate units?

   F. $\sqrt{33}$
   G. $\sqrt{53}$
   H. $\sqrt{65}$
   J. $\sqrt{67}$

7. In the figure, X is on $\overline{WZ}$. If the angle measures are as shown, what is the degree measure of ∠YXZ ?

   A. $37\frac{1}{2}°$

   B. $65\frac{1}{2}°$

   C. $112\frac{1}{2}°$

   D. $114\frac{1}{2}°$

   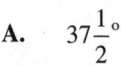
   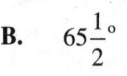
   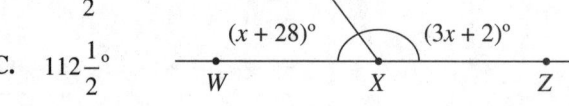

8. Circle A has its center at point (−5,2) with a radius of 2, and circle B is represented by the equation $(x + 4)^2 + (y − 2)^2 = 9$. Where is point (−2,2) located?

   F. Inside circle A only
   G. Inside circle B only
   H. Inside both circle A and circle B
   J. Outside both circle A and circle B

9. What is the degree measure of an angle that measures $\frac{7\pi}{15}$ radians?

   A. $\left(180 - \frac{7\pi}{15}\right)°$

   B. $252°$

   C. $84°$

   D. $12°$

10. *RST* is a right triangle with side lengths of r, s, and t, as shown. What is the value of $\cos^2 S + \cos^2 R$?

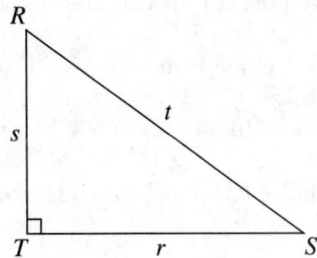

   F. $\dfrac{1+\sqrt{2}}{3}$

   G. $\dfrac{\sqrt{2}}{2}$

   H. $\sqrt{2}$

   J. 1

11. In isosceles triangle *ABC* shown, the measures of $\angle BAC$ and $\angle BCA$ are equal and $\overline{DE} \parallel \overline{AC}$. The diagonals of trapezoid *DECA* intersect at *F*. The lengths of $\overline{DF}$ and $\overline{EF}$ are 6 centimeters, the length of $\overline{DE}$ is 9 centimeters, and the length of $\overline{AC}$ is 27 centimeters. What is the length, in centimeters, of $\overline{FC}$?

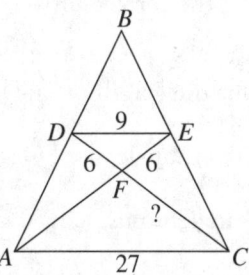

   A. 12
   B. 15
   C. 18
   D. 33

12. In the figure shown, lines *p* and *q* are parallel and angle measures are as marked. If it can be determined, what is the value of *a* ?

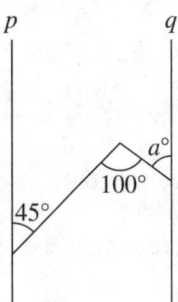

   F. $45°$
   G. $55°$
   H. $100°$
   J. Cannot be determined from the information given

GEOMETRY DRILL 2 EXPLANATIONS

1. **C** The question asks for the measure of the vertex angle. If the base angles, which are equal, are x, then the vertex angle can be written as $4x$. The sum of the angles in a triangle is 180°, so for this triangle, $x + x + 4x = 180$. Simplify the equation to $6x = 180$, and then divide both sides by 6 to get $x = 30$. Choice (A) gives the value of x (which also is the measure of each base angle), but the question asks for the vertex angle. This value is $4(30) = 120$. Choice (B) gives the sum of the base angles, and (D) subtracts the value of only one base angle from 180. The correct answer is (C).

2. **F** The question asks for the length of one leg of a right triangle. Given the length of one side and the measure of an angle of the triangle, use SOHCAHTOA. The length of the hypotenuse is provided, and $\overline{BC}$ is adjacent to the 70° angle, so use $\cos 70° = \dfrac{\text{adjacent}}{\text{hypotenuse}} = \dfrac{\overline{BC}}{13}$. Use the given decimal value for $\cos 70°$ to get $0.3420 = \dfrac{\overline{BC}}{13}$; then multiply both sides of the equation by 13 to get $\overline{BC} = 13(0.3420) \approx 4.4$. Choices (H) and (J) are the result of using either the sine or the tangent functions. Choice (G) may be the result of assuming that the figure is a 5:12:13 right triangle. The correct answer is (F).

3. **C** The question asks for the equation of the line passing through the given points. Use the two points given to find the slope of the line: $m = \dfrac{y_2 - y_1}{x_2 - x_1} = \dfrac{17 - (-7)}{2 - (-2)} = \dfrac{24}{4} = 6$. Manipulate the answer choices to match the slope-intercept form of a line, where $y = mx + b$. For (C), add y and subtract -5 from both sides to get $6x + 5 = y$, or $y = 6x + 5$. In this equation, the slope, m, is 6, which is the correct slope. None of the other lines have this slope. Choice (B) confuses signs in calculating the slope. Choice (A) confuses the slope and y-intercept. It is also possible to solve this question by testing the answers: simply plug in the (x, y) values of the two provided points into the answers to see which equation is true for both points. The correct answer is (C).

4. **J** The question asks for the number of tiles needed to cover the surface of the box. Work through the question one step at a time. The tiles must equal the surface area of the box, which is the sum of the areas of all six faces. There are three sets of faces: front/back, top/bottom, and the two sides. The sum of the areas of the faces is $2(4 \times 9) + 2(3 \times 9) + 2(3 \times 4) = 72 + 54 + 24 = 150$. Because each tile covers 1 cm², the artist must have 150 cm² ÷ 1 cm² = 150 tiles, (J). Choice (F) finds the area of only three faces, and (G) and (H) account for only two of the three pairs of faces. The correct answer is (J).

5. **D** The question asks for the height of the boulder, which is the same as a short leg of a right triangle. Use SOHCAHTOA. The length of the ramp is the hypotenuse of the triangle, and the height of the boulder is the side opposite the angle of 32°. Use sine with these two sides to get $\sin 32° = \dfrac{\text{opposite}}{\text{hypotenuse}} = \dfrac{h}{10}$. Multiply both sides by 10 to get $h = 10 \sin 32°$. The correct answer is (D).

6.   **H**   The question asks for the distance between two points. Use the distance formula: $d = \sqrt{(x_2 - x_1)^2 + (y_2 - y_1)^2}$. Plug in the points to get $d = \sqrt{(-1 - 3)^2 + (9 - 2)^2} = \sqrt{(-4)^2 + (7)^2} = \sqrt{16 + 49} = \sqrt{65}$. The correct answer is (H).

7.   **D**   The question asks for the measure of $\angle YXZ$. Since $\angle YXZ$ is clearly larger than 90°, eliminate (A) and (B). Now solve for x. Since there are 180° in a straight line, the sum of the two angle measures must be equal to 180. Therefore, $(3x + 2) + (x + 28) = 180$. Simplify the equation to get $4x + 30 = 180$; then subtract 30 from both sides to get $4x = 150$. Divide both sides by 4 to find that $x = 37.5$. To find the measure of $\angle YXZ$, substitute this value of x in $3x + 2$ to get $3(37.5) + 2 = 112.5 + 2 = 114.5°$. The correct answer is (D).

8.   **G**   The question asks for the location of a point in relation to two circles. Draw the two circles on the coordinate plane and plot the point $(-2, 2)$. The equation of a circle is $(x - h)^2 + (y - k)^2 = r^2$, where (h, k) is the center of the circle and r is the radius. Thus, circle B has its center at $(-4, 2)$ with a radius of 3. A drawing of this will show that the point lies outside circle A and inside circle B.

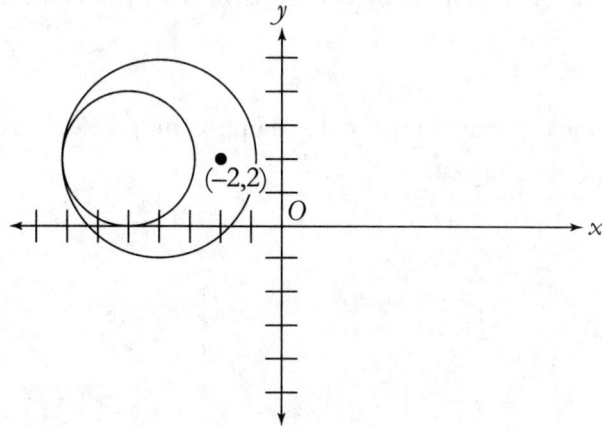

The correct answer is (G).

9.   **C**   The question asks for the equivalent measure in degrees of an angle measure in radians. Degree measurements should not be in terms of π, so eliminate (A). Now, multiply by a conversion factor to change units. The relationship between degrees and radians is $180° = \pi$ radians. Substitute 180 for π to get an angle measure of $\dfrac{7(180)}{15} = \dfrac{1,260}{15} = 84°$. The correct answer is (C).

10. **J** The question asks for the value of an expression involving cosine. The definition of cosine is $\cos\theta = \dfrac{\text{adjacent}}{\text{hypotenuse}}$. In this triangle, $\cos S = \dfrac{r}{t}$ and $\cos R = \dfrac{s}{t}$. Therefore, $\cos^2 S + \cos^2 R = \dfrac{r^2}{t^2} + \dfrac{s^2}{t^2}$, or $\dfrac{r^2 + s^2}{t^2}$. Since ΔRST is a right triangle, use the Pythagorean Theorem to determine that $r^2 + s^2 = t^2$. Substitute t^2 for $r^2 + s^2$ to find that $\cos^2 S + \cos^2 R = \dfrac{t^2}{t^2} = 1$. The correct answer is (J).

11. **C** The question asks for the length of a line segment. First, label the figure with information from the question. Trapezoid $DECA$ is isosceles because ΔABC is isosceles and, since $\overline{DE}\parallel\overline{AC}$, line segments $\overline{AD}$ and $\overline{CE}$ have equal lengths. Since the trapezoid is isosceles, the diagonals are congruent. Thus, ΔDFE and ΔAFC are similar. Set up a proportion to find the missing side: $\dfrac{9}{6} = \dfrac{27}{FC}$. Cross-multiply to get $9\overline{FC} = 162$; then divide both sides of the equation by 9 to find that $\overline{FC} = 18$. Choice (A) is the short side of ΔDFE multiplied by 2. Choice (B) is $9 + 6$. Choice (D) is $27 + 6$. The correct answer is (C).

12. **G** The question asks for the measure of angle a. To complete this problem, extend the left transversal to form a triangle with a as one of its angles:

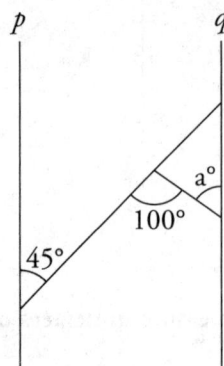

First, find that the supplement of $100°$ will be $80°$. Note that because lines p and q are parallel, the uppermost angle of this triangle will be $45°$. Now, find a by subtracting the two known angles from the total angle measure of the triangle: $180° − 45° − 80° = 55°$. Choice (F) cannot work because a does not lie along the same transversal as $45°$; (H) cannot work because the $100°$ angle and a do not share any parallel lines; and (J) cannot work because the value can be determined. The correct answer is (G).

STATISTICS AND PROBABILITY

These questions test knowledge and application of statistical measures—primarily mean, median, mode, and standard deviation—and the ability to work with probabilities. Many questions present the information in a figure or a word problem. The final subcategory of Preparing for Higher Math, Statistics & Probability questions make up 12–15% of the ACT Math Test.

There are two Statistics and Probability Drills on the following pages, with easy to medium questions in the first drill and medium to hard questions in the second drill.

STATISTICS AND PROBABILITY DRILL 1

1. For each of 3 years, the table gives the number of different routes a runner ran, the number of runs she ran, and the total number of miles she ran.

Year	Routes	Runs	Total miles run
2005	12	395	1,255
2006	12	396	1,014
2007	11	368	1,898

To the nearest tenth of a mile, what is the average number of miles the runner ran per run in 2005 ?

A. 2.5
B. 2.6
C. 3.2
D. 4.8

2. Stacie has a bag of solid colored jellybeans. Each jellybean is orange, purple, or pink. If she randomly selects a jellybean from the bag, the probability that the jellybean is orange is $\frac{2}{9}$, and the probability that it is purple is $\frac{1}{3}$. If there are 72 jellybeans in the bag, how many pink jellybeans are in the bag?

F. 24
G. 32
H. 40
J. 48

3. Susie has three T-shirts: one red, one blue, and one black. She also has three pairs of shorts: one red, one blue, and one black. How many different combinations are there for Susie to wear exactly one T-shirt and one pair of shorts?

A. 3
B. 6
C. 8
D. 9

4. Each of the following values could represent a probability EXCEPT:

F. 0.00004

G. 0.7

H. $\frac{51}{60}$

J. $\frac{5}{4}$

5. At a school picnic, 150 children scored points in a game, as shown in the table below. The lowest number of points was 2 points and the highest was 7 points. What is the probability that a child would have scored 5 points or more, rounded to the nearest hundredth?

Number of Points	Number of children
2	15
3	45
4	43
5	17
6	14
7	16

A. 0.09
B. 0.11
C. 0.20
D. 0.31

6. A college student's ID is required to contain 4 single-digit numbers alternating with 4 letters: for example, Q1P3R5S7. Only odd numbers from 1 to 9, inclusive, can be used, and none of the 5 vowels can be part of the student ID. Otherwise, each letter and each digit can be used up to 4 times. Which expression accurately represents the number of student IDs that can be generated using these requirements?

F. 21(5)(20)(5)(19)(5)(18)(5)
G. 21(5)(21)(5)(21)(5)(21)(5)
H. 21(9)(20)(8)(19)(7)(18)(6)
J. 26(9)(26)(9)(26)(9)(26)(9)

7. In a data set of 5 points, the mean, median, and mode are each equal to 8. Which of the following could be the data set?

    A. {5, 7, 8, 8, 12}
    B. {7, 7, 8, 8, 12}
    C. {7, 8, 8, 8, 12}
    D. {7, 8, 8, 10, 12}

8. The stem-and-leaf plot below shows the scores for each golfer in a recent tournament at the Lehigh Valley Golf Club. There were 13 golfers participating in the tournament.

Stem	Leaf
6	6, 7
7	1, 2, 2, 3, 5, 7, 9
8	2, 3, 3, 7

(Note: For example, a score of 72 would have a stem value of 7 and a leaf value of 2.)

Which of the following is closest to the mean score of all the golfers in the tournament?

    F. 72.0
    G. 74.4
    H. 75.0
    J. 75.9

STATISTICS AND PROBABILITY DRILL 1 EXPLANATIONS

1. **C** The question asks for the average number of miles run in 2005. Divide the total number of miles the runner ran in 2005 by the number of runs she ran in that year to find the average number of miles per run: $\frac{1,255}{395} = 3.177$, which rounds to 3.2 miles. Be careful when finding the numbers within the table: there is more data than is required to answer the question. The correct answer is (C).

2. **G** The question asks for the number of pink jellybeans in the bag. When dealing with probabilities, the total of all possible outcomes must equal either 100% or 1, so use the provided probabilities to find the chance of selecting a pink one. The probability of pink, $1 - \frac{2}{9} - \frac{1}{3}$, can be rewritten with common denominators as $\frac{9}{9} - \frac{2}{9} - \frac{3}{9}$, so the probability of picking a pink jellybean must be $\frac{4}{9}$. Since probability is defined as $\frac{\text{number of desired outcomes}}{\text{number of total outcomes}}$, find the number of pink jellybeans by setting the probability of $\frac{4}{9}$ equal to $\frac{x}{72}$ and solving. Given $\frac{4}{9} = \frac{x}{72}$, cross-multiply to get $9x = 288$, which solves to $x = 32$. The correct answer is (G).

3. **D** The question asks for the number of combinations of two things. Susie has 3 options for her T-shirt and 3 options for her pair of shorts. Susie can combine any of the T-shirts with any of the pairs of shorts, so there are 3×3, or 9, combinations. Choices (A) and (B) do not account for all possible combinations. Choice (C) is 2^3 rather than 3^2. The correct answer is (D).

4. **J** The question asks which number could NOT represent a probability. By definition, probability can be no less than 0% and no greater than 100%. As such, any probability p must be $0 \le p \le 1$. Choices (F), (G), and (H) are all numbers between 0 and 1, but (J) would equal 1.25 if converted to a decimal. The correct answer is (J).

5. **D** The question asks for a probability, which is defined as $\frac{\text{number of desired outcomes}}{\text{number of total outcomes}}$. Read the table carefully to find the numbers to make the probability. The question asks for the probability that a child scored 5 points or more. The *number of desired outcomes* is the sum of the numbers of children who scored 5 or more points, or $17 + 14 + 16 = 47$. The *number of total outcomes* is the total number of children in the table, or 150 as stated in the question. Place the numbers into the probability definition to get $\frac{47}{150} = 0.313$. The question asks for the probability *rounded to the nearest hundredth*, which is 0.31. The correct answer is (D).

6. **G** The question asks for the total number of possible letter/number combinations in a given scenario. The question says that the student's ID needs to alternate between four single digit numbers and four letters. The question also states that *Only odd numbers from 1 to 9, inclusive, can be used, and none of the 5 vowels can be part of the student ID.* Since there are five odd numbers from 1 to 9, eliminate (H) and (J) because they use all nine numbers from 1 to 9, not just the odd numbers. Because each letter and digit can be used up to four times, the number of options for each letter or number in each space should stay the same. Eliminate (F) because the number in each space where a letter would go decreases. The correct answer is (G).

7. **A** The question asks for the data set that fits certain requirements—the mean (average), median (middle value), and mode (number that appears most often) all equal 8. Start with the easiest terms to calculate and use Process of Elimination. All four answer choices have a median of 8, but (B) can be eliminated because its mode is not 8. Calculate the mean of the remaining answer choices by adding the numbers and dividing by the number of terms. The mean of (A) is $\frac{5 + 7 + 8 + 8 + 12}{5} = \frac{40}{5} = 8$. The means of (C) and (D) are 8.6 and 9, respectively. The correct answer is (A).

8. **J** The question asks for the mean of the data set. To find the mean, add all the scores: $66 + 67 + 71 + 72 + 72 + 73 + 75 + 77 + 79 + 82 + 83 + 83 + 87 = 987$. Divide this number by the total number of scores, 13, to find $\frac{987}{13} \approx 75.9$. Choice (H) gives the median instead of the mean, and (G) takes the mean of the stems and leaves as separate elements instead of in their combined integer form. The correct answer is (J).

STATISTICS AND PROBABILITY DRILL 2

1. Two fair six-sided dice are repeatedly rolled simultaneously. What is the probability that both dice land with the number six facing up on the 48th roll?

A. $\dfrac{1}{4}$

B. $\dfrac{1}{36}$

C. $\dfrac{1}{48}$

D. $\dfrac{1}{192}$

2. At a fundraiser, participants can trade tickets for a chance to spin a wheel that has 9 equal sections. One of the sections is labeled $9.00, three of the sections are labeled $3.00, and the remaining five sections are labeled $0.00. The participant will win the amount of money indicated by the section on which the wheel lands. To the closest penny, what is the expected value a participant will win by spinning the wheel one time?

F. $0.33
G. $1.33
H. $2.00
J. $4.00

3. A bowler's average score for the season is calculated based on the bowler's scores in ten games. Each game has a maximum score of 300 points. If Stacey has an average score of exactly 240 points in the first seven games of the season, how many points must she average in the last 3 games to earn an average score of 252 points exactly?

A. 264
B. 270
C. 276
D. 280

4. The distribution of a set of 14 integers is shown in the bar chart below. Which of the following is true about the mean, mode, and median of the numbers in the set?

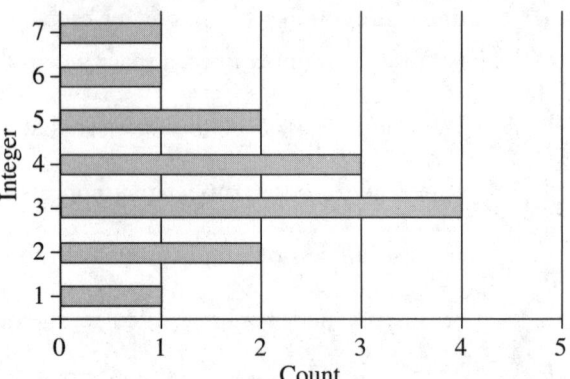

F. The mean is the greatest of the three, and the median is the least of the three.
G. The mean is the greatest of the three, and the mode and median are equal.
H. The mean is the greatest of the three, and the mode is the least of the three.
J. The mean and median are equal, and the mode is the least of the three.

5. Jonathan, Ellery, and 3 other groomsmen are rehearsing for a wedding by walking down an aisle one at a time, one groomsman in front of the other. Each time all 5 walk down the aisle, the groom tells them to walk in a different order from first to last. What is the greatest number of times the groomsmen can walk down the aisle without walking in the same order twice?

A. 3,125
B. 120
C. 100
D. 25

6. A game involves rolling two dice that have an equal chance of landing on any of their sides. One of the dice has 6 sides numbered 1, 2, 3, 4, 5, and 6. The other die has 8 sides numbered 1, 2, 3, 4, 5, 6, 7, and 8. Players roll the dice and multiply the two numbers shown on the dice together. What is the probability that the product of the numbers rolled on the two dice is odd?

F. $\dfrac{1}{4}$

G. $\dfrac{3}{7}$

H. $\dfrac{1}{2}$

J. $\dfrac{4}{7}$

7. The standard (x,y) coordinate plane below shows the graph of a function with standard normal distribution ($\sigma = 1$ and $\mu = 0$). In any normal distribution, 68% of the data is within how many standard deviations of the mean?

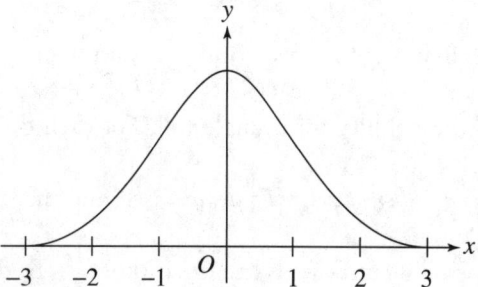

A. 0.5
B. 1
C. 1.5
D. 2

8. Gopi took 5 quizzes for which the scores are integer values ranging from 0 to 10. The median of her scores is 9. The mean of her scores is 8. The only mode of her scores is 10. Which of the following *must* be true about her quiz scores?

F. Her lowest score is 5.
G. The median of the 3 lowest scores is 6.
H. The sum of the 5 scores is 50.
J. The sum of the 2 lowest scores is 11.

STATISTICS AND PROBABILITY DRILL 2 EXPLANATIONS

1. **B** The question asks for a probability, which is defined as $\frac{\text{number of desired outcomes}}{\text{number of total outcomes}}$. The results of the first 47 rolls have no impact on the probability of the 48th roll ending up a certain way, so calculate the probability for a single roll. For each die, there is 1 side that could have *the number six, face up*, so the *number of desired outcomes* is 1, and there are 6 sides, so the *number of total outcomes* is 6. The probably of rolling a six with one die is thus $\frac{1}{6}$. To determine the chance that both will end up with the number six face up, multiply the probabilities together to get $\left(\frac{1}{6}\right)\left(\frac{1}{6}\right) = \frac{1}{36}$. The correct answer is (B).

2. **H** The question asks for the expected value of an outcome. The expected value is found by taking the product of each value and the probability of its occurrence, then adding those results. There are 9 equal spaces on the wheel, which means that the probability of landing on any single space is 1 in 9. There is one space labeled $9.00, three labeled $3.00, and five labeled $0.00. Therefore, the probability of landing on $9.00 is $\frac{1}{9}$, the probability of landing on $3.00 is $\frac{3}{9}$, and the probability of landing on $0.00 is $\frac{5}{9}$. Therefore, the expected value is $\frac{1}{9}(\$9.00) + \frac{3}{9}(\$3.00) + \frac{5}{9}(\$0.00)$ = $1.00 + $1.00 + $0.00 = $2.00. The correct answer is (H).

3. **D** The question asks for the average score a bowler must earn in her last three games to earn a specific average for the 10-game season. The question says that *Stacey has an average score of exactly 240 points in the first seven games of the season*. The question also says Stacey must *earn an average score of 252 points exactly*. For averages, use the formula $T = AN$, in which T is the *total*, A is the *average*, and N is the *number of things*. To determine the total number of points Stacey earned in the first seven games, the formula becomes $T = 240(7) = 1,680$ points. To determine the total number of points Stacey must earn in the entire 10-game season, the formula becomes $T = 252(10) = 2,520$ points. Subtract the 7-game total from the 10-game total to determine the total number of points Stacey must earn in the final 3 games of the season: $2,520 - 1,680 = 840$ points. Divide this total by 3 to determine the average number of points she must earn in each of the final 3 games: $\frac{840}{3} = 280$. The correct answer is (D).

4. **H** The question asks which statement about the relationship between the mean, mode, and median of a set of numbers is true. The mode of a set of numbers is the number that appears most often. Looking at the table, this is 3, which appears four times. The median of a list of numbers is the middle number when all values are arranged in order. In lists with an even number of items, the median is the average of the middle two numbers. There are 14 integers in total in the list, so the median will be the average of the seventh and eighth numbers. The integers are already listed in order, so start counting from the least integer, which is 1. The second and third integers are 2. The fourth, fifth, sixth, and seventh integers are 3, and the eighth integer is 4. The average of the seventh and eighth integers is $\frac{3+4}{2} = \frac{7}{2} = 3.5$. This is greater than the mode, so eliminate (F) and (G). To find the mean, or average, use the formula $T = AN$, in which T is the *total*, A is the *average*, and N is the *number of things*. To find the total of the integers, multiply each integer by the number of times it occurs and add the results. This becomes $(1 \times 1) + (2 \times 2) + (3 \times 4) + (4 \times 3) + (5 \times 2) + (6 \times 1) + (7 \times 1)$, which is $1 + 4 + 12 + 12 + 10 + 6 + 7 = 52$. The average formula becomes $52 = A(14)$. Divide both sides by 14 to get $3.7 \approx A$. This is greater than the median, so eliminate (J). The correct answer is (H).

5. **B** The question asks for the number of possible orders in which the five groomsmen could walk down the aisle. Figure out how many different groomsmen can go in each position. For the first position, any of the 5 groomsmen can go. For the second position, there are only 4 groomsmen remaining. For the third position, there are 3, for the fourth position, there are 2, and for the fifth position, there is only one. To get the total possible permutations, multiply these values together to get $5 \times 4 \times 3 \times 2 \times 1 = 120$ possible orders. The correct answer is (B).

6. **F** The question asks for the probability that the product of rolling two dice is odd. A product is odd when both numbers being multiplied together are odd. Find the probability that the number rolled on each die is odd. Probability is defined as $\frac{\text{number of desired outcomes}}{\text{number of total outcomes}}$. For the first die, there are 6 possible numbers, so that is the *number of total outcomes*. Of these, 3 are odd, so that is the *number of desired outcomes*. Therefore, the probability that the first die is odd is $\frac{3}{6} = \frac{1}{2}$. For the second die, there are 8 possible numbers, so that is the *number of total outcomes*. Of these, 4 are odd, so that is the *number of desired outcomes*. Therefore, the probability that the second die is odd is $\frac{4}{8} = \frac{1}{2}$. The probability that two independent events happen is the product of the probabilities of the two events happening separately. Thus, the probability that both dice are odd is $\frac{1}{2} \times \frac{1}{2} = \frac{1}{4}$. The correct answer is (F).

7. **B**   The question asks about the number of standard deviations that represent a percent of the data. Although there are very few questions about standard deviation on the ACT, the topic does come up once in a while. For these questions, it is helpful to know the percent of the data that each standard deviation encompasses. When a data set has a normal distribution, the standard deviation function is generally broken up like this:

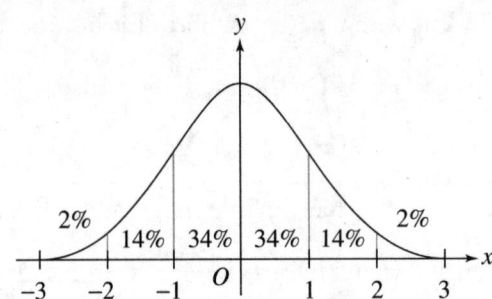

Therefore, 34% of the values are within 1 standard deviation above the mean and 34% of the values are within 1 standard deviation below the mean. The question refers to *68% of the data*, which is the sum of 34% and 34%, which means that 68% of the data is *within* 1 standard deviation of the mean. The correct answer is (B).

8. **J**   The question asks for the statement that *must* be true for Gopi's quiz scores. If the quiz scores are listed from lowest to highest, the middle score, the median, is 9. The two highest scores are both 10. Since the only mode of the quiz scores is 10, the remaining two scores must be distinct integers. The mean of the 5 scores is 8, so the sum of the five scores is 8 × 5 = 40. The sum of the two lowest scores must be 40 − (9 + 10 + 10) = 11. Choices (F) and (G) *could* be true because the quiz scores could be, for example, (5, 6, 9, 10, 10). Choice (H) is the number of scores multiplied by the mode. The correct answer is (J).

INTEGRATING ESSENTIAL SKILLS

The previous drills were from the Preparing for Higher Math category. The other category of ACT Math questions is Integrating Essential Skills. This category accounts for approximately 20% of the ACT Math Test.

Questions in this category often combine two skills or topics and tend to deal with relationships between numbers or shapes. It might not be obvious whether a question is considered Preparing for Higher Math or Integrating Essential Skills, but don't worry! Apply the same careful approach to every question, eliminate answers whenever possible, and look for the most efficient way to get questions correct.

There are three Integrating Essential Skills drills on the following pages, increasing from easy to medium to hard.

INTEGRATING ESSENTIAL SKILLS DRILL 1—EASY

1. A magician performing at children's birthday parties charges $120.00 total for a one-hour performance with 10 goody bags for children at the party. She will provide additional goody bags for $2.50 each. For an additional $25.00, she will also present a 15-minute laser light show. The magician is always paid on the day of the show, receives no tips or other additional payments, and never varies the length of the show. If the magician performs exactly four shows one weekend, presents the light show at three of those performances, and collects $635.00 total, how many additional goody bags did she provide?

   A. 26
   B. 32
   C. 48
   D. 86

2. Which of the following inequalities represents the graph shown below on the real number line?

   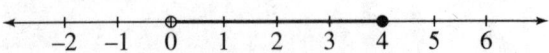

   F. $0 < x < 5$
   G. $0 < x \le 4$
   H. $0 \le x < 4$
   J. $-2 < x \le 4$

3. For the rectangle shown in the standard (x,y) coordinate plane below, what are the coordinates of the unlabeled vertex?

   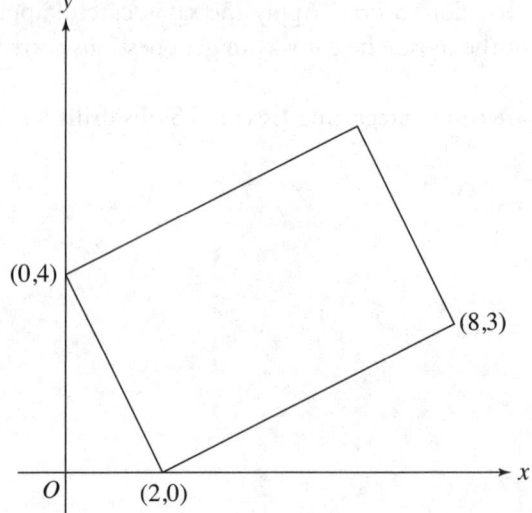

   A. $(4,5)$

   B. $\left(5, \dfrac{7}{2}\right)$

   C. $(6,7)$

   D. $(10,4)$

4. Three friends agree to share the work on a job that they know will take a total of 6 hours to complete. Jurnee works on the job by herself for $1\dfrac{4}{5}$ hours, then Jacob works by himself for another $2\dfrac{3}{5}$ hours. If Jones will complete the rest of the job by himself, how many hours will he need to work?

   F. $4\dfrac{2}{5}$

   G. $2\dfrac{4}{5}$

   H. $1\dfrac{4}{5}$

   J. $1\dfrac{3}{5}$

5. 20% of 20 is equal to 50% of what number?

   A. 4
   B. 8
   C. 10
   D. 200

6. There are 45 musicians in an orchestra, and all play two instruments. Of these musicians, 36 play the piano, and 22 play the violin. What is the maximum possible number of orchestra members who play both the piano and the violin?

   F. 9
   G. 13
   H. 22
   J. 36

7. The Northampton Volunteer Association has built a rectangular sandbox for a local elementary school and is ready to fill it with sand. The sandbox is 60 inches wide, 72 inches long, and will be filled 18 inches deep. Under the assumption that 1 bag of sand can fill 3,600 cubic inches of the sandbox, what is the minimum number of bags of sand they will need in order to fill the sandbox?

   A. 7
   B. 12
   C. 21
   D. 22

8. Salvador is trying to scale his rectangular self-portrait down to postcard size. The painting is 9 feet wide by 16 feet long. He is using a scale of $\frac{1}{3}$ inch = 1 foot for the postcard-sized self-portrait. What will be the dimensions, in inches, of Salvador's postcard-sized self-portrait?

   F. $1\frac{1}{3}$ by 4

   G. 3 by $5\frac{1}{3}$

   H. 3 by 4

   J. 27 by 48

9. Phil earned $800 at his summer job and saved all of his earnings. He wants to buy a deluxe drum kit that is regularly priced at $925 but is on sale for $\frac{1}{5}$ off. The drum kit is subject to 5% sales tax after all discounts are applied. If Phil buys the kit on sale and gives the sales clerk his entire summer earnings, how much change should he receive?

   A. $23
   B. $37
   C. $77
   D. None; Phil still owes $171.25.

10. The circumference of a car tire is 75 inches. About how many revolutions does this car tire make traveling 225 feet (2,700 inches) without slipping?

   F. 3
   G. 14
   H. 36
   J. 432

11. At Fatima's Fruits, a bag of eight grapefruits costs $4.40. At Ernie's Edibles, a bag of three grapefruits costs $1.86. How much cheaper, per grapefruit, is the cost at Fatima's Fruits than at Ernie's Edibles?

   A. $0.07
   B. $0.35
   C. $0.59
   D. $1.17

INTEGRATING ESSENTIAL SKILLS DRILL 1 EXPLANATIONS

1. **B** The question asks for the number of additional goody bags the magician provided. The magician receives $4(\$120) + 3(\$25) = \$555$ in payment for performances and light shows, leaving $\$635 - \$555 = \$80$ in payment for additional goody bags. Since each costs $2.50, she provides $\frac{80}{2.5} = 32$ bags. Choice (A) calculates all 4.75 hours worked at the $120 rate. Choice (C) divides the $120 and $2.50 from the problem without answering the question, and (D) miscalculates based on three performances instead of four. The correct answer is (B).

2. **G** The question asks for the inequality that describes the graph. Use Process of Elimination. Start by looking at the endpoints on the number line and match those up with the inequality signs in the answer choices. The left circle at 0 is an open circle, so this corresponds to <, eliminating (H). The right circle at 4 is a closed circle, so this corresponds to ≤, eliminating (F). Now look at the range of values covered in the line: 0 to 4—a range that does not include –2, as (J) suggests. The correct answer is (G).

3. **C** The question asks for the coordinates of the unlabeled vertex of the rectangle. Use Process of Elimination. Because the unlabeled point is higher up on the graph than the point on the y-axis, the y-coordinate must be larger than 4; eliminate (B). The unlabeled point is to the left of the point (8, 3), so the x-coordinate must be less than 8; eliminate (D). The unlabeled point is not in the center of the rectangle horizontally (i.e., halfway between 0 and 8 on the x-axis), so eliminate (A). Alternatively, since the figure is a rectangle, opposite sides must be equal in length and parallel, meaning they have the same slope. The slope of the side between the points (2, 0) and (8, 3) is 6 units right and 3 units up. The side between the point (0, 4) and the unlabeled point will have the same length and slope, so the coordinates of the unlabeled point are (0 + 6, 4 + 3) = (6, 7). The correct answer is (C).

4. **J** The question asks how long it will take Jones to complete the job by himself. Start by adding together the number of hours that Jurnee and Jacob worked. Add the whole numbers and the fractions separately to avoid making a mistake: $1\frac{4}{5} + 2\frac{3}{5} = (1+2) + \left(\frac{4}{5} + \frac{3}{5}\right) = 3 + \frac{7}{5} = 4\frac{2}{5}$. Now subtract $4\frac{2}{5}$ from 6 to get Jones's time as $1\frac{3}{5}$ hours. The correct answer is (J).

5. **B** The question asks for the value of a series of percents. Use the words in the problem to create an equation: *percent* means "divide by 100," *of* means "multiply," and *what number* means "use a variable." The resulting equation is $\frac{20}{100} \times 20 = \frac{50}{100} \times y$. Do the multiplication to find $4 = 0.5y$; then divide both sides by 0.5 to get $y = 8$. Be careful of (A), which is 20% of 20, and (C), which is 50% of 20. The correct answer is (B).

6. **H** The question asks for the maximum number of orchestra members who play both instruments. Use Process of Elimination. The number of piano players exceeds the number of violin players; thus, the number of musicians who play both instruments cannot exceed the number who play violin, eliminating (J). Since all 22 musicians who play the violin could also play the piano, (H) gives the maximum possible number. The correct answer is (H).

7. **D** The question asks for the total number of sand bags required to fill the sandbox. First, find the volume of the sandbox by substituting the provided dimensions into the formula for the volume of a rectangular prism, $V = lwh$: the equation becomes $V = (60)(72)(18)$ and solves to $V = 77{,}760$. Now, find the number of sand bags required by dividing this volume by the volume of sand in a single bag: 77,760 cubic inches ÷ 3,600 cubic inches per bag = 21.6 bags required. Since more than 21 bags would be required to fill the sandbox, round up to the nearest integer to get a final answer of 22. The correct answer is (D).

8. **G** The question asks for the dimensions of Salvador's self-portrait when shrunk to postcard size. Use proportions to convert from the original to the scaled size. Since 1 foot of original size will become $\frac{1}{3}$ inch when scaled, the new width can be found by solving $\frac{\frac{1}{3} \text{ inch}}{1 \text{ foot}} = \frac{x \text{ inches}}{9 \text{ feet}}$. Cross-multiply to find that $1x = 9 \times \frac{1}{3}$, so $x = 3$. Since the width is 3, eliminate (F) and (J), which give incorrect widths. Repeat this process to find the height: $\frac{\frac{1}{3} \text{ inch}}{1 \text{ foot}} = \frac{x \text{ inches}}{16 \text{ feet}}$, which cross-multiplies to $1x = 16 \times \frac{1}{3}$ and solves to $x = 5\frac{1}{3}$. The correct answer is (G).

9. **A** The question asks how much change Phil receives. Work through the problem one step at a time. First, find the sale price of the drum kit: $\frac{1}{5} \times \$925 = \$185$, so the sale price of the drum kit is $\$925 - \$185 = \$740$. Since the sales tax is $0.05 \times \$740 = \$37$, the total owed is $\$740 + \$37 = \$777$. Phil receives back the amount he gave the sales clerk minus the amount he owes: $\$800 - \$777 = \$23$. Choice (B) is the amount of tax paid. Choice (C) resembles numbers from steps within the problem, and (D) calculates the taxed price without applying the sale discount. The correct answer is (A).

10. **H** The question asks for the number of tire rotations needed to travel 225 feet or 2,700 inches. Since the circumference is given in inches, use the distance of 2,700 inches. For every single revolution, the tire will travel a horizontal distance equivalent to that tire's circumference. To find how many revolutions this tire makes, simply divide 2,700 inches ÷ 75 inches = 36 revolutions. Choice (F) incorrectly pairs units by dividing 225 *feet* by 75 *inches*, and (J) confuses the units for 2,700 *inches* and treats that measure as if it were given in feet. The correct answer is (H).

11. **A** The question asks for the difference in the prices of grapefruits at the two stores. Work through the problem one step at a time. Find the cost per grapefruit at each store by dividing the cost of each bag by the number of grapefruits in each bag. The cost per grapefruit at Fatima's is $4.40 ÷ 8 = $0.55, while the cost per grapefruit at Ernie's is $1.86 ÷ 3 = $0.62. Find the difference: $0.62 − $0.55 = $0.07. Choice (B) comes from multiplying $0.07 by the difference in the number of grapefruits (8 − 3 = 5). Choice (C) comes from averaging $0.55 and $0.62. Choice (D) comes from adding $0.55 and $0.62. The correct answer is (A).

INTEGRATING ESSENTIAL SKILLS DRILL 2—MEDIUM

1. Jasper wants to measure the altitude of his kite. He ties the kite string to a spike driven into the ground and measures the angle between the string and the ground. Then, he creates two similar triangles by adjusting the distance between an 8-foot pole and the spike until the angle created by a piece of string tied to the top of the pole and to the spike in the ground is the same as the angle he measured previously. The length of the string to the kite is 85 feet and the length of the string to the pole is 17 feet. Which of the following is closest to the height, in feet, that the kite is above the ground?

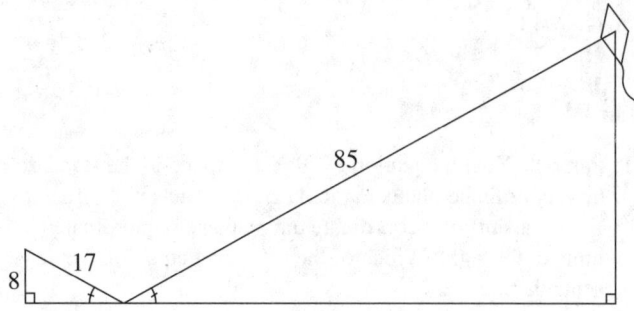

A. 25
B. 40
C. 102
D. 181

2. What is the y-intercept of the line given by the equation $7x - 3y = 21$?

F. -7

G. $-\dfrac{7}{3}$

H. $\dfrac{7}{3}$

J. 7

3. A company will reimburse its employees' personal expenses on weekend business trips. It will reimburse $0.80 for every $1.00 an employee spends, up to $100.00. For the next $200 an employee spends, the company will reimburse $0.70 for every $1.00 spent. For each additional dollar spent after that, the company will reimburse $0.60. If an employee was reimbursed $400.00, approximately how many dollars must she have spent on a weekend business trip?

A. 667
B. 600
C. 500
D. 367

4. The following table shows the ages of all the attendees of Camp Wannaboggin.

Age	9	10	11	12	13
Percent of campers	10%	24%	21%	37%	8%

What percent of the Wannaboggin campers are at least 11 years old?

F. 34%
G. 45%
H. 55%
J. 66%

5. Which of the following geometric figures has at least 1 rotational symmetry and at least 1 reflectional symmetry?

(Note: The angle of rotation for the rotational symmetry must be less than 360°.)

A. ▱

B. ◁

C. ⬡

D. ⏢

6. In rectangle *ABCD* below, $\overline{BC}$ is 16 inches long and $\overline{CD}$ is 12 inches long. Points *E*, *F*, and *G* are the midpoints of $\overline{AD}$, $\overline{AB}$, and $\overline{BC}$, respectively. What is the perimeter, in inches, of pentagon *CDEFG* ?

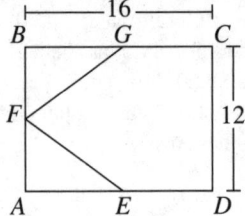

- **F.** 48
- **G.** 56
- **H.** 96
- **J.** 192

7. The ratio of a side of square *X* to the length of rectangle *Z* is 3:4. The ratio of a side of square *X* to the width of rectangle *Z* is 3:2. What is the ratio of the area of square *X* to the area of rectangle *Z* ?

- **A.** 1:1
- **B.** 2:1
- **C.** 9:4
- **D.** 9:8

8. What is the least common multiple of 8, 2, 3*a*, 6*b*, and 4*ab* ?

- **F.** 16*ab*
- **G.** 24*ab*
- **H.** 24*a²b*
- **J.** 54*ab*

9. A rectangular piece of paper has 2 adjacent sides represented by $5d + 4$ inches and $d + 3$ inches. What is the area, in terms of *d*, of the rectangle in square inches?

- **A.** $5d^2 + 19d + 12$
- **B.** $5d^2 + 19d + 7$
- **C.** $5d^2 + 9d + 12$
- **D.** $5d^2 + 12$

10. Evan purchased 6 boxes of sugar cookies, each box containing 10 snack bags and each bag containing 12 cookies. Evan could have purchased the same amount of cookies by buying how many family-sized packs of 30 cookies each?

- **F.** 24
- **G.** 48
- **H.** 72
- **J.** 180

11. Parabola Y with equation $y = 9x^2$ is graphed in the standard (x,y) coordinate plane. Parabola Z is the image of Parabola Y after a shift of 2 coordinate units up and 6 coordinate units to the right. Which of the following equations represents Parabola Z ?

- **A.** $y = 9(x - 6)^2 - 2$
- **B.** $y = 9(x - 6)^2 + 2$
- **C.** $y = 9(x + 6)^2 - 2$
- **D.** $y = 9(x + 6)^2 + 2$

INTEGRATING ESSENTIAL SKILLS DRILL 2 EXPLANATIONS

1. **B** The question asks for the vertical height of the kite. Since the triangles are similar, set up a proportion: $\frac{8}{17} = \frac{x}{85}$. Cross-multiply to get $17x = 680$; then divide both sides by 17 to find that $x = 40$. Choice (A) is $17 + 8 = 25$. Choice (C) is $85 + 17 = 102$. Choice (D) flips one side of the proportion: $\frac{8}{17} = \frac{85}{x}$. The correct answer is (B).

2. **F** The question asks for the y-intercept of the given line. One way to solve this problem is to rewrite the equation in the slope-intercept form, $y = mx + b$. First, subtract $7x$ from both sides of the equation to get $-3y = -7x + 21$. Then divide both sides by -3 to get $y = \frac{7}{3}x - 7$. In this equation, -7 is the value of b, the y-intercept. Alternatively, plug $x = 0$ into the equation as-is, since the y-intercept occurs at $x = 0$. The equation becomes $7(0) - 3y = 21$. Solve for y: the equation becomes $-3y = 21$ and dividing both sides by -3 results in $y = -7$. Choice (H) is the slope of the line, and the other choices do not modify the equation correctly. The correct answer is (F).

3. **B** The question asks for the total amount of money spent by the employee. For the first $100.00 spent, multiply $100.00 × $0.80 = $80.00 that the company will reimburse. For the next $200.00 spent, multiply $200.00 × $0.70 = $140.00. So far, for $300.00 spent, the company will have reimbursed $80.00 + $140.00 = $220.00. Subtract $400.00 – $220.00 = $180.00 that the employee was reimbursed. To find the additional amount of money the employee must have spent, set up an equation with x as the additional number of dollars. The reimbursement rate on the remaining money is $0.60 per dollar spent, so the equation is $0.60(x) = $180. Divide both sides by $0.60 to find that $x = $300.00. Finally, add all of the dollars spent: $100.00 + $200.00 + $300.00 = $600.00. The correct answer is (B).

4. **J** The question asks for the percentage of campers who are at least 11 years old. The campers who are *at least 11 years old* include the 11-, 12-, and 13-year-olds. Because all the values in the chart represent percents of the same number, simply add them together to get $21 + 37 + 8 = 66\%$, or (J). Choice (F) counts only the 9- and 10-year-old percentages; (G) counts the percentage of everyone older than 11 (12- and 13-year-olds); and (H) counts ages up to and including 11. The correct answer is (J).

5. **C** The question asks for the shape that has both reflectional and rotational symmetry. A geometric figure has rotational symmetry if it looks the same after a certain amount of rotation. A geometric figure has reflectional symmetry when one half is the reflection of the other half. The shape in (D) has reflectional symmetry if cut vertically in half, but (C) is the only figure that has rotational and reflectional symmetry. The correct answer is (C).

6. **F**   The question asks for the perimeter of the pentagon. Use the Pythagorean Theorem to find the length of $\overline{EF}$. The midpoints cut each side of the rectangle in half, so $AF = 6$ and $AE = 8$. Right triangle AFE, then, is a 6:8:10 triangle, and $EF = 10$. FG is also 10, and the perimeter of the pentagon is $10 + 10 + 8 + 12 + 8 = 48$ inches. Choice (G) is the perimeter of the rectangle. Choice (H) is the area of a triangle with the same base and height as the rectangle. Choice (J) is the area of the rectangle. The correct answer is (F).

7. **D**   The question asks for the ratio of the areas of two shapes. Substitute in a real value for the side length of square X to find the measure of the sides for rectangle Z, and then find the area of each shape using those values. The easiest thing to do is to use the numbers in the ratios if possible. If each side of square X measured 3 units, then the 3:4 ratio of the side of X to the length of Z gives the rectangle a length of 4. The 3:2 ratio between the side of X and the width of Z gives the rectangle a width of 2. Using these same numbers, the area of the square, s^2, is $(3)^2$ or 9; the area of the rectangle, lw, is 4×2 or 8. The ratio of the area of the square to the area of the rectangle is 9:8. The correct answer is (D).

8. **G**   The question asks for the least common multiple of the given numbers. First, factor each number. In this problem, the given numbers are all products of 2, 3, a, and b. To find the least common multiple of the given values, figure out the maximum number of times each component (2, 3, a, and b) appears in any one of the given values. $8 = 2 \times 2 \times 2$, so the lowest common multiple must have $2 \times 2 \times 2$ as a factor. No value has more than one factor of 3, so the number is required to have only one factor of 3. Finally, the least common multiple must have one a and one b. Multiply the mandatory factors together, $2 \times 2 \times 2 \times 3 \times a \times b$, to get $24ab$. The correct answer is (G).

9. **A**   The question asks for the area of a rectangle. The question says the sides are *represented by 5d + 4 and d + 3 inches*. The formula for the area of a rectangle is $A = lw$, so plug in the expressions given in the question to get $A = (5d + 4)(d + 3)$. Use FOIL to get $A = 5d^2 + 15d + 4d + 12$, then combine like terms to get $A = 5d^2 + 19d + 12$. The correct answer is (A).

10. **F**   The question asks for the amount of family-sized packs of cookies that would have given Evan the same number of cookies as his original purchase. If Evan purchased 6 boxes with 10 bags in each box and 12 cookies in each bag, he will have purchased $6 \times 10 \times 12 = 720$ cookies. Dividing 720 by 30 will give the number of family packs with 30 cookies that he could have purchased instead: $720 \div 30 = 24$. The correct answer is (F).

11. **B**   The question asks for the equation of a parabola that is shifted from another parabola. The equation of a parabola is represented as $y = a(x - h)^2 + k$ in which (h, k) is the vertex. Translate the question one piece at a time. One piece of information says *Parabola Z is a shift of 2 coordinate units up.* Up means along the vertical axis, and k is the y-coordinator of the vertex. To shift up 2 units, the equation should have $k = 2$, so eliminate (A) and (C). Another piece of information says *Parabola Z is a shift of 6 coordinate units to the right.* Unlike transformations that move up or down, shifts to the left or the right have the opposite sign of the direction in which the graph moves. The equation should have $h = 6$, with subtraction between the x and the 6 in parentheses, so eliminate (D). If transformation of graphs gets tricky, another option is to graph $y = 9x^2$ on a graphing calculator. Then graph the equations in the answers to see which one moved in the correct way. Either way, the correct answer is (B).

INTEGRATING ESSENTIAL SKILLS DRILL 3—HARD

1. A basketball player has attempted 30 free throws and made 12 of them. Starting now, if he makes every free throw attempted, what is the *least* number of additional free throws he must attempt to raise his free-throw percentage to at least 55% ?

   (Note: Free-throw percentage =

   $\dfrac{number\ of\ free\ throws\ made}{number\ of\ free\ throws\ attempted} \times 100$)

   A. 5
   B. 10
   C. 16
   D. 29

2. During a daily training race, Carl has to stop to tie his shoes. Melissa, whose shoes are Velcro, continues to run and gets 20 feet ahead of Carl. Melissa is running at a constant rate of 8 feet per second, and Carl starts running at a constant rate of 9.2 feet per second to catch up to Melissa. Which of the following equations, when solved for s, gives the number of seconds Carl will take to catch up to Melissa?

   F. $8s + 20 = 9.2s$
   G. $8s - 20 = 9.2s$
   H. $8s = 20$
   J. $9.2s = 20$

3. The point $(24,3)$ on a standard (x,y) coordinate plane is halfway between points $(z,2z + 1)$ and $(15z,z - 4)$. What is the value of z ?

   A. 1
   B. 1.5
   C. 3
   D. 7

4. If $X = \begin{bmatrix} 1 & 0 \\ -2 & -1 \end{bmatrix}$, $Y = \begin{bmatrix} 3 & 1 & 0 \\ 1 & 2 & 6 \end{bmatrix}$, and $Z = \begin{bmatrix} 1 & 2 \\ 0 & -1 \\ 1 & 3 \end{bmatrix}$, then what is the value of $YZ + X$, if it can be calculated?

   F. $\begin{bmatrix} 4 & 5 \\ 5 & 17 \end{bmatrix}$

   G. $\begin{bmatrix} -5 & -4 \\ 2 & -1 \end{bmatrix}$

   H. $\begin{bmatrix} 3 & 2 \\ 0 & -2 \\ 0 & 18 \end{bmatrix}$

   J. $YZ + X$ cannot be calculated.

5. As shown in the (x,y,z) coordinate space below, the cube with vertices L through S has edges that are 2 coordinate units long. The coordinates of Q are $(0,0,0)$, and S is on the positive x-axis. What are the coordinates of O ?

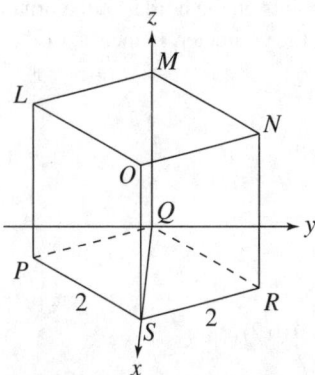

   A. $(2,0,2)$

   B. $(2,2,2)$

   C. $(2\sqrt{2},0,2)$

   D. $(2\sqrt{2},0,2\sqrt{3})$

6. A marathon runner records her speed in kilometers per hour while running in a marathon for 5 hours. According to the chart of the data she recorded below, what was her speed's rate of change, in kilometers per hour, between hours 1 and 3 ?

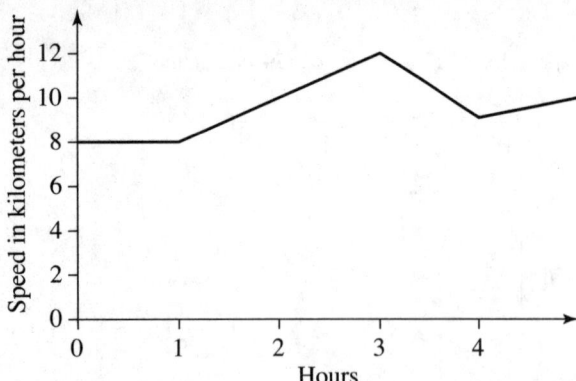

F. 1
G. 2
H. 4
J. 12

7. A heart-shaped ornament is made from a square and two semicircles, each of whose diameter is a side of the square. The ornament is shown in the standard (x,y) coordinate plane below, where 1 coordinate unit represents 1 inch. The coordinates of six points on the border of the ornament are given. What is the perimeter, in inches, of the ornament?

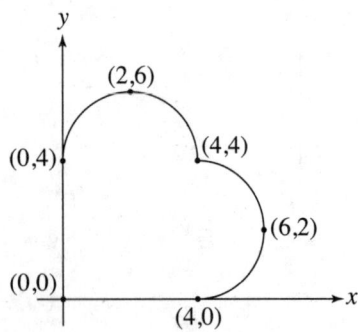

A. $4 + 2\pi$
B. $8 + 4\pi$
C. $8 + 8\pi$
D. $16 + 8\pi$

8. The measure of the sum of the interior angles of a regular n-sided polygon is $(n-2)180°$. A regular octagon is shown below. What is the measure of the designated angle?

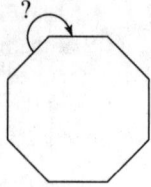

F. 135°
G. 144°
H. 200°
J. 225°

9. What values of x satisfy the equation $x^2 - 4x + 13 = 0$?

A. $2 \pm 3i$
B. $2 \pm \left(\sqrt{17}\right)i$
C. $2 \pm 6i$
D. $4 \pm 6i$

10. An angle in the standard (x,y) coordinate plane has its vertex at the origin and its initial side on the positive x-axis. If the measure of an angle in standard position is $(1,314°)$, it has the same terminal side as an angle of each of the following measures EXCEPT:

F. 594°
G. 314°
H. −126°
J. −486°

11. An artist creates a new sculpture that consists of tangent spheres. The top view, front view, and left side view are shown below, with labels to show where the top (T), front (F), and left (L) sides are in relation to each perspective. If the radius of one of the spheres is 1 m, what is the combined surface area of the spheres in the sculpture, in meters squared?

Note: the surface area of a sphere is given by the equation $4\pi r^2$.

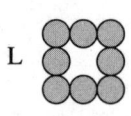

top

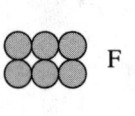

front   left

A. 24π
B. 36π
C. 44π
D. 72π

INTEGRATING ESSENTIAL SKILLS DRILL 3 EXPLANATIONS

1. **B** The question asks for the least number of additional free throws the basketball player must make to raise his free-throw percentage to 55%. If the basketball player made 12 out of his 30 shots, he currently has a free-throw percentage of 40%. Use the answers to calculate the least number of additional free throws he must make. Make sure to add the number to both the numerator and denominator, since any additional free throws are both attempted and made. Choice (B) gives $\frac{12+10}{30+10} \times 100 = 55\%$. Choice (A) is the result of adding 5 only to the numerator. Choice (C) approximates 55% of 30 free throws. Choice (D) incorrectly raises the percentage *by* 55% rather than *to* 55%. The correct answer is (B).

2. **F** The question asks for the equation that correctly describes the scenario. To solve this problem, use the distance formula $d = rt$. If both runners start from the point at which Carl had to stop to tie his shoes, and d represents the distance each person has run when they meet, then Carl will run $d = 9.2s$ and Melissa will run $d = 8s + 20$ because she has a 20-foot head start. Because d is the same for each equation, simply set these equations equal to each other to find $8s + 20 = 9.2s$. Choice (G) gives Carl the 20-foot head start instead of Melissa. The correct answer is (F).

3. **C** The question asks for the value of z. If (24,3) is the midpoint of the other two points, then the average of the two x-values should be 24. This becomes $\frac{z+15z}{2} = 24$ or $\frac{16z}{2} = 24$. Multiply both sides by 2 to get $16z = 48$, so $z = 3$, or (C). Choice (B) mistakenly calculates $z + 15z = 24$ (so $z = 1.5$). The other choices mistakenly set point values equal to each other. Choice (A) calculates $2z + 1 = 3$ (so $z = 1$), and (D) calculates $z - 4 = 3$ (so $z = 7$). The correct answer is (C).

4. **F** The question asks for the value of an expression involving matrices. Start by using Process of Elimination. When doing multiplication on matrices, the resulting matrix will have the same number of rows as the first matrix and the same number of columns as the second matrix. The matrix YZ will have 2 rows and 2 columns and will retain these dimensions when matrix X is added. Eliminate (H), which does not have these dimensions. Now calculate YZ. To multiply matrices, take the products of each number in the first row of the first matrix and each number in the first column of the second matrix, then add the results to get the number in the upper left of the resulting matrix. Then continue this process with each row and column. Often it will not be necessary to completely multiply the matrices together to get the correct answer. For YZ, the number in the upper left is $3(1) + 1(0) + 0(1) = 3 + 0 + 0 = 3$. When adding matrices, just add the numbers in corresponding positions. The number in the upper left of $YZ + X$ will be $3 + 1 = 4$. Eliminate (G). Also eliminate (J) because these matrices are the correct dimensions to multiply and add, so the value of $YZ + X$ can be calculated. The correct answer is (F).

5. **C**   The question asks for the three-dimensional coordinate of point O. Compare point O to the answer choices, watching the order of the three axes. Point O shifts neither to the left nor right in the y direction, so the y-value will be 0, eliminating (B). The height of the cube is 2 units and side $\overline{OS}$ starts where z is 0, so the z-coordinate of O is 2, eliminating (D). The distance along the x-axis from Q to S is the diagonal of square $PQRS$. The diagonal of a square is the value of its side times $\sqrt{2}$, which in this case is $2\sqrt{2}$, meaning that the x-value of O is $2\sqrt{2}$, eliminating (A). The correct answer is (C).

6. **G**   The question asks for the rate of change of a marathon runner's speed between hours 1 and 3. *Rate of change* means slope. Use the slope formula to calculate the slope between hours 1 and 3. The equation for slope is $slope = \dfrac{y_2 - y_1}{x_2 - x_1}$. Read the figure carefully to find the points to use in the slope formula. The speed at 1 hour is 8, so the coordinates at hour 1 are (1, 8). The speed at 3 hours is 12, so the coordinates at hour 3 are (3, 12). Plug these into the formula to get $slope = \dfrac{12 - 8}{3 - 1} = \dfrac{4}{2} = 2$. The correct answer is (G).

7. **B**   The question asks for the perimeter of a figure. The perimeter is the distance around the shape's outline. There are two straight lines: from (0, 0) to (0, 4) and from (0, 0) to (4, 0), each with a length of 4. The straight lines total 8, eliminating (A) and (D). The curved parts are two semicircles, and two semicircles make one complete circle, so find the circumference of one circle with radius 2: $C = 2\pi r = 2\pi(2) = 4\pi$. The entire perimeter is thus $8 + 4\pi$. The correct answer is (B).

8. **J**   The question asks for the measure of the indicated angle. First, use Process of Elimination: since the angle shown is clearly larger than 180°, eliminate (F) and (G). Octagons have 8 sides, so using the formula in the question, the sum of the interior angles measures $(8 - 2)180 = 1,080$. The angles of regular polygons are equal, so divide by 8 to find the measure of each angle: $\dfrac{1,080}{8} = 135°$. The designated angle in the figure is an exterior angle, and there are 360° in a circle, so subtract the interior angle from 360° to find the measure of the designated angle: $360° - 135° = 225°$. The correct answer is (J).

9. **A**   The question asks for the values of x that satisfy the equation. The fact that the answers have the $\pm$ symbol is a clue that the quadratic formula will be needed. This formula for quadratics in standard form $ax^2 + bx + c = 0$ gives the solutions as $x = \dfrac{-b \pm \sqrt{b^2 - 4ac}}{2a}$. For the given equation, $a = 1$, $b = -4$, and $c = 13$. Plug these into the formula to get $x = \dfrac{-(-4) \pm \sqrt{(-4)^2 - 4(1)(13)}}{2(1)}$. This simplifies to $x = \dfrac{4 \pm \sqrt{16 - 52}}{2} = \dfrac{4 \pm \sqrt{-36}}{2}$. Simplify further by splitting the right side into two fractions to get $x = \dfrac{4}{2} \pm \dfrac{\sqrt{-36}}{2}$. The first fraction on

the right will reduce to 2, so (D) can be eliminated. Rewrite $\sqrt{-36}$ as $\sqrt{(-1)(36)}$, which becomes $6\sqrt{-1}$.

The square root of −1 is i, so the equation becomes $x = 2 \pm \dfrac{6i}{2}$ or $x = 2 \pm 3i$. The correct answer is (A).

10. **G** The question asks for the angle that does NOT have the same terminal side as 1,314°. Since terminal angles are defined as angles that are at the same rotational position on a circle, find these matching terminal angles by repeatedly subtracting full revolutions of 360° from the original angle. Begin with 1,314° − 360° = 954° and continue subtracting by 360° to get other terminal angles: 954° − 360° = 594°, eliminating (F); 234° − 360° = −126°, eliminating (H); and −126° − 360° = −486°, eliminating (J). The correct answer is (G).

11. **C** The question asks for the total surface area of the spheres in the sculpture. Start by trying to draw a 3-dimensional image of the sculpture to determine how many spheres it contains. The top view shows that there is a base layer of 8 spheres.

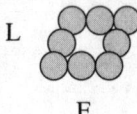

The front view shows that there must be at least one sphere in the top layer along the left side of the base, but it is not clear if it is in the front, middle, or rear position or even if there is more than one in that row. The left view shows that there are spheres in the front, middle, and back of the top layer in the row on the left. The sculpture must look like this:

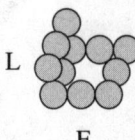

Therefore, there are 11 total spheres. Use the formula for the surface area to find the surface area of 1 sphere. The radius is 1 m, so the surface area is $4\pi(1)^2 = 4\pi$. Multiply this by 11 to get the total surface area of all the spheres as $11(4\pi) = 44\pi$. The correct answer is (C).

Reading Drills

A NOTE ON HIGHLIGHTING

If you are taking your ACT online, any references to specific lines (such as "in line 2" or "based on lines 11–15") or paragraphs (such as "according to the seventh paragraph") will instead be presented as highlighted text, and the passage will automatically jump to the highlighted text within the passage once you reach any question with highlighted text. This will make it slightly easier to locate the relevant portion of the passage. Otherwise, there are no major differences to the presentation of Reading between the paper-and-pencil and the online ACT.

KEY IDEAS AND DETAILS

The Key Ideas and Details reporting category accounts for 44–52% of the Reading questions you will encounter on your ACT. These questions assess your ability to determine central ideas and themes, summarize information from the passage, understand relationships in the passage, and make logical conclusions from the passage. Simply stated, these questions are rather directly about the informational content present in the passage. They are not asking why the author included something or how the passage might be analyzed. The following pages contain six Key Ideas and Details passages, each with 8 or 9 questions that you can practice on if this category is an area of focus for you.

KEY IDEAS AND DETAILS DRILL 1

PROSE FICTION: This passage is adapted from the short story "Ruby" by Tristan Ivory (©2007 by Tristan Ivory).

Ruby's Downhome Diner was an institution. If you only spent one night in Franklin, Texas, someone would inevitably direct you right off Highway 79 and Pink Oak Road to Ruby's Downhome Diner, Ruby's, or The Down-
5 home; whatever name the locals gave you, there was always something there that you would enjoy.

Ruby's was named after Ruby Sanders, my grandmother. She had opened the diner with money she saved from cleaning houses and with personal loans from friends. By the time
10 I was born, Ruby's did enough business to pay off all debts and obligations. It didn't take long before my grandmother was a person of considerable stature in and around Robertson County, just like the restaurant that bore her name.

Ever since I was knee-high, I spent each sweltering
15 summer with my grandmother. This, truth be told, meant that for all practical purposes I lived at Ruby's Downhome. Time familiarized me with all nuances within the diner: there were five steps and four ingredients that separated peach preserves from peach cobbler filling; Deputy Sheriff Walter Mayes pre-
20 ferred his eggs, always cooked over-easy, to finish cooking on the top of his ham before it was transferred to his plate; Mr. Arnold delivered the milk and the buttermilk on Mondays, Thursdays, and Saturdays; and there were days when I would need to go to the general store to pick up whatever was in
25 short supply. By the time I entered high school, I could have run the diner from open to close if my Grandmother were absent, but she never was.

Perhaps the single greatest contributing factor to the success of Ruby's Diner was the omnipresent personality of
30 its namesake. Even the most hopelessly spun-around visitor who happened inside those doors would know who Ms. Ruby was. There were no sick days, vacations, or holidays. Between 5 A.M. and 9 P.M., you knew where Ruby Sanders could be found. If the diner were a sort of cell, then my grandmother was
35 its nucleus; without the nucleus, the cell would surely perish.

The people who worked at Ruby's were as dedicated as Ruby herself. There were the regulars: Del (short for Delmont) did double duty as a short-order cook and janitor, while Marlene and Deborah waited tables. Extra help would
40 be hired from time to time depending on the season and individual need. No matter how long those extra helpers stayed, they and everyone else who worked at the Downhome were family, and no one ever fell out of touch.

Ruby's did the things you'd expect a diner to do, as
45 well as the things you wouldn't. You could stop in and get yourself a nice cool drink for the road. Or you could pull up a stool at the counter and grab a steaming hot bowl of red pepper chili with a slice of corn pone or a dish of chilled and creamy homemade ice cream. Or better still, you could
50 grab a booth and try any number of full-plate entrees made to order. But you could also order a wedding cake a week in advance, take a weekend course in food preparation, or, when the time came, have your wake catered with dignity and grace.

When I was very young, I would spend most of my time
55 exploring every inch of Ruby's until the entire layout was printed indelibly in my mind. I could walk blindfolded from the basement where the dry goods were kept, up to the kitchen with the walk-in refrigerator filled with perishables, over to the main restaurant with row after row of booths and counter and stools,
60 well-worn but always cleaned after each patron had finished, and finally to the front porch, with its old wooden swing. I can see my grandmother moving from her station near the door to the kitchen, over to the counter and tables, and then back to the front again. Even now, I can see Del speedily making a double
65 order of hash, Deborah picking up a generous tip, and Marlene topping off a customer's sweet tea. Every summer sunset from that porch seemed to be more magnificent than the last.

As I got older, I took on more responsibility. There were fewer sunsets to watch and more work to be done. It was hard
70 but never dull work. The company kept me coming back despite the increasing allure of summer football leagues and idle moments with friends or girls. After all, the woman who built Ruby's was strong enough to make me forget those things, if only for the summer. I didn't know that I would never return
75 after my sophomore year of college, and for that, I am glad—I could not have asked for a better end to my long history at Ruby's. It warms my heart when I think of the last memory of Ruby Sanders: tying her silver hair into a tight bun, hands vigorously wiping down tables with a rag, enjoying a story
80 and a laugh as we closed for the night.

1. Based on the narrator's characterization, Ruby Sanders would best be described as:

   A. always at the diner, though she often preferred to be absent.
   B. the main force holding the diner and its employees together.
   C. carefree, particularly when it came to hearing humorous stories.
   D. the only woman the narrator had ever respected.

2. Information in the last paragraph most strongly suggests that the narrator felt his last summer at the diner to be:

   F. disappointing because he didn't know it would be his last.
   G. something he was forced to do when he would rather have been playing football.
   H. pleasant although he did not know it would be his last.
   J. exhausting because of all his new responsibilities.

3. According to the narrator, working at Ruby's Diner was:

   A. easy but tedious.
   B. difficult but enjoyable.
   C. hard and monotonous.
   D. unpredictable and overwhelming.

4. According to the narrator, his grandmother was like the diner in that she had:

   F. a position of high standing within the community at large.
   G. a desire to make all people feel comfortable no matter who they were.
   H. an ability to make money within the community.
   J. a refusal to settle for anything but the best.

5. The statement in lines 44–45 most strongly suggests that the Downhome Diner:

   A. served the community in ways beyond simple dining.
   B. was the most significant place within Robertson County.
   C. gave the people who worked there great importance in Robertson County.
   D. was a place where the waiting times were often unpredictable.

6. The narrator describes Ruby's Downhome Diner as providing all of the following EXCEPT:

   F. cooking classes.
   G. football leagues.
   H. wedding cakes.
   J. corn pone.

7. The passage indicates that one of the ways in which the narrator was familiar with Ruby's Downhome Diner was shown by his:

   A. ability to teach the cooking classes held on the premises.
   B. awareness of the habits of visitors to Robertson County.
   C. detailed memory of the layout of the kitchen and the restaurant.
   D. unwillingness to leave at the end of each summer before his return to school.

8. According to the narrator, which of the following most accurately represents the reason he was able to forget the summer activities outside while working at his grandmother's restaurant?

   F. His tips and wages helped to contribute to his college tuition.
   G. His grandmother's restaurant was chronically understaffed.
   H. It helped him to gain stature in and around the community.
   J. He admired his grandmother's strength.

KEY IDEAS AND DETAILS DRILL 1 EXPLANATIONS

1. **B** The question asks how best to describe Ruby Sanders. Because this is a general question, it should be done after all the specific questions. The fourth paragraph describes how Ruby was *omnipresent* at the diner, but there is no indication that she *preferred to be absent;* eliminate (A). Lines 34–35 use the metaphor of a cell to describe Ruby's importance to the diner: *without the nucleus* (that is, Ruby), *the cell* (the diner) *would surely perish.* This supports the idea in (B). Lines 79–80 describe Ruby *enjoying a story and a laugh,* but this is one small detail, not the main characterization of her; eliminate (C). The passage does not discuss any women other than Ruby at any length, so it is not possible to say whether Ruby was *the only woman the narrator had ever respected;* eliminate (D). The correct answer is (B).

2. **H** The question asks how the narrator felt about his last summer at the diner based on the last paragraph. Read the last paragraph. Lines 74–76 state that the narrator *didn't know that [he] would never return,* and that *[he] could not have asked for a better end.* There is no indication that it was *disappointing,* so eliminate (F). There is also no indication that he was *forced* to do anything, so eliminate (G). Choice (H) is supported by lines 74–76. Line 68 says that the narrator *took on more responsibility,* but there is no indication of that responsibility being *exhausting;* eliminate (J). The correct answer is (H).

3. **B** The question asks what working at Ruby's Diner was like. Look for the word *work* to find the answer to the question. Lines 69–70 say *It was hard but never dull work.* Choice (A) is the opposite of this idea, so eliminate it. Choice (B) matches lines 69–70. *Monotonous* is also contradicted by *never dull,* so eliminate (C). There is no indication of either *unpredictable* or *overwhelming,* so eliminate (D). The correct answer is (B).

4. **F** The question asks for a comparison that the narrator makes between his grandmother and the diner. Look for comparative language in the passage. In lines 11–13, the narrator says that Ruby *was a person of considerable stature in and around Robertson County, just like the restaurant that bore her name,* which matches (F). Eliminate (G) because it describes Ruby, but not the diner. Eliminate (J) for the same reason; it could describe Ruby, but not the diner. Choice (H) is the opposite; it could describe the diner, but not Ruby. Eliminate (H). The correct answer is (F).

5. **A** The question asks what is suggested about the Downhome Diner by lines 44–45, so read a window around those lines. The sixth paragraph, which starts on line 44, describes the wide array of services the diner offered, which supports (A). No other places in Robertson County are discussed, so eliminate (B). The only person whose stature in Robertson County is discussed is Ruby, and that discussion is in lines 11–13, not lines 44–45; eliminate (C). There is no discussion of *waiting times,* so eliminate (D). The correct answer is (A).

6. **G** The question asks what Ruby's Downhome Diner does not provide. When a question asks which answer is **not** in the passage, eliminate answers that **are** in the passage. Use words from the answer choices to locate the relevant portions of the passage. The sixth paragraph describes *cooking classes, wedding cakes,* and *corn pone* as things that Ruby's Diner offers, so eliminate (F), (H), and (J). *Football leagues* are mentioned in the last paragraph, but they are not something offered at the diner. The correct answer is (G).

7. **C** The question asks how the passage indicates the narrator's familiarity with the diner. Lines 55–56 state that *the entire layout [of the diner] was imprinted indelibly in [the narrator's] mind. Cooking classes* are mentioned in the sixth paragraph, but there is no indication that the narrator taught them; eliminate (A). *Visitors to Robertson County* are mentioned in the first and fourth paragraphs, but their *habits* are not described, so eliminate (B). Choice (C) is supported by lines 55–56. The last paragraph talks about a *summer before [the narrator's] return to school,* but there is no indication of *unwillingness to leave,* so eliminate (D). The correct answer is (C).

8. **J** The question asks what allows the narrator to forget the summer activities outside while working at his grandmother's restaurant. Look for the words *summer* and *work,* which appear in the last paragraph. Lines 70–74 say that *The company kept [the narrator] coming back,* and that *the woman who built Ruby's was strong enough to make [him] forget* summer activities. There is no discussion of *tips and wages,* so eliminate (F). There is no indication the diner was *understaffed,* so eliminate (G). There is no discussion of the narrator's *stature in…the community,* so eliminate (H). The paragraph does discuss *his grandmother's strength.* The correct answer is (J).

KEY IDEAS AND DETAILS DRILL 2

SOCIAL SCIENCE: This passage is adapted from the entry "Happiness" from *The Psychologist's Scientific Encyclopedia* (© 2004 by The Scientific Press of Illinois).

Lee D. Ross, a psychologist at Stanford University, has a friend who lost both her parents in the Holocaust. According to the woman, the awful events of the Holocaust taught her that it was inappropriate to be upset about trivial things in
5 life and important to enjoy human relationships. Even though the circumstances of her life were tragic, the woman was extremely happy, perhaps due to an innate sense of well-being.

According to psychologists, most of our self-reported level of happiness, a measure researchers call "subjective
10 well-being," seems to be genetically predetermined, rather than caused by experience. A study carried out by Auke Tellegen and David Lykken of the University of Minnesota compared the subjective well-being scores of both fraternal and identical twins, some of whom were raised together and
15 some of whom were separated and raised in different families. By comparing the scores of the twins, Tellegen and Lykken determined that most of the differences in people's levels of happiness are determined by differences in genetic makeup.

A genetic predisposition toward a certain level of hap-
20 piness means that regardless of what happens in a person's life, he or she will eventually adjust to the new circumstances and report the same level of subjective well-being as before. The tendency for people to maintain a consistent level of happiness despite their circumstances, known as "hedonic
25 adaptation," benefits those whose life-experiences are beset by adverse conditions, such as permanent disability or sudden loss of income. Because they return to a "genetic set point," they eventually feel just as happy as they did before the unfortunate event.

30 However, hedonic adaptation also affects the happiness of people who experience positive changes in their lives. For example, in one study conducted in the 1970s among lottery winners, it was found that a year after the winners received their money, they were no happier than non-winners.

35 Despite the quantity of research that supports hedonic adaptation, there is still some debate within the scientific community over how much people can change their baseline happiness. Kennon M. Sheldon, a psychologist at the University of Missouri-Columbia, explains that many research
40 psychologists hypothesized that certain behaviors, such as choosing particular goals in life, could affect long-term happiness. However, scientific literature suggests that these behaviors provide only a temporary increase in subjective well-being.

45 Sheldon worked alongside Sonja Lyubomirsky of the University of California at Riverside and David A. Schkade of the University of California at San Diego to determine exactly what is known about the science of happiness. They compiled the findings of existing scientific studies in the field
50 of happiness and determined that 50 percent of subjective well-being is predetermined by the genetic set point, while only about 10 percent is influenced by circumstances.

However, people are not completely at the mercy of their genes. Lyubomirsky notes that 40 percent of what con-
55 tributes to people's happiness is still unexplained, and she believes that much of this may be attributable to what she calls "intentional activity," which includes mental attitudes and behaviors that people can modify and improve. Conscious choices such as demonstrating kindness, fostering optimism,
60 and expressing gratitude may work to influence subjective well-being in much the same way that diet and exercise can affect a person's inherited predisposition toward heart disease. Lyubomirsky hopes to learn the specific mechanisms by which these conscious strategies counteract genetic forces. She and
65 Sheldon are currently expanding their study of subjective well-being to large groups of subjects to be observed over extended periods of time. Using these longitudinal studies, the researchers hope to discover the inner workings of the correlations between behaviors and mood.

70 Lyubomirsky and Sheldon's studies have found that simply choosing "happy" activities may not be the most effective way to increase happiness. Lyubomirsky says that other factors, such as variation and timing of intentional activities, are crucial in influencing happiness. For example, one study
75 has shown that subjects who varied their acts of kindness from one day to the next experienced greater happiness than those who repeated the same kind act many times. Another study demonstrated that writing a list of things to be grateful for only once a week was more effective in improving levels
80 of happiness than keeping a gratitude journal every day.

The study of happiness is still a relatively new area of psychological research. Traditionally, much more psychological research focused on depression and other disorders associated with destructive mental health, leading some psychologists
85 to suspect that overall levels of subjective well-being are low. But now that more studies are focused on positive psychology, there is evidence to the contrary. Researchers have discovered not only that personal choices improve subjective well-being from a genetic set point, but also that this level is higher than
90 traditionally expected. According to surveys conducted by the University of Chicago, only about one in ten people claim to be "not too happy." Most Americans describe themselves as "pretty happy," and 30 percent as "very happy," even without using intentional activities specifically to improve
95 their well-being.

1. The passage's focus is primarily on the:

   A. search for the specific genes known to cause hedonic adaptation.

   B. scientific studies investigating various influences on happiness.

   C. attempts by experimental psychologists to develop cures for depression.

   D. conflicting opinions of psychologists regarding the influence of genes on happiness.

2. Based on the passage, the subjects in the studies by Tellegen and Lykken and the subjects in studies by Lyubomirsky and Sheldon were similar in that both groups were:

   F. part of large groups studied over an extended time.

   G. intentionally engaged in acts of kindness.

   H. asked to describe their own subjective well-being.

   J. either identical or fraternal twins.

3. Which of the following questions is NOT answered by the passage?

   A. To what extent is a person's level of happiness determined by his or her circumstances?

   B. According to Lyubomirsky and Sheldon's studies, what are some specific things people can do to improve their subjective well-being?

   C. Does the choice of specific life goals affect happiness over a lifetime?

   D. According to Tellegen and Lykken, were twins who were raised together happier than twins who were raised apart?

4. The passage most strongly suggests that the primary goal of Lyubomirsky and Sheldon's research is to:

   F. discover the specific mechanisms that may help people overcome the level of happiness determined by their genetic set point.

   G. contradict Tellegen and Lykken's findings that genes are the primary determinant in a person's overall level of happiness.

   H. find out whether keeping a gratitude journal or engaging in kind acts is more effective at improving happiness.

   J. determine which behaviors most completely eliminate hedonic adaptation.

5. Which of the following statements best summarizes the findings of the University of Chicago surveys on happiness?

   A. Earlier psychologists were mistaken to believe people are generally depressed and experience low levels of happiness.

   B. Depression and other destructive mood disorders are uncommon in America.

   C. People are happier if they do not try to improve their subjective well-being by writing in a gratitude journal.

   D. Most people report a level of happiness higher than was traditionally expected by psychologists and researchers.

6. According to the passage, all of the following are true of the Lykken and Tellegen study EXCEPT:

   F. The subjects were paired groups of twins.

   G. Subjects rated their happiness.

   H. The twins studied were all raised together.

   J. The study found happiness is genetic.

7. According to the passage, "hedonic adaptation" (lines 24–25) is a useful trait because it can help people to:

   A. restore levels of happiness that have been interrupted or altered by tragic events.

   B. forget that they have suffered a permanent disability or loss of income.

   C. adjust quickly to positive circumstances like winning the lottery and become happier.

   D. identify with immediate family members who share their genes and choose those who are more inclined to be happy.

8. According to the passage, which of the following researchers have an ongoing collaboration?

   F. Tellegen and Lykken

   G. Sheldon and Schkade

   H. Sheldon and Lyubomirsky

   J. Schkade and Lykken

KEY IDEAS AND DETAILS DRILL 2 EXPLANATIONS

1. **B** The question asks for the primary focus of the passage. Because this is a general question, it should be done after all the specific questions. The passage describes a variety of studies on the question of happiness. There is no mention of a *specific gene*, and *hedonic adaptation* is only part of the focus of the passage, so eliminate (A). Choice (B) accurately summarizes the passage. The passage discusses possible ways to increase happiness, but not *cures for depression*, so eliminate (C). None of the psychologists disagree on *the influence of genes on happiness*, so eliminate (D). The correct answer is (B).

2. **H** The question asks for a similarity in the subjects of the studies by two pairs of researchers. Look for the words *Tellegen and Lykken* and *Lyubomirsky and Sheldon* in the passage. Tellegen and Lykken's study is described in the second paragraph, which states that their study *compared the subjective wellbeing scores of both fraternal and identical twins.* Lyubomirsky and Sheldon's study is described in the sixth through eighth paragraphs. Lines 65–67 mention their subjects, when it says the researchers are *expanding their study of subjective well-being to large groups of subjects to be observed over extended periods of time.* Eliminate (F) and (J) as each of those choices describes only one of the pairs of researchers. The eighth paragraph describes one of Lyubomirsky and Sheldon's studies in which participants *intentionally engaged in acts of kindness,* but again, this is just one pair of researchers. Eliminate (G). Both pairs of researchers depended on *subjective well-being,* so the correct answer is (H).

3. **D** The question asks which question is *NOT* answered by the passage. When a question asks which answer is **not** in the passage, eliminate answers that **are** in the passage. Use words from the answer choices to locate the relevant portions of the passage. Line 52 states that *about 10 percent [of subjective well-being] is influenced by circumstances,* which effectively answers the question in (A); eliminate (A). Lines 72–74 state that *Lyubomirsky says that...variation and timing of intentional activities, are crucial in influencing happiness,* which effectively answers the question in (B); eliminate (B). Lines 41–44 mention that *choosing particular goals in life* is one of several things that *provide only a temporary increase in subjective well-being,* which effectively answers the question in (C); eliminate (C). The passage does not provide details about the question posed in (D). The correct answer is (D).

4. **F** The question asks for the primary goal of Lyubomirsky and Sheldon's research. Look for the words *Lyubomirsky* and *Sheldon* in the passage: their research is described in the sixth through eighth paragraphs. Lines 63–64 say that *Lyubomirsky hopes to learn the specific mechanisms by which these conscious strategies counteract genetic forces,* which supports (F). Lines 50–51 state that Lyubomirsky and Sheldon *determined that 50 percent of subjective well-being is predetermined by the genetic set point,* which agrees with, rather than contradicts, Tellegen and Lykken's findings; eliminate (G). *Keeping a gratitude journal* and *engaging in kind acts* are both examples given in the eighth paragraph of activities that subjects in Lyubomirsky and Sheldon's studies engaged in, but they did not study the relative effects of the two activities, so eliminate (H). The studies aimed to *counteract genetic forces,* not to *completely eliminate* them, so eliminate (J). The correct answer is (F).

5. **D**   The question asks for a summary of the University of Chicago surveys on happiness. Look for the words *University of Chicago* in the passage. Lines 90–95 describe the surveys, and lines 89–90 indicate that the results were unexpected, in that the genetic set point of well-being *is higher than traditionally expected.* Although the survey results were unexpected, the surveys themselves did not reference *earlier psychologists,* so eliminate (A). There is no indication of the rates of *depression and other destructive mood disorders... in America,* so eliminate (B). The survey results indicate that people are generally happy *even without using intentional activities specifically to improve their wellbeing,* but it does not compare those who engage in activities such as *writing in a gratitude journal* to those who do not, so eliminate (C). Choice (D) is supported by lines 89–90. The correct answer is (D).

6. **H**   The question asks what is not true of Lykken and Tellegen's study. When a question asks which answer is **not** in the passage, eliminate answers that **are** in the passage. Look for the words *Lykken* and *Tellegen* in the passage; their study is described in the second paragraph. Lines 13–14 indicate that they studied twins, so eliminate (F). Line 13 indicates that the study used *subjective well-being,* which in lines 8–9 is defined as *self-reported levels of happiness,* so eliminate (G). Lines 14–15 states that *some of [the twins] were raised together and some...were separated and raised in different families,* which contradicts (H). Lines 17–18 say that the researchers *determined that most of the difference in people's levels of happiness are determined by differences in genetic makeup,* so eliminate (J). The correct answer is (H).

7. **A**   The question asks why hedonic adaptation is helpful. Read a window around the given lines. Lines 25–29 describe how hedonic adaptation *benefits those whose life-experiences are beset by adverse conditions* because it allows them to *return to a "genetic set point"* of happiness, which means that *they eventually feel just as happy as they did before the unfortunate event.* This explanation supports (A). There is no indication that people regain happiness because they *forget that they have suffered,* so eliminate (B). Choice (C) can be eliminated because, while *winning the lottery* is discussed in lines 32–34, the passage says that *a year after the winners received their money, they were no happier than non-winners,* which contradicts (C). The discussion of hedonic adaptation makes no mention of *family members who share...genes,* so eliminate (D). The correct answer is (A).

8. **H**   The question asks which pair of researchers has an ongoing collaboration. Use the names in the answer choices to find the relevant portions of the passage. *Tellegen* and *Lykken's* study is described in the past tense in the second paragraph, so eliminate (F). *Sheldon* is paired with *Lyubomirsky,* not with *Schkade,* so eliminate (G). Lines 64–65 say that *[Lyubomirsky] and Sheldon are currently expanding their study,* which supports (H). *Lykken* is paired with *Tellegen,* not with *Schkade,* so eliminate (J). The correct answer is (H).

KEY IDEAS AND DETAILS DRILL 3

HUMANITIES: This passage is adapted from the entry "How Songs Make Meaning" from the volume *How to Listen to Music Like a Conductor* (© 2007 by Air Guitar Press).

I used to have to feel pain in order to write songs.

Normally, this inspiration took the form of wanting or losing a girl. My heartsickness would reach a state of such unwieldy gloom that words and melodies would coalesce
5 and fall like raindrops to relieve the stress of carrying such a heavy cloud of misery. I think many of us mainly write songs for relief. It's unhealthy to keep swallowing unspoken words. Keep them on the tip of your tongue and they'll fester like bacteria. Stash them all in a song and you suddenly have an
10 emotional storage unit, which un-clutters your inner world.

The first "songs" we ever write are just exaggerated expressions of our stream of consciousness. We create theme songs while jostling with action figures, concoct mocking serenades to annoy our siblings, or narrate our inner lives
15 to a random tune. We have all been yelled at by a frustrated audience of our friends, acquaintances, and family members to cease our incessant noise making. While many learn to keep their songs to themselves as they master the rules of polite etiquette, songwriters apparently never learn. Instead, we begin
20 to turn our songs into something people will be happy to hear.

Music somehow makes people feel unashamed about being completely expressive. In speech, someone melodramatically complaining about all the injustices of his world would probably be chastised for lacking self-control. However,
25 in song, a proclamation of suffering is received as an almost heroic attempt to overcome adversity. Songs boldly broadcast a description of someone's inner world. Why do people want to tune into someone else's emotional episodes?

There's a balance of two opposing forces that we enjoy
30 in music. One force soothes, the other agitates. As music plays, the actual frequencies of the individual notes are constantly lining up in different mathematical relations to each other. When they are proportional to each other, we hear chords, harmony, and unison. Songs normally end on this
35 sort of relationship because it conveys closure, completion, resolution. Other combinations create a sense of tension, discomfort, and anticipation. Successful songs win over listeners just as successful stories do. They normally introduce a protagonist and take the listener along to experience some
40 of his/her setbacks and triumphs. Even instrumental pieces often introduce a central melody and then explore its travels through different passages of the song's structure.

Young children often enjoy hearing soothing lullabies as a way to be distracted from anxiety or coaxed into a peace-
45 ful slumber. They take great pleasure in singing agitating songs, such as the "nenny nenny boo boo" melody that can be customized into any taunt. Similarly, adults have classical, smooth jazz, and easy listening styles of music when they want to be relaxed or distracted, and they have the more provocative
50 extremes of punk, rap, and metal when they want to use music to express irreverence or rebellion.

We become much more selective in our musical tastes as we age. As children, we passively accept and learn to love our parents' music just like we do their cooking. It's not that
55 a parent necessarily cooks "better" than other parents, but through sheer familiarity a child will greatly prefer her parents' cooking to that of others. Similarly, the cultural backdrop of a child's upbringing calibrates her listening tastes to a given set of rhythms, instruments, harmonic scales, and song structures.
60 As adolescents, though, we begin to choose our own songs just as we would choose our friends. We identify with artists based on their dress, their politics, their mood, and their popularity. We look to find personal meaning in lyrics and to latch onto songs that seem to broadcast our private thoughts. Despite
65 not being the author of our favorite songs, we wear our songs like trinkets of personal expression, telltale accessories that describe to others important parts of our psychology. When we develop a kinship with a song, we feel waves of euphoria as it plays, the feeling of our inner world radiating out.

70 As songwriters, we must aspire to this private release in every song we write. However, sometimes we fear that if we express ourselves too specifically, we will deny listeners the opportunity to mold our song into something they can claim as their own. We often replace specific details with general
75 symbols, preserving for ourselves the original meaning of a lyric while infusing it with enough flexibility that someone else can derive a different significance.

The one thing we must be sure of as performers is that a song means *something* to us. Through observation of other
80 artists, we learn to mimic expressions of joy and anguish. It becomes easy for us to write and perform songs without any genuine attachment to their emotional content. Nevertheless, just as audiences can distinguish between good and bad acting, so too will audience members feel a difference between
85 a contrived and an authentic performance.

1. When the writer refers to "the rules of polite etiquette" in (lines 18–19), he is most likely referring to rules that:

   A. diminish the role of imagination in playing with action figures or other toys.
   B. are taught to children when they are enrolled in behavior modification classes.
   C. are too restrictive and demanding for songwriters to abide by.
   D. limit certain personal behaviors that others might find irritating or discomforting.

2. In the third paragraph (lines 11–20), the author says that a songwriter aspires to write songs people will be "happy to hear." It can reasonably be inferred that which of the following is NOT a characteristic of such songs?

   F. Mimicking joy and anguish
   G. Blending comfort and tension
   H. Fostering a kinship with the listener
   J. Allowing for different interpretations

3. When the author states a songwriter must aspire to "this private release" (line 70), he is most directly referring to the idea that a songwriter must:

   A. describe her experiences with very specific details.
   B. outwardly project a genuine internal emotional state.
   C. force listeners to develop a kinship with the song.
   D. focus on the emotions of joy or anguish.

4. The author states that, unlike children, adolescents approach songs with a goal of:

   F. feeling a sense of belonging and familiarity.
   G. discovering new trends in fashion and politics.
   H. departing from the cultural backdrop of their upbringing.
   J. deriving some personal meaning from those songs.

5. The author states that our process of selecting songs can be compared to that of selecting all of the following EXCEPT:

   A. our friends.
   B. our parents' cooking.
   C. our favorite authors.
   D. personal trinkets.

6. According to the passage, the divergent songwriting purposes of "soothes" and "agitates" (line 30) differ from one another in that:

   F. soothing songs, unlike agitating ones, have a mellowing effect that is often enjoyable to adults but annoying to younger audiences.
   G. soothing songs are associated with inducing sleep or reducing distress, while agitating songs can be used to convey ridicule.
   H. agitating songs, unlike soothing songs, are often used by relatives to coax a child out of a state of slumber.
   J. agitating songs distract us from the things that we passionately hate, while soothing songs are very gentle to our ears.

7. According to the author's analogy, acting and performing music:

   A. are completely different.
   B. share at least one important characteristic.
   C. are more convincing expressing anguish than joy.
   D. are completely identical.

8. Based on the passage, the cultural backdrop of a child's upbringing is significant to her appreciation of music because it:

   F. predisposes the child to prefer the musical ingredients customary in that culture's music.
   G. gives the child a model of what to avoid in order to stand out as an original songwriter.
   H. instructs the child concerning the proper structure and political content of songs.
   J. will later be the primary basis through which the child is able to make friends.

KEY IDEAS AND DETAILS DRILL 3 EXPLANATIONS

1. **D**   The question asks which rules the writer is referring to with the phrase *"the rules of polite etiquette."* Read a window in the passage around the given lines. Lines 15–17 state, *We have all been yelled at by a frustrated audience of our friends, acquaintances, and family members to cease our incessant noise making,* and the next lines say that *many learn to keep their songs to themselves as they master the rules of polite etiquette.* The rules of polite etiquette are therefore rules that discourage people from behavior that others may find annoying. The passage doesn't say that people use less *imagination* when *playing,* so eliminate (A). There is no mention of *behavior modification classes,* so eliminate (B). Lines 19–20 indicate that songwriters never learn to keep their songs to themselves, but instead turn the *songs into something people will be happy to hear.* However, this does not imply that songwriters don't *abide by* the *rules of polite etiquette,* so eliminate (C). Keep (D), since it is supported by lines 15–19. The correct answer is (D).

2. **F**   The question asks what is NOT a characteristic of the songs that a songwriter aspires to write. When a question asks which answer is **not** supported, eliminate answers that **are** supported. Use words from the answer choices to locate the relevant portions of the passage. Lines 78–85 state that songwriters *learn to mimic expressions of joy and anguish* and *to write and perform songs without any genuine attachment to their emotional content.* However, the author says that audiences *can feel a difference between a contrived and an authentic performance.* This implies that *mimicking joy and anguish* is not something that songwriters should aspire to, so keep (F). Lines 29–31 explain that *There's a balance of two opposing forces that we enjoy in music. One force soothes, the other agitates.* This indicates that *people will be happy to hear* songs that blend *comfort and tension,* so eliminate (G). Lines 67–69 state that *When we develop a kinship with a song, we feel waves of euphoria as it plays.* This indicates that *people are happy to hear* songs that foster *a kinship with the listener,* so eliminate (H). Lines 70–77 state that songwriters don't want to *deny listeners the opportunity to mold our song into something they can claim as their own,* so the songwriters make efforts to give a song *enough flexibility that someone else can derive a different significance.* This indicates that songwriters aspire to write songs that allow *for different interpretations,* so eliminate (J). The correct answer is (F).

3. **B**   The question asks what the author is referring to with the statement that a *songwriter must aspire to "this private release."* Read a window in the passage around the given line. Lines 67–71 state, *When we develop a kinship with a song, we feel waves of euphoria as it plays, the feeling of our inner world radiating out. As songwriters, we must aspire to this private release in every song we write.* Lines 71–74 explain that songwriters *often replace specific details with general symbols* in order to allow *listeners the opportunity to mold our song into something they can claim as their own,* so eliminate (A). Keep (B) since it conveys the idea of *the inner world radiating out.* The author doesn't advocate that songwriters *force listeners to develop a kinship* with their songs, so eliminate (C). *Joy* and *anguish* are mentioned as two expressions that songwriters can *learn to mimic* (lines 79–80); they are not emotions the author says songwriters must *focus on,* so eliminate (D). The correct answer is (B).

4. **J**   The question asks for a goal with which *adolescents approach songs* that differs from that of children. Look for the words *children* and *adolescents* in the passage. Lines 52–59 discuss how children approach music, and lines 60–69 discuss how adolescents differ in their approach, saying, *We look to find personal meaning in lyrics and to latch onto songs that seem to broadcast our private thoughts.* The passage emphasizes *familiarity*

as a quality that children prefer, so eliminate (F). The passage says that adolescents *identify with artists based on their dress, their politics,* but it does not say that adolescents are trying to discover *new trends,* so eliminate (G). The passage indicates that *the cultural backdrop of a child's upbringing calibrates her listening tastes,* and that an adolescent's preferences are influenced by other things. However, it does not say that adolescents have a *goal* of *departing from* their *cultural backdrop,* so eliminate (H). Keep (J) because it is supported by lines 63–64. The correct answer is (J).

5. **C** The question asks what selection process cannot be compared to our *process of selecting songs.* When a question asks which answer is **not** supported, eliminate answers that **are** supported. Look for references to selecting songs in the passage. Lines 52–69 discuss the ways we select songs as children and adolescents. Lines 60–61 say, *we begin to choose our own songs just as we would choose our friends,* so eliminate (A). Lines 53–54 say, *we passively accept and learn to love our parents' music just like we do their cooking,* so eliminate (B). The word *author* appears in line 65, but the phrase says, *Despite not being the author of our favorite songs;* this is not a comparison with choosing *our favorite authors,* so keep (C). Lines 65–66 say, *we wear our songs like trinkets of personal expression, telltale accessories that describe to others important parts of our psychology,* so eliminate (D). The correct answer is (C).

6. **G** The question asks how the *divergent songwriting purposes of "soothes" and "agitates" differ from one another.* Read a window in the passage around the given line. Lines 43–47 state, *Young children often enjoy hearing soothing lullabies as a way to be distracted from anxiety or coaxed into a peaceful slumber. They take great pleasure in singing agitating songs, such as the "nenny nenny boo boo" melody that can be customized into any taunt.* There is no indication that soothing songs are *annoying to younger audiences,* so eliminate (F). Keep (G) because it is supported by lines 43–47. *Agitating songs* are not related to *slumber* in the passage, so eliminate (H). The passage says that *soothing* songs can distract children from anxiety; it does not say that *agitating songs distract us from the things that we passionately hate,* so eliminate (J). The correct answer is (G).

7. **B** The question asks what the author's analogy conveys about *acting and performing music.* Look for the words *acting* and *performing* in the passage. Lines 83–85 state that *just as audiences can distinguish between good and bad acting, so too will audience members feel a difference between a contrived and an authentic performance.* The author is highlighting a similarity between acting and performing, so eliminate (A) and keep (B). There is no contrast made between *expressing anguish* and *joy;* both are listed as expressions that performers *learn to mimic,* so eliminate (C). The author only mentions one shared aspect of acting and performing; there is no support for the statement that they are *completely identical,* so eliminate (D). The correct answer is (B).

8. **F** The question asks why *the cultural backdrop of a child's upbringing is significant to her appreciation of music.* Look for the words *cultural backdrop of a child's upbringing* in the passage. Lines 57–59 state that *the cultural backdrop of a child's upbringing calibrates her listening tastes to a given set of rhythms, instruments, harmonic scales, and song structures.* Keep (F) because it is a paraphrase of lines 57–59. This paragraph is not discussing *what to avoid in order to stand out as an original songwriter,* so eliminate (G). *Political content* is not mentioned in relationship to cultural backdrop, and there is no discussion of what is *proper,* only what is familiar; eliminate (H). The passage does not state that a child's cultural backdrop is a *basis through which the child is able to make friends,* so eliminate (J). The correct answer is (F).

KEY IDEAS AND DETAILS DRILL 4

NATURAL SCIENCE: This passage is adapted from the article "Fair-Weather Warning" by Julia Mittlebury (© 2007 by Julia Mittlebury).

Could the sun be causing epidemics? Take cholera, for example, an often fatal disease caused by the bacterium *Vibrio cholerae* (*V. cholerae*). Every so often, coastal areas suffer massive outbreaks of cholera due to infected food or water.
5 Where do these outbreaks come from?

The bacterium that causes cholera is found in areas that contain the copepod, a certain type of crustacean. The copepod depends on zooplankton for nourishment, and these zooplankton in turn depend on phytoplankton for their nourish-
10 ment. Phytoplankton use photosynthesis to feed on sunlight. Although one might need to go to the bottom of the food chain, the evidence shows that an increase in sunlight might mean an increase in the potential for cholera.

Interested in this correlation, Rita Colwell and her fel-
15 low researchers at the University of Maryland are studying ways to use satellite measurements of sea temperatures, sea height, and chlorophyll concentrations in order to predict when conditions favoring a cholera outbreak are more likely. As sea temperatures rise, photosynthetic organisms such as
20 phytoplankton become more abundant. As sea levels rise, the phytoplankton, zooplankton, copepods, and, by extension, the cholera bacterium are all brought closer to the shore. This increases the likelihood of food and water contamination.

By monitoring the cholera food chain in reverse, Colwell
25 and her colleagues believe they can predict the emergence of cholera 4 to 6 weeks in advance. Colwell's model predicted the rate of infection during one recent cholera outbreak in Bangladesh with 95 percent accuracy. Unfortunately, because this field of study is so new and its insights are so specula-
30 tive, local public health officials have not yet begun to base any preventative measures on these satellite-based forecasts.

Just up the road from Colwell and the University of Mary-
land, Kenneth Linthicum is leading similar efforts at the NASA Goddard Space Flight Centre in Greenbelt, Maryland. He has
35 designed a model to analyze the spread of Rift Valley fever, a mosquito-spread virus that killed about 100,000 animals and 90,000 people back in December 1997.

Scientists observed that prior to the outbreak, the equatorial region of the Indian Ocean saw a half-degree increase in
40 surface temperature. Although half of a degree sounds like only a slight difference, the temperature of an ocean does not change easily. Warmer ocean water in this region corresponds

with strong and prolonged rains, increased cloud cover, and warmer air over equatorial parts of Africa. These characteris-
45 tics favor the proliferation of mosquitoes and help keep them alive long enough for the virus to become easily transmittable.

In September 2007, Linthicum and his team became alerted to similar environmental changes. Over the next few months, they warned local health officials in Kenya, Somalia,
50 and Tanzania that conditions were ripe for a mosquito-based outbreak. As a result, only 300 lives were lost, an almost miraculous improvement from the devastation of the 1997 outbreak. While it is impossible to know if this outbreak would have been as far-reaching as that of 1997, it seems likely that
55 the advance warning succeeded in saving thousands, if not tens of thousands, of lives.

Similarly, a study by David Rogers at Oxford University has helped to predict outbreaks of sleeping sickness, a parasitic disease caused by West African tsetse flies. Here, Rogers first
60 calibrated regional levels of photosynthesis to the size of a vein in the wings of the flies. The vein size is a good measure of how numerous and robust the tsetse fly population is. Today, by reading the photosynthetic levels from satellite data, even researchers outside of West Africa can predict potential
65 epidemics in the region.

This type of research is encouraging to many in the disease prevention field, because traditional methods involve slow, costly research. The newfound ability to cull massive amounts of meteorological data from satellites and to run that
70 data through computer models has been much more efficient.

The goal of these models is to study the relationships between disease data and climate data. However, to do so requires decades', if not centuries', worth of high quality data to identify correlating factors with accuracy. Currently,
75 the climatic data is much more reliable than the disease data. Nevertheless, excitement about the potential usefulness of satellite-based predictions is persuading health agencies to compile and integrate their disease data more efficiently to give easier access to those trying to discover climate-disease links.

80 It may still take a good deal of time and energy before this technology is ready for practical application. Critics claim that the number of variables underlying the spread of disease are too numerous and varied for a climate-based approach ever to be reliable. Fluctuations in the immunity of local populations,
85 human and animal migrations, and the resistance to drugs used to commonly treat certain diseases could confuse climate-based models. Advocates respond, though, that these non-climatic factors can similarly be incorporated into their research as long as the relevant data is collected, and the resulting models will
90 have even better accuracy.

1. The passage mentions that all of the following are variables that could confuse climate-based models EXCEPT:

   A. ocean temperature.
   B. resistance to drugs.
   C. animal migration.
   D. fluctuations in immunity.

2. According to the sixth paragraph (lines 38–46), scientists have concluded that a half-degree increase in surface temperature in the Indian Ocean corresponds with:

   F. increased cloud cover and warmer air over the ocean.
   G. warmer rains at the equator.
   H. strong and prolonged mosquito clouds.
   J. higher populations of mosquitoes carrying the Rift Valley fever virus.

3. The correlation described in the third paragraph (lines 14–23) can be most accurately described as linking which of the following?

   A. Copepods and crustaceans
   B. Contamination of food and water
   C. Sunlight and cholera
   D. Photosynthesis and the food chain

4. According to the passage, the vein size of tsetse flies can help predict sleeping sickness outbreaks because:

   F. it affects the level of photosynthesis that causes the disease.
   G. the parasite that causes the disease can only live in large veins.
   H. it is a good measure of how numerous and robust the fly population is.
   J. satellite data can read the level of parasites in the veins.

5. Information in the ninth and tenth paragraphs (lines 66–79) regarding the relationships between disease data and climate data indicates that:

   A. climate data needs to be better integrated before it can be used in conjunction with disease data.
   B. studying disease data alone is faster and cheaper than studying climate data alone.
   C. studying climate data alone is faster and cheaper than studying disease data alone.
   D. disease data needs to be better integrated before it can be used in conjunction with climate data.

6. The passage indicates that satellite-based forecasts have not been acted upon by local health officials in:

   F. Kenya.
   G. Bangladesh.
   H. Somalia.
   J. Tanzania.

7. According to the passage, all of the following are part of a copepod's food chain EXCEPT:

   A. sunlight.
   B. phytoplankton.
   C. chlorophyll.
   D. zooplankton.

8. According to the passage, the author describes satellite measurements of sea temperatures, sea height, and chlorophyll concentrations because they can be used for which of the following?

   F. A survey of the food chain in coastal areas
   G. An analysis of how sea temperature affects copepods
   H. An estimation of how much sunlight phytoplankton need to survive
   J. A prediction of when a cholera outbreak is likely

9. In the last paragraph, the author expresses the belief that the practical application of climate data to disease prevention is:

   A. sure to provide better accuracy than using disease data alone.
   B. likely to require significant time and energy.
   C. the best course of action for epidemiologists to follow.
   D. unlikely to succeed because of fluctuations in immunity.

KEY IDEAS AND DETAILS DRILL 4 EXPLANATIONS

1. **A**   The question asks which answer choice is not a variable that could confuse climate-based models. When a question asks which answer is **not** supported, eliminate answers that **are** supported. Look for the words *climate-based* in the passage. Lines 84–87 state, *Fluctuations in the immunity of local populations, human and animal migrations, and the resistance to drugs used to commonly treat certain diseases could confuse climate-based models.* These lines include the variables given in (B), (C), and (D), so eliminate these choices. *Ocean temperature* is discussed in lines 38–46; the passage states that *Warmer ocean water…corresponds* with conditions that *favor the proliferation of mosquitoes and help keep them alive long enough for the virus to become easily transmittable* (lines 42–46). The next paragraph gives an example of a disease outbreak that was successfully predicted based on *similar environmental changes.* This is evidence that *ocean temperature* is a useful variable for prediction, and would not *confuse a climate-based model,* so keep (A). The correct answer is (A).

2. **J**   The question asks what scientists think corresponds with a half-degree increase in surface temperature in the Indian Ocean. The question references the sixth paragraph, so read lines 38–46, and a few lines before or after this paragraph if needed. Lines 39–46 state that *a half-degree increase in surface temperature* of the ocean corresponds with conditions that *favor the proliferation of mosquitoes and help keep them alive long enough for the virus to become easily transmittable.* The virus is identified in the previous paragraph as *Rift Valley fever,* a mosquito-spread virus. The passage describes *increased cloud cover…over equatorial parts of Africa,* not over *the ocean,* so eliminate (F). The passage mentions *warmer air* and *prolonged rains,* but not *warmer rains,* so eliminate (G). The passage states that *rains* are *strong and prolonged,* not that *mosquito clouds* are, so eliminate (H). Choice (J) is supported by the fifth and sixth paragraphs. The correct answer is (J).

3. **C**   The question asks what two things are linked in the correlation described in the third paragraph. The question references the third paragraph, so read lines 14–23, and a few lines before or after this paragraph if needed. The reference to *this correlation* is in line 14; the word *this* indicates that the *correlation* is discussed just before this in the passage. Lines 12–13 state that *an increase in sunlight might mean an increase in the potential for cholera.* Line 7 simply states that the *copepod* is a type of *crustacean;* this is not the *correlation* the researcher is interested in, so eliminate (A). *Food and water contamination* are treated as a single variable in line 23; this is not the *correlation* the author is interested in, so eliminate (B). Keep (C) because it is supported by lines 11–13. Although there is a link between *photosynthesis* and the *food chain,* this is not the *correlation* that is discussed in line 14, so eliminate (D). The correct answer is (C).

4. **H**   The question asks why the vein size of tsetse flies can help predict sleeping sickness outbreaks. Look for the words *tsetse flies* and *sleeping sickness* in the passage. Lines 57–62 state that sleeping sickness is *a parasitic disease caused by West African tsetse flies,* and that *vein size is a good measure of how numerous and robust the tsetse fly population is.* Sleeping sickness is caused by a parasite, not by *photosynthesis,* so eliminate (F). The passage does not mention the parasite's living conditions, so eliminate (G). Choice (H) is supported by lines 61–62, so keep (H). *Satellite data* is used to read *photosynthetic levels,* not *vein size,* so eliminate (J). The correct answer is (H).

5. **D** The question asks what is indicated by information regarding the relationships between disease data and climate data. The question references the ninth and tenth paragraphs, so read lines 66–79. Lines 76–79 state that health agencies are working to *integrate their disease data…to give easier access to those trying to discover climate-disease links.* Lines 74–75 state that *Currently, the climatic data is much more reliable than the disease data,* so eliminate (A). The paragraphs discuss using the two types of data together, rather than using either type *alone,* so eliminate (B) and (C). Choice (D) is supported by lines 76–79. The correct answer is (D).

6. **G** The question asks where satellite-based forecasts have not been acted upon by local health officials. Look for the words *satellite-based forecasts* and *local officials* in the passage. Lines 24–31 state that *Colwell's model predicted the rate of infection during one recent cholera outbreak in Bangladesh with 95 percent accuracy,* and it goes on to say that *local public health officials have not yet begun to base any preventative measures on these satellite-based forecasts.* Lines 47–56 describe how a satellite-based forecast of an outbreak in *Kenya, Somalia, and Tanzania* helped local health officials save *thousands, if not tens of thousands, of lives.* The countries in (F), (H), and (J) are mentioned as places where *local health officials* have acted on *satellite-based forecasts,* so eliminate these choices. Choice (G) is supported by lines 24–31. The correct answer is (G).

7. **C** The question asks what is NOT part of a copepod's food chain. When a question asks which answer is **not** supported, eliminate answers that **are** supported. Look for the word *copepod* in the passage. Lines 6–10 describe the copepod's food chain: *The copepod depends on zooplankton for nourishment, and these zooplankton in turn depend on phytoplankton for their nourishment. Phytoplankton use photosynthesis to feed on sunlight. Sunlight, phytoplankton,* and *zooplankton* are all included in this description, so eliminate (A), (B), and (D). Keep (C) because *chlorophyll* is not included in the description. The correct answer is (C).

8. **J** The question asks what potential use for satellite measurements of sea temperatures, sea height, and chlorophyll concentrations caused the author to discuss them. Look for the words *satellite measurements of sea temperatures, sea height, and chlorophyll concentrations* in the passage. Lines 14–18 state that researchers are *studying ways to use satellite measurements of sea temperatures, sea height, and chlorophyll concentrations in order to predict when conditions favoring a cholera outbreak are more likely.* Although the *food chain, copepods,* and *phytoplankton* are related to the correlation that researchers are interested in, the purpose of taking the measurements is to predict cholera outbreaks, so eliminate (F), (G), and (H). Keep (J) because it is supported by lines 14–18. The correct answer is (J).

9. **B** The question asks what belief about a practical application of climate data to disease prevention the author expresses in the last paragraph. The question references the last paragraph, so read lines 80–90. Lines 80–81 state, *It may still take a good deal of time and energy before this technology is ready for practical application.* The last sentence states that incorporating *non-climatic factors* will give climate-based models *even better accuracy,* but this is not comparing using *climate data* with using *disease data alone,* so eliminate (A). Keep (B) because it is supported by lines 80–81. Although the author feels that climate data can be useful, there is no comparison with another *course of action* in the last paragraph, so the phrase *best course of action* is not supported; eliminate (C). Although *fluctuations in immunity* are mentioned as a potential challenge in using climate data, the last sentence indicates that incorporating that kind of *non-climatic factor* with other data will lead to *even better accuracy*; the author doesn't think *the practical application of climate data to disease prevention* is *unlikely to succeed,* so eliminate (D). The correct answer is (B).

KEY IDEAS AND DETAILS DRILL 5

PROSE FICTION: This passage is adapted from the short story "Into the Past" by Amanda C. Thomas (© 2004 by Amanda C. Thomas).

Even at eight in the morning, the thermometer was heading up towards 80 degrees when my mother put me and my brother Kiran on the southbound bus heading from our home in New York City to our aunt and uncle's place in North
5 Carolina. Her new job on the third shift of the garment factory gave us the potential for a better life ahead, but she was wary about leaving us alone at home in the evenings and overnight. I had never been outside of New York City before, so I was nervous about moving, not to mention that I had never met
10 my aunt and uncle before.

"Now Essie, you be on your best behavior, mind your elders and watch out for your little brother, you hear me?" Her words were admonishments, but I saw the tear in the corner of her eye and knew that she'd miss us over the next
15 three months. She stood still, arm upraised in farewell, until her lemon-yellow dress became no more than a pinprick in the distance.

Kiran and I had promised each other that we would notice all the things that were different from New York while
20 we were on our trip. In the bus, the heat of the road was balanced to some degree by the breeze blowing in through the windows. We pressed our noses up to the glass, peering out as the dense thicket of buildings thinned, then disappeared altogether as we hit the unfamiliar farm country in the South.
25 We chewed the soggy pickle and butter sandwiches our mother had packed for us, sucking the juice out from between the slices of white, soft bread and watched the green fields rush by.

We were greeted at the bus station by Uncle Desmond, a quiet man whose skin shone dark from working out in the
30 sun. He said almost nothing as he took us back to his neat, white house with its red barn that looked just like my mother's descriptions of it and the pictures in books I'd seen when I was younger. At first glance, Aunt Millie seemed the polar opposite of my mother. Where my mother was all sharp lines
35 and tight angles, Aunt Millie was almost blurred, her hair looser and her hips more ample. Still, her kind face and shrewd glance at our city outfits showed the same deep intelligence.

"We're gonna have to see if some of your cousins' old overalls can be taken up for you. Don't want to get your nice
40 things scuffed up. Farm life's not easy on fancy dresses and patent leather shoes and you'll both be doing your share of the chores around here, that's for sure! Now your cousin Ike'll show you where to go to get washed up for dinner."

I had never seen so much food in my life before that
45 first meal at the farm. Collard greens, biscuits with red-eye gravy, fried chicken, macaroni and cheese—I'd eaten most of these dishes at home, but here they tasted different in a way that was hard to put a finger on at first. As though they were *from* somewhere, instead of appearing magically on our
50 kitchen table. They tasted the way the farm smelled—of the animals and the earth. I glanced over at Kiran, and he was digging in hungrily.

The next day, Kiran and I were roused early by Aunt Millie carrying two smaller versions of what, presumably,
55 had been Ike's old overalls. Ike and Desmond, who had both been awake hours earlier, came by carrying pails of warm milk, some of which would be put to household use while the main load was put by to be picked up by a cheese-making facility in Virginia.

60 Ike then taught us to gather eggs from the chickens in the henhouse. This quickly became my favorite task over that summer. I loved going out into the early dawn, the air still cool and damp and feeling my bare feet sink into grass wet with dew. I'd approach the coop with great care not to
65 disturb the slumbering ladies, as I thought of them, making sure not to betray my presence by any quick movement or careless noise. Then, with infinite gentleness, I'd reach out, my hands rustling under the soft feathers of the hens, sensing their respiration, their warmth, feeling for the smooth white
70 eggs and placing each one I found carefully into my basket.

At night I would take a bath and Aunt Millie would take time away from her evening chores to braid my hair. But instead of the intricate patterns my mother liked to make, Aunt Millie gave me looser plaits and even sometimes gathered them
75 into a single tail inching down my neck. Sometimes, when Aunt Millie seemed in an especially good mood, we would condition it with egg yolk and milk, which Aunt Millie would work into my hair gently massaging each strand, working the mixture deep into the roots. Afterwards I was pleased to see
80 how the brittle, frizzy ends softened.

My body became loose-limbed from the outdoor exercise and I noticed Kiran growing stronger and bolder as he ran through the fields with Ike. In the afternoons when it was too hot to do anything else, we'd lie in the shade of the huge oak
85 tree, chewing on grass stems, lost in the sweet, green taste and our own thoughts.

1. It can most reasonably be inferred from the passage that the narrator:

   A. thinks New York City is superior to the farm.
   B. has never visited Uncle Desmond and Aunt Millie's farm before.
   C. sees the visit to the farm as the most important event in her life.
   D. loves her Aunt Millie more than her mother.

2. In line 35 the narrator describes Aunt Millie as "blurred," which most nearly suggests that:

   F. unlike the narrator's mother, Aunt Millie doesn't have sharp features.
   G. Aunt Millie is older than the narrator's mother, so she has a bad memory and forgets things.
   H. Essie doesn't see well because she often reads books under her bedcovers.
   J. Aunt Millie doesn't have as distinctive a personality as the narrator's mother does.

3. It can reasonably be inferred from the passage that which of the following events happened first in the narrator's life?

   A. She learned to collect eggs from the henhouse.
   B. She met her Aunt Millie and Uncle Desmond.
   C. She visited North Carolina for the first time.
   D. She lived in New York City.

4. It can reasonably be inferred from the passage that the narrator views life on the farm as:

   F. requiring a great deal of hard work that is not appreciated by her aunt and uncle.
   G. an escape from the difficulties of living in impoverished, restrictive conditions in New York City.
   H. a place where daily chores, even those that require that the narrator wake up early, can be enjoyable and satisfying.
   J. a place where the physical nature of the local recreational activities are more suited to boys than to girls.

5. As depicted in the ninth paragraph (lines 71–80), the relationship between the narrator and Aunt Millie is best described by which of the following statements?

   A. Aunt Millie feels close to the narrator, as shown in the way she puts aside other tasks to braid and condition Essie's hair.
   B. Aunt Millie feels emotionally cut off from the narrator because of the young girl's city manners.
   C. Aunt Millie loves the narrator in spite of their different ways of seeing the world.
   D. Aunt Millie is indifferent toward the narrator, seeing her as another part of her daily work.

6. Which of the following statements most nearly captures the sentiment behind the narrator's comment that the food at the farmhouse tastes like it is "*from* somewhere" (line 49)?

   F. "The food tasted just like the food I had in New York."
   G. "The food tasted fresh from the fields, instead of from a supermarket."
   H. "The food tasted like no other food that I had ever tasted."
   J. "The food tasted strongly of the rich soil that Uncle Desmond tilled."

7. Details in the second paragraph (lines 11–17) most strongly suggest that the narrator's mother:

   A. hopes her children will have a good time on the farm, enjoying their summer vacation before school starts again.
   B. feels saddened by the children's departure and will miss them while they're away.
   C. believes that life on the farm will teach them the self-discipline they need to survive in the city.
   D. is afraid for them during the long bus ride and hopes the children will not speak to strangers.

8. Which of the following statements about why the narrator and Kiran will spend the summer on the farm is supported by the passage?

   F. The narrator is weak and sickly, needing the fresh air of the farm to recover her health.
   G. Aunt Millie and Uncle Desmond will teach the children valuable work skills.
   H. The narrator and Kiran wanted to develop a relationship with their cousins.
   J. The children's mother worried about leaving them alone while she worked.

KEY IDEAS AND DETAILS DRILL 5 EXPLANATIONS

1. **B**   The question asks what can be inferred about the narrator. Because this is a general question, it should be done after all the specific questions. The passage doesn't indicate that the narrator *thinks New York City is superior to the farm,* so eliminate (A). Line 8 says, *I had never been outside of New York City before,* and lines 30–33 say that the farmhouse *looked just like my mother's descriptions of it and the pictures in books I'd seen when I was younger,* so it is reasonable to infer that the narrator has never visited the farm before; keep (B). The narrator does not indicate that she *sees the visit to the farm as the most important event in her life,* so eliminate (C). There is no comparison made between the narrator's love for *her Aunt Millie* and *her mother,* so eliminate (D). The correct answer is (B).

2. **F**   The question asks what is suggested by the narrator's description of *Aunt Millie* as "*blurred.*" Read a window in the passage around the given line. Lines 33–36 state, *At first glance, Aunt Millie seemed the polar opposite of my mother. Where my mother was all sharp lines and tight angles, Aunt Millie was almost blurred, her hair looser and her hips more ample.* Keep (F), since it is supported by these lines. In lines 36–37, Aunt Millie is described as *shrewd* and having *deep intelligence,* so there is no support for the idea that she *has a bad memory and forgets things;* eliminate (G). There is no mention that Essie *often reads books under her bedcovers,* and the many visual details given throughout the passage suggest that Essie has good eyesight: the word *blurred* doesn't indicate that Essie can't see her Aunt clearly, so eliminate (H). The description *blurred* is used to refer to Aunt Millie's physical appearance, and she is described as *kind, shrewd,* and having *deep intelligence,* so there is no evidence that she *doesn't have as distinctive a personality as the narrator's mother;* eliminate (J). The correct answer is (F).

3. **D**   The question asks which event occurred first in the narrator's life. Use words from the answer choices to locate the relevant portions of the passage. In lines 1–10, the narrator recounts, *when my mother put me and my brother Kiran on the southbound bus heading from our home in New York City to our aunt and uncle's place in North Carolina…I had never been outside of New York City before, so I was nervous about moving, not to mention that I had never met my aunt and uncle before.* Lines 60–61 say, *Ike then taught us to gather eggs from the chickens in the henhouse.* This occurs after the narrator arrives at the farm. These two parts of the passage establish that the narrator *lived in New York City* before she *visited North Carolina for the first time, met her Aunt Millie and Uncle Desmond,* or *learned to collect eggs from the henhouse,* so eliminate (A), (B), and (C), and keep (D). The correct answer is (D).

4. **H**   The question asks what can be inferred about how *the narrator views life on the farm.* Because this is a general question, it should be done after all the specific questions. There is no evidence that the narrator's work on the farm is unappreciated by her aunt and uncle, so eliminate (F). Lines 5–6 say that the narrator's mother's *new job on the third shift of the garment factory gave us the potential for a better life ahead,* but the passage doesn't indicate that the narrator has been living in *impoverished, restrictive conditions* in New York City, so eliminate (G). In lines 60–62, the narrator states that gathering eggs *quickly became my favorite task over that summer. I loved going out into the early dawn.* This indicates that a *chore* requiring *that the narrator wake up early* was *enjoyable,* so keep (H). There is no discussion of a *recreational activity* that was *more suited to boys than to girls,* so eliminate (J). The correct answer is (H).

5. **A** The question asks which statement best describes *the relationship between the narrator and Aunt Millie*. The question references the ninth paragraph, so read lines 71–80. Lines 71–78 state, *Aunt Millie would take time away from her evening chores to braid my hair…Sometimes, when Aunt Millie seemed in an especially good mood, we would condition it with egg yolk and milk, which Aunt Millie would work into my hair gently massaging each strand.* Keep (A), since it is supported by these lines. There is no indication that *Aunt Millie feels emotionally cut off from the narrator,* or that the narrator has *city manners,* so eliminate (B). There is no discussion of these characters having *different ways of seeing the world,* so eliminate (C). These lines state that Aunt Millie *would take time away from her evening chores,* indicating that she does not see the narrator *as another part of her daily work,* so eliminate (D). The correct answer is (A).

6. **G** The question asks which statement *captures the sentiment behind the narrator's comment that the food at the farmhouse tastes like it is "from somewhere."* Read a window in the passage around the given line. Lines 46–51 state, *I'd eaten most of these dishes at home, but here they tasted different in a way that was hard to put a finger on at first. As though they were from somewhere, instead of appearing magically on our kitchen table. They tasted the way the farm smelled—of the animals and the earth.* The narrator says that *here they tasted different,* so the food does not taste *just like the food* she *had in New York;* eliminate (F). Keep (G), since it is supported by the phrases *They tasted the way the farm smelled—of the animals and the earth,* and *instead of appearing magically on our kitchen table.* Although the food tastes different to her, the narrator indicates that *I'd eaten most of these dishes at home,* so eliminate (H). The food does not literally taste like *soil,* so eliminate (J). The correct answer is (G).

7. **B** The question asks what is suggested about the *narrator's mother* by details in the second paragraph, so read lines 11–17. Lines 13–15 state, *Her words were admonishments, but I saw the tear in the corner of her eye and knew that she'd miss us over the next three months.* The previous paragraph indicates that the children are going to the farm because of their mother's *new job,* rather than for *vacation;* there is also no mention here of the mother hoping they *will have a good time,* so eliminate (A). Keep (B) since it is supported by lines 13–15. There is no mention of the children learning *the self-discipline they need to survive in the city,* so eliminate (C). The previous paragraph mentions that the mother is *wary* of leaving the children *alone at home in the evenings and overnight* (lines 6–7), but not of *the long bus ride* or talking to *strangers,* so eliminate (D). The correct answer is (B).

8. **J** The question asks *why the narrator and Kiran will spend the summer on the farm.* Look for references to reasons the children leave their home to travel to the farm. Lines 2–7 recount, *my mother put me and my brother Kiran on the southbound bus heading from our home in New York City to our aunt and uncle's place in North Carolina. Her new job on the third shift of the garment factory gave us the potential for a better life ahead, but she was wary about leaving us alone at home in the evenings and overnight.* There is no indication that *the narrator is weak and sickly,* so eliminate (F). Although the children do learn to do chores on the farm, there is no evidence that this is the reason they travel to the farm, so eliminate (G). Similarly, although the *cousins* are mentioned in the passage, there's no indication that *developing a relationship* with them is the reason the children visited the farm, so eliminate (H). Keep (J) because it is supported by lines 2–7. The correct answer is (J).

KEY IDEAS AND DETAILS DRILL 6

NATURAL SCIENCE: This passage is excerpted from the article "Alternative Medicines: A New Perspective" by Audrey C. Tristan (© 2004 by Audrey Tristan).

The view of health as a holistic and integrative state of physical, spiritual, and emotional well-being is deeply rooted in mind-body philosophies that have survived thousands of years. Traditional *mindful movement* therapies found in
5 *yoga, tai chi,* and *qigong,* for example, couple aerobic and anaerobic exercise with mental focus. These practices, which originated in Eastern medicine, guide participants through a series of specialized movements synchronized to the breath and mental images. Involving more than cardiovascular activ-
10 ity, these exercise routines are said to improve overall health by bringing deeper awareness to the body and promoting strength, flexibility, and balance.

Modern Western biomedicine, on the other hand, has advanced largely by splitting the mind and body to allow for
15 the objective study of health and disease mechanisms, and thus has been slow to embrace the implications of mind-body health. However, as alternative and traditional therapies have become increasingly more popular and available in the West, researchers have begun to delve deeper into mind-body
20 therapy efficacy, that is, the ability to consistently produce a desired, therapeutic effect.

There is particularly solid research to support the use of mind-body therapy to counteract the debilitating effects of stress. Certain mind-body therapies may alter the way
25 we experience pain and manage stress through the use of conscious strategies to avert automatic responses. Stress, as defined in biomedical terms, is the physiological response to a perceived threat. It is not to be confused with the common usage of the term, which generally equates stress with those
30 activities that provoke a stress response (these are deemed *stressors*). When the central nervous system perceives a threat, the sympathetic division of the autonomic nervous system is engaged, signaling the release of stress hormones such as epinephrine and cortisol into the bloodstream that in
35 turn activate particular physiological responses: heart and respiratory rate acceleration, muscle tension, perspiration, indigestion, and pupil dilation.

This "fight-or-flight" response alludes to the conditions of ancestral humans and the presumed adaptive function of
40 such a response in evolutionary history. The response, how-ever, does not occur only in reaction to isolated incidences. Indeed, most stressors today, related to work, family, school, and interpersonal relationships, are prolonged, and the fight-or-flight responses are thus sustained. This continual state
45 of arousal results in deleterious effects on health over time,

such as high blood pressure, cardiovascular disease, diabetes, digestive disorders, and suppressed immune response.

Mind-body therapies, such as guided imagery and medita-tion, essentially work by altering responses to stressors. The
50 simple act of breathing deeply and focusing on the breath will, in contrast to a stress response, engage the parasympathetic division of the autonomic nervous system, which lowers blood pressure, heart, and respiratory rates, and decreases muscle tension, thus counteracting the negative consequences of
55 fight-or-flight response.

Other mind-body therapies alter the experience of pain itself. Pain is a multidimensional experience that traverses four physiological pathways. *Transduction* occurs first, as sensory neurons, the *nociceptors*, detect potentially damaging
60 stimuli and transmit signals from affected tissue to neural activ-ity. The next step is *transmission*, in which the pain messages are exchanged between the nociceptors and the spinal cord. *Central representation* follows as the information is relayed from the spinal cord through the thalamus to the limbic and
65 cortical structures of the brain, which identify the sensations relayed. *Modulation,* the last step, is a descending pathway in which the brain sends signals back to the spinal cord to moder-ate the sensation of pain, basically "numbing" the pain. Since the limbic system is also the brain center for emotion, memory,
70 and autonomic nervous system integration, the experience of pain is ultimately mediated by emotions, an individual's own past experiences, and present external environment.

In clinical hypnosis, or *hypnotic analgesia,* patients are taught alternative skills to alter the experience of pain.
75 Hypnotic analgesia produces psychophysiological effects as patients are taught to consciously re-evaluate and manage a painful stimulus, using visual imagery and positive emotional reinforcement. A recent review of controlled studies of hyp-notic analgesia suggests that the treatment can reduce pain
80 in chronic conditions resulting from osteoarthritis, cancer, fibromyalgia, and disability. The authors cautioned, however, that a number of questions remain unanswered.

Mind-body research has provided important insights into both the efficacy of such therapies and our understanding of
85 the cognitive and physiological perception of pain. More investigation is needed, however, to ascertain if outcome expectations influence the success of particular therapies, if response rates differ as a result of pain type or pain diagnosis, and to what degree variation in individual response, and if
90 research design should preclude broader inferences.

1. The studies reviewed in the seventh paragraph (lines 73–82) have shown that hypnotic analgesia may be effective in:

   A. restructuring the brain non-invasively.
   B. fighting cancer and fibromyalgia.
   C. decreasing depression in patients.
   D. altering the experience of pain.

2. According to the sixth paragraph, (lines 56–72), when a door slams on a person's hand, the detection of pain results from:

   F. the transmission of nerve signals from damaged tissue to the spinal cord and sympathetic nervous system.
   G. the transmission of nerve signals from damaged tissue to the spinal cord and brain.
   H. the sympathetic nervous system releasing chemical hormones, which reach the heart via the bloodstream.
   J. the sympathetic nervous system releasing chemical hormones, which reach the brain via the spinal cord.

3. According to the passage, overall health may be improved in part through any of the following EXCEPT:

   A. exercise combined with mental focus.
   B. cardiovascular activity combined with nutritious diet.
   C. awareness of the body.
   D. movement synchronized with breath and mental imagery.

4. According to the passage, the limbic system would be directly involved in all of the following EXCEPT:

   F. pain modulation.
   G. stress management.
   H. muscle movement.
   J. memory.

5. Information in the second paragraph indicates that mind-body therapies in Western medicine have been:

   A. increasingly used in place of biomedicine.
   B. rejected because there have not been enough clinical studies.
   C. an emerging field of scientific investigation.
   D. successful in curing many conditions and diseases.

6. The mind-body therapies mentioned in the fifth paragraph (lines 48–55) function by:

   F. preventing stress hormones from activating negative physiological responses.
   G. engaging the sympathetic nervous system to reduce stress responses.
   H. effectively eliminating emotional stressors.
   J. counterbalancing the effects of flight or fight responses.

7. According to the passage, stress responses with adaptive functions, as would have evolved in ancestral conditions, can be expected to:

   A. increase cortisol levels in the blood.
   B. suppress immune activity.
   C. perceive threats.
   D. decrease muscle tension.

8. In the last paragraph, the author expresses the belief that mind-body therapy should be further investigated because results from research are:

   F. carefully controlled to yield results consistent with expectations.
   G. valid only when analyzing Western-originating therapies.
   H. susceptible to external variables, the effects of which are yet to be determined.
   J. proof of the effectiveness in fighting stress and eliminating pain.

9. According to the passage, healthy mind-body therapies would have been deemed ineffective if which of the following effects occurred after patients engaged in positive meditation to manage work-related stress?

   A. Nociceptive signals were transmitted.
   B. The parasympathetic nervous system was engaged.
   C. The fight-or-flight response was prolonged.
   D. Spinal cord activity diminished.

KEY IDEAS AND DETAILS DRILL 6 EXPLANATIONS

1. **D** The question asks what the studies reviewed in the seventh paragraph have shown that *hypnotic analgesia may be effective in*. The question references the seventh paragraph, so read lines 73–82. These lines indicate that *in hypnotic analgesia, patients are taught alternative skills to alter the experience of pain*, and that a *recent review of controlled studies of hypnotic analgesia suggests that the treatment can reduce pain in chronic conditions resulting from osteoarthritis, cancer, fibromyalgia, and disability*. There is no discussion of *restructuring the brain*, so eliminate (A). The passage states hypnotic analgesia can *reduce pain…resulting from…cancer and fibromyalgia*, but not that it treats these conditions themselves, so eliminate (B). There is no discussion of *depression*, so eliminate (C). Keep (D) because it is supported by the seventh paragraph. The correct answer is (D).

2. **G** The question asks what the detection of pain results from *when a door slams on a person's hand*. The question references the sixth paragraph, so read lines 56–72. These lines describe the process that occurs as pain *traverses four physiological pathways*. First, *the sensory neurons, the nociceptors…detect potentially damaging stimuli*. Next, the *pain messages are exchanged between the nociceptors and the spinal cord*. Then, *the information is relayed from the spinal cord through the thalamus to the limbic and cortical structures of the brain*. The *sympathetic division of the autonomic nervous system* and *stress hormones* are mentioned in lines 22–37 as part of the body's response to *stress*, not *pain*, so eliminate (F), (H), and (J). Keep (G) because it is supported by the sixth paragraph. The correct answer is (G).

3. **B** The question asks what does not improve *overall health*. When a question asks which answer is **not** supported, eliminate answers that **are** supported. Look for the words *improve overall health* in the passage. Lines 4–12 discuss *mindful movement therapies* that are said to *improve overall health*. Lines 5–6 state that the therapies *couple aerobic and anaerobic exercise with mental focus*, so eliminate (A). There is no mention of *diet*, so keep (B). Lines 10–11 state that the therapies *improve overall health by bringing deeper awareness to the body*, so eliminate (C). Lines 6–9 state that *These practices…guide participants through a series of specialized movements synchronized to the breath and mental images*, so eliminate (D). The correct answer is (B).

4. **H** The question asks what the *limbic system* would not be directly involved with. When a question asks which answer is **not** supported, eliminate answers that **are** supported. Look for the words *limbic system* in the passage. The *limbic system* is mentioned in line 64 in a discussion of the pathways involved in the experience of pain; one of the pathways is *modulation*, so eliminate (F). Lines 69–70 identify the limbic system as the *brain center for autonomic nervous system integration*, and the *autonomic nervous system* is identified as part of the stress response in lines 32–33. Therefore, the limbic system would be involved in *stress management*, so eliminate (G). There is no mention of *muscle movement* in connection with the limbic system, so keep (H). Line 69 states that the *limbic system is also the brain center for…memory*, so eliminate (J). The correct answer is (H).

5. **C** The question asks what information in the second paragraph indicates about *mind-body therapies in Western medicine*. The question references the second paragraph, so read lines 13–21. Lines 17–21 say *that as alternative and traditional therapies have become increasingly more popular and available in the West, researchers have*

begun to delve deeper into mind-body therapy efficacy. The passage doesn't state that mind-body therapies are being used *in place of biomedicine* in the West, so eliminate (A). The passage states that more research is being done and that *alternative and traditional therapies have become increasingly more popular,* so eliminate (B). Keep (C) because it is supported by lines 17–21. There is no discussion in this paragraph about whether mind-body therapies are *successful in curing* disease, so eliminate (D). The correct answer is (C).

6. **J** The question asks how the *mind-body therapies* mentioned in the fifth paragraph function. The question references the fifth paragraph, so read lines 48–55. These lines state that *Mind-body therapies…essentially work by altering responses to stressors…thus counteracting the negative consequences of fight-or-flight response.* There is no indication that these therapies *prevent stress hormones from activating negative* responses; the passage simply says that the therapies counteract these responses, so eliminate (F). Lines 51–52 say the therapies *engage the parasympathetic,* not the sympathetic, nervous system; eliminate (G). The passage doesn't indicate that the therapies *eliminate* the stressors; it says they work by *altering responses* to them; eliminate (H). Keep (J) because it is supported by the lines 54–55. The correct answer is (J).

7. **A** The question asks what *stress responses with adaptive functions, as would have evolved in ancestral conditions,* can be expected to do. Look for the words *adaptive functions* and *ancestral* in the passage. Lines 38–40 state that *This "fight-or-flight" response alludes to the conditions of ancestral humans and the presumed adaptive function of such a response in evolutionary history.* The word *this* indicates that the fight-or-flight response is discussed just before this line, so read the previous paragraph. Beginning on line 26, the passage explains that *Stress…is the physiological response to a perceived threat…When the central nervous system perceives a threat, the sympathetic division of the autonomic nervous system is engaged, signaling the release of stress hormones such as epinephrine and cortisol into the bloodstream.* Keep (A) since *increase cortisol levels in the blood* is supported by these lines. *Suppressed immune response* is mentioned in line 47 as a result of modern-day stressors, not ancestral conditions, so eliminate (B). The passage indicates that the stress response is a *response to a perceived threat*; perceiving threats is not something the stress response would *do,* so eliminate (C). Lines 35–36 indicate that a stress response will *activate…muscle tension,* not *decrease* it, so eliminate (D). The correct answer is (A).

8. **H** The question asks for the characteristic of research results that causes the author to believe that *mind-body therapy should be further investigated.* The last paragraph is referenced, so read lines 83–90. Lines 85–90 state, *More investigation is needed…to ascertain if outcome expectations influence the success of particular therapies, if response rates differ as a result of pain type or pain diagnosis, and to what degree variation in individual response, and if research design should preclude broader inferences.* These lines indicate that research results may be affected by factors that haven't been accounted for in the studies and that, for this reason, the author believes more investigation is needed. The author indicates that *outcome expectations* might influence results but doesn't say that the *research results are carefully controlled to yield results consistent with expectations,* so eliminate (F). There is no indication that the author believes research results are *valid only when analyzing Western-originating therapies,* so eliminate (G). Keep (H) because it is supported by lines 85–90. The author says that *Mind-body research has provided important insights into…the efficacy of such therapies* but advocates further investigation to confirm the results. Therefore, the author doesn't believe the results are *proof of the effectiveness,* so eliminate (J). The correct answer is (H).

9. **C** The question asks which effect, if it had *occurred after patients engaged in positive meditation to manage work-related stress*, would have caused *healthy mind-body therapies to be deemed ineffective*. Look in the passage for references to effects caused by work-related stress. Lines 42–44 state that *most stressors today, related to work, family, school, and interpersonal relationships, are prolonged, and the fight-or-flight responses are thus sustained.* This indicates that if a therapy intended to manage work-related stress was ineffective, fight-or-flight responses would continue. *Nociceptors signals* are mentioned in lines 59–60 as part of the pain response; they are not related to stress, so eliminate (A). Lines 48–55 explain that mind-body therapies counteract stress by engaging *the parasympathetic division of the autonomic nervous system.* If the *parasympathetic nervous system was engaged*, it would be a sign that the meditation was effective, not ineffective, so eliminate (B). Keep (C) because it is consistent with the explanation in lines 42–44. The passage doesn't give details about how *spinal cord activity* is related to stress, so eliminate (D). The correct answer is (C).

CRAFT AND STUCTURE

The Craft and Structure reporting category accounts for 26–33% of the Reading questions you will encounter on your ACT. These questions ask you to determine the meaning of words or phrases within the passage, understand the author's purpose and rhetorical decisions made when writing the passage, differentiate between various perspectives and points of view, and articulate the general structure of the passage. Simply stated, these questions ask why the passage was written the way it was and how the author's choices affected the finished product. They are not asking only for details or central themes. The following pages contain seven Craft and Structure passages, each with 4 or 5 questions that you can practice on if this category is an area of focus for you.

CRAFT AND STRUCTURE DRILL 1

PROSE FICTION: This passage is adapted from the short story "Going Home" by Lucretia Prynne (© 2007 by Lucretia Prynne).

Summers in Alabama had always been hot. My child-hood memories are filled with days spent floating in the pond, sitting on the porch swing, lying sprawled in front of any source of moving air, trying in vain to get, and stay, cool.
5 But when I walked out of the airport, already tired from a three-hour flight that had been delayed by over half an hour, laden with suitcases and dressed for an overly air-conditioned office climate, the heat came over me like a blanket. An old, unwashed woolen blanket that had been soaked in water,
10 allowed to dry crumpled on the floor, then resoaked and thrown at me in all of its mildewed glory. The short walk to the car-rental agency felt like a trek through the jungle; by the time I got to my rental, my shirt was soaked through in patches, my hair was limp and sticky, and my mood was foul.

15 During the hour-long drive home, I had plenty of time to think. About why I had left, about all the things I had chosen to leave behind, about the life I had built for myself far away from this world of heat and poverty and depression. Lost in my thoughts, I found myself driving up the gravel road lead-
20 ing to my childhood home before I realized where I was. The clapboard house looked the same as it had when I had left ten years earlier, save for a slight accumulation of the junk common to front yards in this part of the world. The old tire swing still hung askew from the hickory tree, half the ropes
25 worn away from constant use. On the porch sat a rocker that had once been my grandmother's and a watering can that looked almost as old. Parking off to the side, I grabbed my bags anxiously, trying to calm my nerves, and braced myself.

No one ever used the front door to the house. I remem-
30 bered that, of course, and walked instead to a side door that opened onto the kitchen. The door itself was propped open to allow for whatever breeze might meander by, the screen door shut to keep out the mosquitoes, giving me a view of the room. There was the kitchen table, covered in dents and scratches
35 but polished to a high sheen; behind and to the right, the pantry, no doubt stocked full of the jars of preserves that my mother would have been making all summer; and straight ahead, my mother, standing at the sink. She had aged during the years of my absence. I could see it in the way she stood, slightly
40 hunched over the sink, and in the color of her hair, pulled back

as always. She had to have heard me coming—gravel roads announce visitors from miles away—but she showed no sign that she knew I was standing there in the doorway, debating whether or not to knock.

45 "Mother? It's me. I'm here."

Her back straightened as she replied, though she never turned or left the sink.

"Come on in, and be sure to close the screen door behind you. It's been a bad year for bugs."

50 I opened the door and stepped back in time. When I had announced my plan to go away for school, she had asked me how I thought I was going to pay for it. When the holidays came around, and I told her I wasn't going to be able to come home, she didn't ask why, and when I stopped calling on a
55 regular basis, she didn't ask then either. How many nights had I spent, hating her for making those decisions so hard for me? Already I could feel the anger rising, that she could act so unconcerned at my arrival, standing at the sink shelling peas. Her only daughter, whom she hadn't seen for a decade.

60 As I approached the sink, ready to demand an explana-tion, I saw that her hands were shaking, the peas falling into the sink as much as the bowl. She looked so much older, aged even more than I had thought, in the same faded dress she'd probably worn for five years. It suddenly hit me that all
65 that time, she hadn't called not because she didn't care, but because she did. She had never been able to leave, but I had, and she understood that I needed to strike out on my own, far from here. Now here I was, in my fancy city clothes, with my college degree and impressive job, and she didn't know what
70 to say. I bridged the gap the only way I knew how: I rolled up my sleeves, and started to help with the peas.

1. The primary purpose of the first paragraph is to:

   A. describe the narrator's transition from her every day, working life in the city to the world of her rural childhood.
   B. explain why the narrator becomes so frustrated when she arrives at her mother's house in the countryside.
   C. give the reader enough background about the setting of the story to explain the events of the later parts of the passage.
   D. foreshadow the narrator's feelings of abandonment as described in the last paragraphs of the passage.

2. The primary function of the description of the narrator's reaction to seeing her childhood home in the second paragraph (lines 15–28) is:

   F. to express her surprise at the dilapidated state of the building.
   G. to emphasize her frustration and anger toward her mother.
   H. to clarify that the joy she feels is tinged with fatigue due to her travels.
   J. to indicate both her familiarity and nervousness regarding her current situation.

3. The best description of the point of view from which this passage is told is that of a:

   A. daughter describing her thoughts during an event in her adult life.
   B. daughter reminiscing about her distant childhood in Alabama.
   C. mother remembering her daughter's visit to the family home.
   D. mother who longs to visit her adult daughter but cannot.

4. As it is used in line 28, the word *braced* most nearly means:

   F. fastened.
   G. straightened.
   H. prepared.
   J. supported.

5. The emotional states of the characters are primarily conveyed by the author's use of:

   A. metaphorical descriptions of the setting.
   B. subtle but emotionally charged dialogue.
   C. visual descriptions and narrative reflections.
   D. detailed psychological portraits by an objective narrator.

CRAFT AND STRUCTURE DRILL 1 EXPLANATIONS

1. **A** The question asks for the primary purpose of the first paragraph. Read the first paragraph. The paragraph describes the narrator's return to Alabama. She first recounts some of her *childhood memories*. Then she refers to herself as *dressed for an overly air-conditioned office climate* and mentions her rental car and her delayed flight, all things that relate to her life in the city. Choice (A) accurately describes the first paragraph, so keep (A). Choice (B) can be eliminated; the last sentence says *my mood was foul*, but the narrator is frustrated before arriving at her mother's house. This answer also does not address the change from the city to the country. The first paragraph does not describe the setting of the bulk of the passage; eliminate (C). Eliminate (D) because the first paragraph does not foreshadow a feeling of abandonment; the narrator's difficult relationship with her mother is in her past. The correct answer is (A).

2. **J** The question asks the primary function of the description of the narrator's reaction to seeing her childhood home in the second paragraph. Read the second paragraph. Lines 20–22 state that the narrator's *childhood home…looked the same as it had when [she] had left ten years earlier*. Lines 27–28 state that she had to *calm [her] nerves* and that *she grabbed [her] bags anxiously*. The word *surprise* in (F) is contradicted because she describes the house as virtually unchanged; eliminate (F). In these lines, the narrator is anxious, not angry or frustrated, so eliminate (G). The second paragraph does not mention that *joy* or *fatigue* was associated with the narrator's travels in the first paragraph; eliminate (H). Choice (J) references both the narrator's recognition of the house and her nervousness. The correct answer is (J).

3. **A** The question asks about the point of view from which the passage is told. Because this is a general question, it should be done after all the specific questions. The narrator describes visiting her family home and seeing her mother after having moved away ten years earlier. She mentions moving away for college and having worked in an office, which matches (A). Choice (B) focuses on the narrator's childhood, which is mentioned only briefly and is not the main theme of the passage; eliminate (B). Eliminate (C) and (D) because they incorrectly identify the mother as the narrator. The correct answer is (A).

4. **H** The question asks what the word *braced* means in line 28. Go back to the text, find the word *braced* and mark it out. Carefully read the surrounding text to determine another word that would fit in the blank based on the context of the passage. Lines 27–28 say *I grabbed my bags anxiously, trying to calm my nerves, and braced myself.* The narrator is getting ready to enter her mother's house, and she is nervous, so *braced* could be replaced with "readied." *Fastened* means "attached," which does not match "readied," so eliminate (F). *Straightened* means "untwisted" or "made tidy," neither of which match "readied," so eliminate (G). *Prepared* means "readied," so keep (H). *Supported* means "helped up," which does not match "readied," so eliminate (J). The correct answer is (H).

5. **C** The question asks how the author conveys the characters' emotional states. Because this is a general question, it should be done after all the specific questions. Most of the passage is told from the point of view of the narrator, as she reflects on her journey, so her own emotions are conveyed in her thoughts: *my mood was foul; I grabbed my bags anxiously, trying to calm my nerves; I could feel the anger rising.* When she first encounters her mother, however, she notices *that her hands were shaking...She looked so much older...in the same dress she'd probably worn for five years.* From those sights, the narrator determines her mother's emotions: *she understood that I needed to strike out on my own.* The emotional states of the characters are not conveyed through the *setting*, so eliminate (A). The dialogue is limited to two lines, so eliminate (B). Choice (C) matches the ways that the narrator's and mother's emotions are conveyed. Eliminate (D) because the narrator describes her own emotional experiences and cannot be said to be *objective*. The correct answer is (C).

CRAFT AND STRUCTURE DRILL 2

SOCIAL SCIENCE: This passage is adapted from the article "Slang: Why It's Totally Sweet" by Patrick Tyrrell (© 2008 by Patrick Tyrrell).

Tony Thorne's email inbox is bloated with messages from teenagers and college students around the world explicating the meaning behind local terms such as "toop," "tonk," and "chung." Why would the Director of the Language Center at
5 King's College of London concern himself with seemingly nonsensical linguistic inventions?

Thorne is busy compiling a current dictionary of slang from around the English-speaking world. Although *neologisms*, new adaptations or inventions of words, are normally
10 born out of a specific geographic and cultural context, the ease of worldwide communication ushered in by the technological age has made slang an instantly exportable commodity. College students in Iowa are just as likely to use British slang like "bum" (one's posterior) as British homemakers are to employ
15 American slang like "dust bunny," since both groups are exposed to each other's movies, TV, music, and other media.

In the world of linguistics, slang is often viewed condescendingly as an affliction of vulgar speech, its users condemned for their intellectual laziness. Early 20th century
20 linguist Oliver Wendell Holmes described slang as "at once a sign and a cause of mental atrophy." Meanwhile, Thorne points out, some legendary authors such as Walt Whitman elevated the status of slang, referring to it as "an attempt by common humanity to escape from bald literalism, and express
25 itself illimitably."

What are the origins of most slang words? Many philologists, those who attempt to study and determine the meaning of historical texts, believe that slang is created as a response to the status quo, that its usage represents a defiant opposition
30 of authority. For example, many Americans use the phrase *a cup of joe* to refer to a cup of coffee; however, few know that it originated from one Admiral Joe Daniels who in 1914 denied his sailors wine. As a result, they decided their strict leader was a fitting namesake for the terribly acidic black
35 coffee they were forced to drink instead.

Thorne, however, would point out that most slang is derived for much more innocent purposes. For example, terms like "ankle-biters" (infants), "ramping up" (on the job training), and "Googling" (searching on the Internet) do not involve
40 opposition to authority. Usually, slang evolves out of very insular groups with specific needs for informative or vibrant expressions that normal language does not encapsulate. It is the marriage of jargon, nuance, and effective imagery. While

traditional hotbeds of slang have been the military, industrial
45 factories, and street markets, most modern slang comes from such arenas as corporate offices, college campuses, and users/designers of computers.

In determining the sources of slang terms, Thorne and his contemporaries repeatedly refine their definition of "slang" as
50 distinctive from "idioms," "euphemisms," "hyperbole," and other instances of conventional figurative language. Many linguists consider slang the polar opposite of formal speech, with other figurative language devices falling somewhere in between. Whereas a "colloquialism" still indicates a mea-
55 sure of respect owed to the expression's regional usefulness, "slang" brands a word as having fallen into a state of overused emptiness.

How do we know when a word has become overused or empty? Much slang is attached to some sense of style or fad
60 and therefore risks being as short-lived in nature as the trend upon which it is based. However, some terms such as "punk" and "cool" have been in common use for a century or more and have completely assimilated into the acceptable mainstream dialect. Clearly, then, some words fall into a gray area
65 between slang and proper language. Although lexicologists like Thorne attempt to define and apply standard principles in their classification of slang, there is definitely some subjectivity involved in determining whether a term deserves the maligning moniker.

70 Furthermore, intellectuals who would categorically denounce slang struggle with the fact that slang, when first conceived, involves as much inherent creativity and word play as the figurative language revered in poetry. It is ultimately how the word survives, or rather who continues to use it, that
75 determines its stature as artful rhetoric or the dreaded slang. If "respectable" people continue to use an expression for its conceptual vivacity, then the word was a clever invention worth enriching a nation's lexicon. If the "common man" uses a term and uses it too liberally, the word is deemed slang,
80 and an eloquent speaker will have the tastefulness to avoid it.

Whatever slang's level of social esteem, Thorne believes that it is an essential project to compile accurate modern dictionaries of its usage. When one considers the large amount of written artifacts our present world creates on a daily basis,
85 it is reasonable to also consider providing future generations (or civilizations) of humans with an effective way of decoding our meaning, which could easily be confused by our prevalent use of slang. Imagine how much less debate there would be over the meaning of some Shakespearean verses if we had a
90 detailed description of his contemporary slang. Because of this need to inform future scholars, Thorne's dictionary of slang attempts to not only define each term but also to explain its origins, connotations, and typical conversational uses.

1. The author includes the information in the last paragraph primarily to:

   A. criticize Thorne for being too subjective with which words he chooses to include in his dictionary.
   B. illustrate how a future scholar might be able to use Thorne's dictionary as a resource.
   C. identify the ways Thorne uses Shakespearean slang to describe modern terms.
   D. argue that Thorne's dictionary should be the primary focus of modern linguistics.

2. The quotation marks around the phrase "common man" in line 78 primarily serve to:

   F. emphasize the subjective and somewhat derogatory process of categorizing people and the words they use.
   G. reveal the author's suspicion that the man in question is not common at all.
   H. introduce a demeaning term the author believes is appropriate to describe users of slang.
   J. show how an inventive term may enjoy popularity briefly but ultimately does not have the proper usage to survive.

3. As it is used in line 18, the word *vulgar* most nearly means:

   A. sickening.
   B. malicious.
   C. unsophisticated.
   D. profane.

4. The main purpose of the first paragraph in relation to the passage is to:

   F. acquaint the reader with some examples of slang.
   G. establish that British scholars are the leaders in slang research.
   H. introduce slang as a possibly surprising topic of academic study.
   J. outline Tony Thorne's problems with managing his email inbox.

CRAFT AND STRUCTURE DRILL 2 EXPLANATIONS

1. **B** The question asks why the author includes the information in the last paragraph, so read lines 81–94. This paragraph states *Thorne believes that it is an essential project to compile accurate modern dictionaries of [slang's] usage,* in order to provide *future generations (or civilizations) of humans with an effective way of decoding our meaning.* Specifically, the paragraph mentions the *need to inform future scholars.* There is no criticism of Thorne or any indication that he is *subjective with which words he chooses to include in his dictionary,* so eliminate (A). Keep (B) because it is consistent with the discussion of *the need to inform future scholars.* The reference to *Shakespearean verses* is an analogy illustrating why a slang dictionary might be useful for future scholars; there's no mention of Thorne using *Shakespearean slang to describe modern terms,* so eliminate (C). The author doesn't make an argument about what the *primary focus of modern linguistics* should be, so eliminate (D). The correct answer is (B).

2. **F** The question asks for the primary purpose of the quotation marks around the phrase *common man.* Read a window in the passage around the given line. Lines 67–69 make the point that *there is definitely some subjectivity involved in determining whether a term deserves the maligning moniker [slang].* In the next paragraph, the author states that *intellectuals who would categorically denounce slang struggle with the fact that slang…involves as much inherent creativity and word play as the figurative language revered in poetry.* Despite this similarity, the author notes that *it is who continues to use [a term] that determines its stature as artful rhetoric or the dreaded slang.* Therefore, the author is arguing against categorizing words and the people who use them; he puts the terms *"respectable people"* and the *"common man"* in quotation marks to indicate that these categories are subjective. Keep (F) because it is supported by the discussion in these lines. The phrase *common man* does not refer to one particular man, so eliminate (G). The author is opposed to using *a demeaning term to describe users of slang,* so eliminate (H). The passage discusses the people who continue to use a term, so the author does not believe that slang terms do *not have the proper usage to survive;* eliminate (J). The correct answer is (F).

3. **C** The question asks what the word *vulgar* means in line 18. Go back to the text, find the word *vulgar* and mark it out. Carefully read the surrounding text to determine another word that would fit in the blank based on the context of the passage. Lines 17–19 state, *In the world of linguistics, slang is often viewed condescendingly as an affliction of vulgar speech, its users condemned for their intellectual laziness.* The word *vulgar* could be replaced with the word "unrefined." *Sickening* means "repulsive"; it doesn't match "unrefined," so eliminate (A). *Malicious* means "intentionally harmful"; it doesn't match "unrefined," so eliminate (B). Keep (C) because *unsophisticated* matches "unrefined." *Profane* means "sacrilegious" or "secular"; it doesn't match "unrefined," so eliminate (D). The correct answer is (C).

4.   **H**   The question asks for the main purpose of the first paragraph in relation to the passage. Because this is a general question, it should be done after all the specific questions. The passage as a whole discusses slang, in particular, a linguist's efforts to compile *a current dictionary of slang* (line 7). The question references the first paragraph, so read lines 1–6. These lines say that Tony Thorne receives many emails *explicating the meaning behind local terms,* and asks, *Why would the Director of the Language Center at King's College of London concern himself with seemingly nonsensical linguistic inventions?* This paragraph gives a few *examples of slang,* but the question at the end suggests that the paragraph's main purpose is not simply introducing the examples, so eliminate (F). Although the paragraph indicates that Thorne is from London, the author does not try to *establish that British scholars are the leaders in slang research,* so eliminate (G). Keep (H), since the phrase *a possibly surprising topic of academic study* is supported by the question about *why* Thorne would *concern himself* with the slang terms. Although the passage describes Thorne's email inbox as *bloated,* the author never discusses Thorne *struggling to manage his email inbox,* so eliminate (J). The correct answer is (H).

CRAFT AND STRUCTURE DRILL 3

NATURAL SCIENCE: This passage is adapted from the article "A Tree Frog Grows Up in Hawaii" by Ashley C. Tulliver (© 2005 by Ashley Tulliver).

As night falls on Hawaii's Big Island, a low, jarring sound begins. It is a faint murmur at first, but as the darkness deepens, the sound grows louder, rending the stillness of the evening. These deep cries, from male *E. coquí* frogs, are met
5 with lower, guttural croaks from their prospective mates; during this time, the sound for which the coquí is named (ko-KEE) fills the air. This sound has become the theme song of a growing environmental problem: invasive species' threat to ecological biodiversity.

10 Native to Puerto Rico, the small tree frogs—measuring about five millimeters long—probably arrived in Hawaii as passengers aboard potted plants imported from the Caribbean. Once coquíes explored their new environment, they found an abundance of food, including insects, tiny spiders, and mites.
15 In addition, they faced little ecological competition, as there are no other amphibians native to the islands, nor are there the snakes, tarantulas, or other Caribbean hunters that usually serve to keep the coquí population in check.

The way the coquí hatch also gives the coquí an advan-
20 tage in Hawaii's ecosystem. Frogs usually hatch into tadpoles, which require a consistent and substantial amount of water to survive. By contrast, the coquí emerges from the egg as a tiny but fully formed frog, which allows it to thrive in saturated moss, the dampened plastic that importers wrap around plants,
25 or even a drop of water on a plant leaf. Moreover, young coquíes don't begin to emit their signature calls until they are about a year old; consequently, avian predators are unable to locate the tiny frogs by sound.

Perhaps the coquí's most noteworthy feature is its ex-
30 tremely loud calling song. To a listener one to two feet away, a single coquí can produce a mating call up to 100 decibels. The unusual volume of the frog's call is compounded by two other factors. First, coquíes congregate closely on relatively small parcels of land; one recent survey found 400 adult frogs
35 in one 20-by-20-meter plot. This degree of concentration amplifies the sound the frogs make. Second, coquíes tend to overlap their calls, with a single coquí seeking to fill gaps in other frogs' songs with its own effort to attract a mate. As a result, coquíes create a "wall of sound" that is even more
40 pronounced because Hawaii boasts few other night-calling species. For these reasons, human residents of Hawaii tend to regard coquíes as nuisances, polluting the air with their incessant noise.

Conservationists worry about other ramifications of the
45 coquí's invasion of the Hawaiian ecosystem. One problem is that while the coquí receives the bulk of residents' attention because of its nocturnal serenades, another, quieter genus of the frog—the greenhouse frog—represents an equal threat to the biodiversity of the island. As voracious insectivores,
50 coquíes and greenhouse frogs are threatening the survival of arthropods (invertebrate animals with jointed legs, including insects, scorpions, crustaceans, and spiders), whose populations are already close to extirpation due to other foreign predators. Ornithologists fear that depleting the insect population
55 could result in serious consequences for Hawaii's food web, especially considering that the birds native to the islands are also insectivores.

Symbiotic interactions between the coquí and other in-vasive species pose another ecological threat. The presence
60 of coquíes could permit the flourishing of other so-called "dissonant" species, such as non-native snakes that prey upon the frogs. Herpetologists have speculated that nematodes and other types of vertebrate parasites can be transported with coquíes and can infect indigenous fauna. Furthermore, many
65 ecologists believe the proliferation of these frogs will further homogenize the island's biota.

Debate persists about how best to reduce or even eradicate the population of coquíes and their cousins in Hawaii. Hand-capturing the tiny frogs is probably the most environmentally
70 sensitive way to remove them from their habitat, but their sheer number renders this approach inefficient. The maximum con-centration of pesticides that would not damage fauna or flora has not been potent enough to kill the frogs. Seeking a more creative solution, scientists have had some success treating the
75 frogs with caffeine citrate, a drug typically prescribed to treat breathing and metabolic abnormalities in humans. Caffeine citrate can penetrate the coquí's moist skin, and the drug's high acidity essentially poisons the animal and inactivates its nervous systems. From a biodiversity standpoint, this
80 technique has the added benefit of posing almost no danger to plants, which lack a nervous system, or to insects, which have an impenetrable, hard exoskeleton.

Even if new techniques finally exterminate the coquí, experts are skeptical that the invader's current effects on the
85 1,000 acres of Hawaii's ecosystem can be reversed. This patch of land is not expansive in comparison to Hawaii's total 4.1 million acres, yet it is an indication of potential widespread disaster: since the habitat and its native residents have thus far been able to adjust to the presence of coquíes, eliminating the
90 frogs could yield unintended and far-reaching consequences to the biodiversity of the habitat beyond arthropods. For now, scientists are likely to continue the delicate balancing act of limiting the coquí's population growth while preventing further damage to Hawaii's ecosystem.

1. The primary purpose of the third paragraph (lines 19–28) is to:

   A. describe wet weather conditions in Hawaii necessary for the coquí to breed.
   B. provide a physical description of the coquí's habitat in Hawaii compared to that in Puerto Rico.
   C. explain the ecological and behavioral advantages that permit the coquí to thrive in Hawaii.
   D. give an overview of the amphibian life cycle, from the tadpole to frog stage.

2. Compared to the language of the first paragraph, the language of the sixth paragraph (lines 58–66) is more:

   F. opinionated.
   G. scientific.
   H. optimistic.
   J. casual.

3. As it is used in line 53, the word *extirpation* most nearly means:

   A. competition.
   B. extinction.
   C. overpopulation.
   D. pursuit.

4. The author includes the discussion of the greenhouse frog in order to:

   F. establish a contrast between the preferred habitat of the greenhouse frog and that of the coquí.
   G. explain that the greenhouse frog can be as detrimental to the environment as the coquí despite the former's smaller population.
   H. clarify that the greenhouse frog does not pose as dangerous a threat to the Hawaiian ecosystem as the coquí does.
   J. emphasize the greater difficulty in locating greenhouse frog populations, as they do not make loud mating calls like the coquí do.

CRAFT AND STRUCTURE DRILL 3 EXPLANATIONS

1. **C** The question asks for the primary purpose of the third paragraph, so read the third paragraph. The paragraph says that *the way the coquí hatch also gives the coquí an advantage in Hawaii's ecosystem*, and that *young coquíes don't begin to emit their signature calls until they are about a year old; consequently, avian predators are unable to locate the tiny frogs by sound*. Lines 23–25 emphasize the small amount of water coquíes need to survive: *saturated moss, the dampened plastic that importers wrap around plants, or even a drop of water on a plant leaf*. This contradicts (A), so eliminate (A). Puerto Rico is mentioned in the second paragraph, not the third, so eliminate (B). Choice (C) is supported, so keep it. The paragraph discusses coquíes (which do not have a tadpole stage) in particular, not amphibians in general, so eliminate (D). The correct answer is (C).

2. **G** The question asks for the difference in the language used in the sixth paragraph as compared to the first paragraph. Read both paragraphs. The first paragraph uses descriptive language to evoke the sense of the coquí's call: *a low, jarring sound begins…the sound grows louder, rending the stillness of the evening*. The sixth paragraph uses words like *symbiotic, "dissonant" species, herpetologists, vertebrate parasites, indigenous fauna,* and *biota*. These words are not *opinionated*, so eliminate (F). They are *scientific*, so keep (G). The paragraph discusses *another ecological threat*, so it is not *optimistic;* eliminate (H). The words used are formal, not *casual*, so eliminate (J). The correct answer is (G).

3. **B** This question asks what the word *extirpation* means in line 53. Go back to the text, find the word *extirpation*, and mark it out. Carefully read the surrounding text to determine another word that would fit in the blank based on the context of the passage. Lines 50–51 say that *coquíes…are threatening the survival of arthropods*. The phrase *already close to* indicates that *extirpation* is similar to *threatening the survival*, so *extirpation* could be replaced with "dying out." *Competition* means "rivalry," which does not match "dying out," so eliminate (A). *Extinction* means "dying out," so keep (B). *Overpopulation* is the opposite of "dying out," so eliminate (C). *Pursuit* means "following," which does not match "dying out," so eliminate (D). The correct answer is (B).

4. **G** The question asks why the author included the discussion of the greenhouse frog. Look for the phrase *greenhouse frog* in the passage. Lines 47–49 state that *another, quieter genus of the frog—the greenhouse frog—represents an equal threat to the biodiversity of the island*. There is no discussion of where the greenhouse frog prefers to live, so eliminate (F). Choice (G) is supported by lines 47–49. Choice (H) says the opposite of lines 48–49, so eliminate it. Although the passage says the greenhouse frogs are *quieter* than coquíes are, it does not state that the greenhouse frog is more difficult to locate, so eliminate (J). The correct answer is (G).

THIS PAGE IS INTENTIONALLY LEFT BLANK.

CRAFT AND STRUCTURE DRILL 4

PROSE FICTION: This passage is adapted from the novel *A Passage to America* by Aditi C. Thakur (© 2003 by Aditi Thakur).

I'm shivering in the air conditioning. I've never gotten used to the swirl of chilled air in the apartment. I'd like to open the window, to welcome in the hot bright yellow sun, but the superintendent has painted all the building's windows
5 shut for some unexplained reason.

Ramesh won't be home from the university for several hours, I know. The project he's working on is keeping him at the lab until later in the evenings these days. Still shivering, I mull the choices for our evening meal, scanning the vegetables,
10 herbs, and spices I collected at the specialty food market this morning. Even after five years in the United States, I find I still seek the patterns of our life in India, including my daily morning visits to the market to do the day's food shopping.

As I pore over the curled turmeric roots and the bright
15 orange and red mangoes—both of which appeared in the market's bins today for the first time—I remember the first time I went to an American-style supermarket. Intimidated by the unfamiliar streets and landmarks of our new city, Ramesh and I had spent the first month of our American life eating all
20 our meals at restaurants within walking distance of the flat. Ramesh had concocted his lunches from items purchased at the university's "convenience store"; he joked that convenience was really the only desirable thing the shop offered. Once we had exhausted the menus at each of the nearby restaurants,
25 I promised that I would brave the supermarket so we could both have a taste of the home we'd been aching for.

Naturally—or rather, unnaturally—the store was cold, and I was glad I had decided to bring along my *dupatta* to shield my otherwise bare shoulders.

30 At first, the enormous quantity of goods and the wildly varied colors everywhere I looked were impressive. But then I noticed that the produce section—it seemed surprisingly tucked away on the end farthest from the doors, as if the store were somehow ashamed of it—lacked items we considered
35 favorites or even staples: no dried lentils or chickpeas, no cherimoyas or pomegranates. I wandered up and down the aisles, wondering at the slabs of meat sealed within cocoons of plastic, and at the seemingly infinite rows of boxes, each of which somehow housed "dinner for the whole family."
40 Unable after a time to focus on the boxes' labels, I turned to a gangly, uniformed teenager who was pretending to straighten the ginger ale bottles on the bottom shelf.

"Excuse me, please, I am wondering whether you could help me find…" I began.

45 He glanced up at me, noting my *sari* with an eye that felt at once piercing and uncritical. "Aisle 7, on the right," he squeaked, with a wide, unexpectedly amiable grin.

My irritation at having been so easily categorized faded somewhat at discovering two shelves' worth of jars of chutneys
50 and mixes, including one imported tandoori paste that had been one of our favorites back in India. But as I unsteadily but successfully navigated the checkout lines and paid for my few, familiar products, I observed that the supermarket's fluorescent ceiling bulbs effectively bleached out the shelves'
55 contents. The bottles and boxes no longer seemed exotic or glamorous. It seemed to me that no matter how insistently the labels tried to draw attention to the wonders within their containers, the vividness of their colors would inevitably appear flat and lifeless under the homogenizing light.

60 I still go to the supermarket sometimes, but recently a colleague of Ramesh's recommended that we go to the outskirts of the city to shop at a new Indian market, where I went this morning. The old woman who manages the place moves quickly from stall to stall, urging customers to sample
65 pieces of fruit or explaining how adding one more ingredient will perfect the planned dish. She reminds me, almost painfully, of my grandmother, who was similarly convinced that she could make others' lives better through shared food or wisdom—my grandmother, to whose image I've often come
70 back whenever I've needed consolation or company.

I trace my finger along the beige granite countertop, as if conjuring up the rough wooden surface in my grandmother's kitchen. As a child, I'd believed the dark wood had retained every nick from every vegetable chopped, and every stain
75 from every fruit that had yielded its sticky sweetness to my grandmother's swift, sure knife. I think of the fourteen distinct spices, each with its own grainy texture and subtle but memorable color, that she pounded into dust with her mortar and pestle. Then I recall the grayish, unfriendly curry powder
80 I'd seen in the American supermarket, so unlike the familiar result of my grandmother's efforts. I sigh.

I don't really need to begin to prepare our dinner yet. I've learned to combine the specialty market's fresh produce with the supermarket's "quick prep" sauces and pastes, so making
85 dinner isn't the all-day task it often was for my grandmother and even my mother. Even so, I decide to ward off the cold by shrugging on a sweatshirt embossed with the university's logo, and I set myself to work.

1. As presented in the passage, how does the narrator's attitude toward living in the United States change from when she was a recent arrival until the present day?

   A. At first, she was intimidated by unfamiliar surroundings, but she has since learned to blend Indian and American ways.
   B. At first, she was excited about the prospect of learning new ways, but she has since become disillusioned by the people she meets.
   C. At first, she enjoyed eating out at restaurants with her husband, but she has begun to miss him as he increasingly works late.
   D. At first, she is thrilled by the supermarket displays, but she now refuses to leave her apartment.

2. How can the conversation between the narrator and the supermarket clerk (lines 40–47) best be characterized?

   F. The narrator is pleased that the clerk is friendly and able to tell her where to find the items she's looking for.
   G. The narrator is shocked and upset by the clerk's hostility toward her.
   H. The narrator is annoyed that the clerk knew what she wanted before she asked.
   J. The narrator wishes the clerk had been more cooperative instead of being distracted by her clothing.

3. The narrator refers to the supermarket's "fluorescent ceiling bulbs" (line 54) in order to:

   A. draw a contrast between the supermarket and the outdoor markets she remembers from India.
   B. explain how her perception of the store's offerings had changed.
   C. suggest one reason that the supermarket terrified her.
   D. describe why she was able to see the fruits and vegetables more clearly.

4. As it is used in line 79 the word *unfriendly* most nearly means:

   F. neutral.
   G. unfamiliar.
   H. unbalanced.
   J. bleak.

CRAFT AND STRUCTURE DRILL 4 EXPLANATIONS

1. **A**   The question asks how the narrator's attitude toward living in the United States changed from her arrival until the present day. Since this is a general question, it should be done after all the specific questions. The narrator is initially *Intimidated by the unfamiliar streets and landmarks of our new city* (line 18), but in lines 82–88 she says that she has *learned to combine the specialty market's fresh produce with the supermarket's "quick prep" sauces,* which implies that she has become more comfortable. Keep (A), since it is supported by these references. The narrator was *intimidated* at first, not *excited,* and she is *irritated,* but not *disillusioned* by the grocery store clerk she meets in lines 43–50, so eliminate (B). The discussion of eating at restaurants in lines 18–26 doesn't indicate that the narrator *enjoyed* them, and though the first paragraph does mention that her husband works late, there is no mention of *missing* him; eliminate (C). The passage indicates that the narrator goes out shopping, so it's not true that *she now refuses to leave her apartment;* eliminate (D). The correct answer is (A).

2. **H**   The question asks how the conversation between the narrator and the supermarket clerk can be characterized. Read a window in the passage around the given lines. Lines 45–51 describe the clerk's *amiable grin* and indicate that he helped the narrator find what she was looking for. However, the narrator experienced brief *irritation at having been so easily categorized.* The reference to her *irritation* indicates that the narrator is not entirely *pleased,* so eliminate (F). The clerk does not show any *hostility,* and the narrator is not *shocked,* just *irritated,* so eliminate (G). Keep (H), since it is supported by line 48. The clerk is *cooperative* and he is not *distracted* by her clothing, so eliminate (J). The correct answer is (H).

3. **B**   The question asks why the narrator refers to the supermarket's *fluorescent ceiling bulbs.* Read a window in the passage around the given lines. Lines 53–59 state that the fluorescent ceiling bulbs effectively *bleached out the shelves' contents. The bottles and boxes no longer seemed exotic or glamorous,* and *the vividness of their colors would inevitably appear flat and lifeless under the homogenizing light.* The passage never mentions *outdoor markets in India,* so eliminate (A). Keep (B) because the contrast of *exotic or glamorous* with *flat and lifeless* indicates a change in the narrator's *perception of the store's offerings.* Earlier in the passage the narrator says, *I would brave the supermarket* (line 25). Though this indicates that she was initially intimidated by the prospect of going to the supermarket, the lighting is not what intimidates her, and *terrified* is too strong in any case, so eliminate (C). Lines 53–59 indicate that the lighting made the products *flat and lifeless,* not more clearly visible, and the fruits and vegetables are not discussed in this part of the passage, so eliminate (D). The correct answer is (B).

4. **G**   This question asks what the word *unfriendly* means in line 79. Go back to the text, find the word *unfriendly,* and mark it out. Carefully read the surrounding text to determine another word that would fit in the blank based on the context of the passage. Lines 80–81 say that the grayish, unfriendly curry powder was *so unlike the familiar result of my grandmother's efforts.* Since the curry powder made by the narrator's grandmother is described as *familiar* and the grocery store curry powder is *so unlike* it, *unfriendly* could be replaced with "strange." *Neutral* means "impartial," which does not match "strange," so eliminate (F). *Unfamiliar* means "strange," so keep (G). *Unbalanced* means "uneven," which does not match "strange," so eliminate (H). *Bleak* means "dreary," which does not match "strange," so eliminate (J). The correct answer is (G).

THIS PAGE IS INTENTIONALLY LEFT BLANK.

CRAFT AND STRUCTURE DRILL 5

NATURAL SCIENCE: This passage is adapted from the entry "Migration" from *Wallace Wimpole's Bird Book* (© 1998 by Wallace Wimpole).

It has been well known among even casual observers of the natural world that many bird species make seasonal trips between cooler breeding grounds in the spring and summer, and warmer locations in the autumn and winter. Migration is 5 a part of the annual cycle of over 50 billion individual birds worldwide. (This is not to say all birds migrate; there are many species, particularly in the tropics, that maintain a single residence year-round.) However, the biological mechanisms that prompt birds to choose a particular date to begin migra-10 tion are complex and seem to be influenced by many factors.

The most obvious pressure on the timing of seasonal bird migration is the weather. As the weather cools and precipitation increases, birds living in temperate climates move in the direction of warmer weather. However, seasonal weather pat-15 terns are notoriously unpredictable. Cloud cover can obscure even reliable measures of the seasons, such as the position of the sun and the stars. Therefore, it is clear that birds must rely more heavily on an internal clock to time their seasonal movements. In fact, biologists have observed a phenomenon known 20 as "migratory restlessness" in caged birds at the same time the wild members of their species set off on seasonal migrations.

For most migratory birds, food supply is a major factor that contributes to the need to move from one location to another. Birds must have ample nutrition to reproduce, and 25 seasonal changes in weather affect the availability of berries, nuts, insects, rodents, and other sources of nourishment. Furthermore, birds must store a great deal of energy in the form of body fat to fuel their migration, so they have to leave while their reserves are high, before changes in weather cause 30 the food supply to dwindle. Many species seem to anticipate changes in weather and food sources, and adjust their migration schedules to accommodate significant variations in weather and food supply that occur from year to year, causing scientists to speculate that unknown internal stimuli may have a strong 35 effect on the timing of the migration decision.

In 1967, Russian ornithologists Viktor Dolnik and Tatiana Blyumental collected chaffinches as they migrated along the Baltic Coast. By examining the fat content and food in the gut of the carcasses of birds gathered at different 40 stages of the waves of migration, and then comparing these findings to the number of birds out of the total population yet to migrate, the scientists determined the social influence fat, healthy birds have on the remaining population that was not as physically fit for migration. Dolnik and Blyumental found 45 that on the first day of each wave of migration, only very fat

birds flew. These birds left at sunrise, on days when weather conditions were favorable. They did not feed before beginning their migratory flight, instead relying on stored fat for energy.

On the second day, the chaffinch migration began again 50 in the morning with fat birds. By the afternoon the migration volume peaked, as more and more lean birds began to migrate, many with the morning's food still in their stomachs. By the third day, almost all the birds that began to migrate were very lean. These birds began their migration only after 55 feeding in the morning. Often these leaner birds began their migration despite inclement weather. Dolnik and Blyumental suggested that the social pressure exerted by the large volume of healthier birds in the flock that had already begun to migrate was an influence strong enough to override the lean birds' 60 poor physical readiness and the adverse conditions as factors in their decision to migrate. The scientists conducted their experiment on only one species, and though chaffinches are typical of diurnal migratory land birds, they do not accurately represent sea birds, raptors, or nocturnal species. Nonetheless, 65 Dolnik and Blyumental's work suggests that social pressure could explain why many different species of birds choose to migrate at apparently unfavorable times.

Some migratory birds travel much further than chaffinches. Most migrants spend a great deal of time storing energy 70 to make trips that take a matter of days or weeks to complete, and travel tens to hundreds of kilometers, spending most of their lives in residence at their breeding grounds and their winter habitats. A few species, however, can spend months of each year en route between residences continents apart, and 75 expend little more energy flying than sitting still. Wandering albatrosses spend almost all their time in the air, either migrating or foraging over oceans, moving up to 2000 kilometers on a single foraging expedition, and flying over 250,000 kilometers in a year (a distance equivalent to 4.6 times around the 80 Earth's equator). Such sea birds rely on their specialized wing structure to hold them aloft in air currents that transport them long distances, and some travel back and forth along the same paths on schedules dictated by the prevailing winds.

1. The main purpose of the passage is to:

    A. discuss the research techniques of scientists studying bird migration.
    B. provide data on the distances traveled seasonally by various migratory bird species.
    C. describe various factors that stimulate migratory behavior in birds.
    D. prove the effects of weather on bird migration.

2. The author uses the information in parentheses in lines 6–8 primarily to:

    F. prevent readers from misunderstanding the statistic cited in the previous sentence.
    G. debunk claims that the biological mechanism for migration is complex.
    H. imply that ornithologists disagree about whether birds choose their migration schedule.
    J. prove the assertion that the migration cycle is changing due to global warming.

3. The main purpose of the third paragraph (lines 22–35) is to:

    A. specify the many sources of food birds use as energy to fuel their migratory movements.
    B. document the weather conditions that impact birds' ability to fly.
    C. present a variety of reasons why the availability of nourishment is important in the timing of bird migration.
    D. summarize several scientific principles discovered by observing migratory birds.

4. The author includes the statement in lines 44–46 in order to:

    F. introduce an assumption based on a small sample of a few captured chaffinches.
    G. describe a characterization based on the comparison of the fat content of the bodies of many individual chaffinches.
    H. make an observation based on the visual appearance of chaffinches as they flew over the Baltic Coast.
    J. offer an opinion based on the personal preferences of Dolnik and Blyumental.

CRAFT AND STRUCTURE DRILL 5 EXPLANATIONS

1. **C** The question asks for the main purpose of the passage. Since this is a general question, it should be done after all the specific questions. Lines 8–10 indicate the main focus of the passage: *However, the biological mechanisms that prompt birds to choose a particular date to begin migration are complex and seem to be influenced by many factors.* Although the passage does describe some *research techniques*, describing them is not the main purpose of the passage, so eliminate (A). Similarly, although the passage does provide some *data on the distances traveled* by *various migratory bird species,* this is not the passage's primary purpose, so eliminate (B). Keep (C) since this is a paraphrase of the focus outlined in lines 8–10. The passage does not *prove the effects of weather on bird migration,* so eliminate (D). The correct answer is (C).

2. **F** The question asks why the author uses the information in parentheses in lines 6–8. Read a window in the passage around the given lines. Beginning on line 4, the passage states, *Migration is a part of the annual cycle of over 50 billion individual birds worldwide. (This is not to say all birds migrate; there are many species, particularly in the tropics, that maintain a single residence year-round.)* The information in the parentheses clarifies a potential *misunderstanding* about the *statistic* given in the previous sentence, so keep (F). Lines 8–10 state that *the biological mechanisms that prompt birds to choose a particular date to begin migration are complex,* so the author is not trying to *debunk claims that the biological mechanism for migration is complex;* eliminate (G). This paragraph doesn't indicate that *ornithologists disagree,* so eliminate (H). This paragraph also doesn't discuss *the migration cycle changing due to global warming,* so eliminate (J). The correct answer is (F).

3. **C** The question asks for the main purpose of the third paragraph. Read lines 22–29. These lines state, *For most migratory birds, food supply is a major factor that contributes to the need to move from one location to another. Birds must have ample nutrition to reproduce, and seasonal changes in weather affect the availability of…sources of nourishment. Furthermore, birds must store a great deal of energy in the form of body fat to fuel their migration, so they have to leave while their reserves are high.* Lines 25–26 list several of the birds' *sources of food,* but listing them is not the main purpose of the passage, so eliminate (A). *Changes in weather* are mentioned in the paragraph, but it does not *document the weather conditions that impact birds' ability to fly,* so eliminate (B). Keep (C), since lines 22–29 give *reasons why the availability of nourishment is important in the timing of bird migration.* The study that involved *observing migratory birds* is discussed in the fourth paragraph, not the third paragraph, so eliminate (D). The correct answer is (C).

4. **G** The question asks why the author includes the statement in lines 44–46. Read a window in the passage around the given lines. The paragraph that begins on line 36 describes what researchers observed when they *collected chaffinches as they migrated along the Baltic Coast.* They examined *the fat content and food in the gut of the carcasses of birds gathered at different stages of the waves of migration* and compared *these findings to the number of birds out of the total population yet to migrate.* The statement in lines 44–46 is, *Dolnik and Blyumental found that on the first day of each wave of migration, only very fat birds flew.* This was an observation, not an *assumption,* so eliminate (F). Keep (G) because it matches the description of the study found in lines 38–42. The researchers observed *the fat content and food in the gut of the carcasses of birds;* they did not observe *the visual appearance of chaffinches as they flew over the Baltic Coast,* so eliminate (H). The researchers' *personal preferences* are never mentioned, so eliminate (J). The correct answer is (G).

THIS PAGE IS INTENTIONALLY LEFT BLANK.

CRAFT AND STRUCTURE DRILL 6

PROSE FICTION: This passage is adapted from the short story "A Prisoner in His Castle" by Curtis Longweather (© 2008 by Curtis Longweather).

Since he returned from the hospital, he has been unable to reclaim his speaking voice. That is not to say that he can't make sounds, but that he often can't make his thoughts into sounds like words and sentences. Something is polluting the
5 chemistry that distills mental language into vocal output. His mind lights up with ideas just like mine does, but his ideas cannot escape. His thoughts are dispatched like knights to battle only to find they are unable to cross the moat that surrounds their castle. They are held prisoner in their own home,
10 quarantined in frustrated isolation from the outside world.

"I fear that I will eventually choke on my own thoughts," he worries aloud to me in one of his desperate letters.

"Then expel them all on to the page," I remind him. He is a volcano with no air vents to relieve the pressure of the heat
15 churning in his belly. His insides roil with fire, occasionally bubbling to the surface. His core vibrates with tightly coiled anticipation, the roof of his head eventually shedding off all shingles as a prelude to its propelling explosively into the atmosphere.

20 I tell him that his speaking voice may be like the oceanic cloud of dust and debris that the volcano spews into the air, but his writing can flow like omni-directional lava, indiscriminately absorbing everything in its path. Eventually, the continents that form as this lava cools will be fertile grounds
25 for his readers. Each of his letters stands proudly as an island within the sloshing seas of his mind, and his clarity of prose allows us explorers to navigate him.

"There is plenty of solace in writing," he acknowledges, but maintains, "never explain to someone who can't run that
30 at least he can drive a car."

He will always hear his thoughts as an echo, either reverberating within his own skull or as a crude imitation when transferred by pen.

I concede that the Page's shortcoming is a lack of dy-
35 namic human ears, but I optimistically point to the fact that written language has the potential to be seen by *countless* human eyes. It has the potential to be richly revered classical music, not just catchy pop expressions that inspire bystanders to twitch in accordance. It has the advantage of being me-
40 thodically composed and purposefully orchestrated. However, it can be spontaneous and stream-of-consciousness as well.

"A verbal speech can be a symphony of thought just as an essay can be an improvisational blunder." He responds. "You are wrongly contrasting two styles of music when the more
45 appropriate comparison is two very different instruments."

His distinction is a valid one, but I continue to stubbornly assert the superiority of literary communication. When we *speak* to convey meaning, I argue, we can too easily get away with lazy word choice by using context, body language, tone,
50 and other non-verbal devices to supplement our stated words. In a piece of writing, the words exist in isolation from their author. They belong only to each other, like pirates who share a common destiny but no longer pledge allegiance to any sovereign entity. Judge them by your own standards
55 if you wish to be confused, but realize that the only telling diagnosis rests in the internal consistency of their ways. Do the various tensions created by the professed actions, ideas, and feelings of the writing allow the reader to vicariously behold the mental state of the author? If so, then the reader
60 has the satisfying experience of being simultaneously in the audience and backstage as well.

He enjoys coming to watch me during my trials. Sometimes I look over at him while I am delivering my closing arguments to a jury, and I see the mix of pride and pain in
65 his eyes as he listens to me express myself more lucidly than he may ever be able to again. If my profession would allow it, I would gladly yield my voice to him and become a mere puppet for his ideas, just so he could again experience the instant gratification of vocal persuasion. (I frequently wonder
70 if my friendship with him will ultimately venture into the territory of Cyrano de Bergerac, who so wished to woo the heart of a woman that he enlisted the help of a friend to speak his thoughts aloud to her.)

It is not the organization of thought that he treasures in
75 listening to my courtroom orations. It is the expressiveness that a human voice can add to the meaning of words that he deeply misses. He will occasionally have me rehearse my speeches to him and never permits me to begin reciting my words too mechanically. The moment I begin *reading* and not
80 *speaking*, he will clap his hands and signal me to return back to the beginning of the idea.

In this way, just as I continue to remind him of the unspeakable value of written language, he continues to remind me of the irreplaceable value of the human voice.

1. As it relates to his friend's fear as described in the third paragraph, the narrator's description of a volcano (lines 13–19) most serves to:

   A. elaborate the friend's inner torment.
   B. speculate that his friend's thoughts will be unleashed.
   C. explain why the friend is unable to speak.
   D. imply the friend needs to be more patient.

2. Which of the following best describes the structure of the passage?

   F. A detailed character study of two close friends by means of describing one extended argument between them
   G. A debate about a topic during which the two main characters take equal turns discussing their positions and reasons
   H. An exploration of the author's experience of his friend's speech impairment using their verbal and written exchanges as a primary source
   J. The depiction of a unique friendship that allows the narrator to explain his successes and struggles as a lawyer

3. The erupting volcano simile refers to a dust cloud and a lava flow to portray:

   A. intuition and logic.
   B. simplicity and complexity.
   C. instinct and deliberation.
   D. vocal and non-vocal expression.

4. Based on the passage, which of the following statements most clearly portrays the respective attitudes of the narrator and his friend?

   F. The friend is argumentative and cynical; the narrator is jaded and indifferent.
   G. The friend is scornful and depressed; the narrator is apologetic and idealistic.
   H. The friend is anxious and despondent; the narrator is sympathetic and encouraging.
   J. The friend is shy and reclusive; the narrator is outgoing and nonchalant.

5. As it is used in (line 68), the word *puppet* most nearly means:

   A. entertainer.
   B. conversationalist.
   C. toy.
   D. mouthpiece.

CRAFT AND STRUCTURE DRILL 6 EXPLANATIONS

1. **A**   The question asks what purpose the narrator's *description of a volcano* serves, as it relates to his friend's fear. The question references the third paragraph, so read lines 13–19, and a few lines before and after if needed. The first paragraph describes the experience of the narrator's friend, who *has been unable to reclaim his speaking voice*, although…*his mind lights up with ideas*. The friend's fear is expressed in lines 11–12: *"I fear that I will eventually choke on my own thoughts."* In lines 13–19, the narrator compares the friend to *a volcano with no air vents to relieve the pressure of the heat churning in his belly*. The narrator uses the metaphor of the volcano to illustrate the friend's difficult experience. Keep (A), since the volcano is an illustration of *the friend's inner torment*. The narrator is not speculating about what will happen, so eliminate (B). The explanation of *why the friend is unable to speak* is in the first paragraph; that is not the purpose of the description of the volcano, so eliminate (C). The author does not *imply the friend needs to be more patient,* so eliminate (D). The correct answer is (A).

2. **H**   The question asks for a description of the structure of the passage. Because this is a general question, it should be done after all the specific questions. The passage focuses on the narrator's experience with a friend who loses his ability to speak, recounting some of their conversations and letters in which they compare spoken and written communication. The passage is not a character study, since it focuses on ideas about communication rather than on the personalities of the two friends; additionally, their exchanges are not best described as an *argument,* so eliminate (F). The passage is mostly written from one perspective; there are brief excerpts from a letter from the author's friend, but they don't *take equal turns discussing their positions,* so eliminate (G). Keep (H) because it captures the main topic as well as *the verbal and written exchanges* included in the passage. The author's successes and struggles as a lawyer are not discussed, so eliminate (J). The correct answer is (H).

3. **D**   The question asks what the *dust cloud* and *lava flow* portray in the *erupting volcano simile*. Look for the words *dust cloud* and *lava flow* in the passage. Lines 20–23 state *I tell him that his speaking voice may be like the oceanic cloud of dust and debris that the volcano spews into the air, but his writing can flow like omni-directional lava, indiscriminately absorbing everything in its path*. There is no comparison of *intuition and logic* in these lines, so eliminate (A). There is also no discussion of *simplicity and complexity,* so eliminate (B). In lines 39–45, the author and the friend discuss *methodically composed* and *spontaneous* communication, but the dust cloud and lava flow don't portray *instinct and deliberation,* so eliminate (C). Keep (D) because the phrase *vocal and non-vocal expression* is supported by *his speaking voice* and *his writing*. The correct answer is (D).

4. **H**   The question asks which statement most clearly portrays the respective attitudes of the narrator and his friend. Because this is a general question, it should be done after all the specific questions. At the beginning of the passage, the friend shows anxiety in his statement, *"I fear that I will eventually choke on my own thoughts,"* (line 11) and later the passage refers to a *mix of pride and pain in his eyes* (lines 64–65) and says that he *deeply misses* the *expressiveness that a human voice can add to the meaning of words* (lines 75–77). The narrator is sympathetic to his friend's experience, as indicated by statements such as, *"If my profession would allow it, I would gladly yield my voice to him* (lines 66–67). The narrator is also encouraging, as in lines 35–37: *I optimistically point to the fact that written language has the potential to be seen by countless human*

eyes. Though the author and the friend debate, the friend *acknowledges* that *There is plenty of solace in writing* (line 28) and helps the narrator with his speeches (lines 77–81). Therefore, he is not *argumentative* or *cynical.* Based on the references above, the narrator is not *jaded* or *indifferent;* eliminate (F). The friend is not *scornful* or *depressed,* and there's no indication that the narrator is *apologetic,* so eliminate (G). Keep (H) because it is supported by the lines cited above. The friend doesn't speak because he has lost his voice, not because he is *shy,* and he comes to the narrator's trials (line 62), so he is not *reclusive.* In the passage, the narrator only speaks to his friend and in court, so there is no evidence that he is *outgoing,* and the effort he puts into the debate with his friend indicates that he is not *nonchalant;* eliminate (J). The correct answer is (H).

5. **D** The question asks what the word *puppet* means in line 68. Go back to the text, find the word *puppet,* and mark it out. Carefully read the surrounding text to determine another word that would fit in the blank based on the context of the passage. In lines 66–69, the narrator says *If my profession would allow it, I would gladly yield my voice to him and become a mere puppet for his ideas, just so he could again experience the instant gratification of vocal persuasion.* The phrase *become a mere puppet for his ideas* refers to *yield my voice to him,* so *puppet* could be replaced with the phrase "one who speaks another's words." An *entertainer* is a person who "performs for others' amusement"; it doesn't match "one who speaks another's words," so eliminate (A). A *conversationalist* is a person who "converses often or well"; it doesn't match "one who speaks another's words," so eliminate (B). A *toy* is a "plaything"; it doesn't match "one who speaks another's words," so eliminate (C). A *mouthpiece* is a "one who expresses another's views"; this matches "one who speaks another's words," so keep (D). The correct answer is (D).

CRAFT AND STRUCTURE DRILL 7

NATURAL SCIENCE: This passage is adapted from "A Comment on Comets" by Dr. Anatole C. Thierry (© 2002 by Weak Alliteration Press).

Comets are solid masses of dust and frozen gases with diameters of only a few kilometers that revolve in highly eccentric orbits around the Sun. As a comet approaches the Sun, a very small portion of the frozen matter evaporates. This
5 creates a shroud of gas and dust, called a coma, enveloping an area up to a million kilometers around the solid nucleus of the comet. Solar winds and radiation pressure from the Sun can blow the material of the coma away from the comet's nucleus, creating a tail, which is sometimes longer than the
10 distance from the Earth to the Sun. However, the appearance of comets is misleading; they cast no light of their own. Though the comas and tails of the brightest comets can be seen with the naked eye in cities with heavy light pollution, the nucleus of a comet cannot be detected even with the most
15 powerful telescopes. This is not only because the solid portion of a comet is so small, but also because the highly reflective nature of the coma's material obscures the view to the nucleus.

The brightness of a comet depends primarily on two factors: its distance from the Sun and its distance from the
20 Earth. When comets are at their closest approach to the Sun, called perihelion, evaporation of the icy material occurs at a greater rate and volume, and the solar forces that scatter the gas and dust are stronger. However, when comets are far from the Sun, they become less active and are often undetectable.
25 Because comets come from the farthest reaches of the solar system, most take over 200 years to orbit the Sun, and most of the time they are so far away that the solar influence does not create a coma or tail, causing the comets to become invisible.

The stronger determinant of a comet's brightness is its
30 distance to Earth, especially in relation to its perihelion. If a comet passes its nearest point to Earth after the comet's perihelion, it will be much brighter than if it reaches its closest point to Earth while it is still relatively cold and solid, before the Sun evaporates much of the comet's matter. This explains
35 why Halley's Comet, which was very bright during its first observed pass near Earth in 1910, was so disappointing to astronomers when it returned, this time much further from the Earth, in 1986. The distance from the Earth also determines a comet's speed as observed by astronomers—the closer a
40 comet comes to the Earth, the more quickly it moves across the sky. Typically, comets move about one or two degrees per day—much too slow to be perceived by the naked eye—and can remain visible for months. However, when comet IRAS-Araki-Alcock, the closest comet to pass the Earth in modern
45 times, appeared in 1983, it looked both very bright and very fast. This comet moved so quickly that observers compared its motion to that of the minute hand on a clock, and it had twice the apparent diameter of the Moon.

Even dedicated sky watchers and professional astrono-
50 mers are more likely to discover a comet by chance than by exacting calculations, because comets are only detectable for such a short portion of their orbits, and because it is so infrequent that the comets pass near enough to the Earth to be observed. However, astronomers' interest in comets lies in
55 characteristics beyond the novelty of these comets. Comets are believed to be remnants of the original disc of chemical material that formed the solar system about four billion years ago. Because comets spend most of their time in the very cold areas barely within the Sun's gravitation, they are believed to
60 have remained relatively unchanged during that time, and can thereby serve as a sort of "fossil record" of the solar system.

For this reason, planetary scientists have a great deal of interest in studying comets directly, rather than merely through telescopic observation. By studying the specific chemical comp-
65 osition of comets, scientists hope to learn more about the chemical origins of the solar system. Explorations of comets can provide glimpses into this past. For example, a recent collection of tiny dust particles left in the Earth's stratosphere by the passage of comet 26P/Grigg-Skjellerup has led to the discovery of a previ-
70 ously unknown mineral that had not been predicted by scientists to have been formed in the solar nebula. This highly unusual substance generates strong scientific interest because it, along with other new materials that may be found in comets, may cause scientists to reconsider models of how the solar system formed.
75 Future missions are planned to retrieve material directly from comets. Some scientists, who hypothesize that water and some organic compounds may have been delivered to Earth by colli-sions between comets and our planet in its earliest days, hope that comet material may reveal information about the origins
80 of life on Earth.

1. The primary purpose of the passage is to:

   A. persuade readers that astronomers have not yet done adequate studies to discover the origins of the solar system.
   B. encourage readers to learn to use telescopic equipment to aid in the search for new comets.
   C. describe the characteristics of comets currently known by astronomers and the motivation for their research.
   D. catalogue the experiments planetary scientists have done to determine the composition of comets.

2. In the context of the third paragraph (lines 29–48), lines 34–38 primarily serve to emphasize the:

   F. relationship a comet's apparent speed has to its other visual characteristics, such as its apparent diameter.
   G. influence a comet's distance from Earth with regard to its perihelion has on a comet's apparent brightness.
   H. disappointment astronomers feel when highly anticipated celestial events do not live up to their expectations.
   J. difficulty in predicting when comets will be visible in the sky because of their highly eccentric orbits.

3. The author uses the phrase "characteristics beyond the novelty of these comets" (line 55) most likely to:

   A. evaluate the likelihood of discovering new comets.
   B. explain the difficulties present in detecting distant comets.
   C. introduce the subject of the chemical composition of comets.
   D. emphasize the scope of research required to determine a comet's age.

4. The main purpose of the last paragraph is to:

   F. describe particular experiments that have been performed on comets as they pass near the Earth.
   G. convince readers that comets are responsible for the evolution of intelligent species.
   H. discuss the reasons planetary scientists are interested in pursuing direct study of comet material.
   J. contradict outdated information about the origin of the solar system.

CRAFT AND STRUCTURE DRILL 7 EXPLANATIONS

1. **C**   The question asks for the primary purpose of the passage. Because this is a general question, it should be done after all the specific questions. The first three paragraphs of the passage discuss some of the characteristics of comets, including what factors affect *the brightness of a comet,* and the last two paragraphs discuss the reasons for *astronomers' interest in comets.* The last paragraph says that discoveries about comets *may cause scientists to reconsider models of how the solar system formed* (lines 73–74). However, this is discussed in only one paragraph, so it is not the primary purpose of the passage; eliminate (A). The author does not *encourage readers to learn to use telescopic equipment,* so eliminate (B). Keep (C) since it includes both *the characteristics of comets currently known by researchers* and the *motivation for their research.* The passage mentions only one study that has already been done (lines 67–71), so the passage's purpose is not to *catalogue the experiments planetary scientists have done;* eliminate (D). The correct answer is (C).

2. **G**   The question asks what lines 34–38 emphasize *in the context of the third paragraph,* so read lines 29–48. Lines 34–38 give an example about *Halley's comet,* beginning with the phrase *This explains why.* The word *this* indicates that the explanation is given just prior to the example, and lines 30–34 state, *If a comet passes its nearest point to Earth after the comet's perihelion, it will be much brighter than if it reaches its closest point to Earth while it is still relatively cold and solid, before the Sun evaporates much of the comet's matter.* These lines do not mention *a comet's apparent speed* or *apparent diameter,* so eliminate (F). Keep (G) because it matches lines 30–34. Although the passage says that the Halley's comet was *disappointing to astronomers when it returned,* the surrounding context does not focus on this, so eliminate (H). The paragraph also doesn't discuss *difficulty in predicting when comets will be visible* or *highly eccentric orbits,* so eliminate (J). The correct answer is (G).

3. **C**   The question asks what the phrase *characteristics beyond the novelty of these comets* in line 55 is used to do. Read a window in the passage around the given line. Lines 54–58 state, *astronomers' interest in comets lies in characteristics beyond the novelty of these comets. Comets are believed to be remnants of the original disc of chemical material that formed the solar system about four billion years ago.* These lines don't refer to *the likelihood of discovering new comets,* so eliminate (A). The paragraph starts with a discussion of the difficulty and rarity of detecting or observing a comet, but the sentence in question begins with the word *However,* and states that the interest lies *beyond the novelty of these comets,* so the interest is not in the *difficulty present in detecting distant comets;* eliminate (B). Keep (C) because *the chemical composition of comets* is supported by the reference to the *original disc of chemical material that formed the solar system.* Although the comets' *age* is part of what makes them a *possible "fossil record" of the solar system,* their age or the *scope of research* required to determine their age is not mentioned as something that interests the scientists, so eliminate (D). The correct answer is (C).

4. **H**   The question asks for the main purpose of the last paragraph, so read lines 62–80. This paragraph discusses scientists' *interest in studying comets directly* and the topics that *scientists hope to learn more about.* The paragraph gives only one example of an experiment that has been performed, so eliminate (F). The scientists hope that *comet material may reveal information about the origins of life on Earth,* but the author does not try to *convince readers that comets are responsible for the evolution of intelligent species,* so eliminate (G). Keep (H), since it is supported by the discussion of scientists' *hope to learn more about the chemical origins of the solar system* and *information about the origins of life on Earth.* The passage states that discoveries made in studying comets directly *may cause scientists to reconsider models of how the solar system formed,* but the purpose of the paragraph is not to *contradict outdated information,* so eliminate (J). The correct answer is (H).

INTEGRATION OF KNOWLEDGE AND IDEAS

The Integration of Knowledge and Ideas reporting category accounts for 19–26% of the Reading questions you will encounter on your ACT. These questions ask you to understand the author's claims, differentiate between facts and opinions, and analyze the connections between multiple passages. Any question asking about both Passage A and Passage B falls into this category, as well as any question asking you to categorize a statement from the passage or that asks you to determine which point a piece of evidence is intended to support. The following pages contain four Integration of Knowledge and Ideas passages, each with five questions, that you can practice on if this category is an area of focus for you.

INTEGRATION OF KNOWLEDGE AND IDEAS DRILL 1

HUMANITIES: Passage A is adapted from "Living Between Worlds: Searching for Identity" by Kenora Crowfeather (© 1998 by Birch Bark Press). Passage B is adapted from *American Indian Stories* by Zitkala-Sa (Gertrude Simmons Bonnin), 1921.

Passage A by Kenora Crowfeather

As I gaze at the picture of Zitkala-Sa that confronts me from the cover of her collected writings, *American Indian Stories*, I see a beautifully proud Sioux woman. Long, glossy black braids frame her serious and unflinching face, hang like
5 heavy silken cords in front of her traditional dress, and end somewhere out of the bottom of the frame, past her waist I imagine. It is hard to make myself believe that the woman in this picture was named Gertrude Simmons Bonnin; Zitkala-Sa (Red Bird) was her pen name.

10 Zitkala-Sa's life-long struggle with the clash between Native American culture and white men has intrigued me for the better part of two decades since I first began reading her essays. Returning home after a long trip and feeling unsettled is not unique to her experience, but the clash between
15 Native Americans and the "pale-faces" who misunderstood and exploited them adds fire to Zitkala-Sa's chronicles of her school years, which might otherwise have been written by any angst-filled teenager.

The daughter of a white man and a Sioux woman,
20 Zitkala-Sa spent the first years of her life firmly ensconced in Native American life with her mother on the Pine Ridge Reservation in South Dakota. She chose to leave home at age eight to go to a missionary school in Indiana. Her memoirs describe her unhappiness at school: her dismay at having her
25 hair cut and her moccasins taken away and her rage at the unjust rules and willful neglect on the part of the teachers. Yet when she returned home, she remained unsatisfied. She was able to wear her beloved moccasins again, but she felt friendless and misunderstood. She had discarded her school
30 clothes and so was ill-equipped to socialize with the young people on the reservation who had adopted that style of dress.

Her return to school and the white man's world for a time confused me, despite my understanding of her urge to leave. How could she have gone to work at an institution so
35 like her first, hated school? How could she have abandoned her mother and her heritage?

In the midst of my indignation, I forgot that Gertrude Bonnin was the daughter of a white man. Her mother, though she never learned English, married three different white men
40 over the course of her life. The clash between the two cultures began deep within Gertrude before she was even born. She was destined to feel like an outsider anywhere, and leaving home allowed her to embrace her Sioux identity. Pursuing education among white men was not, in the end, abandoning
45 her culture, but rather a step in her journey towards becoming an advocate for Native American rights.

Passage B by Zitkala-Sa (Gertrude Simmons Bonnin)

After my first three years of school, I roamed again in the Western country through four strange summers.

During this time I seemed to hang in the heart of chaos,
50 beyond the touch or voice of human aid. My brother, being almost ten years my senior, did not quite understand my feelings. My mother had never gone inside of a schoolhouse, and so she was not capable of comforting her daughter who could read and write. Even nature seemed to have no place for me.
55 I was neither a wee girl nor a tall one; neither a wild Indian nor a tame one. This deplorable situation was the effect of my brief course in the East, and the unsatisfactory "teenth" in a girl's years.

It was under these trying conditions that, one bright af-
60 ternoon, as I sat restless and unhappy in my mother's cabin, I caught the sound of the spirited step of my brother's pony on the road which passed by our dwelling.

I met him there with a hurried greeting, and, as I passed by, he looked a quiet "What?" into my eyes.

65 "No, my baby sister, I cannot take you with me to the party to-night," he replied. Though I was not far from fifteen, and I felt that before long I should enjoy all the privileges of my tall cousin, Dawée persisted in calling me his baby sister.

That moonlight night, I cried in my mother's presence
70 when I heard the jolly young people pass by our cottage. They were no more young braves in blankets and eagle plumes, nor Indian maids with prettily painted cheeks. They had gone three years to school in the East, and had become civilized. The young men wore the white man's coat and trousers, with
75 bright neckties. The girls wore tight muslin dresses, with ribbons at neck and waist. At these gatherings they talked English. I could speak English almost as well as my brother, but I was not properly dressed to be taken along. I had no hat, no ribbons, and no close-fitting gown. Since my return
80 from school I had thrown away my shoes, and wore again the soft moccasins.

While Dawée was busily preparing to go I controlled my tears. But when I heard him bounding away on his pony, I buried my face in my arms and cried hot tears.

1. The author makes the statement "It is hard to make myself believe that the woman in this picture was named Gertrude Simmons Bonnin" (lines 7–8) to support her point that:

   A. she is confused by the incongruity between the picture of a Sioux woman and a white woman's name.
   B. Bonnin's use of a pen name caused some confusion among critics.
   C. Bonnin had been incorrectly identified as individual in the picture.
   D. she has a preference for Bonnin's traditional Sioux name.

2. In the context of the passage, the narrator's statement in lines 55–56 is used to support the idea that:

   F. she considers one of her physical features to be average.
   G. she desires to forget the awkwardness of her teenage years.
   H. she felt a distinct sense of not belong in her teenage years.
   J. she was rejected by members of her family.

3. Both passages emphasize Zitkala-Sa's:

   A. refusal to fit in on the reservation after she returned home from school.
   B. desire to become an advocate for sending Native Americans to school.
   C. difficulty getting along with her mother as a teenager.
   D. sense of not belonging either at home or in the world of white men.

4. In both passages, moccasins function as a symbol of:

   F. the oppression of Native Americans by white men.
   G. Zitkala-Sa's frustration at being caught between two cultures.
   H. Native American culture.
   J. comfortable and practical footwear.

5. The author of Passage A would most likely view the events described in Passage B as:

   A. a struggle that ultimately led Zitkala-Sa to have a strong sense of identity.
   B. an emotional outburst by Zitkala-Sa typical of a teenage girl.
   C. a time when Zitkala-Sa came to fully appreciate Sioux culture.
   D. a period of conflict.

INTEGRATION OF KNOWLEDGE AND IDEAS DRILL 1 EXPLANATIONS

1. **A** The question asks what point the statement is used to support. Read a window in the passage around the given lines. Before the statement in lines 3–5, the author describes a picture of *a beautifully proud Sioux woman,* including details of her *long, glossy black braids* and *traditional dress.* The author then says *it was hard to make myself believe that the woman in this picture was named Gertrude Simmons Bonnin.* The contrast between the appearance of the Sioux woman and her name supports (A). There is no indication that the pen name caused *confusion,* so eliminate (B). There is also no indication that the author believes that *Bonnin had incorrectly identified in the picture,* so eliminate (C). The author mentions Bonnin's Sioux name, but never expresses a *preference* for it, so eliminate (D). The correct answer is (A).

2. **H** The question asks what idea the statement is used to support. Read a window in the passage around lines 55–56. Lines 49–55 describes how the author was *beyond the touch or voice of human aid,* and that *even nature seemed to have no place for [her].* Although one of her *physical* features, her height, is mentioned (*I was neither a wee girl nor a tall one),* this is just a detail and not the *idea* the detail was used to support; eliminate (F). Similarly, the author describes her teenage years negatively in lines 57–58, but does directly say that *she desires to forget the awkwardness* of them; eliminate (G). Choice (H) is supported by the entire second paragraph, so keep it. Although lines 50–53 say that the narrator's *brother…did not quite understand my feelings* and that her mother *was not capable of comforting her daughter,* that does not mean that her family *rejected* her, so eliminate (J). The correct answer is (H).

3. **D** The question asks what both passages emphasize about Zitkala-Sa. Eliminate any answer choices that misrepresent either passage. Both passages discuss her difficulties fitting in when she returned from school, but neither passage indicates that there was a *refusal* to do so; eliminate (A). Although Passage A says that Zitkala-Sa went *to work at an institution…like her first…school,* there is no indication that she became *an advocate for sending Native Americans to school;* eliminate (B). Passage B says that Zitkala-Sa's mother *was not capable of comforting her,* but that is not the same as *difficulty getting along with her mother;* eliminate (C). Lines 41–42 in Passage A say that Zitkala-Sa *was destined to feel like an outsider anywhere,* and line 54 says that *Even nature had no place for [her],* both of which support the idea of *not belonging* in (D). The correct answer is (D).

4. **H** The question asks what moccasins are a symbol of in both passages. Look for the word *moccasins* in both passages. In Passage A, lines 23–26 describe Zitkala-Sa's *unhappiness at school,* and that fact that *her moccasins [were] taken away* is an example of what made her unhappy. When she returned home, *she was able to wear her beloved moccasins again.* Passage B also describes her wearing moccasins at home, in lines 79–81: *Since my return from school I had thrown away my shoes, and wore again the soft moccasins.* While the taking away of moccasins might symbolize oppression, the moccasins themselves cannot symbolize oppression since they are described as *beloved* and *soft;* eliminate (F). Similarly, the moccasins do not symbolize *frustration,* so eliminate (G). The moccasins are mentioned in both passages in the context of Zitkala-Sa not being dressed like the other young people who wore their school clothes, so they could be a symbol of Native American culture; keep (H). The moccasins are described as *soft,* which could support the idea of *comfortable,* but they **are** comfortable footwear, not a *symbol* of it, so eliminate (J). The correct answer is (H).

5.   **A**   The question asks how the author of Passage A would view the events in Passage B. Eliminate any answer choices that don't agree with the main idea of Passage A. Passage A continually refers to the *clash between Native American culture and white men*, and lines 42–43 state that *leaving home allowed [Zitkala-Sa] to embrace her Sioux identity*. This supports the ideas of a *struggle* and a *strong sense of identity* in (A). Lines 16–18 say that the clash of culture *adds fire to Zitkala-Sa's chronicles...which might otherwise have been written by any angst-filled teenager;* in other words, the author is saying she is **not** a typical teenager, so eliminate (B). Lines 43–46 say that *Pursuing her education...was...a step in her journey towards becoming an advocate for Native American rights*. Thus, her school years were only the beginning of her appreciation of Sioux culture, so eliminate (C). Passage A makes no mention of Zitkala-Sa's relationships with her mother and brother, so eliminate (D). The correct answer is (A).

INTEGRATION OF KNOWLEDGE AND IDEAS DRILL 2

SOCIAL SCIENCE: Passage A is adapted from "Let Me Think About It: Plants and Consciousness" by Andres C. Tejada (© 2010 by Andres Tejada). Passage B is adapted from "The Great Debate: Recent Developments in Plant Consciousness Research" by Nicole Fiori (© 2012 by Nicole Fiori).

Passage A by Andres Tejada

Sheila Jennings was making her rounds at the Boston Botanical Gardens, gently humming songs to the lilies she was watering and speaking directly to a patch of ferns into which she was scooping fertilizer. To a casual observer, she
5 appeared to be entertaining herself during her morning routine, but Sheila's friendly behavior around the plants is actually called "social reinforcement" and is one of her job requirements. The idea that interacting with these plants will help them flourish has been common sense to gardeners for ages,
10 but it has attained some scientific credibility mainly since the work of Clive Buckner first came to light.

Forty years ago Buckner conducted a series of experiments on his plants using "lie-detectors," polygraph galvanometer equipment. These experiments led him to conclude
15 that plants possess a means of perception that allows them to react to human thoughts.

The scientific community was shocked. It is already hard enough to prove that higher order mammals have consciousness, despite many experiments that seem to prove the
20 ability of non-human animals to learn and perform complex, non-instinctive behaviors. To contend that plants have some mechanism of mind-reading goes so far beyond the orthodoxy of modern scientific beliefs that anyone suggesting they might was instantly considered a heretic.

25 However, a steady flow of research over the next two decades would continue to revisit and replicate Clive Buckner's hypothesis. During his original experiment, Buckner noticed that his plant would produce a sharp and immediate response when he attempted to visualize the act of burning the plant's
30 leaves. Botanists at Kansas State found they could produce a similar response by cutting the leaves of an adjacent plant. Researchers in Wyoming discovered that plants respond to the distress signals of a spider in the room. A New Jersey scientist was able to cause a plant to trigger a switch on an
35 electric train set every time he gave himself a painful shock to the finger. One of Buckner's colleagues showed him how she was able to keep a detached leaf moist and lush for two months through daily positive encouragement while a control leaf which received no positive attention had completely
40 withered to a dry, brittle brown.

Although these experiments seem to add fuel to the flames of Buckner's speculations about plant consciousness, he is willing to acknowledge the scientific issues involved

in replicating the experiments. "Many others have failed to
45 produce the same effects," he says. "The outcomes of the experiments seem very dependent on the experimenter's relationship to his plants." But at the same time, Buckner believes these problems actually strengthen his theories. "We are trying to demonstrate the fact that plants develop subtle
50 yet meaningful connections with their caretakers, so the fact that the outcomes of experiments are varied is actually in *support* of our notion that plant behavior is dynamic and responsive to a given individual."

Passage B by Nicole Fiori

The world of botany has recently been buzzing with news
55 of an unconventional experiment that produced seemingly ground-breaking results: a plant in a lead box (shut off from all electromagnetic radiation) was able to react to a human thought. Max Crusella, a plant researcher at the Marina Del Rey Plant Laboratory, is one of those who believe that this
60 is only a small part of the mountain of evidence that plants are sensitive to their environments in ways that traditional science is not equipped to describe. "It's possible that these particular researchers have proposed overzealous explanations for their observations," Crusella said at a recent symposium
65 on the subject, "but it is completely well-grounded to believe that there needs to be *some* kind of new scientific explanation for what are otherwise mysterious phenomena."

Sitting across the table from Crusella, both literally and figuratively, is Cornell University professor Betty Wilkinson.
70 She points out that the lead box experiment failed to register any plant reaction when it was replicated by a different researcher. In her view, it is clear that plants are responsive to certain kinds of interaction, but she questions the reasons and means attributed to plants by other researchers. She believes
75 the interpretations of experiments into plant consciousness are too dependent on the philosophical and metaphysical beliefs of the interpreter. "Many people without any botanical credentials are anxious to latch onto these experiments to support ideas they may have about the holistic interconnectivity
80 of the universe," she says.

Those on Wilkinson's side are concerned that such experimenters may be merely interpreting the reactions of plants to agree with their premeditated goal of finding consciousness (scientists call this *confirmation bias*), or that they
85 are ignoring the possibilities of alternative explanations for the sake of justifying their faulty hypotheses (scientists call this *self-deception*).

Steve Karnell, a writer for a leading scientific journal, agrees with Wilkinson. "Lacking in this so-called 'experi-
90 ment' are ingredients fundamental to the scientific method like control groups and blind studies," he complains. "Work like this opens up a Pandora's box of bad science."

Question 1 asks about Passage A.

1. In lines 48–53, Clive Buckner's comment could best be described as:

   A. an oddity.
   B. an excuse.
   C. a justification.
   D. a fact.

Question 2 asks about Passage B.

2. As presented in the passage, Steve Karnell's statement in lines 88–92 is best described as:

   F. an opinion based on how the process utilized during research can affect its findings.
   G. a judgment based on the lack of comprehension that some scientists have regarding the scientific method.
   H. an observation based on the ability of blind studies to prove a hypothesis.
   J. an assumption based on the relative ease with which the error of confirmation bias can be made.

Questions 3–5 ask about both Passages.

3. Clive Buckner's observation of his plant as mentioned in the fourth paragraph of Passage A would most likely be described by Betty Wilkinson and Steve Karnell as which of the following?

   A. Evidence that plants possess a sense of memory
   B. A subtle connection between plant and caretaker
   C. Something that other researchers may have trouble duplicating
   D. An example of a plant's ability to perceive distress

4. Based on the information in Passage A, how would Clive Buckner most likely respond to the criticism of Betty Wilkinson as described in the second paragraph of Passage B (lines 68–80)?

   F. By providing specific examples that defend his theory of plant consciousness
   G. By suggesting that he does not believe that Wilkinson's criticism is a legitimate one
   H. By stating his complete indifference toward Wilkinson's scientific concerns
   J. By outlining how he could counsel other experimenters on how to be better caretakers of plants in order to better replicate certain results

5. Both Passage A and Passage B emphasize:

   A. the importance of replicating the results of plant consciousness experiments.
   B. the dramatic difference that social reinforcement makes in how well a plant grows.
   C. the difficulties of interpreting the results of experiments into plant consciousness.
   D. the dangers presented by confirmation bias and how to avoid them when designing an experiment.

INTEGRATION OF KNOWLEDGE AND IDEAS DRILL 2 EXPLANATIONS

1. **C**   The question asks what *Clive Buckner's comment* in lines 48–53 could best be described as. Read a window in the passage around lines 48–53. Lines 47–48 state that *Buckner believes these problems actually strengthen his theories.* The description *beyond the orthodoxy of modern scientific* beliefs, which could describe an oddity or something strange, is mentioned in lines 22–24, but it is attributed to the *scientific community,* not to Buckner's comment in lines 48–53, so eliminate (A). Though Buckner acknowledges *scientific issues involved in replicating the experiments,* the passage states that *Buckner believes these problems actually strengthen his theories.* He is not making *an excuse* for the issues encountered by others, so eliminate (B). Keep (C), since the phrase *the outcomes of the experiments seem very dependent on the experimenter's relationship to his plants* is something Buckner claims is *actually in support* of his theory. Since Buckner *is willing to acknowledge the scientific issues involved in replicating the experiments,* he is not certain his theory should yet be taken as *fact,* so eliminate (D). The correct answer is (C).

2. **F**   The question asks what *Steve Karnell's* statement in lines 88–92 could be best described as, so read lines 88–92. The quotation states, *"Lacking in this so-called 'experiment' are ingredients fundamental to the scientific method like control groups and blind studies…Work like this opens up a Pandora's box of bad science."* Keep (F), since *ingredients fundamental to the scientific method* matches *the process utilized during research* and *opens up a Pandora's box of bad science* matches *can affect its findings.* The quotation states that *control groups* are *lacking,* not that *some scientists* have a *lack of comprehension,* so eliminate (G). The quotation states that *blind studies* are one of the *ingredients fundamental to the scientific method,* but it does not indicate that a blind study alone would *prove* a hypothesis, so eliminate (H). Karnell does not reference how easy it is to make an *error of confirmation bias,* so eliminate (J). The correct answer is (F).

3. **C**   The question asks how *Betty Wilkinson and Steve Karnell* would describe *Clive Buckner's observation of his plant.* The question references the fourth paragraph of Passage A, so read lines 25–40. Lines 27–30 describe Clive Buckner's observation: *During his original experiment, Buckner noticed that his plant would produce a sharp and immediate response when he attempted to visualize the act of burning the plant's leaves.* Next, look for the names *Betty Wilkinson* and *Steve Karnell* in Passage B. Lines 68–72 present Betty Wilkinson's point of view: discussing an experiment similar to Buckner's, *She points out that the…experiment failed to register any plant reaction when it was replicated by a different researcher.* Lines 88–89 indicate that *Steve Karnell… agrees with Wilkinson.* Both Wilkinson and Karnell point out flaws in experiments like Buckner's, so they are not likely to draw conclusions about plants based on Buckner's observations. Choices (A), (C), and (D) each draw a conclusion about the plant, so eliminate these choices. Keep (C), since this is supported by the statement in lines 70–72. The correct answer is (C).

4. **G**   The question asks how *Clive Buckner* would respond to *Betty Wilkinson's criticism.* The question references the second paragraph of Passage B, so read lines 68–80. Discussing an experiment with results similar to those of Buckner's experiment, Wilkinson *points out that the…experiment failed to register any plant reaction when it was replicated by a different researcher.* Next, look for references to *Clive Buckner* in Passage A. Lines 44–53 indicate that Buckner acknowledges that other researchers have failed to replicate the results of his study and that the *outcomes of the experiments seem very dependent on the experimenter's relationship*

to his plants. However, he goes on to say that *these problems actually strengthen his theories. "We are trying to demonstrate the fact that plants develop subtle yet meaningful connections with their caretakers, so the fact that the outcomes of experiments are varied is actually in support of our notion that plant behavior is dynamic and responsive to a given individual."* This indicates that Buckner would not see Wilkinson's objection as a valid criticism. Buckner is not likely to respond simply by providing *specific examples* to support his theory: Wilkinson is criticizing the validity of such an example, and additional examples would be vulnerable to the same criticism; eliminate (F). Keep (G), since it is supported by Buckner's statements in lines 47–54. Buckner responded to criticisms similar to Wilkinson's, so he would probably not state *complete indifference* to her concerns; eliminate (H). Buckner doesn't *counsel other experimenters on how to be better caretakers of plants,* so eliminate (J). The correct answer is (G).

5. **C**   The question asks what is emphasized by both Passage A and Passage B. Because this is a general question, it should be done after all the specific questions on both passages. Eliminate any answer choice that misrepresents either passage. Both passages discuss experiments that seem to demonstrate plant consciousness, as well as challenges presented by these experiments' methodology. Both passages discuss *replicating results of plant consciousness experiments,* but they disagree on its importance, so eliminate (A). The effect of *social reinforcement* on *how well a plant grows* is not discussed in Passage B, so eliminate (B). Keep (C), since both passages discuss *difficulties of interpreting the results of experiments.* Passage A does not discuss *confirmation bias,* nor does either passage discuss *how to avoid* confirmation bias, so eliminate (D). The correct answer is (C).

INTEGRATION OF KNOWLEDGE AND IDEAS DRILL 3

HUMANITIES: Passage A is adapted from the essay "Listening" by Nicolas Lloyd (© 2003 by Nicolas Lloyd). Passage B is adapted from the essay "Music from the Heart" by Noël Kelley (© 1996 by Noël Kelley).

Passage A by Nicolas Lloyd

I have early memories of lying in my crib, listening to the lush, powerful voices of the great Wagnerian singers that my parents played most nights after they put me to bed. The sound, building and growing in dramatic energy, would envelop
5 me as I fell asleep, and became the soundtrack of my dreams.

I never learned to read music or play an instrument, but the primal emotions expressed in opera are part of a universal language. The forces of good and evil, love and hate, desire and revenge, emanate from the music like smells from an
10 oven. Just as a sniff lets us know whether there is a cake or lasagna baking, a single chord can elicit a strong reaction, even to the untrained ear.

The words of Tristan and Isolde may be different from those of Mimi and Rodolfo, and Wagner's application of
15 musical conventions distinct from Puccini's, but they come from the same place. Star-crossed lovers have existed for at least as long as the human race. While words can be used to express the combination of longing, joy, and sorrow that the lovers feel, music adds depth; it communicates those com-
20 mon feelings above and beyond what is possible with spoken language alone.

As Victor Hugo wrote, "Music expresses that which cannot be said and on which it is impossible to be silent."

All of the major events in my life have soundtracks, though
25 they are not all operatic. Sometimes the music is what was playing: I met my wife for the first time at an outdoor cafe when we were in college, and some street musicians were performing "O Sole Mio" nearby. I hear that song every time I see her again after we've been separated, whether it's been
30 an hour or a week.

Other times, my life soundtrack comes from the emotions of the event. When my mother was dying, excerpts from Mozart's *Requiem* played over and over again in my head as I sat by her bedside.

35 Wagner's music continues to feature prominently in my dreams. It takes me back to the beginning of consciousness. I know it is the beginning of my own consciousness, but it feels bigger than that, as if the music expresses the beginning of the world, the beginning of life.

Passage B by Noël Kelley

40 My parents were professional musicians. I have friends who are music teachers who enjoy having two weeks off for the winter holidays and who spend their entire summers on the beach. But holidays are busy for professional musicians. Brass players, as my parents were, are in high demand for
45 Christmas and 4th of July concerts and summer weddings. My parents never took vacations, and we rarely had normal holiday celebrations.

When I went to college, my roommate was a music major. I rarely saw her, and she was always harried-looking
50 when I did. She was constantly hurrying from one rehearsal to another. I quit singing in choirs, stopped practicing the piano, and declared an engineering major. I wanted to have a "regular" life, with weekends and vacations.

I had that life for a while, and then I got married and
55 had a baby. He was chubby and bald with serious, dark eyes that studied me intently. I sang to him all day long because it made me feel more connected to him. I sang nursery rhymes while we played, old country ballads while I bathed him, hymns when we went for walks in the woods, and lullabies
60 to soothe him to sleep. After his sister was born, I no longer wanted my "regular" life. I wanted to be with my babies, and to fill their days with song.

My parents had become musicians because it was a way of earning a living. They ran themselves ragged during
65 the holiday season, squeezing in one more church service, one more concert, because it meant extra money that they could put towards their five children's college tuitions or the mortgage on the house that held all of us. I became a music therapist because I knew first-hand as a mother how deeply
70 song could influence my children. It became my mission to share its healing power with others.

I have had some incredible successes. I've helped stroke victims regain the ability to speak and given children tools to manage their ADHD without medication.

75 But it isn't always easy. Sometimes, when I come home at the end of a long day, I'm tired and cranky, and I wonder why I do it. I have learned that I can't heal everyone, even my own children. As they've grown and become more independent, life has dealt them disappointment and heartache that doesn't
80 go away simply by playing a silly song or dancing around the kitchen the way I did when they were little.

My parents both died before it occurred to me to ask them whether their hard work as musicians ever brought them joy. I recently came across an old picture of my mother, sitting in
85 a rocking chair with my oldest sister who couldn't have been more than a few weeks old. There was something about the picture that was very comforting to me. It took me a while to realize why, but I finally saw it. My mother is singing in the picture. She looks happy.

Question 1 asks about Passage A.

---

1. Lloyd quotes Victor Hugo to support his point that:

   A. music expresses more than words can alone.
   B. Wagner's music represents the beginning of conscious thought.
   C. all major events in one's life should have a soundtrack.
   D. unrequited love is best expressed through music.

Question 2 asks about Passage B.

---

2. Compared to her parent's motivations, Kelley's motivations for becoming a music therapist were:

   F. similar; Kelley valued having a steady income.
   G. similar; Kelley prioritized making the most of her time.
   H. different; Kelley was uncertain about the profitability of her career.
   J. different; Kelley understood how music could impact children.

Questions 3–5 ask about both Passages.

---

3. One way the perspectives of the authors differ is that Lloyd:

   A. enjoys music for its beauty, while Kelley uses music as a tool in her job out of financial necessity.
   B. is not a musician, so he lacks Kelley's deeper understanding of how music can affect a person's emotions.
   C. arrived at his love for music all on his own, while Kelley learned about music from her parents who were professional musicians.
   D. is a music aficionado that has always felt a strong connection to music, while Kelley is a musician that went through a period during which she distanced herself from music.

4. Which of the following do both authors use to support their ideas?

   F. Specific song titles
   G. Detailed explanation of performance technique
   H. Recollections from childhood
   J. Comparisons of different music genres

5. Based on these two passages, which of the following best relates Lloyd's relationship with music to Kelley's?

   A. Impassioned amateur versus appreciative professional
   B. Casual listener versus intent performer
   C. Curious outsider versus jaded singer
   D. Enthusiastic supporter versus disillusioned pianist

INTEGRATION OF KNOWLEDGE AND IDEAS DRILL 3 EXPLANATIONS

1. **A**   The question asks what point the author is supporting with the reference to Victor Hugo. Look for the name *Victor Hugo* in Passage A. Lines 17–23 state, *While words can be used to express the combination of longing, joy, and sorrow that the lovers feel, music adds depth; it communicates those common feelings above and beyond what is possible with spoken language alone. As Victor Hugo wrote, "Music expresses that which cannot be said and on which is it impossible to be silent."* Keep (A), since it is supported by these lines. The references to *Wagner's music* and *the beginning of conscious thought* are in the last paragraph; this is not the point the author is making when he quotes Victor Hugo, so eliminate (B). The sentence after the Victor Hugo quote says, *All of the major events in my life have soundtracks,* but it does not say that life events *should* have soundtracks; this is also not the point that the Hugo quote emphasizes, so eliminate (C). The author is not making a claim about the *best* way to express *unrequited love,* so eliminate (D). The correct answer is (A).

2. **J**   The question asks how Kelley's motivations for choosing her career compare to those of her parents. Look for references to where Kelley's and her parents' careers are discussed together in the passage. Lines 63–71 state that *My parents had become musicians because it was a way of earning a living* and later that Kelley *became a music therapist* because she *knew first-hand as a mother how deeply song could influence* her children. These are different motivations, so eliminate (F) and (G). Kelley never discusses the *profitability* of her career, so eliminate (H). Keep (J) because it is supported by the discussion of Kelley's career in lines 68–71. The correct answer is (J).

3. **D**   The question asks about one way that the perspectives of the authors differ. Since this is a general question, it should be done after all the specific questions on both passages. Eliminate any answer choices that misrepresent either passage. In lines 54–71 and in lines 82–89, Kelley discusses feeling *connected* to her *baby* and her *mother* through music; it is not simply *a tool* she uses *in her job out of financial necessity,* so eliminate (A). Lloyd discusses how *a single chord can elicit a strong emotion* (line 11) and he gives examples throughout Passage A of how music has affected him personally, so eliminate (B). Lloyd says his earliest memory of music was of opera that *my parents played most nights after they put me to bed;* he did not *arrive at his love for music all on his own,* so eliminate (C). In line 24, Lloyd says, *all the major events in my life have soundtracks;* in lines 51–53, Kelley says, *I quit singing in choirs, stopped practicing the piano, and declared an engineering major.* Choice (D) reflects this difference between the two authors. The correct answer is (D).

4. **H**   The question asks what both authors use to support their ideas. Eliminate any answer choices that misrepresent either passage. Since this is a general question, it should be done after all the specific questions on both passages. There are no specific *song titles* in Passage B, so eliminate (F). Neither author gives a *detailed explanation of performance technique,* so eliminate (G). Lloyd mentions *early memories of lying in my crib, listening to* music that *my parents played* (lines 1–3). Kelley says that *My parents were professional musicians... [they were] in high demand for Christmas and 4th of July concerts and summer weddings. My parents never took vacations, and we rarely had normal holiday celebrations.* Since both authors use *recollections from childhood,* keep (H). Although both authors mention *different music genres,* neither uses a *comparison* of these genres, so eliminate (J). The correct answer is (H).

5. **A**   The question asks how Lloyd's relationship with music relates to Kelley's. Since this is a general question, it should be done after all the specific questions on both passages. In line 6, Lloyd states, *I never learned to read music or play an instrument,* yet the passage as a whole reflects the importance of music in his life. In lines 68–70, Kelley states, *I became a music therapist because I knew first-hand as a mother how deeply song could influence my children.* Keep (A) because it captures this relationship between Lloyd as an *impassioned amateur* and Kelley as an *appreciative professional.* Passage A doesn't support describing Lloyd's relationship to music as *casual,* and Kelley says, *I quit singing in choirs, stopped practicing the piano* (lines 51–52) and *I became a music therapist* (lines 68–69), indicating that she is not an *intent performer,* so eliminate (B). Although Kelley distanced herself from music for a time, in lines 69–71 she says, *I knew first-hand as a mother how deeply song could influence my children. It became my mission to share [music's] healing power with others.* This indicates that she is not *jaded,* nor is *outsider* an apt description for Lloyd's relationship to music, so eliminate (C). The same lines from Passage B rule out *disillusioned* as a description for Kelley, so eliminate (D). The correct answer is (A).

INTEGRATION OF KNOWLEDGE AND IDEAS DRILL 4

HUMANITIES: Passage A is adapted from the article "Harper Lee's Bold Beginnings" by Jason Schampfter. (Used with permission from the author.) Passage B is adapted from the article, "Marja Mills addresses Harper Lee controversy at literary event" by Courtney Crowder. (From Chicago Tribune. © 2014 Chicago Tribune. All rights reserved. Used under license.)

Passage A by Jason Schampfter

Nearly seven decades have passed since its 1960 publication, but the story of how *To Kill a Mockingbird* came to be still captivates readers. Originally a set of loosely related anecdotes titled *Go Set a Watchman*, the future bestseller intrigued an edi-
5 tor, Tay Hohoff, at the J.B. Lippincott company. She embarked on a long series of conversations and edits with the unpublished author Nelle Lee (who was 34 years old and chose to use her middle name Harper for publication). Lee herself had studied law at the University of Alabama but had dropped out of classes a few
10 credits short of graduation, to the disappointment of her father, an attorney and state legislator.

There were many reasons why the novel succeeded so massively, winning a Pulitzer Prize in 1961. One was the public's growing awareness of racial injustice in the Deep South, thanks
15 to the growing civil rights movement. In 1954, *Brown v. Board of Education* desegregated American schools, later leading to the Little Rock Nine crisis. The next year, a 14-year-old boy named Emmett Till was abducted, tortured, and lynched in rural Mississippi after supposedly insulting a white woman in a grocery store.

20 Many of the details of the story had been drawn from Lee's own life. Like Atticus Finch, her own father had defended a pair of black men who'd been accused of rape. When he lost the case, they were hanged. Scout's friend Dill was based on Lee's own childhood friend, the writer Truman Capote, who later acknowl-
25 edged that the character of Boo Radley had been based on one of their spooky neighbors.

Lee's book has become one of the most widely read novels dealing with race in America, and it was voted the "Best Novel of the Century" in a poll conducted by *Library Journal* in 1999.
30 Interestingly, the story accomplishes such a serious aim while also serving as both a coming-of-age story and a Southern Gothic tale. It touches on themes ranging from class to compassion, from adolescence to anger, and from laws to liberties.

Lee's layered, nuanced novel is an American story, a
35 portrayal of a town in Alabama in the 1930s. Marja Mills probed the reality of this portrayal as paralleled by Lee's own life in an insightful 2002 article in the *Chicago Tribune*. Mills continued her analysis of the connection between Lee's childhood and writing in the 2015 book *The Mockingbird Next Door*. While opinions on
40 this later work of Mills are quite divided, the very fact that Mills explored the subject multiple times is testament to the intrigue surrounding the inspirations for *To Kill a Mockingbird* to this day.

Passage B by Courtney Crowder

Less than a week after the publication of Marja Mills' memoir, *The Mockingbird Next Door*, her story of befriend-
45 ing the famously reclusive 88-year-old author Harper Lee, the book remains embroiled in controversy. On July 14, the day before the book's publication date, Lee, author of the American classic *To Kill a Mockingbird*, issued a statement refuting the memoir's main narrative: that Mills was allowed
50 unique access to the author and her sister, Alice Lee, 102, and that the sisters told her stories with the knowledge that Mills was going to use them in a book. "Rest assured, as long as I am alive any book purporting to be with my cooperation is a falsehood," Lee's statement said.

55 On Monday at a sold-out Tribune-sponsored book discussion at Tribune Tower, Mills, a former Tribune reporter, addressed the dispute: Lee "had always been encouraging and also quite specific about stories that she was sharing for the book and those that were to remain private, and I did respect
60 those…I can only speak the truth, that Nelle Harper Lee and Alice F. Lee were aware I was writing this book and my friendship with both of them continued during and after my time in Monroeville." …

Mills' journey to the center of Lee's social circle began
65 in 2001, when the Tribune assigned her to capture the spirit of Monroeville, Ala., Lee's hometown, when the Chicago Public Library selected *To Kill a Mockingbird* as the first pick for the One Book, One Chicago program. After the exhaustive and meticulously researched Tribune article was published in
70 2002, Mills remained friends with the sisters, although Harper Lee, characteristically, had declined to comment for the article. In 2004, Mills moved into the house next door to them with their blessing, according to the book jacket. For the next 18 months, from fall 2004 to spring 2006, Mills accompanied
75 the sisters as they ate, explored and even did their laundry.…

Mills described her book as focusing on "the last chapter of life as (the Lees) knew it." In 2007, Harper Lee had a serious stroke and had to move into an assisted-living facility. Soon after, Alice Lee also moved out of the house they had
80 both lived in for nearly all their lives. "So much that has been said about (the Lees) has been secondhand or speculated," Mills said. "I just wanted to get out of the way. I wanted to show them sitting at the kitchen table, listening to Nelle tell stories, or being in the car with them as they talked about the
85 Monroeville of 1930 versus now."

Question 1 asks about Passage A.

1. In the context of Passage A, the references to Dill and Boo Radley in the third paragraph are intended to support the claim that:

    A. Lee had considered a career as a lawyer prior to becoming an author.
    B. Lee based the character Atticus Finch on a famous defense attorney.
    C. Lee was distressed by the criminal activity in her neighborhood while growing up.
    D. Lee used her own history as an inspiration for her novel.

Question 2 asks about Passage B.

2. Based on Passage B, Harper Lee's reaction to Mills's book could best be described as:

    F. an admonishment based on Lee's wishes to have greater input on the book.
    G. a dismissal based on Lee's refusal to collaborate with Mills.
    H. a criticism based on the pride Lee takes in remaining private.
    J. an approval based on Lee's intent to share her story before she passed.

Questions 3–5 ask about both Passages.

3. Which statement most accurately compares the content of the two passages?

    A. Both present information about awards and tributes Lee received for *To Kill a Mockingbird*.
    B. Both analyze Lee's readers but draw different conclusions about their motivations.
    C. Both describe first-hand accounts of contact with Lee that had different outcomes.
    D. Both explore the psychological motivations for Lee's self-identification with a bird.

4. Based on the passages, it's most likely that Schampfter and Crowder would agree that Marja Mills' publications were:

    F. impactful: Mills' works increased the popularity of *To Kill a Mockingbird*.
    G. insightful: the Chicago Tribune article was carefully researched while *The Mockingbird Next Door* covered details of the Lees' life.
    H. falsified: they were based on knowledge that only Lee herself would know.
    J. factual: the origins of *To Kill a Mockingbird* are found in Lee's family's history.

5. It can most reasonably be inferred from the passages that:

    A. Harper Lee should have written more books.
    B. Marja Mills' publications were controversial.
    C. the success of *To Kill a Mockingbird* was based on style.
    D. *To Kill a Mockingbird* is not relevant today.

INTEGRATION OF KNOWLEDGE AND IDEAS DRILL 4 EXPLANATIONS

1. **D** The question asks what claim the references to Dill and Boo Radley were intended to support. Locate where Dill and Boo Radley are discussed in the passage, which is in lines 20–26. While a legal case is discussed in these lines, the passage does not say that Lee *considered a career as a lawyer* or was *distressed by the criminal activity in her neighborhood*. Eliminate (A) and (C). The lines imply that the character *Atticus Finch* was based on aspects of Lee's *own father*, a lawyer, but not that her father was a *famous* defense attorney. So, eliminate (B). Lines 20–21 say that *Many of the details of the story had been drawn from Lee's own life* and both Dill and Boo Radley are based on people from *Lee's own childhood*, so keep (D). The correct answer is (D).

2. **G** The question asks how Harper Lee's reaction to Mills's book could best be described. Look for references to Lee's reaction in Passage B. Lines 47–54 indicate that Lee *issued a statement refuting* the claim that Mills's book was written with Lee's cooperation. There is no indication that Lee wished *to have greater input* on Mills's book, so eliminate (F). Keep (G) because it is supported by lines 47–54. There is no indication that Lee took *pride* in remaining private, so eliminate (H). The information in lines 47–54 contradicts the idea that Lee gave Mills any type of *approval*, so eliminate (J). The correct answer is (G).

3. **A** The question asks which statement accurately compares the content of the two passages. Eliminate any answer choice that misrepresents either passage. Both passages discuss accolades given to Lee for *To Kill a Mockingbird*. Passage A states that the novel won a *Pulitzer Prize*, while Passage B states that *the Chicago Public Library selected* To Kill a Mockingbird *as the first pick for the One Book, One Chicago program*. This is consistent with the *awards and tributes Lee received* in (A), so keep (A). There is no analysis of *Lee's readers* in either passage, so eliminate (B). Passage B describes Mills' contact with Lee, but Passage A doesn't describe any first-hand accounts of contact with Lee. Passage A only references certain individuals who knew her in childhood or at the start of her career. Eliminate (C). Neither passage mentions any *psychological motivations for Lee's self-identification with a bird*, so eliminate (D). The correct answer is (A).

4. **G** The question asks for a statement about Marja Mills' publications that Schampfter and Crowder would agree with. Eliminate any answer choice that misrepresents either passage. In Passage A, Schampfter says that *Mills probed the reality of this portrayal as paralleled by Lee's own life in an insightful 2002 article in the* Chicago Tribune. *Mills continued her analysis of the connection between Lee's childhood and writing in the 2015 book* The Mockingbird Next Door. Similarly, Crower in Passage B states that the Tribune article was *exhaustive and meticulously researched* and that The Mockingbird Next Door was *Mills' memoir* that focused on *"the last chapter of life as (the Lees) knew it."* Choice (F) states that Mills' work is *impactful*, but neither passage indicates how much of an impact Mills' works made, particularly regarding if her *works increased the popularity of* To Kill a Mockingbird. Eliminate (F). Choice (G) states that Mills' works are insightful and that the Tribune *article was carefully researched, while* The Mockingbird Next Door *covered details of the Lees' life,* which is consistent with both passages. Keep (G). Choice (H) states that Mills' works were *falsified*, and while both authors indicate at different points that there is some controversy surrounding Mills' works for different reasons, neither author claims anything as extreme as her works being *falsified*—in fact, both indicate her work is either *insightful* or *exhaustive*. Eliminate (H). Choice (J) states Mills' works are factual,

which is supported by both passages, but only Passage A supports that the *origins of* To Kill a Mockingbird *are found in Lee's family history.* Passage B does not mention any such connections, so eliminate (J). The correct answer is (G).

5. **B** The question asks what can reasonably be inferred from both passages. Eliminate any answer choice that mispresents either passage. Choice (A) states that *Harper Lee should have written more books,* but while Passage A is definitely positive toward Lee's novel, neither passage offers any opinion if Lee should have written more books. Eliminate (A). Choice (B) states that *Marja Mills' publications were controversial.* Passage A states that *opinions on this later work of Mills are quite divided* in its last paragraph, while Passage B in its first paragraph states Mills' *story of befriending the famously reclusive 88-yeard-old author Harper Lee...remains embroiled in controversy.* Keep (B). Choice (C) states that *the success of* To Kill a Mockingbird *was based on style.* Passage A attributes the success of the novel to the *public's growing awareness of racial injustice* and its ability to touch on a wide range of themes, not to *style.* Passage B makes no mention of what made *To Kill a Mockingbird* successful. Eliminate (C). Choice (D) states that To Kill a Mockingbird *is not relevant today,* which goes against Passage A, which states that *nearly seven decades* since its 1960 publication, *the story of how* To Kill a Mockingbird *came to be still captivates readers.* Eliminate (D). The correct answer is (B).

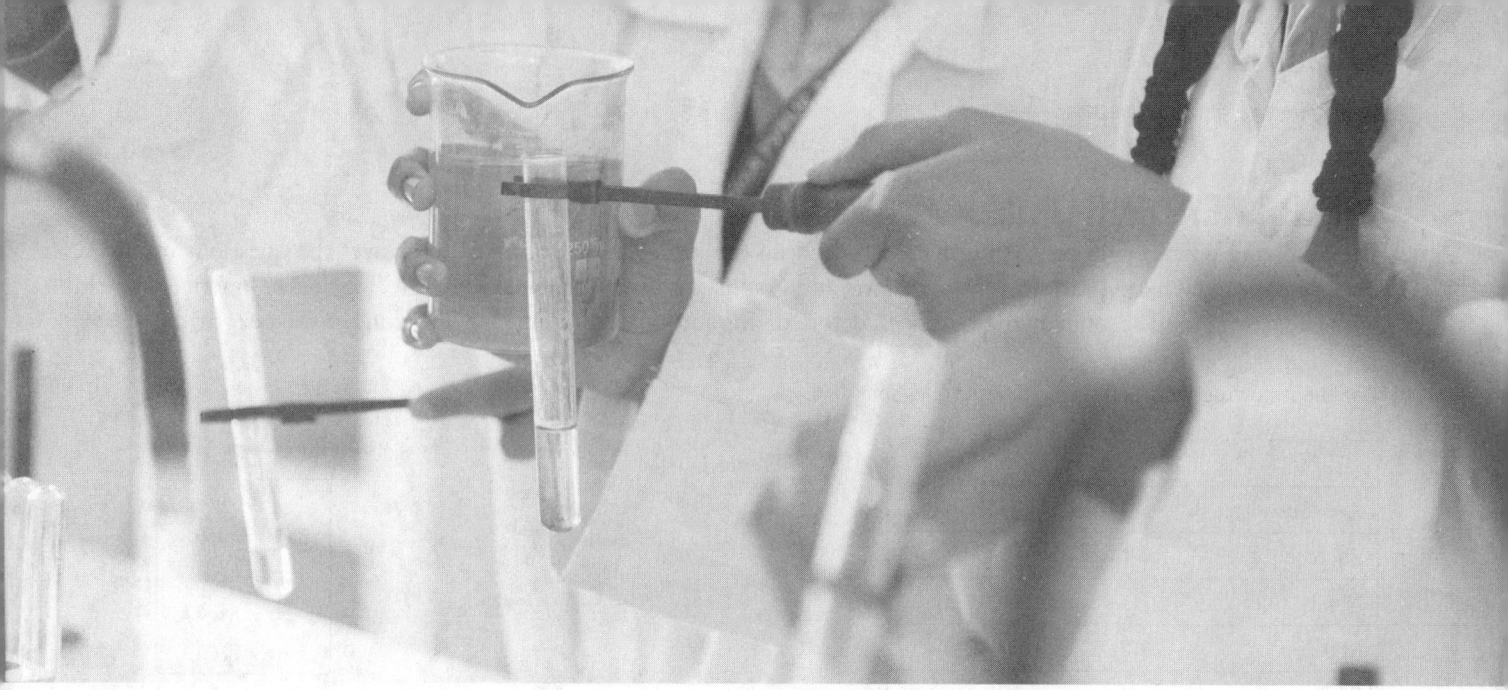

Science Drills

GRAPH READING DRILL

The following passage will help you get used to finding the information you need to answer the questions on an ACT Science passage. Reading various types of charts and graphs is a fundamental skill for ACT Science. Practice your skills with the passage and accompanying questions before diving into real ACT Science questions in the next drill.

Use the following table and illustration for questions 1–4.

Table 1	
Substance	van 't Hoff factor *
Sucrose	1.0
NaCl	1.9
$MgCl_2$	2.7
$FeCl_3$	3.4
*Values at 300 K	

Figure 1

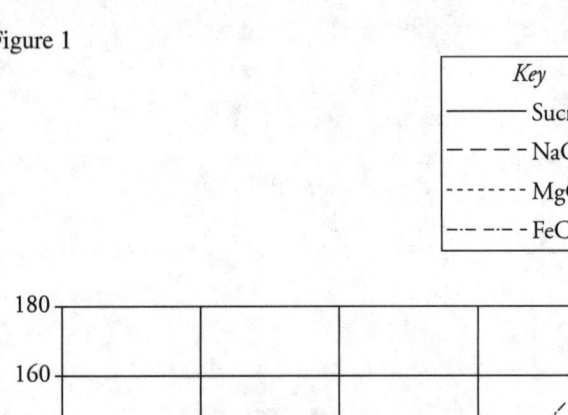

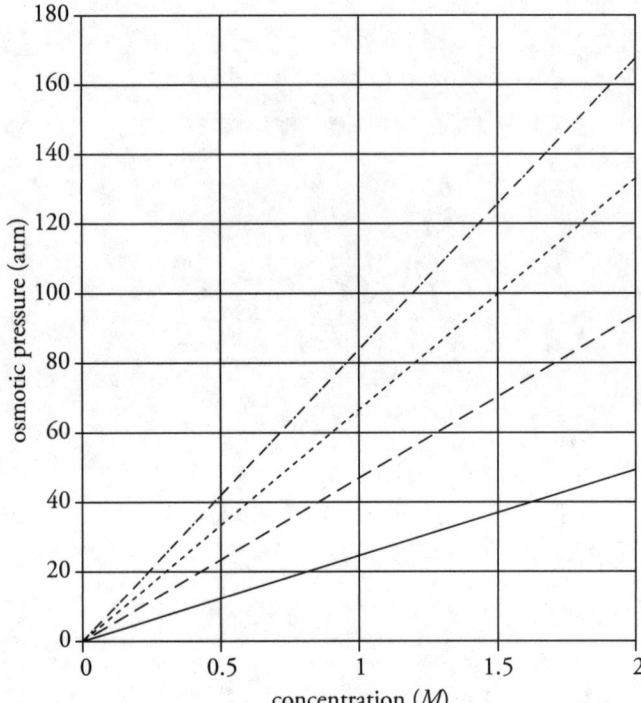

1. What do the different lines on Figure 1 show?

2. What is the relationship between concentration and osmotic pressure?

3. What do Table 1 and Figure 1 have in common?

4. What is the relationship between van 't Hoff factor and osmotic pressure at concentration of 1 *M*?

Use the following table and illustration for questions 5–8.

Figure 2

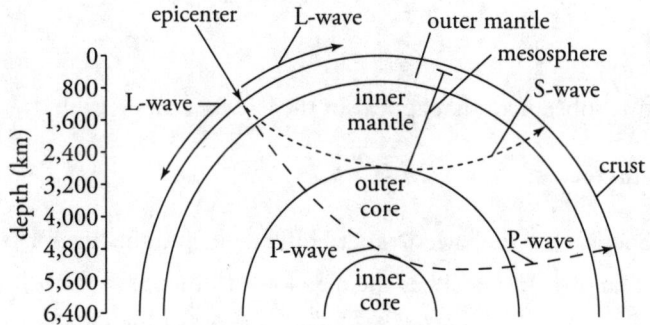

Table 2		
Seismic wave	Depth range (km)	Crust velocity (m/s)
L-wave	0–10	2.0–4.5
S-wave	0–2,921	3.0–4.0
P-wave	0–5,180	5.0–7.0

5. What does Figure 2 show?

6. What do Figure 2 and Table 2 have in common?

7. Which types of waves could occur in the outer mantle?

8. Which types of waves could occur in the inner core?

GRAPH READING DRILL EXPLANATIONS

1. **Difference substances**

   Use the key above Figure 1 to see what the lines represent. According to the key, they are sucrose, NaCl, $MgCl_2$, and $FeCl_3$, which are different substances.

2. **Direct**

   A direct relationship is one in which both variables follow the same trend—as one increases, the other also increases, or vice versa. As concentration increases, osmotic pressure also increases, since the lines are all headed upward to the right. Thus, this is a direct relationship.

3. **Substances**

   The key in Figure 1 shows that the figure has the same substances that appear in the left column of Table 1.

4. **As van 't Hoff factor increases, osmotic pressure increases**

   Compare the van 't Hoff factors of the substances. Sucrose has the lowest van 't Hoff factor, and the line for sucrose is the lowest line on Figure 1 at a concentration of 1 M. NaCl has the next lowest van 't Hoff factor, and it is the next lowest line. The other two lines continue in the same fashion, so a substance with a higher van 't Hoff factor has a higher osmotic pressure at a given concentration.

5. **A cross-section of a planet**

   While this information would be provided in the text, common sense or outside knowledge can also reveal what this figure shows. The figure displays areas that can be recognized as components of a planet, such as inner core, outer core, crust, and mantle.

6. **Depth and waves**

   Figure 2 shows depth in kilometers on the vertical axis, and this is also provided in the second column of Table 2. The seismic waves shown in the first column of Table 2 are also labeled on Figure 2. Crust velocity, the third column of Table 2, does not appear in the figure, nor do any of the other features from the figure appear in the table.

7. **S and P**

   Find the outer mantle, which is the outermost section on Figure 2. L-waves appear to be outside the outer mantle, so they would not be included as an answer. The curve with the short dashes labeled as S-wave does pass through the outer mantle. The same is true for the P-wave curve made of long dashes.

8. **None**

   None of the lines for the three waves pass through the inner core, which is the innermost section of the figure, so the answer is none.

LOOK IT UP

Look It Up questions are questions that can be answered directly from the figures with minimal need for interpretation, synthesis, or additional reading. These questions should be the first questions you answer on any passage. The key on Look It Up questions is to take your time to make sure you are checking the correct variable, graph, or experiment: you don't want to lose any of the points simply because you read the data for Trial 3 instead of Trial 4!

LOOK IT UP DRILL 1

Yellow Fever is caused by a virus transmitted by mosquitoes from monkeys to humans. Figure 1 shows the life cycle of the mosquitoes who carry this disease. These mosquitoes' eggs do not hatch unless there is enough water for the next two stages of their life cycles. Yellow Fever is passed when an adult of these mosquitoes first bites a monkey that is infected with the virus and then bites a human. Two studies were done on the incidence of Yellow Fever in a particular jungle.

Figure 1

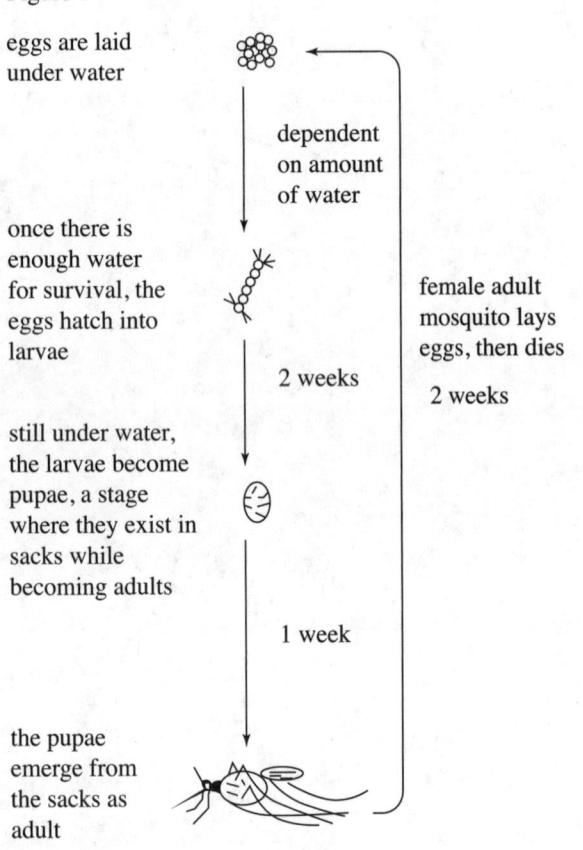

Study 1

For one year, researchers collected data on the monthly rainfall and the number of new cases of Yellow Fever that occurred in a village in the jungle. The results are shown in Figure 2.

Figure 2

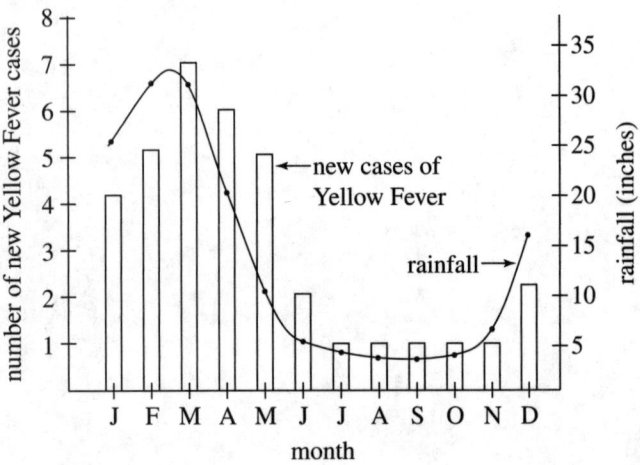

Study 2

Five ecologists conducted a study in five separate villages in the same jungle. Each ecologist moved into the village for one year to collect data. Table 1 shows the population of each village, the number of water sources within 2 miles of the center of the village, the average number of monkeys seen by the ecologist each month, the number of mosquito bites received by the ecologist over the course of the year, and the percentage of the village that was infected with Yellow Fever at some point over the year.

Table 1					
Village	Population	Number of water sources	Average number of monkeys seen	Number of mosquito bites	Percent of village infected with Yellow Fever
A	910	2	36	100	10%
B	1,012	4	20	156	18%
C	1,109	7	43	210	29%
D	811	11	38	220	38%
E	913	15	58	338	52%

1. Based on Table 1, the average percent of villagers affected by the Yellow Fever virus was closest to:

   A. 20%.
   B. 30%.
   C. 60%.
   D. 80%.

2. Suppose additional data had been gathered in Study 2 about the number of mosquito bites per month. Based on Figure 2 and Table 1, in which of the following months would you expect to have the largest total of mosquito bites per month?

   F. April
   G. June
   H. August
   J. November

3. According to Figure 2, the amount of rainfall was different for each of the following pairs of months EXCEPT:

   A. May and December.
   B. February and March.
   C. January and October.
   D. April and May.

4. Based on Table 1, as the number of water sources increased, the number of monkeys seen:

   F. increased only.
   G. decreased only.
   H. increased, then decreased.
   J. varied with no consistency.

5. An extended drought in the jungle leads to a 3-month period with no mosquito bites or new Yellow Fever cases in the surrounding jungle towns. Based on Figure 1, what is most likely the *minimum* amount of time that the ecologists would expect to pass between the first rainfall and the first recurrences of mosquito bites?

   A. Less than 1 week
   B. Between 1 and 2 weeks
   C. Between 2 and 3 weeks
   D. At least 3 weeks

LOOK IT UP DRILL 1 EXPLANATIONS

1. **B** The question asks for the approximate average percent of villagers affected by Yellow Fever, based on Table 1. Refer to Table 1 and examine the percentages of villagers affected for each village. To help find the average, round each value. Village A has about 10% affected. Village B has about 20% affected, and Village C has about 30% affected. Village D has about 40% affected. Village E has about 50% affected. Eliminate (C) and (D) because these are both higher than any of the values in the table. Look at the remaining answers. The averages of three of the towns are all well above 20%, and only village A is well below 20%. The average has to be higher than this, so eliminate (A). The correct answer is (B).

2. **F** The question asks which month would be expected to have the *largest total of mosquito bites per month,* given the data in Study 2 and Figure 2. Since number of mosquito bites per village was measured in Study 2, look here first. As the number of mosquito bites increases, the percentage of the group affected by Yellow Fever increases. Therefore, the greatest number of mosquito bites would be expected in months with the greatest number of Yellow Fever cases. Refer to Figure 2 and find the month with the greatest number of new Yellow Fever cases. In April there were 6 new Yellow Fever cases, and in June there were 2 new Yellow Fever cases. Eliminate (G). In both August and November there was only 1 new Yellow Fever case. Eliminate (H) and (J). The correct answer is (F).

3. **B** The question asks for which pair of months was the amount of rainfall NOT different. The question states that each of the pairs of months have different amounts of rainfall except for one. The correct answer will be the pair with the same amount of rainfall. Use Figure 2 and work through the answer choices. Start with (A). In May the rainfall was 10″, and in December the rainfall was 16″. Since these are different, eliminate (A). For (B), both February and March had about 32″ of rainfall. These are the same, so keep (B). Since January and October had different rainfalls (25″ versus 4″), eliminate (C). Since April and May also had different rainfalls (20″ versus 10″), eliminate (D). The correct answer is (B).

4. **J** The question asks about the relationship between the number of water sources and the number of monkeys seen. Refer to Table 1, which shows that the number of water sources increases from Village A to Village E. Meanwhile, the number of monkeys neither consistently increases nor decreases. Since there is no distinct pattern, the correct answer is (J).

5. **D** The question asks about the minimum amount of time expected to pass between the first rainfall and the first reoccurrence of mosquito bites after an extended drought, according to Figure 1. The figure indicates that mosquito eggs will not hatch unless there is sufficient water; this would represent the first rainfall after a drought. At this point, it takes 2 weeks for the hatched eggs to progress from larvae to pupae. It then takes an additional week for pupae to emerge from their sacks and become adult mosquitoes. At this point the mosquitoes will begin biting and infecting people. Therefore, after an extended drought, it would take a minimum of 3 weeks before the first reoccurrence of mosquito bites. The correct answer is (D).

THIS PAGE IS INTENTIONALLY LEFT BLANK.

LOOK IT UP DRILL 2

Soil salinity is the concentration of potentially harmful salts dissolved in the groundwater that fills soil pores. Salinity is determined by measuring a soil's *electrical conductivity (EC)* and *exchangeable sodium percentage (ESP)*. High EC indicates a high concentration of dissolved salt particles; ESP indicates the proportion of electrical conductivity that is due to dissolved sodium ions.

Soil samples were collected from five different distances west of a particular river. Figure 1 shows the electrical conductivity of the soil samples (in milli-Siemens per centimeter, mS/cm) at four different depth ranges measured.

Figure 1

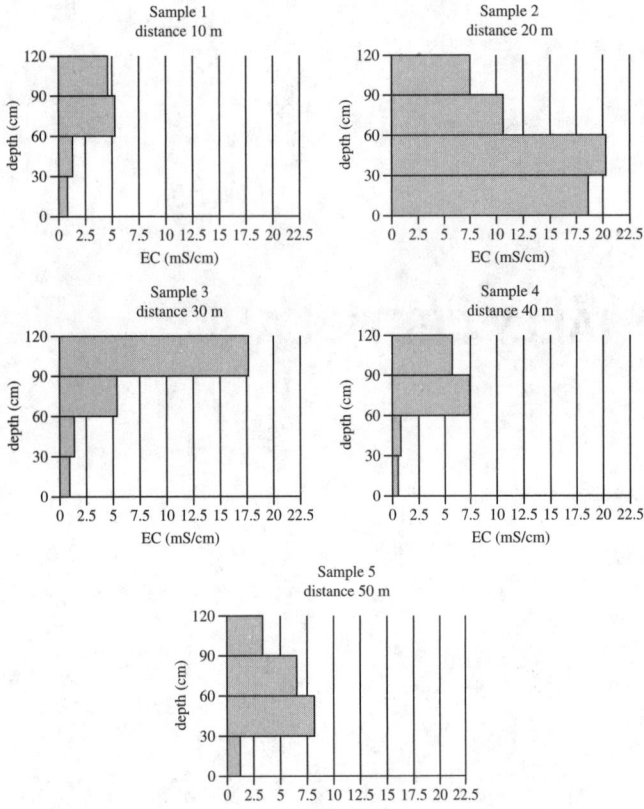

Figure 2 shows the exchangeable sodium percentage of the five sites at different depths.

Figure 2

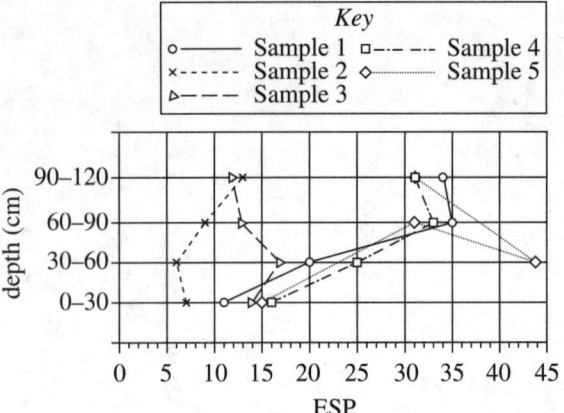

1. In Sample 2, as the EC increases from its lowest value to its highest value, the ESP:

    A. increases only.
    B. decreases only.
    C. increases and then decreases.
    D. decreases and then increases.

2. Figure 2 indicates that, compared with the soil tested in Sample 1, the soil tested in Sample 4 contains:

    F. a higher percentage of sodium ions throughout.
    G. a lower percentage of sodium ions throughout.
    H. a higher percentage of sodium ions at shallower depths only.
    J. a lower percentage of sodium ions at shallower depths only.

3. According to Figure 2, in the soil collected in Sample 3 at a depth of 30–60 cm, approximately what percent of the soil conductivity is due to sodium ions?

    A. 14%
    B. 17%
    C. 24%
    D. 44%

4. Based on Figures 1 and 2, the electrical conductivity due to sodium ions in the sample collected 40 m west of the river was:

    F. greatest at a depth of 0–30 cm.
    G. greatest at a depth of 90–120 cm.
    H. least at a depth of 0–30 cm.
    J. least at a depth of 30–60 cm.

5. Based on Figure 2, which of the following figures best represents the exchangeable sodium percentage for the five soil samples collected at a depth of 90–120 cm ?

A.
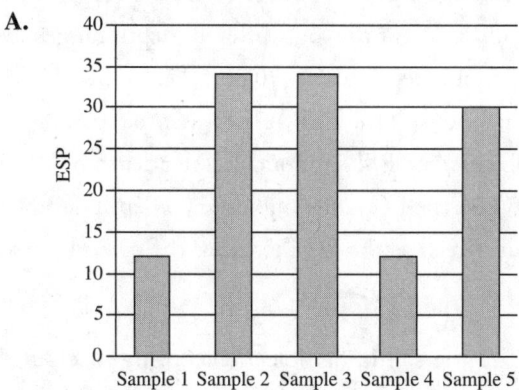

B.
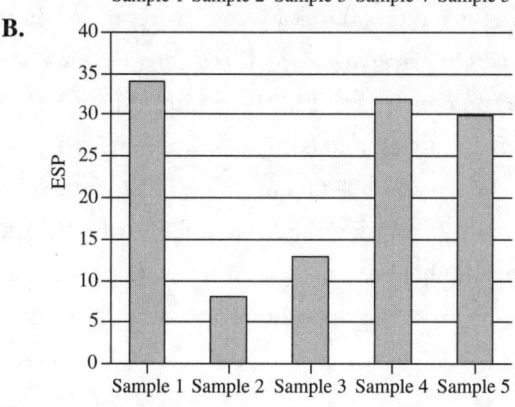

C.
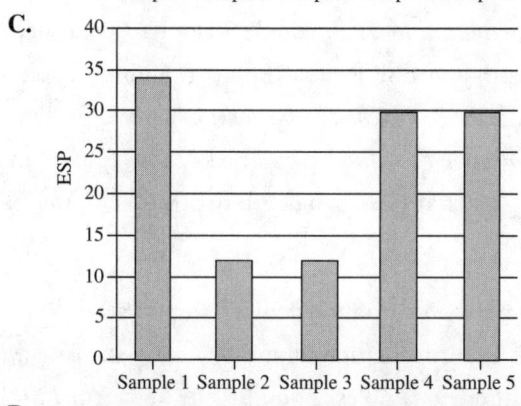

D.
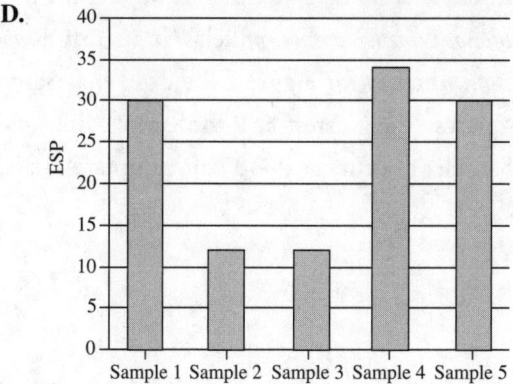

6. A student claimed that as soil moves away from a major water source, such as a river, the salinity of the soil increases. Is this claim supported by Figures 1 and 2 ?

F. No; the electrical conductivity and exchangeable sodium percentage both decreased from Sample 1 to Sample 5.

G. No; there was no consistent trend for electrical conductivity and exchangeable sodium percentage.

H. Yes; the electrical conductivity and exchangeable sodium percentage both increased from Sample 1 to Sample 5.

J. Yes; the electrical conductivity increased and exchangeable sodium percentage decreased from Sample 1 to Sample 5.

LOOK IT UP DRILL 2 EXPLANATIONS

1. **B** The question asks what happens to the ESP as the EC increases from its lowest to its highest value in Sample 2. Refer to Sample 2 in Figure 1 and look at the trend for EC at the four different depth ranges. EC is the lowest at a depth of 90–120 cm. The next highest EC is at a depth of 60–90 cm, then 0–30 cm. The highest EC is at a depth of 30–60 cm. Now examine what happens to the ESP at these depths in Sample 2 of Figure 2. At a depth of 90–120 cm, when the EC is the lowest, the ESP is about 13. At a depth of 60–90 cm, the ESP is 9 and at a depth of 0–30 cm, the ESP is 7. When the EC is the highest, at a depth of 30–60 cm, the ESP is the lowest, at 6. Since the ESP continually decreases as the EC increases, the correct answer is (B).

2. **H** The question asks about the soil in Sample 4, as compared to the soil in Sample 1, according to Figure 2. Look at Figure 2, which shows depth and ESP for five different samples. Look for the key term *ESP* in the passage; the first paragraph says that *ESP* is *exchangeable sodium percentage,* which *indicates the proportion of electrical conductivity that is due to dissolved sodium ions,* so compare the ESP for Samples 1 and 4. The key indicates that Sample 1 is represented by the solid line with circles, and Sample 4 is represented by the alternating dash and dot line with squares. At depths of 0–30 cm and 30–60 cm, the ESP for Sample 1 is lower than that for Sample 4. At depths of 60–90 cm and 90–120 cm, the ESP for Sample 1 is higher than that for Sample 4. Eliminate (F) and (G) because the relationship between the two samples is not consistent at all depths. Choice (H) is consistent with the data, and (J) gives the opposite relationship. The correct answer is (H).

3. **B** The question asks for the percent of soil conductivity *due to sodium ions* for Sample 3 at a particular depth, according to Figure 2. Look at Figure 2. Figure 2 shows depth and ESP for five different samples. Look for the key term *ESP* in the passage; the first paragraph says that *ESP* is *exchangeable sodium percentage,* which *indicates the proportion of electrical conductivity that is due to dissolved sodium ions.* The key for Figure 2 indicates that Sample 3 is represented by the long-dashed line with triangles. At a depth of 30–60 cm, the ESP for Sample 3 is 17. The correct answer is (B).

4. **H** The question asks for the *electrical conductivity due to sodium ions* in a particular sample, according to Figures 1 and 2. Look at both figures. Only Figure 1 has any information about *distance;* Sample 4 was located at 40 m. Figure 2 shows depth and ESP for five different samples. Look for the key term *ESP* in the passage; the first paragraph says that *ESP* is *exchangeable sodium percentage,* which *indicates the proportion of electrical conductivity that is due to dissolved sodium ions.* The key for Figure 2 indicates that Sample 4 is represented by the alternating dash and dot line with squares. The greatest ESP for Sample 4 occurs at 60–90 cm, so eliminate (F) and (G). The lowest ESP for Sample 4 occurs at 0–30 cm; eliminate (J). The correct answer is (H).

5. **C** The question asks for the best representation of *exchangeable sodium percentage* of the five samples at a particular depth, in bar graph form. Look for the key term *exchangeable sodium percentage* in the passage; the first paragraph says that *ESP* is an abbreviation for *exchangeable sodium percentage*. Figure 2 shows depth and ESP for the five different samples, so look at Figure 2. At a depth of 90–120 cm, Samples 2 and 3 both have ESPs between 10 and 15. Eliminate (A) and (B) because they give the wrong value for one or both of those samples. Figure 2 shows that Sample 1 has the highest ESP at a depth of 90–120 cm, so eliminate (D). The correct answer is (C).

6. **G** The question asks whether the proposed claim that the salinity of soil increases as the soil moves away from a major water source is supported by Figures 1 and 2. Eliminate any answer choices that do not accurately describe both figures. Neither Figure 1 nor Figure 2 shows a consistent decrease from Sample 1 to Sample 5, so eliminate (F) and (J). Neither figure shows a consistent increase either, so eliminate (H). Choice (G) is consistent with the data because there is no consistent trend from Sample 1 to Sample 5 in either figure. The correct answer is (G).

OUTSIDE KNOWLEDGE DRILL

On every ACT Science Test, you can expect to see several Outside Knowledge questions. These questions relate to the passage but require background knowledge that isn't provided in the passage itself. There is no reason to try to take a crash course in physics or chemistry, though! These questions make up a small portion of the test, and many involve basic topics that you may already be familiar with. For any topics you are unfamiliar with, there are usually ways to use Process of Elimination to improve your odds of guessing correctly. The following drill provides some examples of the kinds of outside knowledge questions that you may see on the Science Test. Make sure to read through the explanations for any questions about concepts or terms you aren't familiar with, as several of these topics make frequent appearances on the Science Test!

Questions 1 and 2 relate to the following reaction.

$$6CO_2 + 6H_2O \xrightarrow{\text{light}} C_6H_{12}O_6 + 6O_2$$

1. Which of the following is true of all organisms that utilize the process represented by the reaction above?

   A. They are autotrophs that contain chlorophyll.
   B. They are autotrophs that do not contain chlorophyll.
   C. They are heterotrophs that contain chlorophyll.
   D. They are heterotrophs that do not contain chlorophyll.

2. The primary product of the reaction shown above is a:

   F. lipid.
   G. sugar.
   H. protein.
   J. enzyme.

Questions 3–5 refer to the following experiment.

Experiment 1

Researchers selected twenty 5 m^2 plots with similar conditions throughout a local community with a large population of both honeybees and bumblebees. The twenty plots were divided into 4 groups of 5 plots. The researchers planted a local non-flowering grass in all twenty plots and then added additional flowering plants (either Plant A, Plant B, or both Plant A and B) to three of the four groups. After the plants began flowering, they selected a 3-hour observation window and recorded the number of bee visits to each plot, the types of bees that visited each plot, and the amount of time spent in the plot by each bee. Only bumblebees and honeybees were seen visiting the plots. The results for each group were then averaged. The results are shown in Table 1.

Table 1			
	Number of bee visits	Ratio of bumble-bees to honeybees	Average time spent in plot per bee
Flowering Plant A only	50	7:3	58 min
Flowering Plant B only	64	3:5	41 min
Both Plant A and Plant B	70	2:3	35 min
No flowering plants	11	5:6	10 min

3. Which of the following is a dependent variable in Experiment 1?

   I. Type of vegetation in the plot
   II. Ratio of bumblebees to honeybees
   III. Average number of bee visits

   A. I only
   B. III only
   C. II and III only
   D. I, II, and III

4. Are the organisms listed in Table 1 eukaryotic or prokaryotic?

   F. The vegetation is prokaryotic, while the two bee species are eukaryotic.
   G. The vegetation is eukaryotic, while the two bee species are prokaryotic.
   H. Both the vegetation and the two bee species are prokaryotic.
   J. Both the vegetation and the two bee species are eukaryotic.

5. Studies have shown that the reproductive rates of Plant A and Plant B fall to almost zero in the absence of bees. Is the primary form of reproduction for Plants A and B most likely asexual reproduction or sexual reproduction?

A. Asexual reproduction; the bees assist through pollination.

B. Asexual reproduction; the bees assist in vegetative propagation.

C. Sexual reproduction; the bees assist through pollination.

D. Sexual reproduction; the bees assist in vegetative propagation.

Question 6 refers to the following information.

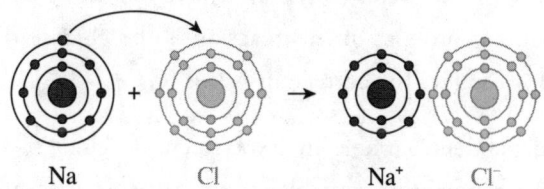

Na   Cl   Na⁺   Cl⁻

6. In the ionic bonding of sodium chloride, the sodium atom:

F. donates an electron to the chlorine atom, resulting in a positively charged sodium ion.

G. donates an electron to the chlorine atom, resulting in a negatively charged sodium ion.

H. donates a proton to the chlorine atom, resulting in a positively charged sodium ion.

J. donates a proton to the chlorine atom, resulting in a negatively charged sodium ion.

Questions 7–8 refer to the following information.

An experiment is set up to look at the physics of a bouncing ball as shown in Figure 1.

Figure 1

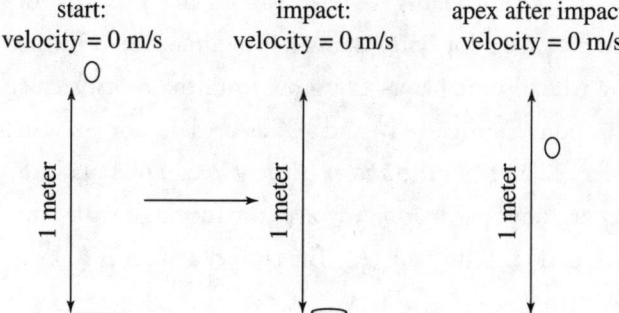

Figure 2 shows the velocity of a ball versus time for balls with various weights dropped from 1 meter height.

Figure 2

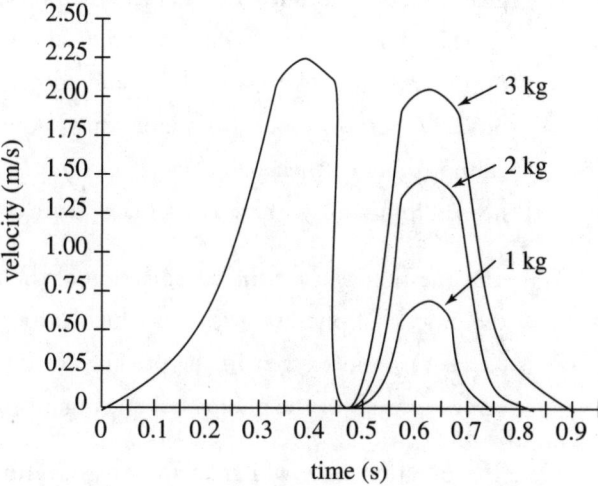

7. Which of the following describes how the kinetic and potential energy of the ball changes in the first 0.35 seconds after the ball is initially dropped? From a time of 0 seconds to a time of 0.35 seconds, the potential energy of the ball:

A. increases as the kinetic energy decreases.

B. decreases as the kinetic energy increases.

C. increases as the kinetic energy also increases.

D. decreases as the kinetic energy also decreases.

8. A student suggests that denser balls reach a *lower* apex after impact. If all 3 balls depicted in Figure 2 have the same radius, do the results shown in Figure 2 support this hypothesis?

F. Yes; density and mass are directly proportional, so the 3 kg ball is the densest ball.

G. Yes; density and mass are inversely proportional, so the 1 kg ball is the densest ball.

H. No; density and mass are directly proportional, so the 3 kg ball is the densest ball.

J. No; density and mass are inversely proportional, so the 1 kg ball is the densest ball.

OUTSIDE KNOWLEDGE DRILL EXPLANATIONS

1. **A** The question asks which of the following is true of all organisms that utilize the process shown in the given reaction. The reaction depicts the process of photosynthesis in which carbon dioxide (CO_2) and water (H_2O) are converted into glucose ($C_6H_{12}O_6$) and oxygen (O_2) in the presence of light. Photosynthetic organisms, such as plants, algae, and some bacteria, are known as *autotrophs* or *primary producers* that produce their own food from inorganic resources. Eliminate (C) and (D) as *heterotrophs* are *consumers* that cannot produce their own food. *Chlorophyll* is the pigment that helps autotrophs absorb the light energy needed for photosynthesis. Eliminate (B) as chlorophyll is vital to photosynthesis. The correct answer is (A).

2. **G** The question asks for the classification of the primary product shown in the reaction. The reaction depicts the process of photosynthesis in which carbon dioxide (CO_2) and water (H_2O) are converted into glucose ($C_6H_{12}O_6$) and oxygen in the presence of light. The primary product of this reaction is the glucose that serves as food for the photosynthetic organism. Glucose is a sugar. The correct answer is (G).

3. **C** The question asks which of the answer choices is a dependent variable in Experiment 1. Use Process of Elimination. A *dependent variable*, sometimes called a measured variable, is the variable measured or observed for any changes caused by the manipulation of the independent variable. In Experiment 1, researchers directly manipulated the type of vegetation in each plot, so the type of vegetation is an *independent variable*. Eliminate (A) and (D) as they include statement (I). Both the ratio of bumblebees to honeybees and the average number of bee visits are variables that were measured in response to the differing vegetation, so both are dependent variables. Eliminate (B) as it does not include statement (II). The correct answer is (C).

4. **J** The question asks if the organisms listed in Table 1 are eukaryotic or prokaryotic. The organisms listed in Table 1 include some plant species (grass and two flowering plants) as well as two animal species (bumblebees and honeybees). A prokaryotic organism is a single-celled organism without a nucleus or other membrane-bound organelles. Only organisms within the domains of Bacteria and Archaea are prokaryotic. All plants, animals, fungi, and protists are *eukaryotic* and contain a nucleus and membrane-bound organelles. Therefore, all the species shown in Table 1 are eukaryotic. The correct answer is (J).

5. **C** The question asks whether the primary form of reproduction for Plants A and B is most likely asexual or sexual reproduction. The question states that reproductive rates for both plants fall to almost zero in the absence of bees. *Vegetative propagation* is a process by which some plants can grow from the roots, stems, or leaves of a parent plant without the need for fertilization. Eliminate (B) and (D) as bees do not assist in vegetative propagation. Bees are *pollinators* that transfer pollen from the *anther* (male gamete) of a plant to the *stigma* (female gamete) so that fertilization can occur. Since pollination involves the fusion of male and female gametes, this process is considered sexual reproduction. Eliminate (A). The correct answer is (C).

6. **F** The question asks what happens to the sodium atom during the ionic bonding of sodium chloride. On the left side of the figure, the sodium atom (Na) is neutrally charged prior to bonding. After ionic bonding, the sodium is now a positively charged ion (Na^+). Eliminate (G) and (J) because both claim the sodium ion is negatively charged. Some students may be aware that only electrons can be donated or accepted by atoms

as both protons and neutrons are located inside the nucleus. However, even without this outside knowledge, the question can still be answered with a more common piece of outside knowledge: *protons* have a positive charge, while *electrons* have a negative charge. Since the neutral Na atom becomes a positively charged Na$^+$ ion, it must have donated a negatively charged electron to chlorine. This resulted in a positively charged sodium ion and a negatively charged chloride ion (Cl$^-$). The correct answer is (F).

7. **B** The question asks how the kinetic and potential energy of the ball changes in the first 0.35 seconds after the ball is dropped. The *potential energy* is the stored energy that an object possesses due to its position or state. In the case of the ball, it has already been lifted above the ground and has stored energy in the form of gravitational potential energy that will cause movement as soon as it is released. As it falls toward the ground in the first 0.35 seconds, this stored energy decreases as it returns to ground level. Eliminate (A) and (C) as they incorrectly state that the potential energy increases during the descent. Now, consider the kinetic energy. As the ball falls during those initial 0.35 seconds, the velocity of the ball increases. *Kinetic energy* is the energy an object possesses due to its motion. Kinetic energy is directly related to velocity, so as the velocity increases, the kinetic energy increases. Therefore, during the initial 0.35 seconds from the time the ball is dropped until just before impact with the ground, the potential energy decreases while the kinetic energy increases. The correct answer is (B).

8. **H** The question asks if the hypothesis that denser balls reach a lower apex is supported by Figure 2. Density is mass divided by volume, so if volume is held constant, then a higher mass corresponds to a higher density. Eliminate (G) and (J) as both incorrectly identify the 1 kg ball as the densest ball. Now, refer to Figure 2. The 3 kg ball reaches the highest apex, which is the opposite of the hypothesis in the question. Eliminate (F) as this data does not support the hypothesis. The correct answer is (H).

MULTIPLE VIEWPOINTS

Each ACT Science Test has one Multiple Viewpoints passage that contains 2 to 5 different viewpoints. Unlike the rest of the Science passages, this passage should be read in its entirety. Use the following strategy for Multiple Viewpoints:

1. **Preview the passage.** Read the introduction and familiarize yourself with the topic that the viewpoints are addressing. Then, quickly preview the questions and make a notation to keep track of those that relate to only one specific viewpoint.
2. **Work a viewpoint.** Read one viewpoint: look for the main idea rather than focusing on the details. Then work any questions that relate to that viewpoint only.
3. **Rinse, repeat.** Repeat step 2 with the remaining viewpoint(s). As you read each viewpoint, focus on the key differences between this viewpoint and the other(s).
4. **Synthesize.** Tackle the remaining questions with a heavy dose of Process of Elimination!

MULTIPLE VIEWPOINTS DRILL 1

Students studying gravity and motion were given the following information:

- *Gravity* is an attractive force between two bodies that is directly related to their *mass* and indirectly related to the square of the *distance* between their centers.

- *Acceleration due to gravity* is the acceleration of an object that results from the *force* of gravity.

- *Weight* is the *force* on an object that results from *gravity*, and is not the same as *mass*.

- *Drag* is a force directly related to the *velocity* of a moving object and which results from air resistance and acts to *slow* an object down.

- When the *drag* on a free-falling object is equivalent to the *weight* of that object, the object maintains a constant velocity called *terminal velocity*.

The students' teacher then described the following experiment:

The experimenter dropped a ball from a known height and recorded the time it took to hit the ground. In a second location, a second ball was dropped from the same height and the experimenter observed that it took a longer time to fall to the ground.

Providing no additional information, the teacher asked her three students to provide an explanation of the experimental conditions that would account for the different times it took the two balls to fall.

Student 1

Both trials were conducted in air with the same atmospheric properties. The balls had the same mass and weight, but the second ball had a larger radius and *surface area*. Therefore, the second ball was subjected to more drag and reached a lower terminal velocity than the first. This resulted in an increased fall time.

Student 2

Each ball had identical dimensions, but the first ball was made of a denser material giving it both greater mass and weight. Each ball was dropped through air with the same atmospheric properties. Since the second ball was subjected to less gravitational force and weighed less, it reached a lower terminal velocity compared to the first. Therefore, the second ball took more time to hit the ground.

Student 3

Both balls had the same dimensions and mass. The first ball was dropped above the Earth, while the second ball was dropped above the Moon. The first ball reached terminal velocity in the Earth's atmosphere. The second ball was not subjected to any atmosphere or air resistance. However, there was substantially less gravitational force on the second ball and subsequently it weighed less than the first ball. The overall net result was that the second ball fell more slowly and took longer to hit the ground.

1. What are the students attempting to explain?

_____

_____

2. In just a few words, what is the main point of Student 1's explanation?

_____

_____

3. What is the main point of Student 2's explanation?

_____

_____

4. What is the main point of Student 3's explanation?

_____

_____

5. The teacher added another question to the students' assignment: Suppose the experimenter repeated the experiment by dropping two balls at the same time from the same height in a single *vacuum*, where no air resistance was present. The balls have different dimensions but identical weights, and they hit the ground at the same time. This new result is consistent with the explanations of which student(s)?

   A. Student 1 only
   B. Student 2 only
   C. Students 1 and 2 only
   D. Students 1, 2, and 3

6. According to Student 2, which of the following graphs demonstrates the velocity of the two balls as time increases?

   F.
   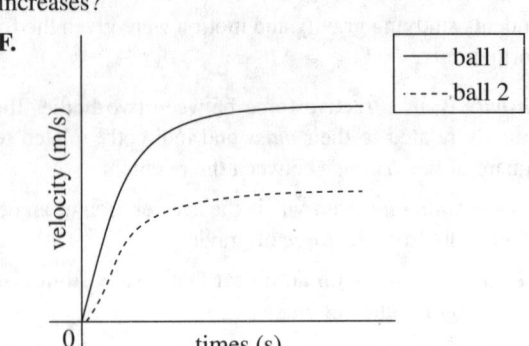

   G.
   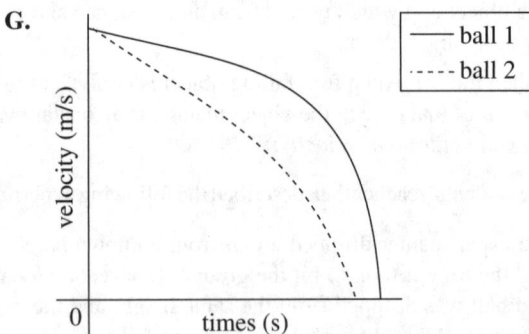

   H.
   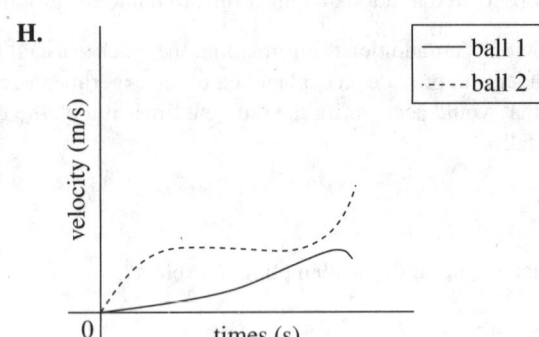

   J.
   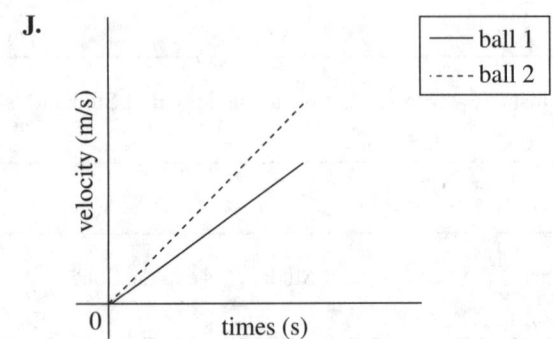

7. According to Student 1, did the surface area of the second ball have an effect on its terminal velocity?

   A. Yes; as the surface area of a ball decreases, its terminal velocity decreases only.

   B. Yes; as the surface area of a ball increases, its terminal velocity decreases only.

   C. No; as the surface area of a ball increases, its terminal velocity decreases, then increases.

   D. No; as the surface area of a ball increases, its terminal velocity is not affected.

8. Assuming that Student 3's explanation is correct, once the second ball starts falling, does it reach terminal velocity?

   F. Yes, because the weight of the ball was constant and drag force increased.

   G. Yes, because the weight of the ball decreased and no drag force was present.

   H. No, because the weight of the ball decreased and drag force was constant.

   J. No, because the weight of the ball was constant and no drag force was present.

9. The 3 explanations of the motion of the balls are similar to each other in that all 3 explanations suggest that:

   A. differences in the gravitational force are responsible for the change in falling times.

   B. increases in velocity result from gravity.

   C. drag plays only a small part in determining how long it takes an object to fall.

   D. a lead ball would have fallen faster.

10. Based on the explanations of the 3 students, what did all 3 students assume about the first ball?

   F. The velocity did not change.

   G. The velocity increased only.

   H. The velocity decreased only.

   J. The velocity increased for a time, and then reached terminal velocity.

MULTIPLE VIEWPOINTS DRILL 1 EXPLANATIONS

1. The students are attempting to explain the conditions that account for the different times it took for the two balls to fall.

    The final sentence of the introduction states that *the teacher asked her three students to provide an explanation of the experimental conditions that would account for the different times it took the two balls to fall.*

2. Ball 2 had higher surface area and more drag.

    Student 1's explanation states that the second ball had a *larger radius and surface area*, which led to more drag and *a lower terminal velocity.*

3. Ball 1 was denser and weighed more.

    Student 2's explanation states that the first ball was a *made of a denser material giving it both greater mass and weight.* The student explains that since the second ball was weighed less, there was less gravitational force and *a lower terminal velocity.*

4. Ball 2 was dropped on the moon with less gravity.

    Student 3 states that *the second ball was dropped above the moon* and *there was substantially less gravitational force on the second ball.*

5. **D** The question asks which students' explanations would be consistent with the results of a new trial, in which two balls were dropped *at the same time from the same height in a single vacuum, where no air resistance is present* and with balls that *have different dimensions but identical weights.* By placing two balls in a vacuum, where no air resistance is present, the experimenter would have eliminated the effects of drag. This suggests that air resistance had an effect on the results, which supports Student 1. Eliminate (B) because it does not include Student 1. The new experiment uses balls with identical weights, which suggests that weight can affect the results, which supports Student 2. Eliminate (A) because it does not include Student 2. This experiment also placed both balls in the same location with the same force of gravity. This suggests that gravitational force can play a role, which supports the views of Student 3. Eliminate (C) because it does not include Student 3. The correct answer is (D).

6. **F** The question asks which graph *demonstrates the velocity of the two balls as time increases,* according to Student 2. Look for the key word *velocity* in the explanation provided by Student 2. It states that *the second ball...reached a lower terminal velocity compared to the first,* which implies that both balls reached terminal velocity. Look for the term *terminal velocity* in the passage. The fifth bullet point defines *terminal velocity* as *a constant velocity* that is reached *when the drag on a free-falling object is equivalent to the weight of that object.* The only graph that shows velocity reaching a terminal level and holding constant is in (F). The correct answer is (F).

7. **B**   The question asks whether *the surface area of the second ball [had] an effect on its terminal velocity,* according to Student 1. Look for the key words *surface area* in Student 1's explanation. It states *the second ball had a larger radius and surface area...therefore, the second ball...reached a lower terminal velocity than the first.* Therefore, Student 1 believes that as surface area increases, terminal velocity decreases. Eliminate (C) and (D) because they state that surface area had no effect on terminal velocity. Choice (A) states the opposite relationship, so eliminate (A). The correct answer is (B).

8. **J**   The question asks whether the second ball reaches terminal velocity, according to Student 3's explanation. Look for the key words *second ball* in the explanation provided by Student 3. It states that *the second ball was not subjected to any atmosphere or air resistance.* According to the introduction of the passage, drag force results from air resistance. Therefore, there is no drag force; eliminate (F) and (H). Student 3 states that the second ball *weighed less than the first ball* but does not say that *the weight decreased;* eliminate (G). Choice (J) is consistent with Student 3's explanation. The correct answer is (J).

9. **B**   The question asks in what way *the 3 explanations of the motion of the balls are similar to each other.* Eliminate (A) because only Student 3 discusses *differences in the gravitational force.* Keep (B) because all three students imply that the balls accelerate until they reach terminal velocity. Eliminate (C) because *drag* is the primary cause of the slower falling time for Student 1. Eliminate (D) because only Student 2 discusses different *material.* The correct answer is (B).

10. **J**   The question asks what all three students assumed about the first ball, based on the explanations of all three students. All three students believe that the first ball reached *terminal velocity.* Look for the term *terminal velocity* in the passage. The fifth bullet point defines *terminal velocity* as *a constant velocity* that is reached *when the drag on a free-falling object is equivalent to the weight of that object.* Velocity would need to increase in order to reach a *terminal velocity,* so eliminate (F) and (H). Eliminate (G) because it does not match the definition of *terminal velocity* in the passage. The correct answer is (J).

MULTIPLE VIEWPOINTS DRILL 2

Taraxicum, the common dandelion, can reproduce both through spreading seeds and through vegetative reproduction. To spread its seeds, the dandelion grows seed pods shaped like globes, in which the seeds are loosely attached to a central ball; each seed grows a parachute-like tuft that lets it travel long distances on the wind (or when blown upon by humans). In vegetative reproduction, a new dandelion stalk and leaves can grow up from an existing root system. Two students discuss the spread of dandelion populations.

Student 1

In *Taraxicum*, vegetative reproduction and seed distribution make up the only means of growing new plants. Each accounts for 50% of the growth of new dandelions.

Taraxicum grows throughout North America. In many places there is very little wind. Therefore, *Taraxicum* must have a non-wind-based means of spreading itself. While blowing dandelion seeds is a common pastime among humans, this human influence is very recent in evolutionary terms; it is very unlikely that *Taraxicum* evolved to rely on humans to distribute its seeds.

The way *Taraxicum* grows in a typical field shows that both vegetative reproduction and seed distribution are at work. While seeds scatter over the whole field, the dandelions tend to grow together in clumps. This suggests that individual seeds sprout the first new dandelions, which then grow several more through vegetative reproduction.

Student 2

Seed distribution is the main way *Taraxicum* spreads itself. Without seed distribution, there are very few new dandelions. *Taraxicum* does use vegetative reproduction, sending new stalks from existing roots, but this is mainly to replace the above-ground plant if it has been cut or eaten. This allows the plant to survive threats in the environment but does not allow for the growth of new plants.

Plant studies show that plants which rely on vegetative reproduction to spread themselves tend to have large, complex root networks or underground root clusters. *Taraxicum* plants, however, each have a single large, deep taproot. This makes them very difficult to uproot, but it also means that their roots do not spread out underground, so any new plants growing from the roots would compete with each other for sunlight. Even a slight breeze or the brush of a passing animal is enough to spread dandelion seeds to a new area. Additionally, all known types of *Taraxicum* produce seed globes. If half the new dandelions grew from vegetative reproduction, then a seedless dandelion should not be at a competitive disadvantage and should be commonly observed in the wild.

Experiment

The students proposed 3 trials using an introduced *Taraxicum* population in three fields in a windy area where *Taraxicum* can naturally thrive (see Table 1).

Table 1	
Trial	Procedure
1	Several *Taraxicum* plants are planted in the soil of a field with no other *Taraxicum* plants. They are allowed to grow and spread normally.
2	*Taraxicum* specimens are planted in the soil of a similar field with no other *Taraxicum* plants. Their flowers are covered with plastic bags once they have grown seeds.
3	*Taraxicum* specimens are planted in large glass jars, which are then buried in a third similar field. Seeds are allowed to blow normally, but the plant roots cannot grow out of the glass jars.

1. Suppose an experiment were performed in which several new *Taraxicum* plants were planted in a field with their roots in glass jars and with plastic bags over the flowers. Assuming that Student 1's hypothesis is correct, the number of new dandelions in the field would most likely be what percent of the number in a control field?

   A. 0%
   B. 25%
   C. 50%
   D. 100%

2. Which of the following trials most likely provided the control group in the students' experiment?

   F. Trial 1, in which *Taraxicum* specimens are planted in the soil of a field with no other *Taraxicum* plants
   G. Trial 1, in which *Taraxicum* specimens are planted in large glass jars, which are then buried in the soil of a field with no other *Taraxicum* plants
   H. Trial 2, in which *Taraxicum* specimens are planted in the soil of a field similar to that of Trial 1
   J. Trial 3, in which specimens are planted in large glass jars in a field similar to that of Trial 1

3. Student 1 states that dandelions growing in clumps "suggests that individual seeds sprout the first new dandelions, which then grow several more through vegetative reproduction." Which of the following indicates why Student 2 believes this cannot be true? Student 2 says:

   A. *Taraxicum* tends to grow from a root network, while vegetative reproducers grow from single roots.
   B. *Taraxicum* tends to grow from a single root, while vegetative reproducers grow from root networks.
   C. *Taraxicum* has seeds that are attached loosely to the stem, a fact that suggests they are not important to *Taraxicum*'s reproductive strategy.
   D. *Taraxicum* has seeds that are attached loosely to the stem, but vegetative reproducers tend not to have seeds at all.

4. With regard to the experiment described in the table, Students 1 and 2 would most likely agree that the increase in the *Taraxicum* population would be greatest in a field where:

   F. neither plastic bags nor glass jars were used.
   G. plastic bags were used, but not glass jars.
   H. glass jars were used, but not plastic bags.
   J. both plastic bags and glass jars were used.

5. Suppose Trial 3 of the experiment was performed as described. Based on Student 1's hypothesis, the resulting population would be closest to what percentage of a control population?

   A. 0%
   B. 25%
   C. 50%
   D. 100%

6. Suppose the 3 trials were performed as described. Student 2's hypothesis about the way *Taraxicum* reproduces would be best supported if the number of new dandelions fit which of the following patterns?

   F. The field in Trial 3 had roughly the same number of dandelions as the field in Trial 1, both of which had fewer dandelions than the field in Trial 2.
   G. The field in Trial 1 had more dandelions than the field in either Trial 2 or Trial 3, while the fields in Trials 2 and 3 had roughly equal numbers of dandelions.
   H. The field in Trial 2 had fewer dandelions than the field in Trial 3, which had more dandelions than the field in Trial 1.
   J. The field in Trial 3 had slightly fewer dandelions than the field in Trial 1, both of which had many more dandelions than the field in Trial 2.

MULTIPLE VIEWPOINTS DRILL 2 EXPLANATIONS

1. **A** The question asks what percent of the number of dandelions in a control field would the number of new dandelions be if another experiment were conducted, *in which several new Taraxicum plants were planted in a field with their roots in glass jars and with plastic bags over the flowers,* assuming that Student 1's hypothesis is correct. Look at Student 1's explanation. The first paragraph of Student 1's explanation states that *in Taraxicum, vegetative reproduction and seed distribution make up the only means of growing new plants. Vegetative reproduction* is described in the introduction as a process in which *a new dandelion stalk and leaves can grow up from an existing root system.* The new experiment described would prevent vegetative reproduction with the glass jars. It would also prevent seed distribution with the plastic bags, so no new plants would ever grow. The correct answer is (A).

2. **F** The question asks which trial *provided the control group in the students' experiment.* A control group is one that is left alone, with no variables. According to Table 1, Trial 1 was performed *in the soil of a field with no other Taraxicum plants,* and the new *Taraxicum* plants *are allowed to spread normally.* Trial 1 is the control, so eliminate (H) and (J). Eliminate (G) because it mentions glass jars, which were not used in Trial 1. The correct answer is (F).

3. **B** The question asks why Student 2 does not believe Student 1's statement *that dandelions growing in clumps* "suggests that individual seeds sprout the first new dandelions, which then grow through vegetative reproduction." Look for words from the answer choices in Student 2's explanation. Eliminate (A) because the second paragraph of Student 2's explanation states that the roots of *Taraxicum* plants *do not spread out underground.* Keep (B) because the second paragraph of Student 2's explanation states that *Taraxicum...each have a single large, deep taproot* and that *plants which rely on vegetative reproduction...tend to have large, complex root networks.* Eliminate (C) because, according to Student 2, *seed distribution is the main way Taraxicum spreads itself* and so seeds **are** important to *Taraxicum's reproductive strategy.* Eliminate (D) because Student 2 states in paragraph 6 that *all known types of Taraxicum produce seed globes.* The correct answer is (B).

4. **F** The question asks under which conditions of the experiment the *Taraxicum* plants would be greatest in number, according to Students 1 and 2. Student 1 believes *vegetative reproduction and seed distribution make up the only means of growing new plants.* Student 2 believes *seed distribution is the main way Taraxicum spreads itself,* but that *Taraxicum does use vegetative reproduction.* They would both agree that plastic bags would prevent *seed distribution,* so eliminate (G) and (J). *Vegetative reproduction* is described in the introduction as a process in which *a new dandelion stalk and leaves can grow up from an existing root system.* Both students would therefore agree that glass jars would limit *vegetative reproduction;* eliminate (H). Choice (F) is the only option that uses neither. The correct answer is (F).

5. **C** The question asks what percentage of a control population the resulting population of Trial 3 would be, according to Student 1. In paragraph 2, Student 1 states that *vegetative reproduction* and *seed distribution... each accounts for 50% of the growth of new dandelions. Vegetative reproduction* is described in the introduction as a process in which *a new dandelion stalk and leaves can grow up from an existing root system.* Look at Table 1. Trial 3 prevented *vegetative reproduction* by placing the roots in a glass jar. Therefore, the plants would be half as likely to reproduce. The correct answer is (C).

6. **J** The question asks which pattern would support *Student 2's hypothesis about the way Taraxicum reproduces*. Student 2's explanation states that *seed distribution is the main way Taraxicum spreads itself* even though it *does use vegetative reproduction*. Eliminate (F) and (G) because Trial 2 would prevent *seed distribution* so, according to Student 2, it would have fewer plants than Trials 1 and 3. Eliminate (H) because the seeds were not covered in Trial 3, so according to Student 2, it should have the same number of dandelions as Trial 1. Keep (J) because Student 2 believes that the glass jar would prevent a few dandelions from growing in Trial 3, and Student 2 also believes that the plastic bags in Trial 2 covering the seeds would prevent *many more dandelions* from growing. The correct answer is (J).

THIS PAGE IS INTENTIONALLY LEFT BLANK.

NOW PASSAGES

Now passages are the passages you should tackle first in the Science Test. Good Now passages contain easy-to-read figures and several Look It Up questions. Many answer choices contain numbers or phrases such as "increases only" or "increases and then decreases."

As you work the Now passages, remember to apply the Basic Approach:

1. **Work the Figures.** Familiarize yourself with the variables represented in each figure and any trends or relationships depicted among those variables.
2. **Work the Questions.** Start with the Now questions: questions that ask for values or contain trend phrases such as "increases only" or "decreases only." Make sure to read the question carefully to identify the relevant experiment, figure, and/or variable. Then, refer back to relevant data to find the answer. If any reading is required outside of the figures, skim the text for the key terms from the question to identify the specific text you need to read.
3. **Work the Answers.** Use Process of Elimination when necessary. Ideally, many of the answers will come directly from the figures on a Now passage, but Process of Elimination is still necessary at times.

Make sure to answer every question before moving on to another passage as you won't have time to return to passages once you have moved on. Enter a guess answer if one Later or Last question is dragging you down on a Now passage. You don't want to waste too much time on one question if you have already completed all the other questions on that passage!

NOW PRACTICE PASSAGE 1

In recent years, the technology of magnetic levitation ("maglev") has been investigated to provide an alternative rapid transportation option. Using repulsion of magnetic fields, maglev trains can be pushed forward at speeds of up to 300 miles per hour. One specific type of magnetic levitation currently being investigated is electrodynamic suspension (EDS).

In EDS, magnetic rods are located at the bottom of the maglev train and within the track underneath the train. An electric current can induce a magnetic field in the magnets of the track. If this magnetic field can be induced to repel constantly the magnet in the maglev train, then the train will maintain a distance above the track known as an "air gap" and move forward. Theoretically, the maglev train in EDS should travel at least 4 inches above the track, so there would be virtually no energy lost to friction. If the system does lose energy, it will be in the form of thermal energy.

Figure 1

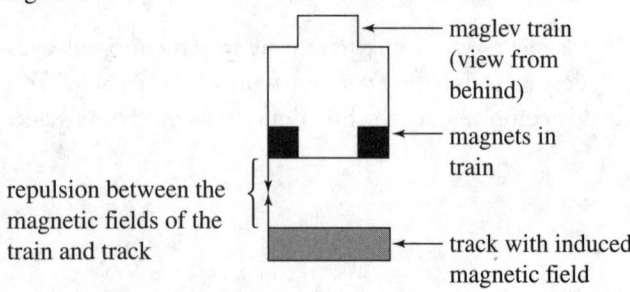

Under controlled conditions, scientists conducted tests on an experimental maglev track oriented in an east-to-west direction.

Study 1

A maglev train with magnetic rods of fixed length was moved along the experimental track from east to west at various velocities v. The current I in the track required to induce these velocities was measured in amperes (A).

Table 1		
Trial	v (m/s)	I (A)
1	40	50
2	80	100
3	120	150
4	160	200
5	200	250

Study 2

The maglev train was run in five trials with varying lengths, L, of the magnetic rods, and run at a constant velocity of 40 m/s. The current I in the track required to induce this velocity given the different lengths of the rods was recorded.

Table 2		
Trial	L (m)	I (A)
6	0.6	50
7	0.8	67
8	1.0	84
9	1.2	100
10	1.4	116

Study 3

The magnetic field, B, measured in tesla (T), was varied in the maglev track. The current running through the maglev track was then measured in five new trials. Throughout these trials, the lengths of the magnetic rods and the maglev train velocities were kept constant.

Table 3		
Trial	B (T)	I (A)
11	5.90×10^{-4}	300
12	7.87×10^{-4}	400
13	9.84×10^{-4}	500
14	1.05×10^{-3}	600
15	1.20×10^{-3}	700

Study 4

The maglev train with magnetic rods of fixed length was moved along the experimental track from west to east at various velocities, and the current in the track required to induce these velocities was measured. The magnetic field was kept constant for each of these trials.

Table 4		
Trial	v (m/s)	I (A)
16	40	−50
17	80	−100
18	120	−150
19	160	−200
20	200	−250

1. In Study 1, *I* would most likely have equaled 500 A if *v* had been:

   A.   40 m/s.
   B.   125 m/s.
   C.   200 m/s.
   D.   400 m/s.

2. In Study 2, as the length of the magnetic rods in the maglev train increased, the amount of the current required to induce the train's velocity:

   F.   increased only.
   G.   decreased only.
   H.   remained constant.
   J.   varied, but with no consistent trend.

3. During each trial, an electrical current moves through the magnetic track because a nonzero voltage was produced in the track. During which of the following trials in Study 3 was the voltage greatest?

   A.   Trial 11
   B.   Trial 12
   C.   Trial 13
   D.   Trial 14

4. In which of the studies, if any, did the electrical current flow in the opposite direction as compared with the other studies?

   F.   Study 1 only
   G.   Study 4 only
   H.   Studies 1 and 3 only
   J.   None of these studies

5. The results of Study 3 are best represented by which of the following graphs?

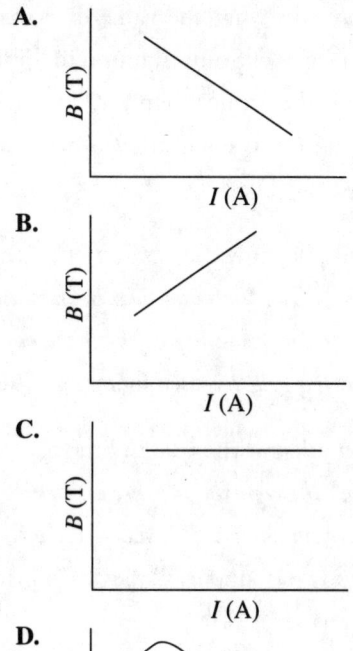

6. Based on the results of Studies 1 and 2, the length of the maglev trains used in Study 1 was most likely:

   F.   0.6 m.
   G.   0.8 m.
   H.   1.0 m.
   J.   1.2 m.

NOW PRACTICE PASSAGE 1 EXPLANATIONS

1. **D** The question asks what the value of v would have been if I had equaled 500 A, according to Study 1. Look at the results of Study 1, found in Table 1. As v increases, so does the value of I. If I is greater than 250 A, then v must be greater than 200 m/s. Eliminate (A) and (B) because they are less than 200 m/s. Eliminate (C) because it is equal to 200 m/s. Keep (D) because it is the only value greater than 200 m/s. The correct answer is (D).

2. **F** The question asks how *the amount of current required to induce the train's velocity* changed *as the length of the magnetic rods in the maglev train increased,* according to Study 2. Look at the results of Study 2, found in Table 2. As the value for L, *the length of the magnetic rods,* increases, *I, the amount of current required to induce the train's velocity,* also increases. The correct answer is (F).

3. **D** The question asks for the trial in Study 3 with the greatest voltage, given that *during each trial, an electrical current moves through the magnetic track because a nonzero voltage was produced in the track.* This suggests that the *electrical current* is directly related to the *voltage,* and Study 1 proves this relationship. Look at the results of Study 3, found in Table 3. Choose the answer choice with the electrical current, which is Trial 14. The correct answer is (D).

4. **G** The question asks for the studies in which *the electrical current flowed in the opposite direction as compared with the other studies.* Look at the values listed for the *electrical current (I)* in the results of each study. Tables 1, 2, and 3 show all positive values, while Table 4 shows negative values. The *electrical current* must have flowed in the opposite direction in Study 4. The correct answer is (G).

5. **B** The question asks which graph accurately represents the data found in the results of Study 3. Look at Table 3. As B increases, I also increases. The only graph that reflects this relationship is the one found in (B). The correct answer is (B).

6. **F** The question asks about the length of the maglev trains used in Study 1, based on the results of Studies 1 and 2. Study 1 used maglev trains of fixed length and measured current with varying velocities. No current is given in Table 2, but the passage states that in Study 2 the maglev trains were run at a *constant velocity of 40 m/s.* This matches up with Trial 1 in Table 1, which found that at a velocity of 40 m/s, the current measured was 50 A. In Study 2, the trial that produced a current of 50 A was Trial 6, which was performed with a maglev train with a length of 0.6 m. Therefore, the maglev trains in Study 1 must have been 0.6 m. The correct answer is (F).

THIS PAGE IS INTENTIONALLY LEFT BLANK.

NOW PRACTICE PASSAGE 2

Metals differ in their relative abilities to conduct electricity. *Resistance* is a measurement in ohms (Ω) of how much a metal opposes electric current at a particular voltage.

A scientist performed 3 experiments using the circuit shown in Figure 1.

Figure 1

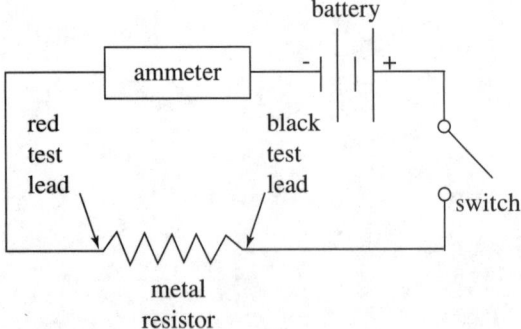

The *metal resistor* consisted of a coil of metallic wire with a known cross-sectional area and length (see Figure 2).

Figure 2

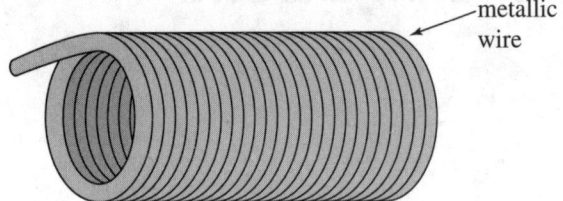

metallic wire

At the outset, the switch was open and no current flowed through the circuit. A 9-volt battery was used, and the black and red test leads of the circuit were attached to a metal resistor. When the switch was closed, electrons (negatively charged) flowed away from the negative battery terminal, through the circuit, and back to the positive battery terminal. The magnitude of current (charge per unit time) from this electron flow was measured by an *ammeter*, and was 1.0×10^{-3} coulombs/second for the first trial of each experiment. The resistance (R) of the metal resistor was calculated in ohms (Ω) from the resulting values for voltage (V) and current (I).

Experiment 1

Three nickel resistor coils, each with a cross-sectional area of 7.61×10^{-10} m^2 but with different lengths, were attached separately to the circuit. Results were recorded in Table 1.

Table 1		
Resistor length (m)	I (coulombs/second)	R (Ω)
100	1.0×10^{-3}	9,000
50	2.0×10^{-3}	4,500
25	4.0×10^{-3}	2,250

Experiment 2

Three gold resistor coils of varying cross-sectional areas were tested. Each resistor coil had a measured length of 100 m. The results were recorded in Table 2.

Table 2		
Resistor cross-sectional area (m^2)	I (coulombs/second)	R (Ω)
2.7×10^{-10}	1.0×10^{-3}	9,000
8.0×10^{-10}	3.0×10^{-3}	3,000
2.4×10^{-9}	9.0×10^{-3}	1,000

Experiment 3

Three coils made of different metals were tested. Each resistor had a cross-sectional area of 2.67×10^{-10} m^2 and a length of 100 m. The value ρ is related to each metal's inherent *resistivity* to current flow. Results were recorded in Table 3.

Table 3			
Metal	ρ	I (coulombs/second)	R (Ω)
Gold	2.4×10^{-8}	1.0×10^{-3}	9,000
Nickel	6.9×10^{-8}	4.4×10^{-4}	25,690
Tin	1.1×10^{-7}	3.4×10^{-4}	41,250

1. If Experiment 1 had been conducted with gold resistors, at each resistor length:

   A. the resistance would be lower than shown in Table 1, and the current would be higher.
   B. the resistance would be higher than shown in Table 1, and the current would be lower.
   C. the resistance would be lower than shown in Table 1, and the current would remain the same.
   D. the resistance would be the same as shown in Table 1, and the current would be lower.

2. Which of the following is the manipulated variable in Experiment 2?

   F. Identity of the metal coil
   G. Cross-sectional area of the coil
   H. Length of the coil
   J. Value ρ of the metal composing the coil

3. Assume that as ρ increases, a metal's ability to conduct current decreases. Based on the results of Experiment 3, which of the following correctly lists gold, nickel, and tin in order of increasing ability to conduct electrons when shaped as a wire coil?

   A. Gold, nickel, tin
   B. Gold, tin, nickel
   C. Tin, nickel, gold
   D. Tin, gold, nickel

4. Based on the results of the 3 experiments, the resistor with which of the following values of length, cross-sectional area, and metal type will have the highest current at a given voltage?

	Length (m)	Cross-sectional area (m²)	Metal
F.	100	2.00×10^{-10}	nickel
G.	50	2.00×10^{-10}	tin
H.	50	4.00×10^{-10}	gold
J.	50	2.00×10^{-10}	gold

5. In Experiment 1, the current across the circuit increased and the resistance of the resistor decreased as the:

   A. value ρ of the metal resistor increased.
   B. cross-sectional area of the metal resistor decreased.
   C. length of the metal resistor increased.
   D. length of the metal resistor decreased.

6. When the switch is closed in the circuit described in the passage, the battery caused electrons to flow in the direction(s) shown by which of the following diagrams?

F.
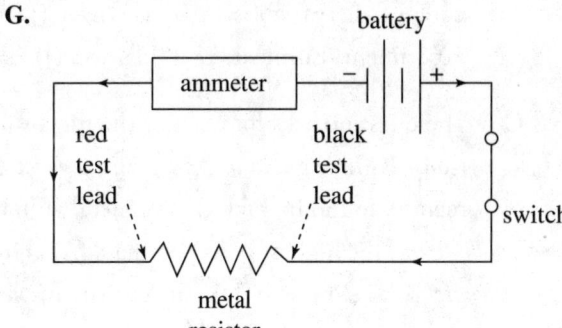

G.
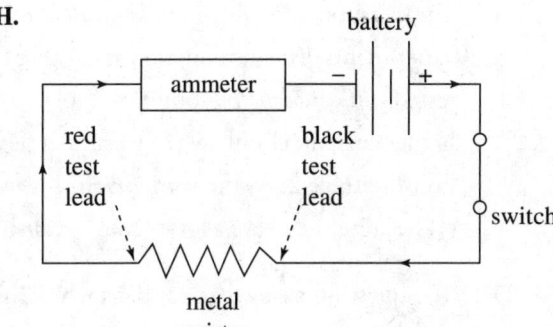

H.
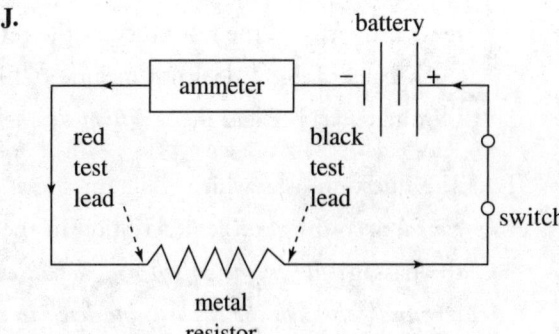

J.

NOW PRACTICE PASSAGE 2 EXPLANATIONS

1. **A** The question asks what would happen if Experiment 1 were conducted with gold resistors. Experiment 1 was initially conducted with nickel resistors. For information about resistors made of different metals, refer to Table 3. According to Table 3, resistors made of gold will have much lower resistances than those made of nickel (25,690 Ωs compared to 9,000 Ωs). This means if Experiment 1 were repeated with gold resistors, the resistance would be lower. Use this information to eliminate (B) and (D). Table 3 also indicates that current (*I*) would also be lower with gold resistors. The correct answer is (A).

2. **G** The question asks for *the manipulated variable* in Experiment 2. Look at the results of Experiment 2 in Table 2. The only variable from the answer choices that appears in the table is *cross-sectional area*. Since none of the variables in (F), (H), or (J) appears in the table, they must have been held constant in the experiment. Eliminate (F), (H), and (J). The correct answer is (G).

3. **C** The question asks for a list of the metals used in Experiment 3, *in order of increasing ability to conduct electrons*, assuming *that as ρ increases, a metal's ability to conduct current decreases*. Look at the results of Experiment 3, found in Table 3. The metal with the highest *ability to conduct electrons* is the one with the lowest ρ. *Tin* has the highest ρ, so eliminate (A) and (B). The metal with the next highest *ability to conduct electrons* is *nickel,* so eliminate (D). The correct answer is (C).

4. **H** The question asks which resistor *will have the highest current at a given voltage,* based on the results of the three experiments. The introduction states that *current* is referred to as *I.* Look at the results of Experiment 1, which tested *different lengths,* found in Table 1. As lengths decrease, current increases. A shorter resistor will have a higher current; eliminate (F) because it has the longest length. Experiment 2 tested *varying cross-sectional areas.* Look at Table 2. As the *resistor cross-sectional area* increases, the current also increases. Eliminate both (G) and (J) because they have a lower *cross-sectional area* than that of (H). The correct answer is (H).

5. **D** The question asks what happens when the *current across the circuit increased and the resistance of the resistor decreased* in Experiment 1. Look at the results of Experiment 1 in Table 1, which shows that as the current, *I,* increased, the resistance of the resistor, *R,* decreased, and the resistor length decreased. Eliminate (A) because Table 1 does not include ρ. Eliminate (B) because Table 1 does not include *cross-sectional area.* Eliminate (C) because the *length of the metal resistor decreased.* The correct answer is (D).

6. **J** The question asks which diagram shows the electrons flowing in the right direction *when the switch is closed,* according to the description in the passage. Look for the word *switch* in the passage. According to the passage, *when the switch was closed, electrons (negatively charged) flowed away from the negative battery terminal, through the circuit, and back to the positive battery terminal.* The diagrams in each answer choice have arrows running along the circuit. Look at the negative side of the battery. In order to be consistent with the passage, the arrows should point away from the negative terminal of the battery and continue in the same direction toward the positive terminal of the battery. Eliminate (F) and (G) because the arrows do not continue in the same direction around the current. Eliminate (H) because the arrows are pointing in the opposite direction, away from the positive terminal and toward the negative terminal. Choice (J) is consistent with the description in the passage. The correct answer is (J).

THIS PAGE IS INTENTIONALLY LEFT BLANK.

NOW PRACTICE PASSAGE 3

A scientist studying hemoglobin investigated the impact of temperature and carbon dioxide (CO_2) partial pressures on the binding capacity of oxygen (O_2). The scientist observed the binding of oxygen to hemoglobin molecules as the partial pressure of oxygen was increased. The temperature and CO_2 were varied to identify their direct impact on the binding capacity of O_2.

Figure 1 displays the impact of changes in temperature on the binding (percent of hemoglobin saturated) of oxygen when the partial pressure of carbon dioxide is held constant. Figure 2 displays the impact of varying carbon dioxide partial pressures on oxygen binding when the temperature is held constant. Under normal conditions, the core body temperature is 37°C, and the carbon dioxide and oxygen partial pressures are 40 mmHg and 100 mmHg, respectively.

Figure 1

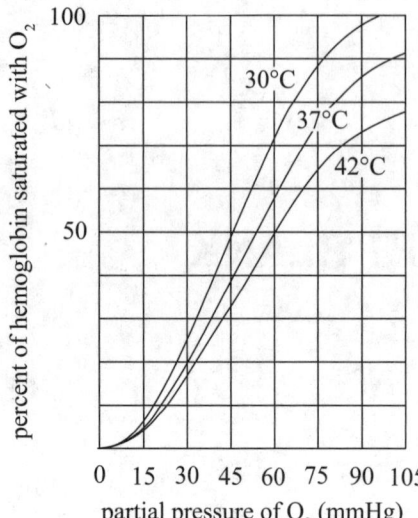

Figure 2

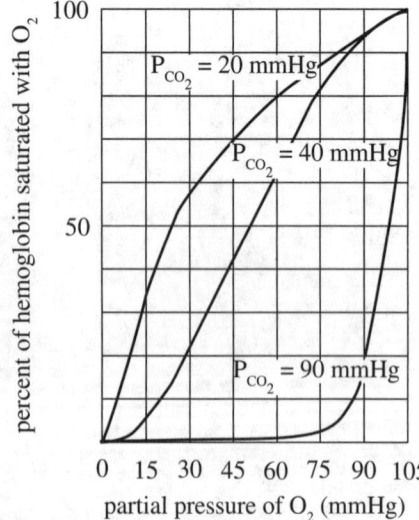

1. Assume the data in Figure 2 was collected at a constant temperature of 37°C. Based on the information in Figures 1 and 2, the data in Figure 1 was most likely collected when the P_{CO_2} was:

   A. less than 20 mmHg.
   B. between 20 and 40 mmHg.
   C. between 40 and 90 mmHg.
   D. greater than 90 mmHg.

2. According to Figure 1, if the temperature is 42°C, which of the following changes in partial pressure of oxygen will cause the least increase in the percent of hemoglobin saturated with O_2?

   F. 0–15 mmHg
   G. 15–30 mmHg
   H. 30–45 mmHg
   J. 45–60 mmHg

3. According to Figure 1, which of the following sets of temperature and partial pressure of oxygen results in the lowest hemoglobin saturation with oxygen?

	temperature (°C)	partial pressure of oxygen (mmHg)
A.	37	45
B.	37	60
C.	42	45
D.	42	60

4. According to Figure 1, if the partial pressure of oxygen is 100 mmHg and 65% of hemoglobin molecules are saturated with oxygen, then the core body temperature is most likely within which of the following ranges?

   F. Less than 30°C
   G. 30°C–37°C
   H. 37°C–42°C
   J. Greater than 42°C

5. Based on Figure 2, if an individual has 70% of his hemoglobin molecules saturated at a partial pressure of 75 mmHg of oxygen, then the individual's carbon dioxide partial pressure is most likely closest to which of the following?

   A. 30 mmHg
   B. 50 mmHg
   C. 70 mmHg
   D. 90 mmHg

6. According to Figure 2, at a CO_2 partial pressure of 90 mmHg, as the partial pressure of O_2 is increased from 45 mmHg to 90 mmHg, the percent of hemoglobin saturated with oxygen:

   F. increases slowly, then increases more rapidly.
   G. increases slowly, then decreases slowly.
   H. increases rapidly, then remains constant.
   J. decreases slowly, then increases rapidly.

NOW PRACTICE PASSAGE 3 EXPLANATIONS

1. **C** The question asks about the P_{CO_2} of Figure 1, given that the values in Figure 2 were obtained at a temperature of 37°C. To answer this, start by examining the curve for 37°C in Figure 1. Notice that at its highest point (when the partial pressure of O_2 is at 105 mmHg), the percentage of hemoglobin saturated with O_2 is slightly greater than 90%. Also notice that at an O_2 partial pressure of 60 mmHg, the percentage of hemoglobin saturated with O_2 is slightly less than 60%. Compare this curve and these points to the curves in Figure 2. While the 37°C curve in Figure 1 most closely resembles the 40 mmHg P_{CO_2} curve in Figure 2, the values noted in the 37°C curve are slightly less. This indicates that the P_{CO_2} at 37°C must be somewhere between 40 mmHg and 90 mmHg. The correct answer is (C).

2. **F** The question asks which change *in the partial pressure of oxygen will cause the least increase in the percent of hemoglobin saturated with O_2* at 42°C, according to Figure 1. Look at Figure 1. The *partial pressure of O_2* is on the *x*-axis and the *percent of hemoglobin saturated with O_2* is on the *y*-axis. The lowest curve represents conditions at 42°C. Look up each range of partial pressure in the answer choices to find *the percent of hemoglobin saturated with O_2*. In order to evaluate (F), find 0–15 mmHg on the *x*-axis; the 42°C curve increases from 0 percent to about 5 *percent of hemoglobin saturated with O_2*. This is an increase of 5%. To evaluate (G), find 15–30 mmHg on the *x*-axis; the 42°C curve increases from 5 percent to about 15 *percent of hemoglobin saturated with O_2*. This is an increase of 10%. Eliminate (G) because the increase is greater than that in (F). To evaluate (H), find 30–45 mmHg on the *x*-axis; the 42°C curve increases from 15 percent to about 32 *percent of hemoglobin saturated with O_2*. This is an increase of 17%. Eliminate (H) because the increase is greater than that in (F). To evaluate (J), find 45–60 mmHg on the *x*-axis; the 42°C curve increases from 32 percent to about 50 *percent of hemoglobin saturated with O_2*. This is an increase of 18%. Eliminate (J) because the increase is greater than that in (F). The correct answer is (F).

3. **C** The question asks which conditions would result in the *lowest hemoglobin saturation with oxygen,* according to Figure 1. First, look at Figure 1 to determine the relationship between hemoglobin saturation and temperature. At any given partial pressure, greater than zero, the *percent of hemoglobin saturated with O_2* decreases as temperature increases. Eliminate (A) and (B) because a temperature of 37°C always has a higher percent of hemoglobin saturated with O_2 than a temperature of 42°C does. Next, look at Figure 1 to determine the relationship between the partial pressure of oxygen and *hemoglobin saturation with O_2*. At 45 mmHg, the *percent of hemoglobin saturated with O_2* is lower for all temperatures than at 60 mmHg. Eliminate (D). The correct answer is (C).

4. **J** The question asks what the core body temperature would most likely be if the *partial pressure of oxygen is 100 mmHg and 65% of hemoglobin molecules are saturated with oxygen,* according to Figure 1. Look at Figure 1. Find 100 mmHg on the *x*-axis and draw a vertical line to the top of the graph. Find 65 percent on the *y*-axis and draw a horizontal line across the graph at this value. Circle the intersection of these two lines. This point is below the 42°C curve. Compare the 30°C, 37°C, and 42°C curves. As the temperature increases, the curve location gets lower, so the temperature at this point on the graph would be higher than 42°C. The correct answer is (J).

5. **B**   The question asks what the carbon dioxide partial pressure would be closest to if 70% of *hemoglobin molecules are saturated at a partial pressure of 75 mmHg of oxygen,* according to Figure 2. Look at Figure 2. Find 70% on the *y*-axis and draw a horizontal line to the other side of the graph. Find 75 mmHg on the *x*-axis and draw a vertical line to the top of the graph. Circle the intersection of this point. The carbon dioxide partial pressure increases from the left-hand line to the right-hand line. The intersecting point is slightly to the right of the 40 mmHg curve and so therefore must be slightly larger than 40. Eliminate (A) because it is smaller than 40. Keep (B) because it is slightly larger than 40. Eliminate (C) and (D) because they are too large. The correct answer is (B).

6. **F**   The question asks how the percentage of hemoglobin saturated with O_2 changes as the partial pressure of oxygen increases from 45 mmHg to 90 mmHg for the P_{CO_2} = 90 mmHg in Figure 2. Go to Figure 2 and locate the curve for P_{CO_2} = 90 mmHg. Follow the curve and notice that the curve first increases very slowly until a partial pressure of about 75 mmHg of O_2, at which the curve begins to increase more rapidly. This trend is best described in (F). The correct answer is (F).

THIS PAGE IS INTENTIONALLY LEFT BLANK.

LATER PASSAGES

Later passages are the passages you tackle after you have finished all the Now passages. Compared to Now passages, Later passages have more complicated figures, less consistent relationships among variables, longer questions and answers, and/or require more reading. Focus on using your time most strategically and trying to get as many points as possible.

Apply the Basic Approach to Later passages:

1. **Work the Figures.** Make an effort to familiarize yourself with the variables represented in each figure and any trends and relationships depicted among those variables. If you're struggling to find trends or decipher the data, go ahead and move to step 2.
2. **Work the Questions.** Start with the Now questions. As you answer the Now questions, you should become more familiar with the figures and what they represent. The remaining questions should be easier to tackle afterwards. If any reading is required outside of the figures, skim the text for the key terms from the question to identify the specific text you need to read.
3. **Work the Answers.** On Later passages, you should rely heavily on Process of Elimination!

LATER PRACTICE PASSAGE 1

Bats of the family *Vespertilionidae* (Vesper bats) are commonly found in North America. A guide for identifying Vesper bats found in Utah is presented in Table 1.

Students observed Vesper bats in a Utah nature reserve and recorded descriptions of them in Table 2.

Table 1			
Step	Trait	Appearance	Result
1	If the ears are	longer than 25 mm	go to Step 2
		shorter than 25 mm	go to Step 5
2	If the dorsum (back) has	3 white spots	*Euderma maculotum*
		no spots	go to Step 3
3	If the ears are	separated at the base	*Antrozous pallidus*
		not separated at the base	go to Step 4
4	If the muzzle has	well-defined skin glands	*Idionycteris phyllotis*
		ill-defined skin glands	*Corynorhinus townsendii*
5	If the uropatagium* is	heavily furred	go to Step 6
		not heavily furred	go to Step 7
6	If the fur color is	pale yellow at the base	*Lasiurus cinereus*
		dark with silver tips	*Lasionycteris noctivagans*
		brick red to rust	*Lasiurus blossevillii*
7	If the tragus** is	< 6 mm and curved	go to Step 8
		> 6 mm and straight	go to Step 9
8	If the forearm length is	> 40 mm	*Eptesicus fuscus*
		< 40 mm	*Pipistrellus hesperus*
9	If there is an obvious fringe of fur	on the edge of the uropatagium	*Myotis thysanodes*
		between the elbows and knees	*Myotis volans*
*Wing-like tissue between hind legs **Cartilage structure in the ear			

Table 2				
Bat	I	II	III	IV
Ears	20 mm long, separate at base	18 mm long	30 mm long, joined at base	15 mm long
Dorsum	no spots	no spots	no spots	no spots
Muzzle	ill-defined skin glands	ill-defined skin glands	well-defined skin glands	ill-defined skin glands
Uropatagium	not heavily furred	not heavily furred; only an obvious fringe of fur on its edge	not heavily furred	heavily furred
Fur	brown	brown	olive	black with silver tips
Tragus	4 mm, curved	7 mm, straight	9 mm, curved	4 mm, curved
Forearm	50 mm long	25 mm long	30 mm long	20 mm long

1. Based on the information in Tables 1 and 2, *Idionycteris phyllotis* most likely has an average forearm length that is:

   A. greater than 40 mm; Bat I has a forearm length greater than 40 mm.
   B. greater than 40 mm; Bat III has a forearm length less than 40 mm.
   C. less than 40 mm; Bat I has a forearm length greater than 40 mm.
   D. less than 40 mm; Bat III has a forearm length less than 40 mm.

2. Based on the given information, which of the following characteristics distinguishes Bat IV from a *Pipistrellus hesperus*?

   F. 4 mm and curved tragus
   G. 15 mm long ears
   H. 20 mm long forearm
   J. Heavily furred uropatagium

3. Based on Table 1, Bats I and II share the same results through Step:

   A. 1.
   B. 5.
   C. 7.
   D. 9.

4. Which of the following best describes the family *Vespertilionidae*?

   F. Mammals
   G. Protists
   H. Lampreys
   J. Birds

5. Based on Table 1, which of the following is likely to be most genetically similar to Bat II ?

   A. *Lasiurus blossevillii*
   B. *Idionycteris phyllotis*
   C. *Lasionyceris noctivagans*
   D. *Myotis volans*

LATER PRACTICE PASSAGE 1 EXPLANATIONS

1. **D** The question asks for the average forearm length of *Idionycteris phyllotis* based on Tables 1 and 2. Find *Idionycteris phyllotis* in Table 1 and circle it. *Idionycteris phyllotis* appears in Step 4, with the option of *well-defined skin glands*. In Table 2, only Bat III has *well-defined skin glands*, so look at the information about the forearm given for Bat III. Since Bat III has a forearm length that is 30 mm long, eliminate (A) and (B). The data about Bat I is not relevant to *Idionycteris phyllotis*, so eliminate (C). The correct answer is (D).

2. **J** The question asks which characteristic *distinguishes Bat IV from a Pipistrellus hesperus*. Check each answer choice against the information given about Bat IV and *Pipistrellus hesperus*. Bat IV is listed in in Table 2, and it has all the characteristics given in the answer choices. *Pipistrellus hesperus* is located in Step 8 of Table 1. Step 8 indicates *forearm length*, and *Pipistrellus hesperus* has a *forearm length* of *<40 mm*, which is consistent with (H). Eliminate (H) since this does not indicate a difference between the two bats. Step 7 indicates *tragus*. A measurement of *<6 mm and curved* gives the option of going to Step 8 where *Pipistrellus hesperus* is located. This is consistent with (F), so eliminate (F). The *uropatagium* is in Step 5. A *heavily furred uropatagium* leads to Step 6, which does not include *Pipistrellus hesperus*, so (J) describes a difference between the two bats. The *ears* are in Step 1; ears *shorter than 25 mm* lead to Step 5. From Step 5 it is possible to get to Step 7, and then Step 8, and to *Pipistrellus hesperus*, which is consistent with (G). Eliminate (G). The correct answer is (J).

3. **B** The question asks for the step number through which Bats I and II share the same results, according to Table 1. Check each answer choice against the information in the table. Step 1 indicates ear length. Bat I has ears that are 20 mm long and Bat II has ears that are 18 mm long. These are both *shorter than 25 mm*, so both bats share the same results. Next, look at Step 5, which indicates the *uropatagium*. Both Bats I and II share the trait of a *not heavily furred uropatagium*, so they share the same results through Step 5. For this reason, eliminate (A). Next, look at Step 7, which indicates the *tragus*. Bat I has a 4 mm curved *tragus* and Bat II has a 7 mm straight *tragus*. This difference leads to different results, so eliminate (C) and (D). The correct answer is (B).

4. **F** The question asks for the best description of the family *Vespertilionidae*. The word *Vespertilionidae* appears in the introduction, which indicates that it is a family of *Vesper bats*. The passage does not give any further information about the family, so this is an outside knowledge question. Bats are not *protists*, *lampreys*, or *birds*, so eliminate (G), (H), and (J). Bats are *mammals*. The correct answer is (F).

5. **D** The question asks for the bat that is *most genetically similar to Bat II*, according to Table 1. In Table 1, circle the names of the bats in the answer choices, and check their characteristics against those given for Bat II in Table 2. *Idionycteris phyllotis* appears in Step 4, as a result of choosing *well-defined skin glands*. Since Bat II has *ill-defined skin glands*, eliminate (B). Both *Lasionycteris noctivagans* and *Lasiurus blossevillii* appear in Step 6 of Table 2. All characteristics of those two bats up to Step 6 must be the same, and neither of those bats has the same *fur color* as Bat II, which means that neither of those bats could be *more genetically similar* to Bat II than the other; eliminate (A) and (C). *Myotis volans* appears in Step 9 of Table 1. To get to Step 9, a bat must have ears *shorter than 25 mm* from Step 1, a *not heavily furred uropatagium* from Step 5, and a *>6 mm and straight* tragus from Step 8. Bat II has all these characteristics, so it is *genetically similar* to *Myotis volans*. The correct answer is (D).

THIS PAGE IS INTENTIONALLY LEFT BLANK.

LATER PRACTICE PASSAGE 2

The *Citric cycle* is an essential process used to transform carbohydrates, lipids, and proteins into energy in aerobic organisms. If yeast is unable to produce *succinate*, it cannot survive. The Citric cycle steps leading to the creation of succinate in yeast are shown in Figure 1. Each step in this cycle is catalyzed by an enzyme, which is essential to overcome the energy barrier between reactant and product. In the first step, Enzyme 1 is the enzyme, citrate is the reactant, and isocitrate is the product.

Figure 1

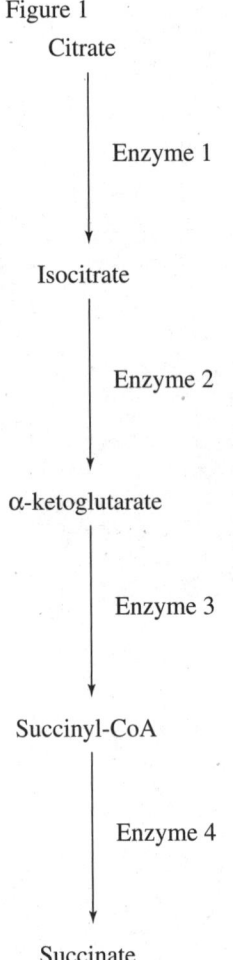

Citrate

Enzyme 1

Isocitrate

Enzyme 2

α-ketoglutarate

Enzyme 3

Succinyl-CoA

Enzyme 4

Succinate

Experiment

A scientist grew four strains of yeast on several different growth media. Each strain was unable to produce succinate because it lacked one of the enzymes required for the reaction pathway shown in Figure 1. Table 1 shows the results of the scientist's experiment: "Yes" indicates that the strain was able to grow in the basic nutrition solution (BNS) + the particular chemical. An undamaged strain of yeast would be able to grow in the basic nutrition solution without any additional chemical. If a strain was able to grow in a given growth medium, then it was able to produce succinate from the additional chemical added to the basic nutrition solution.

Table 1				
Growth medium	Yeast strain			
	W	X	Y	Z
BNS				
BNS + Isocitrate	Yes			
BNS + α-ketoglutarate	Yes	Yes		
BNS + Succinyl-CoA	Yes	Yes	Yes	
BNS + Succinate	Yes	Yes	Yes	Yes

If certain genes are damaged, the essential enzymes cannot be produced, which means that the reactions that the enzyme catalyzes cannot occur. Table 2 lists the genes responsible for the enzymes in the steps of the Citric cycle leading to succinate production in yeast. If an enzyme cannot be produced, then the product of the reaction that enzyme catalyzes cannot be synthesized and the reactant in that reaction will become highly concentrated. If a gene is damaged, then it is notated with a superscript negative sign, as in Cat3⁻; if a gene is not damaged, it is notated with a superscript positive sign, as in Cat3⁺.

Table 2	
Gene	Enzyme
Cat1	Enzyme 1
Cat2	Enzyme 2
Cat3	Enzyme 3
Cat4	Enzyme 4

1. Based on the information in the passage, which of the following is the correct notation for yeast Strain Y ?

   A. $Cat1^- \ Cat2^+ \ Cat3^- \ Cat4^+$
   B. $Cat1^- \ Cat2^- \ Cat3^+ \ Cat4^+$
   C. $Cat1^+ \ Cat2^+ \ Cat3^- \ Cat4^-$
   D. $Cat1^+ \ Cat2^+ \ Cat3^- \ Cat4^+$

2. Based on the information presented, the highest concentration of isocitrate would most likely be found in which of the following yeasts?

   F. Yeast that cannot produce Enzyme 1
   G. Yeast that cannot produce Enzyme 2
   H. Yeast that cannot produce Enzyme 3
   J. Yeast that cannot produce Enzyme 4

3. According to the information in the passage and Table 2, a strain of yeast that is $Cat1^+ \ Cat2^- \ Cat3^- \ Cat4^+$ *cannot* produce:

   A. Enzyme 1 and Enzyme 2.
   B. Enzyme 1 and Enzyme 4.
   C. Enzyme 2 and Enzyme 3.
   D. Enzyme 3 and Enzyme 4.

4. Strain X yeast was most likely unable to synthesize:

   F. isocitrate from citrate.
   G. α-ketoglutarate from isocitrate.
   H. succinyl-CoA from α-ketoglutarate.
   J. succinate from succinyl-CoA.

5. One of the growth media shown in Table 1 was a control that the scientist used to demonstrate that all four strains of yeast had genetic damage that prevented the reactions shown in Figure 1, the reactions which are responsible for the synthesis of succinate. Which growth media was used as a control?

   A. BNS
   B. BNS + succinate
   C. BNS + isocitrate
   D. BNS + succinyl-CoA

6. For each of the four strains of yeast, W–Z, shown in Table 1, if a given strain was able to grow in BNS + succinyl-CoA, then it was also able to grow in:

   F. BNS.
   G. BNS + isocitrate.
   H. BNS + α-ketoglutarate.
   J. BNS + succinate.

LATER PRACTICE PASSAGE 2 EXPLANATIONS

1. **D** The question asks for the correct notation of yeast Strain Y. In the second paragraph of the passage, it says that *each strain was unable to produce succinate because it lacked one of the enzymes required for the reaction pathway*. According to the information preceding Table 2, a damaged gene that does not produce an enzyme is denoted with a negative superscript. Therefore, the correct answer should have only one negative superscript since the passage states that each strain is missing only *one* enzyme. Eliminate (A), (B), and (C). The only answer that shows only one damaged gene is (D). Choice (D) indicates that Cat3 is damaged. If Enzyme 3 is not produced, then a yeast is unable to produce Succinyl-CoA and would therefore grow only if it were provided with Succinyl-CoA or the final product, succinate. This matches the information in Table 1 for Yeast Y. The correct answer is (D).

2. **G** The question asks which yeast would most likely contain *the highest concentration of isocitrate*. Since there is no information about *highest concentration* in any of the figures, look for these key words in the description of the experiment. Paragraph 3 says that a *reactant becomes highly concentrated if an enzyme cannot be produced* and *the product of the reaction that the enzyme catalyzes cannot be synthesized*. According to Figure 1, isocitrate is a reactant in the second step and it will become *highly concentrated* if Enzyme 2 cannot be produced. Choice (G) is consistent with this information. The correct answer is (G).

3. **C** The question asks which enzymes cannot be produced by a strain of yeast that is $Cat1^+$ $Cat2^-$ $Cat3^-$ $Cat4^+$, according to the passage and Table 2. Look for the key words *cannot produce* in the passage text above Table 2. Paragraph 3 says, *if certain genes are damaged, the essential enzymes cannot be produced*. It goes on to say that *if a gene is damaged, then it is notated with a superscript negative sign, as in $Cat3^-$; if a gene is not damaged, it is notated with a superscript positive sign, as in $Cat3^+$*. This means that $Cat2^-$ and $Cat3^-$ are both damaged and cannot produce their essential enzymes. Look at Table 2. The essential enzymes associated with $Cat2^-$ and $Cat3^-$ are Enzymes 2 and 3. The correct answer is (C).

4. **G** The question asks what *Strain X yeast was most likely unable to synthesize*. The yeast strains are shown in Table 1. Circle the column labeled Strain X. According to the explanation of the experiment above, *"Yes" indicates that the strain was able to grow in the basic nutrition solution (BNS) + the particular chemical*. Strain X was unable to grow in the BNS until α-ketoglutarate was added. This indicates that α-ketoglutarate could not be made naturally by Strain X. The only choice consistent with the data is (G). The correct answer is (G).

5. **A** The question asks *which growth media, shown in Table 1, was used as a control*. A control is an unaltered factor in an experiment that can be used as a standard of comparison against the groups in which another variable is altered. Look at Table 1. Each of the growth mediums contains BNS, and in four of the five media, something else was added to BNS. Because BNS is present in all of the media, the medium with only BNS must be the control. The correct answer is (A).

6. **J** The question asks which growth medium a strain of yeast would also be able to grow in if it had been able to grow in BNS + Succinyl-CoA, according to Table 1. Strains W, X, and Y were all able to grow in BNS + Succinyl-CoA, and every strain was able to grow in BNS + Succinate. The correct answer is (J).

NOW, LATER, LAST/NEVER

Remember that the passages on the ACT do not need to be completed in the order they are given. Start with the passages that you can complete quickly and with greater accuracy, and save the more complicated passages for later. If you run out of time, just pick a letter and use it to answer all questions on the harder passages you saved for last. You're bound to score points on at least some of them!

Some things to look for in a good **Now** passage include:

- short answer choices
- short question stems
- easy-to-spot trends in relationships between variables
- easy-to-read tables and graphs
- topics of particular interest to you

Use the following set of seven drill passages to work on your passage selection skills. Before completing each passage, take a few seconds to classify it as a **Now, Later,** or **Last/Never** passage. Then, start a stopwatch before completing the drill. Mark down the time spent on each passage in the space provided.

SCIENCE PASSAGE DRILL 1

Now   Later   Last/Never

Time Spent: _____

In agriculture, soils can be classified based on *mineral content* (the amount of various metals present in the soil), and *organic content* (the percent of soil volume occupied by material made by living organisms). Ideal concentrations of various minerals are given in parts per million (*ppm*) in Table 1. If the concentrations of different minerals, relative to their ideal concentrations, are all similar to each other, the soil is said to be *well defined*. If the concentrations of different minerals in a soil vary widely relative to each other, the soil is said to be *poorly defined*.

Table 1	
Mineral	Ideal concentration (ppm)
Nitrogen	22
Phosphorus	14
Potassium	129
Chloride	12
Sulfur	88
Iron	6.9
Manganese	2.7

Study 1

Soil was taken from 5 different farms to a laboratory. The soils were *desiccated* (all water was removed), and a 1 L sample of each soil was prepared. In order to make sure that no minerals were trapped within the organic matter of a soil, the organic matter of each soil was burned by heating the soil to 500°C for 20 minutes. The ash of the organic matter was removed, and the remaining soil analyzed for the concentration of various minerals. The results are shown, as percent of ideal concentration, in Table 2.

Table 2					
Mineral	Concentration of minerals (% of ideal concentration)				
	Farm 1	Farm 2	Farm 3	Farm 4	Farm 5
Nitrogen	89	112	160	78	210
Phosphorus	76	19	212	94	34
Chloride	124	106	64	87	65
Sulfur	290	97	189	102	112
Iron	57	26	73	91	165
Manganese	86	45	89	97	109

Study 2

To determine the percentage of the mass of each soil composed of organic matter, the above procedure was repeated, with the soil weighed before being heated to 500°C and after having the ash removed. The number of live cells (bacteria, fungi, etc.) in a cubic millimeter of each soil was determined by microscopic analysis. The results are presented in Table 3.

Table 3		
Farm	% organic matter	# living cells per mm³
1	7.1	2,964
2	8.9	3,920
3	4.8	1,642
4	6.6	2,672
5	18.9	9,467

1. Based on Table 1 and Table 2, the concentration, in ppm, of sulfur measured in the soil of Farm 1 was closest to:

   A. 88 ppm.
   B. 170 ppm.
   C. 255 ppm.
   D. 290 ppm.

2. Soils with more living cells per mm^3 generally consume more oxygen than soils with fewer living cells. Based on this information, the soil of which farm would be expected to consume the most oxygen?

   F. Farm 1
   G. Farm 2
   H. Farm 3
   J. Farm 5

3. If, in Study 2, before and after heating a soil sample to 500°C for 20 minutes and removing the ash, the mass of the sample was approximately the same, which of the following is the most reasonable conclusion?

   A. There was little or no water in the soil.
   B. There was a large quantity of water in the soil.
   C. There was little or no organic matter in the soil.
   D. There was little or no mineral content in the soil.

4. In Study 2, before heating the sample to 500°C, it was necessary for the scientists to desiccate the soil in order to ensure that:

   F. the water was not mistaken for a mineral.
   G. the water was not consumed by the living cells.
   H. it was possible to count live cells by making sure the soil didn't stick together.
   J. the mass of the water was not mistaken for organic matter.

5. Based on Study 2, if the scientists took a soil sample from another farm, and the number of living cells per mm^3 was determined to be 2,100, the % organic matter in that soil would most likely be:

   A. less than 4.8.
   B. between 4.8 and 6.6.
   C. between 6.6 and 7.1.
   D. greater than 7.1.

6. The soil of which of the farms would likely be considered the most well defined, based on the information in Study 1 ?

   F. Farm 1
   G. Farm 2
   H. Farm 3
   J. Farm 4

SCIENCE PASSAGE DRILL 1 EXPLANATIONS

1. **C**   The question asks for the concentration of sulfur in ppm in the soil on Farm 1. Refer to Table 2, which shows the concentration of minerals in each farm, *expressed as a percentage of the ideal concentration*. The concentration of sulfur in the soil on Farm 1 is 290% of the ideal concentration. To find the ideal concentration, refer to Table 1. According to Table 1, the ideal concentration of sulfur is 88 ppm. Since the concentration of sulfur in the soil on Farm 1 is almost 300% of this ideal concentration, the concentration of sulfur will be about *three times* the ideal concentration. Since 88 ppm × 3 is approximately 260 ppm, the best answer is 255 ppm. The correct answer is (C).

2. **J**   The question asks which farm's soil *would be expected to consume the most oxygen* based on the fact that *soils with more living cells per mm³ generally consume more oxygen than soils with fewer living cells.* Look at Table 3, which shows the number of *living cells per mm³* of the soil collected at the five different farms. The largest number under the heading *# living cells per mm³* is 9,467, which was collected at Farm 5. The correct answer is (J).

3   **C**   The question asks which conclusion would be the most reasonable if *the mass of the [soil] sample was approximately the same before and after heating a soil sample to 500°C for 20 minutes and removing the ash,* based on Study 2. Look for the key word *mass* in the description of the study to find out how this process affects the soil and its mass. It says that *to determine the percentage of the mass of each soil composed of organic matter,* the samples were *weighed before being heated to 500°C and after having the ash removed.* Choices (A) and (B) mention *water* but not *organic matter,* so eliminate them. Choice (C) mentions *organic matter,* so keep it. Choice (D) mentions *mineral content* but not *organic matter;* eliminate (D). The correct answer is (C).

4. **J**   The question asks why the scientists desiccated the soil in Study 2. Look for the key word *desiccate* in the description of Study 2. There is no mention of it; however, it does say that *the above procedure was repeated to determine the percentage of the mass of each soil composed of organic matter,* so look for the key word *desiccate* in the description of Study 1. It says that *the soils were desiccated,* which means *all water was removed.* Eliminate (F) because it refers to *minerals* and not *organic matter.* The text makes no mention of water being *consumed,* so eliminate (G). Eliminate (H) because the text never states anything about the soil sticking together. Choice (J) is consistent with the purpose of the study, to measure the organic matter. The correct answer is (J).

5. **B**   The question asks what the *% organic matter* in a soil sample with 2,100 *living cells per mm³* would be, according to Study 2. Look at the results of Study 2 found in Table 2. Look for numbers of *living cells per mm³* closest to 2,100. Farm 3 had 1,642 and Farm 4 had 2,672. So, *% organic matter* for this new soil sample should fall within the range of the *% organic matter* found on Farms 3 and 4, between 4.8 and 6.6. The correct answer is (B).

6. **J** The question asks which of the farms would likely be considered *the most well defined,* according to Study 1. Since there is no mention of *well defined* in the description of Study 1, look for those key words in the introduction. Paragraph 1 states that *if the concentrations of different minerals, relative to their ideal concentrations, are all similar to each other, the soil is said to be well defined.* Look for the farm that has mineral percentages most similar to each other in Table 2. The smallest range of mineral concentration is present in Farm 4. The correct answer is (J).

SCIENCE PASSAGE DRILL 2

Now   Later   Last/Never

Time Spent: _____

There are four planets in our solar system called gas giants: Jupiter, Saturn, Uranus, and Neptune. They are so named because they are composed largely of gases rather than solids. Figure 1 shows how temperatures of the atmospheres of Jupiter, Neptune, and Saturn vary with altitude in relation to the cloud tops. Table 1 gives the composition of the planets in both relative abundance of gases and the altitude at which those gases are most abundant. Table 2 gives what the temperature at the cloud tops would be without greenhouse warming.

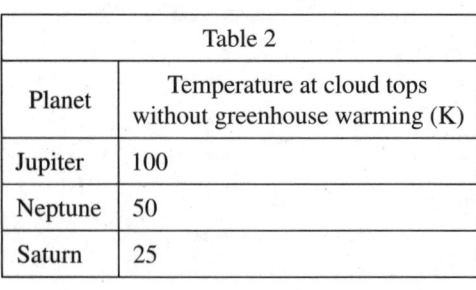

Table 2	
Planet	Temperature at cloud tops without greenhouse warming (K)
Jupiter	100
Neptune	50
Saturn	25

Figure 1

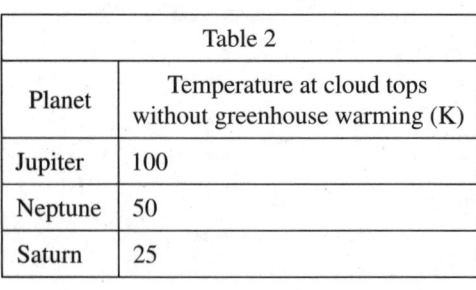

Table 1						
	Relative abundance (%)			Altitude above cloud tops where gas is most abundant (km)		
Gas	Jupiter	Neptune	Saturn	Jupiter	Neptune	Saturn
H	86.1	79.0	96.1	−1,000 to −70,000	−10,000 to −23,000	−1,000 to −60,000
He	13.6	18.0	3.3	−500 to −1,000	−500 to −10,000	−500 to −900
CH_3	0.2	3.0	0.4	0 to 300	−100 to 0	0 to 200
NH_3	0.0045	0	0.0035	0 to −100	–	−50 to −200
H_2O vapor	0.0055	0	0.0065	−50 to −100	–	−200 to −300

1. According to Figure 1, the temperature of Jupiter changes the most between:

   A. −150 km and −50 km.
   B. −50 km and 50 km.
   C. 50 km and 100 km.
   D. 100 km and 200 km.

2. Considering only the gases listed in Table 1, which gas is more abundant in the atmosphere of Jupiter than in the atmosphere of either Neptune or Saturn?

   F. H
   G. CH_3
   H. NH_3
   J. He

3. Based on Table 2, the average temperature at Saturn's cloud tops *without* greenhouse warming is how many degrees cooler than the temperature given in Figure 1 ?

   A. 5 K
   B. 25 K
   C. 75 K
   D. 150 K

4. Which of the following statements about H and He in the atmospheres of the 3 planets is supported by the data in Table 1 ?

   F. Both Saturn and Neptune have a higher relative abundance of He than of H.
   G. Both Saturn and Jupiter have a higher relative abundance of He than of H.
   H. Both Jupiter and Neptune have an equivalent relative abundance of He and H.
   J. Both Saturn and Neptune have a lower relative abundance of He than of H.

5. A researcher states that Neptune, Saturn, and Jupiter all exhibit greenhouse warming at the cloud tops. Does the information in the passage support this statement?

   A. Yes; all three planets are between 25 K and 100 K warmer at the cloud tops than they would be without greenhouse warming.
   B. Yes; all three planets are between 25 K and 100 K cooler at the cloud tops than they would be without greenhouse warming.
   C. No; Neptune is 50 K warmer at the cloud tops than it would be without greenhouse warming.
   D. No; Neptune is the same temperature at the cloud tops as it would be without greenhouse warming.

SCIENCE PASSAGE DRILL 2 EXPLANATIONS

1. **A** The question asks which range of altitudes has the largest temperature change on Jupiter, according to Figure 1. Look at Figure 1 and use the values in the answer choices to determine the temperature change within each range of altitudes. Choice (A) shows a range of –150 km to –50 km. Between those altitudes, the temperature on Jupiter ranges from about 150 K to 300 K, a difference of 150 K. Choice (B) shows a range of –50 km to 50 km. Between those altitudes, the temperature on Jupiter ranges from about 150 K to 200 K, a difference of 50 K. This temperature change is smaller than that of (A), so eliminate (B). Choice (C) shows a range of 50 km to 100 km. Between those altitudes, the temperature on Jupiter ranges from about 200 K to 210 K, a difference of 10 K, which is smaller than that of (A), so eliminate (C). Choice (D) shows a range of 100 km to 200 km. Between those altitudes, the temperature on Jupiter ranges from about 190 K to 200 K, a difference of 10 K, so eliminate (D). The largest temperature change occurred in the range of altitudes in (A). The correct answer is (A).

2. **H** The question asks *which gas is more abundant in the atmosphere of Jupiter than in the atmospheres of either Neptune or Saturn,* according to Table 1. Look at Table 1. Use the answer choices to find the *relative abundance* of each gas on Jupiter and compare the value to that found on the other two planets. The amount of H is greater on Saturn than on Jupiter, so eliminate (F). The amount of CH_3 is greater on both Neptune and Saturn than on Jupiter, so eliminate (G). The amount of NH_3 is greatest on Jupiter, so keep (H). The amount of He is greatest on Neptune, so eliminate (J). The correct answer is (H).

3. **C** The question asks for the difference between *the average temperature at Saturn's cloud tops without greenhouse warming,* given in Table 2, and *the temperature given in Figure 1.* Look at Table 2. The *temperature at cloud tops* on Saturn is 25 K. Look at Figure 1. Find the curve that represents the temperature on Saturn. Altitude is located on the y-axis; find 0 km above cloud tops. Draw a line to meet Saturn's curve, and then draw a line down to the x-axis to determine the temperature at the cloud tops, which is 100 K. The difference between 25 K and 100 K is 75 K, (C). The correct answer is (C).

4. **J** The question asks which statement about H and He is supported by the data in Table 1. Look at Table 1 and eliminate any answers that contradict the given data. Choice (F) states that *both Saturn and Neptune have a higher relative abundance of He than of H.* The relative abundance of He on Saturn is 3.3%, and the relative abundance of H on Saturn is 96.1%. The relative abundance of He is not higher than that of H, so eliminate (F). Choice (G) also states that Saturn has *a higher relative abundance of He than of H,* so eliminate (G). Choice (H) states that *both Jupiter and Neptune have an equivalent relative abundance of He and H.* The relative abundance of He on Jupiter is 13.6% and on Neptune it is 18%. They are not equivalent, so eliminate (H). Choice (J) is consistent with the data in Table 1. The correct answer is (J).

5.   **D**   The question asks if the passage supports the statement that *Neptune, Saturn, and Jupiter all exhibit greenhouse warming at the cloud tops*. The cloud top temperatures for the three planets without greenhouse warming are 100 K for Jupiter, 50 K for Neptune, and 25 K for Saturn. Now look at Figure 1 to find the actual temperatures for the three planets at the cloud tops. Draw a horizontal line across the 0 km point on the graph. Find the points of intersection for each planet. The cloud top temperatures for the three planets are 50 K for Neptune, 100 K for Saturn, and 150 K for Jupiter. Notice that the temperature on Neptune is the same in both Figure 1 and Table 2. Therefore, the statement in the question is *not* supported by the passage. Eliminate (A) and (B). The reason the statement is false is because Neptune's observed temperature remains the same as that without greenhouse warming. The correct answer is (D).

SCIENCE PASSAGE DRILL 3

Now   Later   Last/Never

Time Spent: _____

Pressure, temperature, volume, and amount of reactant are four variables that affect the rate at which a reaction in the gas phase occurs. A change in any of these variables changes the likelihood of particles running into each other and reacting.

Pressure is measured in atmospheres, atm, where 1 atm is the sea level pressure of Earth's atmosphere. Volume is measured in liters, L. The amount of reactant is measured in moles, where 1 mole is 6.02×10^{23} molecules.

Figure 1 shows how pressure affects the gaseous reactants in an experiment. Figures 2 and 3 show how the rate of Reaction A is affected by pressure and temperature, respectively.

Figure 1

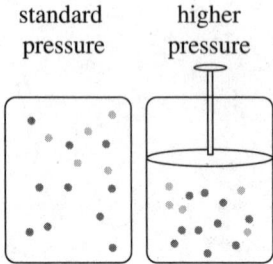

standard pressure   higher pressure

as pressure increases, the concentration of particles increases

Figure 2

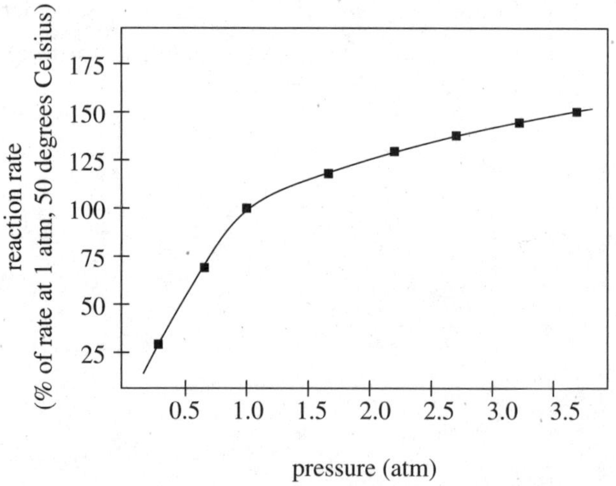

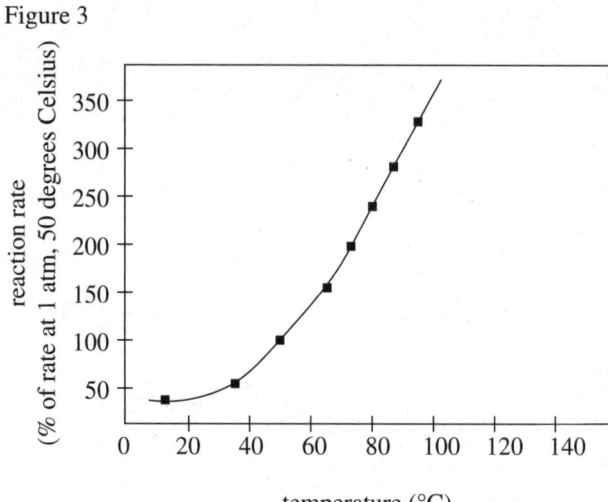

pressure (atm)

Figure 3

temperature (°C)

1. A scientist claimed that increasing temperature increases the rate at which Reaction A occurs and increasing pressure increases the rate at which Reaction A occurs. Is the scientist's claim supported by the data in Figures 2 and 3 ?

   A. Yes; the rate at which Reaction A occurred increased as temperature increased and increased as pressure increased.
   B. Yes; the rate at which Reaction A occurred increased as pressure decreased.
   C. No; the rate at which Reaction A occurred increased as temperature increased, but decreased as pressure increased.
   D. No; the rate at which Reaction A occurred decreased as pressure increased.

2. According to Figures 2 and 3, the reactions occur at the same rate at what pressure and temperature?

   F. 20°C and 2.0 atm
   G. 40°C and 1.5 atm
   H. 50°C and 1.0 atm
   J. 70°C and 1.5 atm

3. The amounts of reactants in Reaction A are 1 mole/L of Compound Y and 2 mole/L of Compound Z. According to the passage, the number of molecules of Compound Y is:

   A. one-quarter of the number of molecules of Compound Z in the reactants.
   B. one-half the number of molecules of Compound Z in the reactants.
   C. equal to the number of molecules of Compound Z in the reactants.
   D. twice the number of molecules of Compound Z in the reactants.

4. A scientist tests a new Reaction B. This reaction is conducted with the same gas phase reactants, volume, and temperature as Reaction A, but the amounts (moles) of reactants are doubled. Based only on the information in the passage and Figures 1–3, how will the rate of Reaction B compare with the rate of Reaction A ?

   F. Reaction B will be slower than Reaction A because temperature will be lower.
   G. Reaction B will be faster than Reaction A because temperature will be lower.
   H. Reaction B will be faster than Reaction A because the concentration of reactants is greater, so the likelihood of reactant molecules colliding and reacting is greater.
   J. Reaction B will be slower than Reaction A because the concentration of reactants is greater, so the likelihood of reactant molecules colliding and reacting is greater.

5. Based on the data in Figures 2 and 3, which of the following changes would lead to the greatest increase in the reaction rate of Reaction A ?

   A. Decreasing the pressure from 1 atm to 0.5 atm
   B. Increasing the pressure from 1 atm to 3 atm
   C. Decreasing the temperature from 50°C to 20°C
   D. Increasing the temperature from 50°C to 100°C

6. Which of the following is true of the volume of the gas in Figure 2 as the pressure increases from 1.0 atm to 2.0 atm ?

   F. It increases by 50% because pressure and volume are inversely proportional.
   G. It decreases by 50% because pressure and volume are inversely proportional.
   H. It increases by 50% because pressure and volume are directly proportional.
   J. It decreases by 50% because pressure and volume are directly proportional.

SCIENCE PASSAGE DRILL 3 EXPLANATIONS

1. **A**   The question asks whether a scientist's claim that *increasing temperature increases the rate at which Reaction A occurs and increasing pressure increases the rate at which Reaction A occurs* is consistent with Figures 2 and 3. Figure 2 shows that as pressure increases, reaction rate also increases. Figure 3 shows that as temperature increases, reaction rate also increases. The scientist's claim is true, so eliminate both (C) and (D). Eliminate (B) because it inaccurately states that *the rate at which Reaction A occurred increased as pressure decreased.* The correct answer is (A).

2. **H**   The question asks, *according to Figures 2 and 3,* at *what pressure and temperature* do the reactions occur *at the same rate.* Look at Figure 2. According to the label on the *y*-axis, the temperature is constant at 50°C in this figure. Eliminate (F), (G), and (J), because the only possible temperature in Figure 2 is 50°C. Therefore, the only point in common between the two figures occurs at 50°C and 1.0 atm, where the reaction rate is 100%. The correct answer is (H).

3. **B**   The question asks how *the number of molecules* in 1 mole/L *of Compound Y* compares to *the number of molecules* in 2 mole/L *of Compound Z,* according to the passage. Look for the words *molecule* and *mole* in the passage. Paragraph 2 states that *1 mole is 6.02×10^{23} molecules.* Since Compound Y contains 1 mole, it has 6.02×10^{23} molecules. Compound Z has 2 moles, so it has 12.04×10^{23} molecules. Compound Y has half as many molecules as Compound Z. The correct answer is (B).

4. **H**   The question asks how the rate of Reaction B compares to that of Reaction A, when Reaction B *is conducted with the same gas phase reactants, volume, and temperature as Reaction A, but the amounts (moles) of reactants are doubled,* based on the information in the passage and Figures 1–3. Eliminate (F) and (G) because the question says that temperature does not change. Look for information in the passage about *reactants.* The first paragraph states that *pressure, temperature, volume, and amount of reactant are four variables that affect the rate at which a reaction in the gas phase occurs* and that *a change in any one of these variables changes the likelihood of particles running into each other and reacting.* Reaction B will be faster than Reaction A because it has more reactants. Eliminate (J) because it states the opposite. The correct answer is (H).

5. **D**   The question asks which change would lead to the greatest increase in the reaction rate of Reaction A, based on the data in Figures 2 and 3. According to Figure 2, reaction rate increases with increasing pressure, so eliminate (A). According to Figure 3, reaction rate also increases with increasing temperature, so eliminate (C). In Figure 2, increasing the pressure from 1.0 atm to 3.0 atm as suggested in (B) causes only modest increases in reaction rate (from 100% to about 140%). Meanwhile, increasing the temperature from 50°C to 100°C would cause the reaction rate to increase drastically (from 100% to about 325%). Therefore, this is the change that would lead to the greatest increase in the reaction rate of Reaction A. The correct answer is (D).

6. **G**   The question asks about the volume of the gas in Figure 2 as the pressure increases from 1.0 atm to 2.0 atm. Figure 1 shows that as pressure increases, the concentration of particles increases and the volume decreases. Therefore, as the pressure increases from 1.0 atm to 2.0 atm, the volume will decrease. Eliminate (F) and (H). This relationship is inversely proportional (one value increases as the other decreases), so eliminate (J). The correct answer is (G).

THIS PAGE IS INTENTIONALLY LEFT BLANK.

SCIENCE PASSAGE DRILL 4

Now   Later   Last/Never

Time Spent: _____

Many viruses are known to persist more prevalently during certain times of the year. A study of four relatively unknown viruses was conducted to examine their annual rate of prevalence and mortality in a host population. A large survey was conducted of a local population for the presence of antigen markers indicative of viral exposures to the four virus types (Viruses A–D). Measurements were acquired monthly beginning in January of 2000 and concluding two years later. All monthly measurements were averaged for comparison.

Figure 1 shows the incidence (cases per 1,000 individuals studied) of viral infections attributed to each viral type over the duration of the study. Figure 2 shows the number of deaths (per 1,000 individuals studied) attributed to Virus A and D infections.

Figure 1

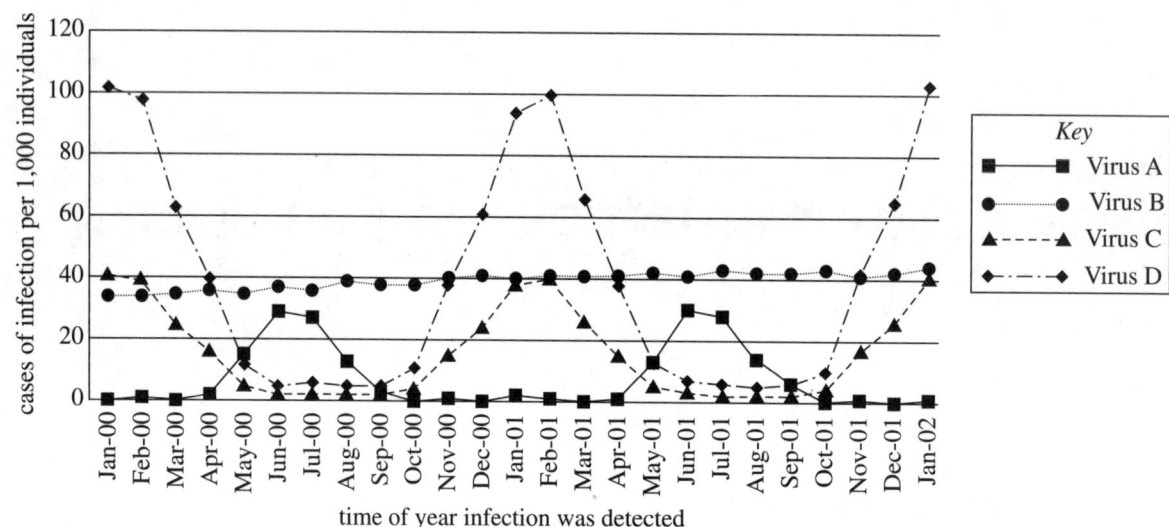

Figure 2

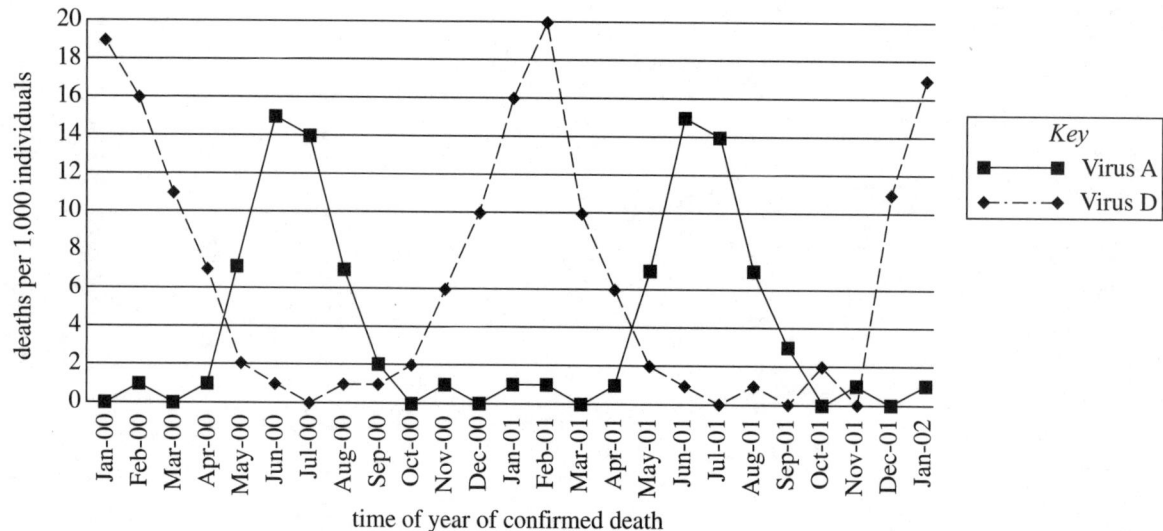

1. A study shows that many seasonal flu viruses thrive in the winter because they are more stable in cold temperatures and the lower humidity allows the particles to remain air-borne longer. Changes in temperature and humidity likely have the *least* effect on which of the following viruses?

   A. Virus A
   B. Virus B
   C. Virus C
   D. Virus D

2. In a previous study, a virologist claimed that the incidence of Virus B has always exceeded the incidence of Virus C. As shown in Figure 1, the data for which of the following months is *inconsistent* with the virologist's claims?

   F. January 2000
   G. February 2001
   H. August 2001
   J. December 2001

3. If approximately 800 cases of Virus B were recorded in the surveyed population in November 2000, which of the following is closest to the total population surveyed?

   A.   320
   B.   2,000
   C. 20,000
   D. 32,000

4. During both years of the survey, in one month every year, 7 out of 1,000 individuals died as a result of infection with Virus A and 2 out of 1,000 individuals died as a result of infection with Virus D. According to Figure 2, these data most likely were obtained during which of the following months?

   F. January
   G. March
   H. May
   J. October

5. The *case fatality rate* of a virus is the percentage of in-fected individuals that die from the illness. Based on the information in Figures 1 and 2, compared to Virus A, the case fatality rate of Virus D is:

   A. higher; there are more total deaths from Virus D than from Virus A.
   B. lower; approximately half of the cases of infection from Virus A lead to death.
   C. higher; approximately half of the cases of infection from Virus A lead to death.
   D. lower; there are more total deaths from Virus D than from Virus A.

SCIENCE PASSAGE DRILL 4 EXPLANATIONS

1. **B** The question asks which virus would be the least affected by temperature and humidity. According to the question, temperature and humidity vary by season, but by looking at Figure 1, the number of infected cases from Virus B (circle data points) remain unchanged throughout the year, independent of the season. Therefore, the correct answer is (B).

2. **F** The question asks which data is inconsistent with the virologist's claim that *the incidence of Virus B has always exceeded the incidence of Virus C*. Examine Figure 1, and look for time points when the incidence of Virus C (triangle data points) was actually *higher* than the incidence of Virus B (circle data points). Use the answer choices to help. Start with (F), which points to January of 2000. Since the triangle data point is *higher* than the circle data point, the incidence of Virus C is actually *higher* than the incidence of Virus B. Since this time point is inconsistent with the virologist's claim, the correct answer is (F).

3. **C** The question asks what value is the closest to the total population surveyed in November of 2000 given that 800 cases of Virus B were recorded during this month. According to the data in Figure 1, 40 cases of infection of Virus B were recorded for every 1,000 individuals surveyed in November of 2000. Set up a proportion to find the total population surveyed: $\frac{40}{1,000} = \frac{800}{x}$. Cross-multiply to get $40x = 800,000$. Divide both sides by 40 to find that $x = 20,000$. The correct answer is (C).

4. **H** The question asks during which months the data in Figure 2 shows that 7 of 1,000 individuals died as a result of infection with Virus A and 2 out of 1,000 individuals died as a result of infection with Virus D. Refer to Figure 2 and find which months show 7 individuals died from Virus A (square data points). In both May and August of both years, 7 individuals died from Virus A. Since August is not an answer choice, the correct answer must be (H). Double-check by confirming that 2 individuals died from Virus D (diamond data points) in May of both years. The correct answer is (H).

5. **B** The question asks about the *case fatality rate* of Viruses A and D and defines case fatality rate as *the percentage of infected individuals who die from the illness*. Start by examining Virus A in both graphs. In Figure 1, the largest incidence of infection for Virus A occurred during June and July, with approximately 30 cases per 1,000 individuals. Now look at Virus A in Figure 2. During June and July, there were approximately 15 deaths from infection with Virus A. This means that the case fatality rate of Virus A was about 50%. Now compare this to Virus D. In Figure 1, the largest incidence of infection for Virus D occurred during January of 2001, with approximately 100 cases per 1,000 individuals. Now look at Virus D in Figure 2. During January of 2001, there were approximately 20 deaths from infection with Virus D. This means that the case fatality rate of Virus D was about 20%. Therefore, the case fatality rate of Virus D is *lower* than that of Virus A. Eliminate (A) and (C). Since (B) gives the correct explanation that approximately half of the cases of infection from Virus A lead to death, the correct answer is (B).

THIS PAGE IS INTENTIONALLY LEFT BLANK.

SCIENCE PASSAGE DRILL 5

Now   Later   Last/Never

Time Spent: _____

Methane (CH_4) is an important energy source and a powerful greenhouse gas. CH_4 levels in the atmosphere are increasing, largely as a result of increasing livestock populations and energy emissions. Two scientists debate possible consequences of rising levels of atmospheric methane.

Scientist 1

Increasing CH_4 levels are a serious concern because, in the atmosphere, CH_4 can be converted into *formaldehyde* (H_2CO). H_2CO is a dangerous chemical, banned in some countries and used as an embalming fluid in others.

When *ozone* (O_3) is struck by solar radiation (light) in the presence of water, *hydroxyl radicals* ($\cdot OH$) are created (Reaction 1):

(1) $$light + O_3 + H_2O \rightarrow 2 \cdot OH + O_2$$

When $\cdot OH$ comes into contact with CH_4, another radical, $\cdot CH_3$, is formed (Reaction 2):

(2) $$\cdot OH + CH_4 \rightarrow \cdot CH_3 + H_2O$$

In the presence of oxygen (O_2) and nitric oxide (NO), the highly reactive $\cdot CH_3$ is converted into H_2CO (Reaction 3):

(3) $$\cdot CH_3 + NO + 2O_2 \rightarrow H_2CO + NO_2 + HO_2$$

The product HO_2 is unstable and reacts with NO, yielding more $\cdot OH$ (Reaction 4):

(4) $$HO_2 + NO \rightarrow NO_2 + \cdot OH$$

Together, Reactions 2–4 are called a *chain reaction* because the $\cdot OH$ formed in Reaction 4 can react with another CH_4 molecule in Reaction 2:

(2) $$\cdot OH + CH_4 \rightarrow \cdot CH_3 + H_2O$$

(3) $$\cdot CH_3 + NO + 2O_2 \rightarrow H_2CO + NO_2 + HO_2$$

(4) $$HO_2 + NO \rightarrow NO_2 + \cdot OH$$

As a result, one $\cdot OH$ can convert a great deal of CH_4. At current CH_4 levels, this chain reaction is the primary fate of atmospheric $\cdot OH$, making the formation of H_2CO an urgent concern.

Scientist 2

H_2CO is a dangerous chemical, but atmospheric formaldehyde levels will not increase dramatically due to methane emissions. *Carbon monoxide* (CO) generation may be the greater concern. Hydroxyl radicals can break down methane, leading to the formation of H_2CO and nitric oxide, as in Reactions 1–4; in the presence of light, however, H_2CO quickly decomposes to CO and *hydrogen*, H_2 (Reaction 5):

(5) $$H_2CO \rightarrow H_2 + CO$$

Furthermore, the $\cdot OH$ generated by Reactions 1 and 4 will react rapidly with any H_2CO in the atmosphere to produce CO and water (Reaction 6):

(6) $$H_2CO + 2 \cdot OH \rightarrow CO + 2H_2O$$

In addition to reducing the amount of H_2CO by breaking down the H_2CO molecule, this reaction removes OH from the atmosphere, inhibiting the chain reaction of Reactions 2–4.

1. Which of the following substances do the two scientists agree must be present in order for $\cdot CH_3$ to be generated by atmospheric methane?

   A. H_3O^+
   B. NO_2
   C. HNO_3
   D. O_3

2. Which of the following graphs reflects Scientist 1's hypothesis of how levels of H_2CO in the atmosphere will change as more CH_4 is released into the atmosphere?

F.

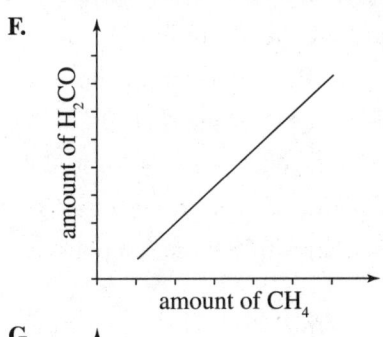

G.

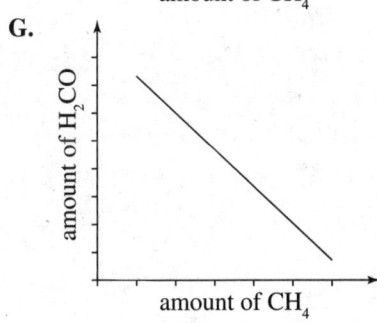

H.

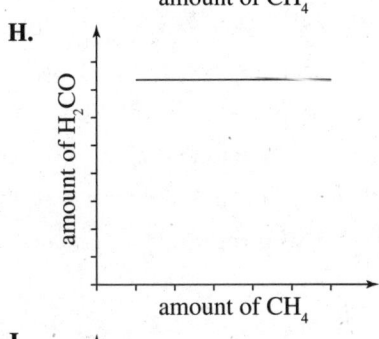

J.

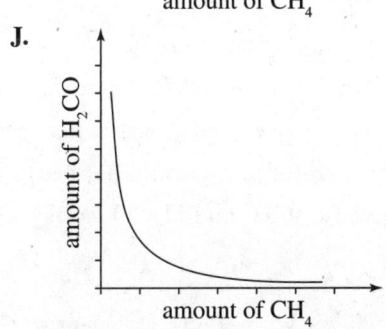

3. A student suggested that the molecular mass of either product in Reaction 5 would be greater than the molecular mass of the reactant in Reaction 5. Is he correct?

A. No; H_2CO is composed not of molecules, but of atoms.
B. Yes; the mass of a molecule of H_2CO is greater than the mass of either reactant.
C. No; the mass of a molecule of H_2CO is greater than the mass of either product.
D. Yes; the mass of a molecule of CO is greater than the mass of a molecule of H_2.

4. In certain parts of the atmosphere, the amount of O_3 is decreasing. As O_3 levels decrease, which of the following would Scientist 1 *most strongly agree with* regarding the levels of $\cdot CH_3$ and H_2CO in the atmosphere?

F. The amount of $\cdot CH_3$ would increase and the amount of H_2CO would decrease.
G. The amount of $\cdot CH_3$ would decrease and the level of H_2CO would remain constant.
H. The amounts of $\cdot CH_3$ and H_2CO would both decrease.
J. The amounts of $\cdot CH_3$ and H_2CO would both increase.

5. Of the following statements, with which would Scientist 2 *most strongly disagree*?

A. O_3 is involved in the generation of H_2CO in the atmosphere.
B. $\cdot OH$ is contributing to the formation of carbon monoxide in the atmosphere.
C. Solar radiation contributes to the breakdown of CH_4.
D. As CH_4 emissions increase, levels of H_2CO will rise dramatically.

6. After examining Scientist 1's hypothesis, Scientist 2 claimed that Reaction 3 would lead to increased levels of carbon monoxide. By which of the following explanations would Scientist 2 most likely support this argument?

F. Reaction 3 reduces the amount of NO present, inhibiting Reaction 4.
G. Reaction 3 produces H_2CO, which can react in Reaction 5 and Reaction 6.
H. Reaction 3 produces HO_2, which can react with H_2CO to produce CO.
J. Reaction 3 reduces the amount of O_2 present, making it more difficult for CO to form.

SCIENCE PASSAGE DRILL 5 EXPLANATIONS

1. **D** The question asks which substances both scientists agree must be present for $\bullet CH_3$ *to be generated by atmospheric methane.* Look at each scientist's explanation one at a time, and use Process of Elimination. The generation of $\bullet CH_3$ is described by Scientist 1 in Reaction 2, and one of the important components of Reaction 2, $\bullet OH$, is generated in Reaction 1. Neither Reaction 1 nor Reaction 2 includes H_3O^+, NO_2, or HNO_3, so eliminate (A), (B), and (C). O_3 is one of the reactants of Reaction 1, so keep (D). Scientist 2 does not explicitly discuss the generation of $\bullet CH_3$ but does say that *the $\bullet OH$ generated by Reactions 1 and 4 will react rapidly with any H_2CO in the atmosphere,* which means Scientist 2 believes that those reactions occur. The correct answer is (D).

2. **F** The question asks which graph shows Scientist 1's idea of the relationship between H_2CO and CH_4. Look for the key terms H_2CO and CH_4 in Scientist 1's hypothesis. Reactions 2 and 3 show that CH_4 starts a chain of reactions that increases H_2CO. Thus, if CH_4 levels rise, H_2CO levels will also rise. Keep (F) because it accurately describes this relationship. Eliminate (G) and (J) because they both show H_2CO decreasing as CH_4 rises. Eliminate (H) because it shows H_2CO levels remaining constant. The correct answer is (F).

3. **C** The question asks whether the student's suggestion is correct. The suggestion is that *the molecular mass of either product in Reaction 5 would be greater than the molecular mass of the reactant in Reaction 5.* Look at Reaction 5. Because both sides of the reaction contain the same atoms, the reactant (that is, the left side) is heavier than either product (the right side) because the reactant contains all the atoms in the reaction, while each product contains only a portion of them. Thus, the student's suggestion is wrong; eliminate (B) and (D). Although the reason in (A) is true (H_2CO is a molecule that is made up of atoms), it does not describe why the student is incorrect. Eliminate (A). Choice (C) accurately describes why the student is incorrect. The correct answer is (C).

4. **H** The question asks which statement Scientist 1 would *most strongly agree* with, based on decreasing O_3. Look for the key terms O_3, $\bullet CH_3$, and H_2CO in Scientist 1's hypothesis. O_3 appears in Reaction 1, the beginning of a series of reactions that increase first $\bullet CH_3$ and then H_2CO. Thus, there is a direct relationship between O_3 and $\bullet CH_3$ and H_2CO, so if O_3 *decreases,* the other two will also decrease. Eliminate (F) and (G) because O_3 does not have different effects on $\bullet CH_3$ and H_2CO. Eliminate (J) because $\bullet CH_3$ and H_2CO would not *increase.* The correct answer is (H).

5. **D** The question asks which statement Scientist 2 would *most strongly disagree* with. Look at Scientist 2's hypothesis. Scientist 2 states that *atmospheric formaldehyde levels will not increase dramatically due to methane emissions.* O_3 is described in Reaction 1, and Scientist 2 indicates that Reaction 1 does occur, so eliminate (A). Scientist 2 states that *$\bullet OH$ generated by Reactions 1 and 4 will react rapidly with any H_2CO in the atmosphere to produce CO,* which supports (B). Eliminate (B). *Solar radiation* and CH_4 are described in Reactions 1 and 2, and Scientist 2 believes Reaction 1 happens and never specifically mentions Reaction 2; eliminate (C). Choice (D) is directly contradicted by Scientist 2. The correct answer is (D).

6. **G**   The question asks how Scientist 2 would support the new claim that Reaction 3 leads to increased levels of carbon monoxide. Look at Scientist 2's hypothesis and at Reaction 3. Scientist 2 never discusses NO, so eliminate (F). Choice (G) accurately describes Reactions 3, 5, and 6, so keep (G). Choice (H) accurately describes Reaction 3, but Scientist 2 never discusses HO_2, so eliminate (H). Choice (J) also accurately describes Reaction 3, but Scientist 2 never discusses O_2, so eliminate (J). The correct answer is (G).

SCIENCE PASSAGE DRILL 6

Now   Later   Last/Never

Time Spent: _____

The 4 different blood types in sheep are A, B, AB, and O. The blood type of an offspring is determined by the blood types of its parents. Each parent contributes one version of a gene, or an *allele*, to its offspring. The *genotype* of an offspring refers to the combination of the offspring's two alleles, each of which came from one parent. The *phenotype* refers to the observable characteristics of a trait.

There are three possible alleles of this gene: the type-A blood allele (I^A), the type-B blood allele (I^B), and the type-O blood allele (I^O). Both I^A and I^B are *dominant* to I^O, and I^O is *recessive* to I^A and I^B. This means that an individual with one I^A and one I^O will have type-A blood, and an individual with one I^B and one I^O will have type-B blood. When an individual has one I^A and one I^B allele, this individual will have type-AB blood, due to the *codominance* of the I^A and I^B alleles.

Table 1	
Blood Type	Possible Genotypes
A	$I^A I^A$ or $I^A I^O$
B	$I^B I^B$ or $I^B I^O$
AB	$I^A I^B$
O	$I^O I^O$

To explore the inheritance patterns of blood types in sheep, researchers conducted 4 analyses. In each analysis, male and female sheep of differing blood types were mated and the resultant blood types of their offspring recorded.

Analysis 1

One thousand males with type-O blood were mated with 1,000 females with type-AB blood. The following blood types were observed in the offspring:

Type A: 50%
Type B: 50%

Analysis 2

Two hundred of the type-A offspring from Analysis 1 were mated with 200 type-O mates from no previous experiment. The following blood types were observed in the offspring:

Type A: 50%
Type O: 50%

Analysis 3

One hundred of the type-A offspring from Analysis 1 parented children with 100 type-B offspring from Analysis 1. The following blood types were observed in the offspring:

Type A: 25%
Type B: 25%
Type AB: 25%
Type O: 25%

Analysis 4

Twenty-five of the type-A offspring from Analysis 3 were mated with type-B mates with Genotype $I^B I^B$ who were not from any previous analysis. The following blood types were observed in the offspring:

Type AB: 50%
Type B: 50%

1. Which of the following is true of the offspring produced in Analysis 4 ?

   A. Some of the offspring have both the same genotype and phenotype as one of their parents.
   B. Some of the offspring have the same genotype as one of their parents, but no offspring have the same phenotype as a parent.
   C. Some of the offspring have the same phenotype as one of their parents, but no offspring have the same genotype as a parent.
   D. None of the offspring have the same phenotype or genotype as one of their parents.

2. The ratio of blood types containing at least one I^A allele to the blood types containing at least one I^B allele produced in Analysis 3 was:

   F. 1:0.
   G. 1:1.
   H. 2:1.
   J. 3:1.

3. An offspring whose blood type exhibits codominance has which of the following genotypes?

   A. $I^B I^B$
   B. $I^B I^O$
   C. $I^A I^B$
   D. $I^A I^O$

4. In Analysis 3, the offspring used from Analysis 1 most likely had which of the following genotypes?

   F. $I^A I^O$ and $I^B I^B$
   G. $I^A I^O$ and $I^B I^O$
   H. $I^A I^A$ and $I^B I^B$
   J. $I^A I^A$ and $I^B I^O$

5. Some or all of the offspring had 1 allele for type-O blood in Analyses:

   A. 1 and 2 only.
   B. 2 and 3 only.
   C. 1, 2, and 4 only.
   D. 1, 2, 3, and 4.

6. Suppose that 300 offspring were produced in Analysis 3. Based on the results, the number of offspring with type-B blood produced in Analysis 3 would most likely have been closest to:

   F. 25.
   G. 50.
   H. 75.
   J. 100.

SCIENCE PASSAGE DRILL 6 EXPLANATIONS

1. **C** The question asks about the offspring produced in Analysis 4. The passage states that *phenotype refers to the observable characteristics of a trait*, which is the blood type in this case. In Analysis 4, the phenotypes of the parents were type-A and type-B. Meanwhile, the phenotypes of the offspring were type-AB and type-B. Since some of the offspring have the same phenotype as a parent (type-B), eliminate (B) and (D), which contradict this information. Since the remaining choices ask for a comparison between the genotypes of the parents and their offspring, it is important to figure out genotypes for both parents and their offspring. The study states that the type-B parent is $I^B I^B$, but the choices in Table 1 indicate that the type-B offspring can either be $I^B I^B$ or $I^B I^O$. All of the offspring must have inherited one I^B allele from their type-B parent. However, since the other parent is type-A, the only alleles these offspring could have inherited from their type-A parent are I^A or I^O. Accordingly, all of the offspring are either $I^A I^B$ (type-AB) or $I^B I^O$ (type-B). Since the two different types of offspring all have different genotypes as both of their parents, eliminate (A). The correct answer is (C).

2. **G** The question asks for the *ratio of blood types containing at least one I^A allele to the blood types containing at least one I^B allele produced in Analysis 3*. Look at Analysis 3. There are two types that contain I^A: type-A (25%) and type-AB (25%). Together, they make up 50% of the offspring. There are two types that contain I^B, type-B (25%) and type-AB (25%). Together, they make up 50% of the offspring. Because they each represent 50% of the offspring, it is a 1:1 ratio. The correct answer is (G).

3. **C** The question asks which genotypes would exhibit *codominance*. Since there is no information about *codominance* in the table, look for the key word *codominance* in the text of the passage. The second paragraph says, *when an individual has one I^A and one I^B allele, this individual will have type-AB blood, due to the codominance of the I^A and I^B alleles*. Choice (C) contains $I^A I^B$, which is type-AB blood. The correct answer is (C).

4. **G** The question asks about the genotypes of *the offspring...from Analysis 1* that were used in Analysis 3. Look at Analysis 1. The explanation says that *one thousand males with type-O blood were mated with 1,000 females with type-AB blood*. Look at Table 1 to find possible genotypes for these blood types. The males with type-O blood must have had $I^O I^O$ genotype. The females with type-AB blood must have had $I^A I^B$ genotype. As offspring receive one gene from each parent, mating would produce offspring with $I^A I^O$ and $I^B I^O$ genotypes. The correct answer is (G).

5. **D** The question asks which analyses produced offspring that *had 1 allele for type-O blood*. Look at Table 1. Table 1 shows which alleles are present in each blood type. Type-O blood has a genotype of $I^O I^O$, so all offspring from a type-O parent will receive an allele for type-O blood. Analysis 1 and Analysis 2 both involve a type-O parent, so eliminate (B). Since the parents in Analysis 3 came from Analysis 1, the genotypes of the parents both had to include a type-O allele: $I^A I^O$ and $I^B I^O$. Since there is only one parental type-A allele and one parental type-B allele, the type-A and type-B offspring in Analysis 3 must also be $I^A I^O$ and $I^B I^O$, respectively. Eliminate both (A) and (C) because they do not include Analysis 3. The correct answer is (D).

6. **H** The question asks about *the number of offspring with type-B blood* that would have been produced in Analysis 3 had there been a total of 300 offspring. Look at the percentages of offspring produced in Analysis 3. According to the data, 25% of the offspring would be type-B. 25% of 300 is 75. The correct answer is (H).

THIS PAGE IS INTENTIONALLY LEFT BLANK.

SCIENCE PASSAGE DRILL 7

Now   Later   Last/Never

Time Spent: _____

Chemical researchers studied the *viscosity* (a fluid's resistance to flow) for several liquids. Highly viscous fluids take more time to flow through a vessel than do fluids with lower viscosities. They measured the viscosity in *centipoise* (cP) (.01 grams per centimeter per second). Some solutions were treated with chemical additives before the fluids were heated. The results are shown in Figures 1–3.

Figure 1

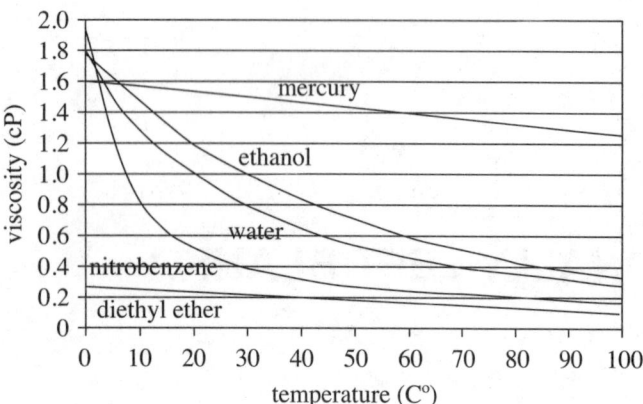

Figure 2

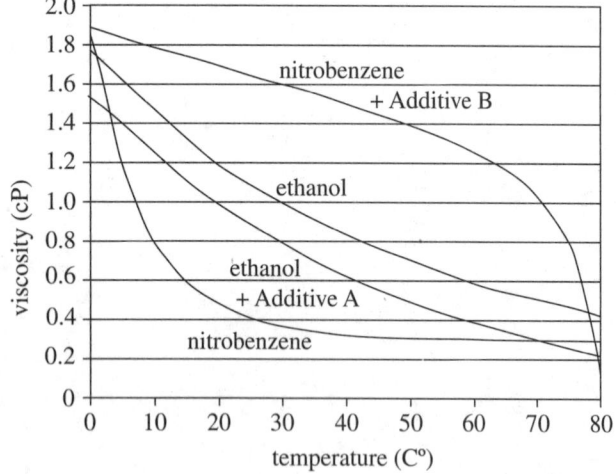

Figure 3

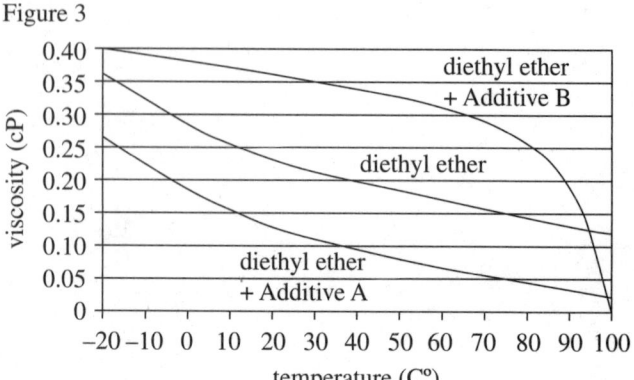

1. For which of the 3 figures did at least one sample fluid have a viscosity greater than 1.0 cP at a temperature of 0°C ?

   A. Figure 1 only
   B. Figure 3 only
   C. Figures 1 and 2 only
   D. Figures 1, 2, and 3

2. According to Figure 2, for the sample that contained nitrobenzene without Additive B, the greatest decrease in fluid viscosity occurred over which of the following intervals of temperature change?

   F. From 0°C to 10°C
   G. From 10°C to 20°C
   H. From 30°C to 40°C
   J. From 40°C to 50°C

3. According to Figure 1, after water was heated to reach a temperature of 70°C, the viscosity was closest to which of the following?

   A. 0.2 cP
   B. 0.4 cP
   C. 0.7 cP
   D. 1.0 cP

4. Based on the information given, which of the following best describes and explains the experimental results presented in Figure 2? As the temperature increased, the time required for the sample fluids to flow out of their containers:

   F. decreased, because heating the fluids increased each fluid's viscosity.
   G. decreased, because heating the fluids decreased each fluid's viscosity.
   H. increased, because heating the fluids increased each fluid's viscosity.
   J. increased, because heating the fluids decreased each fluid's viscosity.

5. A researcher hypothesized that a solution of nitrobenzene treated with Additive A would have a lower viscosity at 60°C than would untreated diethyl ether at that same temperature. Do the results in the figures confirm this hypothesis?

   A. Yes; according to Figure 2, at 60°C, nitrobenzene had a higher viscosity than did nitrobenzene treated with Additive B.
   B. Yes; according to Figure 3, at 60°C, diethyl ether had a higher viscosity than did diethyl ether treated with Additive A.
   C. No; according to Figure 2, at 60°C, nitrobenzene had a higher viscosity than did nitrobenzene treated with Additive B.
   D. No; according to Figures 1–3, samples of nitrobenzene treated with Additive A were not tested for viscosity.

6. Researchers conducted a study in which they suspended a capped funnel with 100 mL of solution over a beaker, as shown in Figure 4.

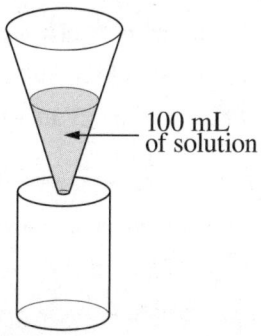

100 mL of solution

Figure 4

After removing the funnel cap, they recorded the amount of time elapsed until the solution in the beaker reached 50 mL. If this process was repeated for each solution shown in Figures 1–3, which of the following solutions, at 10°C, would reach 50 mL in the shortest amount of time?

   F. Diethyl ether
   G. Nitrobenzene
   H. Diethyl ether + Additive A
   J. Nitrobenzene + Additive B

SCIENCE PASSAGE DRILL 7 EXPLANATIONS

1. **C** The question asks for the figures in which at *least one sample fluid had a viscosity greater than 1.0 cP at a temperature of 0°C.* Look at Figure 1. At 0°C, four *sample fluid[s] have a viscosity greater than 1.0 cP.* Eliminate (B) because it doesn't include Figure 1. Look at Figure 2. At 0°C, all four *sample fluid[s] have a viscosity greater than 1.0 cP.* Eliminate (A) because it doesn't include Figure 2. Look at Figure 3. At 0°C, no *sample fluid[s] have a viscosity greater than 1.0 cP;* eliminate (D) because it includes this sample. The correct answer is (C).

2. **F** The question asks for the interval of *temperature change* that had *the greatest decrease in fluid viscosity* for *the sample that contained nitrobenzene without Additive B,* according to Figure 2. Look at Figure 2 and locate the curve that represents the data regarding *nitrobenzene without Additive B.* From 0°C to 10°C, there is a slightly more than 1.0 cP change in *viscosity.* From 10°C to 20°C, there is about a 0.2 cP change in *viscosity;* eliminate (G) because this is less than the change in (F). From 30°C to 40°C, there is a less than 0.1 cP change in *viscosity;* eliminate (H) because this is less than the change in (F). From 40°C to 50°C, there is almost no change in *viscosity;* eliminate (J). The correct answer is (F).

3. **B** The question asks for the *viscosity* of water after it *was heated to reach a temperature of 70°C,* according to Figure 1. Look at Figure 1 and locate the curve that represents the data regarding water. At 70°C, the water had a *viscosity* of 0.4 cP. The correct answer is (B).

4. **G** The question asks for an explanation of the relationship between *temperature* and *the time required for the sample fluids to flow out of their containers,* according to Figure 2. Look at Figure 2. As *temperature* increases, *viscosity* decreases. Since Figure 2 does not show *time,* look for the word *time* in the passage. The passage says that *highly viscous fluids take more time to flow through a vessel than do low viscous fluids.* So, as *viscosity* increases, *the time required for the sample fluids to flow out of their containers* also increases. Therefore, as *temperature* increases, *the time required for the sample fluids to flow out of their containers* decreases. Eliminate (H) and (J) because they state that the time increased, which is the opposite relationship. Eliminate (F) because it erroneously states that as *temperature* increases, *viscosity* also increases. The correct answer is (G).

5. **D** The question asks whether *a solution of nitrobenzene treated with Additive A would have a lower viscosity at 60°C than would untreated diethyl ether at that same temperature,* according to the results in the figures. Look for *nitrobenzene treated with Additive A* in Figures 1–3. Since it has not been tested, the results of the figures cannot confirm the hypothesis put forth in the question stem. Eliminate (A) and (B) because they both state that the hypothesis is confirmed. Eliminate (C) because the hypothesis was not about *nitrobenzene treated with Additive B.* The correct answer is (D).

6. **H**   The question asks which of the solutions listed would fill the beaker in Figure 4 to 50 mL in the shortest amount of time at a temperature of 10°C. The figures do not give any data about time, so look for the word *time* in the passage. According to the passage, fluids with a higher viscosity *take more time to flow through a vessel than do fluids with lower viscosities*. Therefore, the fluid with the lowest viscosity at 10°C will fill the beaker in the shortest amount of time. Choice (F), diethyl ether, is shown in Figure 1 and has a viscosity of about 0.3 cP at 10°C. Choice (G), nitrobenzene, is also shown in Figure 1 and has a viscosity of about 0.8 cP at 10°C. Eliminate (G) because it has a higher viscosity than (F) does. Choice (H), diethyl ether + Additive A, is shown in Figure 3 and has a viscosity of about 0.15 cP at 10°C. This is lower than diethyl ether alone, so eliminate (F). Choice (J), nitrobenzene + Additive B, is shown in Figure 2 and has a viscosity of about 1.8 cP at 10°C. This is higher than diethyl ether + Additive A so eliminate (J). The correct answer is (H).

Writing Drills

WRITING DRILL 1

Directions

This is a test of your writing skills. You will have forty (40) minutes to read the prompt, plan your response, and write an essay in English. Before you begin working, read all material in this test booklet carefully to understand exactly what you are being asked to do.

You will write your answer on the lined pages in the answer document provided. Your writing on those pages will be scored. You may use the unlined pages in this test booklet to plan your essay. Your work on these pages will not be scored.

Your essay will be evaluated based on the evidence it provides of your ability to:

- clearly state your own perspective on a complex issue and analyze the relationship between your perspective and at least one other perspective

- develop and support your ideas with reasoning and examples

- organize your ideas clearly and logically

- communicate your ideas effectively in standard written English

Lay your pencil down immediately when time is called.

DO NOT OPEN THIS BOOK UNTIL YOU ARE TOLD TO DO SO.

Composition paper for the essay can be found beginning on page 414.

The Banishment of Cigarettes

Over the last several decades, society has become increasingly aware of the detrimental effects of tobacco products. A person is far more likely to see an anti-smoking advertisement on television that illustrates the harmful effects of the product than to see one that is in favor of it, and print ads are accompanied by large warnings from the surgeon general. Some argue that even though they increase awareness of tobacco's harmful side effects, these advertisements are still advocating for the purchase of the product. Because of the findings, some maintain that cigarettes and other tobacco products should be banned.

Read and carefully consider these perspectives. Each suggests a particular way of thinking about the conflict over whether cigarettes should be banned.

Perspective One	Perspective Two	Perspective Three
Dangerous drugs are already banned by the federal government. While marijuana is illegal in many parts of the United States, many argue that cigarettes are worse than marijuana for a variety of reasons. Cigarettes have a negative effect on individuals and society as a whole and should be banned.	The government cannot ban everything that carries a risk. Unhealthy foods have led to diseases such as diabetes and obesity, yet people are still free to enjoy the plethora of options available to them. A ban on cigarettes is unnecessary and infringes on an individual's right to control his or her own life.	In history, Prohibition was largely unsuccessful and led to social uprising. Certain historians argue that because of this failure, the ban would be largely unsuccessful and potentially dangerous.

Essay Task

Write a unified, coherent essay in which you evaluate the multiple perspectives on the banishment of cigarettes. In your essay, be sure to:

- clearly state your own perspective on the issue and analyze the relationship between your perspective and at least one other perspective
- develop and support your ideas with reasoning and examples
- organize your ideas clearly and logically
- communicate your ideas effectively in standard written English

Your perspective may be in full agreement with any of the others, in partial agreement, or wholly different. Whatever the case, support your ideas with logical reasoning and detailed, persuasive examples.

The Princeton Review
Diagnostic ACT Form

ESSAY

Begin your essay on this side. If necessary, continue on the opposite side.

The Princeton Review
Diagnostic ACT Form

Continued from previous page.

The Princeton Review
Diagnostic ACT Form

Continued from previous page.

The Princeton Review
Diagnostic ACT Form

Continued from previous page.

WRITING DRILL 2

Directions

This is a test of your writing skills. You will have forty (40) minutes to read the prompt, plan your response, and write an essay in English. Before you begin working, read all material in this test booklet carefully to understand exactly what you are being asked to do.

You will write your answer on the lined pages in the answer document provided. Your writing on those pages will be scored. You may use the unlined pages in this test booklet to plan your essay. Your work on these pages will not be scored.

Your essay will be evaluated based on the evidence it provides of your ability to:

- clearly state your own perspective on a complex issue and analyze the relationship between your perspective and at least one other perspective

- develop and support your ideas with reasoning and examples

- organize your ideas clearly and logically

- communicate your ideas effectively in standard written English

Lay your pencil down immediately when time is called.

DO NOT OPEN THIS BOOK UNTIL YOU ARE TOLD TO DO SO.

Composition paper for the essay can be found beginning on page 420.

Dress Codes in Schools

Some parents have advocated for the enforcement of strict dress codes in schools. Student organizations and groups have argued against this, citing that such an act stifles individuality and denies freedom of expression. Private institutions have rules about what students may or may not wear, with a number of those institutions requiring uniforms. When public schools have tried to implement and recommend reform, they have been met with resistance from the student body.

Read and carefully consider these perspectives. Each suggests a particular way of thinking about the conflict over whether dress codes should be implemented by schools.

Perspective One	Perspective Two	Perspective Three
The unconstitutionality of the dress code is the reason that it cannot be put into effect. This would violate the individualistic right to expression. Though some articles of clothing may be controversial, many individuals like to express their views and feelings through the clothing they wear.	While the ability to express oneself is an inalienable right, it does carry some limits. Schools have the authority to ban articles of clothing that are hindering the learning process. A dress code is the surest way to maintain the primary focus of learning.	Dress codes have the potential to be sexist, especially if they affect some students more than others. Many students have called for gender-equal dress codes to allow for fairness and to not just restrict the rights of one group.

Essay Task

Write a unified, coherent essay in which you evaluate multiple perspectives on dress codes in schools. In your essay, be sure to:

- clearly state your own perspective on the issue and analyze the relationship between your perspective and at least one other perspective
- develop and support your ideas with reasoning and examples
- organize your ideas clearly and logically
- communicate your ideas effectively in standard written English

Your perspective may be in full agreement with any of the others, in partial agreement, or wholly different. Whatever the case, support your ideas with logical reasoning and detailed, persuasive examples.

The Princeton Review
Diagnostic ACT Form

ESSAY

Begin your essay on this side. If necessary, continue on the opposite side.

The Princeton Review
Diagnostic ACT Form

Continued from previous page.

_____

_____

_____

_____

_____

_____

_____

_____

_____

_____

_____

_____

_____

_____

_____

_____

_____

_____

_____

_____

_____

_____

_____

_____

**PLEASE PRINT
YOUR INITIALS**

First	Middle	Last

The Princeton Review
Diagnostic ACT Form

Continued from previous page.

The Princeton Review
Diagnostic ACT Form

Continued from previous page.

_____

_____

_____

_____

_____

_____

_____

_____

_____

_____

_____

_____

_____

_____

_____

_____

_____

_____

_____

_____

_____

**PLEASE PRINT
YOUR INITIALS**

First	Middle	Last

WRITING DRILL 3

Directions

This is a test of your writing skills. You will have forty (40) minutes to read the prompt, plan your response, and write an essay in English. Before you begin working, read all material in this test booklet carefully to understand exactly what you are being asked to do.

You will write your answer on the lined pages in the answer document provided. Your writing on those pages will be scored. You may use the unlined pages in this test booklet to plan your essay. Your work on these pages will not be scored.

Your essay will be evaluated based on the evidence it provides of your ability to:

- clearly state your own perspective on a complex issue and analyze the relationship between your perspective and at least one other perspective

- develop and support your ideas with reasoning and examples

- organize your ideas clearly and logically

- communicate your ideas effectively in standard written English

Lay your pencil down immediately when time is called.

DO NOT OPEN THIS BOOK UNTIL YOU ARE TOLD TO DO SO.

Composition paper for the essay can be found beginning on page 426.

Increase the Driving Age

Because of the rising incidence of accidents among teenage drivers, many have sought to increase the legal driving age. With the increased dependence on technology, there are many proposing this ramification. An influential auto safety group in Chicago is calling on states to raise the age for getting a driver's license to 17 or even 18. Some have even commissioned reports calling for a 12-month learner permit that requires at least 120 hours of practice.

Read and carefully consider these perspectives. Each suggests a particular way of thinking about the conflict over whether the driving age should be raised.

Perspective One

Operating a vehicle requires a maturity that is simply not acquired by an individual at the tender age of 16. To join the armed services and to vote, the legal age is 18. To be able to rent a car, an individual must be 25 years old. At 16 years of age, a person is not prepared to operate a vehicle.

Perspective Two

Increasing the driving age will not reduce the number of traffic accidents. Instead, by making it more difficult to get experience driving, it will just make it harder for those who are "of age" to get behind the wheel. This, in turn, will increase the number of accidents among older drivers.

Perspective Three

A driving curfew could be an effective deterrent. This act would distribute 120 practice hours: 100 during the day and 20 at night, all under the supervision of a licensed driver for at least three years. This would see the roads clear of newly qualified drivers between 10 P.M. and 5 A.M.

Essay Task

Write a unified, coherent essay in which you evaluate multiple perspectives on the issue of increasing the legal driving age. In your essay, be sure to:

- clearly state your own perspective on the issue and analyze the relationship between your perspective and at least one other perspective
- develop and support your ideas with reasoning and examples
- organize your ideas clearly and logically
- communicate your ideas effectively in standard written English

Your perspective may be in full agreement with any of the others, in partial agreement, or wholly different. Whatever the case, support your ideas with logical reasoning and detailed, persuasive examples.

The Princeton Review
Diagnostic ACT Form

ESSAY

Begin your essay on this side. If necessary, continue on the opposite side.

Continue on the opposite side if necessary.

The Princeton Review
Diagnostic ACT Form

Continued from previous page.

_____

_____

_____

_____

_____

_____

_____

_____

_____

_____

_____

_____

_____

_____

_____

_____

_____

_____

_____

_____

_____

_____

PLEASE PRINT
YOUR INITIALS

First	Middle	Last

The Princeton Review
Diagnostic ACT Form

Continued from previous page.

The Princeton Review
Diagnostic ACT Form

Continued from previous page.

ESSAY CHECKLIST

1. The Introduction
   Did you:
   o start with a topic sentence that paraphrases or restates the prompt?
   o clearly state your position on the issue?

2. Body Paragraph 1
   Did you:
   o start with a transition/topic sentence that discusses the opposing side of the argument?
   o give an example of a reason that one might agree with the opposing side of the argument?
   o clearly state that the opposing side of the argument is wrong or flawed?
   o show what is wrong with the opposing side's example or position?

3. Body Paragraphs 2 and 3
   Did you:
   o start with a transition/topic sentence that discusses your position on the prompt?
   o give one example or reason to support your position?
   o show the grader how your example supports your position?
   o end the paragraph by restating your thesis?

4. Conclusion
   Did you:
   o restate your position on the issue?
   o end with a flourish?

5. Overall
   Did you:
   o write neatly?
   o avoid multiple spelling and grammar mistakes?
   o try to vary your sentence structure?
   o use a few impressive-sounding words?